San Francisco

Tom Downs

LONELY PLANET PUBLICATIONS
Melbourne • Oakland • London • Paris

San Francisco
3rd edition – January 2002
First published – February 1996

Published by
Lonely Planet Publications Pty Ltd ABN 36 005 607 983
90 Maribyrnong St, Footscray, Victoria 3011, Australia

Lonely Planet Offices
Australia Locked Bag 1, Footscray, Victoria 3011
USA 150 Linden St, Oakland, CA 94607
UK 10a Spring Place, London NW5 3BH
France 1 rue du Dahomey, 75011 Paris

Photographs
Many of the images in this guide are available for licensing from Lonely Planet Images.
email: lpi@lonelyplanet.com.au
Web site: www.lonelyplanetimages.com

Front cover photograph
Golden Gate Bridge (Christoph Wilhelm/FPG International)

Map section photograph
San Francisco by night (John Elk III)

ISBN 1 86450 309 2

Printed by The Bookmaker International Ltd
Printed in China

Contents

The Author

Tom Downs

Tom, caught chowing on a bowl of Taiwanese noodles in the adjacent photo, began traveling out of necessity – as is the lot of many fledgling accordion players, he wasn't allowed to stay in one town for very long. When Tom came to Lonely Planet a few years back, we agreed to let him keep the accordion if he took some lessons, but the hobo suit and the avaricious little monkey had to go. Since then, Tom has contributed to a variety of Lonely Planet books, including *New Orleans* and *Louisiana & the Deep South*. This is his second turn at the helm of *San Francisco*. Tom lives in Chinatown with his wife, Fawn, and their kids, Mai and Lana.

FROM THE AUTHOR

Fawn, I couldn't have conjured up a dreamier gal to tumble through life with. Soon as I finish typing this, let's get out the ice crusher and that bottle of Bombay. Little pecks to Sugar Pie and Pinky, who road-tested all of San Francisco's swing sets and carousels.

Cheers to Elaine Merrill and Sarah Hubbard for an exceptional Excursions chapter. I'll be relying on that chapter myself on future getaways! Tim Kingston's special section on queer San Francisco shows a dazzling mastery of language and an equally impressive know-how about San Francisco's gay scenes. The Places to Eat chapter benefited tremendously from the discriminating advice of Michele Posner, Wendy Taylor, Kim Zetter and the *Out to Eat* crew. Thanks to Marcel Gaston and Nadine Fogale and their army of reformatters, who primed the text for a much-needed overhaul.

I owe a debt of gratitude to my Lonely Planet shipmates. Senior Editor Maria Donohoe cast an ever-steady gaze on the horizon, and with her bare hands she wrassled many a giant sea monster to the deck. Editor Rachel Bernstein navigated through the ceaseless storms and stopped up a multitude of holes that threatened to suck our leaky vessel down to the shadowy depths. Cartographers Monica Lepe, Tracey Croom, Naoko Ogawa and Stephanie Sims tirelessly pored over maps to ensure we didn't get lost at sea. Managing Editor Kate Hoffman stood by my side as I babbled away a fever that very nearly meant a watery grave for me, and Publisher Mariah Bear proved her mettle against a band of thieves intent on having my gold teeth. Proofer Valerie Sinzdak tugged our exhausted little galleon back in through the Golden Gate. In dry dock, Designer Josh Schefers mended the sails and meticulously repainted the bowsprit. I'd walk the plank for any of you.

Only a few years ago, it was considered uncouth to call San Francisco 'Frisco.' The city has changed much in a short period of time, and the argument against Frisco no longer seems relevant – which leads me to believe that the city of old somehow really was Frisco, and the city we are left with is just San Francisco. I'm indebted to friends and family who are longtime residents and knew Frisco and taught me much about the city: Margaret, Dorothy, Jim, Chris, Mark, Al, Randall, John and Beca.

This Book

The 3rd edition of *San Francisco* was updated by Tom Downs, with Sarah JH Hubbard, Tim Kingston and Elaine Merrill contributing.

FROM THE PUBLISHER

This book was a labor of love for Lonely Planet's Oakland office. Rachel Bernstein edited *San Francisco* with the invaluable help of Valerie Sinzdak. Senior Editor Maria Donohoe's support was priceless, as was her native perspective on the Bay Area. Valerie redefined 'proofing' with her thorough, thoughtful work on the text. Managing Editor Kate Hoffman went beyond the call of duty with her attention to the project and Michele Posner's last-minute help kept the book on track. Gabi Knight, Elaine Merrill, Pelin Thornhill and China Williams fact-checked and phone-called. Ken DellaPenta created the index.

The spectacular maps were drawn by Naoko Ogawa and Stephanie Sims with Tracey Croom's oversight. When Nao was forced into an overseas adventure, Steph calmly stepped into the lead cartographer role to keep things on track. A cartographic crew of Sean Brandt, John Culp, Monica Lepe, Herman So and Eric Thomsen pitched in along the way.

Josh Schefers laid out *San Francisco* with patience and humor; Margaret Livingston, Daniel New and Susan Rimerman watched his back. Josh, Daniel and Wendy Yanagihara spent endless hours improving the book's internal design and Wendy designed the cover. Andreas Schueller pulled together all the editorial, design and technical pieces like nobody else could. Justin Marler drew the delightful chapter ends and, along with Hugh D'Andrade and Hayden Foell, graced this book with absolutely fabulous illustrations. Justin and the ever-witty Beca Lafore coordinated the illustrations.

Down in Australia, Nadine Fogale, Marcel Gaston and their gang of Knowledge Bank folk, with patience and flexibility, turned codes and gibberish into organized files.

Tim Kingston contributed his delightful perspective on the area's swingin' queer life. A skilled team of three LP editors switched roles to update *San Francisco* with all the attention to detail *their* editor could ask; the editorial team sends out a loud and appreciative round of applause to Tom Downs, Elaine Merrill and Sarah Hawkins Hubbard for their excellent writing and willingness to do things differently, and for their support along the way.

ACKNOWLEDGMENTS

Grateful acknowledgment is made to the Bancroft Library for the use of their historic photos.

Foreword

ABOUT LONELY PLANET GUIDEBOOKS

The story begins with a classic travel adventure: Tony and Maureen Wheeler's 1972 journey across Europe and Asia to Australia. Useful information about the overland trail did not exist at that time, so Tony and Maureen published the first Lonely Planet guidebook to meet a growing need.

From a kitchen table, then from a tiny office in Melbourne (Australia), Lonely Planet has become the largest independent travel publisher in the world, an international company with offices in Melbourne, Oakland (USA), London (UK) and Paris (France).

Today Lonely Planet guidebooks cover the globe. There is an ever-growing list of books, and there's information in a variety of forms and media. Some things haven't changed. The main aim is still to help make it possible for adventurous travelers to get out there – to explore and better understand the world.

At Lonely Planet we believe travelers can make a positive contribution to the countries they visit – if they respect their host communities and spend their money wisely. Since 1986 a percentage of the income from each book has been donated to aid projects and human-rights campaigns.

Updates Lonely Planet thoroughly updates each guidebook as often as possible. This usually means there are around two years between editions, although for more unusual or more stable destinations the gap can be longer. Check the imprint page (usually following the color map at the beginning of the book) for publication dates.

Between editions up-to-date information is available in two free newsletters – the paper *Planet Talk* and email *Comet* (to subscribe, contact any Lonely Planet office) – and on our Web site at www.lonelyplanet.com. The *Upgrades* section of the Web site covers a number of important and volatile destinations and is regularly updated by Lonely Planet authors. *Scoop* covers news and current affairs relevant to travelers. And, lastly, the *Thorn Tree* bulletin board and *Postcards* section of the site carry unverified, but fascinating, reports from travelers.

Lonely Planet gathers information for everyone who's curious about the planet – and especially for those who explore it first-hand. Through guidebooks, phrasebooks, activity guides, maps, literature, newsletters, image library, TV series and Web site we act as an information exchange for a worldwide community of travelers.

Correspondence The process of creating new editions begins with the letters, postcards and emails received from travelers. This correspondence often includes suggestions, criticisms and comments about the current editions. Interesting excerpts are immediately passed on via newsletters and the Web site, and everything goes to our authors to be verified when they're researching on the road. We're keen to get more feedback from organizations or individuals who represent communities visited by travelers.

Research Authors aim to gather sufficient practical information to enable travelers to make informed choices and to make the mechanics of a journey run smoothly. They also research historical and cultural background to help enrich the travel experience and allow travelers to understand and respond appropriately to cultural and environmental issues.

Authors don't stay in every hotel because that would mean spending a couple of months in each medium-size city and, no, they don't eat at every restaurant because that would mean stretching belts beyond capacity. They do visit hotels and restaurants to check standards and prices, but feedback based on readers' direct experiences can be very helpful.

Many of our authors work undercover; others aren't so secretive. None of them accept freebies in exchange for positive write-ups. And none of our guidebooks contain any advertising.

Production Authors submit their manuscripts and maps to offices in Australia, the USA, UK or France. Editors and cartographers – all experienced travelers themselves – then begin the process of assembling the pieces. When the book finally hits the shops, some things are already out of date, we start getting feedback from readers and the process begins again…

WARNING & REQUEST

Things change – prices go up, schedules change, good places go bad and bad places go bankrupt – nothing stays the same. So, if you find things better or worse, recently opened or long since closed, please tell us and help make the next edition even more accurate and useful. We genuinely value all the feedback we receive. A well-traveled team reads and acknowledges every letter, postcard and email and ensures that every morsel of information finds its way to the appropriate authors, editors and cartographers for verification.

Everyone who writes to us will find their name listed in the next edition of the appropriate guidebook. They will also receive the latest issue of *Planet Talk*, our quarterly printed newsletter, or *Comet*, our monthly email newsletter. Subscriptions to both newsletters are free. The very best contributions will be rewarded with a free guidebook.

We may edit, reproduce and incorporate your comments in all Lonely Planet products, such as guidebooks, Web sites and digital products, so let us know if you don't want your comments reproduced or your name acknowledged.

Send all correspondence to the Lonely Planet office closest to you:

Australia: Locked Bag 1, Footscray, Victoria 3011
USA: 150 Linden St, Oakland, CA 94607
UK: 10a Spring Place, London NW5 3BH
France: 1 rue du Dahomey, 75011 Paris

Or email us at: talk2us@lonelyplanet.com.au

For news, views and updates, see our Web site: www.lonelyplanet.com

HOW TO USE A LONELY PLANET GUIDEBOOK

The best way to use a Lonely Planet guidebook is any way you choose. At Lonely Planet, we believe the most memorable travel experiences are often those that are unexpected, and the finest discoveries are those you make yourself. Guidebooks are not intended to be used as if they provided a detailed set of infallible instructions!

Contents All Lonely Planet guidebooks follow roughly the same format. The Facts about the Destination chapters or sections give background information ranging from history to weather. Facts for the Visitor gives practical information on issues like visas and health. Getting There & Away gives a brief starting point for researching travel to and from the destination. Getting Around gives an overview of the transport options when you arrive.

The peculiar demands of each destination determine how subsequent chapters are broken up, but some things remain constant. We always start with background, then proceed to sights, places to stay, places to eat, entertainment, getting there and away, and getting around information – in that order.

Heading Hierarchy Lonely Planet headings are used in a strict hierarchical structure that can be visualized as a set of Russian dolls. Each heading (and its following text) is encompassed by any preceding heading that is higher on the hierarchical ladder.

Although inclusion in a guidebook usually implies a recommendation, we cannot list every good place. Exclusion does not necessarily imply criticism. In fact there are a number of reasons why we might exclude a place – sometimes it is simply inappropriate to encourage an influx of travelers.

Entry Points We do not assume guidebooks will be read from beginning to end, but that people will dip into them. The traditional entry points are the list of contents and the index. In addition, however, some books have a complete list of maps and an index map illustrating map coverage.

There may also be a color map that shows highlights. These highlights are dealt with in greater detail in the Facts for the Visitor chapter, along with planning questions and suggested itineraries. Each chapter covering a geographical region usually begins with a locator map and another list of highlights. Once you find something of interest in a list of highlights, turn to the index.

Maps Maps play a crucial role in Lonely Planet guidebooks and include a huge amount of information. A legend is printed on the back page. We seek to have complete consistency between maps and text and to have every important place in the text captured on a map. Map key numbers usually start in the top left corner.

HOW TO USE A LONELY PLANET GUIDEBOOK

Introduction

JOHN ELK III

Head up to San Francisco's Twin Peaks on a summer evening when the city is not shrouded in its famous fog, and you'll see a postcard-perfect view: rows of Victorian houses stretching over more than 40 hills, a curvaceous bay speckled with sailboats, two of the world's best-loved bridges, and, if you're lucky, a few harmless shreds of fog colored in shades of red and pink by the setting sun as they glide through downtown skyscrapers. No other city in the USA can offer such a seductive sight. And yet, if you ask San Franciscans what their city has to offer, few begin with that singular image. There are so many other things to love about this town.

Like all great cities, San Francisco is an amalgam of distinct neighborhoods – but here, these vital urban pockets are compressed within the 7-by-7-mile thumbnail at the tip of a peninsula. Contrasts from one street to the next are intriguing and delightful. Not surprisingly, the best way to explore San Francisco is on foot.

A leisurely stroll through North Beach, with its relaxed European charm, leads smack into bustling Chinatown, which often seems more Chinese than does Hong Kong. A hike up hoity-toity Nob Hill segues down to the troubled Tenderloin and on past the ornamental old theaters of Geary St, the department stores and fashion billboards of Union Square, and the sleek towers of the Financial District. South of Market offers its own contrasts; a busy warehouse district during the day, it transforms into nightclub central at night. The Mission District embodies several personalities: along many of its streets it remains the city's Latino enclave, which it has been for more than four decades, but a continuous flow of hip young invaders has redefined many of the district's crossroads. The nearby Castro was claimed by gay men in the 1970s, and it remains predominantly gay today, projecting an assured, almost mainstream air.

The city abounds with creative energy, feeding on the richness of its diverse cultures and lifestyles. No aspect of San Francisco life better reflects this cultural exchange than its cuisine. The restaurants for which the city is so famous liberally mix traditions from every continent on the planet. But there are other examples of San Francisco's multicultural and artistic leanings. In the Mission District, for example, many streets and alleys have been transformed into galleries of colorful murals depicting an array of local and international themes. Creativity practically oozes from the buildings.

San Francisco can probably coast a bit in the wake of the dot-com bonanza of the late 1990s. New museums, planned during the boom time, will continue to open over the next few years; meanwhile, established museums might want to catch their breaths after recent spending frenzies that brought many great works of art to San Francisco. An economic slowdown will purge the city of a few excess restaurants, but San Francisco has always had more than a few to spare. The best places to eat will remain, since San Franciscans can't seem to resist the pleasures of dining out.

The city has so much to offer, it seems visitors can't help but want to move here. Spend just a few days roaming its neighborhoods, and it's difficult not to start considering which part of town you want to live in. If that's your inclination, be warned: in recent years so many people have been trying to get into San Francisco, the cost of real estate and rentals has skyrocketed. It is much easier – and cheaper – to remain contented with a brief visit!

Facts about San Francisco

HISTORY

The knob of earth and sand now called San Francisco has probably been inhabited by human beings for 15,000 years, though little history over that span is actually known. Only to the past 150 years can we with any certainty apply Rudyard Kipling's famous 1889 assessment, 'San Francisco is a mad city – inhabited for the most part by perfectly insane people.'

The First San Franciscans

When the Civic Center BART station was under construction in 1970, workers discovered the thigh bone of a young woman, dating to about 3000 BC. This bone is the earliest evidence of human life to be uncovered in San Francisco, although the shell mounds left behind by people who subsisted on mussels and other seafood indicate the area was populated long before that. By 1000 BC, the last native group to reside here, the Ohlone people, had constructed temporary villages in the marshlands near the bay shore and along inland creeks. The Ohlone lived in simple huts, and they relied on the surrounding waters, woods, and sand dunes for their food, which consisted of acorns (their staple ingredient), mussels, shark, rabbit, and an occasional grizzly bear. They maintained this way of life, continually picking up and transporting their villages from marsh to marsh, until California fell under Spanish rule.

The Europeans Arrive

The Portuguese navigator Juan Rodríguez Cabrillo, employed by the Spanish, anchored in San Diego Bay in 1542, thus becoming the first European to set eyes on what is now California. Thereafter, many European ships probed the California coast in search of an ideal harbor, but persistent fog and the narrowness of the Golden Gate kept San Francisco Bay hidden from them for more than two centuries. Even Francis Drake missed it. Drake, in 1579, landed just 35 miles north of the Golden Gate, near present-day Point Reyes, which he claimed for England. (Today, that bay is known as Drakes Bay.)

Though San Francisco Bay remained unknown to Europe, the Spanish were certainly not idle in the New World, having built an empire that included Mexico, Central America, and most of South America. Not until the late 18th century, when Russian fur trappers began to make forays into California, did the Spanish turn their attention to their own claims there. In 1769, Gaspar de Portolá, governor of Baja California, and Father Junípero Serra, founder of the missions of Baja California, accompanied by soldiers, clerics, and Indian servants, began to proceed slowly up the California coast. Their goal was to eventually make it as far as Drakes Bay, establishing missions, presidios (military posts), and pueblos along the way. After founding the first mission, at San Diego, Serra boarded a ship headed for Monterey Bay, where the second mission was to be built. Portolá and his men continued overland but, somehow missing Monterey entirely, proceeded too far and inadvertently stumbled across San Francisco Bay. (It was actually a detachment of Portolá's party, led by Sergeant José Ortega, that first set eyes on the bay.) Having little use for a harbor, and possibly fearing a bleak winter (they had no knowledge of the local climate), Portolá's group turned back.

In 1772, two years after the mission and presidio were established in Monterey, a second party, led by Don Pedro Fages and one Father Crespi, set off to have a better look at the bay Ortega had discovered. They were understandably impressed with what they saw: as Crespi noted, 'It is a harbor such that not only the navy of our most Catholic Majesty but those of all Europe could take shelter in it.'

Spanish San Francisco

Still, another three years would pass before any ship would enter the Golden Gate. In 1775, Juan Manuel de Ayala, aboard a

Legends of the Barbary Coast

San Francisco hadn't been around very long before it had earned a reputation as a fairly rough and rowdy port of call. In the very heart of the city, just east of Portsmouth Square, was the notorious Barbary Coast, where the local citizenry enjoyed or suffered every vagary that has plagued ports everywhere since the beginning of time.

The Barbary Coast tag was decided on more or less by a worldwide consensus that the neighborhood bore some resemblance to the pirate-plagued coast of North Africa, home of the Berbers. (No doubt, the pirates' colorful, rum-soaked patois was responsible for the evolution of 'Berbers' into 'Barbary.') Naturally, violence, sex, gambling, and music characterized the neighborhood. The corner of Jackson and Kearny Sts became known as Killer's Corner; the center of the district was Devil's Acre, described in 1869 as a 'cesspool of rottenness' by the *San Francisco Chronicle;* and other landmarks on the neighborhood map included Deadman's Alley and Murder Point. As the *Chronicle* reported rather vividly: 'Ribald song and bawdy jest float through the polluted atmosphere with the squeal of fiddles and tumming of banjoes. Sometimes in the midst of the noise there is a shot, a curse, a shriek, a groan, and another hulk whirls down the dark whirlpool of death.'

The main function of the Barbary Coast was to separate men from their money, and that was accomplished through a variety of one-two punches, usually entailing some sort of entertainment followed by the unsuspected knockout blow. A grand time was had by all, but the hangovers were particularly nasty.

In 1917, California invoked its Red-Light Abatement Act, and police blockaded the Barbary Coast, effectively shutting down 83 brothels and 40 saloons all at once. But old habits die hard. Jackson Square retained some of its boisterous past even into Prohibition, with a smattering of speakeasies and underground jazz clubs. The striptease craze of the early 1960s turned Broadway into a modern, if tamer, Barbary Coast, and neon signs overhanging that era's tattered remnants still fill the night sky with the promise of sin.

Here's a brief hornbook highlighting some useful Barbary Coast terminology and some of the district's more infamous legends:

Melodeons The throbbing heart of the Barbary Coast was in its burlesque dance halls, which Victorians, with their penchant for pretentious language, called 'melodeons.' Music, laughter, and general caterwauling spilled out from these establishments. At the time, women were so scarce in California that one could attract a male crowd merely by walking down the street. The melodeons

modest vessel called the *San Carlos,* barely weathered the treacherous currents through the gate's narrow passage. But his became the first European ship to explore the bay. Ayala, echoing Father Crespi, marveled at the 'pocketful of ports.' He was followed by the overland arrival, in June 1776, of Captain Juan Bautista de Anza and Father Francisco Palou. They soon established a presidio at the southern side of the Golden Gate and the Misión San Francisco de Asís beside a swampy pond. Their party included more than 200 men, women, and children who were persuaded to leave their homes in Sonora and Sinaloa, Mexico, to settle and farm the lands around the new mission.

The Ohlone at first did not resist the Spaniards' efforts to Christianize and 'civilize' them. But, housed in austere stone and adobe barracks and obliged to labor as farmhands, many of them gradually grew weary of the mission routine of work and prayer. Many deserted, and though some were caught and punished, others resumed their traditional way of life. Introduced diseases and the shock of the arduous lifestyle cut the native population by half during the 50 years of Spanish rule in California.

Legends of the Barbary Coast

capitalized on that phenomenon with scant embellishment. Most of the singers and dancers had minimal training – licentiousness and profanity were generally considered adequate substitutes for real talent – but they drew huge crowds of lonely, easily excited men into the doors.

Cribs Brothels did a brisk business on the Barbary Coast. The population of early San Francisco consisted largely of free-spending men between the ages of 18 and 40; prostitutes, at first a rare commodity, commanded far higher prices here than they did in other hotbeds of sin, such as New Orleans or Paris. But soon thousands of harlots flowed into town, and the cost of an hour with a strumpet quickly dropped to a few dollars. To make ends meet, prostitutes often collaborated with shanghaiers (see below).

Crimping For some 60 years, the San Francisco waterfront was controlled by 'crimps,' proprietors of boardinghouses who did a lucrative business providing crews to ships through highly nefarious means. Men with colorful names that seemed designed to advertise their untrustworthiness, such as Smoothy Gus, Blinky Tom, Chicken Jim, and Whale-Whiskers Kelley, nevertheless succeeded in hoodwinking their fair share of innocents. Their seafaring boarders would be allowed to run up exorbitant tabs on wine, women, and song until they were indebted to the crimp. Through arrangements with ship captains, the crimps would essentially sell seamen's debts to the ships in exchange for advances on the seamen's wages; when a vessel set sail from San Francisco, it was often with a crew of indentured servants. During the height of crimp power, the boardinghouses had a virtual monopoly on San Francisco's maritime employment, and sailors had little choice but to accept their terms. As one 19th-century sailor put it, 'A seaman spent his life, both ashore and afloat, in a state of servitude to those who preyed upon him.'

Shanghaiing The most notorious practice of the crimps was known as 'shanghaiing,' because victims of this scam were treated to a free – albeit unplanned – trip to Shanghai or some other far-flung port. Saloon keepers treated a sailor fresh in town to free drinks containing 'knockout drops,' sometimes followed by a blow to the back of the head; the sailor was then relieved of his money and possessions and eventually awoke with an unwanted job aboard a ship already on its way to China. When experienced sailors couldn't be coaxed into the shanghaiers' dens, unsuspecting landlubbers were doped and carted off instead. (One smooth operator, named Calico Jim, reputedly shanghaied six policemen, but as the story goes, he was eventually found and gunned down by one of them.)

Yerba Buena

The mission settlement never really prospered. The sandy, scrubby fields were difficult to farm and yielded only enough food to sustain those who had cultivated them. The presidio rarely exceeded more than 20 soldiers, the harbor saw little trade, and no pueblo was established. It wasn't until after Mexico gained its independence from Spain that the local economy, based on the hide and tallow trade, began to show signs of life. Yerba Buena Cove – where the Financial District now stands, and named by the Spanish for the 'good herb' *(Satureja douglasii)* that grew wild there – became a regular port of call. Soon trading posts, houses, grocery stores, and grog shops appeared on the slopes that rose from the bay.

The handful of Yankee residents in the tiny town, along with a rising clamor in Washington, DC, to fulfill the USA's manifest destiny by acquiring California, might well have warned Mexican authorities that their hold on the northern territories was growing tenuous. In 1835, a US dignitary, acting on behalf of President Andrew Jackson, made a formal offer of $500,000 to buy Northern California, but the offer was declined. During the 1840s, US-Mexican relations steadily deteriorated. Rumors breezed through the pillars and podiums of Washington about Mexico's impending sale of California to the British. In a near panic, Washington stepped up its naval presence in the North Pacific. One American commander, Commodore Thomas Catesby Jones, acting under the assumption that the two countries were at war, actually invaded Monterey; two days later, after realizing his mistake, he apologized and returned to his ships.

In 1846, war did break out. The Mexican-American War lasted for two years, ending with the Treaty of Guadalupe Hidalgo, which formally ceded California and the present-day southwest states to the US. Before the ink was dry on that document, Yerba Buena was renamed San Francisco so that the growing town would benefit from the worldwide renown of the bay.

More significantly, gold was discovered in the Sierra foothills in January 1848.

Boom Town

The discovery of gold just 120 miles away made a city out of San Francisco. The first few flakes were chanced upon by James W Marshall, who was building a sawmill for Captain John Sutter near present-day Placerville. Sutter ordered his employees to start panning, and although he attempted to keep the gold strike a secret, within a few months newspaper publisher Sam Brannan was at the mill, checking on the rumors that were spreading around San Francisco. When Brannan returned to the city, he was too ecstatic to wait to break the big news in print; instead, he reportedly ran down Montgomery St holding up a bottle filled with gold flakes, shouting, 'Gold! Gold! Gold on the American River!' The gold rush was on.

The immediate impact on San Francisco was that its citizens closed up shop and headed for the diggings, leaving the town virtually deserted. But it wasn't long before many San Franciscans realized that the smart money was in supplying materials for the miners, business best conducted right there in town. They returned to the city, and their numbers quickly multiplied. News of the discovery spread to the East Coast, Europe, Australia, and China. Soon ships arrived daily at the once-sleepy port, their crews and captains leaping over the bulwarks to get to the nearest shop selling shovels, picks, and pans. A tent city, comparable in size to the actual city, arose along the waterfront and around the base of Telegraph Hill.

In the harbor, abandoned ships began to rot. Many of the empty wooden hulls were ground down to create landfill; Yerba Buena Cove, whose waters once lapped the edge of Montgomery St, gradually shrank back until no cove remained. Still other deserted ships served to make up for the shortage of buildings. Some of them were rammed into the waterfront and became shops; others became hotels. One brig, the *Euphemia*, served as the city's first prison.

By 1850, the year California was admitted as the 31st state in the union, San Francisco's population had grown to an estimated 25,000, up from just 800 a year earlier. The newcomers, called '49ers, were mostly men under the age of 40. To keep them entertained, some 500 saloons and 20 theaters opened in the space of five years. Miners ready to take their diggings back home usually waited for weeks in San Francisco for a ship, giving them plenty of time to disperse all their earnings among the casinos and bordellos that had sprouted off the waterfront. Naturally, currency in this flurry of spending was gold dust, which fluctuated wildly in value, from $6 to $12 an ounce.

The city was fast gaining a reputation for raucousness, pyromania, and general lawlessness. Certain sin-loving streets in the vicinity of the port were well on their way to earning the sobriquet 'Barbary Coast.' Large sections of town regularly burned to the ground – indeed, in more than one instance the entire city was reduced to ashes. On many occasions in 1851 and '56, hastily formed vigilante committees stormed the jail and dragged a prisoner up Russian Hill, where citizens gathered to watch a quick trial, followed directly by a hanging. As if to provide the necessary tonic that would

Map of the city, 1854 – note the original shoreline.

make a civilized city of San Francisco, in 1859 the Comstock Lode was struck.

The Comstock Lode

During the 1860s and '70s, silver deposits unearthed in the High Sierra, around Virginia City, Nevada, yielded more than $300 million, far more than was earned during the gold rush, and profits from the bonanza flowed into San Francisco. Anyone who possessed a little cash to speculate took a piece of the action. The lush new mansions adorning Nob Hill announced that a blessed few – the 'Silver Kings,' who included two former San Francisco barkeeps – had become the city's first multimillionaires. A financial district shot up along Montgomery and California Sts, new canneries and packinghouses sprawled from present-day North Beach to China Basin, streets were graded and paved, and scores of French restaurants opened to satisfy the palates of the nouveau riche.

The Civil War (1861–65) profited San Francisco as well, as industry was diverted there from factories on the East Coast burdened by the war effort. Fort Point was completed to calm the fears of San Franciscans, who, in their isolation from the warring states back east, felt vulnerable to foreign invasion by passing European warships. Although California remained officially loyal to the Union side, many prominent San Franciscans were Confederate sympathizers, and on several occasions authorities broke up crackpot Rebel conspiracies that aimed to capture the state and all its wealth.

Growing Pains

To consolidate the Union during the war, Congress approved funding for the building of a transcontinental railroad. Extending the range of the 'iron horse' westward ended the era of stagecoaches and of arduous sea voyages around Cape Horn, thus making the journey several months shorter between California, which was solidifying its trade ties to Asia, and the East Coast. But though the 'Big Four' railroad barons – Leland Stanford, Collis P Huntington, Mark Hopkins, and Charles Crocker (see 'The Railroad Barons' boxed text in Things to See & Do) – amassed huge fortunes, for the rest of San Francisco the anticipated economic boom failed to pan out.

Laying the railroad tracks was accomplished primarily through the recruitment of thousands of Chinese workers. At the height of construction, an estimated 12,000 Chinese laborers (of the Central Pacific Railroad Company's 14,000 total) were blasting a right of way through the Sierra Nevada. Upon completion of the railroad, the majority of these laborers settled in San Francisco, where they faced little opportunity besides menial jobs at low wages. During the depression of the 1870s they would face greater indignities as the scapegoats for hard times. In 1877, anti-Chinese riots shook San Francisco, and in 1882 Congress passed the Chinese Exclusion Act, which stopped the flow of Chinese people entering the country. Among other things, it prevented Chinese immigrants, the vast majority of whom were men, from bringing their wives into the US. The act remained on the books until 1943.

The City Beautiful

By the turn of the century, San Francisco's population surpassed 300,000. To accommodate so many people, new neighborhoods sprang up in the former cattle-grazing pastures of the Western Addition (the area west of Van Ness Ave, including present-day Pacific Heights and Cow Hollow) and the Mission District.

While San Francisco continued to grow as it prospered with the country's increased trade in the Pacific, the city's politics remained a tawdry, backroom affair that more often than not served the needs of tycoons like the Big Four and promoted seamy dealings that profited the politicians. Abe Ruef, the city's notorious political boss, and his handpicked mayor, Eugene Schmitz, were eventually indicted on charges of extorting huge sums of money from whorehouses. Meanwhile, public works were completely neglected. City streets followed a basic grid system that mulishly flouted the dramatic topography, and the most heavily populated sections of the city lacked attractive public spaces. Many prominent citizens – among them James Phelan, who would eventually become mayor and a US senator – considered City Hall's awkward agglomeration of classic architectural styles an embarrassment to the fledgling world capital.

To boost the city's reputation, Phelan commissioned Chicago architect Daniel Burnham, in the vanguard of the urban planning movement called 'city beautiful,' to give San Francisco a civic aesthetic to rival that of Baron Haussmann's Paris. Burnham drew up ambitious plans that included a public library, an opera house, new avenues radiating from the Civic Center, new streets that followed the contours of the city's hills, and a panhandle extending all the way from outlying Golden Gate Park to Van Ness Avenue. Ironically, this elaborate plan had just been finalized in April 1906, on the eve of the city's biggest disaster.

Quake! Fire!

San Francisco had suffered major earthquakes before, most notably in 1868, but the quake of April 18, 1906, centered 25 miles north of San Francisco near Point Reyes, is estimated to have measured 8.3 on the Richter scale (although that system of rating quake magnitude had not yet been invented), a magnitude still unmatched in California temblor history. For 47 seconds, streets buckled and buildings toppled. When the shaking stopped, the city's infrastructure and government buildings, including City Hall, lay in ruins.

The greatest damage, however, came from the ensuing fires, ignited by toppling chimneys and fueled by fractured gas mains and the wooden structures the quake had reduced to kindling. One such fire, known as the 'ham and eggs fire,' began as a woman prepared breakfast on a damaged stove in her home a few blocks west of City Hall. Because her neighbors' houses had become tinderboxes, a spark carried off by a slight breeze soon set the entire neighborhood around Civic Center ablaze. Broken water mains left the fire department unable to douse the flames. Under the direction of General Frederick Funston, firebreaks were created by dynamiting entire city blocks. But rather than contain the conflagration, the dynamiting set off several new fires. Many citizens took refuge on Potrero Hill, to the south, and watched their city go up in columns of smoke. When it was all over, after three days and two nights, 4½ sq miles of the city – from Van Ness Ave to the waterfront and along Dolores St – lay in a smoldering black heap.

Some 3000 people died in the disaster. To offer temporary refuge for the more than 100,000 left homeless, tent cities were established in parks and on the burnt-out lot of Charles Crocker's Nob Hill estate. Many more people, taking advantage of the free rail transit offered to quake victims, left San Francisco for good. Despite relief efforts, the city became a hotbed for disease. Bubonic plague broke out, and although it never reached epidemic proportions – 77 deaths from the plague were reported – authorities carried out an intensive rat hunt that lasted three years.

The city reconstructed itself at an astounding pace, largely ignoring Burnham's elaborate designs. Each day saw the completion of 15 more buildings – characterized, some felt, by an austere uniformity – along streets that still adhered to the old grid pattern. Knowing that its reemergence would coincide with the completion of the Panama Canal, San Francisco campaigned successfully to be the site of the 1915 Panama-Pacific International Exposition.

Geary and Kearny Sts just weeks before the 1906 quake

COURTESY OF THE BANCROFT LIBRARY

Market and New Montgomery Sts after the quake

The Depression & WWII

The Great Depression of the 1930s brought hardship and strife to San Francisco. Striking longshoremen shut down the waterfront for two months in 1934. Attempting to break the strike on July 5 – a date now known as 'Bloody Thursday' – police cracked down on the strikers. When two longshoremen were killed in the violence, laborers throughout the Bay Area went on strike, bringing the local economy to a halt for three days.

As it did in other cities during the Great Depression, the federal government initiated large-scale public-works projects in San Francisco to create jobs. And the Bay Area certainly got its money's worth: the Oakland–San Francisco Bay Bridge, completed in 1936, and the Golden Gate Bridge, finished the following year, ensured that San Francisco's growth would not be stemmed by the limits of ferry trafficking. Both bridges stand as apt symbols of the city.

The distant thunder of WWI had had little impact on San Francisco, but WWII was a different story. The Bay Area was a major launching point for military operations in the Pacific, and shipyards sprang up around the bay. The Kaiser Shipyard in Richmond employed more than 100,000 people; the workers at Marinship of Sausalito turned out 93 ships during the war. This and other wartime industries attracted huge numbers of workers to the Bay Area, including a sizable number of blacks, most of whom settled in Oakland (see the Oakland section in the Excursions chapter).

It was during WWII and its aftermath that a visible gay community began to form in San Francisco. The armed forces had conducted purges of gay servicemen and servicewomen, dishonorably discharging scores of them, and because the naval fleets were arriving and departing from San Francisco, it was here that these people found themselves. Many stayed, forming the foundation of what would later become the world's largest and strongest gay community.

The city's population jumped by nearly 140,000 during the war years, reaching its highest level ever (more than 775,000) by the early 1950s.

A City in Transition

The postwar years proved to be a time of transition. The city's bridges had already spelled the end for the bay's ferry services, which had transported 50 million passengers a year from points around the bay to San Francisco's Ferry Building. The bridges made commuting more attractive than living in the city to a great many middle-class families, thus setting the stage for the phenomenon of 'white flight' in the 1950s. Many of the city's central neighborhoods – including much of the Western Addition – were deserted by whites making decent wages and became slums as the blacks who still lived there lost their wartime jobs.

By the late '50s, the city's piers, which still sprocket out from the crescent-shaped waterfront, had become outdated. The old break-bulk method of cargoing was giving way to higher-volume and labor-saving container shipping, which required more space for storage than was available around San Francisco's heavily developed downtown district. The shipyards of West Oakland were better suited to modern trade, and as shipping shifted across the bay, San Francisco's life as a port city drew to a close. As if to hasten that end, the Embarcadero Freeway was constructed, symbolically cutting the waterfront off from the rest of the city.

The hallmarks of postwar America – conformity, conservatism, and a growing obsession with security – were primarily evidenced in the suburbs around San Francisco. In the city itself, quite a different trend emerged. Following the decline in population and standard of living, rents dropped in highly livable neighborhoods such as North Beach and the Haight, and bohemian poets, novelists, and artists started to move in. The writers who converged on San Francisco – most notably transplanted East Coasters Jack Kerouac and Allen Ginsberg – spearheaded an influential social and literary movement that came to be known as the Beat Generation.

In contrast to the values of mainstream white America, Kerouac and Ginsberg promoted a life unbound by convention and motivated by spontaneous creativity rather than greed or ambition. They frequently smoked marijuana and experimented with peyote and mescaline, and Ginsberg and others were openly gay. Their work, notably Kerouac's iconoclastic novel *On the Road* and Ginsberg's controversial poem 'Howl,' constituted a watershed in American literature; along with poets Kenneth Rexroth and Lawrence Ferlinghetti, they put San Francisco on the literary map.

But the Beats did not settle permanently in San Francisco. Of the core group of poets, only Ferlinghetti established himself as a longtime resident of the city.

For many years, the influence of the Beats lingered in San Francisco like the bouquet of a cheap Chianti. The scenesters and bongo players who followed the poets to the city were dubbed 'beatniks,' which was meant as a put-down. They converted ennui into street theater along the avenues of North Beach, turning the neighborhood, with all its cafés and bars, into America's Left Bank. Though few of these eccentrics had ever published poetry, the national media took notice. Very quickly San Francisco became known worldwide as a tolerant, creative city. That reputation lives on, and the city continues to attract its share of people living alternative lifestyles. (For more on the Beats, see the Literature section of this chapter; also see North Beach in Things to See & Do.)

Drugs & Revolution

The bipolar forces of the 1960s were probably more evident in San Francisco than anywhere else in the US. In the months leading up to the psychedelic decade, revolution and tradition converged on the city. The Beats and baseball, the 'national pastime,' came to San Francisco almost simultaneously – the Giants and their Hall of Fame slugger Willie Mays moved to San Francisco from New York in 1958. And at the same time that big business was exerting its control over City Hall – instigating the high-rise development that would Manhattanize San Francisco's Financial District – a crystalline compound called lysergic acid diethylamide – that is, LSD or 'acid' – began hitting the streets up in the Haight. By the middle of the 1960s, baby boomers were tripping in San Francisco on a regular basis, and soon 'free love' and 'flower power' were a way of life in the neighborhood. In January 1967, 20,000 'hippies' – the term was originally a put-down coined by beatniks who didn't dig these younger hipsters – congregated in Golden Gate Park for a free concert kicking off the 'Summer of Love,' making San Francisco ground zero for yet another countercultural scene.

Across the bay, however, peace and love were not the order of the day. While hippies in the Haight were dropping out, the Berkeley revolutionaries were leading the worldwide student upheavals of the late '60s, slugging it out with the cops and the university administration over civil rights. In Oakland, Huey Newton and Bobby Seale founded the Black Panther Party for Self-Defense, the most militant of the groups involved in the black-power movement of that era. (For more '60s history, see the Haight section of Things to See & Do.)

Gay Pride

Though in most people's minds the '60s belonged to student protesters and hippies, the decade was also significant for the gay community. In the early 1950s, a chapter of the Los Angeles–based Mattachine Society, the first serious homosexual rights organization in the US, opened in San Francisco, and in 1955 the Daughters of Bilitis, the nation's first lesbian organization, was founded here. These were the beginnings of what was known as the homophile movement, a precursor to the modern gay rights movement.

In San Francisco, gay issues took the political stage in 1959, when mayoral candidate Russ Wolden accused incumbent mayor George Christopher of turning San Francisco into 'the national headquarters of the organized homosexuals in the United States.' Christopher was reelected, but he wasn't about to foster the reputation of being soft on queers. Instead he initiated a massive police crackdown on gay cruising areas. The raids resulted in a public blacklist of gay citizens.

Wolden's negative campaign was a backhanded acknowledgment that gays were becoming a significant force in the city, and it probably helped coalesce the political movement that followed. When, in 1961, a female impersonator named José Sarria ran for the San Francisco Board of Supervisors, he received 5600 votes. The gay voting block had arrived.

But police harassment continued. In 1965, a dance sponsored by the Council on Religion and the Homosexual was raided by the police, and everyone in attendance was arrested and photographed. The media denounced the behavior of the police, helping to turn around the city's perception of its gay community. The crackdown on gay bars stopped, and a gay representative was appointed to sit on the police community-relations board.

In 1964, a *Life* magazine article featured a photo essay on San Francisco that labeled the city the 'gay capital' of the US. For gays, the growing recognition spearheaded a decade of gay rights protests. In 1969, the Stonewall Riots took place in New York's Greenwich Village, where random police raids on gay bars were still commonplace. That event is widely considered to be the spark of the modern gay rights movement, but San Francisco's gay community by that time had already enjoyed considerable success rebuffing police harassment through effective political organizing. The 1970s would be the banner decade for the gay community nationwide, especially in San Francisco.

Decade of Turmoil

The turbulence of the late '60s carried over into the 1970s, which were a decade-long bad trip in San Francisco. For many people, Charles Manson, a former resident of the Haight-Ashbury who ritualistically murdered two women in Southern California in 1969, epitomized how the '60s had gone wrong. Local newspapers would feature disturbing headlines for years. A serial killer calling himself the Zodiac corresponded regularly with the local newspapers and gripped the Bay Area in a panic for most of the decade. He murdered at least 50 people and was never caught. In 1974, Patty Hearst, granddaughter of newspaper magnate William Randolph Hearst, was kidnapped by the Symbionese Liberation Army (SLA), who held her captive in a San Francisco studio apartment. One of the SLA's demands was met by the Hearst papers, which begrudgingly published the organization's absurd propaganda (one slogan was 'Crush the fascist insect'). In an odd twist, Patty joined her captives' ranks and participated in the armed robbery of a Sunset District bank.

The dementia of the '70s came to a head in November 1978. On November 18, a San Francisco–based cult called the People's Temple, led by the Reverend Jim Jones, committed the largest mass suicide in modern times. More than 900 followers drank Kool-Aid laced with cyanide at Jonestown, the cult's South American commune. In his last testimonial, Jones said the suicide was a statement 'protesting the conditions of an inhumane world.' As if to underscore Jones' point, nine days later Dan White, a former member of the San Francisco Board of Supervisors, entered City Hall and shot Mayor George Moscone and gay supervisor Harvey Milk to death. White, whose lawyers contrived the notorious 'Twinkie defense,' in which they said the Twinkies he had eaten earlier that day had given him a sugar high he couldn't control, was convicted of manslaughter rather than murder and served a soft jail sentence for his crime. On the night of White's conviction, May 21, 1979 – now known as 'White Night' – gays outraged over the lenient verdict rioted around City Hall, causing more than $1 million in damage to public property.

The Yuppies & other Plagues

Throughout the 1980s, the get-rich-quick delirium of Reaganomics helped boost the city's restaurant industry, and San Francisco established itself as an internationally recognized culinary force. In neighborhoods such as the Marina, young urban professionals, derisively called 'yuppies,' revived the notion that urban living was something to aspire to, rather than avoid. Although recession at decade's end let the air out of the economic balloon, the city was once again considered a desirable place to live by the middle class.

But yuppie delirium alone did not define the 1980s. During the decade, San Francisco was hit by plagues approaching biblical proportions. The first cases of AIDS – at the time known as GRID, Gay-Related Immune Deficiency – were reported in 1981. By the end of the 1980s, AIDS had claimed thousands of lives, and it continues to evade researchers searching for a cure. A more startling, but shorter-lived catastrophe came at 5:04pm on October 17, 1989. The Loma Prieta earthquake measured 7.1 on the Richter scale, and its damage was far-reaching. A section of the upper level of the Bay Bridge slumped down to the lower deck, and fires fed by fractured gas mains burned down many homes in the affluent Marina District. The quake's worst disaster was the collapse of a double-decker section of I-880 in Oakland, which killed 42 people. In all, 67 people died in the earthquake.

MONICA J MEARES

Golden Gate Park's AIDS Memorial Grove

The death toll might have been worse were it not for that evening's World Series game between the National League's San Francisco Giants and the American League's Oakland A's. When the quake struck, a large proportion of the Bay Area's population was at home watching the third game of the series on TV, greatly reducing rush-hour traffic.

Invasion of the Dot-Coms

The Reaganomics recession lasted longer locally than in other parts of the nation. In the early '90s, the Clinton administration pulled the plug on federal military spending, much of which had been directed to Bay Area technology firms and military base contractors. But San Francisco and nearby Silicon Valley, 50 miles to the south, were primed to ride the crest of the multimedia wave that would carry the stock market to unprecedented heights.

What followed was a period of prosperity not seen since the days of the Comstock Lode, and consumer giddiness perhaps not seen ever before. While Silicon Valley remained the epicenter of the communications revolution, San Francisco's South of Market area was invaded by internet start-up firms that could generate absurd amounts of investment capital on the flimsiest of business plans. (At least one start-up was launched with *no* stated purpose, other than to 'be flexible' to market needs.) And, in a reversal of its traditional role, San Francisco became the industry's bedroom community, as thousands of dot-commers making their fortunes down the Peninsula showed a preference for the big-city lifestyle.

While some surfed the multimedia wave, others were ground under by the real estate glacier that tore through the city. Rents, much higher than the national average to begin with, doubled, then tripled and quadrupled in just a few months, and many tenants were forced out of the city as their homes were sold from under them. Neighborhoods metamorphosed as longtime residents and established businesses lost leases.

The dot-com boom was destined to go bust, and shortly after the turn of the millennium the industry indeed took an awkward swan dive (the water level turned out to be much higher than anticipated) – but not before billions of dollars had changed hands.

Brown's Town

A sizable portion of the dot-com money ultimately ended up in the pockets of real estate speculators and developers, many of whom were, suspiciously, friends of the city's mayor, Willie Brown. When Brown took office in 1995, he did so with a vague but unmistakable mandate to stir things up in a city long frustrated by ineffective leadership. When the city voted Brown in, it also passed new legislation granting the mayor unprecedented power. Voters expected to see an end to bureaucratic gridlock, and that's pretty much what they got. However, most were sadly disappointed with the results.

Wheelin' and dealin' Willie Brown

Brown, who had served as Speaker in the California State Assembly prior to his run for mayor, was already well known for his insider deal-making skills and back-room politics, and he quickly established a political machine in San Francisco. He put friends on the city payroll and allegedly exchanged favors with the city's power-brokers and developers. The city skyline, especially South of Market, underwent a noticeable transformation as Brown's machine smoothed the way for builders. A 1999 FBI probe revealed that many of these developers and their lobbyists had direct ties to Brown.

The central city is indeed *looking* better than it has in many decades. Financial District streets, always plagued by potholes, have been resurfaced; the Yerba Buena Gardens area, after three decades of grindingly slow progress, is finally starting to look cohesive; the airport is undergoing badly needed expansion; and the Mission Bay area, around the new baseball stadium, is becoming a vital part of the city after a generation of neglect.

Some of these improvements, of course, are the result of Brown's behind-the-scenes wheeling and dealing. But too much change too fast is not what San Franciscans had hoped for. Many seemingly solvable issues, like the flagging performance of the city's bus system, continue to exasperate citizens. And, in San Francisco's increasingly monoclass society, the poor, the homeless and other unfortunates are feeling less represented than before.

Repeatedly over the last 150 years, the city has shown a tendency to transform itself dramatically. And, in an ongoing tug of war, mutually opposed forces – vital cultural waves and cold-hearted economic surges – have by turns defined the city. Boom periods have always drawn get-rich-quick hoards, and in recessions the city tends to cultivate its creative side. Communities come and go. That, like it or not, is America for you.

CLIMATE

San Francisco is famous for its summer fog, which can bring the temperature down in a hurry and make tourists' knees shake in their short pants. Although recent summers in the city haven't been as chilly as the notorious 'coldest winters' that Mark Twain ever spent, summers in San Francisco are still mild at best. Inland summer heat draws the fog in from the sea, and as it rolls across the city the temperature plummets and the wind picks up. In winter, when the contrast between land and sea temperatures is less extreme, the fog is less frequent, the temperatures are more stable, and the weather is more reliable.

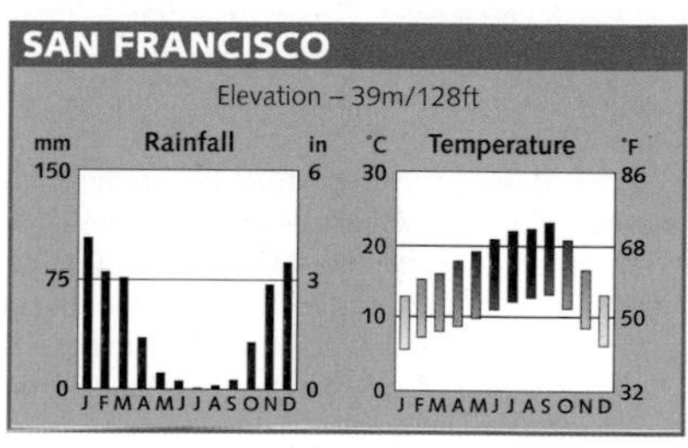

But the city does have its microclimates, many of them nestled in the protective cover of its hills. A well-placed hill can neatly redirect the fog as it rolls across the city, and one area may consistently be sunny and fog-free while the next is in the mist. Basically, the area from Twin Peaks to the ocean gets most of the fog, while the bay side of the city stays sunny but still gets windy.

You can expect afternoon temperatures to range between 55° and 70°F most of the year, with highs above 80°F occurring unpredictably from spring through fall. San Francisco receives the most rain from December to March; it gets particularly wet during 'El Niño' years, which occur every three to five years (the last occurrence being 1997–98).

To be prepared for any kind of weather, dress in layers and never venture out without a sweatshirt – or you'll probably end up buying one.

GEOGRAPHY

At 49 sq miles, San Francisco is the second smallest major city in the US – and that's

Earthquakes

Earthquakes are the tangible evidence of what sounds like a dry subject: plate tectonics. The earth's crust is made up of a number of large plates that are frequently shifting in relation to one another. When one plate rubs up against another, the shift is not a gradual or gentle one, and the results are often disastrous for those of us on the surface. San Francisco is particularly susceptible to occasional shakes because it straddles the San Andreas Fault, which divides the Eastern Pacific and North American plates. Half the Bay Area is on its way north to Alaska, while the other half isn't.

Earthquakes are measured on the Richter scale, which records the total amount of energy released in a quake. Developed in 1935, it's a logarithmic scale, which means that each step up the scale is 10 times as powerful as the last. (The scale runs from 0 through 9.) A magnitude 5 earthquake is 10 times as powerful as a magnitude 4. The 1906 quake measured approximately 8.3, the 1989 quake 7.1. Geologists estimate that over millions of years California has sustained tens of thousands of quakes of a magnitude equal to the one that struck in 1906, suggesting that the impending 'big one' that makes many San Franciscans so nervous will come not just once but many times.

The ground on which structures are built has a lot to do with how well they hold up under such pressure. In an earthquake zone, the best foundation is bedrock. The 1989 quake damaged the Oakland side of the Bay Bridge, which was built on squishy bay-bottom mud, but the San Francisco side, strung between bedrock foundations on San Francisco and Yerba Buena Island, sustained no major damage. In the city itself, much of the underlying strata consists of landfill and sand. Neighborhoods such as the Marina, built on reclaimed wetlands, do not hold up nearly as well as do inland areas such as Nob Hill.

With the constant threat of earthquakes, it is essential that buildings be of sound construction, and an alarming number of San Francisco's older structures are not. Around town you are likely to run across a sign in the doorway of an old apartment building announcing that the building is constructed of unreinforced concrete or brick, making it vulnerable to collapse in the event of an earthquake. Gradually, these weaker buildings are being augmented with internal and external reinforcements, but other facets of the city's infrastructure, such as streets, sidewalks, and gas and water lines, remain vulnerable. Modern buildings – including all skyscrapers – are constructed with steel-reinforced concrete, which combines strength with flexibility and is supposed to absorb the shock of a major quake.

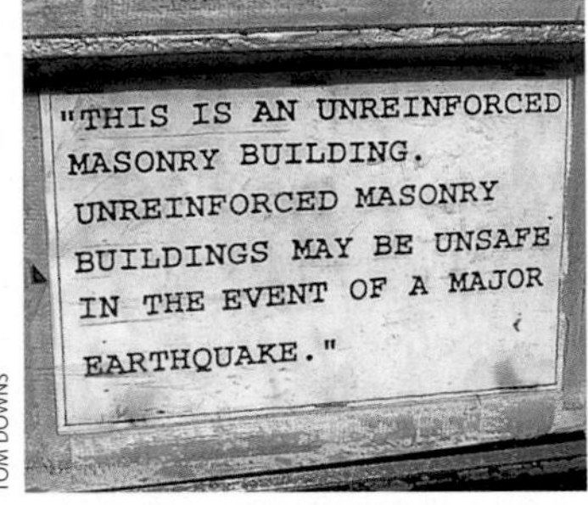

TOM DOWNS

only if Buffalo, NY, is included in the 'major city' category. By virtue of its location at the northern tip of a peninsula between San Francisco Bay and the Pacific Ocean, its shape and topography are determined by hills and water. The city has 43 hills, the highest being Mt Davidson, 938 feet above sea level.

ECOLOGY & ENVIRONMENT

San Franciscans are generally sympathetic to environmental concerns, and although the city is not one of the country's major culprits when it comes to toxic-waste production, the San Francisco Commission on the Environment in 1997 drafted a 177-page 'Sustainability Plan' calling for citywide ecological improvements. In strong, intelligent terms, the plan outlines objectives for improving the quality of the city's air and water and reducing traffic and solid waste. Endorsed by the Board of Supervisors, the plan advances the idea that for a sustainable future, San Francisco will need to eliminate automobile traffic – a concept that many of the city's bike riders have been promoting for years. (It isn't likely to happen anytime soon.)

San Francisco already has one of the state's most successful curbside recycling programs, but at 30% participation, there's clearly room for improvement. It is hoped that in the future compost waste will be separated out for reuse much in the manner that paper, glass, and plastic are now.

San Francisco Bay, part of the West Coast's largest estuary, supports a rich ecosystem that has been battered over the years by urbanization and human use of the waterway – shipping, recreational boating, fishing, and bay-side farming and industry all have taken their toll. Much of the city's storm-water runoff goes directly into the bay – you'll notice stenciled warnings on city sidewalks advising not to pour pollutants down the gutter. As the Bay Area's population continues to grow at an astounding rate, added measures will be needed to protect the region's signature natural feature.

GOVERNMENT & POLITICS

The City and County of San Francisco function as a single unit, and in fact they cover roughly the same terrain. The city government consists of a mayor and an 11-member Board of Supervisors. Like the mayor, the supervisors serve four-year terms and are limited to two terms.

Although the city has its conservative pockets, San Francisco tends to vote overwhelmingly Democratic, and it is not uncommon for the mayor and all 11 supervisors to be affiliated with the Democratic Party. The Board of Supervisors otherwise tends to reflect the city's diverse population, with women, gays and lesbians, Chinese, Latinos, and African Americans represented pretty equally, though no system is in place to ensure such representation. In November 2000, when elections by district were put into effect, diversity on the board seemed secure. The startling result of that election, though, was the emergence of several new and independent supervisors who were expected to diminish the influence of Mayor Willie Brown.

RICK GERHARTER

City Hall

ECONOMY

San Francisco remains the center of the Bay Area's economy, but in recent decades successful new industries have spawned hubs in the South Bay and inland counties. In a reversal of the traditional suburb-to-metropolis commute, many San Franciscans now commute to jobs outside the city, in industrial centers such as Silicon Valley.

The city's oldest and most influential companies are rooted in industries such as finance, insurance, and real estate. Banking has occupied a large sector of the city's economy since the gold rush. Montgomery St, which was originally designed for financial institutions wanting out of the young town's rowdier quarters, is still known as the Wall St of the West.

In the 1990s, the fast-growing multimedia industry dominated the local economy, with a profusion of start-up companies setting up shop in SoMa, Potrero Hill, and the Mission District. Many fortunes were won and lost within a few short years – with stock market traders and real estate investors taking a generous share of the winnings.

With some 16.4 million visitors spending around $12 billion annually, tourism accounts for nearly half the city's economy. Although many of those visitors come for conventions and business, San Francisco is consistently rated among the top vacation destinations in the US.

POPULATION & PEOPLE

In the latter half of the 20th century, San Francisco's population held steady at more than 700,000. During the same decades, however, the city's population shifted from white homogeneity (89% white in 1950) toward a diversity that challenges the ethnic 'mosaics' of New York and Los Angeles, albeit on a smaller scale. Statistics from the 2000 census suggest that whites make up almost 50% of the population (that category including large numbers of Irish and Italians, as well as Jews and recent immigrants from Russia), Asians nearly 31% (mostly Chinese, joined by smaller numbers of Japanese, Filipinos, and Vietnamese), and Latinos 14% (mostly Mexicans and Central Americans).

Unlike Oakland, San Francisco has never been home to a large community of blacks, who make up less than 8%. Native Americans, who left the city in droves after the establishment of Mission Dolores (those who remained were all but wiped out by disease), now maintain a possibly greater number than they did prior to the Spanish conquest, even though they compose a barely perceptible 0.4% of San Francisco's population.

ARTS

The Bay Area is culture conscious: a lot of books get written and read here, the proliferation of galleries around the city shows an avid interest in art, and the city's symphony, opera, and ballet are world class.

Literature

It's hardly surprising to learn how much has been written about the Bay Area, given its many excellent bookstores, its reputation as an important US publishing center, and its place in American history as the spawning ground of some significant social and literary movements. To visit some notable sites in the area's literary history, grab a copy of *The Literary World of San Francisco and Its Environs,* by Don Herron, which shows you where many of the following writers lived and worked, as well as the places they wrote about.

GOLD RUSH TO THE 1920s The colorful mining era of the 1850s and '60s attracted writers to chronicle San Francisco's frontier history. The ever-popular Mark Twain made his journalistic debut in the Bay Area, reporting on pioneering life at the Comstock Lode silver mines. His book *Roughing It,* published in 1872, covered his westward stagecoach journey and the mining days.

Bret Harte, a contemporary of Twain's (and some say the editor of 'Jim Smiley and His Jumping Frog,' Twain's first published short story), was also one of the most popular writers of the era. The distinctly Western flavor of Harte's work in stories such as 'The Luck of Roaring Camp' and 'The Outcasts of Poker Flat' – both published in the *Overland Monthly,* the celebrated magazine Harte edited – gave rise to the 'local color' movement, putting the Pacific Coast on the map with a bona fide regional identity.

Best known today for his *Devil's Dictionary,* Ambrose Bierce was the world's first newspaper columnist. Penning the 'Prattles' column in the *Sunday Examiner,* he earned the nickname 'Bitter Bierce' for his rapier-like wit and unfailing eye for controversy.

Scottish-born Robert Louis Stevenson lived briefly in Monterey and San Francisco and honeymooned by an abandoned silver mine in nearby Calistoga. This stay led to his 1872 book *The Silverado Squatters.*

While Stevenson, Bierce, and Twain were imports, professional hell-raiser Jack London was San Francisco born and Oakland bred. In the early 20th century, London turned out a massive volume of writings, including the immensely popular novel *The Call of the Wild* and his own – suitably fictionalized –

story under the title *Martin Eden.* Another Oakland-raised author, Gertrude Stein, recalls her time there in *The Making of Americans.*

THE CRIME WRITERS San Francisco owes its strong tradition in crime writing to one author: Dashiell Hammett. Hammett, who briefly worked for the San Francisco branch of the Pinkerton National Detective Agency, is credited with fathering the modern American detective novel. Sam Spade, hero of Hammett's 1930 *Maltese Falcon,* remains the ultimate American private eye: an unsentimental character in a cutthroat world. Summertime walking tours that highlight Hammett sites around Union Square and the Tenderloin often attract contemporary mystery writers, who come to pay their respects.

Charles Willeford, another pulp writer, rented a furnished room on Powell St in the early '50s. Willeford's *High Priest of California* and *Pickup* portray the hopeless and sometimes amusing daily vagaries of San Francisco lowlifes in the middle of the 1900s.

THE SAN FRANCISCO RENAISSANCE & THE BEATS Poet Kenneth Rexroth began his Bay Area tenure of literary prominence in 1940 with his first collection, *In What Hour.* Also an influential critic, Rexroth was at the center of a fledgling poetry scene that called itself the San Francisco Renaissance, which evolved into the Beat scene after Jack Kerouac and Allen Ginsberg arrived from New York. Michael McClure – an original member of Rexroth's San Francisco Renaissance and another of the earliest Beats – is famed for his scandalous 1965 play *The Beard.* Other San Francisco poets of the era are Philip Whalen *(On Bear's Head),* Philip Lamantia, Gary Snyder *(Myths and Texts),* Lawrence Ferlinghetti *(A Coney Island of the Mind),* Joanne Kyger *(The Tapestry & the Web),* and Peter Orlovsky *(Clean Asshole Poems and Smiling Vegetable Songs).* Rexroth preferred to distance himself from the Beats, but the rest of these poets are now commonly identified with them.

The Beats pioneered the concepts of jazz poetry and bop prose, styles of writing that relied heavily on spontaneity (much of it fueled by mescaline, Benzedrine, and booze). Kerouac's *On the Road* (1957), which he wrote in New York and polished in San Francisco, became the bible for a generation of disaffected American youth, and Ginsberg's performance of 'Howl' at a now legendary reading at the Six Gallery on Fillmore St in 1955 is widely considered the signifying moment of the Beat era. Kerouac also wrote the lovely poem 'San Francisco Blues,' about a period during which he lived

Literary Streets of San Francisco

In January 1988, the San Francisco Board of Supervisors approved poet Lawrence Ferlinghetti's proposal to rename 12 city streets in honor of famous artistic figures from the city's past. All but two were writers. The signs were unveiled in North Beach outside Ferlinghetti's City Lights Bookstore, at the corner of Columbus Ave and what that day became Jack Kerouac Alley. The 11 other honorees were writers Mark Twain, Jack London, Richard Henry Dana, Dashiell Hammett, William Saroyan, Frank Norris, Ambrose Bierce, Bob Kaufman, and Kenneth Rexroth; dancer Isadora Duncan; and sculptor Beniamino Bufano. Ferlinghetti himself has since been honored with a small alley, Via Ferlinghetti, in North Beach.

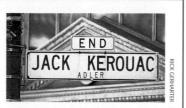

RICK GERHARTER

on the city's skid row, and his reading of the poem can still be heard on a recording from the early 1960s. His contemporary Bob Kaufman is best known for *Solitudes Crowded with Loneliness,* which includes his poems honoring musicians Charles Mingus and Ray Charles.

THE '60s Ken Kesey's novel *One Flew Over the Cuckoo's Nest* (1962) pits a freethinker against stifling authority. For this, his most popular book, Kesey drew on his own experiences at a Bay Area psychiatric ward.

Richard Brautigan's curious novels haven't aged too well, but they had a major cult following in their time. *Trout Fishing in America* (1967) is one of the best of them. East Bay writer Philip K Dick is chiefly remembered for his science fiction, notably *Do Androids Dream of Electric Sheep?* (1968), which became the classic sci-fi film *Blade Runner.* Dick's *Man in the High Castle* (1962) envisions a Japanese-dominated San Francisco after Japan and Germany have won WWII and divided the US between them. Frank Herbert, author of *Dune,* was also a local during these years, as was Thomas Pynchon, whose *Crying of Lot 49* (1966) takes place in '60s Berkeley. Josephine Miles, a respected poet and critic and the author of *Civil Poems* (1966), taught at the University of California, Berkeley from 1940 to 1985.

CONTEMPORARY WRITERS No writer watched San Francisco's gay fraternity emerge from the closet with clearer vision than Armistead Maupin. His 'Tales of the City' series, which in 1979 began as a newspaper serial, became a smash-hit collection of literary soap operas, light as a feather but a great-to-read romp. The late Randy Shilts, author of *And the Band Played On* (1987), a moving account of the early years of AIDS awareness, also wrote for the *San Francisco Chronicle* – where 'Tales of the City' got its start – and the *Examiner*.

Today, the San Francisco literary community is stronger than ever, with many prominent writers making their homes here, including Alice Walker, Pulitzer Prize–winning author of *The Color Purple* (1988); Chilean novelist Isabel Allende, author of *The House of the Spirits* (1985); Dorothy Allison, whose novel *Bastard Out of Carolina* (1992) won the National Book Award; and romance novelist Danielle Steel, who bought one of sugar baron Adolph Spreckels' mansions in 1990. Michelle Tea's widely acclaimed *Valencia* is a blunt, funny look inside the Mission's 20-something lesbian community in the '90s.

The area's vital Asian community has yielded an impressive lineup of writers. Amy Tan's best-selling *The Joy Luck Club* (1989) looks back on the lives of four Chinese women and their American-born daughters. Another Chinese American, Maxine Hong Kingston, wrote the National Book Critics' Circle Award–winning *The Woman Warrior: Memoir of a Girlhood among Ghosts* (1976), a lyrical account of a Chinatown childhood. *Bone* (1993), by San Francisco native Fae Myenne Ng, is an intricate tour of life in Chinatown.

Local favorite Anne Lamott sets her poignant and witty novels in Marin County;

Author and former Mission District resident Michelle Tea

her autobiographical *Operating Instructions* (1993), written in diary form, recounts the joys and horrors of motherhood. Postmodernist author Kathy Acker *(Blood and Guts in High School,* 1989), lived in San Francisco and taught at the Art Institute before her death in 1997 from cancer.

The disturbed literary progeny of the likes of Nelson Algren and Hubert Selby Jr, is Seth Morgan, whose *Homeboy* (1990) is a gritty ride through the city's underworld.

There's an impressive group of contemporary poets in the Bay Area as well. Former US poet laureate Robert Hass, whose works include *Human Wishes* (1990), is a professor at the University of California's Berkeley campus. Czech Nobel laureate Czeslaw Milosz also teaches at Berkeley, and the two have teamed up on translations of Milosz's poetry, which includes *The Witness of Poetry* (1983).

Painting

The Bay Area's small Native American population was disappearing even before the Spanish and Mexican eras ended. Nevertheless, traces of their artwork survive, blended with Spanish colonial design in murals on the walls and ceilings of mission churches.

Painters, inspired by the state's dramatic scenery and financed by San Francisco's nouveau riche art collectors, arrived in San Francisco soon after the gold rush. The San Francisco Art Institute and the MH de Young Memorial Museum were both in operation before the beginning of the 20th century, and after the 1906 earthquake artists dispossessed by the disaster moved south to establish Carmel as an artists' colony, a role it continues to play in a rather exclusive fashion.

Early in the century, a California version of the impressionist plein air movement celebrated the state's natural scenery and clear light. The social realist movement of the 1930s had a major impact on San Francisco, and an original work by Diego Rivera, a major proponent of the style, graces the Diego Rivera Gallery at the Art Institute. The Depression-era Work Projects Administration (WPA) sponsored other painters who worked in the mural tradition, and you'll find fine examples of it at Coit Tower and in the Rincon Annex Post Office, near the Embarcadero.

In the late 1950s and early '60s, local painters were among the first to reject the orthodoxy of abstract expressionism in favor of a loose, painterly, representational art known as Bay Area figurative painting. Its chief practitioners were Richard Diebenkorn, David Park, and Elmer Bischoff. The San Francisco Museum of Modern Art (SFMOMA) is a worthy home for the city's collection of figurative painting, and across the bay the Oakland Museum of California has a permanent exhibition featuring most of the area's styles and movements (see the Excursions chapter).

Photography

Bay Area photographers played an important role in elevating photography to an art form, particularly San Francisco native Ansel Adams, whose landscape photographs from the 1940s heightened the world's appreciation of some of California's natural wonders, such as Yosemite. Adams was also a prolific writer, and his books and work have had a profound influence on photographers worldwide. Dorothea Lange, who for many years was based in San Francisco, brilliantly photographed Californians coping with hardship. Her photo 'Migrant Mother, Nipoma, California, 1935' is the most indelible image of the Great Depression, and her photos of Japanese Americans being forced to leave their San Francisco homes during the WWII internment cast a tragic light on that dark moment in US history.

Architecture

The Bay Area is architecturally diverse, with buildings reflecting the region's Spanish and Mexican heritage, its strong links with Asia, and its own homegrown style. The mission and presidio built by the Spanish were San Francisco's first 'permanent' structures, and some of these adobe (mud brick) buildings still stand in the city and elsewhere in California.

Public Art in the City

Many of San Francisco's most prominent and important works of art are public murals, mosaics, sculpture, and graffiti adorning walls, indoors and out, throughout the city. In many instances, they can be viewed free of charge.

RICK GERHARTER

Diego Rivera mural at the Art Institute

In the 1930s, Mexican artist Diego Rivera painted several murals in San Francisco. The most accessible one is at the **Diego Rivera Gallery**, on the Art Institute campus in Russian Hill. Another is in the **City Club**, upstairs from the Pacific Stock Exchange at 155 Sansome St. This building is not open to the public; to see the mural you have to make a reservation for a tour of the Stock Exchange (☎ 415-285-0495), which takes place the first Wednesday of every month at 3pm and costs $5. A third Rivera mural is at the Diego Rivera Theater at **City College** (closed to the public during the school's summer break), in the southwestern Ingleside neighborhood.

San Francisco has some stellar examples of WPA art from the 1930s and '40s, many of them easy to see. The main level of **Coit Tower**, free and open to the public, is embellished with a series of frescoes that constituted the first WPA mural project nationwide (and provided 25 local artists with regular work and pay at a time when that was unheard of). Reflecting their era, many of the frescoes convey strong socially conscious messages, particularly one by John Langely Howard called *Social Revolution*. When completed in 1934, the project sparked instant controversy. Fearing the murals would heighten social unrest as the tempestuous political climate of the period turned violent, the city's art commission actually closed Coit Tower for awhile.

On the western edge of Golden Gate Park, the **Beach Chalet** features frescoes of a very different temperament. Painted in 1936 by French-born artist Lucien Labaudt, they present a series of leisurely San Francisco scenes. Although some of the murals portray people at work, none of the strife of the Coit Tower murals is evident here. Still, Labaudt's simple, realistic style of painting is very much in the spirit of WPA art.

In the late 1970s, the **Rincon Annex Post Office** was saved from demolition just to

RICK GERHARTER

Maritime Museum

Public Art in the City

preserve the exceptional murals in its lobby. These same murals, completed in 1948 by Russian-born artist Anton Refregier, had been threatened once before. They trace California history in straightforward images, and in the 1950s reactionary pro-McCarthy politicians wanted them destroyed for being too 'communistic' in tone.

RICHARD I'ANSON

The Mission's Balmy Alley

The **Maritime Museum**, near Ghirardelli Square, contains one of the city's most diverse collections of public artwork. Departing significantly from the realism of traditional public art, the building's extravagant beauty begins with the flowing carvings by African American artist Sargent Johnson on the green slate above the front entrance. Johnson, a prolific and exceptionally versatile artist, also completed the beautifully abstract fish mosaic on the building's back veranda. That mosaic is joined by two smoothly polished Beniamino Bufano sculptures of a seal and a toad. The centerpiece of the building, however, is Hilaire Hiler's abstract floor-to-ceiling foyer mural of a highly imaginative underwater scene that includes the lost continent of Atlantis.

The Mission District mural movement began in the 1960s and is still going strong. Most murals in the neighborhood are community efforts on outer walls of buildings, fully visible to the public. Early and contemporary murals, many of which reflect Latino political activism over the past 30 years, line the back fences and garage doors of **Balmy Alley**, off 24th St between Treat Ave and Harrison St. *Maestrapeace,* a collaboration by seven women painters, spectacularly tattoos the entire facade of the **Women's Building**, on 18th St between Valencia and Guerrero Sts; the intensely colorful building is a striking sight to behold. **Clarion Alley**, between Mission and Valencia Sts, is lined by the work of diverse artists exhibiting a variety of individual styles that frequently depart from traditional mural subjects.

FRANK CARTER

Mural on the Women's Building

In recent years, the notion of public art has moved in new directions, most visibly in the work of Rigo and Barry McGee. Rigo, whose provocative *One Tree* mural covers the entire side of a SoMa building at the corner of 10th and Bryant Sts, communicates social messages in a style that suggests roots in comic books. McGee is a graffiti artist more commonly known as Twist. His droopy-eyed characters, also comic-book inspired, appear around the city on vacant buildings and other sites of his choosing.

The American takeover of California and the gold rush brought rapid changes in building styles and techniques. Sawed timber, ready-made components, and even prefabricated houses arrived from Australia and the East Coast. As San Francisco evolved from a temporary settlement to a permanent town, rows of Victorian houses were built, similar to one another in general design and usually made of wood but remarkably varied in their appearance and embellishments (see the boxed text 'The Victorians').

Toward the beginning of the 20th century, more new techniques and styles developed. Championed by architect Daniel Burnham, the classical beaux arts, or city beautiful, style was adopted for the Civic Center buildings; at the same time, the folksy Arts and Crafts movement was adapted to California in the many private homes designed by Berkeley-based architect Bernard Maybeck. Julia Morgan, a pioneer woman architect, created a landmark in the Fairmont Hotel before being recruited to design newspaper magnate William Randolph Hearst's mansion at San Simeon.

Steel-frame construction also started to appear at this time, and the successful performance of these new buildings in the 1906 earthquake led to larger and higher steel-framed buildings in the city's reconstruction. Willis Polk was one of the city's busiest

The Victorians

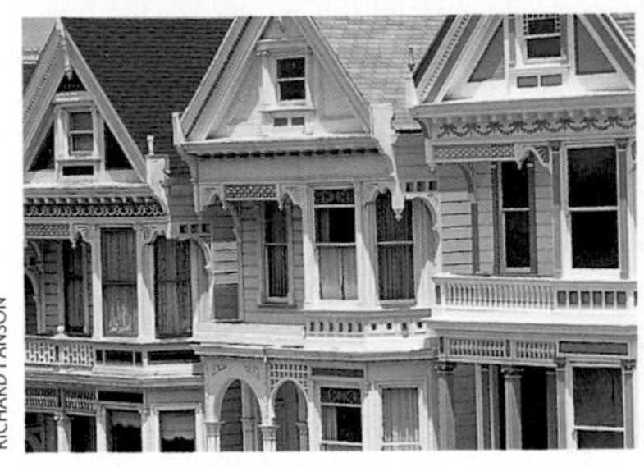
RICHARD I'ANSON

San Francisco's downtown leaves some architecture enthusiasts cold. The 1906 quake and fire destroyed many of the central city's 19th-century treasures, and fear of quakes arrested high-rise development here at a time when the New York and Chicago skylines were reaching for the stars. The real gems in town are the ornate and picturesque Victorian homes, found in great quantity in neighborhoods that were spared the wrath of the 1906 quake and fire. Pacific Heights and the Haight are both pedestrian-friendly neighborhoods with some spectacular architectural sights. The Mission District also has some well-preserved Victorians.

The best way to get really familiar with Victorian architecture is to stay in one of the B&Bs in Pacific Heights or the Mission (see Places to Stay). But even if that's not your cup of tea, it's worth boning up on Victorian architecture before setting out to admire the buildings. A few key styles predominate in San Francisco, though often you'll see combinations of several styles.

Italianate Italianate houses, which began appearing in the city in the late 1860s, are often simple and comparatively severe, by Victorian standards. They're generally flat-fronted, with no visible roof line but with a deep cornice around the top of the building.

Gothic Revival Gabled roofs, pointed arches over the windows, and verandas or porches running the width of the house are all Gothic signatures.

Eastlake Increased ornamentation and a variety of wooden flourishes characterize the delicate-looking Eastlake style, named after English furniture designer Charles Eastlake. Because of its vertical sticklike patterning, this style is also commonly referred to as the 'stick' style.

Queen Anne San Francisco architecture reached the height of its exuberance in the 1880s and '90s, with the arrival of the Queen Anne Victorians. Architects pulled out all the stops, furnishing homes with balconies, towers, turrets, chimneys, bay windows, and gables. The Haas-Lilienthal House, in Pacific Heights, is a fine example of this period's design.

architects; one of his best-known buildings is the Hallidie Building, on Sutter St, the first-ever glass curtain–walled building. Population growth and the movement to the suburbs inspired the California bungalow, a small and simple single-story design that was soon popping up all around the world.

The 1920s brought the mission revival style, a nostalgic look back at the state's Spanish heritage. San Francisco architects played with art deco and streamlined moderne styles, but the Depression years of the 1930s and then the WWII era were relatively static; the city skyline scarcely changed for almost 30 years, until the early '60s, when San Francisco's downtown suddenly started to soar skyward.

Film

Some of filmdom's most important studios are camped in the Bay Area, and the local film industry is frequently referred to as 'Hollywood North.' In San Francisco, Francis Ford Coppola's company, American Zoetrope, is headquartered in his Sentinel Building, in North Beach. Coppola's tenants in the tower include filmmaker Wayne Wang *(Chan Is Missing,* 1978; *Smoke,* 1996), who rents office space for his company, Chrome Dragon Productions; and actor Sean Penn, who moved to San Francisco to start his own film company, Clyde Is Hungry Productions. Philip Kaufman, director of *Invasion of the Body Snatchers* (1978), *The Right Stuff* (1983), and *The Unbearable Lightness of Being* (1988), also lives and frequently works in San Francisco.

Producer Saul Zaentz maintains his company headquarters in Berkeley. Zaentz, founder of the renowned jazz label Fantasy Records, began his film career in 1975 with the Oscar-winning *One Flew Over the Cuckoo's Nest* and hasn't faded at all – in 1997, his production of Michael Ondaatje's novel *The English Patient* won him yet another Best Picture award.

The biggest Bay Area movie force is George Lucas, whose films *American Graffiti* (1973), the *Star Wars* trilogy (1977–83), and *Raiders of the Lost Ark* (1981) are among the most influential and profitable films ever made. Lucas' contracting firms sometimes seem to have a hand in every big-budget film coming out of Hollywood. His Skywalker Ranch, in San Rafael (in Marin County, just minutes from San Francisco), is home to three companies, among them the subsidiaries Skywalker Sound and Industrial Light and Magic, which have garnered 24 Academy Awards for technical achievements.

San Francisco has made a great backdrop for an amazing number of movies. Many are available on video. For an intensive San Francisco movie experience, you can stay at the Phoenix Motel (see Civic Center in Places to Stay), which has a library of San Francisco films for guests' enjoyment.

You can relive San Francisco history in period pieces such as David Niven's *Barbary Coast* (1935), Clark Gable's *San Francisco* (1936; catch the re-creation of the 1906 quake), or Jack Nicholson's *Psyche-Out* (1968; relive the hippie era in Haight-Ashbury). More recent chronicles of the city's history include *Patty Hearst* (1988), a recap of the weird '70s kidnapping case; for Hollywood, this dramatization was a surprisingly long time in coming. The Oscar-winning *Life and Times of Harvey Milk* (1986) tells the story of the murder of Mayor Moscone and openly gay city supervisor Milk. In *Common Threads* (1989) Dustin Hoffman narrates the story behind the AIDS quilt and the city's AIDS battle.

Alcatraz Island is a natural for prison movies; John Frankenheimer's 1962 work *Birdman of Alcatraz,* with Burt Lancaster, was filmed there, as was the Clint Eastwood vehicle *Escape from Alcatraz* (1979). *The Rock* (1997), starring Nicolas Cage and Sean Connery, is probably the loudest film ever made in San Francisco. The film's main event is the improbable car chase through Nob Hill that attempts to top the car chase in *Bullitt,* the 1968 San Francisco thriller starring Steve McQueen.

Clint Eastwood's Dirty Harry character found San Francisco familiar territory. The maverick cop started his long film career there with the 1971 *Dirty Harry,* in which he hunts for an elusive serial killer; the story is loosely based on that of the Zodiac killer, who continued to terrorize the Bay Area for several years after this film was made. The suspenseful 1974 Francis Ford Coppola film *The Conversation* stars Gene Hackman as a surveillance expert who does his spying from the St Francis Hotel. Paul Verhoeven's raunchy 1992 thriller *Basic Instinct* ran fast and furiously through its Bay Area locations. The club scenes in the film were filmed at Rawhide in the SoMa district.

Alfred Hitchcock's movies often make use of San Francisco locales. You can stay in the York Hotel, on Sutter St, famous for its 1958 *Vertigo* stairway sequences. The most famous San Francisco private eye was Dashiell Hammett's Sam Spade. His screen double, Humphrey Bogart, appears in *The Maltese Falcon* (1941), a classic film noir murder mystery.

The 1967 hit *The Graduate* pays several visits to Berkeley and is notable for Dustin Hoffman's unique ability to head toward Berkeley by crossing the Bay Bridge in the wrong direction: speeding across the bridge in a red Alfa Romeo simply looks better on the top deck – never mind that the top deck leads to San Francisco. In *Foul Play* (1978), Chevy Chase and Goldie Hawn combine thriller with comedy and throw in a few more car chases and some great scenes at the San Francisco Opera House.

Theater

In the 1960s, San Francisco was fertile soil for cutting-edge theater. Grassroots companies such as the San Francisco Mime Troupe combined avant-garde theater with the burlesque and a healthy dose of radical politics. Peter Coyote began his acting career as a member of the Mime Troupe, which continues to set up its traveling stage show in parks around the city each summer.

By the end of the '60s, the Magic Theatre had established itself as one of the most important companies in the US. Playwrights Michael McClure and Sam Shepard, writer in residence at the Magic for much of the 1970s, put San Francisco theater on the map. In recent years, the American Conservatory Theater (ACT) has taken the forefront on the local theater scene, largely on the strength of its actors. Many film stars have worked for ACT before making their mark in Hollywood (ACT alumni include Denzel Washington, Danny Glover, and Annette Bening). Likewise, many Broadway productions are born here before heading to New York.

Dance

In dance, San Francisco's claim to fame is that Isadora Duncan (1877–1927), widely credited with originating modern dance, was born just a few blocks west of Union Square. However, she grew up in Oakland and shocked and delighted dance fans from New York City to Europe. An alley off Taylor St between Post and Geary, near her birthplace, now bears her name.

Today, San Francisco has a respected ballet company, the San Francisco Ballet, and several smaller companies that also enjoy good critical reception.

Music

CLASSICAL MUSIC & OPERA The San Francisco Symphony has established itself as one of the country's best since conductor Michael Tilson Thomas took the helm in 1995. Thomas' innovative programming, emphasizing American composers, has drawn the envy of New York critics, who complain that their renowned city's music scene has grown staid. Tilson Thomas and the San Francisco Symphony record regularly and won a Grammy for Best Orchestral Performance in 1996.

And of course, the San Francisco Opera is world class.

ROCK In all likelihood, San Francisco will always be known for the psychedelic bands that came out of the Haight in the 1960s: the Charlatans, Jefferson Airplane and the Grateful Dead. The San Francisco sound was a unique, drug-influenced brand of rock and roll that perfectly complemented the times. Haight residents Janis Joplin and Big Brother and the Holding Company also helped define the era's music. Guitar legend Carlos Santana whose music blends Latin-influenced

Carlos Santana

rhythms with blues and rock and roll, was raised in the Mission District and still calls the Bay Area home.

For decades, the Grateful Dead refused to die, and its nonstop tour never lost popularity: the band gained new fans – many of whom hadn't even been born when the Summer of Love happened in 1967 – until the death of leader Jerry Garcia in 1995, which finally brought the Dead caravan to a halt.

In the 1970s and '80s, San Francisco didn't project a particularly flattering rock and roll image, with local bands like Journey and Pablo Cruise dominating the national airwaves. Thankfully, Steve Perry's ode to the 'sit-tay by the bay' is now fading from memory (although a 'retro-Journey' trend will no doubt rear its ugly head in the near future). But the city's vital punk scene unleashed some major artists in the '70s and 80s, including the Dead Kennedys, whose singer, Jello Biafra, actually ran for mayor of San Francisco in 1980 (he finished fourth in an election won by Dianne Feinstein). Tribe 8 and Pansy Division and a number of other 'queercore' bands grew out of the sometimes-overlapping gay and punk scenes that flourished here. Faith. No More – probably the only band to put a period in its name – was on the fringe of the punk scene before losing faith in punk and transforming into a powerhouse rock band in the late 1980s. Retro crooner Chris Isaak is based in San Francisco, but of late he seems to record only to support his surfing habit – you're far more likely to see him out at Ocean Beach than in a local club. Counting Crows also got their start in San Francisco.

Tom Waits' move to the Bay Area in the early '90s helped a sophisticated alternative scene to coalesce.

JAZZ The Barbary Coast played an active role in the spread of jazz, as ragtime pianists were able to get ample work in raucous San Francisco saloons. For many decades, the city maintained a preference for 'trad' jazz; the Dixieland band of Turk Murphy remained extremely popular here long after jazz had evolved to bebop. Another legendary traditionalist, Earl 'Fatha' Hines, tickled the ivories at San Francisco's Club Hangover for years. Bop and later styles of jazz were frequent imports. Miles Davis recorded in San Francisco, innovators such as Billie Holiday made regular stops here, and the legendary bop jams in places like Jimbo's Bop City were infectiously chronicled in Jack Kerouac's novel *On the Road*.

ANDREW DEAN NYSTROM

Jazz history mural in North Beach

A recent, largely local innovation is acid jazz, a form difficult to define. Bands such as Alphabet Soup combined rap and jazz, while other groups, such as the Broun Fellinis, stayed close to the '60s blend of jazz and funk grooves. Following a more straightforward vein, jazz guitarist Charlie Hunter blasted onto the national jazz scene in the mid-'90s, but his success ultimately led him to relocate to New York.

The odd phenomenon that was the post-punk swing revival is bigger in San Francisco than anywhere else. Swing is so popular that the Hi-Ball Lounge in North Beach books nothing but swing artists. Some bands that play regularly in venues throughout the city are Lee Press-On and the Nails, Vice Grip and the Ambassadors of Swing, the New Morty Show, and crooner Lavay Smith and her Red Hot Skillet Lickers.

RELIGION

San Francisco is predominantly Christian, but the Bay Area also features just about every

Go to Church!

San Francisco has a pair of dynamic and unconventional religious congregations that will lift even the staunchest atheist's spirits with soul-stirring music and progressive sermons.

Glide Memorial United Methodist Church MAP 3
330 Ellis St ☎ 415-771-6300 ⏲ 9am Sun 🚌 27 Muni ♿
www.glide.org

Glide Memorial, near the corner of Ellis and Taylor Sts in the Tenderloin, embraces a liberal theology that begins 'with the human condition, not the Bible.' The church offers drug counseling and a food program; the church's recently retired minister, Cecil Williams, also performed holy union ceremonies for gay couples. Glide's Sunday morning services are enlivened by a gospel choir, jazz band, and psychedelic slide shows. Often 1500 people come for services – not a bad turnout.

St John Coltrane's African Orthodox Church MAP 10
930 Gough St ☎ 415-621-4054 ⏲ 11:45am-2:45pm Sun 🚌 5, 31 Muni ♿
www.saintjohncoltrane.org

That this church has a different approach to worship becomes obvious as soon as Bishop Franzo King, wearing the long robe and skullcap befitting a bishop of the African Orthodox Church, steps up to the pulpit and begins blowing a tenor sax. The music of John Coltrane – who died in 1967 and was canonized a saint by the African Orthodox Church in 1982 – serves as gospel. Every service begins with Coltrane's 'Africa Brass,' followed by a 60-minute rendition of 'A Love Supreme,' Coltrane's spiritual 1964 composition. By the time the bishop finally puts his horn down, the congregation has reached a state of exaltation. Bishop King's sermons often riff on the concept of reaching enlightenment through 'practicing your horn.' Clearly, Coltrane's spiritual quest lives on at the corner of Gough and Turk. Services begin every Sunday at 11:45am and last about three hours.

other religion you'd care to mention. There are Chinese temples in Chinatown, Japanese temples in Japantown, a Hindu temple in Pacific Heights, a Zen Buddhist retreat near Muir Beach (in Marin County), and a Mormon Temple overlooking the entire East Bay. There is also a sizable Jewish community. If the Bay Area has a religious specialty, however, it's the controversial and bizarre. The Reverend Jim Jones was an influential public figure in San Francisco in the mid-1970s, before leading his followers to mass suicide in Jonestown, Guyana; Anton LaVey, leader of the Church of Satan, remains a presence in the city. One of the city's most inspired churches is the African Orthodox Church of St John Coltrane, on Gough St (see the boxed text 'Go to Church!').

LANGUAGE

The Bay Area speaks a whole dictionary of languages apart from traditional English. You can roll out your Cantonese in Chinatown, practice your Italian in North Beach, listen for a whole range of Latin American Spanish dialects in the Mission, and hear every possible Asian language in distinct enclaves around the city.

Facts for the Visitor

WHEN TO GO

San Francisco is a popular location any time of the year, but it is best to avoid visiting during the summer. That is the prime tourist season, so prices are higher, lines are longer, and parking is more difficult. In terms of weather, summer in San Francisco can be foggy and cold (see Climate, later, for details), while inland or north in the Wine Country it is often too hot and dusty for comfort. You're more likely to find the Bay Area's climate hospitable at other times of the year, especially in September and October, which can be the nicest months.

ORIENTATION

The city of San Francisco is a compact area, covering the tip of a 30-mile-long peninsula with the Pacific Ocean on one side and San Francisco Bay on the other. The city can be simply divided into three sections, each containing a multitude of distinct neighborhoods. The central part resembles a generous slice of pie, with Van Ness Ave and Market St marking the two sides and the Embarcadero bend serving as the outer edge of crust. Squeezed into this compact area are Union Square, the Financial District, Civic Center, Chinatown, North Beach, Nob Hill, Russian Hill, and Fisherman's Wharf.

South of Market St is SoMa, an upwardly mobile warehouse zone where dot-com start-ups compete for space with so-called 'live-work' lofts inhabited by the city's latest nouveaux riches. Farther south and to the west, SoMa fades into the Mission, where Mexican and Central American immigrants rub shoulders with dot-com hipsters and bohemians. San Francisco's gay community has established itself most famously in the Castro and in Noe Valley, both part of picturesque Eureka Valley, immediately west of the Mission. Overlooking the Castro, Twin Peaks presides over most of San Francisco and often contains the fog that so often creeps into the city from the Pacific Ocean.

The third part of the city – according to this loose breakdown – is the long sweep from Van Ness Ave all the way to the Pacific Ocean. This varied area encompasses the upscale Marina and Pacific Heights, the 'fog belt' (as the Richmond and Sunset Districts are deservedly known), and areas with a flavor all their own, such as the Fillmore, Japantown, and the Haight. The city's three great parks – the Presidio, Lincoln Park, and Golden Gate Park – are also in this area.

MAPS

Lonely Planet publishes a laminated pocket-size map of San Francisco that's widely available in bookstores. Free maps that are generally adequate for most visitors are available from a variety of sources. The excellent *San Francisco Street Map & Visitor Guide* is available at many of the city's hotels, and rental car firms usually offer maps. If you're going to explore the city by public transportation, the Muni *Street & Transit Map* is a wise $2 investment. Get a copy at the Visitors Information Center, at the newspaper kiosk next to the Powell St cable car turnaround, or at any large bookstore in the city.

Rand McNally
595 Market St ☎ 415-777-3131 ⌚ 9am-7pm Mon-Fri, 10am-6pm Sat, 11am-5pm Sun Ⓜ Montgomery St BART & Muni station 🚌 Market St buses ♿
w www.randmcnallystore.com

Thomas Bros Maps
550 Jackson St ☎ 415-981-7520 ⌚ 9:30am-5:30pm Mon-Fri 🚌 15, 41 Muni ♿
w www.thomas.com

Several detailed street atlases to the Bay Area are put out by Thomas Bros Maps. You can pick one up at their store or at most bookstores.

TOURIST OFFICES

The city of San Francisco and the state of California operate information centers in the city to help travelers arrange accommodations and develop itineraries. By checking out their websites and contacting these organizations by phone or mail, you can get pre-trip planning assistance.

San Francisco Convention and Visitors Bureau
PO Box 429097 ☎ 415-974-6900
w www.sfvisitor.org

Although the SFCVB is set up primarily to serve the needs of conventioneers, it does run the useful Visitors Information Center in Hallidie Square (see below) and its website may be of help for pre-trip planning.

San Francisco Visitors Information Center MAP 2
900 Market St ☎ 415-391-2000 events hot line, 415-391-2001 English, 415-391-2003 French, 415-391-2004 German, 415-391-2122 Spanish, 415-391-2101 Japanese
9am-5pm Mon-Fri, 9am-3pm Sat-Sun
Powell St BART & Muni station, Market St buses
w www.sfvisitor.org

This helpful office, operated by the SFCVB, is just a stone's throw from Union Square. It provides practical information for tourists, publishes glossy tourist-oriented booklets, and runs a 24-hour phone events hot line in English, French, German, Spanish, and Japanese. The office also has two internet terminals.

California Welcome Center
Pier 39, 2nd Level ☎ 415-956-3493
11am-5pm daily, 42, F Muni
w gocalif.ca.gov

A wing of the California Division of Tourism, the California Welcome Center has a helpful multilingual staff that will help arrange tours, provide travel information, and help plan itineraries. Information on California tourism can be obtained by mail or through the website.

DOCUMENTS

Passports & Visas

To enter the US, Canadians need only proper proof of Canadian citizenship, such as a citizenship card with photo ID or a passport. Visitors from other countries must have a valid passport and, unless they qualify under the reciprocal visa-waiver program, a US visa.

The reciprocal visa-waiver program allows citizens of certain countries to enter the USA for stays of 90 days or shorter without first obtaining a US visa. Currently these countries are Andorra, Argentina, Australia, Austria, Belgium, Brunei, Denmark, Finland, France, Germany, Iceland, Ireland, Italy, Japan, Liechtenstein, Luxembourg, Monaco, Netherlands, New Zealand, Norway, San Marino, Slovenia, Spain, Sweden, Switzerland, and the United Kingdom. Under this program, you must have a passport and a nonrefundable roundtrip ticket originating outside the USA, and you will not be allowed to extend your stay beyond 90 days.

Other travelers will need to obtain a visa from a US consulate or embassy. In most countries, the process can be done by mail.

Your passport should be valid for at least six months longer than your intended stay in the USA, and you'll need to submit a recent photo that's 1½ inches square (37mm x 37mm) with the application. Documents of financial stability and/or guarantees from a US resident are sometimes

WOODS WHEATCROFT

Bay Bridge at night

required, particularly for those from developing countries.

Visa applicants may also be required to 'demonstrate binding obligations' that will ensure their return to their countries. Because of this requirement, those planning to travel through other countries before arriving in the USA are generally better off applying for their US visa while they are still in their home country – rather than while on the road.

The validity period for US visitor visas depends on what country you're from. The length of time you'll be allowed to stay in the USA is ultimately determined by US immigration authorities at the port of entry.

HIV & Entering the USA

Everyone entering the USA who isn't a US citizen is subject to the authority of the Immigration & Naturalization Service (INS). The INS can keep people from entering or staying in the USA by excluding or deporting them. This is especially relevant to travelers with HIV (human immunodeficiency virus). Though being HIV-positive is not grounds for deportation, it is 'grounds for exclusion,' and the INS can invoke it to refuse admission.

Although the INS doesn't test people for HIV at customs, it may try to exclude anyone who answers 'yes' to this question on the nonimmigrant visa application form: 'Have you ever been afflicted with a communicable disease of public health significance?' INS officials may also stop people if they seem sick, are carrying AIDS/HIV medicine, or, sadly, if the officer happens to think the person 'looks gay,' though sexual orientation is neither legal grounds for exclusion, nor is it connected to HIV infection.

It is imperative that visitors know and assert their rights. Immigrants and visitors who may face exclusion should discuss their rights and options with a trained immigration advocate before applying for a visa. For legal immigration information and referrals to immigration advocates, contact:

National Immigration Project of the National Lawyers Guild
14 Beacon St, Suite 602, Boston, MA 02108 ☎ 617-227-9727

Immigrant HIV Assistance Project, Bar Association of San Francisco
465 California St, Suite 1100, San Francisco, CA 94104 ☎ 415-782-8995

VISA EXTENSIONS Tourists are usually granted a six-month stay on first arrival. If you try to extend that time, the first assumption will be that you are working illegally, so come prepared with concrete evidence that you've been traveling extensively and will continue to be a model tourist. A wad of traveler's checks looks much better than a solid and unmoving US bank account. If you want, need, or hope to stay in the US longer than the date stamped on your passport, go to the immigration office before the stamped date to apply for an extension.

Immigration and Naturalization Service (INS)
630 Sansome St ☎ 800-375-5283 ⌚ 7am-3pm Mon-Tues & Thurs-Fri, 7am-2:30pm Wed Ⓜ Montgomery St BART & Muni station 🚌 42 Muni ♿
w www.ins.usdoj.gov
In San Francisco, visa extensions are handled by this federal service.

Travel Insurance

No sensible visitor will arrive in the USA without the security of a good travel insurance policy. When looking for a policy, coverage for lost baggage, canceled flights, and minor medical bills may be nice to have, but what you're really after is coverage against a true catastrophe. Your travel agent will have some suggestions about travel insurance, and many policies offer higher levels of coverage for the USA. Check the fine print, as some policies may exclude coverage for 'dangerous' activities, which can include scuba diving, motorcycling, skiing, rock climbing, and the like. If you're planning to engage in such sports, you don't want a policy that leaves you in the cold.

For young visitors, insurance policies issued through student travel–oriented organizations like Travel Cuts, STA, Campus Travel, or Council Travel are usually a good value.

If you do require medical attention, be sure to save all invoices and documentation and put in a claim to your insurance company as soon as possible.

Other Documents

You'll need a picture ID to show that you are over 21 to buy alcohol or gain admission to bars or clubs (make sure your driver's license has a photo on it, or else get some other form of ID).

Bring your driver's license if you intend to rent a car; visitors from some countries may find it wise to back up their national license with an International Driving Permit, available from their local auto club. A comprehensive travel or health insurance policy is very important for overseas visitors, and they should bring a membership card or documentation. If you will be staying in an HI-AYH hostel and are already a member, you'll need to bring your membership card to get discount rates.

If you are a student, be sure to obtain an International Student Identification Card (ISIC), available on your campus. Having it with you when you travel can get you discounted admission to museums and plays, as well as discounts on some accommodations, such as the YMCA.

Copies

Before you leave home, you should photocopy all important documents (passport data page and visa page, credit cards, travel insurance policy, air/bus/train tickets, driver's license, etc). Leave one copy with someone at home and keep another with you, separate from the originals.

It's also a good idea to store details of your vital travel documents in Lonely Planet's free online Travel Vault in case you lose the photocopies or can't be bothered with them. Your password-protected Travel Vault is accessible online anywhere in the world – create it at www.ekno.lonelyplanet.com.

EMBASSIES & CONSULATES

US Embassies & Consulates Abroad

US diplomatic offices abroad include the following:

Australia

21 Moonah Place, Yarralumla, ACT 2600
☎ 02 6214 5600 US citizens only fax 02 6214 5970 ⌚ 8am-5pm Mon-Fri
w *www.usis-australia.gov/embassy*

19-29 Martin Place, Level 59, Sydney, NSW 2000 ☎ 02 9373 9200, 1902 941 641 visa inquiries (charges apply) fax 02 9373 9125, 02 9373 9184 consular section
⌚ 8am-5pm Mon-Fri
w *www.usconsydney.org*

553 St Kilda Rd, Melbourne, Victoria 3004
☎ 03 9526 5900, 03 9389 3601 emergency

Your Own Embassy

It's important to realize what your own embassy – the embassy of the country of which you are a citizen – can and can't do to help you if you get into trouble. Generally speaking, it won't be much help in emergencies if the trouble you're in is remotely your own fault. Remember that you are bound by the laws of the country you are in. Your embassy will not be sympathetic if you end up in jail after committing a crime locally, even if such actions are legal in your own country.

In genuine emergencies, you might get some assistance, but only if other channels have been exhausted. If you need to get home urgently, a free ticket home is exceedingly unlikely – the embassy would expect you to have insurance. If all your money and documents are stolen, it might assist you with getting a new passport, but a loan for onward travel is out of the question.

Some embassies used to keep letters for travelers or have a small reading room with home newspapers, but these days most of the mail-holding services have been stopped and even newspapers tend to be out of date.

after hours, fax 03 9525 0769
8:30am-4:30pm Mon-Fri
W *www.usis-australia.gov/melbourne*

Canada
100 Wellington St, Ottawa, Ontario K1P 5T1
☎ 613-238-4470, 613-238-5335
fax 613-238-5720
W *www.usembassycanada.gov*

1095 W Pender St, Vancouver, BC V6E 2M6
☎ 604-685-4311 fax 604-685-5285
W *www.usembassycanada.gov*

1155 St Alexandre St, Montreal, Quebec H2Z 1Z2 ☎ 514-398-9695 fax 514-398-0973, 514-398-0711
W *www.usembassycanada.gov*

France
2 rue St Florentin, 75382 Paris, Cedex 08
☎ 08 36 70 14 88 (charges apply), 01 43 12 48 40 US citizen services fax 01 42 86 82 91
W *www.amb-usa.fr*

Germany
Neustädtische Kirchstrasse 4-5, Berlin 10117
☎ 030 83050, 030 832 9233 US citizen services, fax 030 8305 1215
W *www.usembassy.de*

Ireland
42 Elgin Rd, Dublin 4 ☎ 353 (1) 6687-122, 353 (1) 6688777 fax 353 (1) 6689946
W *www.usembassy.ie*

14 Queen St, Belfast BT1 6EQ Northern Ireland ☎ 1232 241279, 1232 328239 fax 1232 248482

Japan
1-10-5 Akasaka, Minato-ku, Tokyo 107-8420 ☎ 3 5354 2633, 3 3224 5000
8:30am-noon Mon-Fri
W *www.usembassy.state.gov/tokyo*

Mexico
Paseo de la Reforma 305, Mexico City Col Cuauhtémoc 06500 ☎ 01 5211 0042, 01 5209 9100 fax 01 208 3373, 01 511 9980
W *www.usembassy-mexico.gov*

Netherlands
Lange Voorhout 102, The Hague 2514 EJ
☎ 70 310 9209 fax 70 361 4688
W *www.usemb.nl*

Museumplein 19, Amsterdam 1071 DJ
☎ 20 575 5309 fax 20 575 5310, 20 575 5350
8:30am-noon Mon-Fri
W *www.usemb.nl/consul.htm*

New Zealand
29 Fitzherbert Terrace, Thorndon, Wellington ☎ 04 472 2068 fax 04 471 2380
W *www.usembassy.state.gov/wellington*

Scotland
3 Regent Terrace, Edinburgh EH7 5BW
☎ 131 556 8315 fax 131 557 6023

UK
24 Grosvenor St, London W1A 1AE
☎ 0171 499 9000
W *www.usembassy.org.uk*

Consulates in San Francisco

Check either the white or the yellow pages in the telephone book under 'Consulates' for diplomatic representation in San Francisco. Consulates and Consulate Generals include:

Australian Consulate-General & Trade Commission
625 Market St, Suite 200 ☎ 415-536-1970 fax 415-536-1982 8:45am-1pm & 2pm-4:45pm Mon-Fri Embarcadero BART & Muni station Market St buses

Canadian Consulate Trade Office San Francisco/Silicon Valley
555 Montgomery St, Suite 1288 ☎ 415-834-3180 fax 415-834-3189 8:30am-4:30pm Mon-Fri Embarcadero BART & Muni station
W *www.cdntrade.com*

The Canadian Consulate's San Francisco office handles trade and investment only. Travelers with legal emergencies or visa questions should contact the Los Angeles office at ☎ 213-346-2700.

French Consulate-General
540 Bush St ☎ 415-397-4330 fax 415-433-8357 9am-12:30pm Mon-Fri Embarcadero BART & Muni station
W *www.accueil-sfo.org*

German Consulate-General
1960 Jackson St ☎ 415-775-1061 fax 415-775-0187 9am-noon Mon-Fri
W *www.germany-info.org*

Consulate-General of Ireland
44 Montgomery St, Suite 3830 ☎ 415-392-4214 fax 415-392-0885 9am-noon & 2pm-4pm Mon-Fri Montgomery St BART & Muni station
e *IrishCGSF@aol.com*

Consulate General of Japan
50 Fremont St, Suite 2300 ☎ 415-777-3533 fax 415-974-3660 ⌚ 9am-5pm Mon-Fri Ⓜ Embarcadero BART & Muni station ♿
w www.cgjsf.org

General Consulate of Mexico
870 Market St ☎ 415-392-5554 fax 415-392-3233 ⌚ 8am-1pm Mon-Fri Ⓜ Powell St BART & Muni station

Netherlands Embassy
275 Battery St ☎ 415-981-6454 fax 415-399-1249 ⌚ open hours by appointment only Ⓜ Embarcadero BART & Muni station ♿

Honorary Consulate of New Zealand
1 Maritime Plaza, Suite 700 ☎ 415-399-1255 fax 415-399-9775 ⌚ open hours by appointment only Ⓜ Embarcadero BART & Muni station ♿
e rcsears@aol.com

The consulate's mailing address is PO Box 330455, San Francisco, CA 94133-0455.

British Consulate-General
1 Sansome St, Suite 850 ☎ 415-617-1300 fax 415-434 2018 ⌚ 8:30am-1pm & 2pm-5pm Mon-Fri Ⓜ Embarcadero BART & Muni station
w www.britain-info.org/consular/sf/sf.asp

CUSTOMS

US Customs allows each person over the age of 21 to bring 1 liter of liquor and 200 cigarettes duty-free into the USA. Non-US citizens are allowed to bring in $100 worth of gifts duty free. Should you be carrying more than $10,000 in US and foreign cash, traveler's checks, money orders, or the like, you need to declare the excess amount. There is no legal restriction on the amount that may be imported, but undeclared sums in excess of $10,000 may be subject to confiscation.

MONEY

Currency

US dollars are the only accepted currency in San Francisco. The dollar is divided into 100 cents, with coins of one cent (penny), five cents (nickel), 10 cents (dime), 25 cents (quarter), the relatively rare 50 cents (half dollar), and the equally elusive one-dollar coin.

Bills can be confusing to foreign visitors, because they are all the same size and color; get used to checking the corners for amounts. They come in denominations of $1, $2, $5, $10, $20, $50, and $100.

Exchange Rates

At press time exchange rates were:

country	unit		US dollars
Australia	A$1	=	$0.51
Canada	C$1	=	$0.65
euro	€1	=	$0.88
Hong Kong	HK$10	=	$1.28
Japan	¥100	=	$0.81
New Zealand	NZ$1	=	$0.41
UK	£1	=	$1.43

Exchanging Money

There are exchange bureaus at the airport. At press time, they were located at the upper level of boarding area D and the mezzanine level of boarding area F, but things were shifting around due to the recent opening of the new International Terminal. Ask at an information kiosk if you are unable to find a currency exchange counter. That said, the best rates are generally available at banks in the city.

Bank of America
1 Powell St ☎ 650-615-4700 ⌚ 9am-6pm Mon-Fri, 9am-2pm Sat Ⓜ Powell St BART & Muni station 🚌 Market St buses ♿
w www.bankamerica.com

American Express
455 Market St ☎ 415-536-2600 ⌚ 8:30am-5:30pm Mon-Fri, 9:30am-3:30pm Sat Ⓜ Embarcadero BART & Muni station ♿
w www.americanexpress.com/travel

If you have a credit card or traveler's checks from American Express, you can exchange some foreign currencies here.

TRAVELER'S CHECKS In the US, traveler's checks are virtually as good as cash; you do not have to go to a bank to cash a traveler's check, as most establishments will accept them just like cash. The major advantage of traveler's checks over cash is that they can be replaced if lost or stolen. In the

USA, however, the convenience of traveler's checks applies only if they are in US dollars.

If you're bringing your money in the form of traveler's checks, bring it in denominations of US$100. Having to change small US$10 or US$20 checks is inconvenient, and you may be charged service fees when cashing them at banks.

ATMS These are a convenient way of obtaining cash from a bank account back home, whether you're from the USA or abroad. Most banks have these machines, which are open 24 hours a day, except in neighborhoods where street crime is a problem. There are various ATM networks, and most banks are affiliated with several of them. Exchange, Accel, Plus, and Cirrus are the predominant networks. For a nominal service charge, you can withdraw cash from an ATM using a credit card or a charge card. Credit cards usually have a 2% fee with a $2 minimum, and you are charged interest on the withdrawal until you pay it back. Using bank cards linked to your personal checking account is usually far cheaper. Check with your bank or credit card company for exact information. Contact your bank if you lose your ATM card.

CREDIT CARDS Major credit cards are widely accepted by car rental agencies and most hotels, restaurants, gas stations, shops, and larger grocery stores. The most commonly accepted cards are Visa, MasterCard, and American Express. Discover and Diners Club cards are also accepted by a fair number of businesses.

You will find it difficult to make certain transactions without a credit card. Ticket-buying services, for example, won't reserve tickets over the phone unless you offer a credit card number, and it's almost impossible to rent a car without a credit card. Even if you loathe using credit cards and prefer to rely on traveler's checks and ATMs, it's a good idea to carry one (Visa or MasterCard are your best bets) for emergencies.

American Express card holders can obtain cash advances from American Express Travel Services offices (there are five in San Francisco; see the Exchanging Money section or look in the white pages under American Express) or from American Express check dispensers at major airports.

Carry copies of your credit card numbers separately from the cards. If you lose your credit cards or they are stolen, contact the company immediately. Following are toll-free numbers for the main credit card companies.

American Express
☎ 800-528-4800
W www.americanexpress.com

Diners Club
☎ 800-234-6377
W www.dinersclub.com

Discover
☎ 800-347-2683
W www.discovercard.com

MasterCard
☎ 800-826-2181
W www.mastercard.com

Visa
☎ 800-336-8472
W www.visa.com

Security

Be cautious – not paranoid – about carrying money. If your hotel or hostel has a safe, keep your valuables and excess cash in it. It's best not to display large amounts of

cash in public. A money belt worn under your clothes is a good place to carry excess currency when you're on the move or otherwise unable to stash the money in a safe. Avoid carrying your wallet in the back pocket of your pants. That is a prime target for pickpockets, as are handbags and the outside pockets of knapsacks and fanny packs (bum bags).

Costs

The cost of living in San Francisco is high, but how much money you need depends on your traveling style. You can sleep cheap in a hostel and eat cheap at the Mexican taquería in the Mission, or you can quickly run up whopping balances on your credit card by sleeping at palatial Nob Hill hotels and dining at the Bay Area's swanky restaurants.

Car rental typically starts at around $40 per day. In San Francisco, a car is more of a handicap than a help. Free parking is difficult to come by (vigilant parking cops slap $30 fees for overstaying your two-hour time limit during designated hours), and paid parking is often expensive. Cab fare often beats the price of parking, and public transportation is cheap and usually convenient. However, a car is essential for excursions along the coast or up to the Wine Country.

Tipping & Bargaining

Tipping is an American practice that can initially be a little confusing for foreign visitors. Tipping is not really an option – the service has to be absolutely appalling to consider not tipping. In a restaurant, tip your server at least 15% of the bill. In bars, the same 15% rule applies, but by an unspoken protocol the minimum tip – even for one beer – is $1 (the same dollar would be considered a sufficient tip for two beers, so order one for your friend). As the San Francisco consumer tax is 8.25%, you can easily figure out an adequate tip by doubling the tax that appears above the total amount on your bill.

To tip a cabbie, add at least 10% (starting at $1, even for fares under $6) to the taxi fare. Hotel porters who carry bags a long way expect $3 to $5 or add it up at $1 per bag. Valet parking is worth about a $2 tip, to be given when your car is safely returned to you.

Bargaining isn't widely practiced in San Francisco. In shops, prices are very rarely negotiable. When goods are secondhand, sometimes the price is more open to discussion. At flea markets and garage sales, it is often assumed that you will want to negotiate a better price, but even in these contexts vendors still frequently behave as though bargaining violates some sort of social code.

Consumer Taxes

San Francisco's 8.25% sales tax is tacked on to virtually everything, including meals, accommodations, and car rentals. Grocery items are about the only items that are not taxed. Additionally, there's a 14% hotel room tax to take into consideration when booking a hotel room.

POST & COMMUNICATIONS

Post

Postal rates are always subject to increase. At press time, the rate for 1st-class mail within the United States was 34¢ for letters up to 1oz (21¢ for each additional ounce) and 20¢ for postcards.

International airmail rates are 80¢ for a half-ounce letter and 70¢ for a postcard to any foreign country with the exceptions of Canada and Mexico (60¢ for a 1oz letter and 50¢ for a postcard). Postage stamps are available at post offices, supermarkets, and drug stores. Be aware that stamp-dispensing machines can be a rip-off, charging you more than face value for stamps and sometimes not giving change.

The cost for parcels airmailed anywhere within the USA is $3.50 for 1lb or less, and $4 to $7.55 for up to 5lb. Parcels weighing more than 1lb must be checked at a post office, and will not be delivered if deposited in a mailbox.

Civic Center Post Office MAP 3
101 Hyde St ☎ *800-725-2161* ⌚ *9am-5pm Mon-Fri, 9am-1pm Sat* Ⓜ *Civic Center BART & Muni station* ♿
w *www.usps.com*

FACTS FOR THE VISITOR

This is the main San Francisco post office. Mail can be sent to you here marked c/o General Delivery, San Francisco, CA 94142, USA.

Post Office (inside Macy's)
121 Stockton St ☎ 800-275-8777 ⌚ 10am-5:30pm Mon-Sat, 11am-5pm Sun Ⓜ Powell St BART & Muni station 🚌 38 Muni ♿
W www.usps.com

Be advised that any telephone call to the post office will probably result in more time wasted in the system's labyrinthine telephone network than it would take to walk to the nearest PO and ask your questions in person. Addresses of all post offices are listed in the 'Government Listings' section of the white pages.

Telephone

The Pacific Bell Smart Yellow Pages, commonly known as the 'yellow pages,' is the comprehensive telephone directory, organized alphabetically by subject. Hotel rooms generally come equipped with a phone book (if yours doesn't, ask at the front desk for one), and tattered and abused copies can sometimes be found at phone booths.

Area codes in the Bay Area are:

San Francisco	☎ 415
Marin County	☎ 415
East Bay	☎ 510
Wine Country	☎ 707
Peninsula	☎ 650
San Jose	☎ 408
Santa Cruz	☎ 831

When dialing another area code, the code must be preceded by a 1. For example, to dial an Oakland number from San Francisco, start with ☎ 1-510. Local calls from a pay phone usually start at 35¢. Be aware that there are 'nonlocal' calls even within the same area code, and costs jump dramatically when you call to another area code. Hotel telephones will often have heavy surcharges.

Toll-free numbers start with ☎ 1-800 or ☎ 1-888. Phone numbers beginning with ☎ 1-900 usually incur high fees. Dial ☎ 411 for local directory assistance, ☎ 1 + area code + 555-1212 for long-distance directory information, ☎ 800-555-1212 for toll-free number information. Dial ☎ 0 for the operator.

INTERNATIONAL CALLS If you're calling from abroad, the international country code for the USA and Canada is '1.' To call a San Francisco number, simply dial your local international access code + 1 + 415 + number.

To dial an international call direct from the Bay Area, dial ☎ 011 + country code + area code + number. When calling a number in Canada, there's no need to dial the international access code 011. For international operator assistance dial ☎ 00.

As a general rule, it's cheaper to make international calls at night, but this varies with the country you're calling. The exact cost for making an overseas call from a pay phone will depend on the long-distance company and the country in question. For calls to Australia and Europe, typically the cost should be about $1.50 for the first minute and $1 for each subsequent minute. Calling other continents usually costs about twice that.

PHONE CARDS There's a wide range of local and international phone cards. Lonely Planet's eKno Communication Card is aimed specifically at independent travelers and provides budget international calls, a range of messaging services, free email, and travel information – see below.

eKno Lonely Planet's eKno global communication service provides low-cost international calls – for local calls, you're usually better off with a local phone card. The eKno service also offers free messaging services, email, travel information, and an online travel vault, where you can securely store all your important documents. You can join online at www.ekno.lonelyplanet.com or by phone from San Francisco by dialing ☎ 1-800-707-0031. Once you have joined, to use eKno from anywhere in the continental USA, dial ☎ 1-800-706-1333.

Fax

Fax machines are easy to find in the USA at packaging outlets, photocopy services, and hotel business service centers, but be prepared to pay high prices ($1 or $2 a page). The main library (see Libraries, later) also offers fax services.

Mailboxes Etc
588 Sutter St ☎ 415-834-1555 fax 415-834-1772 ⌚ 9am-6pm Mon-Fri, 10am-4pm Sat Ⓜ Powell St BART & Muni station ♿ w www.mbe.com

Mail Boxes Etc offers fax machines and can take care of all your shipping needs.

Email & Internet Access

Most hotels that cater to business travelers make internet access easy – ask when making hotel reservations if your room is equipped with a modem line. For those traveling without such hardware, another way to log on is to stop by any public library branch, all of which are equipped to allow Web browsing and access to chat groups, though not to send or receive email. The main branch at Civic Center has 160 terminals, some of which are available to non-library-card-holding visitors, and they also can provide information on internet access throughout the city.

Internet cafés, so ubiquitous in tourist zones the world over, are to be found in bunches in San Francisco, but they're not obvious. Usually, they simply look like ordinary cafés from the outside, and have just a couple of terminals inside.

New Main Library MAP 3
100 Larkin St ☎ 415-557-4400 ⌚ 10am-6pm Mon, 9am-8pm Tues-Thurs, noon-6pm Fri, 10am-6pm Sat, noon-5pm Sun Ⓜ Civic Center BART & Muni station 🚌 F Muni ♿ w www.sfpl.lib.ca.us

Free internet access is available on a 15-minute basis. The 1st-floor terminals are available to visitors without SFPL library cards. There isn't any email access.

CompUSA MAP 2
750 Market Street ☎ 415-391-9778 ⌚ 8am-8pm Mon-Fri, 9am-8pm Sat, 11am-6pm Sun Ⓜ Montgomery St BART & Muni station 🚌 Market St buses w www.compusa.com

CompUSA offers free email access on fast iMac computers.

DIGITAL RESOURCES

The World Wide Web is a rich resource for travelers. You can research your trip, hunt down bargain airfares, book hotels, check on weather conditions, and chat with locals and other travelers about the best places to visit (or avoid!).

There's no better place to start your Web explorations than the Lonely Planet website (www.lonelyplanet.com). Here you'll find succinct summaries on traveling to most places on earth, postcards from other travelers, and the Thorn Tree bulletin board, where you can ask questions before you go or dispense advice when you get back. You can also find travel news and updates for many of our most popular guidebooks, and the subWWWay section links you to the most useful travel resources elsewhere on the Web.

Since San Francisco is known to be a fairly 'wired' sort of place, most of the city's hotels have websites. It's a good idea to have a look at a hotel's website to see photos of rooms and get additional information. Most websites also provide email links so you can ask any questions you may have.

CitySync San Francisco is Lonely Planet's digital city guide for Palm OS handheld devices. With CitySync you can quickly search, sort, and bookmark hundreds of San Francisco's restaurants, hotels, attractions, clubs, and more – all pinpointed on scrollable street maps. Sections on activities, transportation, and local events give you the big picture plus all the little details. Purchase or demo CitySync San Francisco at www.citysync.com.

BOOKS

Books are usually published in different editions by different publishers in different countries. As a result, a book might be a hardcover rarity in one country but readily available in paperback in another. Fortunately, bookstores and libraries can search by title or author, so your local bookstore or library is the best place to advise you on the availability of the following recommendations. Most of San Francisco's large and medium-size bookstores have a special section reserved for books about the city. See Shopping for bookstore locations.

Lonely Planet

If you came here to do some serious eating, Lonely Planet's *Out to Eat San Francisco* will be an indispensable resource, with in-depth reviews of more than 400 restaurants and informative sidebars on the city's renowned culinary culture.

If you're exploring other parts of California, LP's *California & Nevada* book offers plenty of information to help get you in and out of the state's bounty of natural and unnatural wonders.

Guidebooks

Randolph Delehanty's *San Francisco: The Ultimate Guide* is more than a guidebook – it's an engrossing read for history buffs interested in scrutinizing the city's architecture. The more recently published *National Trust Guide to San Francisco,* by San Francisco author Peter Booth Wiley, is an equally reliable source on San Francisco history and architecture. Both of these titles are easily found in local bookstores.

For the inside dope on all things scatological and kinky, check out Manic D Press' *The Underground Guide to San Francisco*.

Local music critic Joel Selvin's *San Francisco: The Musical History Tour* is a fun and informative guide to colorful and significant music sites around the city.

Two out-of-print guides are well worth seeking out. *The Literary World of San Francisco and Its Environs* (City Lights, 1990) is an unflashy volume that traces the whereabouts of San Francisco literary figures, from Ambrose Bierce to Lawrence Ferlinghetti. The author, Don Herron, also leads the Dashiell Hammett walking tour around Union Square (see Walking Tours in Things to See & Do). Much more offbeat and cantankerous is *A Guide to Mysterious San Francisco* (Barrett-James Books, 1994), by Doctor Weirde. This humorous and sensational guide leads readers down controversial alleys and 'round otherworldly corners throughout the city. Since San Francisco's haunted houses and murder sites haven't gone anywhere, it's surprising this little volume is out of print.

History

There is no definitive, comprehensive book in print on San Francisco history. Rand Richards' thin *Historic San Francisco* is probably a good enough overview for most tourists' needs. Many other books shed shades of light on particular San Francisco subjects. Robert O'Brien's *This Is San Francisco* (first published in 1948) is a bit dated, but it's a colorful rendition of San Francisco's past and an enjoyable read. A more reliable book, with a bias toward maritime history (Shanghaiers, labor strikes, and such), is William Martin Camp's *San Francisco: Port of Gold.* It's out of print, but it frequently shows up in the city's used-book shops. Another indispensable out-of-print source is *The Barbary Coast* (1933), by Herbert Asbury, which, as the title suggests, chronicles the untoward activities of 19th-century gamblers, harlots, opium addicts, and hoodlums of every stripe. Dusty old copies of this book are widely available from the city's used-book sellers.

Gay by the Bay, by Susan Stryker and Jim Van Buskirk, is an illustrated account of the city's gay history, from Barbary Coast gay bars to the pride movement of the '70s and the AIDS epidemic. For more extensive research on gay studies, visit the Gay and Lesbian Center at the new main library, at the corner of Larkin and Grove Sts.

Several books chronicle San Francisco in the 1960s. *The Haight-Ashbury: A History*, by *Rolling Stone* writer Charles Perry, is a highly readable overview of the time. Along similar lines, but with more emphasis on the music scene, is Joel Selvin's *Summer of Love.* Essayist Joan Didion casts a caustic glance at flower power and the Haight-Ashbury in her essay collection *Slouching Towards Bethlehem.* Tom Wolfe also puts the Bay Area during the '60s in perspective with *The Electric Kool-Aid Acid Test,* blending tales of the Grateful Dead, Hell's Angels, and Ken Kesey's band of Merry Pranksters.

The classic Frisco – er, San Francisco – voice is that of Herb Caen, who died in 1997 after penning his daily column, 'Bagdad by the Bay,' for six decades. Although Caen's patter, rife with medium-rare bons mots and boozy one-liners, didn't enjoy a universal appeal, few can deny that Caen knew and loved the city as intensely as anyone. *The World of Herb Caen* is a collection of writings and photos that serves as a fond memory of San Francisco during the heart of the 20th century.

NEWSPAPERS & MAGAZINES

The Bay Area's number-one daily, the *San Francisco Chronicle,* is not one of the USA's great newspapers, but since being bought by Hearst Newspapers in 2000 it has shown an increased interest in investigative journalism. The Sunday edition includes Datebook, a popular entertainment supplement more commonly known as 'the pink section,' for its pink paper. The afternoon daily is *San Francisco Examiner,* founded by George Hearst and then turned over to his more famous son, William Randolph. (Hearst Newspapers sold the *Examiner* after purchasing the *Chronicle.)*

The city's most prominent locally owned free weekly, the *Bay Guardian*, is an excellent source for local news, although its zealous muckraking can be tiresome even to the most devoted news junkie. Casual readers flip straight to the extensive entertainment reviews and listings, or Isadora Alman's 'Ask Isadora' sex-advice column and the personals, which get pretty raunchy and reveal what's really going on in the city.

The *SF Weekly* offers much of the same fare. Dan Savage's riotous 'Savage Love' advice column surpasses Isadora's for scatological curiosity. The *Bay Times* is a free gay publication, issued every other Thursday night.

Most of the locally published periodicals concern themselves with multimedia. The most readable of these is the computer-culture hit *Wired*. Comic-book shops, bookstores, bars, and coffeehouses around town (particularly in the Mission District and the Haight) usually have stacks of small, cutting-edge 'zines. Increasingly, the underground stuff is turning up on the internet rather than in print.

RADIO & TV

Nearly a hundred radio stations in the Bay Area broadcast hip-hop, classic rock (the definition of which gets cloudier all the time), country and western, jazz, classical, Mexican *banda*, college esoterica, news, talk, sports, or Bible thumping. Here's a small selection of what's riding the airwaves:

KQED 88.5 FM – National Public Radio, news and talk

KPOO 89.5 FM – music and news for the black, Latino, and Asian communities

KUSF 90.3 FM – University of San Francisco radio

KALX 90.7 FM – UC Berkeley radio

KCSM 91.1 FM – Bay Area's best jazz station

KPFA 94.1 FM – Pacifica Radio, news and varied music

KDFC 102.1 FM – classical

KFOG 104.5 FM – laid-back classic rock

KITS 105.3 FM – 'alternative' and 'modern' rock, wiseass DJs

KMEL 106.1 FM – current chart hits, hip-hop

There are no exciting television surprises in the Bay Area – public access (on cable just a few hours a day) is hopelessly devoid of the kind of weird creativity one would expect from San Franciscans. Otherwise, television consists of the usual national network affiliates and a proliferation of cable stations. Some local programming can be found on KQED (channel 9), the PBS affiliate.

PHOTOGRAPHY & VIDEO

San Francisco is one of the USA's most photogenic cities, so don't be surprised if you need more film than you packed. There are a couple of reputable shops for camera gear (new and used), equipment rentals, and repairs. One-hour processing, which often means two- or three-hour processing, is widely available in shops along Market St and around Union Square. These shops almost always toss your film into a machine, which yields satisfactory results if you are taking simple snapshots with a flash. Even Walgreen's drugstores, which are all over town, offer speedy, inexpensive printing. If you are particular about your prints, there are many professional labs in town, but same-day 'rush' printing can be very expensive.

Video supplies are often available at the same camera shops. Overseas visitors who are thinking of purchasing videos here should remember that the USA uses the National Television Systems Committee (NTSC) color TV standard, which is not compatible with other standards such as Phase Alternation Line (PAL).

Adolph Gasser MAP 4
181 2nd St ☎ 415-495-3852, 800-994-2773 ⌚ 9am-6pm Mon-Sat Ⓜ Montgomery St BART & Muni station 🚌 Market St buses ♿ W www.gassers.com

Adolph Gasser, conveniently near downtown, is a good place to go for a wide variety of pro and amateur films in all formats at very reasonable prices (35mm print and slide film is cheaper here than at a drugstore, for instance). This store also deals new and used photo and video equipment, and gear can be rented on a daily basis. Film processing services are decent but not exceptional.

Calumet
2001 Bryant St ☎ 415-643-9275 ⌚ 8am-6pm Mon-Fri 🚌 27 Muni ♿ W www.calumetphoto.com

This is another good place for film and supplies.

Photoworks MAP 12
2077-A Market St ☎ 415-626-6800 ⌚ 9am-8pm Mon-Fri, 10am-8pm Sat, 10am-6pm Sun Ⓜ Church St Muni station 🚌 F Muni ♿

Photographers who appreciate careful work by competent professionals recommend Photoworks for prints. Be warned: you pay for quality (up to $23 for a roll of 36, developed and printed 4x6).

New Lab
651 Bryant St ☎ 415-905-8555 ⌚ 8am-10pm Mon-Fri, 10am-4pm Sat 🚌 30 Muni ♿ W www.newlab.com

The New Lab's late-night service and speedy turnaround make it an ideal place for travelers to go for slide processing. It's a state-of-the-art facility with a solid, not unfriendly staff. This is not where you go with print film, however.

TIME

San Francisco is on Pacific Standard Time, three hours behind the East Coast's Eastern Standard Time and eight hours behind Greenwich Mean Time (GMT). In the summer, there's Summer Time in Britain and daylight saving time in the United States, so the eight-hour difference is usually maintained.

ELECTRICITY

Electric current in the USA is 110-115 volts, 60 Hz AC. Outlets may be suited for flat two-prong or three-prong plugs. If your appliance is made for another electrical system, you will need a transformer or adapter; if you didn't bring one along, try Radio Shack (there are several locations – check the yellow pages) or another consumer electronics store.

WEIGHTS & MEASURES

Distances are in feet, yards, and miles; weights are in ounces (oz), pounds (lb), and tons. Gasoline is measured in US gallons, which are about 20% smaller than the imperial gallon and equivalent to 3.79 liters. There is a conversion chart on the inside back cover of this book.

LAUNDRY

Fancier hotels will do laundry, but it isn't cheap. However, since most residents of the city's central enclaves live in apartments too crowded to fit washers and dryers, inexpensive self-service laundries in those areas can be found on nearly every block. Typical costs are around $1.50 to $1.75 for washing and 25¢ per 10-minute drying cycle. If you do your own wash in a laundromat, be aware that theft isn't unheard of. Strange as it sounds, people have complained of having their pants pinched from the dryer while they weren't looking.

Brain Wash MAP 4
1122 Folsom St ☎ 415-431-9274 ⌚ 8am-midnight Mon-Thurs, 8am-1am Fri, 7:30am-midnight Sat, 7:30am-1am Sun 🚌 12 Muni ♿ W www.brainwash.com

To liven up the drudgery of wash day, try Brain Wash, in SoMa, where you can hang out in the café and listen to live music or stand-up comedy while you wait for your clothes. It can be a surreal experience, folding your underwear while the people standing around you groan at bad jokes. Wash and fold service is available (90¢/lb, minimum $9).

TOILETS

Public toilets are not difficult to find in most parts of San Francisco, particularly in heavily touristed areas, though they are not always clean, especially by the end of the day. In Union Square, where a shopper's every need is accommodated, clean toilets can be found in the San Francisco Shopping Centre and in Macy's department store. In the Civic Center area, the new main library has rest rooms, as do public library branches and parks throughout the city – some of these are heavily utilized by the city's sizable homeless population. In many parts of town, the most convenient public toilets are the green sidewalk commodes installed by the city. Use of these self-flushing and usually clean facilities costs just 25¢. Look for them in North Beach, Fisherman's Wharf, the Financial District, and even the Tenderloin.

The Haight-Ashbury and Mission District are woefully lacking in public toilets, and even most shops do not have facilities for customers – you may have to buy a cup of coffee or a beer just to gain access to private 'facilities.' (Please avoid the temptation to wee in public.)

LUGGAGE STORAGE

Hotels will almost always keep an eye on bags for guests, but be sure to remove anything valuable beforehand – hotels will not assume responsibility for lost items.

HEALTH

For most foreign visitors, no immunizations are required for entry, though cholera and yellow fever vaccinations may be required of travelers from areas with a history of those diseases. In San Francisco, there are no unexpected health dangers, excellent medical attention is readily available, and

Medical Kit Checklist

The following is a list of items you should consider including in your medical kit – consult your pharmacist for brands available in your country.

- ❑ **Aspirin or paracetamol** (acetaminophen in the USA) – for pain or fever
- ❑ **Antihistamine** – for allergies (eg, hay fever); to ease the itch from insect bites or stings; and to prevent motion sickness
- ❑ **Cold and flu tablets, throat lozenges, and nasal decongestant**
- ❑ **Multivitamins** – consider for long trips, when your dietary vitamin intake may be inadequate
- ❑ **Antibiotics** – consider including these if you're traveling well off the beaten track; see your doctor, as they must be prescribed, and carry the prescription with you
- ❑ **Loperamide or diphenoxylate** –'blockers' for diarrhea
- ❑ **Prochlorperazine or metaclopramide** – for nausea and vomiting
- ❑ **Rehydration mixture** – to prevent dehydration, which may occur, for example, during bouts of diarrhea; particularly important when traveling with children
- ❑ **Insect repellent, sunscreen, lip balm, and eye drops**
- ❑ **Calamine lotion, sting relief spray, or aloe vera** – to ease irritation from sunburn and insect bites or stings
- ❑ **Antifungal cream or powder** – for fungal skin infections and thrush
- ❑ **Antiseptic (such as povidone-iodine)** – for cuts and grazes
- ❑ **Bandages, Band-Aids (plasters), and other wound dressings**
- ❑ **Water purification tablets or iodine**
- ❑ **Scissors, tweezers, and a thermometer** – note that mercury thermometers are prohibited by airlines

the only real health concern is that, as elsewhere in the USA, a collision with the medical system can cause severe injuries to your financial state.

Insurance

It is a very good idea to have medical insurance when traveling in the US, in case you suffer an unforeseen illness or injury. Many travel insurance policies include medical coverage. See Travel Insurance, earlier in this chapter, for more information.

Medical Services

Check the yellow pages under 'Physicians & Surgeons' or 'Clinics' to find a doctor or under 'Dentists' to see photos of smiling people with perfect teeth (or to find a dentist). Your hotel might be able to make suggestions. In an emergency, go to the emergency room at one of the city's hospitals. Call ☎ 911 for an ambulance.

San Francisco General Hospital MAP 14
1001 Potrero Ave ☎ 415-206-8000 ⌚ 24 hours 🚌 9 Muni ♿

SF General offers 24-hour emergency care.

Haight Ashbury Free Clinic MAP 11
558 Clayton St ☎ 415-487-5632 ⌚ 1pm-9pm Mon, 9am-9pm Tues-Thurs, 1pm-5pm Fri 🚌 7 Muni ♿

For nonemergency situations, there's the Haight Ashbury Free Clinic. The clinic's services are offered by appointment only, but once you're in, a doctor will see you free of charge and will offer advice if further medical attention is needed.

WOMEN TRAVELERS

Women travelers are less likely to encounter problems in live-and-let-live San Francisco than in other US cities, although the usual precautions apply. Since women play a very active and effective role in city politics, women's organizations proliferate in this city, addressing a wide range of concerns, including abortion rights, rape, child care, domestic violence, and self-defense, and providing support for various constituents, such as African American women, Asian women, women in recovery, women over 40, and lesbian mothers. Look in the yellow pages under 'Women's Organizations & Services' for a comprehensive listing.

San Francisco Women's Building MAP 14
3543 18th St ☎ 415-431-1180 ⌚ 9am-5pm Mon-Fri Ⓜ 16th St BART station 🚌 33 Muni ♿

In the Mission District, the Women's Building has offices and meeting rooms for several women's organizations, including the National Organization for Women (NOW), and it also provides numerous resources and services for women.

Planned Parenthood MAP 3
815 Eddy St, Suite 200 ☎ 800-967-7526 ⌚ 9am-5pm Mon-Fri 🚌 2, 3, 4, 42, 47, 49 Muni ♿
w www.plannedparenthood.org

This San Francisco branch provides health-care services for women, including primary care, gynecological care, pregnancy testing, and birth control.

San Francisco Women Against Rape
☎ 415-647-7273 ⌚ 24 hours

Grassroots SFWAR's volunteer-staffed hot line offers counseling and medical and legal advice.

See Dangers & Annoyances for more details on personal security.

GAY & LESBIAN TRAVELERS

San Francisco's small overall size and relatively prominent gay and lesbian population make it the most 'gay' city in the world. Rainbow flags, a symbol of queer pride, appear in apartment windows and over bar entrances in many neighborhoods, and they adorn almost every other building in the Castro, the upscale heart of the gay community. In the Castro, nearly all shops and bars cater to, and many are owned by, gays and lesbians, making this a destination for gay travelers. Seedier Polk Gulch has declined drastically since the late '70s and the onset of AIDS, but it still has a few bars and clubs, and SoMa's leather scene has waned but is not in danger of disappearing any time soon. In the Mission District, a proliferation of bars and other businesses along Valencia St and nearby side streets cater to a lively lesbian scene. Nearby Bernal Heights is another gay and lesbian hub.

Over the years, San Francisco has elected a number of openly gay politicians to local office; gays and lesbians represent a powerful voice in city politics. Still, acceptance is not universal even here. Vandalism to cars bearing rainbow bumper stickers is not unheard of, especially in more suburban parts of the city like the Sunset District, and incidences of gay bashing still occur.

Check the yellow pages under 'Gay & Lesbian Organizations' for the extensive listings of community resources.

A Different Light Bookstore MAP 12
489 Castro St ☎ 415-431-0891 ⌚ 10am-10pm Sun-Thurs, 10am-11pm Fri-Sat Ⓜ Castro St Muni station 🚌 F Muni ♿
w *www.adlbooks.com*

This is the Bay Area's number-one gay bookshop and is a good place to go to start learning your way around.

Gay, Lesbian, Bisexual & Transgender Switchboard Hot Line
☎ 510-841-6224 ⌚ 24 hours

Community United Against Violence
973 Market St, No 500 ☎ 415-333-4357 ⌚ 24 hours Ⓜ Civic Center BART & Muni station 🚌 Market St buses
w *www.xq.com/cuav*

This organization runs a 24-hour crisis line for victims of hate crimes and domestic violence.

AIDS Hot Line
☎ 800-590-2437

Counseling and advice are offered over the phone to people who have, or think they may have, HIV or AIDS.

DISABLED TRAVELERS

Berkeley, across the bay from San Francisco, is home to several pioneering disabled services organizations, so there are a great deal of resources and provisions for disabled travelers in the Bay Area. All the Bay Area transit companies, including BART, Muni, AC Transit, and Golden Gate Transit, offer travel discounts for the disabled, and they have a jointly issued ID card to access these reductions. (See the Getting Around chapter for phone numbers for these agencies.) All Muni Metro and BART stations are wheelchair accessible. Muni's *Street & Transit Map* details which bus routes and streetcar stops are wheelchair friendly. The *San Francisco Bay Area Regional Transit Guide*, published by the Metropolitan Transportation Commission, has a Disabled Services section. The major car rental companies are generally able to supply hand-controlled vehicles with one or two days' notice.

Center for Independent Living
649 Mission St ☎ 415-543-6222, 415-543-6698 TDD ⌚ 9am-5pm Mon-Thurs, 9am-3pm Fri Ⓜ Montgomery St BART & Muni station 🚌 14, 30 Muni ♿
w *www.cilberkeley.org*

Call this Berkeley-based organization's San Francisco office in advance to get information about the wheelchair accessibility of local hotels.

A number of organizations and tour providers specialize in the needs of disabled travelers:

Access-Able Travel Source
PO Box 1796, Wheat Ridge, CO 80034
☎ 303-232-2979
w *www.access-able.com*

Access-Able has a useful directory of tours, hotels, and travel agents around the world. They have a very informative and easy-to-use website.

Mobility International USA
PO Box 10767, Eugene, OR 97440
☎ 541-343-1284
w *www.miusa.org*

The website is a good place to begin pre-trip planning.

Society for the Advancement of Travel for the Handicapped (SATH)
347 Fifth Ave, No 610, New York, NY 10016
☎ 212-447-7284
w *www.sath.org*

SATH is a good resource for those needing travel advice, books, and referrals to tour operators.

SENIOR TRAVELERS

San Francisco is a popular destination for the retired set. Though the age at which senior benefits begin varies, travelers from 50 years and up (though more commonly 65 and up) can expect to receive cut rates at such places as hotels, museums, and restaurants.

Some national advocacy groups that can help seniors in planning their travels are:

American Association of Retired Persons (AARP)
601 E St NW, Washington, DC 20049
☎ *800-424-3410*
w *www.aarp.org*

This is an advocacy group for people 50 years of age and older and is a good resource when looking for travel bargains. A one-year membership costs $10.

Elderhostel
11 Ave de Lafayette, Boston, MA 02111
☎ *877-426-8056 in the US and Canada, 978-323-4141 international, 877-426-2167 TTY*
w *www.elderhostel.org*

This nonprofit organization offers seniors the opportunity to attend academic college courses throughout the USA and Canada. The programs last one to three weeks, include meals and accommodations, and are open to people 55 years and older and their companions.

SAN FRANCISCO FOR CHILDREN

San Francisco is fairly child friendly, and even some of the priciest restaurants are relaxed enough to accept children. Many of the city's sites and museums were designed with children in mind, and a lot of other attractions will appeal to the young 'uns.

TOM DOWNS

Simply getting around San Francisco and the bay aboard cable cars and the ferries can be a fun adventure for children. On Muni, children under five travel free and those age five to 17 travel for just 35¢.

Here's a list of ideas for keeping your juveniles out of trouble (more detailed coverage of these sites can be found in Things to See & Do):

Alcatraz
Basic Brown Bear Factory – Potrero Hill
California Academy of Sciences and Steinhart Aquarium – Golden Gate Park
Exploratorium – the Marina
San Francisco Zoological Gardens, carousel – the Sunset
Metreon, Where the Wild Things Are – SoMa
Randall Museum – the Haight
Sea lions, carousel, Pier 39 – Fisherman's Wharf
Zeum, carousel – SoMa

As you may be aware, idea number one, Alcatraz, is a famous prison. The catch here is that children must be accompanied by an adult, so Mom and Dad can't just send Junior to jail while they stay in Fisherman's Wharf for cocktails and dinner.

Golden Gate Park, Dolores Park, and Portsmouth Square all have nice playgrounds, and there are others scattered throughout the city. The city's charming old carousels, noted in the list above, make great vacation photo-ops. (There's also a carousel in Golden Gate Park.)

There are pizzerias and fake '50s diners, where dining is as fun as it is nourishing, all over town. Restaurant-bars with dining tables (including brewpubs) and café-bars are not always off-limits to children, so parents don't have to write off the nightlife altogether.

If you aren't accustomed to traveling with children, you might find some encouragement in Lonely Planet's *Travel with Children*, by Cathy Lanigan.

LIBRARIES

The San Francisco Public Library has branches all over the city. The state-of-the-art main library, in Civic Center, is the most likely to be of interest to visitors to the city, with its stellar special collections, myriad services, and attractive modern architecture. Collections that distinguish the main library include the African American Collection (3rd floor), the James C Hormel Gay & Lesbian Center (3rd floor), the Art and Music Center (4th floor), and the San Francisco History Center (6th floor). Services include internet access, fax machines, copiers, word processors, and a lunch café. It's also not a bad place to learn about services available in other parts of town, and special events put on here are often worth checking out.

To borrow books, you must have an SFPL card, and only residents of the city are eligible. However, anyone is welcome to visit the libraries and utilize many of their services.

There are 26 branch libraries in the city. A few of the more central ones are listed here.

New Main Library MAP 3
100 Larkin St ☎ 415-557-4400 ⌚ 10am-6pm Mon, 9am-8pm Tues-Thurs, noon-6pm Fri, 10am-6pm Sat, noon-5pm Sun Ⓜ Civic Center BART & Muni station 🚌 F Muni ♿
w *www.sfpl.lib.ca.us*

Free internet access is available on a 15-minute basis. The 1st-floor terminals are available to visitors without SFPL library cards. There's no email access.

Chinatown Branch Library
1135 Powell St ☎ 415-274-0275 ⌚ 1pm-9pm Mon, 10am-9pm Tues-Wed, 10am-6pm Thurs, 1pm-5pm Fri, 10am-6pm Sat, 1pm-5pm Sun 🚌 1, 45, 30 Muni ♿

Eureka Valley/Harvey Milk Memorial Branch Library MAP 12
3555 16th St ☎ 415-554-9445 ⌚ noon-6pm Mon, 10am-9pm Tues, noon-9pm Wed, 10am-6pm Thurs, 1pm-6pm Fri-Sat Ⓜ Castro St Muni station 🚌 22, 24, F Muni

North Beach Branch Library
2000 Mason St ☎ 415-274-0270 ⌚ noon-6pm Mon, 10am-9pm Tues, 1pm-9pm Wed, 10am-6pm Thurs, 1pm-6pm Fri-Sat 🚌 15, 30, 41, 45 Muni 🚋 Powell-Mason cable car ♿

Mission Branch Library
300 Bartlett St ☎ 415-695-5090 ⌚ 1pm-9pm Mon, 10am-9pm Tues-Wed, 10am-6pm Thurs & Sat, 1pm-6pm Fri, 1pm-5pm Sun Ⓜ 24th St BART station 🚌 14, 26 Muni ♿

UNIVERSITIES

San Francisco is oddly lacking in major universities. The Bay Area's big schools are the University of California at Berkeley, in the East Bay, and Stanford University, in Palo Alto. The University of California does have a small extension campus and a medical school in San Francisco.

But there are two universities where students can earn a Bachelor of the Arts degree, and there's one community college as well.

San Francisco State University
1600 Holloway Ave ☎ 415-338-1111 🚌 17, 18, 26, 28, 29, M Muni ♿
w *www.sfsu.edu*

With more than 20,000 undergrads, SF State, in the Sunset District, is the city's largest university.

University of San Francisco
2130 Fulton St ☎ 415-422-5555 ♿
w *www.usfca.edu*

In the Richmond District, USF is a private Jesuit university founded in 1855.

DANGERS & ANNOYANCES

Like most big US cities, San Francisco has its share of homelessness and crime, but prudent travelers are not at any undue risk. Certain neighborhoods are seedier than others and considered relatively 'unsafe,' especially at night and for those walking alone; these include the Tenderloin, parts of the Mission, the Western Addition, and 6th and 7th Sts south of Market. However, these areas are not always sharply defined, and travelers should be aware of their surroundings whenever they walk in the city. After dark, some of the city's parks, particularly Dolores Park and Buena Vista Park, become havens for drug dealing and sleazy sex. The Bayview-Hunters Point neighborhood north of 3-Com (Candlestick) Park, where the 49ers play, is plagued by a high crime rate and frequent violence and is not particularly suitable for wandering tourists.

If you find yourself somewhere you would rather not be, act confident and sure of yourself; then go into a store and call a taxicab.

Panhandlers

Homelessness is a rampant problem in US cities. Tourists in San Francisco are most likely to be approached by strangers panhandling for cigarettes or change around Union Square and the Powell St BART and Muni station, but there are homeless persons throughout the city. Some panhandlers begin with a friendly bit of chatter before getting to the point. If you aren't accustomed to it, these requests can seem threatening, but in nearly every case, all you need to do is give a firm but polite no, or offer some money or food if you can. Some panhandlers are more persistent than others, and in those cases simply keep walking; the person will soon move on.

If you feel moved to do something about the plight of San Francisco's homeless, it is more effective to give money to a local agency than to individuals on the street.

Glide Memorial Church MAP 3
330 Ellis St ☎ 415-674-6000 🚌 27 Muni ♿
w *www.glide.org*

You can make donations to this church (c/o the Development Office), which provides three meals a day to the needy. It also accepts coats, blankets, and sundry items.

Coalition on Homelessness
468 Turk St ☎ 415-346-3740 🕘 9am-5pm Mon-Fri 🚌 31 Muni ♿
w *www.sfo.com/~coh*

This is a good local advocacy group for the homeless, and it publishes *Street Sheet*, a legitimate mouthpiece for the local homeless (many of whom sell the paper for a modest income).

The Sex Trade

Strip joints, peep shows, and adult video stores are concentrated along the eastern edge of the Tenderloin and along Broadway in North Beach. Strip club barkers are a thing of the past, but skimpily clad women – some of them appearing suspiciously young – will stand beneath the marquees trying to entice passing men – along with their wives and girlfriends – to see the show.

The world's oldest occupation continues visibly along Geary and O'Farrell Sts in the Tenderloin, where men can expect greetings such as 'How ya doin' tonight, honey?'

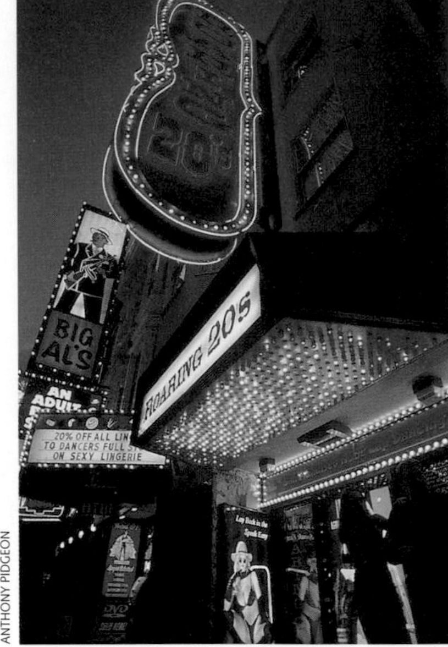

ANTHONY PIDGEON

North Beach offers more than good Italian food.

Transvestites and male hustlers ply their trade nearby, primarily in Polk Gulch. Cars and vans from throughout the Bay Area prowl the area at night, and women walking through these streets alone will probably attract unwanted attention.

Gangs

This book covers some areas where youth gangs exist. These areas include Chinatown, the Tenderloin, and the Mission District (including Mission St and areas to the east). The gangs' most visible signs are the spray-painted signatures – or 'tags' – on garage doors and storefronts. Gang violence, when it occurs, captures local headlines – especially the crimes of Asian gangs in the Tenderloin and Chinatown. Gang members sometimes settle their disputes in public, but shootings out on the street are not common.

Earthquakes

Since the last large earthquake hit San Francisco, in 1989, experts have predicted that the next 'Big One' would occur sometime in the next 30 years. Smaller quakes are more frequent, but they rarely cause much damage. Chances are slim that one will happen while you are here.

However, should the ground begin to shake, keep the following things in mind. The main danger during a big quake is being hit by something falling, whether it's the face of a building or furniture toppling over. If you're indoors, try to get under shelter, such as a strong table or a doorframe. Don't rush outside, where you will be exposed to shattered glass and falling brick. If you're outside, move away from buildings, trees, power lines, signposts, or anything else that might fall on you. If you're in a car, stop if it is safe, but not under bridges, on overpasses, or in tunnels, and be careful not to block the way of rescue vehicles. Reliable information can be difficult to come by during the immediate aftermath of a quake – tune to news radio stations that have their own helicopter crews.

EMERGENCIES

Dial ☎ 911 for all police, fire, and ambulance emergencies. At the front of various Bay Area white pages directories, there's a page of 24-hour 'Emergency Crisis Hotlines.' In San Francisco call the following:

Suicide Crisis Line	☎ 415-781-0500
Drug Treatment	☎ 415-362-3400
Rape Crisis	☎ 415-647-7273

The phone directories also have a First Aid & Survival Guide, which includes advice on surviving an earthquake and a list of steps for performing CPR.

If something is stolen from you, report it to the police; you'll need a police report to make a claim if you have a travel insurance policy. If your credit cards, cash cards, or traveler's checks have been taken, notify your bank or the relevant company as soon as possible. For refunds or lost or stolen traveler's checks (not credit cards), call:

American Express	☎ 800-221-7282
MasterCard	☎ 800-223-9920
Thomas Cook	☎ 800-223-7373
Visa	☎ 800-227-6811

For lost credit cards call:

American Express	☎ 800-233-5432
MasterCard	☎ 800-307-7309
Visa	☎ 800-336-8472

Foreign visitors who lose their passport should contact their consulate. Having a copy of the important pages of your passport will make replacement much easier.

LEGAL MATTERS

There is no reason to expect a run-in with the police force during a visit to San Francisco, unless you blatantly challenge local laws or commit a crime. In recent years the police have cracked down on park squatters…so maybe you should change your plans if you were considering camping in Golden Gate Park. Drinking alcoholic beverages outdoors is not officially allowed, though drinking beer and wine is often permissible at street fairs and other outdoor events; if vendors are selling it, it's safe to assume you can drink it. Although attitudes toward jaywalking (crossing streets where there is no crosswalk) are relaxed and cops usually look the other way if they see you doing it, be advised that it is illegal.

If you are arrested for any reason, you are allowed to remain silent. There is no legal reason to speak to a police officer if you don't wish to, but never walk away from an officer until given permission. All persons who are arrested are legally allowed (and given) the right to make one phone call. If you don't have a lawyer or family member to help you, call your consulate. The police will give you the number on request.

BUSINESS HOURS

Office hours in the Bay Area are commonly 9am to 5pm Monday to Friday, although there can be a variance of half an hour or so. Many shops are open longer hours and through the weekends, and some larger supermarkets are open 24 hours.

Banks are generally open weekdays 8am to 6pm, usually staying open later on one of those evenings. Some are open on Saturday until about noon.

PUBLIC HOLIDAYS

Holidays that may affect business hours and transit schedules include:

New Year's Day – January 1

Martin Luther King Jr Day – 3rd Monday in January

Presidents' Day – 3rd Monday in February

Easter – a Sunday in March or April

Memorial Day – last Monday in May

Independence Day – July 4

Labor Day – 1st Monday in September

Columbus Day – 2nd Monday in October

Veterans Day – November 11

Thanksgiving – 4th Thursday in November

Christmas Day – December 25

SPECIAL EVENTS

San Francisco has a full calendar of festivals and street fairs, with a few stellar highlights, like Chinese New Year and the Gay Pride Parade. Halloween is a popular event in the city; even during the day you may spot masqueraders driving or riding the bus to work. If you're into dressing up, you might also consider coming for the Bay Area's biggest foot race, Bay to Breakers, which is as much a costume party as a sporting event.

For additional events information, contact the San Francisco Convention and Visitors Bureau or visit its website (see Tourist Offices, earlier in this chapter).

JANUARY & FEBRUARY

San Francisco Independent Film Festival

☎ *415-820-3907* W *www.sfindie.com*

Held mid-January since 1998, this nine-day event promotes and celebrates artistic and underground films. Animated shorts are often a festival highlight.

Chinese New Year & Golden Dragon Parade

☎ *415-391-9680* W *www.chineseparade.com*

In January or February, a festive, carnival-like spirit overtakes Chinatown as Chinese New Year is celebrated with color and verve. The nighttime Golden Dragon Parade, led by a 75-foot dragon, is the highlight of the festivities.

MARCH

St Patrick's Day

☎ *415-661-2700*

St Patrick's Day (March 17) is mostly an unorganized affair, but Irish pubs are all too happy to take care of your holiday needs. The city puts on the requisite downtown parade, usually on a Sunday before or after the 17th.

APRIL

Cherry Blossom Festival

☎ *415-563 2313* 🚌 *22, 38 Muni*

The arrival of spring is celebrated in late April in Japantown with martial arts demonstrations, tea ceremonies, and other uniquely Japanese events. Phone for details.

San Francisco International Film Festival

☎ *415-929-5000* W *www.sfiff.org*

In late April or early May, the San Francisco Film Society holds its annual two-week film festival, the longest-running in the country. The program is always exceptional, and tickets can be difficult to come by. Screenings take place at the Castro and Kabuki theaters and elsewhere in the Bay Area.

MAY

Cinco de Mayo

☎ *415-826-1401* W *www.meca.bigstep.com*

RICK GERHARTER

Chinese New Year Parade

The Mexican victory over the French at the Battle of Puebla in 1862 is celebrated the weekend closest to May 5. A festival of music and dancing, with a low-rider and bomb car show, is capped by a vibrant parade down Mission St.

Bay to Breakers
☎ *415-808-5000 ext 2222* Ⓢ *adult $25, child $20*
W *www.baytobreakers.com*

On the third Sunday in May, more than 100,000 Bay Area joggers, many of them in costumes that are not in any way suitable for running, make their way from the bay (the Embarcadero) via Golden Gate Park to the breakers (the Pacific Ocean), a distance of about 7 miles.

Carnaval
☎ *415-826-1401* W *www.meca.bigstep.com*

San Francisco does things its own way, staging a pre-Lenten party long after Lent has ended – on Memorial Day weekend, to be precise. But the requisite exotic dancers and a celebratory Latin American spirit prevail on the streets of the Mission.

JUNE

San Francisco International Lesbian and Gay Film Festival
☎ *415-703-8650* W *www.frameline.org*

The premier independent queer film festival in the world has been held for more than 25 years. For more information, see the special section 'Out in the Streets: More than the Pride Parade.'

Lesbian, Gay, Bisexual, and Transgender Pride Parade
☎ *415-864-3733* W *www.sfpride.org*

This often-outrageous parade, capping Pride Week, takes place on the last Sunday in June. The evening before the parade is the Dyke March and the Pink Saturday party on Castro St. On Sunday, as many as a half-million people congregate along Market St for the city's biggest annual parade – naturally, hotel rooms can be difficult to come by. For more details, see the special section 'Out in the Streets: More than the Pride Parade.'

North Beach Festival
☎ *415-989-6426* 🚌 *30, 45 Muni*

Held in mid-June, this festival features booths run by some of North Beach's best-loved restaurants, as well as stages where opera, swing, jazz, and other types of music are performed.

Haight St Fair
☎ *415-661-8025* 🚌 *7 Muni*

The spirit of the '60s isn't exactly brought back to life, but this fair does attempt to get back to the neighborhood's creative roots with arts, crafts, and entertainment.

JULY

Independence Day

After dark on July 4, fireworks light up the sky around the bay – a popular place to watch from is Fisherman's Wharf.

Cable Car Bell-Ringing Championship
☎ *415-923-6217*

In mid-July, cable car drivers compete to be the loudest or most tuneful bell ringer.

SEPTEMBER

Opera in the Park
☎ *415-864-3330* Ⓢ *free* 🚌 *7, 71 Muni*

On the first Sunday following the start of the opera season, the San Francisco Opera puts on a free show at Sharon Meadow in Golden Gate Park to mark the beginning of its season.

Fringe Festival
☎ *415-931-1094* W *www.sffringe.org*

Hundreds of dramatic performances are staged around downtown, some of them straight-ahead theater, some of them outrageously experimental.

Shakespeare Festival
☎ *415-422-2221*

Free performances of a different play are put on each year, starting Labor Day weekend in Golden Gate Park and other Bay Area parks.

San Francisco Blues Festival
☎ *415-979-5588* Ⓢ *advance ticket $25, gate ticket $30* 🚌 *22, 47, 49 Muni*
W *www.sfblues.com*

Two days of blues performance take place in Fort Mason's Great Meadow in mid- to late September.

Autumn Moon Festival
☎ *415-982-6306* 🚌 *30, 45 Muni*

Chinatown celebrates this traditional festival

FACTS FOR THE VISITOR

with a large street fair featuring entertainment, lion and dragon dances, and fun for the kids. It takes place in late September.

Folsom St Fair
☎ *415-861-3247* 🚌 *12 Muni*
W *www.folsomstreetfair.com*

In late September, the leather crowd shows up in force – and people who love a spectacle naturally follow – for one of the most outrageous street fairs in the city. For more details, see the special section 'Out in the Streets: More than the Pride Parade.'

OCTOBER

Castro St Fair
☎ *415-467-3354* Ⓜ *Castro St Muni station*
🚌 *F Muni* ♿
W *www.castrostreetfair.org*

Another popular street fair, this one in early October attracts crowds from the gay community. For more details, see the special section 'Out in the Streets: More than the Pride Parade.'

San Francisco Jazz Festival
☎ *415-788-7353, 800-627-5277*
W *www.sfjazz.org*

Throughout the city, catch jazz performances by legendary and up-and-coming artists. The festival takes place in late October and early November.

Halloween

For masqueraders, of whom San Francisco has many, the night of October 31 is the highlight of the year, with hundreds of thousands of costumed revelers taking to the streets, particularly in the Castro. An organized event, with live music, DJs, and bawdy costume contests, is held at Civic Center. For more details, see the special section 'Out in the Streets: More than the Pride Parade.'

October is also the time for the annual Pumpkin Festival at Half Moon Bay (see Excursions).

NOVEMBER

Día de los Muertos
☎ *415-821-1155*
W *latinoartsctr.citysearch.com*

On November 2, Mexico's spirited Day of the Dead is celebrated with arts in the Mission.

WORK

Foreign visitors are not legally allowed to work in the USA without the appropriate working visa, and recent legislative changes are specifically targeting illegal immigrants, which is what you will be if you work here while on a tourist visa. See Visa Extensions in the Documents section for warnings on longer stays.

Getting There & Away

AIR

The Bay Area has three major airports: San Francisco International Airport, on the west side of the bay; Oakland International Airport, only a few miles across the bay on the east side; and San Jose International Airport, at the southern end of the bay. The majority of international flights use the San Francisco airport; at Oakland and San Jose, 'international' usually means Mexico and Canada. All three airports are important domestic gateways. See the Getting Around chapter for information on transportation to and from the San Francisco and Oakland airports.

San Francisco International Airport

☎ *650-876-7809* 🚌 *Muni, SamTrans, various van, limo, and taxi services* ♿
w *www.flysfo.com*

SFO is 15 miles south of San Francisco, just off Hwy 101 near the town of San Bruno. There are three terminals at the airport. The North Terminal is where American, Canadian, and United Airlines are based. The South Terminal is home to Air Canada, Alaska Airlines, America West, Continental, Delta, Southwest, TWA, and US Airways. In December 2000, SFO opened its new International Terminal. The largest international terminal in the US, it's the jumping-off point for all international airlines (except for the Canadian ones), plus the international services of Alaska Airlines, Delta, Northwest, and United.

Information booths are on the lower (arrivals) level of all three terminals and operate daily 8am to 1:30am. These booths can also be contacted from any white courtesy phone in the airport (dial ☎ 7-0018). Travelers' Aid information booths are on the upper level and operate daily 9am to 9pm. ATMs are found in all three terminals. Bank of America has branches in the North Terminal on the mezzanine and in the International Terminal. Currency exchange is available in the International Terminal. Lockers in all boarding areas cost $2 for 24 hours; larger luggage can be stored in the Luggage Storage/Travel Agency area in the upper-level connector between the South and International Terminals. On the lower level of the International Terminal, a medical clinic (white courtesy phone ☎ 7-0444) operates 24 hours daily. Weary travelers arriving between 8am and 6pm can freshen up with a shower at SFO Hairport in Boarding Area C. Smokers desperate for that first deep drag after a long nonsmoking flight must locate one of the smoking rooms upstairs in the North and South Terminals and downstairs in the International Terminal.

Warning

The information in this chapter is particularly vulnerable to change: prices for international travel are volatile, routes are introduced and canceled, schedules change, special deals come and go, and rules and visa requirements are amended. Airlines and governments seem to take a perverse pleasure in making price structures and regulations as complicated as possible. You should check directly with the airline or a travel agent to make sure you understand how a fare (and any ticket you may buy) works. In addition, the travel industry is highly competitive, and there are many lurks and perks.

The upshot of this is that you should get opinions, quotes and advice from as many airlines and travel agents as possible before you part with your hard-earned cash. The details given in this chapter should be regarded as pointers and are not a substitute for your own careful, up-to-date research.

Within North America

The Bay Area is a major hub in North American air traffic, so there should be little trouble finding a flight or connection to just about anywhere on the continent. There are several options for finding the cheapest or most convenient flight.

Regional airlines (those serving fewer destinations than the intercontinental companies) are a good bet, as they tend to fly their routes more often than do their globe-trotting competitors.

United Airlines (☎ 800-241-6522 w www.ual.com) is a major airline that has its hub at SFO and serves a wide range of destinations to and from San Francisco.

Southwest (☎ 800-435-9792 w www.iflyswa.com) covers the western USA fairly completely. It often runs specials with rates undercutting those of other major airlines.

Fares change as often as the winds these days, but nearly all the best fares are available only if you purchase them seven to 21 days before your trip. 'Companion fare' specials, letting two people travel for the price of one, are also worth keeping an eye out for. Roundtrip fares to the East Coast typically cost between $300 and $400. Roundtrip fares to Chicago hover around $300. A jaunt down to Los Angeles or up to Seattle or Portland will cost around $100.

Flights outside the USA also vary depending on the frequency of flights, the time of year, the distance traveled, and the whim of the industry. Some average roundtrip fares to Canada are: Vancouver $200, Edmonton $300, Winnipeg $400, and Montreal $450. Flights to Mexico City average around $400, and the fares rise sharply for destinations farther south. Again, these fares are rough guidelines of what to expect. Bear in mind that fares to Canada tend to go up in summer, after its cities have thawed; fares to Mexico are more likely to rise in winter, when snow-birds travel south. Call a travel agent or check the newspapers for specifics.

ANGUS OBORN

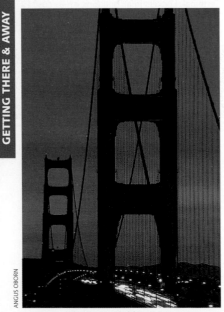

'Open your Golden Gate...'

Scan the Sunday travel section of the *San Francisco Examiner* or the Bay Area's free weekly papers for travel ads and discounted fares out of San Francisco. Good travel agents, both of which also have offices in Berkeley and Palo Alto, include:

Council Travel
530 Bush St ☎ 415-421-3473, 800-226-8624 ⌚ 9am-5pm Mon-Tues & Thurs-Fri, 10am-5pm Wed, 1:30am-2:30pm Sat 🚌 9, 30, 45 Muni ♿
w *www.counciltravel.com*

Council is one of the leading student- and budget-travel agencies, with offices and affiliations throughout the US and Europe.

STA Travel
36 Geary St ☎ 415-391-8407, 800-777-0112 ⌚ 9am-7pm Mon-Fri, 10am-6pm Sat, 10am-5pm Sun Ⓜ Montgomery St BART & Muni station 🚌 38 Muni ♿
w *www.statravel.com*

STA is one of the world's largest international agencies geared toward the needs of young and independent travelers.

To/From Abroad

VISIT USA PASSES Almost all domestic carriers offer Visit USA passes to non-US citizens. The passes are actually a book of coupons – each coupon equals a flight. Typically, the minimum number of coupons you can buy is three or four and the maximum is eight or ten, and they must be purchased in conjunction with a flight on an international airline (Canada and Mexico excluded). Coupons cost anywhere from $100 to $160 each, depending on how many you buy. Most airlines require you to plan your itinerary in advance and complete your flights within 60 days of arrival, but the rules can vary from

Air Travel Glossary

Cancellation Penalties If you have to cancel or change a discounted ticket, there are often heavy penalties involved; insurance can sometimes be taken out against these penalties. Some airlines impose penalties on regular tickets as well, particularly against 'no-show' passengers.

Courier Fares Businesses often need to send urgent documents or freight securely and quickly. Courier companies hire people to accompany the package through customs and, in return, offer a discount ticket which is sometimes a phenomenal bargain. However, you may have to surrender all your baggage allowance and take only carry-on luggage.

Full Fares Airlines traditionally offer 1st class (coded F), business class (coded J) and economy class (coded Y) tickets. These days, so many promotional and discounted fares are available that few passengers pay full economy fare.

Lost Tickets If you lose your airline ticket, an airline will usually treat it like a traveler's check and, after inquiries, issue you with another one. Legally, however, an airline is entitled to treat it like cash: if you lose it, it's gone forever. Take good care of your tickets.

Onward Tickets An entry requirement for many countries is a ticket out of the country. If you're unsure of your next move, the easiest solution is to buy the cheapest onward ticket to a neighboring country or a ticket from a reliable airline that can later be refunded if you do not use it.

Open-Jaw Tickets These are return tickets that permit you to fly into one place but return from another. If available, these tickets can save you backtracking to your arrival point.

Overbooking Because almost every flight has some passengers that fail to show up, airlines often book more passengers than they have seats. Usually excess passengers make up for the no-shows, but occasionally somebody gets 'bumped' onto the next available flight. Guess who it is most likely to be? The passengers who check in late.

Promotional Fares These are officially discounted fares, available from travel agencies or direct from the airline.

Reconfirmation If you don't reconfirm your flight at least 72 hours prior to departure, the airline may delete your name from the passenger list. Call to find out if your airline requires reconfirmation.

Restrictions Discounted tickets often have various restrictions – for example, they may need to be paid for in advance, or altering them may incur a penalty. Other restrictions include minimum and maximum periods you must be away.

Round-the-World Tickets RTW tickets give you a limited period (usually a year) in which to circumnavigate the globe. You can go anywhere the carrying airlines go as long as you don't backtrack. The number of stopovers or total number of separate flights is decided before you set off, and these tickets usually cost a bit more than a basic return flight.

Transferred Tickets Airline tickets cannot be transferred from one person to another. Travelers sometimes try to sell the return half of a ticket, but officials can ask you to prove that you are the person named on the ticket. On an international flight, tickets are compared with passports.

Travel Periods Ticket prices vary with the time of year. There is a low (off-peak) season and a high (peak) season, and often a low-shoulder season and a high-shoulder season as well. Usually the fare depends on your outward flight – if you depart in the high season and return in the low season, you pay the high-season fare.

one airline to another. A few may allow you to use coupons on standby, in which case you should call the airline a day or two before the flight you want and make a 'standby reservation,' which will give you priority over all the travelers who just appear and hope to get on a flight the same day.

ROUND-THE-WORLD TICKETS Round-the-world (RTW) tickets have become very popular in the past few years. They are often real bargains and can work out to be no more expensive than an ordinary roundtrip ticket (sometimes they're even cheaper). The official airline RTW tickets are usually put together by a combination of two airlines, and they permit you to fly anywhere you want on their route systems as long as you do not backtrack. Other restrictions and time limits often apply. An alternative type of RTW ticket is one put together by a travel agent using a combination of discounted tickets. If you're interested in exploring the myriad possibilities afforded by RTW travel, the simplest approach is to contact a travel agent who advertises or specializes in them.

Ticketplanet
59 Grant Ave ☎ 415-288-9999, 800-799-8888 ⏲ 9am-8pm daily Ⓜ Montgomery St BART & Muni station 🚌 15, 30, 38, 45 Muni ♿
w www.ticketplanet.com
San Francisco–based Ticketplanet specializes in helping travelers arrange around-the-world and circle-Pacific itineraries (involving North American, Asian, and Australian destinations).

LATIN AMERICA Most flights to and from Central and South America go via Los Angeles, Miami, or Houston. Most countries' major airlines, as well as US airlines such as United and American, serve destinations in Latin America, with onward connections to San Francisco. Continental has flights to and from about 20 cities in Mexico and Central America.

THE UK Virgin Atlantic consistently offers the cheapest fares between London and San Francisco, with economy roundtrip fares dropping down to around £300 in the off-season and running up to £560 and more in July and August. High-season fares may also apply during the Christmas season. The business of discounting tickets is so well developed in Britain that you can get heavily discounted business-class and 1st-class tickets as well as discounted economy tickets.

The weekly London magazine *Time Out,* the *Evening Standard,* and the various free travel papers are all good sources for cheap-fare ads. Good agents for low-priced tickets in London include:

Council Travel
28A Poland St London W1 England ☎ 020 7437-7767
w www.counciltravel.com

STA Travel
86 Old Brompton Rd London SW7 3LQ England ☎ 020 7581-4132
w www.statravel.com

Trailfinders
215 Kensington High St London W8 7RG England ☎ 020 7937-5400 ⏲ 9am-6pm Mon-Wed & Fri-Sat, 9am-7pm Thurs, 10am-6pm Sun Ⓜ High St Kensington
w www.trailfinders.com

CONTINENTAL EUROPE Many airlines fly between Paris and San Francisco, sometimes offering free stopovers in the US. The lowest roundtrip fares, offered in winter range from around 2700FF to 3000FF. In the summer, look for fares of less than 4800FF; however, it isn't unusual for the best fares to soar above 5000FF for economy-class seats. Northwest Airlines US Airways, Continental Airlines, British Airways, United Airlines, TWA, Air France and American Airlines all fly between Paris and San Francisco, and at a given time any one can offer the best deal.

Other airlines with service to and from Europe include Aeroflot (Moscow), Finnair (Helsinki), KLM (Amsterdam), and Lufthansa (Frankfurt). Although there are good-value charter deals from European cities, the general price of fares will be much higher than fares from London.

Good agents for low-priced tickets elsewhere in Europe include:

Council Travel
Adalbert Strasse 32 Munich 80799 Germany
☎ *89 3883-8970*
w *www.counciltravel.com*

Kilroy Travels
Hardenberger Strasse 9 Charlottenberg D-10623 Germany ☎ *30 3100-040* ⏲ *10am-7pm Mon-Fri, 11am-3pm Sat*
w *www.kilroytravels.com*

Kilroy has offices throughout Scandinavia and northern Europe.

STA Travel
Berger Strasse 118 Frankfurt 1 60316 Germany
☎ *69 430 191*
w *www.statravel.com*

USIT Connect
6 rue de Vaugirard Paris 75006 France
☎ *01 43 29 69 50*

AUSTRALIA & NEW ZEALAND Neither Air New Zealand nor Qantas currently flies direct to San Francisco; their services go to Los Angeles, where you pick up a connecting domestic flight. United Airlines has direct flights to San Francisco from Sydney.

Most services now overfly Hawaii, so the Pacific is crossed in one mighty leap. A flight from Auckland to Los Angeles takes 12 to 13 hours, and from Sydney to Los Angeles 13½ to 14½ hours. Typical roundtrip fares vary from NZ$2000 to NZ$3000 from New Zealand, and A$2150 to A$2700 from Australia's east coast.

Weekend travel sections in major city newspapers in Australia and New Zealand will have ads for travel agents specializing in cheap fares. Flight Centre and STA travel agencies in Melbourne and Sydney have competitively priced tickets. STA also operates an office in Auckland.

ASIA San Francisco's business and cultural ties to Asia are strong, and many US and Asian airlines run frequent flights to and from Hong Kong, Tokyo, Taipei, Singapore, Seoul, Bangkok, Beijing, and Saigon. China Airlines, Asiana, United, Northwest, and Continental are just a few airlines offering daily service across the Pacific. Roundtrip economy fares from Asian capitals fluctuate wildly, from as little as $700 to as much as $1500. Fares often jump around the Lunar New Year.

BUS

Greyhound is the only regular long-distance bus company operating to San Francisco, but there are a variety of bus services between the city and other Bay Area communities.

AC Transit
☎ *510-839-2882, 510-891-4777* ⏲ *24 hours* ♿
w *www.actransit.dst.ca.us*

AC Transit provides service between downtown San Francisco (Transbay Terminal) and the East Bay. After midnight, when BART (the local commuter railway system) stops running, AC Transit or an expensive cab ride are the only options for a stranded carless soul. See Excursions for details.

Golden Gate Transit
☎ *415-923-2000, 415-455-2000, 707-541-2000* ⏲ *6am-8pm Mon-Fri, 7am-8pm Sat-Sun* $ *adult $2.15-4.75, senior $1.05-2.35, child $1.60-3.55* ♿
w *www.goldengatetransit.org*

Golden Gate Transit connects the city to Marin and Sonoma Counties. See Excursions for details.

Greyhound MAP 4
Transbay Terminal, 425 Mission St ☎ *415-495-1575, 800-229-9424* ⏲ *24 hours* ♿
w *www.greyhound.com*

From San Francisco, there are six morning, three afternoon, and five evening Greyhound buses to Los Angeles. The eight- to 12-hour trip costs about $35 to $41 one-way. Roundtrip tickets cost $59 to $76. Greyhound also operates north to Portland (21 to 31 hours, $29 to $105 one-way) and inland to Lake Tahoe (5½ to seven hours, $45 to $70 roundtrip). Fares vary with the season and the day of the week, and you pay less if you purchase your tickets a week or more before your trip.

Green Tortoise MAP 6
494 Broadway ☎ *415-956-7500, 800-867-8647*
w *www.greentortoise.com*

The funky Green Tortoise bus service is a favorite of backpackers and the young at heart. The buses have been converted into rolling lounges, and there are stops along the way for cookouts and dips in hot springs. Destinations are limited but well chosen. The north-south trip runs between Seattle and Los Angeles via

San Francisco. From San Francisco, the fares are: Seattle $69, Portland $59, Eugene $49, and Los Angeles $35. It also has trips to Death Valley (three days, $129) and Yosemite National Park (two days $99, three days $119).

SamTrans
☎ 800-660-4287 ⏲ 6am-2am $ local: adult $2.20, senior 50¢, child 75¢; express: adult $3, senior/child $1.25 ♿
W www.samtrans.com/samtrans

SamTrams is a link to SFO and cities south of San Francisco, including Palo Alto, and it also runs along the Pacific Coast south of the city. See Excursions for details.

TRAIN

Amtrak
☎ 800-872-7245 ⏲ 24 hours ♿
W www.amtrak.com

Amtrak is the national railway system in the US, and its main Bay Area terminal is at Jack London Square in Oakland. A free shuttle bus connects passengers to San Francisco, stopping at the Caltrain station south of Market St and at the Ferry Building on the Embarcadero. Tickets can be purchased at all three locations. If you're traveling north from Los Angeles, it's equally simple to transfer from Amtrak to Caltrain in San Jose and take Caltrain to San Francisco.

Amtrak connects to cities all over the continental United States and Canada. The main services through the Bay Area are the *San Joaquin* route (Oakland-Bakersfield, four times daily), the *Three Capitals* route (San Jose-Oakland-Sacramento-Roseville, several times daily), and the *Coast Starlight* route (Seattle-Oakland-San Jose-Los Angeles, daily).

Rail travel is generally cheaper if you purchase special fares in advance. Roundtrip tickets are the best bargain, but even they are usually as expensive as airfares. The best value overall is the All Aboard America fare, which enables you to travel anywhere on Amtrak's routes within 45 days, with up to three stopovers. (Additional stopovers can be arranged at extra cost.) Your entire trip must be reserved in advance, and seats are limited, so book as far ahead as possible.

For non-US citizens, Amtrak offers a variety of USA Rail Passes that must be purchased outside the United States (check with a travel agent). Prices vary from high to low season, and private sleeping accommodations cost extra. Advanced booking is recommended. Amtrak has sales offices in cities around the world, so check your local listings (or the Amtrak website) to see if there's a representative near you.

Caltrain MAP 4
cnr 4th and King St ☎ 800-660-4287
⏲ 4:30am-10:30am Mon-Fri, 5am-midnight Sat-Sun $ one-way: adult $1.25-6.75, child/senior 50¢-$3.25 🚍 N Muni ♿
W www.caltrain.com

Caltrain operates down the peninsula, linking San Francisco with San Jose and Palo Alto (where Stanford University is). It's the best means of travel along this route.

CAR & MOTORCYCLE

Several freeways crisscross the Bay Area. Hwy 101 runs north-south through San Francisco, continuing south to Los Angeles and north to Eureka and on to Oregon. The bayside stretch of Hwy 101 between San Francisco and San Jose is always busy – sometimes traffic crawls, sometimes it's rather fast-paced, but it's always stressful. I-280, parallel and slightly to the west of Hwy 101, is prettier and much easier on the nerves.

Along the coast north and south of the city, Hwy 1 is a slower but much more scenic road that gets you to the beach communities west of the sparsely populated coastal mountain range. Heading north, Hwys 1 and 101 merge to cross the Golden Gate Bridge but on the Marin County side resume their separate journeys. Just south of San Francisco, Hwy 1 is frequently washed out by rains on the unstable Devil's Slide.

On the east side of the bay, I-80 runs north-south through Berkeley and swings across the Bay Bridge to San Francisco. I-80 also heads inland from the East Bay, passing Sacramento (91 miles), the state capital, on its way to Reno, Nevada (226 miles), and ultimately New York. I-580 swings inland from the East Bay to meet I-5 about 50 miles inland. I-5 is the fastest route south to Los Angeles; the 390-mile trip takes six or seven boring hours. The route inland to Yosemite National Park (210 miles) starts along I-580

HITCHHIKING

Travelers hoping to thumb their way around California may be in for an unpleasant sur prise. On the whole, hitchhiking is much less common in modern-day America than elsewhere in the world, and for good reason. Hitchhiking is never entirely safe, and travelers who decide to do it should understand that they are taking a serious risk.

Officially, hitchhiking is not illegal in California, but it *is* frowned upon by the highway patrol. Pedestrians are not allowed on major highways or on-ramps, and fines are stiff for breaking that law. Local laws may be more even stringent.

Getting Around

San Francisco is not large, and though the locals complain incessantly about the bad public transportation system, city buses will get you almost anywhere.

TO/FROM THE AIRPORTS

San Francisco International Airport

San Francisco International Airport is on the bay side of the peninsula 14 miles south of downtown San Francisco. Highway 101 connects the airport directly to downtown. If you're driving, the trip between the airport and the city can take as little as 20 minutes, but during the morning and evening rush hours it can stretch to 45 minutes or more; at these times, give yourself an hour to be safe.

If you're headed *to* the airport via Hwy 101, don't be tempted by the Airport Rd exit, which just leads to parking lots and warehouses. Be sure to take the San Francisco International Airport exit. (Of course, you may need to exit elsewhere if you're returning a rented car.)

Information on ground transportation is posted throughout the terminals and on the lower-level center islands and is available at airport information booths. Transportation arrives and departs at the upper and lower levels, and color-coded zones identify the correct places to catch buses going to the numerous rental car lots, to the long-term parking lots, to other airports, and to nearby hotels. This can be confusing, so read the terminal signs carefully before stepping outside.

Airport Hot Line

☎ *800-736-2008* ⌚ *7:30am-5pm Mon-Fri*

Call during the given hours for information on ground transportation.

TAXI Cabs operate to and from the yellow zone on the lower level. A taxi to downtown San Francisco will cost around $30 to $35, plus a tip.

TRAIN & BUS Taking the bus from the airport to your hotel in San Francisco almost always means utilizing multiple transit systems (at least SamTrans and Muni, perhaps BART also), which can be confusing and time consuming. But this is by far the thriftiest way to get into the city. BART service from the airport is scheduled to commence in 2002, around the time this book will hit bookstores. If this extension is completed on schedule, it will offer a very attractive alternative to buses.

BART

☎ *650-992-2278* **W** *www.bart.gov*

When the SFO BART extension is completed, travelers will be able to reach several centra stops along Market St without having tc transfer trains or take shuttle buses. The SFC BART station will be near the Internationa Terminal. The ride to downtown San Franciscc will take just 30 minutes and cost around $5 The Powell St station is near Union Square and the Montgomery and Embarcadero stations are in the Financial District.

Caltrain

☎ *800-660-4287* **W** *www.caltrain.com/caltrain*

A free Caltrain shuttle bus takes nine minutes tc reach the Millbrae Caltrain station. The shuttle stops on the lower level at the Central Terminal International Terminal, and North Terminal, anc at the United Airlines Maintenance Operatior Center. Trains take you from Millbrae to Sar Francisco's Caltrain station, a few blocks soutl of Market St, in downtown San Francisco. Fron there, you can catch the Nos 15, 30, 42, 45, anc 76 Muni buses to points dowtown. Train fare: are $2 between 10am and 4pm Monday to Friday, $1.50 at other times.

SamTrans

☎ *800-660-4287*

W *www.samtrans.com/samtrans*

SamTrans (San Mateo County Transit) expres buses depart several times an hour from the lower (arrival) level on the center island at the Central Terminal and curbside at the Nortl and International Terminals. Baggage restrictions – similar to (if not tighter than) those imposed by airlines for carry-on luggage – are enforced at the driver's discretion. Bus KX ($3 takes about half an hour to reach the Trans bay Terminal; bus No 292 ($2.20) is *not* an express and takes twice as long. Bus BX ($1.10) takes 20 minutes to reach the Colma BART station, where you can catch BART to downtown San Francisco ($2.25).

VANS & SHUTTLES Shuttles, coming in various shapes, sizes, and colors, mostly operate to and from the blue, red, and yellow zones on the upper level. A shuttle is a minibus service operating either to specific stops, such as certain downtown hotels, or to any address in the city (door-to-door service). There is no need to book shuttles at the airport – just wait for one to come along. For transportation to the airport, however, you need to phone ahead or ask your hotel to make the booking. Discount coupons are often available for shuttle services, which typically cost $9 to $12 one-way (plus a tip for the driver) and $16 roundtrip.

SFO Airporter
☎ *415-641-3100, 800-532-8405* Ⓢ *one-way $12, roundtrip $20; 12 & younger ride free*
W *www.groundnet.com/sfo-airporter/index.html*

Large Greyhound-size coaches offer three different shuttle services operating every 30 minutes to a number of major hotels.

Super Shuttle
☎ *415-558-8500, 650-558-8500*
Ⓢ *$14.50/person; $8 for additional passenger*
W *www.supershuttle.com*

Blue vans offer door-to-door service, usually with several stops in the city that can prolong your trip to the hotel by as much as an hour. Two passengers going to the same destination get a discounted fare.

Lorrie's Airport Shuttle
☎ *415-334-9000* Ⓢ *to hotels: adult $12, child $7; to private residence: adult $14, child $8*

Red vans offer door-to-door service and discounted rates for downtown hotels.

American Airporter Shuttle
☎ *415-202-0733, 800-282-7758* Ⓢ *adult $14, ages 2-12 $12*

Frequent shuttles drop you off anywhere in the central parts of San Francisco.

Bay Area Shuttle
☎ *650-873-7771* Ⓢ *one-way for Berkeley hotels $22, one-way for Oakland hotels $24*

Shuttles provide service to major East Bay hotels.

Oakland International Airport

Travelers arriving at the Oakland airport will have a little farther to go to reach San Francisco, but it's by no means difficult.

Air-BART
☎ *510-577-4294* ◷ *6:05am-11:50pm Mon-Sat, 8:30am-11:45pm Sun* Ⓢ *adult $2, child 50¢*

Air-BART shuttle buses run between the Oakland Airport and the Coliseum BART station ($2); from there, you can catch a Daly City/Colma BART train to San Francisco ($2.75). Air-BART shuttles have departures every 15 minutes. You must buy tickets from ticket machines inside the terminal before boarding the bus.

SHUTTLE Several companies run door-to-door shuttle services from the Oakland Airport to points throughout the Bay Area. Shuttle stops are located outside of both terminals.

Bayporter Express
☎ *415-467-1800, 877-467-1800* Ⓢ *$15-22*
W *www.bayporter.com*

Shuttles provide door-to-door service to destinations in the East Bay and San Francisco. Prices fluctuate depending on where you're headed.

PUBLIC TRANSPORTATION

A detailed BART and Muni *Street & Transit Map* costs $2 and is available at the tourist information center near the Powell St

BART and Muni station and at many newspaper stands and bookstores. Free timetables, worth having if you're riding a line with irregular service, are available at Muni stations and on some buses. BART schedules are available at all BART stations.

Muni Buses, Streetcars & Cable Cars

☎ *415-673-6864* Ⓢ *general $1, youth/seniors 35¢; cable cars $2*
w *www.sfmuni.com*

San Francisco's principal public transportation system, Muni, operates nearly 100 bus lines (many of them electric trolley buses), metro streetcars, historic streetcars, and the famous cable cars. The system futilely attempts to keep its coaches and trains running according

MONICA J MEARES

Historic F-Market streetcar

to its precise published schedules, but locals have long given up expecting on-time service. Buses that are supposed to arrive at a given stop every 10 minutes are more likely to arrive in packs of two or three every 20 to 30 minutes. Still, the system gets you almost anywhere in the city.

Free transfer tickets are available at the start of your journey, and you can then use them for two connecting trips within 90 minutes or so. They are not transferable to cable cars. Cable car fares are $2; children under five ride free.

A Muni Passport allows unlimited travel on all Muni transports, including cable cars, and offers discounts at several city attractions. Passports are available in one-day ($6), three-day ($10), or seven-day ($15) versions. They are available from the Visitors Information Center at Hallidie Plaza, from the half-price tickets kiosk on Union Square, from a number of hotels, and from businesses that display the Muni Pass sign in their window. A cheaper weekly pass costs $9 and allows bus and railway travel and discounts on cable-car trips. A monthly Fast Pass costs $35 ($8 for seniors 65 and older and youths five to 17) and allows unlimited Muni travel, including the cable cars, and travel on BART within the San Francisco city limits.

Bus lines are noted in this book with the symbol 🚍. Buses display their route number and final destination on the front and side. If the number is followed by a letter (A, B, X, L), then it's a limited-stop or express service. On nine lines an 'owl' service operates from 1am to 5am. Upon boarding the bus, you pay the fare (exact change or a $1 bill) or show your pass to the driver. Ask for a transfer when you board.

Muni Metro streetcars are light-rail cars that run underground below Market St downtown, beginning at the Embarcadero. This book shows the underground Muni stop nearest a site with the symbol Ⓜ; downtown, Muni stations are the same as BART stations.

Beyond the Van Ness Ave station, the Metro cars split into five routes: J-Church, K-Ingleside, L-Taraval, M-Oceanview, and N-Judah. The cars then continue aboveground for most of the remainder of their journeys (although the K, L, and M continue underground through the Church St and Castro St stations) and must negotiate city traffic like the public buses. These lines are noted with the bus information following the symbol 🚍 in this book.

The J and N emerge from the tunnel at Church St. The J-Church bisects the Castro and the Mission on Church St, climbs to Noe Valley, and reconnects with the K and M at Balboa Park station. The N-Judah follows Judah St through Cole Valley and the Sunset District out to the ocean, paralleling the south side of Golden Gate Park. Downtown, the N also continues at street level along the Embarcadero to Pacific Bell Park and the Caltrain station.

The K, L, and M routes continue underground past Castro St station and emerge aboveground at West Portal station, in the Sunset, past which they go their separate ways. The F-Market light-rail line consists of antique streetcars from around the world; these run along Market St from Castro St to the Embarcadero, where they hook left en route to Fisherman's Wharf.

The L and N lines operate 24 hours, but between 12:30am and 5:30am, 'owl' buses replace the streetcars. The other lines operate from between 5am and 6am (a bit later on weekends for the M line) to just after midnight.

There are three **cable car routes** in downtown San Francisco, shown in this guide by a 🚋. There's sitting space for about 30 passengers, but sitters are often outnumbered by the strap-hangers who cling precariously to the outside. In this age of seat belts and air bags, an old-fashioned, open-air, seemingly dangerous cable car ride is all the more fun. Where else can you travel *in* a tourist attraction from one tourist highlight to another?

The starting points, particularly the Hallidie Plaza/Market St turnaround for the

Get on the Bus!

Some of the most important Muni bus routes for visitors include the following:

No 5 – Fulton From the Transbay Terminal, along Market and McAllister Sts to Fulton St, along the north side of Golden Gate Park all the way to the ocean

No 7 – Haight From the Ferry Building, along Market and Haight Sts, through the Haight to the southeast corner of Golden Gate Park; daytime only

No 14 – Mission From the Transbay Terminal, along Mission St through SoMa and the Mission District

No 15 – 3rd St From 3rd St in SoMa, through the Financial District on Kearny St, through North Beach on Columbus Ave, then along Powell St to the Fisherman's Wharf area

No 18 – 46th Ave From the Palace of the Legion of Honor to the Sutro Baths, along the western edge of Golden Gate Park on the Great Hwy, past the San Francisco Zoo and Lake Merced

No 22 – Fillmore From 18th and 17th Sts in Potrero Hill, through the Mission on 16th St, along Fillmore St past Japantown to Pacific Heights and the Marina

No 24 – Divisadero From Noe St in Noe Valley, along Castro St, then Divisadero St in the Western Addition to Pacific Heights

No 26 – Valencia Along Valencia St in the Mission to Market and Polk Sts and through SoMa along Mission St

No 28 – 19th Ave From Fort Mason to the Golden Gate Bridge toll plaza and on through the Presidio, the Richmond District on Park Presidio Blvd, Golden Gate Park, and south on 19th Ave through the Sunset District all the way to the Daly City BART station

No 30 – Stockton From the Caltrain station in SoMa, along 3rd and Market Sts, then on Stockton St through Chinatown and Columbus Ave through North Beach to Fisherman's Wharf, Fort Mason, and the Palace of Fine Arts

No 32 – Embarcadero From the Caltrain station, along the Embarcadero, past the Ferry Building to Fisherman's Wharf

No 33 – Stanyan From Potrero Ave in Potrero Hill, through the Mission on 16th and then 18th Sts, through the Castro up to Market St, up Clayton St above the Haight-Ashbury, down Haight St to Stanyan St on the east edge of Golden Gate Park, to Fulton St and then Arguello Blvd in the Richmond District

No 37 – Corbett A winding route from the Haight via Buena Vista Park to Twin Peaks

No 38 – Geary From the Transbay Terminal, along Market St and then Geary Blvd all the way to the Cliff House at the ocean

No 71 – Haight-Noriega Along Market and Haight Sts, through the Haight, along the south side of Golden Gate Park on Lincoln Way and then down to Noriega St through the Outer Sunset to the ocean

Powell St lines, can be very crowded, entailing a long wait for a ride. Farther down the route, finding space can be a matter of luck. There are cable-car ticket machines at the turnarounds and a ticket conductor on each cable car. The standard fare, irrespective of distance, is $2, but that's just for one ride; there are no transfers on cable cars. An all-day cable car ticket costs $6. The cable cars run from approximately 6am to 12:30am. For more on cable cars, their history, and how they work, see the boxed text 'Cable Cars' in Things to See & Do.

Cable Car Routes

California St This route runs straight up and down California St – from the downtown terminus at Market and Davis Sts through the Financial District, Chinatown, and Nob Hill to Van Ness Ave. There are great views of the bay during the climb up (or drop down) Nob Hill. Although this route is just a straight shot, it does have the shortest lines.

Powell-Mason St From the Hallidie Plaza turnaround at the junction of Market and Powell Sts, the cable car climbs up Powell St past Union Square, then turns west along Jackson St for one block before descending north down Mason, Columbus, and Taylor toward Fisherman's Wharf. On the return trip, it takes Washington St instead of Jackson St and passes by the Cable Car Museum.

ANDREW DEAN NYSTROM

Powell-Hyde St This is a similar route to the Powell-Mason line, but it follows Jackson St west for five blocks and then turns down Hyde St to terminate at Aquatic Park, near Fisherman's Wharf. Along Hyde St, it crosses the top of the famous crooked section of Lombard St. Coming back, it takes Washington St and runs past the Cable Car Museum.

BART (Bay Area Rapid Transit)

☎ *650-992-2278*
W *www.bart.gov*

Lovingly called BART, this underground train system is a fast and convenient link between downtown and the Mission District. It also offers easy transit to Oakland and Berkeley, via a tube that sits on the floor of San Francisco Bay. This book shows the BART stop nearest a site with the symbol Ⓜ.

BART was state of the art when it opened in 1972 and is still convenient, economical, and generally quite safe to use, although caution is required around some BART stations at night. Four of the system's five lines pass through the city before terminating at Daly City or Colma. In the East Bay, the Richmond line serves downtown Oakland and Berkeley, and the Pittsburg/Bay Point line serves downtown Oakland and Rockridge. For the Oakland Coliseum and shuttles to the Oakland airport, take the Dublin/Pleasanton line or the Fremont line.

One-way fares vary from $1.10 to a maximum of $4.70. Popular routes, such as San Francisco to Oakland or Berkeley, are typically $2.20 to $2.70. BART tickets are sold by machines in values of $1.10 up to $40 and are magnetically encoded so that each time you pass through a station entry and exit gate the value of your ride is deducted from the ticket. If your ticket still has value, it is returned to you and can be reused until it is exhausted. If you arrive at an exit gate and your ticket's remaining value is less than is needed, put the ticket in an Addfare machine and pay the appropriate amount (you'll need exact change, but change machines are usually nearby). A monthly Muni Fast Pass (see Public Transportation, earlier) includes BART travel within San Francisco.

BART services operate until at least midnight each night, starting weekdays at 4am, Saturday at 6am, and Sunday at 8am. Bicycles can be carried on BART but not in the commute direction during the weekday commute hours. (See the Bicycle section for more details.)

From the San Francisco BART stations, a transfer is available to Muni bus and streetcar services. In the East Bay, you must get an AC Transit transfer ticket before leaving the station and then pay an additional 60¢.

ADJACENT TRANSPORTATION SYSTEMS

See Getting There & Away if you want to go down the peninsula, across to the East Bay, or north to Marin County. These areas are covered in Excursions, and additional transit information is provided in that chapter.

CAR & MOTORCYCLE

A car is the last thing you want in downtown San Francisco, but if you're traveling farther afield – up to the Wine Country, for example – a car is a necessity. If you're driving into the city and will have a car for the entire length of your stay, it is essential to ask your hotel about parking. Motels typically offer free parking.

Driving in the City

Finding your way around town is not difficult. The city streets are well marked with signs to tourist zones such as North Beach, Fisherman's Wharf, and Chinatown.

If you're driving a stick shift (manual transmission), you'd better have your hill-start technique well honed. Drive carefully; at some of the steepest intersections you're liable to find yourself gazing into space until your car lurches onto the cross street's level.

Parking

Now, the tough part. The search for street parking in pretty much any neighborhood in San Francisco can be excruciating. Desperate motorists often resort to double-parking, or parking in red zones or on sidewalks, but in the city's major hotel zone, around Union Square, trying this for more than a few minutes will surely result in your car being towed.

Parking restrictions are signaled by color-coded sidewalk curbs, which are sometimes long-since faded, and explained by street signs, which can be missing or hidden by trees. Here's a rundown of the system:

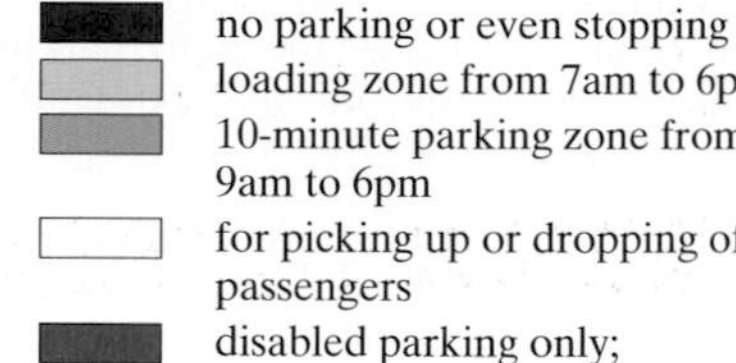
no parking or even stopping
loading zone from 7am to 6pm
10-minute parking zone from 9am to 6pm
for picking up or dropping off passengers
disabled parking only; identification required

Parking tickets run $25 (for an expired meter) to $275 (for blue zone violations). These fines have begun to look mighty lenient to the city's Dept of Parking and Traffic, since San Franciscans so blithely risk getting them, and there have been threats in City Hall of doubling some of the current fines.

Commercial streets typically have metered parking, with varying time limits and costs (usually $1 per half-hour). Usually, meters accept only quarters (25¢ coins), so it's a good idea to have change in your pocket. Even when parking at a meter, you should still read all nearby signs to be sure there are no restrictions.

During the commute hours, parking is forbidden on certain busy streets, and cars violating these rules will be towed. Almost everywhere in the city there are designated hours each week when parking is forbidden because of street cleaning – you won't be towed for obstructing the street-cleaning trucks, but you can expect a $25 fine.

San Francisco's hilly streets have proved too great a challenge for many parking brakes. Consequently, on hill streets (with a grade of as little as 3%), you must 'curb' your wheels, meaning your front tires must ride up against the curb. (The logic is that if your parking break gives out, your car will back into the curb, rather than down the hill.) If you're parked facing downhill, turn your wheels toward the curb; if you're parked facing uphill, turn them away from the curb. Again, the fine for this seemingly innocent infraction is $25.

Parking on residential streets with no meters is the only free parking available in the city, but nonresidents (without city parking stickers) are limited to two hours.

Street parking always entails the risk of break-ins and car theft. The Club is a deterrent, as are alarms, but some thieves will try to break into anything just to see what's in the trunk. Typically, they'll attempt to 'jimmy' the lock by jamming a screwdriver into it – it's a crude method that doesn't always succeed in opening a car door, but it almost always ruins the lock, meaning you'll have to pay about $100 getting it fixed.

Bridge Tolls

The Bay Area's five major bridges all have one-way tolls. The Golden Gate Bridge costs $3 southbound, except for carpoolers (driver plus at least two passengers) on weekdays from 5am to 9am and 4pm to 6pm.

The other four bridges are the Bay Bridge, the Richmond–San Rafael Bridge, the San Mateo–Hayward Bridge, and the Dumbarton Bridge. They all run east-west and have $2 tolls collected from westbound traffic. During the weekday commute hours, 5am to 10am and 3pm to 6pm, a carpool (driver plus two passengers) crosses free. Avoiding the backup at the toll booths is a more important issue than saving the $2 toll.

The safest bet, particularly at night, is to park in a garage. Downtown parking garages usually run $18 to $28 a day, depending on how long (from night 'til dawn, or 24 hours) and whether or not you require in-and-out 'privileges.' For short stops, public garages operated by the city (such as the lots under Union Square and at the corner of 5th and Mission Sts) are cheaper than private garages.

Major parking offenses can result in your car being towed away. If your car is towed, you'll have to call City Tow and pay hefty fees to retrieve it.

City Tow
850 Bryant St, Room 145 ☎ 415-621-8605
24 hours 27, 42 Muni

Call City Tow if you think your car has been towed. The company does all parking-related towing in the city. Above whatever fines you owe for parking violations, you'll also have to fork out a towing and storage fee ($144 for the first day, $27 for every additional day).

American Automobile Association
150 Van Ness Ave ☎ 415-565-2012, 800-222-4357 8:30am-5:30pm Mon-Fri
Civic Center BART & Muni station
Market St buses, 21, 42, 47, 49, F Muni
www.aaa.com

Members can call the 800-number for emergency road service and towing. They can also get travel insurance or stop by for free road maps of the region.

Car & Motorcycle Rentals

All the big rental car operators can be found in the Bay Area, particularly at the airports, along with a host of smaller or local operators. Rates go up and down like the stock market, and it's always worth phoning around to see what's available. Booking ahead usually ensures the best rates, and airport rates are generally better than those in the city. Typically, a small car might cost $35 to $45 a day or $150 to $250 a week, plus the 8.5% sales tax.

On top of that, add in $9 to $12 a day for insurance, called a loss/damage waiver. Some credit cards provide insurance if you charge the car to their account, but it's always wise to check with the card company. Overseas-issued credit cards almost certainly will not offer any insurance coverage. If you have auto insurance at home, check with your insurance company to see if rental is covered. The rental car companies most likely won't explain these alternative insurance policies, as selling insurance is big business.

Most rates include unlimited mileage; if a rate is unbelievably cheap, there is probably a per-mile charge after a certain distance. Though the charge may seem negligible, it's surprising how quickly the miles mount up, even around the city.

Most operators require that you be at least 25 years of age, and if you don't have a suitable credit card, a large cash deposit will be required and you will be treated with great suspicion. Return the car with a full tank of fuel; if you let the operator refill the car for you, the gas price will be much higher.

Some of the larger operators and their main San Francisco outlets are:

Alamo MAP 4
687 Folsom St ☎ 415-693-0191, 800-327-9633 ⌚ 8am-5pm daily 🚌 15, 30, 45, 76 Muni
w www.goalamo.com

Avis
675 Post St ☎ 415-885-5011, 800-831-2847 ⌚ 6am-10pm Mon & Fri-Sun, 6am-8pm Tues-Thurs 🚌 2, 3, 4, 76 Muni
w www.avis.com

Budget
321 Mason St ☎ 415-928-7864, 800-527-0700 ⌚ 6am-8pm daily 🚌 38 Muni
w www.budget.com

Dollar
364 O'Farrell St ☎ 415-771-5301, 800-800-4000 ⌚ 6am-8pm daily 🚌 38 Muni
w www.dollarcar.com

Hertz
433 Mason St ☎ 415-771-2200, 800-654-3131 ⌚ 6am-7pm Mon-Thurs, 6am-10pm Fri-Sun 🚌 2, 3, 4, 38, 76 Muni
w www.hertz.com

Thrifty
520 Mason St ☎ 415-788-8111, 800-367-2277 ⌚ 7am-7pm daily 🚌 2, 3, 4, 76 Muni
w www.thrifty.com

For motorcycle rentals, there's just one place you can call:

Dubbelju MAP 4
271 Clara St ☎ 415-495-2774 🚌 27, 42 Muni
w www.dubbelju.com

If two wheels are more your style, you'll be right at home in this motorcycle-friendly town. Dubbelju stocks BMWs and Harleys. Rates range from $99 to $139 per day for a short trip (three days or less). Call for a brochure. To ride a motorcycle in California, you need to have a valid motorcycle license.

Buying a Car or Motorcycle

One way you might be able to beat the high cost of renting a car is to buy a used vehicle upon your arrival and sell it when you depart. If you go this route, it helps to either have a bit of the auto mechanic in you or find a mechanic you can trust; you won't get much return value on a 'lemon' or a gas guzzler. Don't ask yourself 'Do I feel lucky?' because even minor repairs could cost well over $100.

Once you've purchased the car you must have its emissions smog-tested at a garage and get a certificate that verifies the vehicle meets state standards. You must then purchase a rather costly auto insurance policy and take the smog certificate and proof of insurance, along with the ownership title and bill of sale, to any office of the Dept of Motor Vehicles (DMV). It normally takes a full morning or afternoon to get your auto registration, which will cost anywhere from 7% to 12% of the cost of the car.

As your departure from the USA approaches, you must set aside time to sell the car, perhaps also laying out additional money to place a classified ad in a newspaper.

If you are traveling alone and don't object to a little wind, you might consider buying a motorcycle, which is cheaper than a car and tends to be easier to sell. Be sure to buy a helmet for yourself and any potential passengers: helmets are required by law in California, and the law is strictly enforced.

TAXI

Cabs are usually fairly easy to find in San Francisco, although they do not cruise the streets in the same proliferation as in, say, New York. Fares start at $2.50 at the flag drop and then cost 40¢ for every fifth of a mile thereafter. Add at least 10% to the taxi fare as a tip (starting at $1, even for fares under $6). Credit cards are accepted with increasing frequency, but ask before getting into the cab (otherwise, you can ask the cabbie to stop at an ATM along the way.) Cabs can be found most reliably along downtown streets; elsewhere you may need to phone one of the taxi companies. Complaints can be made to the cab companies or to the Police Dept Taxicab Complaint Line. The main taxi companies are:

DeSoto Cab
☎ 415-970-1300 ⌚ 24 hours

Luxor Cab
☎ 415-282-4141 ⌚ 24 hours
w www.luxorcabsf.com

Veteran's Taxicab Co
☎ 415-552-1300 ⌚ 24 hours

Yellow Cab
☎ 415-626-2345 ⌚ 24 hours

BICYCLE

San Francisco and the Bay Area are great for recreational biking, and for some a bicycle is the ideal method of getting around the city – despite the traffic and all those fearsome hills. A bike is the perfect way to explore Golden Gate Park or the Presidio or to travel across the Golden Gate Bridge to Marin County, birthplace of the mountain bike. For more on city biking, see the Bicycling section under Activities in Things to See & Do; for more on mountain biking in Marin, see Excursions.

Bicycles can be rented for around $25 a day, $30 for mountain bikes. You can also rent by the hour, for around $5 to $7 an hour. Try the following:

Start to Finish Bike Shop MAP 9
2530 Lombard St ☎ 415-202-9830 ⌚ 10am-7pm Mon-Fri, 9am-6pm Sat, 10am-5pm Sun 🚌 28, 30, 43, 76 Muni
w www.starttofinish.com

Start to Finish Bike Shop MAP 11
672 Stanyan St ☎ 415-750-4760 ⌚ 10am-7pm Mon-Fri, 10am-6pm Sat, 10am-5pm Sun 🚌 7, 71 Muni
w www.starttofinish.com

Blazing Saddles
1095 Columbus Ave ☎ 415-202-8888 🚌 30 Muni
w www.blazingsaddles.com

The Bay Area is a good place for buying the very latest in high-tech bicycles. See the Shopping chapter for more on new bicycles.

Bicycles & Public Transportation

Various rules and regulations make life complicated if you want to take your bicycle on the public transit systems. Bikes are allowed on the Golden Gate Bridge, so getting north to Marin County is no problem, but getting to or from the East Bay is more complicated, since cyclists cannot use the Bay Bridge. To transport your bike between the East Bay and San Francisco, you can use BART or Caltrans' Bay Bridge Bicycle Commuter Shuttle. The ferries also allow bikes aboard when space allows.

Muni has racks that can accommodate two bikes on eight of its community-service routes – bus Nos 17, 35, 36, 37, 39, 53, 56, 66, 76, 91, and 108 – but the chances that you'll need those routes while out riding a bicycle are slim.

Bikes are allowed on BART at all hours, but restrictions apply during commute hours. Between 6:30am and 9am, people with bikes are allowed to travel only in the 'reverse commute' direction – from Embarcadero station in San Francisco to points in the East Bay. Between 4pm and 6:30pm, the reverse commute allows people with bikes to travel only from points in the East Bay to San Francisco, and they must exit at Embarcadero station. No restrictions apply on the weekend.

Bay Bridge Bicycle Commuter Shuttle
☎ 510-286-0876 ⌚ 6:30am-8:30am Mon-Fri, 3:50pm-6:50pm Mon-Fri $ $1

Call this number to get information on the Caltrans Bay Bridge shuttle. It's a van that seats 14 and tows a trailer to carry the bikes over the bridge. It operates during commute hours between the Transbay Terminal in San Francisco and the MacArthur BART Station in Oakland.

WALKING

Much of San Francisco is compact enough to make walking a pleasure. What other way is there to explore Chinatown and North Beach? Of course, there are the hills, and sometimes it's worth skirting around them to avoid a lot of exhausting ups and downs. Then again, that isn't always possible or desirable – only by ascending those intimidating inclines will you be rewarded with those magnificent views.

FERRY

Ferry services on the bay were important more than a century ago and reached their peak in the 1930s, when the daily flow of East Bay and Marin County commuters arriving every morning at the Ferry Building on San Francisco's Embarcadero made it one of the busiest transport interchanges in the USA. The opening of the Bay Bridge (in 1936) and the Golden Gate Bridge (in 1937) spelled the near demise of the ferries, although in recent years they have enjoyed a modest revival for both commuters and tourists. For ferry service to Alcatraz and Angel Island, see Things to See & Do.

There are two principal ferry lines serving points scattered around the bay.

Blue & Gold Fleet Ferries
Desk at Pier 39; desk at Pier 41; desk in DFS Galleria at Union Square ☎ 415-705-5555
$ one-way to Oakland $4.75, one-way to Tiburon or Sausalito $6.75
W www.blueandgoldfleet.com

This ferry operates from the Ferry Building at the foot of Market St, and on some runs from Pier 41 at Fisherman's Wharf as well, to Jack London Square in Oakland. Transfers are available to and from Muni and AC Transit buses. There's also service from the Ferry

Critical Mass

On the last Friday of every month, San Francisco motorists have an additional incentive to start their weekends early. In a local twist on rush hour, they hurry to be well clear of downtown before 6pm, when many of the city's primary arteries are transformed into overflowing rivers of festive bicycle traffic. The event is called Critical Mass, and it typically involves more than 2000 cyclists who gather at the foot of Market St and ride, bells ringing, to a different destination each time. There is no organization or committee behind the event, and the whole thing operates without leaders or security in what the *San Francisco Chronicle* has called 'civilized anarchy.'

The celebratory aspect of Critical Mass is not appreciated by everyone, of course. Many motorists have become enraged by the growing popularity of the ride, which typically ties downtown rush-hour traffic in knots. One evening in July 1997, Mayor Willie Brown became one such motorist, and with classic Brown panache he pledged a crackdown on what he termed 'little weenies' and their bikes. During that month's ride, tempers flared on both sides. More than a hundred bicyclists were arrested amid accusations of police misconduct.

In recent years, the city hasn't seen that kind of friction over the pedal-power parade, but Critical Mass remains an issue over which San Franciscans remain divided. Some denounce the ride as disruptive hooliganism; others embrace it as a freewheeling experiment in direct democracy. In any case, the event has done wonders to wake up the bureaucracy to the clout and plight of the city's bicyclists, and the idea of Critical Mass has spread to dozens of other cities around the world.

Visitors to San Francisco will probably consider Critical Mass yet another addition to San Francisco's pantheon of rabble-rousers. To take part, just show up with your bike at Justin Herman Plaza (at the foot of Market St, near the Embarcadero BART station) on the last Friday of the month at 5:30pm – just in time for rush hour.

– Hugh D'Andrade

Building or Pier 41 to Tiburon or Sausalito in Marin County. During the baseball season, Tiburon and Sausalito ferries also stop at a launch just outside Pacific Bell Park before and after Giants games. This is the company that serves Alcatraz and Angel Island.

Golden Gate Transit Ferries MAP 5
☎ *415-923-2000* ⌚ *6am-10pm Mon-Fri, 10am-6pm Sat-Sun* Ⓢ *one-way to Larkspur $2.95 Mon-Fri, one-way to Larkspur $5 Sat-Sun, one-way to Sausalito $5*
W *www.goldengateferry.org*

Part of Golden Gate Transit, these ferries operate regular services from the Ferry Building in San Francisco to Larkspur and Sausalito in Marin County. Transfers are available to Muni bus services, and bicycles are permitted.

ORGANIZED TOURS

Walking tours are a great way to get intimate with the city (see the Walking Tours section in Things to See & Do), but there are other, less energetic tours.

Gray Line
350 8th St ☎ *415-558-7300, 800-826-0202* Ⓢ *4-hour tour $37, various packages at varying prices*
W *www.graylinesanfrancisco.com*

Gray Line has offices at the Transbay Terminal and in a double-decker London bus parked on Union Square at Powell and Geary Sts. Tours aboard its fake-looking motorized cable cars come with superficial patter and unreliable historical narration. Gray Line offers a variety of half-day and full-day tours that travel farther afield. Tours are also offered in Spanish, French, German, and Italian.

Blue & Gold Fleet Ferries
Desk at Pier 39; desk at Pier 41; desk in DFS Galleria at Union Square ☎ *415-773-1188*
Ⓢ *bay cruise: adult $18, senior/ages 12-18 $14, ages 5-11 $10; city tour: adult $30, ages 5-11 $15*
W *www.blueandgoldfleet.com*

The ferry company offers a bay cruise that takes in the city's waterfront and Sausalito's old-world harbor and passes under the Golden Gate Bridge. Also, there's a 3½-hour bus tour that takes in most of the city's essential landlocked sights, departing Pier 41 at 10am and 2pm daily.

Out in the Streets:
More than the Pride Parade

by Tim Kingston

As far as queer street festivities go, there is a lot more to San Francisco than the annual Lesbian, Gay, Bisexual, and Transgender Pride Parade. Pride is indeed a San Francisco symbol known worldwide, a huge flamboyant promenade that attracts a million visitors annually. But have you heard about the Dyke March, which attracts tens of thousands of women every year? Or the International Bear Rendezvous for queer men of the hirsute and hairy persuasion? What about the Folsom St Fair – the world's largest, kinkiest, and friendliest gathering of self-described perverts in the world? Visitors to San Francisco can even attend an Easter egg hunt with the Sisters of Perpetual Indulgence, the only religious order that admits organized religion can be a real drag, particularly when it involves sequins, lots of makeup, and great big mustaches.

San Francisco is home to a host of queer-related street fairs, celebrations, happenings, and just plain excuses for a party. No matter what your gender, orientation, or preference, there is an event at which you'll make a contribution to the city's fractious, turbulent, and demented spirit. Careful, though – you might just have to come back, again and again! For more information on these events and many more, check out the local queer press: *San Francisco Frontiers*, the *Bay Area Reporter*, and the *Bay Times*.

ROBERTO SONCIN GEROMETTA

t: Dykes on (nobody *really* them the ...en's Motorcycle ...ingent) lead the ...al Pride parade.

International Bear Rendezvous

☎ *415-541-5000* W *www.bosf.org*

When: Presidents' Day Weekend, generally the second or third weekend in February

Where: The Castro and the South of Market areas

What: Visitors to the Castro in February can be forgiven for suspecting an invasion of lumberjacks wearing beards, jeans, Pendleton shirts, and leather vests. Don't be alarmed – they are merely bears and bear fanciers in town for the International Bear Rendezvous (IBR). Like their namesakes who terrorized Goldilocks, bears may look threatening, but they frequently have a heart of gold. Their natural habitat tends toward pleasantly grimy bars like the Lone Star Saloon (☎ 415-863-9999, 1354 Harrison St).

IBR is a three-day weekend of activities that attracts 1500 bears and wannabears. Events include the Mr International Bear Competition – where titles like International Bear Cub and Grizzly Bear are awarded. Best of all is a tour of the Basic Brown Bear factory (☎ 415-626-0781, 444 De Haro St). A bunch of butch gay men in a teddy-bear factory is a sight not to be missed! All proceeds go to local AIDS and queer charities.

The Sisters of Perpetual Indulgence Easter Celebration

☎ *415-552-0220* W *www.thesisters.org*

When: Easter Sunday, April

Where: The Castro

What: It's never quite clear what the Sisters of Perpetual Indulgence are going to get up to on Easter Sunday, but it's worth showing up just to see. You might run into an Easter egg hunt or an Easter Bonnet Parade run by men in heels, or even a Hunky Jesus Contest.

The Sisters are a charitable organization of men (and a few women) dedicated to AIDS education and sisterly devotion. Members are marked

RICK GERHARTER

Left: You'd be amaz[ed] by where the Sisters hide their Easter baskets.

by their nuns' habits, fake eyelashes, glitter makeup, and mischievous names – among them Sister Dana Van Iniquity, Sister Lily White Superior Posterior, and Sister Penny Coastal.

The AIDS Candlelight March & Vigil

☎ *415-552-0220* **W** *www.thesisters.org*

When: The third Sunday in May

Where: Starts at Castro and Market Sts and ends at Civic Center Plaza

What: The AIDS Candlelight March & Vigil began in 1983 during the darkest days of the AIDS pandemic, well before former film star and ex-president Ronald Reagan had even mentioned the word. Local AIDS activist Hank Wilson helped organize the first vigil, a bicoastal protest in San Francisco and New York, which has since become an annual tradition drawing several thousand people.

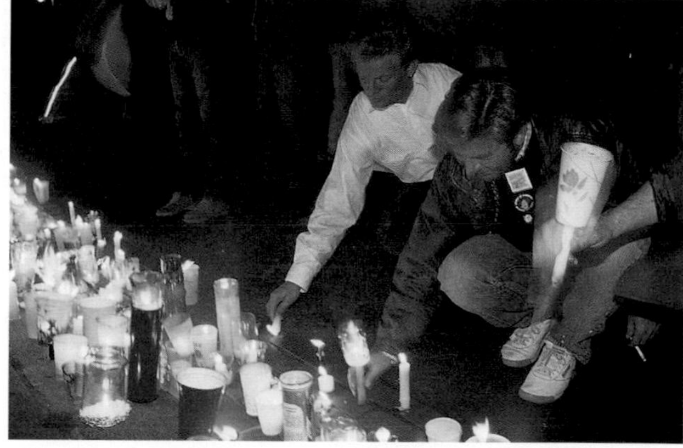

RICK GERHARTER

Right: Loved ones are remembered at the AIDS Candlelight Vigil.

The march begins at twilight. Following a few comments and remembrances of those no longer present, a river of white candles wends its way down Market St. The crowd is quiet and reflective, more reminiscent of a processional than a political rally. Few leave without being touched by the spirit of the evening. Dress warmly, as the evening chill descends rapidly.

The San Francisco Gay & Lesbian Film Festival

☎ *415-703-8650* **W** *www.frameline.org*

When: From mid-June until the end of that month

Where: The Castro Theatre (☎ 415-621-6120, 429 Castro St), the Roxie Cinema (☎ 415-863-1087, 3117 16th St), and other local movie theaters.

What: Billed as the 'world's premiere showcase for lesbian, gay, bisexual, and transgender–themed cinema,' the San Francisco Gay & Lesbian Film Festival lives up to the hype. Two weeks of intensive scheduling give visitors a chance to see the best and worst of queer filmmaking.

Some 250 to 300 films are screened each year. Videos, documentaries, sexy shorts, lesbian processing, and full-on features are present. Past audiences have been the first to see movies by John Waters and Gus Van Sant and crossover programs like the British 'Queer as Folk' TV series. A word to the wise – if you can afford a festival pass, get one. Pass holders can show up at the last minute and avoid the ubiquitous lines.

The Dyke March

☎ *415-241-8882* Ⓦ *www.dykemarch.org*

When: Late afternoon of the last Saturday in June, one day before the Pride parade

Where: Starts at Dolores Park and follows a circuitous route through the Mission District to wind up in the Castro

What: The Dyke March was born at the 1993 LGBT March on Washington, when a bunch of disgruntled dykes were annoyed by the lack of women-specific events. Armed with one bullhorn and the lesbian word-of-mouth telegraph, they announced the first ever Dyke March and, to their shock, thousands showed up. The same group of malcontents then organized San Francisco's first Dyke March the following year.

The event now attracts 50,000 lesbian, bisexual, and transgender women who show up for featured speakers, great music, and far too much fun. (Men are welcome as supporters but not necessarily as marchers.) The march steps off at 7:45pm, headed up by the hundreds-strong Women's Motorcycle Contingent (Dykes on Bikes). Purchase an extremely cool Dyke March T-shirt and see if the apocryphal 'Fudgepackers Salute Muffdivers' poster is still up in an apartment window in the Castro.

The march concludes in the Castro where it joins the Pink Saturday party at Castro and Market Sts. Pink Saturday is one big throng of boys getting all revved up for the big parade the following day. Castro St and upper Market St are both closed for the evening. Entertainment is pro-

RICK GERHARTER

vided by local artists on a sound truck and dancing lasts into the night.

Lesbian, Gay, Bisexual & Transgender Pride Parade

☎ *415-864-3733* **w** *www.sfpride.org*

When: The last Sunday in June

Where: Starts downtown at the Embarcadero and proceeds up Market St

What: This is one of the best-natured crowds you are likely to run into. The first gay-pride parade was in 1971, and each year since it's gotten larger – annual attendance now stands at around one million. Representatives of every portion of the queer community show up from around the world. Sweater queens, crunchy granola lesbians, and queer punks all appear. Participants range from same-sex marriage advocates to polyamorists – not to mention those into Bondage and Discipline. Club kids, gay and lesbian seniors, and queer families all attend, as does PFLAG (Parents and Friends of Lesbians and Gays).

Live music and entertainment is provided on four stages. Usually there is one big disco tent, just in case you get tired of all the speechifying at City Hall. (It should be noted that there have been increasingly loud grumbles in recent years about the growing corporate presence and sponsorship of the event. It seems 'acceptance,' these days, also means corporate intervention.)

RICK GERHARTER

AIDS Walk San Francisco

☎ *415-392-9255* **w** *www.aidswalk.net*

When: The second Sunday in July

Where: Starts in Golden Gate Park at Sharon Meadow

What: For travelers in a charitable mood, there's the AIDS Walk, a sponsored 10km walkathon/stroll through San Francisco's beautiful Golden Gate Park. What better way to do a good deed than to wander through a park along with 30,000 other people? Proceeds go to the San Francisco AIDS Foundation and a host of other local AIDS-related agencies. Bring a sweater; a sunny day chills quickly when the fog rolls in.

Left: Fifty thousand dykes can't be wrong!

ght: A proud dad and n march with PFLAG.

The Dore Alley Fair: Up Your Alley

☎ *415-861-3247* **W** *www.folsomstreetfair.com*

When: The last Sunday in July

Where: The heart of SoMa – Dore Alley and Folsom St between 9th and 10th Sts – is shut down, as are the blocks of 9th and 10th Sts immediately adjacent.

What: The Up Your Alley fair is primarily a local leather-folk event, but that doesn't stop 100,000 people from showing up each year. The atmosphere is distinctly queer with a preponderance of men (and a few women) in leather, all doing their thing, which means some spanking, much gabbing, and a great deal of cruising. For those who want to see leather folk in their natural habitat, this is the place to go. But take heed: this is not a tourist event. Don't show up in khaki shorts and bush hats. (Note to the curious: the black, blue, and white flag with a red heart in its upper left quadrant is indeed the leather folks' flag.)

The East Bay Lesbian, Gay, Bisexual, Transgender & Intersex (LGBTI) Pride Festival

☎ *510-663-3980* **W** *www.eastbaypride.org*

When: The last weekend in August

Where: Downtown Oakland near the Federal Building; nearest BART station is 12th St Oakland.

What: If the San Francisco Pride Parade feels a bit too lily white, try the multihued Oakland one, also called the Oakland Gay Mardi Gras. The East Bay queer community is more relaxed and less hung-up on going to the gym than is San Francisco's, and the East Bay Pride Festival, which attracts 20,000 people, reflects that fact. There are more people of color, more women, and more kids. The whole thing feels very neighborly, so expect less professional entertainment and a more down-home atmosphere. The weather tends to be balmier as well, so wear those shorts and tank tops if you dare!

Folsom St Fair

☎ *415-861-3247* **W** *www.folsomstreetfair.com*

When: The last Sunday in September

Where: The fair eats up most of SoMa; Folsom St and the adjacent blocks of 7th St through 11th St are closed.

What: Astonishingly enough, the Folsom St Fair is the third-largest event in the entire state, trailing only the Tournament of Roses in Southern California and San Francisco's Pride Parade. That's not bad for a gig that started as a small leather-oriented street fair in 1984. An estimated half a million people now attend the all-day event. Given San Francisco's proclivity for mixing music, sex, and parties, it's no surprise the fair exploded in size.

Although hordes of tourists with video cameras now show up alongside those in leather chaps, restraints, and latex skirts, Folsom remains one of the best parties in town. Local and national bands appear. Beer is cheap, and eye candy is everywhere. Much skin is exposed. This can

RICK GERHARTER

be a blessing and a curse, because a variety of physiques are revealed in their entirety.

Castro St Fair

☎ *415-841-1824* **w** *www.castrostreetfair.org*

When: The first Sunday in October

Where: Much of the Castro; Market St is closed from Castro St to Sanchez St, and Castro St is closed from 17th St to 19th St.

What: This is the yin to the Folsom St Fair's yang. Instead of black leathers, think white sweaters. Instead of whips and chains, think stained-glass windows. The Castro St Fair was started by gay political icon and city supervisor Harvey Milk in 1974 as a way to put the nascent gay community on the map. The fair succeeded beyond his wildest dreams, and an estimated 150,000 people now show up. Proceeds fund a variety of queer- and AIDS-related nonprofit groups.

The fair is an all-day event, with bands, emcees, and speakers. The primary activities are endless cruising and shopping, the latter being the favorite activity of the somewhat more conservative gay men and lesbians who attend. Yes, there are gay white male clones out looking for action, but by and large the event is more middle of the road than SoMa's Folsom St Fair.

Halloween

☎ *415-826-1401* **w** *www.latinbayarea.com*

When: October 31, with events scheduled on the closest weekend; check local press for details.

Where: The official party has moved from the Castro to Civic Center, but thousands still flock to the Castro.

Right: Folsom St Fair: your pearls at home.

What: Two words: amateur night. What started in the Castro as the best damn drag and costume show on the face of the planet has been overwhelmed by its own success. Halloween is still the High Holy Day of queer San Francisco, but the drawback is that everyone knows that fact and the holiday draws hordes of gawking bridge-and-tunnel revelers. The whole thing has turned into a zoo. The Castro is jammed with looky-loos, and Civic Center is jammed with drunken straight people.

We cannot in good conscience recommend that visitors attend. The best policy would be show up to the Castro early, check out the costumes, and head to a private event or organize your own party. There are dozens of fancy, pay-for-entry dress, dance, and naughty-behavior parties to choose among. For example, Hell Ball, held the Saturday closest to Halloween, combines all three. Hell Ball is a long-standing techno-house party. The costumes are satanic, the boys are cute (yes, it is mostly boys, but all are welcome), and your main worry will be remembering the name of that new friend the next morning. Hell Ball can be found online at www.hellball.org.

The Harvey Milk & George Moscone Candlelight Memorial March

w *www.milkclub.com*

When: November 27

Where: Starts at 575 Castro St, the site of Supervisor Harvey Milk's former camera store, and proceeds down Market St to City Hall at Civic Center

What: The assassination of Supervisor Harvey Milk and Mayor George Moscone on November 27, 1979, by vengeful city supervisor and ex-cop Dan White, remains a pivotal moment in the history of queer liberation. The night White shot Milk and Moscone, thousands of gays and lesbians gathered at Milk's camera store and marched in a shocked and grieving mass to City Hall.

The twilight candlelight march has been held every November 27

RICK GERHARTER

Left: World AIDS Da[y] in the AIDS Memori[al] Grove

since. The size of the gathering depends largely on the current political climate. The Harvey Milk Lesbian, Gay, Bisexual, Transgender Democratic Club, which organizes the event, requests that people show up at 6pm and that they bring candles. Dress warmly.

World AIDS Day

☎ *415-252-9200* W *www.surviveaids.org*

When: December 1

Where: Proclamations, press conferences, and memorials take place all over the city.

What: World AIDS Day is recognized by scattered press events, ceremonies, and memorials. There is invariably a ceremony and gathering at the AIDS Memorial Grove in a quiet copse at the east end of Golden Gate Park. The AIDS Emergency Fund's Every Penny Counts ceremony is generally held in Union Square. Politicians have their say with speeches at Civic Center, while AIDS activists and the Sisters of Perpetual Indulgence organize more in-your-face activities that include a candlelight vigil.

For further information, check the local alternative and mainstream press or contact the San Francisco AIDS Foundation.

Guerrilla Queer Bar

W *www.guerillaqueerbar.com*

When: There's no telling!

Where: No telling this, either.

What: It's yet another boring Saturday night out in SoMa or the Castro. Or maybe it's not! Guerrilla Queer Bar is determined to fight the boredom described on its website as the 'same music, same neon, same, same, same.' And rarely has the banality of Saturday night been attacked so successfully and with such verve and vigor.

The best way to describe GQB is as a dozens-strong highly mobile roving queer party. It identifies a target bar or area and turns it gay for the night. GQB has shown up in the Tenderloin, downtown, and even at a local sex club (with participants dressed to kill in full circa 1980 preppie gear), with a full complement of queer boys and girls all looking to party, meet, and possibly go home with one another.

Says organizer Barney Schlockum – and no, that is not his real name – 'We were primarily interested in getting ourselves outside of the Castro and SOMA. We wanted an excuse to explore the city.' Under that guise, GQB held a St Patricia's Day event that toured North Beach and Chinatown two weeks before St Paddy's day. Bemused onlookers had to have it explained to them that St Patricia is the 'patron saint of drunken sex mistakes and binge drinking.' At another favorite GQB party, the Financial District's extremely swank W Hotel fell prey to the 'Guerrilla Leather Bar.' The hotel mezzanine was jammed with 'boys and girls getting whipped with bamboo from the flower arrangements in front of a bunch of uptight locals and well-to-do tourists!'

Things to See & Do

Most visitors to San Francisco stay close to the relatively flat, crescent-shaped stretch of land connecting Union Square to Fisherman's Wharf. This area, which includes Chinatown and North Beach, is where the gold-rush boomtown originally sprang up, and it remains the busiest part of San Francisco. Served by the city's quaint cable cars, the zone is compact, safe, and well stocked with colorful history, architecture, and amusements, many of them maintained or designed specifically with tourists in mind. Tourism has had a huge impact on this part of San Francisco, and some longtime residents grumble that it has turned into a theme park. Blatant tourist developments such as Pier 39, exotic lampposts on Grant Ave in Chinatown, and the huge Disney retail store on Union Square all support that view. But this area is still the legitimate heart of San Francisco, its business center and cultural focal point, so tourists need not feel cheated out of an authentic experience.

But you really should try to get out to see other parts of town. The Mission District, where the old Spanish mission still stands, is rich in Mexican American culture, and its bars and restaurants make that neighborhood the city's hottest nighttime scene. The Haight-Ashbury, home to more than a few '60s leftovers (some of them passed out on the sidewalk), still attracts people young and old who are looking for the counterculture that established itself there three decades ago. The Castro – the nation's largest gay enclave – and the former warehouse district now called SoMa are alive with creative energy that transcends sexual boundaries. The Richmond and Sunset Districts have become magnets of ethnic diversity, and between them Golden Gate Park has many worthwhile sights and museums.

Getting around is easy. San Francisco does not sprawl, so wandering the streets by foot is the most effective way of exploring a neighborhood. Buses and streetcars can get you from one neighborhood to another. See Getting Around for more detailed transit information.

The sections in this chapter are organized as much as possible according to distinct, recognizable neighborhoods. Keep in mind that some of these areas, for example SoMa and the Mission, are actually agglomerations of smaller pockets that have character and surprises of their own. And in most cases, neighborhood boundaries are not so cut and dry as maps would suggest.

UNION SQUARE AREA

The blocks surrounding Union Square comprise San Francisco's prestigious shopping district. Macy's, the old stalwart American department store, still presides over the square, as do relative newcomers Saks Fifth Avenue and Neiman-Marcus, but in recent years national chains and commercial outlets such as Disney, Levi's, and Nike have given a new tinge to the cultural hue of the neighborhood by opening shop nearby. These retailers pay preposterous rents in return for their high-profile addresses, and their rooftop billboards vie for ever-greater tracts in the sky in the quest for increased exposure.

That's not to say the area is characterized by an unseemly commercialism. More than anything, the hubbub typical of a thriving city center defines Union Square. Many of the city's old-guard hotels and highly esteemed restaurants grace the fast-paced corridors that converge on the square. Hotel doormen, hilariously attired in period costumes – at the Drake, swashbuckling Spanish conquistador styles are still in vogue, while down the street at the St Francis the dapper duds of the 19th-century English footman are favored – usher guests in and out of hotel lobbies. Their discordant taxi whistles call over the hush and groan of city buses, and cabs obligingly swerve to the curb, where awaiting fares and their luggage obstruct the continuous pedestrian flow. Foot traffic hurries up and down sidewalks, pouring in and out of buildings, veering now and then to avoid panhandlers sitting on the pavement. Autos and pedestrians alike frequently pause for the slow-moving antique cable cars, whose clanging bells are a percussive ornament to the urban clamor.

The Square

The centerpiece of all this activity – Union Square itself – is little more than a glorified parking lot, thanks to a 1942 refurbishment that acknowledged the supremacy of the almighty car. (Here's a little scrap for the trivia buffs: Union Square is the first example of the garage-under-a-park concept.) It's an innovation that is simultaneously celebrated and reviled by local architects and citizens. For years, San Franciscans have bemoaned the square's lack of aesthetic appeal – with its awkward height above street level and with auto entrances cutting it off from the sidewalk, it is not the most inviting of public spaces. Not coincidentally, the garage structure – basically a concrete shell – brings to mind a large public bomb shelter. In the wake of Pearl Harbor, this grim dual purpose seemed sensible to city planners.

The park, *sans garage,* appeared on the original city plan and was laid out in 1850. Union Square acquired its name during the Civil War, when pro-Union rallies took place on the grounds. In 2001, the square was closed so that cosmetic improvements could be made. The new design will transform Union Square into an 'Italian piazza.'

When the square reopens (around the time users of this book start hitting the streets), look for the **Dewey Monument** at the park's center. The monument, erected in 1903, commemorates Admiral George Dewey's 1898 defeat of the Spanish at Manila, which transferred the Spanish colony of the Philippines to the US. Atop the 97-foot granite column is a bronze statue by Robert Aitken. At Christmastime, a tall tree lights up the square, and hordes of determined shoppers swarm the sidewalks, making this the most festive part of town.

The St Francis Hotel

The 1904 St Francis Hotel, a stately but rather austere old hotel, presides over the west side of Union Square. Its grandness is undermined somewhat by the unattractive new wing, added in 1972, which towers over the original, but that doesn't keep visitors from enjoying a visceral kick as well as sweeping views on its newfangled high-speed glass elevators.

ANDREW DEAN NYSTROM

Break time in Union Square

An old San Francisco cliché – 'Meet me at the St Francis' – referred to the genuinely swanky cocktail lounge that formerly stemmed off the lobby. The seductive curves of its bar top and the patent leather covering its walls thoroughly outclassed the hotel's current lounge, the Compass Rose. Today, 'Meet me at the St Francis' is merely an ad slogan.

The St Francis has gained a certain notoriety over the years. In 1921, at a grotesque drunken orgy that spanned three suites in the hotel, the hugely popular comedian Fatty Arbuckle allegedly raped actress Virginia Rappe with a bottle. She subsequently died from her injuries, but Arbuckle escaped conviction. (Years later, the OJ Simpson trial and media frenzy drew comparisons to the Arbuckle case, now long forgotten by most Americans.) More recently, in 1975, former FBI narc and all-around nut Sarah Jane Moore took an unsuccessful shot at President Gerald Ford just outside the St Francis.

Sights on the Square

There aren't many tourist sights around Union Square, but some of the architecture is worth a gander. On the square's southeast corner, the **Neiman-Marcus** department store (150 Stockton St) is not a San Francisco favorite – some old-timers still miss the 1909 City of Paris building it replaced in 1982. You might sympathize with that view after stepping inside the main entrance for a look at the stained-glass dome; a hallmark feature of the City of Paris store, the dome was restored and reinstalled on the newer structure, and it is a sight to behold.

Across the street, New York–based **Macy's** has occupied its building since 1928. Its solid pier-and-spandrel walls reflect the dignified look city planners originally intended for the square, but some of its newer neighbors spoiled that plan. (See Shopping for more on these stores.)

Half a block down Stockton St from Union Square, in the Grand Hyatt plaza, Ruth Asawa's bronze **Children's Fountain** portrays San Francisco's history in intricate and playful detail. Asawa recruited local school children to contribute ideas for the design, making this a particularly interesting stop if you're traveling with kids.

Be sure to venture beyond the square itself for a look at a greater variety of buildings and small districts that are of both historical and ongoing cultural interest.

Powell St Cable Car Turnaround MAP 2
cnr Powell and Market Sts Ⓜ *Powell St BART & Muni station* 🚌 *6, 27, 30, 45, 76, F Muni* 🚋 *Powell-Mason, Powell-Hyde cable cars*

The city's famous cable cars groan along Powell St, on the west side of the square, to and from the turnaround at the corner of Market St. Cable cars on the Powell St line do not travel in reverse, so at the ends of the line (here and at Fisherman's Wharf) they are coasted onto revolving wooden platforms. Cable car drivers and brakemen (and only recently brake*women*) turn the cars around the old-fashioned way – by hand. This is the most popular and crowded spot to catch a cable car.

Nearby, subterranean **Hallidie Plaza**, named after cable car inventor Andrew Hallidie, is a transportation hub (Muni and BART trains stop there) and a daytime hangout for homeless people and alfresco chess players.

MORGAN KONN

James Flood Building MAP 2
cnr Market and Powell Sts Ⓜ *Powell St BART & Muni station* 🚌 *6, 27, 30, 45, 76, F Muni* 🚋 *Powell-Mason, Powell-Hyde cable cars*

This gray, solid building overlooks the cable car turnaround. Occupying most of the triangular block between Market, Stockton, and O'Farrell Sts, it was built in 1904 and survived the 1906 quake. On the street level, it is currently occupied by the Gap's flagship clothing store. In 1921, mystery writer Dashiell Hammett worked for the Pinkerton National Detective Agency, which had its San Francisco offices upstairs.

Eglise Notre Dame des Victoires MAP 2
566 Bush St ☎ *415-397-0113* $ *free* ⏲ *French Mass 10:30am Sun* Ⓜ *Powell St & Montgomery St BART & Muni stations* 🚌 *15, 30, 45 Muni* ♿

Since it was founded in 1855, this Roman Catholic church has been offering services in French. The church was destroyed in the '06 quake and rebuilt in Romanesque style in 1913. The congregation's pride and joy, its grand organ, was installed in 1915 and is the only organ of its type and size still working. Christmas Eve mass at Notre Dame is a lovely way to get away from the commercial Christmas on the square. During the gold rush, this stretch of Bush St was where French argonauts camped. It became known as Frenchmen's Hill, and though that handle has lost its cachet, today the neighborhood still has possibly the greatest concentration of French restaurants in the USA. (Just off Bush, pedestrian Belden St, clogged with café tables, is unofficial headquarters for the city's Francophiliac gastronomes.)

Maiden Lane

Stemming from the east side of the square, historic Maiden Lane is crowded with pricey salons and boutiques. But Maiden Lane's previous incarnation was very different from its present upscale image. San Francisco was not famous for clean living, but before the 1906 earthquake, this street, then called Morton St, was particularly notorious. Topless women stood in bordello windows along the narrow lane, offering their breasts at a nickel a fondle – a mere appetizer for the services rendered indoors. After the rebuilding of San Francisco, the street was renamed twice before city supervisors, intent on changing the street's evil ways, settled on Maiden Lane.

A couple of buildings accessible from this street are of special interest:

Folk Art International MAP 2
140 Maiden Lane ☎ 415-392-9999 $ free ⏲ 10am-6pm Mon-Sat Ⓜ Powell St BART & Muni station 🚌 15, 30, 45, 76 Muni ♿ w www.folkartintl.com

This 1949 structure, with its arched entrance, is the only Frank Lloyd Wright building in San Francisco. You can go inside to have a look at its interior – its spiral walkway suggests that it was the precursor to Wright's later, more famous Guggenheim Museum in New York. The folk art selections within, emphasizing antique handcrafted pieces from Asia and Africa, make this a worthwhile museum stop even if you're not in a buying mood.

Gump's MAP 2
135 Post St ☎ 415-984-9240, 800-766-7628 ⏲ 10am-6pm Mon-Sat Ⓜ Powell St BART & Muni station 🚌 15, 30, 45, 76 Muni ♿

This posh gift emporium, noted for its Asian art and fine jewelry, is a landmark store founded in 1861 by Solomon Gump, who was known to have a discerning eye for decorative arts. It's well worth stopping to view the window displays or stepping inside to ogle the goods.

Theater District

San Francisco's compact Theater District straddles the edge of the Tenderloin and Union Square, with Geary St as its spine. See Entertainment for more information on shows.

Geary Theater MAP 2
415 Geary St Ⓜ Powell St BART & Muni station 🚌 38 Muni ♿

This recently renovated theater is home to San Francisco's most accomplished theater company, the American Conservatory Theater (ACT; see Entertainment for more information). The theater, built in 1909, is worth looking at for its fruit-adorned terra-cotta columns and its classical form.

MONICA J MEARES

The Curran and Geary Theaters

Curran Theatre MAP 2
445 Geary St ☎ 415-551-2000 Ⓜ Powell St BART & Muni station 🚌 38 Muni ♿

This theater, adjacent to the Geary, is managed by the Best of Broadway promotional company. It showcases touring Broadway musicals – for several years, *Phantom of the Opera* played here.

Golden Gate Theatre MAP 3
1 Taylor St ☎ 415-551-2000 Ⓜ Powell St BART & Muni station 🚌 6, F Muni ♿

This theater, designed by FA Lansburgh in the early 1920s, has Moorish and Spanish revival motifs. It attracts middling Broadway productions.

The Warfield MAP 3
982 Market St ☎ 415-567-2060 business office Ⓜ Powell St BART & Muni station 🚌 6, 27, F Muni ♿

Another FA Lansburgh creation, the Warfield is primarily a venue for rock concerts. Bands that ordinarily perform in large arenas sometimes turn up in this relatively intimate theater.

Orpheum Theatre MAP 3
1192 Market St ☎ 415-551-2000 Ⓜ Civic Center BART & Muni station 🚌 6, 19, 26, F Muni ♿

The Orpheum's Moorish façade is one of the more attractive sights on Market St. Originally a Pantages vaudeville theater and later a movie house, the 1926 structure was recently restored to its former splendor, and now Broadway productions are staged here.

Alcazar Theatre MAP 2
650 Geary St ☎ 415-441-6655 business office 🚌 38 Muni ♿

A former Masonic lodge designed to look like a Muslim temple, the Alcazar represents an extravagant architectural departure from the surrounding cityscape.

The 'Tender Nob'

This vague transition zone, roughly west of Taylor St where Nob Hill descends into the Tenderloin, is fast becoming home to an edgy, hip new scene. Much of the urban commotion in the area, most of which commences after dark, has been jump-started by the restoration of several of the neighborhood's art nouveau and art deco hotels. The scene is a healthy mix of young residents – many of them students at the omnipresent Academy of Art College – and out-of-town visitors staying in the area.

The name 'Tender Nob' traditionally has been used by realtors wanting to distinguish their properties from the much maligned Tenderloin, to the immediate south, by modestly suggesting ties to Nob Hill, to the north. It is partly a misnomer, as the hotels abounding in the neighborhood make it clearly an extension of Union Square, but west of Taylor St the main avenues that define the square – Geary and Post Sts, as well as Sutter and Bush – take on some of the Tenderloin's edge. This is one of the best places for young people to stay, as room rates are relatively reasonable and the nightlife is compressed into a fairly small area.

If you spend time here – particularly at night – be careful not to wander off into the Tenderloin without knowing what you're doing. The Powell St BART and Muni station (*not* the Civic Center station) is the safest gateway in and out of the neighborhood. Walking to Market St is best done via Geary St, where the Theater District keeps the sidewalks lively in the evening. A few blocks to the west, Van Ness Ave is a major thoroughfare with a number of bus lines. Call a cab if you're transiting after hours.

A number of the city's blank-faced but powerful social clubs are in this area. The strictly men-only **Bohemian Club** (on the corner of Taylor and Post Sts) is one of the best known. Turn the corner onto Taylor St to spot the club's seal, a bronze cornerstone owl bearing the club's sinister motto, 'Weaving spiders come not here.'

CIVIC CENTER

Comprising several blocks of civic structures built in the early 20th century in the beaux arts style, Civic Center was meant to be the nation's most complete government complex, and although it has long been dragged down by its proximity to the Tenderloin, it may yet realize that ambition. San Francisco has slowly been priming the area, with the restoration of City Hall, completed in 1999, as a key step in that direction. The New Main Library and the forthcoming Asian Art Museum help bolster the neighborhood's traditional stature as the city's cultural focal point. Meanwhile, many of the city's best chefs have opened restaurants in the neighborhood to cater to the symphony and opera crowds pouring out of Davies Symphony Hall and the newly restored War Memorial Opera House.

City Hall MAP 3
400 Van Ness Ave ☎ 415-554-4000, 415-554-6023 tours info $ free ⏲ 8am-5pm Mon-Fri, noon-4pm Sat; tours: 10am, noon, 2pm Mon-Fri, 12:30pm Sat Ⓜ Civic Center BART; Van Ness & Civic Center Muni stations 🚌 5, 21, 47, 49 Muni ♿ w www.ci.sf.ca.us/cityhall

Truly spectacular despite its staid formality, San Francisco's City Hall realized the ambitions of architects John Bakewell and Arthur Brown Jr, who designed its dome to be higher than that of the US Capitol in Washington, DC. Inspiration may also have been taken from the dome at St Peter's Basilica in the Vatican. The structure, which replaced an earlier city hall destroyed in 1906, was completed in 1915 and is in the beaux arts style, with fluted Doric columns and a classic pediment. A brooding statue of Abraham Lincoln ponders the fate of the Union on Polk St. Inside, a dramatic rotunda houses a majestic staircase, and the mayor's office and the local Board of Supervisors' legislative chambers, accessible in public tours, are magnificent. Drab Civic Center Plaza faces the east side of City Hall, which is surrounded by other civic buildings. Free docent tours of City Hall meet at the tour kiosk near the Van Ness entrance and allow visitors access to more of the building. But you can wander the main floor on your own, and the small Museum of San Francisco and a basic café are open to the public.

Museum of the City of San Francisco MAP 3
400 Van Ness Ave ☎ 415-928-0289 $ free ⏲ 10am-4pm Wed-Sun Ⓜ Civic Center BART; Van Ness & Civic Center Muni stations 🚌 5, 21, 47, 49 Muni ♿ w www.sfmuseum.org

This small exhibit inside City Hall showcases some interesting relics from the city's past. The collection includes the severed 3½-foot head of the Goddess of Progress, originally part of a full statue that stood atop the dome of the old City Hall. (Unfortunately, the light bulbs that once illuminated her skull were recently removed.) Most of the other items – photos, old newspapers, scale models of buildings – relate the gold rush and the city's major quakes.

War Memorial Opera House MAP 3
301 Van Ness Ave ☎ 415-864-3330, 415-552-8338 tour info $ tours: adult $5, senior/student $3 ⏲ tours: 10am, 11am, noon, 1pm, 2pm Mon Ⓜ Civic Center BART; Van Ness & Civic Center Muni stations 🚌 5, 21, 47, 49 Muni ♿

Across from City Hall, the Opera House is the venue for performances by the city's acclaimed opera and ballet companies. It was built in 1932 in the beaux arts style. The formal peace treaty between the USA and Japan after WWII was signed here in 1951. Tours of the San Francisco Performing Arts Center (including the Opera House and nearby Davies Symphony Hall and Herbst Theatre) are conducted every Monday except holidays.

RICK GERHARTER
The beaux arts War Memorial Opera House

Veterans Building MAP 3
401 Van Ness Ave ☎ 415-392-4400 $ free ⏲ 9am-5pm Mon-Fri & during shows at the Herbst Theatre Ⓜ Civic Center BART; Van Ness & Civic Center Muni stations 🚌 5, 21, 47, 49 Muni ♿

Adjacent to the Opera House, the nearly identical Veterans Building is home to the Herbst Theatre, a recital hall. The United Nations charter was signed here in 1945. Off the lobby, to the right as you enter, is the San Francisco Arts Commission Gallery (see below). On the lobby's left side, an unsigned iron gate leads to the 'trophy room,' a hidden treasure trove of ancient and modern weaponry that's only open an hour or two on weekday afternoons and before shows at the Herbst. The collection is impressive, containing 18th-century flintlocks and a WWI cannon, along with some chilling antiquities left behind by Roman soldiers and crusaders. See the Opera House, above, for tour information.

San Francisco Arts Commission Gallery MAP 3
401 Van Ness Ave ☎ 415-252-2569 $ free ⏲ 11am-5:30pm Wed-Sat Ⓜ Civic Center BART; Van Ness & Civic Center Muni stations 🚌 5, 21, 47, 49 Muni ♿ w sfac.sfsu.edu/gallery

This gallery inside the Veterans Building puts on small contemporary art exhibits of up-and-coming local artists.

New Main Library MAP 3
100 Larkin St ☎ 415-557-4400 $ free ⏲ 10am-6pm Mon & Sat, 9am-8pm Tues-Thurs, noon-6pm Fri, noon-5pm Sun Ⓜ Civic Center BART; Van Ness & Civic Center Muni stations 🚌 5, 6, 21, 47, 49 Muni ♿ w www.sfpl.lib.ca.us

San Francisco's New Main Library opened in

1995 to mixed reviews. The intriguing interior includes a brightly lit central atrium and a spiral staircase designed by artist Alice Aycock; the staircase runs from the 5th-floor newspaper room to the 6th-floor exhibition gallery. Several of the library's collections reflect the many affinity groups that helped raise money for the new building – comfortable, sleekly lit reading rooms include the African American Center, Chinese Center, James C Hormel Gay and Lesbian Center, and the Center for San Francisco History. However, New Main boosters tend to omit mentioning that the new building turned out to be too small for the library's collection.

Asian Art Museum MAP 3
Civic Center BART; Van Ness & Civic Center Muni stations *5, 6, 21, 47, 49 Muni*
www.asianart.org

The old Main Library is slated to reopen as the new Asian Art Museum in late 2002. With some 2500 objects (statuary and pottery of all types and very few paintings) in its permanent collection, representing countries and cultures across Asia, it will be the premier museum of its kind.

United Nations Plaza MAP 3
free *6am-midnight* *Civic Center BART; Van Ness & Civic Center Muni stations* *5, 6, 21, 47, 49 Muni*

Across Hyde St from the New Main Library, this plaza was built to commemorate the signing of the UN charter in San Francisco. Most days, the plaza is filled with street people sunning themselves, but a farmers' market is held here on Wednesday and Sunday (see Shopping for information).

Bill Graham Civic Auditorium MAP 3
99 Grove St *415-974-4000* *during events* *Civic Center BART; Van Ness & Civic Center Muni stations* *5, 6, 21, 47, 49, F Muni*
www.billgrahamcivic.com

On the south side of Civic Center Plaza, this beaux arts auditorium was built in 1915; Graham's name was added in 1991 to honor the rock-concert impresario, who promoted many of the San Francisco's seminal rock and roll events during the 1960s. The Grateful Dead held many a New Year's Eve concert in the hall, and a fledgling Rock and Roll Walk of Fame is slowly taking shape on the sidewalk in front of the building, with plaques commemorating John Lee Hooker, Carlos Santana, Jerry Garcia, and Janis Joplin.

HAYES VALLEY

West of Van Ness Ave, tiny Hayes Valley blossomed amid the freeway wreckage left by the 1989 quake, and today Hayes St is prime real estate for purveyors of high-end, offbeat fashions. The name honors Colonel Thomas Hayes, whose impressive 19th-century estate was nestled between Duboce Park and Alamo Square. Hayes' grounds included a pleasure garden, an art gallery, and a concert hall. Today, Hayes Valley clings to the stretch of Hayes St between Franklin and Laguna Sts.

Bucheon Gallery MAP 3
540 Hayes St *415-863-2891* *free*
11am-6pm Wed-Sat, noon-5pm Sun
21 Muni
www.bucheon.com

If you are spending an afternoon strolling Hayes St, check out this gallery, which often has interesting art exhibits.

THE TENDERLOIN

The Tenderloin's extents, lacking any natural or structural barriers such as a hill, an overhead freeway, or a tunnel, are not precisely defined. Around its edges are fuzzy transitional zones leading into the Civic Center, Union Square, and the Tender Nob. Suffice it to say, if you start from Hallidie Plaza, at Powell and Market Sts, and head north up Powell, you will enter the posh Union Square area; but if you head due west up Eddy St, you enter the city's most troubled central district, known locally as 'the 'Loin' or the 'TL.' Similarly, if you begin at the corner of Sutter and Jones Sts, in the transitional Tender Nob area, and proceed south down Jones, you will notice that each block, from Post to Geary to O'Farrell, is slightly more dicey than the previous one. By the time you reach O'Farrell, you are definitely in the Tenderloin. At Ellis St, 1 block below O'Farrell, the neighborhood really takes on that troubled air.

Market St between Mason and Larkin is a maligned stretch of what really ought to be a grand avenue through the heart of the city; heading north or west at any corner takes you directly to the TL. If you exit the Civic Center area to the east (on McAllister or Golden Gate) or north (on Polk or Larkin), expect a similar decline.

Such an elaborate description of the neighborhood's extents should serve as warning to visitors heading out on an evening stroll, but that's not at all to say the Tenderloin ought to be dismissed. The area has an interesting history, and walking its streets (preferably during the day) is never dull.

The Tenderloin's troubles go back nearly a century. After the 1906 quake, the district was developed almost exclusively with SRO (single-room-occupancy) hotels and studio apartments, which complemented the city's revolving door of transient laborers and sailors. The area quickly became another of the city's zones of iniquity, as clip joints, brothels, gamy strip joints, and covert gay sailor bars opened up, followed by an increase in crime. The name derives from a similarly beleaguered precinct on the West Side of Manhattan. (There, cops reputedly earned better pay for walking the hazardous beat and could therefore afford choicer cuts of meat – the tenderloins.) Of course, tenderloin is also commonly read as an innuendo for the streetwalkers and massage parlors' that continue the world's oldest trade in the area to this day.

In recent years, the TL has become a neighborhood to watch, as young bohemians invade the area in search of a respite from San Francisco's housing crunch and high rents. The 'Loin has never suffered from a dearth of drinking establishments, and some of the less depressing bars have begun to attract a younger clientele. But the Tenderloin's problems are deeply embedded in its streets, its buildings, and in the destitute lives of many of its residents, and the area will probably continue to defy urban renewal trends for years to come.

One positive development over the last two decades has been the emergence of a cohesive Vietnamese community here. The neighborhood's Vietnamese restaurants and grocery stores are worth scouting out.

Mitchell Brothers' O'Farrell Theater MAP 3
895 O'Farrell St ☎ 415-441-1930 $ $20-40 ⌚ 11:30am-1:30am Mon-Thurs, 11:30am-2:30am Fri-Sat, 5:30pm-1:30am Sun 🚌 19, 38 Muni ♿
w *www.ofarrell.com*

The infamous Mitchell Brothers' O'Farrell Theater strip joint remains open for business, long after one of the founding brothers murdered the other. Jim and Artie Mitchell opened this theater in 1969 and soon began making the pornographic films, some featuring porn legend Marilyn Chambers, that helped launch a multimillion-dollar porn empire. At their prime, the Mitchells owned a film production company and operated 11 theaters in California. But the Mitchell brothers eventually went the way of Cain and Abel, and Jim shot and killed Artie in 1991. He was convicted of voluntary manslaughter and served six years' jail time. Despite its tawdry background, the O'Farrell Theater is generally regarded as a classy sort of place as strip joints go, and fat cats from around the world always drop by when in town.

SOUTH OF MARKET

The area south of Market – 'SoMa,' as it's frequently called – has always been somewhat incongruous with the area north of Market. SoMa streets meet Market St at a right angle, as opposed to the odd angles at which streets from the north meet Market, and the blocks are much longer and less convenient for pedestrians. Nevertheless, much of this vast area is undergoing dramatic gentrification and rebuilding.

The winds of change first blew in the 1970s, when several square blocks of slum housing were demolished to clear the way for Yerba Buena Gardens and Moscone Convention Center, and continued in the 1990s, as dot-com businesses and flimsy-looking live-work lofts redefined the city's image of a district once entirely reserved for warehouses, flophouses for longshoremen, and slums.

The South of Market area actually comprises several unique neighborhoods. South Beach, China Basin, and Mission Bay, along the waterfront, were originally developed with foundries and shipyards that have been replaced by Pacific Bell Park, where the Major League San Francisco Giants play, and by high-priced condominiums and upscale restaurants. Some of the old java houses that once served stevedores still stand, althought a decidedly less boisterous crowd chows in them now. Toward Market St, the ballpark area segues into an extension of the Financial District.

Nearby South Park, a small residential enclave just blocks from the ballpark, is one of many hubs of the South of Market multimedia industry that spread up Potrero Hill and to the Mission District before receding seemingly overnight. E-commerce companies and start-ups continue to operate there but without the investor euphoria and venture capital on which they surged in the late '90s.

Yerba Buena Gardens is the ripening heart of high culture in San Francisco. The success of the San Francisco Museum of Modern Art, which opened in 1995, has led the way for a plethora of museums and galleries opening shop in the area, with more on the way. The Metreon entertainment complex and dozens of esteemed restaurants have further transformed the once sleepy gardens into a place where locals and visitors spend their leisure time.

The unofficial nightclub district, clustered around 11th St, where dance clubs and live music venues have roosted since the 1980s, has survived gentrification, but the dot-com carpe diem mentality has made the strip less a focal point than it once was. Instead, clubs come and go throughout SoMa, with expiring leases and a volatile economy ensuring that nothing is permanent. The South of Market scene reinvents itself constantly.

San Francisco Museum of Modern Art MAP 4
151 3rd St ☎ 415-357-4000 $ adult $9, senior $6, student $5, under 13 free; 6pm-9pm Thurs half-price; 1st Tuesday of the month free ⌚ 11am-6pm Mon-Tues & Fri-Sun, 11am-9pm Thurs Ⓜ Montgomery St BART & Muni station 🚌 14, 40, 45 Muni ♿
W www.sfmoma.org

This is one of the best museums dedicated to modern art in the US, although it doesn't challenge the preeminence of the Museum of Modern Art in New York.

In 1995, SFMOMA moved into its new home, directly across 3rd St from Yerba Buena Gardens. The striking new building, a modernist design by Swiss architect Mario Botta, became an instant South of Market landmark. Its stepped-back brick and granite façade, with a unique truncated white cylinder emerging from its roof, is the most distinctive public structure to appear in San Francisco in quite some time. With 50,000 sq feet and galleries on four floors, the museum has ample space to showcase its permanent collection as well as important touring exhibits.

The permanent collection includes work by all the great American and European artists but is particularly strong in American abstract expressionism, with major works by Clyfford Still, Jackson Pollock, and Philip Guston, and in fauvism, with works such as Henri Matisse's 1905 masterpiece *Femme au chapeau*. The permanent collection also contains several works by Mexican painters Diego Rivera and Frida Kahlo and by Bay Area artists Robert Arneson and Richard Diebenkorn. Willem de Kooning, Marcel Duchamp, Rene Magritte, Robert Rauschenberg, and Andy Warhol are all represented. Since 1995, SFMOMA has aggressively built on its collection, pursuing major works that include Mark Rothko's *No 14, 1960* and Jim Hodges' *No Betweens*.

Perhaps SFMOMA's most distinguishing feature is its photography collection, which is world class. Works by Ansel Adams, Edward Weston, Robert Frank, Dorothea Lange, and William Klein are regularly on view, and the collection is so deep that the museum rarely has to repeat itself. The museum also frequently features multimedia, architecture, and design exhibits.

There are regular free gallery tours, and the museum has an excellent bookstore and a swanky cafeteria eatery.

Yerba Buena Gardens MAP 4
☎ 415-541-0312 $ free ⌚ sunrise-10pm daily Ⓜ Powell St & Montgomery St BART & Muni stations 🚌 14, 40, 45 Muni ♿

Yerba Buena Gardens addresses SoMa's lack of open-air public spaces, and since completion of the buildings that surround it – which include SFMOMA and the Metreon – it has become a very popular place to idle away a lunch hour or a sunny afternoon. Tables and chair

SARAH JH HUBBARD

Yerba Buena's rooftop carousel

or the Metreon food court, a rolling green awn, public sculpture, and a café are all lraws, but the esplanade's pièce de resistance s the sleek Martin Luther King Jr Memorial ountain, a collaboration by sculptor Houston Cornwell and architect Joseph De Pace. Noon-ime concerts are held here in summer.

A pedestrian bridge traverses Howard St, nking the esplanade to a children's play-round and entertainment complex. This in-ludes Zeum (see below), a small bowling lley, an ice rink, and a Looff carousel with omely hand-carved and -painted horses and amels (our six-year-old expert judged the ide too short for the $2 fare). This part of the 'erba Buena complex, which actually sits atop he half-submerged convention center, isn't ery well integrated with the surrounding eighborhood and feels underutilized com-ared to the often crowded esplanade.

Zeum Art & Technology Center MAP 4
21 4th St ☎ 415-777-2800 $ adult $7, enior/student $6, child $5, under 5 free ⌚ 11am-5pm Sat-Sun, Wed-Fri for field ips only Ⓜ Powell St & Montgomery St ART & Muni stations 🚌 14, 30, 45 Muni ♿ w www.zeum.org

eum's mission is to foster the creativity of oung people (primarily ages eight-18), and it oes so with a constantly changing array of xhibits, films, and projects. Children may get to experiment with digital photography, make and record music, or use various technological innovations. Films, plays, and other forms of entertainment contribute to the educational atmosphere. During the school year, it's open to the public only on weekends, but the schedule loosens up during the summer.

Yerba Buena Center for the Arts MAP 4
701 Mission St ☎ 415-978-2710 $ adult $6, senior/student $3 ⌚ 11am-6pm Tues-Wed & Sat-Sun, 11am-8pm Thurs-Fri Ⓜ Powell St & Montgomery St BART & Muni stations 🚌 14, 30, 45 Muni ♿ w www.yerbabuenaarts.org

Two buildings comprise this arts complex, with a museum and performance space occupying separate corners of Yerba Buena Gardens. The focus here is the culturally diverse art and entertainment coming out of the Bay Area. A few years back, for example, costumes from George Lucas' Star Wars films were exhibited in the museum, and more recently the work of San Francisco–based illustrator J Otto Siebold (of 'Space Monkey' renown) were on display. Chinese opera and films and plays with local relevance are the sorts of events staged at the theater. The local connection is sometimes loosely interpreted, enabling the center to display art from just about anywhere in the world.

Metreon MAP 4
101 4th St ☎ 800-638-7366 $ complex free; fees for individual attractions ⌚ 10am-10pm Mon-Thurs & Sun, 10am-11pm Fri-Sat (hours vary for individual attractions) Ⓜ Powell St & Montgomery St BART & Muni stations 🚌 14, 30, 45 Muni ♿ w www.metreon.com

Sony's ultramodern entertainment complex, anchored by a multiplex cinema, attempts to blend commerce and culture in a manner reflecting the multimedia age. The result, due in part to shops that have no walls and to a distinctly cosmopolitan vibe, is something like a futuristic airport where the flights have been canceled to leave more time for shopping. A slew of offbeat specialty shops may succeed in luring you in (see Shopping), and the myriad food options should satisfy your appetites while you're here. There are a few attractions, in addition to the state-of-the art movie theater, that make this a genuine destination.

Where the Wild Things Are brings to life the forests of the picture book by Maurice Sendak, who consulted in the design of this children's fantasyland. Children walk through the forest that grew and grew in Max's room, encountering cleverly mechanized renditions of those mischievous wild things who have made an indelible impression on so many millions of youngsters over the past four decades. Younger tots may be spooked by the funhouse maze if not accompanied by a parent, while older, more cynical tots (in the Harry Potter stage of life) may find it a bit tame. Parents will find it expensive ($6). If this adaptation of the book doesn't quite qualify as a 'wild rumpus,' it's at least a creditable amusement.

Airtight Garage, a darkly lit grotto designed by graphic novelist Jean 'Moebius' Giraud, is sort of a postindustrial video arcade anchored by an unusual new concept: HyperBowl. The virtual bowling alley offers few of the comforts of the real thing – authentic plastic bowling seats were brought in, but the snazzy shoes were left in the nonvirtual realm. But the advantage of virtual bowling ($6) is that instead of straining your wrist rolling heavy balls down a straight wooden lane, you guide an electronic ball through your choice of Roman monuments, the deck of a pirate ship, or the streets of San Francisco (think *Bullitt* but with bowling balls).

St Patrick's Church MAP 4

756 Mission St ☎ 415-421-3730 $ free ⌚ 7am-6pm daily Ⓜ Powell St & Montgomery St BART & Muni stations 🚌 14, 30, 45 Muni ♿ limited

This landmark redbrick cathedral, constructed in 1872, can be admired while lounging on the lawn at Yerba Buena Gardens, but go inside for a look at its marble columns, elaborate stained glass windows, and immense pipe organ. Display cases contain a few interesting artifacts, including raffle tickets from a 1928 charity whist party (grand prize: a Studebaker Dictator sedan). The parish was originally predominantly Irish but today is largely Filipino, and some masses are said in Tagalog.

Ansel Adams Center for Photography MAP 4

655 Mission St ☎ 415-495-7000 $ adult $5, senior $2, student $3 ⌚ 11am-5pm daily Ⓜ Montgomery St BART & Muni station 🚌 30, 45 Muni ♿
w www.friendsofphotography.org

This center is dedicated to photography as art, with an ongoing (but frequently changing) exhibit of Ansel Adams' work and rotating exhibits featuring the work of other notable photographers. San Francisco was a leading center for creative photography during the mid-20th century, with Adams, Edward Weston, Dorothea Lange, and others frequently congregating here. This museum recently moved into its current home on Mission St with hopes that the larger space will allow its curators to promote the art form adequately.

Jewish Museum of San Francisco MAP 4

121 Steuart St ☎ 415-543-8880 $ adult $4, senior/student $3, 12 & younger free ⌚ noon-5pm Sun-Thurs Ⓜ Embarcadero BART & Muni station 🚌 14 Muni ♿
w www.jmsf.org

This very philosophical museum has changing exhibits celebrating Jewish art and culture around the world. In its current one-room space hidden behind the lobby of an office building, the exhibits are modest at best, but expect bigger things when the museum moves into its new home at Yerba Buena Gardens in 2003. (The new site will be on Mission St between 3rd and 4th Sts.)

Mexican Museum MAP 4

718 Mission St ☎ 415-202-9700 Ⓜ Montgomery St BART & Muni station 🚌 14, 30, 45 Muni ♿
w www.thecity.sfsu.edu/users/Mex

When it opened in 1975, this was the first museum in the US dedicated to Mexican art. Long located in a shedlike space at Fort Mason, the Mexican Museum closed its doors before press time, in anticipation of its migration to new quarters at Yerba Buena Gardens. When it opens in 2003, the museum will feature two floors of galleries – room to show off its impressive collection of art from Mexico as well as works by Mexican Americans. Strengths include pre-Columbian art, folk art and modern art.

California Historical Society Museum MAP 4

678 Mission St ☎ 415-357-1848 $ adult $3, senior/student $1 ⌚ 11am-5pm Tues-Sun Ⓜ Montgomery St BART & Muni station 🚌 14, 30, 45 Muni ♿
w www.calhist.org

This historical museum chronicles the gold rush and the rapid growth of the state. Immigration is a natural subtext. The themes are interesting and always pertinent, but the exhib

THINGS TO SEE & DO

is a little staid. Peer in before paying to see if it grabs your interest. A gift shop offers a nice selection of related books.

Society of California Pioneers Museum MAP 4
300 4th St ☎ 415-957-1849 ⓢ adult $3, senior/student $1 ⏲ 10am-4pm Tues-Fri 🚌 12, 76 Muni ♿
w www.californiapioneers.org

The Society of California Pioneers was established in 1850 with the rather exclusive requirement that its members be able to trace their roots in the state to 1849 or earlier. In spite of the dubious value of the society's mission, it has a very nice museum that's well worth visiting, even for newly arrived Californians and tourists. Cohesive exhibits, always concerning significant events in the state's history, are very thoroughly researched and are presented with a variety of media and with an eye for what will hold a modern audience's interest. The upstairs art gallery, though small, displays some outstanding historical paintings.

Cartoon Art Museum MAP 4
1017 Market St ☎ 415-227-8666 ⓢ adult $5, senior/student $3, child $2 ⏲ 11am-5pm Tues-Fri, 10am-5pm Sat, 1pm-5pm Sun Ⓜ Civic Center BART & Muni station 🚌 6, F Muni ♿
w www.cartoonart.org

At press time, this wonderful museum was in transition as it prepared to move into its new Market St space. The museum was founded on a grant from cartoon legend Charles M Schultz, of 'Peanuts' fame, and it features ever-changing exhibits of cartoon art, from the well known to the esoteric. Past exhibits have presented original panels and rarely seen portraits by R Crumb, as well as work by his brother Maxum, who lives just a few blocks away. 'Zippy the Pinhead' creator Bill Griffith, 'Eightball' scribe/penman Daniel Clowes, and 'Chuckling Whatsit' artist Richard Sala, all of whom are based in the Bay Area, have also shown here. Things should be up and running on Market St by the time you read this.

Pacific Bell Building MAP 4
140 New Montgomery St ⓢ free ⏲ 8am-6pm Mon-Fri Ⓜ Montgomery St BART & Muni station 🚌 14 Muni ♿

A striking art deco skyscraper, the terra cotta–clad Pacific Bell Building, designed by Timothy Pflueger (noted for his cinemas, including the Castro), looms over SFMOMA in one of the city's more impressive architectural juxtapositions. You can enter its gorgeous lobby to see its black marble walls, bronze elevator doors, and ceiling resplendent with Chinese mythic figures.

Palace Hotel MAP 4
2 New Montgomery St ☎ 415-512-1111, 800-325-3535 Ⓜ Montgomery St BART & Muni station 🚌 6, F Muni ♿

This luxurious hotel was opened in 1875. The original hotel had 800 rooms and every conceivable luxury, including a fireplace and toilet for each bedroom and five hydraulic elevators. Built right after the disastrous 1868 earthquake, it also featured an exotic array of fire-fighting safeguards; nonetheless, it burned down in the postquake fire of 1906. It was rebuilt and reopened in 1909 with the central Grand Court, where horse-drawn carriages deposited arriving guests. The space later became the glass-domed Garden Court, and afternoon tea in the leafy atrium is the place to contemplate the hotel's 1991 renovation, which cost more than $100 million. The Pied Piper Bar, with its huge 1909 Maxfield Parrish painting *The Pied Piper*, is another relaxing spot.

Old US Mint MAP 4
cnr 5th and Mission Sts Ⓜ Powell St BART & Muni station 🚌 14, 27 Muni

This landmark structure, shuttered since 1995, is a fine and rare example of Greek revival architecture in San Francisco. Built in 1869 with a granite foundation and thick sandstone walls, it originally stored massive quantities of gold and silver mined in the Sierra Nevada. Its graceful front steps now serve primarily as a crash pad for street people.

Rincon Center MAP 4
201 Spear St ☎ 415-243-0473 ⓢ free ⏲ 24 hours 🚌 6, 14, F Muni ♿

Close to the waterfront, the Rincon Center occupies the entire block bounded by Mission, Howard, Steuart, and Spear Sts. A modern complex combining a shopping center (with a notable internal rainfall fountain), an open-air plaza, and office buildings, the center is fronted on Mission St by the Rincon Annex Post Office, a 1939 art deco masterpiece. The post office closed in 1978 but was placed under the protection of the National Register of Historic Places.

The building itself is a treasure (look for the dolphin friezes on the façade), but it was primarily the lobby murals by Anton Refregier that preservationists sought to protect. The murals, which depict the history of California, are the largest single commission by the WPA. They cover more than 400 feet of wall space and were completed in 1948. Display cases exhibit interesting odds and ends found during construction of the modern wing – suggestive finds include bullet shells, a busted harmonica, and fragments of old liquor bottles. Security officers are on duty 24 hours a day, so viewing the murals is easy and free.

Audiffred Building MAP 4
121 Mission St 🚌 *14, F Muni*

The 1889 Audiffred Building stands out with its mansard roof. A saloon popular with sailors and wharf workers occupied the ground floor in 1906, and it's said that the bartender saved the building from the fire department's dynamite crew by bribing them with whiskey and wine. The building now houses the posh Boulevard restaurant.

Pacific Bell Park MAP 4
24 Willie Mays Plaza ☎ *415-972-2000*
$ *game tickets start at $10; tours: adult $10, senior $8, 12 & under $5* ⏲ *game times vary (usually around 1pm or 7pm); tours on the hour 10am-2pm daily, unless events are scheduled* 🚌 *30, 32, 45, N Muni* ♿
w *www.giants.mlb.com*

The San Francisco Giants' new home opened in 2000, and in accordance with current nostalgic trends it was designed to evoke memories of the picturesque ballparks of old, with a redbrick façade and an asymmetrical playing field. Its defining characteristic is a shallow porch in right field that makes it possible for left-handed sluggers to plunk home run balls into the bay (where a labrador in a dinghy awaits, ready to retrieve Big League souvenirs). Games here are much more intimate and appealing to watch than they were at gusty Candlestick Park, but tickets are pricey and not easy to come by. (See Entertainment for tips.) Daily tours of the stadium, when the event schedule allows, are one way to get in, but of course a ballpark without a game is about as compelling as birthday candles without a cake. To make up for this deficiency, the tour pries into areas fans don't ordinarily get to go, such as the press box and the visitors' clubhouse.

GREG GAWLOWSKI

Pacific Bell Park

Lefty O'Doul Bridge
⏲ *24 hours* 🚌 *30, 32, 45, N Muni* ♿

By fortunate coincidence, just outside Pacific Bell Park stands this curious little bridge, long ago named for baseball legend Francis 'Lefty' O'Doul. Built in 1933 to span little Mission Creek, the bridge is a trunnion bascule span – an impressive black snarl of crisscrossing metal beams with an immense concrete weight suspended above one end for balance. It is often cited among the local favorites – not a small compliment, considering the competition, but San Franciscans have always been partial to underdogs. O'Doul (1897–1969), a San Francisco native, was one of the National League's most fiercesome hitters in the late 1920s and early '30s, and he is credited with igniting baseball fever in Japan during a trip to that country in the '50s. Also see Entertainment for details about Lefty's namesake bar.

South Park MAP 4
🚌 *15, 30, 45, N Muni*

This patch of green along South Park Ave is so incongruous with the rest of SoMa that it comes as a shock when you stumble on it. South Park was built in 1852 to replicate a London city square, and in the past decade it was revived as a quiet little restaurant and café quarter in the heart of Multimedia Gulch.

Jack London's Birthplace MAP 4
601 3rd St 🚌 *15, 30, 45, N Muni* ♿

Around the corner from South Park, a plaque on an office building marks the birthplace of

Jack London, esteemed author of *The Call of the Wild, White Fang,* and many other popular adventure stories. London was born in a house on the site on January 12, 1876; he died in Sonoma County in 1916.

FINANCIAL DISTRICT

The compact downtown area spreads east from Union Square and Chinatown to the bay. It's the city's center for banking, which has been San Francisco's true bread and butter ever since banks started to appear in the 1850s to handle the state's mining fortunes. Stock market trading is the district's other hugely prosperous enterprise. Montgomery St is often referred to as 'Wall St of the West.'

Much of the Financial District is built on landfill, some of it founded on the decayed wooden ships abandoned during the gold rush. At one time, Yerba Buena Cove curved inland as far as Montgomery St. The modern shoreline at the Embarcadero was established by the 1880s.

Unless you've arrived with briefcases filled with money, visiting the Financial District is essentially an appreciation of tall buildings. To be sure, the architecture here is not on a par with that in Chicago, New York, or even Los Angeles. Most of the historic structures from the 19th century were reduced to smoldering heaps in the 1906 earthquake, and the greedy real estate moguls who rebuilt the city were too focused on profits to concern themselves with aesthetics or ingenuity. The fear of building too high in earthquake country kept San Francisco out of the skyscraper war that sent the New York and Chicago skylines toward the ozone layer. Consequently, much more style went into Nob Hill and Pacific Heights mansions. But there are a few outstanding structures, and some engineering firsts in the Financial District.

The area is frantically busy during the day, when taxis, buses, delivery trucks, power-dressing businesspeople, and kamikaze bike messengers compete for street and sidewalk space. Come dark, Montgomery St is serenely quiet, and only a handful of restaurants and bars along the district's edges are open. An evening stroll through these urban canyons should not be ruled out – sometimes the dusky air is filled with the mellifluous tones of a solitary tenor saxophonist indulging in the district's echoing acoustics.

Bike Messengers

Bike messengers started to appear downtown in the 1970s, and today they're a familiar sight around the Financial District, often speeding the wrong way down one-way streets or hurtling through red lights, narrowly missing pedestrians and averting near-death experiences. There are probably 300 to 400 bike messengers working the city, with the biggest messenger companies employing about 40 riders and the smallest just a half-dozen. An experienced rider will get through about 25 tags (deliveries) in a day. Bike messengers are a serious city subculture, and they've even got their own fictional hero: the high-tech (and female) Chevette in William Gibson's cyberpunk novel *Virtual Light.*

Modern development and skyscrapers actually spill south of Market St to Howard St, and there are many sights in that pocket that might reasonably be taken in on a day of Financial District walking. See South of Market, earlier, for information on some buildings in that area.

The Embarcadero

The Embarcadero is the wide waterfront thoroughfare from which the old port's now-defunct piers sprocket out into the bay. Once the busiest area of the city, the waterfront has diminished in importance over the years. The completion of the Golden Gate and Bay Bridges in the 1930s ended the ferryboat era, and two decades later the container-ship era made San Francisco's old wharves obsolete. Oakland, with its large tracts devoted to container storage, is now the main port on the bay.

[Continued on page 112]

Skyscraper Walking Tour

Until the 1960s, San Francisco was largely skyscraper free. It was known as the 'white city' because of the city's preponderance of white stucco surfaces. But since engineers figured out how to build up without risk of complete tragedy in an earthquake, the downtown skyline has been thoroughly Manhattanized. All of the following buildings are within a few blocks of one another. A good time to roam the Financial District is midday, when office workers pour from the buildings for lunch. Until then the streets and gray buildings appear relatively subdued, and on the weekend the neighborhood is devoid of life.

There are a few museums and monuments in the Financial District, adding mild seasoning to the architectural meat of this walk. Begin your tour at the foot of Market St, just a block from the Embarcadero BART

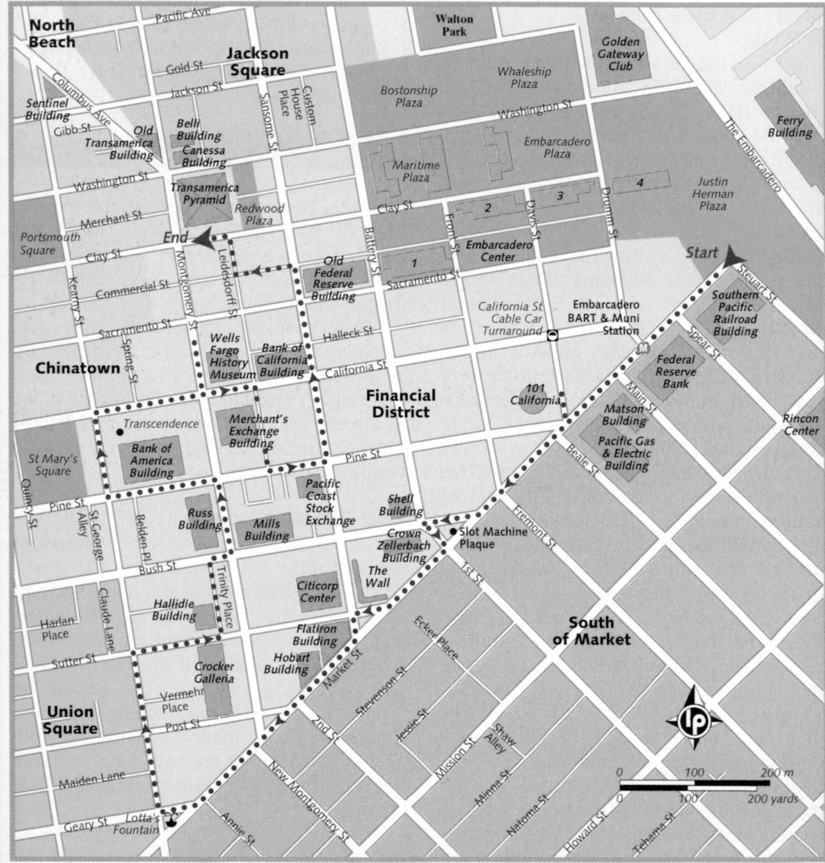

and Muni station. The Ferry Building will be in view on the other side of Justin Herman Plaza.

Southern Pacific Railroad Building *1 Market St* ♿

On the corner, the warm look of this 1916 building belies the raw power this company wielded in California from its creation in 1869 until the early 20th century. SP moved out of the building a few years ago, and the company was absorbed in a merger with Union Pacific.

Matson Building *245 Market St* ♿

A few floors above street level, the façade of this 1921 building is emblazoned with the names of its shipping-company founders. The company's maritime interests are visually represented with waves, fish, and other watery motifs set against a blue-green background.

DAVID TOMLISON

Pacific Gas & Electric Building *245 Market St* ♿

Adjacent to the Matson Building, the PG&E office building dates from 1925 and nicely complements its neighbor. A sculpted bear's head and workmen whose pants are torn to shreds adorn the façade. (You'll notice in many of the district's statues a similar partiality for torn pants.) The great blue-and-gold lanterns flanking the door are impressive too.

Cross where Davis and Pine Sts converge on Market and proceed on Davis to California St.

101 California St *101 California St* ♿

This cylindrical tower, erected in 1982, appears to have had a wedge sliced out of its base. To amateur eyes, the columns supporting the tower will appear too slender for comfort, but the engineers among us just chuckle at such uncertainty.

Return to Market St and continue in the direction you'd been walking. At Bush St, turn right and proceed a half a block to the corner of Battery St.

Right: A quake-proof and Manhattanized downtown

Shell Building *100 Bush St* ♿

This attractive structure went up in 1929 and is an excellent representative of the skyscrapers of that period. The terra-cotta building is adorned with decorative motifs, and the small lobby is worth peeking into.

Return to Market St and continue on it for several blocks.

Crown Zellerbach Building *1 Bush St* ♿

This 1959 building, with its deep-green glass, is a fine example of late '50s architecture. Planters and a 'moat' set this building off from the sidewalk and street, an effect that is somewhat cold and off-putting but frequently copied by modern architects.

On the periphery of the buildings grounds are a couple of curiosities. Across Battery St, next to the exit from the building's underground parking garage, notice the historical landmark slot machine plaque that indicates where, in 1898, Charles August Fey invented the Three-Reel Bell Slot machine, a device that soon came to be known as the 'one-armed bandit.'

Continue on Market (following the sidewalk as it veers up Sutter St), to the other side of the Crown Zellerbach Building, and you'll soon be milling in a crowd of athletic, long-haired, tattooed, and punk-attired men and women.

You are now at 'The Wall.' The Wall is a low-standing concrete fence that's ideal for sitting on, and it has been claimed by the city's bike messengers much the same way the old boat landings at Pier 39 have been claimed by the bay's seals. Comparisons between bike messengers and seals stop there, however. Representing a rogue faction of the city's economic machinery, bike messengers spend most of their time on their bicycles, zipping through dangerous downtown traffic to relay packages from one office to another, and they spend very little time sunning themselves here.

Citicorp Center *1 Sansome St* ♿

The gutted beaux arts façade of the Anglo & London Paris National Bank is now a courtyard entryway for the Citicorp Center, at the corner of Sansome and Sutter. During the day, the marble patio, fenced in by massive columns, is dotted with café tables and chairs generally occupied by well-dressed businesspeople. The bank was originally built in

1910, with additions made in 1921. Citicorp converted the building to suit its own needs in the early 1980s.

Flatiron Building *1 Sutter St* ♿
At one time, stately triangular buildings like this one stood at nearly every corner along Market St. None compared to the Flatiron Building in New York, but they still lent Market St a pleasing uniformity that it lost in the 1960s, when development spelled the end of many of them.

Continue walking along Market St.

Hobart Building *582 Market St* ♿
This idiosyncratic 1916 building is perhaps best viewed from across Market St. Its oddity stems primarily from the demolition of the adjacent building, which exposed the Hobart's western flank. About a dozen flights up, beyond the height of its former neighbor, the Hobart's design changes abruptly from flat and featureless to decoratively rounded, with west-facing windows. The building was designed by Willis Polk, one of the city's most important postquake architects.

RICHARD CUMMINS

At the corner of Geary and Kearny Sts, step out onto the triangular island adorned by a bronze fountain.

Lotta's Fountain
This odd-looking fountain was donated to the city by entertainer Lotta Crabtree in 1875. Crabtree (1847–1924) embarked on her path to fame as an actress and dancer during the Comstock boom years and went on to become the highest-paid female entertainer in the US. At 5am each April 18, survivors of the 1906 earthquake gather at the fountain. You'd think their numbers would have dwindled by now, but a few dozen people show up each year. (Imposters? Set your alarm clock and see for yourself.)

Turn right on Kearny St and turn right again on Sutter St.

Hallidie Building *130 Sutter St* ♿
Named after cable-car inventor Andrew Hallidie, this 1917 building was the world's first glass-curtain-wall building. The technique of hanging a curtain of glass in front of a building's actual structure has become an everyday feature of modern office buildings, but this pioneering example remains a favorite of architects, who often remark on

Top right: The Hobart Building

Bottom right: Lotta Crabtree

RICHARD CUMMINS

the building's elegant fire escapes. Unfortunately, the famed glass curtain is not tinted, and the building's hideous interior, office cubicles and all, is plainly visible. For a good vantage point of the building, go upstairs in the Crocker Galleria, across Sutter St.

Turn left on Trinity St, a narrow alley that rarely sees daylight, and follow it to Bush St. A right turn will lead you to Montgomery St, where two city landmarks face each other.

Russ Building *235 Montgomery St* ♿

With 30 floors, this was San Francisco's tallest building from its creation in 1928 until 1964. It no longer ranks in the top 10. The Russ Building is representative of the architectural school influenced by the elaborate, Gothic-style Tribune Tower in Chicago, completed in 1925. It's more attractive from Bush St.

Mills Building *220 Montgomery St* ♿

The Mills Building is the only prequake skyscraper still standing. Built in 1891 (it gained an additional tower in 1931), it was the first steel-frame building in San Francisco. Its was designed by Chicago architect Daniel Burnham.

Return to Kearny St via Montgomery and Pine and continue to the corner of California St.

Bank of America Building
555 California St ◷ *8am-10pm daily* ♿

The 1969 completion of the Bank of America Building ushered in a new era for San Francisco's previously low-rise skyline. Not only was the 52-story, 761-foot building much higher than any earlier one, its red South Dakota granite looked very different from the consistently pale coloring of the city's other buildings. Collaboratively designed by two architectural firms, the building is fronted by an open plaza that holds a sculpture by Masayuki Nagare, a 200-ton black monolith officially

KIM GRANT

Top left: Crocker Galleria

Bottom left: Bank of America Building

titled *Transcendence* but more popularly known as 'the Banker's Heart.' The views from the top-floor lookout are available only to those drinking or dining in the Carnelian Room (you *might* skirt around that formality if you ask nicely for a brief peek).

RICHARD CUMMINS

The bank's founder, AP Giannini, was born in 1870, cut his business teeth on his stepfather's San Francisco produce operation, and then set out on his own in 1904 to establish the Bank of Italy (which catered at first to the city's Italian immigrants). In 1906, Giannini was able to truck out his bank's assets ahead of the advancing flames following the earthquake. His was the first bank to reopen after the disaster, and he never looked back. In the 1930s, he consolidated his various bank holdings to form the Bank of America, which by 1948 was the largest in the country. Although Bank of America still occupies the California St building, it is no longer the owner. At the end of the 1970s, the bank had accumulated a hefty collection of debts from defaulted third-world loans and was forced to sell the building headquarters to shore up its balance sheet. Two decades later, the bank was bought, and its headquarters are now in North Carolina.

Return to Montgomery via California St. The intersection of these two streets is the epicenter of the Financial District. Turn left.

Wells Fargo History Museum *420 Montgomery St*
☎ *415-396-2619* $ *free* ⏲ *9am-5pm Mon-Fri* ♿

The small museum traces the history of Wells Fargo Bank and the 1849 gold rush. A Wells Fargo stagecoach from around 1865 is the peach of the collection. Wells, Fargo & Co was founded in 1852 by Henry Wells and William Fargo to provide banking, and express and mail delivery services, to businesses in the new state of California (it's the oldest bank in the state). The mining boom was under way, and the new company went where the miners went, starting up stagecoach services throughout the region, buying and selling gold, and transporting mail. The banking and express businesses separated in 1905, and mergers with other banks over the years have made Wells Fargo one of the largest banks in the USA.

Double back and turn left on California St.

Merchant's Exchange Building *465 California St*
☎ *415-421-7730* $ *free* ⏲ *9am-5pm Mon-Fri* ♿

Right: The 200-ton *Transcendence*

Walk through the lobby and into the California Bank & Trust for a look at the series of William A Coulter shipping paintings on the walls. (You may have to sweet-talk the lobby security guard for the privilege.) The paintings are relevant to the building's history. At one time, the comings and goings of ships were monitored from a lookout tower on the roof. The building burned down in the 1906 fire and was subsequently rebuilt.

Turn right on Leidesdorff St, then left onto Pine.

Pacific Coast Stock Exchange *301 Pine St*
☎ *415-285-0495* $ *$5* ⏲ *tours 3pm 1st Wed of the month* ♿

This is a stark mausoleumlike structure with striking statuary that appears strangely out of sync with the building's purpose. Aren't these bold, solid figures the sort of thing one associates with Russian socialism? The stock exchange was built in 1915 and remodeled in 1930, after the stock market crash. Its trading hall and the spectacular City Club upstairs are not ordinarily open to the public, but you can see the interior during a highly recommended tour of the building. The primary purpose of the tour is to showcase a lush stairwell mural by Diego Rivera, who, intriguingly enough, held certain 'communistic' views. Titled *Riches of California,* the mural was Rivera's first in the USA. Call for information.

Continue to the corner of Sansome and California Sts.

Bank of California Building *400 California St*
⏲ *10am-5pm Mon-Fri* $ *free* ♿

Corinthian columns front the templelike 1908 Bank of California. In 1875, the bank's founder, William Ralston, drowned while swimming in the bay. Whether he died by accident or committed suicide is a matter of some speculation. Some suggest he had a heart attack and subsequently drowned. Either cause is probable, as Ralston's empire was crumbling at the time. His bank, the largest financial institution on the West Coast, collapsed when he tried to simultaneously buy the famous Comstock Lode silver mines and build the opulent Palace Hotel on Market St. During business hours, you can admire the cavernous interior and visit the small museum in the basement (see below).

Museum of Money of the American West *400 California St*
☎ *415-765-0400* $ *free* ⏲ *10am-4pm Mon-Fri*

In the basement of the Bank of California Building, this museum recounts the city's long association with money and banking, and gold nuggets found during the gold rush are on display.

Old Federal Reserve Building *400 Sansome St*
⏲ *9am-5pm Mon-Fri*

This former banking institution, now occupied by a law firm, reflects two architectural traditions. The ground level, with its Ionic columns, is from the beaux arts school; the upper level is more in the modern style of the early 20th century. The structure was built in 1924, and in 1985 it was altered to adjoin the Embarcadero Center. Loitering on the building's steps, a bronze sculpture of Dionysius, god of wine, has evidently been slashed to ribbons. He doesn't appear to be thinking 'You should see the other guy,' but if you want to, go to the building's Battery St steps for a look at Hermes, god of commerce, who has been similarly sliced. Step into the lobby to view the giant 1915 painting

Traders of the Adriatic, by Jules Guerin.

Cross to Commercial St and follow it to Leidesdorff, then turn right. The Transamerica Pyramid looms strikingly before you.

JOHN ELK III

Transamerica Pyramid
600 Montgomery St ⓢ *free*
⏲ *9am-6pm Mon-Fri* ♿

At 853 feet, this is San Francisco's tallest building. It was completed in 1972 and quickly became a modern symbol of the city. It is the single feature that makes the San Francisco skyline instantly recognizable. At the time of its construction, architect William Pereira was roundly reviled; the mere fact that he came from Los Angeles implied he was not to be trusted. But gradually the pyramid gained acceptance in the city as a landmark, and it's no longer referred to as 'Pereira's Prick.'

Form definitely wins the battle with function at the pyramid: neatly undermining the old equation that the higher the floor, the higher the rent is the fact that the offices on the higher floors have a smaller square footage than the ones lower down. The 48-story structure is topped by a 212-foot spire, which encloses mechanical equipment in its lower part but is hollow at the top.

There's no observation deck, but in the building's lobby visitors can look at four live video monitors for a 'virtual view.' Buttons let you control the sophisticated zoom lenses and pan back and forth. Adjacent to the building is a half-acre stand of redwood trees, called Redwood Plaza, where Friday lunchtime concerts take place from May through September.

Between 1853 and 1959, the Transamerica Pyramid's site was occupied by the Montgomery Block, an office block with a ground-floor saloon that became a favorite of journalists, artists, and poets. Bret Harte, Mark Twain, and Robert Louis Stevenson all passed through the saloon's swinging doors. While Sun Yat-sen plotted the demise of the Manchu Dynasty, he published the newspaper *Young China* and drafted the Proclamation of the Republic of China in a 2nd-floor office there. When rents dropped, the Montgomery Block's chambers became artists' studios and residences, and Ambrose Bierce, Frank Norris, and Jack London all resided there at one time or another. After the demolition of this historic building, the site was a parking lot for 10 years.

ight: The Transamerica Pyramid and the Sentinel Building

[Continued from page 103]

The elevated Embarcadero Freeway, constructed in the late 1950s, effectively obscured the waterfront from San Francisco's consciousness, and the area declined steadily. Salty old longshoremen's taverns such as Red's Java House slumbered amid the always dark and seedy wharves, and shady hotels beneath the massive freeway were hotbeds of crime and prostitution.

The Embarcadero gained new life when the 1989 Loma Prieta earthquake damaged the freeway beyond repair, and three years later, the remains of the wreckage were cleared. At the corner of Broadway and Sansome, part of an off-ramp still stands in a state of ruin, a reminder of the Embarcadero's dark age.

Still, the fate of the old piers remains uncertain. Some of them serve as warehouses, others house offices for architecture and law firms. But clearly the waterfront area is being groomed for a rebirth. Tourism and entertainment figure to play a prominent role, as they already do at Pier 39 and Fisherman's Wharf, but residents are understandably wary of more of that type of development. A ballot initiative proposing a touristy commercial plan was voted down, signaling that the waterfront's future will have to serve the needs of people who live here.

Newly laid streetcar tracks run the length of the Embarcadero, linking Fisherman's Wharf with Market St.

Ferry Building MAP 5
Ⓜ *Embarcadero BART & Muni station* 🚌 *2, 6, 7, 9, 14, 21, 31, 32, 66, 71, F Muni*

Completed in 1898 and once serving a very significant role as the city's primary transportation hub, the Ferry Building was at one time the city's most recognizable building. It enjoyed its heyday in the 1920s and '30s, when it was the arrival and departure point for ferries shuttling across the bay. At the time, it was one of the world's busiest transport interchanges. The landmark tower is modeled on the Moorish Giralda tower in Seville, Spain, and at 240 feet it was for some time the tallest building in San Francisco. By the late '50s, its stature had diminished significantly, and it could barely be seen from behind the Embarcadero Freeway. Ever since the freeway's demise, the city has debated future uses of the building. At press time, the Ferry Building was receiving a badly needed restoration.

STEPHEN SAKS
The Ferry Building

You can still catch a ferry here. It's the least expensive way to get out on the bay, which, on a warm sunny day, might qualify as one of the highlights of your visit. (If boats make you uncomfortable, there's a bar on board.) Ferries go to Jack London Square in Oakland and to Sausalito and Tiburon in Marin County. See Getting Around for details.

Embarcadero Center MAP 5
☎ *415-772-0500* $ *free* ⏲ *10am-7pm Mon-Fri, 10am-6pm Sat, noon-5pm Sun; call for restaurants' hours* Ⓜ *Embarcadero BART & Muni station* 🚌 *1, 41, 42 Muni* ♿
w *www.embarcaderocenter.com*

One of the city's most ambitious real-estate developments, the Embarcadero Center aspires to be to San Francisco what Lincoln Center is to Manhattan. Comprised of four skyscrapers linked with pedestrian walkways, the complex serves as a shopping center on the two lowest floors and offers some choice office space upstairs. But as the Embarcadero really isn't a central location, the center has never figured very prominently in city life. The movie complex, one of the city's best for independent and foreign films, is one of the only reasons people come here on their own time. (Most of the shopping is done by people on their lunch break.) The four main buildings of the center (Embarcadero Center One through Four) are uniform in style, and together they cut an impressive figure in the city's skyline, especially around Christmas, when lights outline them at night. The complex includes two of the city's 10 highest buildings. Skydeck, a viewing platform atop Embarcadero Center One, is currently closed to the public.

RICHARD CUMMINS

Embarcadero Center

Justin Herman Plaza MAP 5
Embarcadero BART & Muni station *1, 14, 41, 42, F Muni*

Justin Herman Plaza received a huge boost when the Embarcadero freeway went down in 1989. Suddenly, the Ferry Building entered its view, and the new openness and relative quiet made it a more appealing place to hang out. It's a popular outdoor lunch spot for Financial District suits, and skateboard punks like it here, too. Lunchtime concerts are sometimes held during the spring and summer, and in the winter an outdoor ice rink draws crowds not seen the rest of the year. Vaillancourt Fountain, the plaza's ungainly centerpiece, looks like it's made of leftovers from the demolition of the Embarcadero Freeway, but the unfortunate truth is it was here before the freeway tumbled down. When the fountain is dry, usually due to water shortages, it is a pretty dismal sight to behold. Having it at full flow makes all the difference, and walking from step to step behind the fountain's gushing spouts is a small adventure, particularly for the young 'uns.

Broadway Pier
free *24 hours* *32, F Muni*

Most of the old wharves along the Embarcadero shield the bay from view, but this small open pier at the foot of Broadway exists solely to encourage San Franciscans to get in touch with their body of water. It's often crowded with people casting fishing lines into the murky waters below – the object being to see who can reel in the least edible fish. This stretch of the Embarcadero is one of the city's most popular walking, jogging, and skating routes. Also worth temporary stops are the historical markers that jut out of the sidewalk to relate the colorful history of the Barbary Coast to unsuspecting passersby. Nearby, the Filbert St steps are an attractive route from the Embarcadero to North Beach (see the North Beach section for more information).

JACKSON SQUARE

This is the city's first historic district. Initially a central commercial area, it foundered on the tawdry edge of the Barbary Coast for many decades until bohemians, followed by architects and gallery owners, began to appreciate its well-preserved brick and cast-iron buildings, many of which date to the gold rush. By 1971, Jackson Square was officially protected, and as if to signify its treasured status, many of the storefronts have since been taken over by upscale antiques dealers.

[Continued on page 117]

Barbary Coast Walking Tour

The old brick structures of Jackson Square have hosted some of the city's defining events. This was, after all, the edge of one of America's most hedonistic quarters. Spend a little time in San Francisco and you'll begin to sense that the city is rather proud of its decadent history. Many of the buildings still standing in the Jackson Square Historic District were occupied at one time or other by a bordello, a dance hall, or a bawdy saloon. The district is small, and a very quick walk will take it all in. Begin the tour at the Old Transamerica Building, just opposite the much newer pyramid, and start up Montgomery.

Old Transamerica Building *4 Columbus Ave*

This 1909 structure, originally home to the Fugazi Bank, is of interest primarily as a study of contrasts. Its white terra-cotta tile façade lends the modest structure an old-world elegance lacking in the modern Transamerica Pyramid, across the street.

Canessa Building *710 Montgomery St*

It's not a quake survivor (it was built late in 1906), but the Canessa Building was home to the legendary Black Cat bar. The Black Cat, one of the neighborhood's landmark bohemian hangouts, was very popular among gay people. After ongoing police harassment, the club won a landmark California Supreme Court case in 1951 that allowed

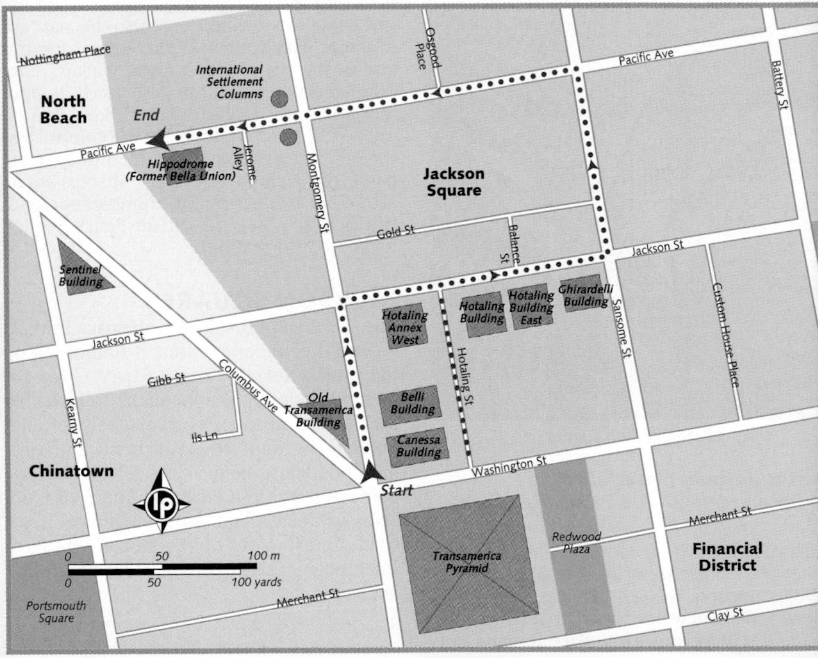

gays to congregate in bars. The original Black Cat closed its doors in 1963, but a new Black Cat (a jazz supper club; see Places to Eat) recently opened a few blocks away, on Broadway.

Belli Building *722 Montgomery St*
This building dates to 1851, and its current decrepit condition is hardly suitable for such a historic structure. It served first as a tobacco warehouse, then as a Barbary Coast cabaret, and finally as the office of renowned lawyer Melvin Belli, who represented the Rolling Stones after their Altamont fiasco. Belli died in 1996, and since then the building has been pretty much left to rot.

Turn right onto Jackson St. Half a block down, the entrance to the alley Hotaling Place is flanked by the Hotaling Buildings.

Hotaling Building *451–55 Jackson St*
On the eastern corner of Hotaling Place and Jackson St, the original, Italianate Hotaling Building is distinguished by cast-iron pilasters and heavy iron shutters; it dates to 1866. The adjacent building, and another just opposite on the western corner, each date to 1860. The owner of these buildings, Anson Parsons Hotaling, traded in liquor, among other things. When his buildings survived the 1906 quake and fire, they inspired a local wit named Charles Field to compose a smart retort, in verse form, to evangelical warnings borne on the echoing thunder of the quake:

> If, as they say, God spanked the town
> For being over frisky,
> Why did He burn His churches down
> And spare Hotaling's whiskey?

Take a quick detour down Hotaling Place and have a look at the ancient back sides of the buildings that overlook this old alley. Then continue on Jackson St.

Ghirardelli Building *415–31 Jackson St*
Until the company's move in 1894 to the Fisherman's Wharf area, this 1853 building was the Ghirardelli chocolate factory. When you try to picture what this lusty neighborhood was like in its heyday, imagine a hint of chocolate in the air. Bas-relief heads above the ground floor create the sensation you're being watched as you walk by.

Turn left on Sansome and left again onto Pacific. These next 2 blocks were the heart of the Barbary Coast.

Pacific Ave
Although the fire of '06 decimated the unseemly businesses that had by that time lined the street for half a century, Pacific St quickly bounced back. The façades were lit up with tawdry signs, strip-show barkers and flirtatious women stood in every doorway, and wicked laughter and the tinkling of pianos rang out from saloons. Ragtime, precursor to jazz, found an early home here.

Two rusted metal columns flank the western corners of the intersection of Pacific Ave and Montgomery St. They once held the arched neon sign for the International Settlement, an ambitious enterprise of the 1940s that attempted to revive the Barbary Coast nightclub district without the whorehouses. WWII curfews put a stop to that, but

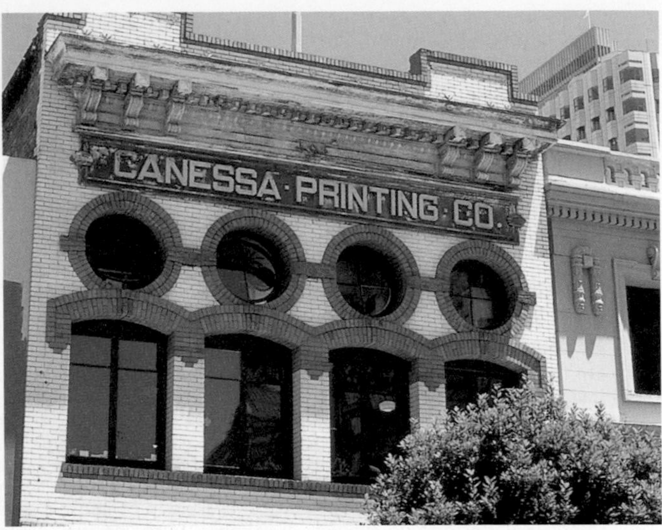

KIM GRANT

for some reason these old columns still stand. Otherwise, very little remains of the street's bawdy past.

Hippodrome *555 Pacific Ave*

The single outstanding remnant of the Barbary Coast is the well-endowed façade of this former melodion, now occupied by a furniture retailer. Peer into the front entrance, where bas-relief sculptures on the sides depict dancing nude nymphs and the pilasters are topped with bare-breasted women – an authentic legacy of a raucous and violent period.

Left: Canessa Building

King of Eccentric

Emperor Norton I was born Joshua Abraham Norton in 1819. He came to San Francisco as a young man and made a fortune off the city's boomtown economy, but in 1852 he lost everything in a business gamble and never recovered. After eight years of increasing poverty, he snapped, at least in one key respect: he declared himself the Emperor of the United States, and within a month he added the title Protector of Mexico.

Norton spent the next 20 years becoming an icon and widely loved mascot of San Francisco, living an oddly dignified life and causing no one any harm. He never appeared without his uniform, with its bulky epaulets and plumed hat, and a sword at his hip. He issued his own scrip in 50¢, $5, and $10 denominations, and though it became mainly a collector's item, it was good-naturedly accepted by many shopkeepers. Among the many decrees Norton made as emperor, such as one dissolving the republican form of government in the US, was his famous injunction against the use of the word 'Frisco.'

COURTESY OF THE BANCROFT LIBRARY

> Whoever after due and proper warning shall be heard to utter the abominable word 'Frisco,' which has no linguistic or other warrant, shall be deemed guilty of a High Misdemeanor, and shall pay into the Imperial Treasury as penalty the sum of $25.

In 1880, thousands of people attended his funeral. He now rests in Colma Cemetery under a prominent headstone unambiguously affirming his status in death, as in life, 'Emperor of the United States & Protector of Mexico.'

– Chris Carlsson

[Continued from page 113]

The architectural cohesiveness of the district is what makes Jackson Square one of the city's distinctive pockets. By fluke, these 4 square blocks – bounded by Washington St, Columbus Ave, Pacific Ave, and Sansome St – were largely spared by the 1906 earthquake and fire, which obliterated nearly every other downtown neighborhood.

CHINATOWN

While other ethnic enclaves fade away as their residents become more affluent and move to less crowded parts of town or to the suburbs, Chinatown continues to grow. That's because as better-off Chinese people leave Chinatown, new immigrants from China move in. The neighborhood is home to some 30,000 Chinese people, most of whom speak Cantonese as a first language. Tourism is obviously a major source of income, as evidenced by the tacky curio shops along Grant Ave, but most of the businesses on the other Chinatown streets serve the daily needs of people whose tastes and lifestyles are distinctly un-Westernized.

The neighborhood seems to have its public face and an elusive private side. Perhaps that is what continues to make Chinatown so alluring to visitors. There are no essential sights in Chinatown, no single place that any visitor absolutely must see, but it's a great place for casual wandering.

[Continued on page 123]

Chinatown Walking Tour

Visitors are really best off just wandering the main drag, Grant Ave, and exploring the myriad side streets and alleys. But if you're starting from the Chinatown Gate, here's a little tour offering some neighborhood history and behind-the-scenes information.

Chinatown Gate

Chinatown visits often begin here. Constructed in 1971, the gate's drab minimalism seems more a nod to modern architecture than to traditionally ornate Chinese styles. But the ceramic dragons that guard it make it pretty clear that this is, indeed, an entrance to Chinatown.

Proceed up Grant Ave.

RICK GERHARTER

Grant Ave

Packed with shops and restaurants, Grant Ave has had a colorful history from its inception as Calle de la Fundacio, the main street in the Spanish village of Yerba Buena. Renamed Dupont St when the US took the city – and known as 'Du Pon Gai' to the Chinese – it became synonymous with brothels, gambling dives, opium dens, and brawling tongs. It was renamed once again in 1885 for US president and Civil War hero Ulysses S Grant, who had died that year. The street is lined with colorful buildings and lampposts, and during holiday times bright yellow and red flags and banners make this the city's most festive thoroughfare. The corner of California St, with three impressive structures, is the architectural hub of Chinatown.

RICHARD CUMMINS

Sing Fat Building *597 California St*

This building, along with the Sing Chong Building across the street, set the tone for the future of Chinatown after the 1906 quake. Designed by T Patterson Ross and AW Burgren and built in 1908, these structures represent the faux pagoda style so prevalent along Grant Ave.

Sing Chong Building *601 Grant Ave*

Like its twin, the Sing Fat building, this structure has shapely pagodalike contours. It's best viewed from across the street – when the cable car goes by you don't have to see the McDonald's restaurant that occupies the building's street level.

St Mary's Square *🕘 sunrise-sunset daily ♿*

Across California St from St Mary's Cathedral is one of Chinatown's few open spaces. It's surrounded by high-rises, making it somewhat claustrophobic, but it is a popular spot for early-morning tai chi and a nice place to relax. Presiding over St Mary's Square like a wise old tin

Top right: Chinatown Gate

man is the serene-looking stainless steel statue of Doctor Sun Yat-sen. It's one of local sculptor Beniamino Bufano's best works.

Old St Mary's Church *660 California St ☎ 415-986-4388*
$ free ⏰ 7am-5:30pm Mon-Fri, 11am-7pm Sat, 7:30am-4pm Sun ♿

St Mary's was the first Roman Catholic cathedral on the West Coast, and its 90-foot tower made it the tallest building in the city when it was completed in 1854. Modeled after a Gothic church in Spain, it was built on foundation stones shipped from China and with bricks brought around the horn from New England.

Turn left at Sacramento St.

Chinese Playground *⏰ sunrise-sunset daily* ♿

This is a handkerchief of open space where toddlers play on a jungle gym and students sometimes play a spirited game of badminton. The benches on alleylike Hang Ah St are a good place for a short stop to absorb the Chinatown atmosphere.

Turn right on Stockton St.

Stockton St markets *⏰ hours vary* ♿ *limited*

Grant Ave may be the essential promenade for tourists, but for an inside view of daily life in Chinatown, go to Stockton St. If you're looking for exotic sights, check out some of the delicacies available in the fish markets and butcher shops. While you're walking Stockton St, some revelations will become abundantly clear: the Chinese waste nothing and they'll eat pretty much anything. Occasionally armadillos – yes, for human consumption – are available.

RICHARD I'ANSON

Left: The heart of Chinatown

Kong Chow Temple *855 Stockton St*
☎ 415-434-2513 ⏰ hours vary

Visitors are welcome at this temple, four flights above the post office. The current building was erected in 1977, but the original Chinese altar, which the people at the temple claim is the oldest in the US, has been preserved. It was before this altar that, in June 1948, Mrs Harry Truman had her fortune told.

DOUG MCKINLAY

Chinese Consolidated Benevolent Building
843 Stockton St

This building, with a pair of lions guarding the entrance, houses its namesake organization, also known as the Six Companies. During the 19th century, the Six Companies wielded tremendous power in Chinatown. They fought for Chinese legal rights, served as an arbitrator in disputes between Chinese people, and helped the Chinese bury their dead.

Turn right down Clay St (toward the Transamerica Pyramid) and left into Waverly Place.

Waverly Place

Colorful Waverly Place has many open balconies and upstairs temples. Temple hours are erratic, and the temples don't have that much to see, but for the curious among us it's always difficult to pass on the chance to go upstairs and see what's hidden behind Chinatown's façade.

Tien Hau Temple *125 Waverly Place*
Ⓢ *donations (free)* ◷ *hours vary*

This old temple, on the top floor, is dedicated to Tien Hau, goddess of heaven and the sea. Chinese immigrants, grateful for their safe passage across the Pacific, built San Francisco's first Tien Hau Temple in 1852. A small donation, polite behavior, and respectful attire are generally expected of visitors.

Turn right onto Washington St.

Sam Wo's *813 Washington St*
☎ *415-982-0596* ◷ *11am-3am Mon-Sat*

This is an old hole-in-the-wall Chinese restaurant once renowned for a gruff waiter who called himself Edsel Ford. The cheap, greasy chow served here was favored by Beat writers and poets, and Jack Kerouac supposedly learned how to use chopsticks in the cramped upstairs dining room. See Places to Eat for more information.

Head in the opposite direction along Washington St and turn right into Ross Alley.

Ross Alley

This is one of Chinatown's darkest and most mysterious alleys, making it a necessary detour for amateur gumshoes. Like nearly every other street in the vicinity, in the late 19th century Ross was lined with 'high-class' opium dens and brothels. Now, it's home to a popular fortune cookie shop (see below).

Golden Gate Cookie Company *56 Ross Alley*
☎ *451-781-3956* ◷ *10am-7pm daily* ♿

Right: Kong Chow Temple

Step into this steamy, dimly lit shop to buy a bag of fortune cookies and set your peepers on its old-fashioned factory works. It's intriguing to watch how the cookies are artfully shaped by adept hands before they cool and harden. As a nod to the alley's notorious past, this shop sells 'French Adult' cookies with risqué fortunes. If you're squeamish about such things, the non-French variety is also available. Incidentally, fortune cookies are a San Francisco invention, not a Chinese one; they were dreamed up for the Japanese Tea Garden in Golden Gate Park.

Turn right onto Jackson St and then right again onto Grant Ave. Turn left onto Washington St and head down hill.

Bank of Canton *743 Washington St*

Another pagodalike building, this one built in 1909, the Bank of Canton once housed the Chinatown telephone exchange. Unfortunately, when it was refitted with teller booths and bank vaults, the building lost its gorgeous interior. The ostentatious roof looks a little out of sorts atop the bank's lackluster accoutrement.

DOUG MCKINLAY

Portsmouth Square ⓢ *free* ⊙ *24 hours* ♿

Portsmouth Square is often called Chinatown's 'living room' because so many of the neighborhood's residents lack a spare room of their own to hang out in and so convene here instead. The square is always crowded with people young and old engaged in fevered games of checkers, chess, or mah-jongg or playing on the square's playground. Some serious betting goes on among the old men. Portsmouth Square, once the heart of the city, got its name from John B Montgomery's sloop, the *Portsmouth*. Montgomery arrived in 1846 to claim the city for the USA, and a plaque commemorates the spot where the Stars and Stripes was first raised in San Francisco. Two years later Sam Brannan, whose newspaper offices overlooked the square, sparked the gold rush by running a newspaper headline announcing that gold had been discovered in the Sierra foothills. During the boom that followed, the square was surrounded by gambling parlors, where many a miner's fortune was lost.

[Continued from page 117]

Roam through the narrow alleys that many locals rely on to avoid the crowds on Stockton and Grant; on quiet afternoons, you'll typically hear old women clacking their mah-jongg tiles from behind screen doors, as well as the little electric-sounding 'snaps' that children toss off the sidewalks echoing within the alley walls.

The most festive time to visit Chinatown is during the Chinese New Year, in late January or early February, when there's a parade, fireworks, and other festivities. The Moon Festival, in the fall, is also an exciting time here. But the day-to-day bustle of Chinatown is reason enough to visit anytime.

History

Of all the city's neighborhoods, Chinatown has perhaps the most interesting history. Chinese people started to flood into California during the 1849 gold rush, and more came with the construction of the transcontinental railroad in the 1870s. These immigrants weren't popular – as the 1882 Chinese Exclusion Act made clear – and in San Francisco anti-Chinese sentiments contributed to Chinatown's almost fortresslike feel. In the 19th century, Chinese people rarely crossed Broadway, the traditional line between Chinatown and North Beach, or Powell St, which divided Chinatown from Nob Hill. Meanwhile, people from other parts of the city freely roamed the streets of Chinatown, where they could gawk at its residents and their 'unusual' ways, much as tourists still do today.

The Chinese Exclusion Act prevented Chinese people from entering the United States in the late 19th century. As a result, residents of Chinatown – mostly men cut off from their wives and families in China – bonded together according to family associations. These loose organizations evolved into the neighborhood's notorious tongs.

Between the 1880s and the 1920s, Chinatown was in the grip of ongoing tong warfare, with rival associations running operations in gambling, prostitution, extortion,

COURTESY OF THE BANCROFT LIBRARY

Chinese fortune-teller

and the opium trade. Much of the neighborhood's mystique derived from this criminal activity. White men regularly came to Chinatown to slum it for a night in an opium den or in the company of a Chinese prostitute.

When the 1906 quake and fire laid waste to the entire neighborhood, many prominent San Franciscans, including former mayor James Phelan, wanted to move the Chinese residents from this central location to Hunters Point. The Chinese avoided eviction by rebuilding quickly. The new pagodalike structures made it clear the Chinese had no intention of leaving, and soon any thought of moving the Chinese community was forgotten.

The earthquake had another, even greater impact on Chinatown. All immigration records had gone up in flames along with City Hall, making it possible for noncitizens

The Death of Miles Archer

Burritt St is a tiny, nondescript alley off Bush St near the stairs that lead up from the Stockton Tunnel. On the wall of a building near the entrance to the alley, look for the plaque that reads:

> On approximately this spot, Miles Archer, partner of Sam Spade, was done in by Brigid O'Shaughnessy.

This bit of intrigue – for those who haven't read the book – is a reference to Dashiell Hammett's classic detective novel *The Maltese Falcon*. (Our apologies for revealing this integral plot twist.)

to claim citizenship; this allowed the Chinese to send for their offspring in China, because although the Chinese Exclusion Act forbade Chinese immigrants from bringing their families over, it did not prevent US citizens from doing so. Thousands of new Chinese poured into Chinatown for the first time since the act had gone into effect, ensuring that the neighborhood would not die out. That many of the newcomers – referred to as 'paper sons and daughters' – were not actually related to Chinese people already in San Francisco was a secret safe in Chinatown.

Today, the neighborhood remains somewhat cut off from adjacent parts of the city, and its residents still sometimes quietly refer to outsiders as *low faan*, meaning 'barbarians.' Its entrance arches, at Grant Ave and Bush St, separate it from Union Square, as does the Stockton Tunnel, a block over. But Chinatown has grown to the north, nudging beyond Broadway along Stockton and Powell Sts, and to the west, up and over the slope of Nob Hill all the way to Larkin St.

Chinatown Museums

Chinatown has several cultural museums that each tell part of the story of this unique neighborhood.

Chinese Culture Center MAP 5
750 Kearny St, 3rd floor ☎ 415-986-1822 $ donations (free) ⌚ 10am-4pm Tues-Sat, noon-4pm Sun 🚌 1, 15, 41 Muni ♿ w www.c-c-c.org

The center has changing exhibits on traditional and contemporary Chinese American art and culture, usually with a local slant.

Chinese Historical Society Museum MAP 5
965 Clay St ☎ 415-391-1188 $ free ⌚ 10:30am-4pm Mon & Wed-Fri, 1pm-4pm Tues 🚌 1, 9, 30, 45 Muni ♿ w www.chsa.org

This museum has an impressive collection of historical artifacts and photos that tell the story of Chinese migration to the US and their way of life here since the gold rush. Items on display, like mining tools and an 1880 Buddhist altar, help bring the message home: the Chinese played a significant part in California's history. The building the museum occupies is also of interest. Designed by Julia Morgan with elegant Chinese features, it was originally a YWCA. It was built in 1932.

Pacific Heritage Museum MAP 5
608 Commercial St ☎ 415-399-1124 $ free ⌚ 10am-4pm Tues-Sat 🚌 1, 12, 42 Muni ♿

In the Old Mint Building (with the monstrous Bank of Canton built right on top of it), this museum aims to promote San Francisco's Asian cultural ties. To that end, it exhibits work by artists from the broad Pacific Rim region.

NORTH BEACH

Despite gentrification and the onslaught of tourist-oriented restaurants, North Beach retains much of its old neighborhood feel. It is traditionally a working-class Italian neighborhood, and though North Beach is now mixed and more upscale than it once was, you are still likely to hear Italian spoken when you enter its cafés and delis.

This is San Francisco's most intimate quarter, particularly on weekdays when the locals set the pace. Then you are likely to notice nondescript old-world bakeries such as Liguria, where only focaccia is made, or to observe elderly Chinese practicing tai chi in Washington Square or to encounter old

[Continued on page 130]

North Beach Walking Tour

North Beach's spirited history is palpable. Its residents and businesses preserve the neighborhood's traditions. In a single, unstrenuous walk you can take in all of the neighborhood's sights. You can really spend an entire day in this interesting enclave: in addition to checking out the sights described here, stop for a midday coffee or a light lunch, hike up to Coit Tower, peruse the shops on Grant St and the bookstores that abound in the neighborhood, have an afternoon beer, and cap the day off with an Italian dinner and some live music. Begin at the Transamerica Pyramid and stroll up Columbus Ave. Keep your eyes peeled for street signs: many streets in the area have been named after writers and poets to commemorate the neighborhood's distinguished literary past.

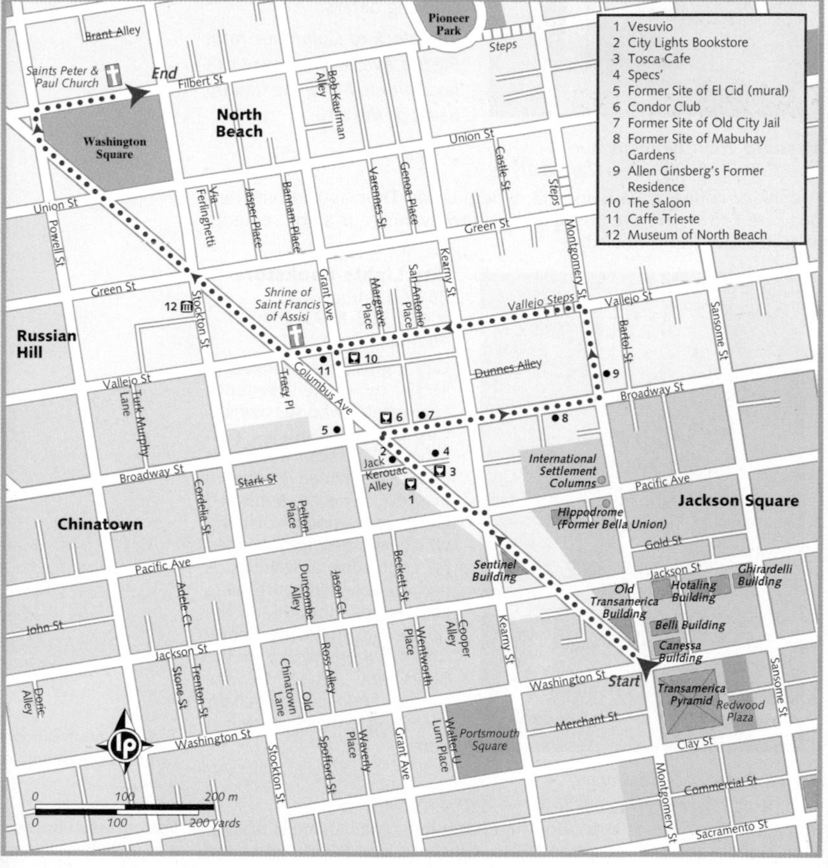

TOM DOWNS

Sentinel Building
916 Kearny St

One of the neighborhood's more stylish buildings is this triangular 1905 structure with a lovely green copper cupola. It is owned by filmmaker Francis Ford Coppola, and offices for his film company, Zoetrope, are in the building. Coppola's winery, Niebaum-Coppola, operates a café on the ground level, and the revolving wooden entrance to this small eatery is yet another of the building's eye-catching details.

The block of Columbus from Pacific Ave to Broadway can lay claim to being the literary heart of the city.

Vesuvio *255 Columbus Ave*
☎ 415-362-3370 ⏲ 6am-2am daily ♿

A drink or coffee at Vesuvio café, where Dylan Thomas and Jack Kerouac are known to have pissed away a few evenings, is a fine segue to a visit to City Lights Bookstore.

TOM DOWNS

City Lights Bookstore
261 Columbus Ave
☎ 415-362-8193 ⏲ 10am-midnight daily

City Lights was founded in 1953 by poet Lawrence Ferlinghetti, who still owns it. City Lights Publishers, with offices upstairs from the bookstore, gained its renown in 1957, when it published Ginsberg's poem 'Howl,' which was promptly banned for containing obscenities. A highly publicized court ruling allowed distribution of the poem. Go up to the Poetry Room, where works of the Beats and others fill the shelves, and tables and chairs invite you to make yourself at home.

Top left: Francis Ford Coppola's Sentinel Building

Bottom left: Vesuvio, a favorite Beat haunt

Tosca Cafe *242 Broadway*
☎ 415-391-1244, 415-986-9651 ⏲ 5pm-2am daily ♿

Tosca is a North Beach institution that has a long and illustrious history. One night in the mid-'60s, Bob Dylan, Ginsberg, and Ferlinghetti were

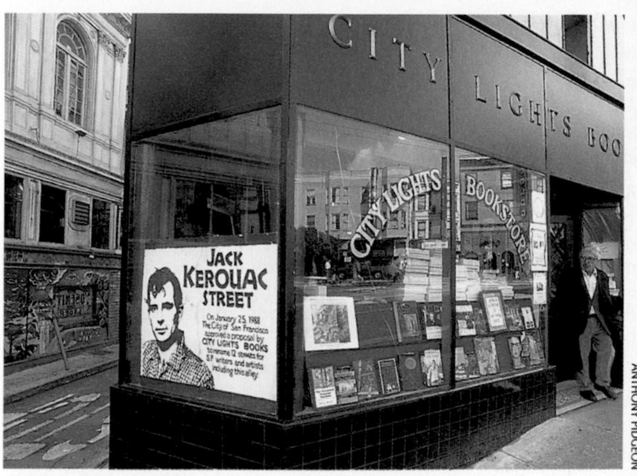

ANTHONY PIDGEON

thrown out of Tosca when another man in their party walked into the women's rest room.

Specs' *12 William Saroyan Place*
☎ *415-421-4112* ⏲ *4:30pm-2am Mon-Fri, 5pm-2am Sat-Sun* ♿
This dimly lit tavern has always been a favorite among literary types and others who appreciate idiosyncratic bars. The trademark logo of a San Francisco book publisher, Chronicle Books, appears to have been inspired by the signature eyeglasses belonging to Specs (that's the owner's nickname); the glasses are roughly sketched beneath signs advising patrons not to fight in the bar. Over the years, the bar's regular cast of characters – including a troupe of Irish musicians and a man who wore a backpack with live bunny rabbits peering out over the top – has dwindled somewhat, but it's still one of the neighborhood's more colorful spots.

Condor Club *300 Columbus Ave*
☎ *415-781-8222* ⏲ *2pm-2am daily* ♿
In its previous incarnation as a strip joint, this now-bland sports bar earned its status as a historic San Francisco cultural site. The Condor is where 'world-famous' Carol Doda made a sensation by dancing in her birthday suit. A plaque on the former strip joint's Columbus Ave façade solemnly declares that Doda first went topless there on June 19, 1964, and bottomless on September 3, 1969, each time setting new American standards in the field of exotic dancing. She soon had plenty of competition – dozens of clubs in the neighborhood followed suit, so to speak, including El Cid, across the street, where Gaye Spiegleman, the 'topless mother of eight,' headlined. The Condor's infamous electric sign, which featured a cartoony likeness of Doda with flashing red light bulbs for nipples, was brought down in 1991. Reportedly the sign was smashed to bits by a reform-minded demolition crew, and never assumed its rightful place in a museum.

Right: The city's most famous bookstore

Stroll east on Broadway for a couple of blocks. The strip has a long, tawdry history. In the evening, it's still lit up with the marquees of strip joints and sex paraphernalia shops, but it isn't particularly dangerous.

Former Site of Old City Jail *540 Broadway*

On the north side of the street, on the side of Black Oak Books, a plaque indicates where the city jail once stood. In the 19th century, condemned criminals were unceremoniously hanged on the site.

Mabuhay Gardens *443 Broadway*

This bright red building once housed one of the USA's great punk rock clubs. The 'Mab' started out as a Filipino restaurant, but business was slow so the owner began booking bands and comedians. Soon, the club regularly featured touring acts such as Blondie, the Ramones, and Devo, along with a nonstop parade of local punk bands. The Mab closed in the 1980s.

Continue down Broadway and turn left on Montgomery St.

Allen Ginsberg's former residence *1010 Montgomery St*

This is the apartment building that Ginsberg lived in for several months in 1955 as he wrote his breakthrough poem 'Howl.' How much of the poem was written in the apartment is open to debate, as Ginsberg, who was fond of hallucinatory substances, was known to pace the streets of the neighborhood, spouting poetic lines as the muse struck. The bespectacled poet just may have composed some lines while shouting at befuddled strip-joint barkers: 'Moloch! Solitude! Filth! Ugliness!'

RICK GERHARTER

Continue up Montgomery to the Vallejo St steps, a half-block away on the left, interspersed with flower gardens and trees. You'll be rewarded by a good view of the bay by peering back over your shoulder as you ascend the steps, and then a nice perspective of North Beach as you reenter the neighborhood on the way back down the hill. Continue down Vallejo to Grant Ave, which will lead you to a choice of restaurants, bars, cafés, and shops.

The Saloon *1232 Grant Ave*
☎ *415-989-7666* ⏲ *noon-2am daily* ♿

This 1861 saloon – which indeed looks like its been around that long – is one of the few North Beach buildings to survive the 1906 earthquake and fire. It was once called Wagner's Beer Hall, but over the years the name was reduced to The Saloon.

Left: The Vallejo St steps

Caffè Trieste *601 Vallejo St* ☎ *415-392-6739*
🕘 *6:30am-11pm daily, open until midnight Fri-Sat* ♿

This comfortable café has been a North Beach gathering spot since 1956. It has always attracted a mixed crowd, from old Italian men to amateur opera singers to Beat poets and artists. Francis Ford Coppola is said to have drafted parts of his screen adaptation of Mario Puzo's *The Godfather* at a table beneath the back wall's mural depicting a quaint Sicilian fishing village.

Shrine of St Francis of Assisi *610 Vallejo St*
☎ *415-983-0405* $ *free* 🕘 *hours vary*

This attractive church was built in 1860 and rebuilt in 1913 after suffering heavy damage in 1906. It was the first American-built Catholic church in the city.

Cross Columbus Ave and turn right on it.

Museum of North Beach *1435 Stockton St, mezzanine*
☎ *415-391-6210* $ *free* 🕘 *9am-5pm Mon-Thurs, 9am-6pm Fri*

Worth a short visit, this modest museum has photographs and memorabilia tracing the history of the neighborhood in the late 19th and early 20th centuries, particularly around the time of the '06 quake.

Head back to Columbus Ave, which continues on its northwesterly course. Along the way, Columbus trims off a corner of Washington Square, which is presided over by Saints Peter & Paul Church. The Square is a good place to stop, rest your boots, feed the pigeons, play bocce, what have you.

RICHARD CUMMINS

Right: Saints Peter & Paul Church

[Continued from page 124]

winos and mad poets, who are likely to say something for you to puzzle over, in Specs' and The Saloon.

Bohemians, artists, writers, and revolutionaries have inhabited the area since the

turn of the 20th century, when Montgomery Block, where the Transamerica Pyramid now stands, served as the city's creative lightning rod. When Jack Kerouac and Allen Ginsberg arrived from New York in the early '50s, joining forces with local poets, the so-called 'Beat Generation' was headquartered in this part of town. (Kerouac is credited with coining the name; he said he was inspired by poet and ex-con Herbert Huncke, who once was tired and said, 'Man, I'm *beat.*')

Excited by the media frenzy that followed the legal battle over publication of Ginsberg's poem 'Howl' (see the North Beach Walking Tour) and the sensation caused by Kerouac's novel *On the Road*, thousands of eccentrics descended on North Beach in the late '50s, filling its bars and cafés with philosophical patter and benzedrine-fueled verse. Grant Ave north of Columbus became known across the country as a 3-block-long, open-air insane asylum, with hangouts like the Coexistence Bagel Shop, where bagels were never available, and the Place, a bar that provided a soapbox on open-mic 'Blabbermouth' nights. Gay bars opened in the neighborhood, and in fact many of the Beat poets were openly gay. Local columnist Herb Caen, noting that the Beats and the Soviet satellite Sputnik, which had recently been launched, were equally 'far out,' coined the term 'beatnik' to refer to the North Beach denizens. Remarkably, the name stuck.

Remnants of the Beat heyday still exist in North Beach. Lawrence Ferlinghetti's bookstore and publishing house, City Lights, is alive and well, and Ferlinghetti is often seen dropping off letters in nearby mailboxes or lunching in neighborhood restaurants. Some of the old bars and cafés are still open for business, with more than a few aged beatniks occupying the stools.

Washington Square MAP 6
15, 30, 41, 45 Muni

With a corner chopped off by Columbus Ave, Washington Square doesn't quite make it as a square, but it is North Beach's cultural focal point and its only open public space. In the morning, practitioners of tai chi congregate in the square, and when shreds of fog drift slowly through, it can be a surreal scene to watch. Also in the morning, the sweet aroma of fresh-baked focaccia from Liguria bakery, on the square's northeast corner, is enough to settle any indecision you might have about what to eat for lunch. The square has its share of pigeons, but its trees are also a frequent stop for the city's burgeoning parrot population.

Benjamin Franklin statue MAP 6
15, 30, 41, 45 Muni

This 1897 statue stands in the middle of Washington Square – Ben Franklin sitting in for the nation's first president. It was erected by teetotaling dentist Henry D Cogswell, who made a fortune fitting miners with gold fillings, and the taps around the base falsely advertise mineral water from as far off as Vichy, France. If Cogswell had hoped this promise of imported water would be enough to lure hard-drinking San Franciscans away from the temptation of liquor, he must have been sorely disappointed.

Volunteer Fireman's Memorial MAP 6
15, 30, 41, 45 Muni

This statue, financed by dedicated fire-engine chaser Lillie Hitchcock Coit (see Coit Tower, later), honors the city's firemen.

Saints Peter & Paul Church MAP 6
666 Filbert St ☎ 415-421-0809 ⌚ 6:30am-4pm daily $ free 🚌 15, 30, 41, 45 Muni ♿

From its diabolical address, this church overlooks the square. Built in 1924, it possesses some superb detailing on its two bell towers. Ferlinghetti once dubbed it the Marzipan Church, and its wedding-cake look was clearly appropriate when baseball star Joe DiMaggio and Marilyn Monroe had their wedding photos taken here, though they weren't permitted to marry in the church because both had been divorced (they got hitched at City Hall instead). In Cecil B DeMille's 1923 film *The Ten Commandments*, the scene of the building of the Temple in Jerusalem is actually the construction of the church's foundations. Each October, the procession honoring Santa Maria del Lume (patron saint of fishermen) makes its way down Columbus Ave to Fisherman's Wharf to bless the fishing fleet. Some masses are still given in Italian.

Telegraph Hill

This North Beach hill was called Alta Loma ('high hillock') in Mexican San Francisco, then became Goat Hill around the time of the gold rush. It settled on its current name in the 1850s, when ships approaching the Golden Gate were contacted from its peak by a pioneering semaphore and optical telegraph station. Coit Tower, one of San Francisco's more prominent landmarks, stands in Pioneer Park, atop Telegraph Hill.

Coit Tower MAP 6
Telegraph Hill Blvd ☎ 415-362-0808 $ adult $3, senior/child $2 ⌚ 10am-6pm daily 🚌 39 Muni ♿

The 210-foot tower that stands now was built in 1934, financed by San Francisco eccentric Lillie Hitchcock Coit. Ms Coit, clearly rebelling against the straitlaced Victorian ethos, dressed as a man to gamble in North Beach, wore short skirts to go ice skating, sneaked away on a men's camping trip, and harbored a lifelong passion for a good fire. In 1863 the 15-year-old Lillie was adopted as the mascot of the Knickerbocker Hose Company No 5, and it's said she rarely missed a blaze. Given Coit's partiality for dousing fires, you'd think the spout-like tower was meant to resemble the nozzle of a fire hose. However, the official story is that the tower has nothing to do with firefighters or the tools of their trade. After her husband's death in 1885, Lillie spent most of the rest of her life in Paris, but she left a third of her fortune to build this monument.

Lillie Hitchcock Coit

The interior lobby (free admission) has superb WPA murals. Painted by 25 local artists, they were highly controversial when the project was finished. See the 'Public Art in the City' boxed text in Facts about San Francisco.

The ride to the top will give you great views across the city and the bay, but the view is pretty special even from the bottom.

Although Pioneer Park has parking spots, there's often a logjam of traffic vying for them, especially in summer. The best way to get to Coit Tower is to walk up steep Filbert St from Washington Square.

Filbert Steps MAP 6
$ free 🚌 39 Muni

Filbert St determinedly climbs the western slope of Telegraph Hill, but the road comes to an abrupt halt on the east side, where a cliff would make a paved street pointless. Instead, the street becomes a switchbacking stairway surrounded by coveted cottages and apartments and luxuriant gardens. The trail leads to Levi's Plaza and the Embarcadero. Go early in the morning and you might catch a glimpse of the family of wild red foxes that reputedly lives in the underbrush. This is another stopping ground for parrots. Paralleling the Filbert Steps are the Greenwich Steps.

RUSSIAN HILL

West of North Beach are the roller-coaster streets of Russian Hill, with some of the city's prime real estate and the famous Lombard St switchback. It's said the hill takes its name from the burial site of early-19th-century Russian fur traders, but no remains of the mysterious Russians have ever been found. Like Nob Hill, these heights were populated only after the cable cars began providing transportation. The neighborhood is excellent for walking, if you don't mind scaling steep hills, principally because some of the steeper inclines can be ascended via steps lush with gardens. Through the neighborhood, cable cars run up and down precipitous Mason and Hyde Sts, offering superb bay views.

Lombard St

For 1 block – the 1000 block of Lombard St, between Hyde and Leavenworth – the city's straightforward grid is broken in dramatic fashion. This famous stretch of street, touted by the local tourist board as the 'world's crookedest street,' features eight switchbacks. It's not only a spectacular slalom but also a pretty one, as the redbrick curves are outlined by flowerbeds.

CHRISTINA LEASE

The world's crookedest street

At one time the crooked block was just as straight as any other, but with a 27% incline it was too steep for early cars to manage. (The steepest incline the cable cars have to tackle is 21%.) The curves were added in 1922, but it was not until after WWII, when local resident Peter Bercut personally imported a couple thousand hydrangeas from France, that the world's crookedest street became a postcard favorite.

Stairways & Lookouts

Ina Coolbrith Park MAP 7

Vallejo St 🚋 Powell-Mason cable car

Walk up Vallejo St from North Beach and you'll reach these steps, which carve a crooked path through lovingly tended gardens and ultimately reach the top of Russian Hill. Benches offer walkers a chance to catch their breath and admire views, framed by trees, of North Beach, Telegraph Hill, and the Bay Bridge. Above Taylor, the steps continue before ending at a pocket-size lawn that yields an even wider view. Just above the park, Russian Hill Place and Florence Place are charmed cul-de-sacs that resemble a Mediterranean hilltop hamlet.

Macondray Lane MAP 7

🚌 41, 45 Muni 🚋 Powell-Mason cable car

This steep wooden stairway, the primary access to homes of a few contented hilldwellers, served as Armistead Maupin's model for Barbary Lane in his 'Tales of the City' series. If you've just climbed up the Vallejo steps via Coolbrith Park, this is not a bad way to get back down.

More Sights

Diego Rivera Gallery MAP 7

800 Chestnut St ☎ 415-771-7020 $ free ⏲ 9am-8pm daily fall, winter, & spring; 9am-5pm daily summer 🚌 30 Muni ♿

An entire wall in this small gallery, on the SF Art Institute campus, is occupied by a wonderful 1931 fresco by the Mexican artist Diego Rivera, titled *The Making of a Fresco Showing a Building of a City*. The title pretty much sums up the mural, without noting that Rivera painted himself into the scene. The Art Institute was founded in 1871 and originally occupied the Nob Hill mansion Mark Hopkins built for his wife, Mary. The mansion burned down in 1906, and the Mark Hopkins Hotel now stands on the site. The institute's current collection of cloisters and courtyards dates from 1926, with a 1970 addition. The school has a café and a fine vista over the bay from its terraces.

Jack Kerouac's former house MAP 7

29 Russell St 🚌 41, 45 Muni 🚋 Powell-Hyde cable car

Jack Kerouac worked on *On the Road* and drafted several other works in 1952 while living in this small house with Neal and Carolyn Cassady. It's a private home, so you can only take a look from the sidewalk.

Feusier Octagon House MAP 7

1067 Green St 🚌 41, 45 Muni 🚋 Powell-Hyde cable car

This house, built in 1870, is not open to the public, unlike the city's only other surviving octagon house, in Cow Hollow. It's in an interesting little enclave of Victorian houses on the same block that make up a rare group of 1906 survivors.

Cable Cars

The Transamerica Pyramid and the Golden Gate Bridge make fine city symbols, but San Francisco has another, much older icon, the beloved cable car. Cable cars were conceived by English mining engineer Andrew Hallidie as a replacement for horse-driven trams, which found the city's steep streets difficult and dangerous. From Hallidie's first experimental line on Clay St in 1873, cable cars quickly caught on, and by 1890 there were eight operators, 500 cable cars, and a route network of more than 100 miles. But by the turn of the century, the system was already past its heyday and shrinking in the face of newfangled electric streetcars. The 1906 earthquake didn't help, but real disaster for the cable car system seemed imminent in January 1947, when the mayor announced that the last lines would be replaced by bus services. He hadn't counted on Friedel Klussmann's Citizens Committee to Save the Cable Cars and a groundswell of public support, though; together they rescued the Powell St lines. San Franciscans may have saved the system from politicians and accountants, but saving it from old age became a new problem, as derailments and runaways became increasingly frequent. In 1979, a six-month shutdown for a million dollars' worth of repairs was just a Band-Aid solution. In 1982, the system was closed for a complete, $60 million overhaul. The rebuilt system, which reopened in 1984, consists of 40 cars on three lines covering a total of 12 miles. That may be just a shadow of the system's heyday, but the cable cars are still an enormously popular tourist attraction and much loved by San Franciscans.

RICHARD I'ANSON

How They Work

There are three key elements to the cable car system: the cable, the grip, and the brakes. They're towed up and down the hills of San Francisco by continuous loops of cable, driven by 510-horsepower electric motors housed in the Cable Car Museum.The cables move at a steady 9mph and can stretch 3 to 12 feet as cars grip and ungrip. Cables on the busy Powell St line last only 75 to 90 days before a new $20,000-plus cable must be installed. Cable replacement occurs in the middle of the night. The old cable is cut, and the new one, weighing more than 30 tons on its drum, is temporarily spliced onto one end and pulled right through the system. The cables are inspected daily, and if a broken wire triggers one of the 60 strand alarms, the system is shut down and a repair is made on the spot. The process of grabbing hold of (or 'picking up') the cable to start off, and letting go of (or 'dropping') the cable to stop, is controlled by the gripman on the cable car. The grip, patented in 1877, has metal dies in its jaw that clamp onto the cable when the gripman pulls back on the grip lever. The soft metal dies wear down quickly and must be replaced every four days.

For braking, cable cars have four systems. First there is the grip. As long as the cable car is gripping the cable, it cannot go faster than the cable is moving. Second are cast-iron brake shoes on all eight wheels. Third are four pinewood block brakes, which simply press down on the track; they last only two to four days, and on steep downgrades you can hear them groan and smell the wood smoke. When all else fails, the fourth braking system is a three-piece wedge that slides down into the cable-car slot in the street and jams everything up solid. It's used for emergencies only.

NOB HILL

This area is just what its name suggests, a classy district perched atop one of the city's famous hills. It has been that way ever since the installment of the California St cable car tracks in the 1870s made the 338-foot summit accessible to people not given to hiking. The mansions went up, the robber barons moved in, and the 1906 quake and fire brought the lot down. Eventually several of the burned-out mansions were replaced with hotels, which remain some of the most select and expensive establishments in the city. The Huntington, Mark Hopkins, Stanford Court, and Fairmont are all perched atop Nob Hill. Although there's not much to see on Nob Hill apart from Grace Cathedral, it's worth a wander, a gawk at the elegant marble lobby of the Fairmont, and perhaps a drink in the Mark's top-floor hotel bar.

Pacific-Union Club MAP 7
1000 California St 🚌 *1 Muni* 🚋 *California St cable car*

The sole Nob Hill residence to survive the 1906 earthquake and fire was this 1885 brownstone, built for James C Flood, one of four 'Bonanza Kings' who made a fortune in the Comstock silver mines. It's now home to the private Pacific-Union Club, which bought and rebuilt the house after it was gutted by the fire in '06. Don't expect to pay a visit if you're not in the millionaire class – that is, the *male* millionaire class. Since the club opened in 1911, women have been allowed in only twice, and the last occasion was back in 1953.

The Railroad Barons

Their names pop up all around the Bay Area, and in their heyday, Nob Hill was their stomping ground. Mark Hopkins and Collis P Huntington were the builders who, with financiers Charles Crocker and Leland Stanford, made fortunes from the Central Pacific Railroad, later renamed the Southern Pacific. They founded the railroad company in 1861 and built eastward, meeting the Union Pacific line on its way west in 1869. The names of Stanford, Huntington, and Hopkins were adopted by Nob Hill hotels. Stanford went on to win election as the state's governor and to found Stanford University, and Crocker's name was applied to a bank.

Also known as the 'Big Four' (there's a bar with that name in the Huntington Hotel), they were less kindly referred to as the 'robber barons,' because their business methods were far from scrupulous.

Fairmont Hotel MAP 7
950 Mason St 🚌 *1 Muni* 🚋 *California St cable car* ♿

This hotel, built by the daughter of silver magnate James Grantham Fair, was actually completed a few days before the '06 quake, only to be gutted by the conflagration. It was rebuilt by architect Julia Morgan (who later designed San Simeon for William Randolph Hearst), and it reopened a year to the day after the quake. It has a spectacular lobby that's worth a walk through, and a tiki lounge in the basement that would seem to conflict with Nob Hill tastes. Unfortunately, the hotel has closed its top-floor bar, so its unbeatable views are now off-limits; also see Places to Stay.

Mark Hopkins Hotel MAP 7
999 California St 🚌 *1 Muni* 🚋 *California St cable car* ♿

Built in 1925, this hotel stands on what once was Hopkins' estate. Only the granite retaining wall that surrounded the original flamboyant wooden mansion survives. The top-floor bar, Top of the Mark, is a nighttime destination; also see Places to Stay.

Huntington Park MAP 7
$ *free* 🚌 *1 Muni* 🚋 *California St cable car* ♿

David Colton, lawyer for the Central Pacific Railroad, built his mansion on the ground now serving as this pleasant park, but following his death his estate was sued by the railroad company for embezzlement. His widow retaliated with letters from Collis P Huntington to her husband detailing under-the-table deals with Washington politicians. The mansion was sold in 1880 and bought by none other than Huntington in 1892. The quake destroyed it, and Huntington's widow gave the site to the city in 1915. The park affords a good vantage of Grace Cathedral, has a nice playground, and features a replica of the Tartarughe Fountain in Rome but without the tortoises.

Grace Cathedral MAP 7
1100 California St ☎ 415-749-6300 $ adult $3, child $2 (donation) ⌚ 7am-5pm daily 🚍 1 Muni 🚋 California St cable car ♿ limited

After the big quake, as hotels popped up on other mansion sites, Charles Crocker and his son William turned over their California St sites to the Episcopal Church. It took from 1927 to 1964 to complete Grace Cathedral. Although it's constructed of reinforced concrete, it takes its inspiration from Notre Dame Cathedral in Paris. The awesome bronze doors are casts of Ghiberti's *Gates of Paradise*, in the Cathedral Baptistry of St John in Florence, Italy. Above the doors is a magnificent rose window made in Chartres, France, in 1964.

California Masonic Memorial Temple MAP 7
1111 California St ☎ 415-292-9190 $ free ⌚ 10am-3pm Mon-Fri 🚍 1 Muni 🚋 California St cable car ♿ limited

This marble mausoleumlike structure adds variety to the Nob Hill skyline. The Masons, of course, are that mysterious fraternal order that built lodges in every town in America. (Many of the nation's fathers, including George Washington, were masons, and fez-wearing Shriners are an affiliated group.) You can enter the main lobby for close inspection of stained-glass windows rife with strange Masonic symbolism. Downstairs, a visitors' center reveals some of the society's intriguing secrets and history. (Be warned, enthusiastic docents are always interested in beefing up the society's membership.)

Cable Car Barn & Museum MAP 7
1201 Mason St ☎ 415-474-1887 $ free ⌚ 10am-6pm daily summer, 10am-5pm daily winter 🚋 Powell-Mason, Powell-Hyde cable cars ♿

The Cable Car Barn & Museum is in the city's only surviving cable-car barn. The building's main function is as the power plant that tows all the system's cables. The huge wheels over which the continuous cables whir are an awesome sight – it's 19th-century technology in full glory. The museum's exhibits include Andrew Hallidie's original Clay St cable car.

FISHERMAN'S WHARF

Many San Franciscans avoid Fisherman's Wharf, and their disdain for the area is as passionate as a cat's for water. The minority regard it merely as a necessary evil.

On the plus side of the 'necessary evil' argument, Fisherman's Wharf brings in tourist dollars that the city benefits from, and it concentrates most of the tackiest tourist traps in one part of town. The wharf has more genuine virtues as well: remarkably, in a city set on an attractive bay, this is one of the few waterfront areas that offer pleasant and picturesque public access to the bay. The city's maritime history is celebrated here with a distinguished museum and a collection of historic boats. And of course, to get to the city's coolest tourist draw – Alcatraz – you catch the ferry here. (Credit San Francisco for coming up with the ingenious concept of turning an island prison into the most literal of tourist traps.)

On the heavily weighted minus side, however, anyone looking for a real taste of San Francisco won't find it at Fisherman's Wharf. In fact, visitors will be hard-pressed to find anything remotely resembling reality here. The waterfront's greatest shortcoming

Sea Lions

With all the effort and expense put into luring tourists to Pier 39, it's amusing that the pier's biggest draw simply turned up, unplanned and uninvited. In 1990 or thereabouts, California sea lions began to haul out onto a section of the walkways at the marina beside Pier 39. Their takeover is now complete: the boats have been cleared, and hundreds of sea lions bask in the sun, woofing noisily and engaging in horseplay to the amusement of onlookers. The population varies during the year from a peak of around 600 in January and February to virtually none in June and July, when the sea lions head south for the breeding season. Pier 39's sea lions are almost all male. They're big creatures – a fully grown male can be 7 feet long and weigh more than 800lb. By contrast, a female may reach only 6 feet and 300lb. Of course, the sea lions are for viewing only – do not feed them, even if you happen to have a mackerel on hand.

is that 'attractions' like Pier 39 are nothing more than thinly disguised shopping malls that tempt loose-walleted tourists to exchange their hard-earned money for cartloads of cheap junk.

At one time, the wharf was alive with the hustle and bustle of honest-to-goodness fishermen, and the docks boasted an interesting array of fishing vessels, as Chinese people fished from junks and Italians fished from Genovese feluccas. During the late 19th century, people began to call the wharf 'Italy Harbor,' because the local fishing industry was dominated by Italian fishermen. The wharf's transformation began in the 1930s, when some of the seafood stalls along it, like Fisherman's Grotto, with its kitschy Venetian candyland decor, were converted into tourist-oriented restaurants. The area gradually began trading on its romantic fishing village image and less on fish, and today the redundant curio shops don't leave much room for faux old-world atmosphere either. But hidden away, behind the shops, a small fishing fleet is still moored here. Get up early in the morning to witness the activity around Pier 45, where thousands of tons of seafood are unloaded each year.

Aquatic Park MAP 8
19, 32 Muni · Powell-Hyde cable car · limited

Hyde St Pier and the long curve of Municipal Pier shelter the waters of Aquatic Park, which boasts San Francisco's only bay-front beach. Although there isn't much sand, and the rim of the little cove is cemented over with amphitheater-style seating, you can sit back and watch hardy breaststrokers brave the usually frigid waters. It is actually more pleasant to laze on the grounds of Victoria Park, a grassy knoll just above Aquatic Park, where you can enjoy the views of the Golden Gate Bridge and the city skyline.

Ghirardelli Square MAP 8
900 North Point St ☎ 415-775-5500 · 19, 32 Muni · Powell-Hyde cable car
w www.ghirardellisq.com

There is ample opportunity to empty your pockets at the former Ghirardelli chocolate factory. In 1964, Ghirardelli Square was the first factory to be recycled into a shopping center, establishing a national trend. Italian immigrant Domingo Ghirardelli (pronounced **gear**-ar-deli) arrived in San Francisco in 1849 and began a successful chocolate business. His sons built a huge chocolate factory between 1900 and 1916, but it was closed in the early '60s. Ghirardelli chocolate is still one of San Francisco's signature products, even though the company has moved its headquarters to San Leandro, in the East Bay.

The Cannery MAP 8
2801 Leavenworth St ☎ 415-771-3112
19, 32 Muni · Powell-Hyde cable car
w www.thecannery.com

Formerly a Del Monte fruit-canning factory, the Cannery followed Ghirardelli Square's example in 1967. It's basically a shopping center, but its interior courtyard is a nice place to have an alfresco lunch on a sunny day. Live jazz or Latin music is featured every afternoon when weather permits.

San Francisco Maritime National Historical Park

The National Park system has gradually been collecting historic ships and other memorabilia here. The National Maritime Museum and Hyde St Pier anchor the exhibits.

San Francisco National Maritime Museum MAP 8
900 Beach St ☎ 415-556-3002 · free
10am-5pm daily · 19, 32 Muni · Powell-Hyde cable car
w www.maritime.org

This museum, at the waterfront end of Polk St, overlooks Aquatic Park. The museum's collection recounts the Bay Area's nautical history with a fine collection of mastheads, bowsprits, lifeboats, paintings, and ship models. The building itself is a worthy attraction. Built in 1939 by WPA workers and initially serving as a public bathhouse, the museum boasts a streamlined moderne design that lends a stylish luxury-liner guise, complete with a bridge, tubular steel railings, and portholes. The building also features some of the city's most important public art, distinguished by expressionist styles rarely seen in the public art of its era. The green slate carvings adorning the front entrance are by African American artist Sargent Johnson, as is the abstract fish tile mosaic on the rear veranda. The smoothly polished toad and seal on the veranda are by Italian American sculptor Beniamino Bufano. The main lobby is enlivened by Hilaire Hiler's underwater mural, depicting the lost worlds of Mu and Atlantis.

Hyde St Pier historic ships collection MAP 8
Pier 45 ☎ 415-556-3002 $ adult $5, senior/teen $2, under 12 free ⏲ 9:30am-5pm daily 🚌 19, 32 Muni 🚋 Powell-Hyde cable car ♿ limited
w www.maritime.org

A fine collection of historic ships that have Bay Area connections is moored along Hyde St Pier. The side-wheel steam ferry *Eureka* started life in 1890 as the railway ferry *Ukiah*. At the end of the 19th century, it was the largest ferry in the world. Refitted and renamed, the *Eureka* shuttled back and forth between San Francisco and Sausalito from 1922 to 1941. Though it could carry more than 2000 passengers and 100 cars, it was sidelined after the opening of the Golden Gate and Bay Bridges.

In the latter half of the 19th century, a huge fleet of magnificent sailing ships rounded Cape Horn each year, carrying California grain to Europe. The Scottish-built *Balclutha* of 1886 is a superb example of an iron-hull square-rigger. After its retirement from the grain fleet, it was conscripted for the Pacific Northwest timber trade, carrying lumber south from Washington and Oregon to build the rapidly expanding cities of California. (At one time, 900 sailing ships shuttled back and forth along this route.) The ship also played a starring role in the 1935 film *Mutiny on the Bounty*.

The smaller wooden *CA Thayer*, built in 1895 in California, also worked the Pacific Northwest lumber trade and was later engaged in salmon and cod fishing in Alaska. It survived to be the last commercial sailing ship to operate from a West Coast port.

Ships along the pier include the 1914 *Eppleton Hall*, a British-built side-wheel tugboat, and the 1891 *Alma*, the last scow to operate on the bay. These flat-bottomed sailing vessels once served as essential transport for the farms around the shallow waters of the bay.

USS *Jeremiah O'Brien* MAP 8
Pier 45 ☎ 415-441-3101 $ adult $5, senior/student $3, under 18 $2 ⏲ 9am-4pm daily 🚌 32, F Muni
w www.ssjeremiahobrien.com

During WWII, the United States built more than 2700 cargo-carrying liberty ships, at 10,000 tons each. At the peak of production, they were being turned out faster than the German U-boats could sink them: the incredible production line took only six to eight weeks to build a complete ship. One of many cargo ships to carry troops and supplies to Normandy on D-Day, the USS *Jeremiah O'Brien* is the sole surviving liberty ship in complete working order. On board you can explore the crew area and bridge, dive down into one of the cargo holds, and investigate the engine room, with its awesome 2700-horsepower, triple-expansion steam engine. Daytime cruises ($100 per person) are available twice a year, on Memorial Day weekend (early May) and during Fleet Week (October).

USS *Pampanito* MAP 8
Pier 45 ☎ 415-775-1943 $ adult $7, senior $5, child $4, under 6 free ⏲ 9am-6pm Sun-Thurs, 9am-8pm Fri-Sat fall, winter, & spring; 9am-8pm Mon-Tues & Thurs-Sun, 9am-6pm Wed summer 🚌 32, F Muni
w www.maritime.org/pamphome.htm

This is a WWII-era US Navy submarine. It was built in 1943 and made six Pacific patrols during the last years of the war, sinking six Japanese ships. Among its victims were the *Kachidoki Maru* and the *Rakuyo Maru*, which were carrying British and Australian POWs. The fascinating do-it-yourself audio tour of the 312-foot submarine conveys the incredibly claustrophobic conditions experienced by submariners and explains the operations and capabilities of this kind of sub.

Pier 39

The shops on Pier 39 peddle everything you absolutely must have while you're in that free-spending vacation frame of mind. The merchandise here ranges from lingerie and college sweatshirts to scissors for left-handers and Christmas tree ornaments. Ironically, the most popular attraction won't cost you a dime: the colony of sea lions that has taken over the docks just off the western side of the pier (see the boxed text 'Sea Lions').

Venetian carousel MAP 8
Pier 39 $ $2 ⏲ 11am-7pm daily 🚌 32, F Muni

Out of place amid the non-atmosphere of Pier 39, this is a charming old merry-go-round that was brought over from Italy.

San Francisco Seaplane Tours MAP 8
Pier 39 ☎ 415-332-4843, 888-732-7526
$ adult $119, child $99; sunset champagne

tour $139 ◷ call to reserve 🚌 32, F Muni
w *www.seaplane.com*

These seaplanes, which take off and land in the bay just off Pier 39, will get you up over the city for 35 minutes (50 minutes during the sunset champagne flight). It's a great opportunity for photographers and a pricey thrill for non-shutterbugs.

Underwater World MAP 8
Pier 39 ☎ 415-623-5301, 888-732-3483 ⓢ adult $13, senior/child $6.50 ◷ 9am-8pm daily summer; 10am-6pm Mon-Fri, 10am-7pm Sat-Sun winter 🚌 32, F Muni ♿
w *www.underwaterworldsf.com*

This is an enormous marine aquarium through which a clear pedestrian tunnel passes. Rather than watch sea life from behind the usual two-dimensional glass wall, visitors can experience the sensation of being a part of its environs.

Hokey Museums

Just to prove Fisherman's Wharf really is a tourist trap, Jefferson St between Mason and Taylor features the requisite Wax Museum & Ripley's Believe It or Not! Museum. Admission prices are absurdly high! Check their websites for discounts.

Wax Museum MAP 8
145 Jefferson St ☎ 415-202-0402, 800-439-4305 ⓢ adult $13, senior $10.50, student $10, ages 6-12 $6 ◷ 9am-10pm daily fall, winter, & spring; 9am-11pm daily summer 🚌 32, F Muni ♿
w *www.waxmuseum.com*

As you'd expect, uncanny wax likenesses of the usual movie stars, athletes, and celebrities show up in this museum.

Ripley's Believe It or Not! Museum MAP 8
175 Jefferson St ☎ 415-771-6188 ⓢ adult $10, senior/student $8, child $7 ◷ 10am-10pm Sun-Thurs, 10am-midnight Fri-Sat 🚌 32, F Muni ♿
w *www.ripleys.com*

Ripley's mission to expose vacationers to the strange, the unusual, and the just plain weird is carried out in another of its ubiquitous museums.

THE MARINA & COW HOLLOW

The Marina is a well-to-do neighborhood where the yuppies of the '80s situated themselves, and the district continues to attract young, single professionals working high-paying jobs downtown. The Marina still has its pickup bars, but it's not quite as swinging as it once was. Chestnut St is the main commercial strip of the Marina; a few blocks south, Union St is the spine of Cow Hollow, so named for a local dairy farm that once occupied the area, and between them is motel-lined Lombard St.

The land that is now the Marina materialized when waterfront marshland was filled in (mainly with rubble created by the quake of 1906) to create the grounds for the 1915 Panama-Pacific International Exposition. That expo commemorated the completion of the Panama Canal and San Francisco's phoenixlike rebirth after the quake and fire. When the expo was over, the displays came down, and lucrative real-estate deals began; in addition to expensive residences, up went the ritzy Golden Gate and St Francis Yacht Clubs. When the next big quake came along in 1989, the Marina was the worst-hit neighborhood in San Francisco, proving once again that landfill is not ideal ground for development in earthquake territory.

Visitors staying in the Marina will have easy access to some of San Francisco's great parks, including Fort Mason (where an attractive youth hostel makes it possible to stay very cheaply) and the Presidio. Cyclists, in-line skaters, joggers, and kite flyers all enjoy the waterfront strip of Marina Green.

Palace of Fine Arts MAP 9
Palace Dr ⓢ free 🚌 28, 76 Muni ♿

A rare surviving structure from the 1915 Panama-Pacific International Exposition, Bernard Maybeck's artificial classical ruin was so popular that it was spared from demolition when the exhibition closed. Eventually, the original stucco construction, intended to last only for the duration of the exposition, began to crumble away. It had become a real ruin by the early '60s, when it was rebuilt in durable concrete.

The Panama-Pacific Exposition featured everything from a Turkish mosque to the 432-foot 'Tower of Jewels,' but the only other survivor at the site is the featureless shed that now houses the Exploratorium.

LOUISA PRESTON

The Palace of Fine Arts

The Exploratorium MAP 9
3601 Lyon St ☎ 415-561-0360, 415-563-7337 ⓢ adult $9, senior $7, child $5; 1st Wed every month free ⏲ 10am-6pm Mon-Tues & Thurs-Sun, 10am-9:30pm Wed summer; 10am-5pm Tues & Thurs-Sun, 10am-9:30pm Wed winter 🚌 28, 76 Muni ♿
w *www.exploratorium.edu*

The Exploratorium, behind the Palace of Fine Arts, was established in 1969 as a museum of art, science, and human perception. Enormously popular with children and curious people of all ages, it has hundreds of exhibits with an emphasis on the interactive discovery of scientific principles. The exhibits include the crowd-pleasing Tactile Dome (separate admission, reservations required) and the optical illusions of the Distorted Room.

Fort Mason

Originally the site of a secondary Spanish fort, Fort Mason became a residential area before it was appropriated by the US Army during the Civil War. It remained in military hands through WWII, when it was the transport hub for troops heading to the Pacific theater. Most of the old storage sheds were handed over for civilian use in the 1970s, and now they house a colorful mix of galleries, museums, theaters, and a famous vegetarian restaurant, Greens. A short but sweet walk skirts the fort's grounds along the cliffhanging Golden Gate Promenade between Aquatic Park and the Marina's Safeway supermarket.

The Golden Gate National Recreation Area MAP 9
Building 201 ☎ 415-556-0560 ⓢ free ⏲ 10am-4:30pm Mon-Fri 🚌 28, 30, 42, 47, 49 Muni ♿
w *www.nps.gov/goga*

The Golden Gate National Recreation Area, which is responsible for much of the coastal parkland north and south of the Golden Gate, has its headquarters and visitors' center in Fort Mason. The GGNRA has jurisdiction over the Presidio, Alcatraz, Fort Point, Fort Funston, the Cliff House, Muir Woods, and the Marin Headlands. Maps and information about camping, hiking, and other programs for these and other national parks in the Pacific West region, including Yosemite, can be found here.

Museo ItaloAmericano MAP 9
Building C ☎ 415-673-2200 ⓢ adult $3, senior/student $2, under 12 free; 1st Wed of the month free ⏲ noon-5pm Wed-Sun 🚌 28, 30, 42, 47, 49 Muni ♿
w *www.museoitaloamericano.org*

This cultural center has a modest but very colorful gallery space devoted to Italian and Italian American art.

San Francisco African-American Historical & Cultural Society MAP 9
Building C ☎ 415-441-0640 ⓢ adult/senior $2, child $1, under 12 free; 1st Wed of the month free ⏲ noon-5pm Wed-Sun 🚌 28,

Views of the City

San Francisco's beauty tends to pop out at you as you turn a corner or reach the crest of a hilly street. The following are some great vantage points:

Cable Car Views
Somehow views are enhanced from a cable car; try looking down Hyde St toward Alcatraz, down Washington St to Chinatown and the Financial District, or down California St to the Financial District and the Bay Bridge.

Coit Tower
The views of the bay, North Beach (with Nob and Russian Hills as backdrop), and the Financial District skyline are superb.

Russian Hill Stairways
Hikers scaling the garden steps that grace Russian Hill are always rewarded with a gorgeous perspective of downtown and the bay.

Lincoln Park Coastal Trail
This interesting walk in Lincoln Park takes you from the ruins of the Sutro Baths to Land's End, and it affords some great views of the ocean and the Golden Gate.

Top of the Mark
Ride the elevator to the city's most famous 'view bar' at the top of the Mark Hopkins Hotel, on Nob Hill.

Twin Peaks
This spot offers a fantastic 360° view of the city – a grand sight at night – but is often blustery. It's a bit removed from the bay and downtown.

Golden Gate Vista Point
There are viewpoints at both ends of the Golden Gate Bridge; the northern one gives you not only the bridge but also the San Francisco skyline.

30, 42, 47, 49 Muni ♿
w *www.fortmason.org/museums/index.html*

This cultural center strives to provide accurate accounts of the culture and history of African Americans. Exhibits change regularly but might grab your interest with traditional African folk arts (textiles, masks) or urban African American art forms – for instance, a past exhibit featured hair sculpture.

Museum of Craft & Folk Art MAP 9
Building A ☎ 415-775-0990 $ adult $3, senior/student $1, under 12 free; 10am-noon Sat & the 1st Wed of the month free ⌚ 11am-5pm Tues-Fri & Sun, 10am-5pm Sat 🚌 28, 30, 42, 47, 49 Muni ♿
w *www.mocfa.org*

With no permanent collection, this gallery has continually changing exhibits celebrating human expression, ranging from traditional and contemporary folk pieces to utilitarian items.

Architecture

The Marina and Cow Hollow are largely residential, with commercial strips that offer little in the way of standout architecture. But there are a few buildings deserving of attention, most of them churches that serve a wide range of cultures, despite the neighborhoods' white yuppie reputation.

Octagon House MAP 9
2645 Gough St ☎ 415-441-7512 $ $3 (donation) ⌚ noon-3pm on 2nd & 4th Thurs and the 2nd Sun of each month, closed in Jan 🚌 41, 45 Muni

The 1861 Octagon House is one of only two survivors from the city's craze for octagonal-shaped houses (see Russian Hill for the other). They were designed with eight sides to catch direct sunlight from eight angles, which was believed to be a surefire ticket to good health. The house is owned by the National Society of Colonial Dames and has a collection of colonial and Federal antiques. It's open to the public three days a month.

Vedanta Temple MAP 9
2963 Webster St ☎ 415-922-2323 🚌 22, 41, 45 Muni
w *www.sfvedanta.com*

This 1905 Hindu temple is a curious conglomeration of architectural styles that really stands out amid the Marina's apartments. The Vedanta Society moved to a new temple in

1959 but continues to schedule lectures and events here.

Church of St Mary the Virgin MAP 9
2325 Union St ☎ 415-921-3665 $ free ⏲ hours vary 🚌 22, 41, 45 Muni ♿ w www.smvsf.org

This is a rustic Arts and Crafts–style Episcopal church from 1891. The courtyard fountain is still fed by one of the old farmland springs.

Holy Trinity Russian Orthodox Cathedral MAP 9
1520 Green St ☎ 415-673-8565 ⏲ Sunday services 🚌 30, 42, 47, 49 Muni w www.holy-trinity.org

The Russian Orthodox Church has been established in San Francisco since 1857. This 1909 baroque and Byzantine structure replaced the church's original structure, which was on Washington Square and burned down in 1906. The bell tower has five bells donated by the Emperor Alexander III in 1888, and the interior chandelier was donated by the last czar of Russia, Nicholas II.

PACIFIC HEIGHTS & JAPANTOWN

The wealthy hilltop Pacific Heights area has many of the city's finest old houses, which were spared in 1906 because the fires that consumed most of downtown San Francisco stopped at Van Ness Ave. During the Spanish era, Divisadero St, which climbs north-south over the ridge, was the 'lookout path,' the principal route between settlements at the Presidio and Mission Dolores.

Two parks (Alta Plaza and Lafayette), the best houses, and the best views are along the neighborhood's east-west ridge. Fillmore St, climbing uphill from Cow Hollow and sloping down to Japantown, is the main drag for restaurants and shops.

Opulent Houses

Inspecting the mansions and fine old Victorians of Pacific Heights is principally a wander-and-look operation; only a couple of houses are open to the public, and for quite restricted hours.

Haas-Lilienthal House MAP 10
2007 Franklin St ☎ 415-441-3004 $ adult/senior $5, child $3 ⏲ noon-3pm Wed, 11am-4pm Sun 🚌 12, 30, 42, 47, 49 Muni w www.sfheritage.org/house.html

This stunning house, perhaps the city's best example of the Queen Anne style, was built between 1882 and '86. Built for wealthy merchant William Haas and inherited by his daughter Alice Lilienthal, it stayed with the Lilienthal family until Alice's death in 1972. The one-hour tour allows entry to the beautiful parlors but is tedious, considering there's not *that* much to look at. You can also go online for a virtual tour.

Spreckels Mansion MAP 10
2080 Washington St 🚌 12 Muni

Looking across Lafayette Park, this huge baroque mansion stretches the entire block. It was built in 1913 by George Applegarth, who also created the Palace of the Legion of Honor, for megawealthy sugar magnate Adolph Spreckels. In 1990, after years of decline, this excessively accoutred home (it started life with 26 bathrooms) was bought by romance novelist Danielle Steel.

Whittier House MAP 10
2090 Jackson St 🚌 12 Muni

This large weathered brownstone house was built for William Frank Whittier in 1894–96 by Edward R Swain, who also designed McLaren Lodge, in Golden Gate Park. This building was once open to the public but is now privately owned.

James Leary Flood Mansion MAP 10
2120 Broadway 🚌 22 Muni

Now occupied by a private school, this Edwardian structure was built in 1901 for the son of 'Silver King' James Clair Flood. From the sidewalk you can admire the marble lions and florid cast-iron gate in front.

James Leary Flood's Second Mansion MAP 10
2222 Broadway 🚌 22 Muni ♿

James Leary Flood's second mansion in the neighborhood is a grand Italian palazzo built in 1912. It now houses the Convent of the Sacred Heart and its academy for wealthy girls.

Bourn House MAP 10
2550 Webster St 🚌 22 Muni

This dark and foreboding Georgian house, designed by Willis Polk, was built in 1896. Far from being born with a mere silver spoon in his mouth, William Bourn started out owning one gold mine and became one of the wealthiest men in San Francisco.

Casebolt House MAP 10
2727 Pierce St 🚌 *22, 41, 45 Muni*
Built in 1866 for Henry Casebolt, this is one of the oldest houses in the Pacific Heights and Cow Hollow area. The house was fashioned out of old ships' timbers in an exquisite Italianate design and stands well back from the street.

Gibbs House MAP 10
2622 Jackson St 🚌 *12, 24 Muni*
Visible from Alta Plaza Park, this 1894 house was built by Willis Polk.

Japantown

There have been Japanese in San Francisco since the 1860s, and today only a tiny portion of them live in the compact Japantown area. The Victorian neighborhood – which the Japanese called *Nihonjinmachi* ('Japanese people's town') – became populated by Japanese following the 1906 earthquake.

The area bustled with shops, schools, restaurants, temples, and newspapers. The WWII internment of Japanese and Japanese Americans devastated the community, and many of the former residents were unable to reclaim their homes after the war.

By war's end, the neighborhood had become populated largely by blacks who had come to the Bay Area for jobs in wartime industries. The neighborhood thrived as a center for black culture, and many jazz clubs and juke joints lined Fillmore St, attracting local favorites like the late blues singer John Lee Hooker. Not much remains of the district's lively musical past. (Hooker deserves mention for hipping up the city's official song, 'I Left My Heart in San Francisco,' with his recording of 'Frisco Blues.')

In the late 1960s, the development of the Japan Center once again gave the Japanese a visible presence in the city. But the full-scale clearing of the old Victorian neighborhood for the center displaced thousands of households, forcing most blacks who lived in the area to relocate to isolated Hunters Point. Today, Japantown is primarily a commercial district – it isn't really a neighborhood in the sense that Chinatown is. After three decades, the Japan Center's uninspired stucco architecture, replete with Japanese wood trimming, is already suffering from neglect. Nevertheless, the center, with an atmosphere that feels strangely authentic, succeeds in drawing huge crowds of Asian shoppers and diners.

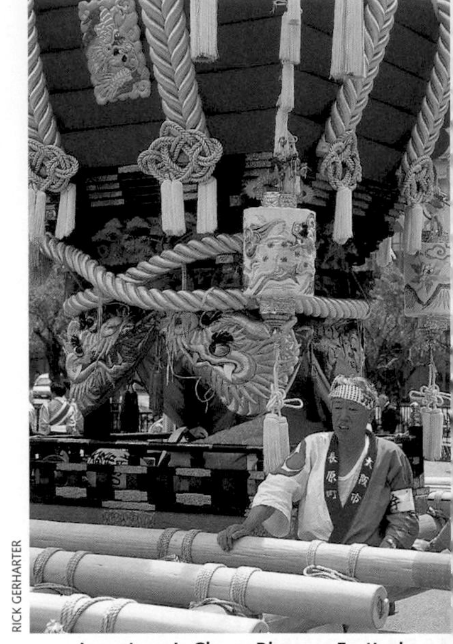

RICK GERHARTER

Japantown's Cherry Blossom Festival

Japantown comes alive during the two-weekend Cherry Blossom Festival in April, with music, dance, a wide variety of demonstrations, a special program for children, a food bazaar, and a Japanese parade. A two-day Nihonmachi Street Fair takes place the first weekend in August.

Some Victorians still survive around Japantown, and it's worth taking a short stroll along Pine and Bush Sts.

Japan Center MAP 10
1625 Post St ☎ *415-922-6776* ⓢ *free*
🕘 *10am-midnight daily, shop hours vary*
🚌 *38 Muni* ♿
W *www.japantown.com*

THINGS TO SEE & DO

This center opened in 1968 around windswept Peace Plaza, with its five-tiered Peace Pagoda. The three shopping centers that make up the Japan Center – the Miyako Mall, Kintetsu Mall, and Kinokuniya Building – are packed with Japanese restaurants and shops, including the excellent Kinokuniya Bookshop and the Maruwa supermarket. The complex also includes the eight-screen Kabuki Theater. More shops and restaurants are in the Buchanan Mall, across Post St from the center. The mall features fountains by sculptor Ruth Asawa that are designed to look as if a stream flows through it. For information on restaurants and shops, see Places to Eat and Shopping.

Kabuki Springs & Spa MAP 10
1750 Geary Blvd ☎ 415-922-6000 $ spa $15-18, other services up to $150 ⏲ 10am-10pm daily 🚌 38 Muni ♿
w www.kabukisprings.com

This spa offers Shiatsu and Swedish massage, acupuncture, and other traditional healing methods that can rejuvenate a weary traveler's body, mind, and soul.

Churches

Lower Pacific Heights offers yet another batch of impressive churches, with several of them clustered together on Cathedral Hill.

Cathedral of St Mary the Assumption MAP 10
1111 Gough St ☎ 415-567-2020 $ free ⏲ 7am-1pm Mon-Fri, 7am-6pm Sat, 8am-3pm Sun 🚌 38 Muni ♿
w www.stmarycathedralsf.org

The modern centerpiece of Cathedral Hill, this striking but ugly 1971 Catholic cathedral is much more impressive inside. Gazing at the heavenward sweep of the ceiling creates a spectacular sensation. This is San Francisco's third St Mary's Cathedral. The original, in use from 1854 to '91, still stands in Chinatown as Old St Mary's. Its replacement, New St Mary's, was on Van Ness Ave, but in 1960 it was completely destroyed by a fire.

RICHARD CUMMINS

Cathedral of St Mary the Assumption

St Mark's Lutheran Church MAP 10
1111 O'Farrell St ☎ 415-928-7770 $ free ⏲ 9am-noon daily 🚌 38 Muni ♿
w www.stmarks-sf.org

This church, built in 1894, contrasts dramatically from the modern St Mary's Cathedral. The Cathedral Hill area that surrounds the church changed dramatically in the 1960s, as old houses were raised to clear the way for high-rise apartments and St Mary's.

Temple Sherith Israel MAP 10
2266 California St ☎ 415-346-1720 $ free ⏲ hours vary 🚌 1, 22 Muni ♿
w www.sherithisrael.org

This impressive sanctuary has a marvelous dome and a spectacular interior. Architectural tours are often available – call to find out when the next one will be.

THE HAIGHT

If it weren't for a few months in 1965, '66, and '67, Haight St would probably just be an ordinary neighborhood shopping strip like 24th St in Noe Valley. Only a few blocks east of Golden Gate Park, the intersection of Haight and Ashbury Sts is San Francisco's most famous crossroads for one reason only: it was ground zero of the Summer of Love.

But the seminal events of San Francisco's hippie scene actually occurred in other parts of town: Ken Kesey's Trips Festival, in which thousands of people dropped acid while the Grateful Dead and other bands played, took place in 1965 at the Longshoremen's Hall, near Fisherman's Wharf; the Gathering of the Tribes–Human Be-In, which ushered in 1967 and the Summer of Love, took place at the Polo Fields in Golden Gate Park. But it was to the somewhat run-down, Victorian Haight-Ashbury that the idealistic 'hippies' gravitated. They were drawn by low rents, proximity to the park, and a pre-existing bohemian community that had grown out of the Beat scene.

[Continued on page 148]

Beatnik-Hippie Walking Tour

The streets of the Haight are lined with old houses and historic Beat and hippie sites and are ideal for walking. This tour starts at the corner of Haight and Fillmore, the hub of the edgy Lower Haight. It's a short walk from the J-Church and N-Judah Muni stop (behind the Market St Safeway). The Lower Haight is best known as a great strip for bars, but there are a few cafés and shops that may also pull you in off the sidewalk.

Walk 6 blocks west on Haight and turn right on Scott; head north a block to Page.

Jack's Record Cellar *254 Scott St*
☎ *415-431-3047* ⏲ *noon-7pm Wed-Sun* ♿

This is the oldest record store still operating in the city. Jack's dusty old shelves are packed tight with highly collectible 78rpm records, and for fans of jazz, rock, and R&B the walls are a breathtaking gallery of original concert posters.

Kenneth Rexroth's former residence *250 Scott St, top floor*

Upstairs from Jack's Record Cellar is the flat in which poet Kenneth Rexroth resided for many years. When East Coasters Jack Kerouac and Allen Ginsberg crashed the San Francisco scene in the '50s, this apartment was already the social epicenter for the city's radicals, poets, artists, and Eastern philosophers.

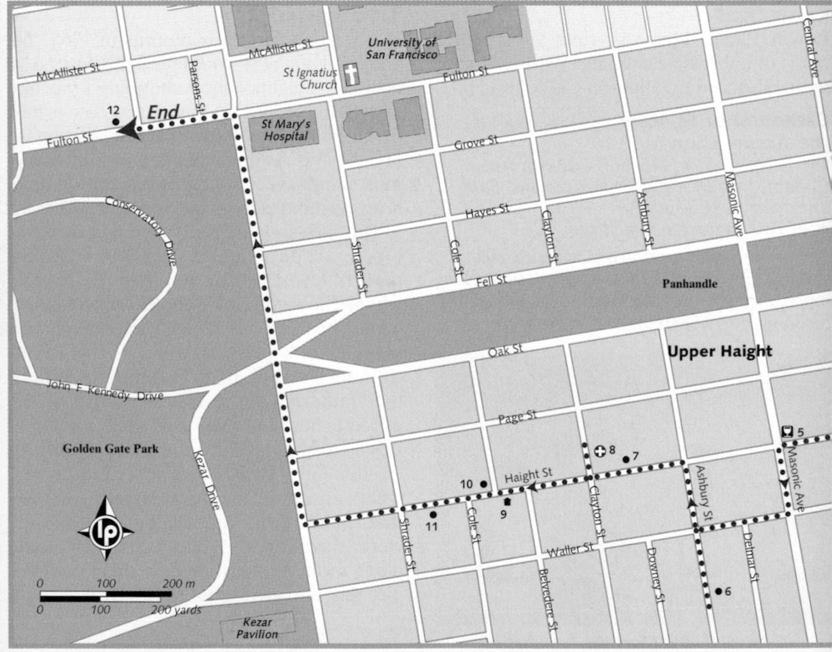

MONICA J MEARES

Right: The '60s live on in the Haight.

Albin Rooming House *1090 Page St*

In the '60s, this house had an informal ballroom of sorts in its basement, and weekend parties here featured rock and roll jam sessions. Out of these jams emerged bands such as Big Brother and the Holding Company.

At Lyon St, head north, toward the Panhandle.

Janis Joplin's former residence *112 Lyon St*

For most of 1967, singer Janis Joplin lived on the 2nd floor of this house, in the front room with the round balcony. She was evicted in 1968 for

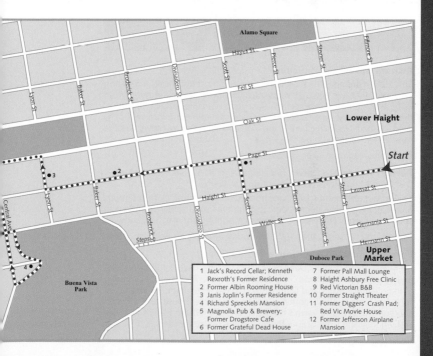

1 Jack's Record Cellar; Kenneth Rexroth's Former Residence
2 Former Albin Rooming House
3 Janis Joplin's Former Residence
4 Richard Spreckels Mansion
5 Magnolia Pub & Brewery; Former Drogstore Cafe
6 Former Grateful Dead House
7 Former Pall Mall Lounge
8 Haight Ashbury Free Clinic
9 Red Victorian B&B
10 Former Straight Theater
11 Former Diggers' Crash Pad; Red Vic Movie House
12 Former Jefferson Airplane Mansion

having a pet dog. (It's unconfirmed whether the dog was forced to leave with her.)

Panhandle

There isn't much to see in the Panhandle, except for dog walkers and joggers, but in the late '60s the Panhandle was the site of several legendary outdoor concerts. In June 1967, the Jimi Hendrix Experience played an impromptu show here. Even if you don't get Hendrix's music, the thought of hearing his voice and guitar riffs echoing off the nearby houses ought to give you an idea of what an exciting place the Haight was during the Summer of Love.

Walk a block west on Oak St and turn left on Central St. At Haight, you'll see the northwest corner of Buena Vista Park.

ANDREW DEAN NYSTROM

Richard Spreckels Mansion *737 Buena Vista Ave W*

This 1897 mansion is the most impressive and most historically interesting on Buena Vista Ave West. It's where Jack London lived while writing *White Fang,* and Ambrose Bierce spent the last years of his life here. In the 1960s, the house contained a small recording studio that numerous local musicians used. Graham Nash lived here in the '70s, and actor Danny Glover was the most recent celebrity to purchase it.

Continue heading east on Haight St.

Former Drogstore Cafe *1398 Haight St ☎ 415-864-7468 $ free ⌚ 11am-11pm Mon-Fri, 10am-11pm Sat-Sun ♿*

This corner restaurant space once housed the Drogstore Cafe, a famous hippie hangout. The name's odd spelling was supposedly contrived to confound Barney Fife types in a time of mounting antidrug crackdowns.

Turn left on Masonic, then right on Waller and left on Ashbury.

Former Grateful Dead house *710 Ashbury St*

Members of the Grateful Dead began moving into this Victorian in 1966, and eventually Jerry Garcia, Bob Weir, and Pigpen lived here, along with managers Rock Scully and Danny Rifkin and a revolving door of characters. In October 1967, antidrug police raided the house and arrested everyone in it (Garcia wasn't home). The Dead left the Haight in 1968, settling in Marin County. The house is still a private residence.

Return to Haight St and turn left.

Left: The Haight, a neighborhood with character

Former Pall Mall Lounge
1568 Haight St ♿

The Pall Mall Lounge was famous for serving 'Love Burgers' in the late '60s. Beef patties on a sesame-seed bun may not be what you'd imagine hippies eating, but these burgers were often given away free. In those idealistic times, free food was often available in the Haight's restaurants. So a poor, hungry flower child, having driven a VW bus from some far-flung commune to San Francisco, could saunter up to the counter and cop a free burger. In the Irish pub that is now open for business here, the Guinness isn't free.

RICK GERHARTER

Haight Ashbury Free Clinic *558 Clayton St ☎ 415-487-5632*
🕘 1pm-9pm Mon, 9am-9pm Tues-Thurs, 1pm-5pm Fri ♿

This is where, true to the spirit of the '60s, you can still see a doctor for free.

Red Victorian B&B *1665 Haight St ☎ 415-864-1978*

This bright red Victorian hotel was built in 1904, but it left its heart in the '60s. You are welcome to enter the lobby and look at the psychedelic paintings and 'peace t-shirts,' created by proprietor Sami Sunchild. Ms Sunchild has been around the block a few times, and if she's around she usually doesn't mind talking about her experiences traveling the globe in search of enlightenment. Judging by the far-off look on her face, she found it here.

Former Straight Theater *1700 Haight St* ♿

Before succumbing to the wrecking ball, the legendary Straight Theater, where the psychedelic San Francisco sound reached its zenith, stood on a corner lot now occupied by a Goodwill store.

Former Diggers' crash pad *1775 Haight St*

A flophouse run by an anarchic group called the Diggers once occupied this address, near the Red Vic theater. During the flower-power years, the Diggers, whose anonymous leaders turned out to be Emmett Grogan and actor Peter Coyote, gave free food, clothing, and lodging to anyone in need.

If you haven't had enough '60s history, turn right at Stanyan St at the end of Haight and take a short walk around the northeast corner of the park to where the Jefferson Airplane Mansion stands.

Former Jefferson Airplane Mansion *2400 Fulton St*

The rock band Jefferson Airplane (which, you'll recall, after making significant technological advances, redubbed itself the Jefferson Starship) bought this attractive mansion in 1968. Grace Slick & Co painted the place black, and unlike most of the neighborhood's other rockers, they continued to live here throughout the '70s.

ight: Haight Ashbury Free Medical Clinic

[Continued from page 143]

The 'San Francisco sound' – the LSD-inspired psychedelic rock typified by such groups as the Charlatans and the Grateful Dead – gestated in Haight St clubs like the Straight Theater. The neighborhood was populated with musicians who would become the legends of the '60s: the Dead, Jefferson Airplane, Janis Joplin, Big Brother

and the Holding Company, and Country Joe and the Fish were all neighbors as Haight-Ashbury reached its full flowering.

The early Haight scene was the most romantic period of the decade. Outdoor rock concerts were free, LSD and marijuana proliferated, public nudity and free love were commonplace rather than shocking, and political dialectics emanated from hangouts like the Psychedelic Shop and Mnasidika boutique. The local economy revolved around what many aptly called the 'Psychedelic Revolution.'

By the time the national media caught on to what was going on in the Haight, thousands of kids from around the country had gravitated to the neighborhood, which spanned just a couple dozen square blocks. The media attention attracted more people wanting to 'turn on' in San Francisco, and the scene quickly began to sour. By late '67, drug overdoses and incidences of violence were increasing among the throngs of hippies, gawkers, media, and police. By the early '70s, Haight St was skid row for burnt-out hippies, and as the '60s hippie scene faded, the street became a hub of gay nightlife.

Today, you'll see only a few remnants of the idealistic side of the '60s on Haight St. The Haight Ashbury Free Clinic is still providing medical care at no charge (see Facts for the Visitor for information, if on reading this you are reminded that you need medical attention). But an unappealing hangover from the '60s is much more evident. Teenage runaway meth-freaks ask for change, and disgruntled winos and LSD casualties shout abusive obscenities at passersby. The eastern edge of Golden Gate Park – which had become a shantytown for street people, some of whom were in the habit of shooting up in the children's playground – was temporarily closed in 1997 to restore it to its former status as a public park.

Beyond Haight St itself, however, the neighborhood has been gentrified. The Victorian houses have been stripped of their psychedelic paint jobs, and a professional class of people has moved in. Many boutiques in the area reflect the presence of this affluent, though still quirky and politically liberal, population.

There isn't really much to do or see in the Haight, but for 8 dense blocks it is certainly one of the more active and interesting streets in San Francisco. The favored activities here are hanging out in funky cafés, people-watching, shopping for nostalgic curios or retro clothing, nosing through leftist bookstores, and absorbing the history of the place. For '60s buffs, a short walk will take you past many places where the famous resided and some of the decade's definitive events occurred. At night, Haight St is somewhat edgy but worth coming to for its handful of idiosyncratic bars.

The Panhandle, a narrow strip of park that forms a handle to Golden Gate Park's pan, 2 blocks from Haight St, makes a natural northern border to the Haight.

East of the Haight-Ashbury, the Lower Haight is a colorful and grungy few blocks of clubs and bars. On one corner of Haight St, a chain pasta restaurant recently opened, possibly a harbinger of blander things to come.

In the southern reaches of the Haight-Ashbury, tiny Cole Valley is the area's most upscale gentrified neighborhood, with some cafés, restaurants, and shops.

Nearby Parks

Alamo Square MAP 11
21 Muni ♿

This park is famous for the 'painted ladies' on Steiner St, an unbroken row of elegant Victorian houses that make a postcard view with the city skyline in the background. You'll see several lovely Queen Anne Victorians on the 600 block of Steiner St. From the corner of Steiner and Fulton Sts, you can catch a flattering glimpse of City Hall. Two of Alamo Square's Victorians have been converted into hotels where Victoriana enthusiasts will surely feel at home (see Places to Stay).

ANDREW DEAN NYSTROM

Alamo Square mural

Buena Vista Park MAP 11
37, N Muni ♿ *limited*

True to its name, this park affords sweeping views of the city, the bay, and parts of Marin County. Like many San Francisco parks, it's great to visit in the daytime but not so wise to enter after dark. Buena Vista Ave West, curving up the hill and around the park, features some fine old houses.

Corona Heights Park MAP 11
37 Muni ♿ *limited*

Overlooking the Castro, this rugged little peak has a few trails and affords some really spectacular views. There's a playground, but the main reason to bring the kids here is the Randall Museum (see below).

Randall Museum MAP 11
199 Museum Way ☎ *415-554-9600*
donations (free) *10am-5pm Tues-Sat*
37 Muni ♿
w *www.randallmuseum.org*

With a kids' petting zoo that houses a variety of small wildlife and domestic animals, the Randall Museum has made it its mission to teach children to respect wildlife and the environment. There are also educational programs for kids that give them hands-on experience in a woodshop, arts and ceramics studios, theater, darkroom, lapidary workshop, greenhouse, and gardens.

THE CASTRO & UPPER MARKET

There aren't many sights in the Castro, and since the 1970s and early 1980s the neighborhood has mellowed considerably, but as the epicenter of the city's sizable and influential gay community, the Castro is definitely worth strolling. Some gay visitors may initially be disappointed by the neighborhood's upper-middle-class urbanity, but with a street scene that seems to buzz at all hours, the Castro is still one of San Francisco's most vital neighborhoods.

The streets that rise to the swoop of Market St on the lower slopes of Twin Peaks – notably 18th and 19th Sts – are distinguished by rows of meticulously painted Queen Anne–style Victorian cottages. The first inhabitants of these quaint structures were working-class families of German, Scandinavian, and Irish descent. On upper Market St, you can still see Scandinavian architectural influence in some of the apartment buildings.

Gay men didn't start moving in until the early 1970s. They came primarily for the houses, which by that time badly needed repainting and restoration. Many earned a good living buying, restoring, and selling the old houses, and the neighborhood rapidly acquired color and energy the city hadn't known since the Barbary Coast days. While the nonstop party of 1970s' gay life was more seedy and outrageous in Polk Gulch (near Civic Center) and on Folsom St south of Market, the Castro projected a certain respectable élan not seen elsewhere. It was in the Castro that most gay political and community organizations formed. Harvey Milk, the first openly gay man elected to public office in the city, called the Castro home. (In front of 575 Castro St, the location of Milk's old camera store and apartment, a plaque honoring him has been embedded in the sidewalk.)

Harvey Milk

The neighborhood was hit hard by the AIDS epidemic, which claimed thousands of lives during the 1980s. But the strength of the community held up and even showed a new resolve during that difficult decade. As the male population declined, many lesbians moved into the neighborhood, and for the first time the two groups – long segregated by gender – began to form a loose coalition here.

The Castro is great for people-watching, stopping for coffee, shopping, or having a leisurely lunch. See Entertainment for more on what to do at night.

Continue south along Castro or Noe Sts and you'll come to **Noe Valley**, another of San Francisco's wonderful small neighborhoods. The mixture of Victorian homes, restaurants, coffeehouses, and eclectic shops gives it a villagey feel. The main drag is 24th St.

Harvey Milk Plaza MAP 12
Castro St Muni station 37, F Muni

The neighborhood's crossroads is marked by small cramped plaza named for Harvey Milk. An enormous rainbow flag raised high on a flagpole flaps in the wind, leaving no doubt that this is a gay neighborhood.

Castro Theatre MAP 12
429 Castro St ☎ 415-621-6120 $ general $7.50, senior/child/matinee $4.50 show times vary Castro St Muni station 37, F Muni ♿ limited
w www.thecastro.com

The beaconlike vertical neon sign of the Castro Theatre is the Castro's most recognizable landmark. The theater, built in 1922, predates the neighborhood's gay community by five decades. The ornate Spanish Renaissance structure has an intact interior that features a pipe organ still regularly used. Seeing a film here is always an event, but the annual highlight is the Gay and Lesbian Film Festival. For more information, see Entertainment and the special section 'Out in the Streets: More than the Pride Parade.'

THE MISSION

The Mission District is a large area with several distinct pockets. Dolores St, where the Mission Dolores has stood for more than two centuries, is a genteel residential street; its graceful undulations, lovely houses, and palm-lined median make it the city's most attractive thoroughfare. Two blocks east, Valencia St is grittier, but its mélange of bars, funky boutiques, coffeehouses, international restaurants, and lesbian-owned businesses are what make the Mission one of the USA's hippest neighborhoods. One more block east, Mission St is beyond a doubt the city's most dynamic and colorful commercial strip, with a lively mix of shops, delis, and taquerías that cater primarily to the district's large Latino community. For more neighborly Latino charm, stroll down shaded 24th St, the heart of the Mission, with mural-covered alleyways branching off it.

Over the years, the Mission District has been home to communities of immigrants from varying parts of the world. Late-19th-century German and Scandinavian immigrants were followed by Irish and Italians. As local Irish Catholics multiplied, their offspring became known citywide as ICBMs, or Irish Catholics Born in the Mission; today there remain a few shops bearing distinctly Irish names on now predominantly Latino strips. It was not until the early 1960s that

Mexican immigrants, along with Central and South American political refugees, asserted a decidedly Latino atmosphere.

Over the last decade, the western half of the Mission – west of Mission St – seems to have hit a new stride, and more recently dot-commers have migrated into the area east of Mission St. New bars and restaurants and live-work lofts reflect a free-spending, modern sensibility. The evolution is undeniably toward gentrification, which makes many long-term residents unhappy. But diversity and alternative lifestyles are still the rule.

The Mission manages relative immunity from San Francisco's fog, so it's one of the warmest areas in the city.

Mission Dolores MAP 14
3321 16th St ☎ *415-621-8203* ⓢ *adult $3, child $2, audio tour $5* ⏲ *9am-4pm daily* Ⓜ *16th St BART station* 🚌 *22 Muni* ♿
w *www.missiondolores.citysearch.com*

The Misión San Francisco de Asis acquired its familiar name from a nearby pond, La Laguna de Nuestra Sende los Dolores (Our Lady of the Sorrows). The pond disappeared long ago, but the mission, with its 4-foot-thick adobe walls, survives as the oldest building in San Francisco. The mission was the sixth in the chain of California missions founded by Father Junípero Serra. Its site was consecrated on June 29, 1776, five days before the colonies on the East Coast declared their independence from Britain. A temporary structure was replaced in 1782 by the permanent building that stands today. Its construction was overseen by Franciscan monks; the actual labor was performed by Ohlone Indians. Today, the mission building is overshadowed by the adjoining basilica, built in 1913.

The mission is entered via a small shop, which leads to the cemetery. It is said that more than 5000 Native Americans were buried here after measles epidemics devastated the Ohlone tribe in 1814 and 1826. The cemetery, watched over by a statue of Junípero Serra, was once much larger, and the international collection of gravestones are more recent, a surprising number of them marking Irish deaths from the gold-rush era. Notable graves in the cemetery include that of Father Francisco Palou, who designed the mission and wrote Serra's biography; Don Luis Antonio Arguello, the first governor of Alta

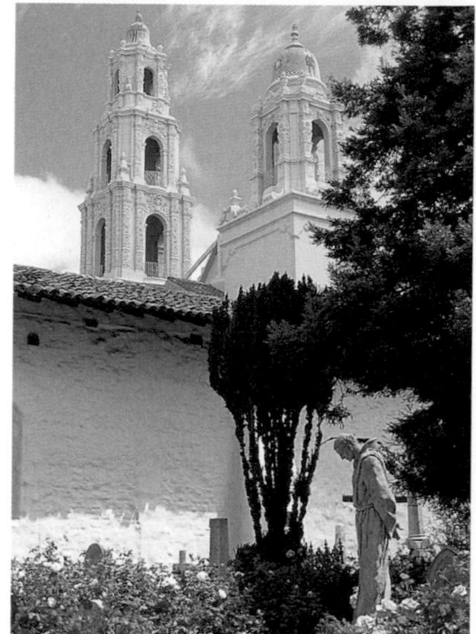
RICK GERHARTER

Mission Dolores

California under Mexican rule; Don Francisco de Haro, first alcalde (mayor) of San Francisco; and James Casey, Charles Cora, and James 'Yankee' Sullivan, 1856 victims of the Vigilance Committee, a lynch-first, ask-questions-later citizens' organization. Hitchcock fan's looking for the grave of Carlotta Valdez will be disappointed – Ms Valdez's tomb, a mere prop for the film *Vertigo,* was removed decades ago. A small museum stands at one end of the mission and includes a tabernacle door brought from the Philippines.

The mission chapel was built in 1782, and it's said that the building's ceiling was originally painted with vegetable dyes by the local Indian tribes. Although it has been repainted, the original designs have been retained. The colorful altars and altar niche statues were brought from Mexico in the early 19th century. Four burial sites are marked within the mission building: those of pioneer entrepreneur William Leidesdorff; the Noe family, whose sizable ranch once comprised the area that still bears the family name; Lieutenant Jose Joaquin Moraga, who led the Spanish expedition of 1776; and Richard Carroll, the first pastor of Mission Dolores after San Francisco became an archdiocese.

The sturdy mission survived the 1906 quake unscathed, but the adjoining church, built to mark the mission's centenary in 1876, was severely damaged. Its replacement dates from 1913 and was designated a basilica by Pope Pius XII after his visit in 1952. The basilica's ornate churrigueresque design is eye-catching, and inside are seven panels, one above the main door and three on the façades of each of the side balconies, depicting the Seven Sorrows of Mary. The choir windows picture St Francis of Assisi, after whom the mission and the city of San Francisco are named. The lower windows show the 21 California missions, plus two more in honor of Father Junípero Serra and Father Francisco Palou.

Mission Dolores Park MAP 14
9am-4pm daily *33 Muni* *limited*

Sloping up from Dolores St between 18th and 20th Sts, Mission Dolores Park is popular with neighborhood dog-walkers, soccer and tennis players, and children who make use of its playground. Over all of this activity presides a statue of Miguel Hidalgo (1753–1811), martyred Mexican priest and revolutionary hero.

RICHARD I'ANSON

Downtown, from atop Dolores Park

The southwest corner inclines steeply to the corner of Church and 20th Sts, where the J-Church streetcar stops. The corner affords a postcard-perfect view of downtown and the Bay Bridge, and on sunny days the grassy slope is popular with gay sunbathers, who have given it the sobriquet 'Dolores Beach.'

Mission High School MAP 14
3750 18th St ☎ *415-241-6240* *33 Muni*

This school was built in the 1920s in the mission revival style and topped by a churrigueresque tower that nicely complements the Mission Dolores basilica, 2 blocks away.

Levi Strauss Factory MAP 14
250 Valencia St ☎ *415-565-9153* *26 Muni*
w *www.levistrauss.com*

The Mission's Levi Strauss factory, built in 1906, was the second established by the San Francisco–based inventor of blue jeans (see the boxed text 'Levi Strauss' in Shopping), and today it is the company's oldest and smallest factory, turning out just 7500 pairs per week. A sign out front advises employees to leave their guns at the door. The factory no longer offers tours.

Mission Murals

The Mission is a gallery of colorful murals depicting San Francisco labor history, Central American revolutions, the women's movement, and local street life. Murals are scattered all over the place, so simply wandering the neighborhood is one way to take them in.

Precita Eyes Mural Arts Center MAP 14
2981 24th St ☎ *415-285-2287* $ *walking tour map $1.50* *10am-5pm Mon-Fri, 10am-4pm Sat, noon-4pm Sun* *48 Muni*
w *www.precitaeyes.org*

This community arts center, under the direction of muralist Susan Cervantes, was founded in the late 1970s to create murals that reflect the community and also involve the community in the artistic process. As a result of the center's efforts, many young people have been encouraged to develop their artistic talents, and schools and public buildings in the neighborhood have been beautified. The center conducts walking tours led by muralists (see Activities, in this chapter) and sells a walking-tour map and postcards of the murals.

Balmy Alley MAP 14
$ *free* *12, 47, 68 Muni*

This narrow street, between Folsom and Harrison Sts and 24th and 25th Sts, is a Mission District landmark. Lined from end to end with murals, it is here that the Mission mural movement began in the early 1970s. Some of the original murals, now fading, still adorn garages and backyard fences in the alley. Over the years new murals have been added, further developing the original themes of family and community values, labor movements, and political activism.

Women's Building MAP 14
3543 18th St ☎ *415-431-1180* *9am-5pm Mon-Fri* *16th St BART station* *33 Muni*
e *sfwctwb@aol.com*

MARIA MACK

Balmy Alley

Thanks to the spectacular mural that covers nearly every inch of its façade, this building is one of the city's most eye-catching structures. The mural, titled *Maestrapeace*, was a collaborative effort (as murals often are) by seven women artists. Heroic bodies and pensive faces swirl dramatically from the sidewalk to the very top of the building, as do the names and portraits of notable women both contemporary and historic.

Art Galleries

There are a number of galleries specializing in Latino art in the Mission.

Galería de la Raza MAP 14
2857 24th St ☎ 415-826-8009 $ free
⌚ noon-6pm Wed-Sun 🚌 27, 48 Muni ♿
w the-city.sfsu.edu/~galeria

This is the best – and most controversial – of galleries specializing in Latino art. The gallery's curators don't shy away from tough issues like racism and homophobia. It has been central to the Latino art scene since 1970.

Mission Badlands MAP 14
2811 Mission St, 2nd floor ☎ 415-920-0896
$ free ⌚ noon-6pm Sat-Sun Ⓜ 24th St BART station 🚌 14, 48, 49 Muni

This gallery specializes in pop art with a Latino twist.

Mission Cultural Center for Latino Arts MAP 14
2868 Mission St ☎ 415-821-1155 $ $2
⌚ 10am-4pm Tues-Sat Ⓜ 24th St BART station 🚌 14, 48, 49 Muni ♿
w www.bayarea.citysearch.com/profile/891391

This community center celebrates Latino arts and culture with a gallery and theater where plays, music, and poetry are performed. The center also makes elaborate floats for the Carnaval parade in the spring and sponsors Día de los Muertos events in the fall.

POTRERO HILL

Potrero Hill is an unsung neighborhood south of SoMa and east of the Mission. Cut off from surrounding areas by freeways on three sides and by the steepness of the streets climbing the hill, Potrero Hill enjoys a small-town quiet without being all that far from the center of things. There's not much in the way of active sightseeing, but the hill does have nice views of the rest of town. A tour of the Anchor Brewery, a drive down Vermont St, and a bite to eat at one of the many restaurants on 18th St and you've pretty much 'done' Potrero. One of the city's better small venues for live music, Bottom of the Hill, is also in this part of town (see Entertainment).

Anchor Brewing Company MAP 14
1705 Mariposa St ☎ 415-863-8350 $ free
⌚ tours 2pm Mon-Fri 🚌 19 Muni ♿
w www.anchorbrewing.com, www.anchorsteambeer.com

This is where the city's fine Anchor Steam beer is brewed. Long before the microbrewery craze hit America, the small Anchor Brewery was supplying San Francisco bars with quality, traditionally crafted beers. All of the Anchor brews are produced at the company's Potrero Hill base. There are small group tours daily; reserve well in advance, especially if you want to get in on Thursday or Friday. Freshly brewed samples – compliments of the house – are poured at tour's end.

McKinley Square MAP 14
🚌 53 Muni ♿ limited

This park and playground sits at the top of the hill and is a great place for a picnic. For those not prone to vertigo, the swings at the ledge of the park provide quite a thrill as they swoop you out into space over the Mission (but adults must be accompanied by a child). Continue down one-way Vermont St toward 20th St on what locals will tell you is the *real* crookedest street in the world. It's less traveled and longer than Lombard St, but not so quaint as its touristy counterpart.

Basic Brown Bear Factory MAP 14
444 DeHaro St ☎ 800-554-1910 $ $12-65 ⏲ 10am-5pm Mon-Sat, noon-5pm Sun 🚌 19 Muni ♿
w www.basicbrownbear.com

This is a popular attraction for the tiny tots. Children can stuff their own bear before it gets stitched up and sent home with them. They also get to make decisions that will determine how the bears are dressed and groomed. Since the bears vary widely in price, the challenge for parents is ensuring their child is happy choosing a bear within the vacation budget.

THE PRESIDIO

The northwest corner of the San Francisco peninsula was for many decades occupied by a rather low-key army base; as a result, it has not been developed extensively, and most of it remains green and parklike. Hwys 1 and 101 meet in the middle of the Presidio and lead to the Golden Gate Bridge, but despite the steady flow of traffic along these arteries the Presidio has remained a refreshingly relaxed escape from the rest of the city. It is deservedly popular for hiking, jogging, and biking.

The Presidio has a long military history. It was established in 1776 by the Spanish as the site of their first fort (*presidio* in Spanish) and was linked with the religious center of Mission Dolores, 3 miles to the south, by Divisadero. It also served the Mexican army for a period of time before the US took over in the 1840s. Under American rule, Fort Point was built at the start of the Civil War, in 1861, to guard the entrance to the bay. The Presidio's military role ended in 1996, when the Golden Gate National Recreation Area (GGNRA) assumed control over the new park. Future development in the park will likely include a campus of offices to house filmmaker George Lucas' empire.

Presidio Visitors Center MAP 16
102 Montgomery St ☎ 415-561-4323 $ free ⏲ 9am-5pm daily 🚌 28, 76 Muni
w www.nps.gov/prsf

Stop by this visitors' center for maps and information on park facilities. There's also a small photo exhibit that is supposed to grow into a full-fledged museum within the next few years.

Fort Point MAP 16
Marin Dr ☎ 415-556-1693 $ free ⏲ 10am-5pm Wed-Sun 🚌 28 Muni ♿ limited

Some of the most spectacular views of the Golden Gate Bridge and the bay are from this lookout. The small Spanish fort that originally occupied the site was replaced, by the US Army, with a much larger, triple-tiered fortress between 1853 and 1861. Though it had 126 cannons, it never saw battle or cannon fire and was abandoned in 1900. The bridge was built right over it, and now it houses displays relating to the Civil War. Battery Chamberlin, with another cannon, is on the bluffs above Baker Beach.

RICHARD CUMMINS

Golden Gate Bridge, from Fort Point

Baker Beach MAP 16
☎ 415-561-4323 ⏲ dawn-dusk daily

Along the ocean side of the peninsula, this is the most picturesque of the city's beaches with craggy rock formations backed up against cliffs. But because of cold water and strong currents, it's not a great swimming beach.

San Francisco National Military Cemetery MAP 16
off Lincoln Blvd ⏲ dawn-dusk daily 🚌 28, 76 Muni ♿ limited

Originally the burying ground for Spanish settlers, this area became a US military cemetery in 1884. It's the resting place for soldiers from the Civil War to the present.

Presidio Pet Cemetery MAP 16
Crissy Field Ave ⌚ dawn-dusk daily 🚌 28, 76 Muni ♿ limited

This is a strange and forgotten patch of ground holding the remains of many army dogs and family pets, their graves marked with sentimental hand-painted tombstones.

THE RICHMOND

Bordered by the green parkland of the Presidio to the north and Golden Gate Park to the south, the uniform rectangles of the Richmond District stretch all the way to the ocean. East of Park Presidio Blvd, in the area known as the Inner Richmond, the restaurants and bookstores along busy Clement St make up the heart of 'New Chinatown.' Farther west, in the Outer Richmond, Geary Blvd becomes a montage of ethnic eateries and shops, including Chinese, Southeast Asian, and Russian establishments. This is one of San Francisco's most diverse strips, and people come here from all over San Francisco just to eat. The Richmond District is home to a couple of interesting religious buildings, as well as the Palace of the Legion of Honor, in Lincoln Park, and the Cliff House.

Cliff House & Sutro Baths

On sunny afternoons, the Cliff House complex, overlooking the Pacific Ocean, and the ruins of the once-grand Sutro Baths are fine for poking around. This is also a good jumping-off point for a day of hiking and exploring the many wonderful trails that pass through.

Cliff House MAP 15
1090 Point Lobos Ave ☎ 415-386-3330
$ free ⌚ see individual sites 🚌 18 Muni ♿ limited
W www.cliffhouse.com

Fires and earthquakes have resulted in multiple incarnations for many San Francisco buildings, but none have come back as often as the Cliff House, originally built in 1863 as an escape from the crowds and hectic pace of the city. The second Cliff House, an elegant eight-story gingerbread resort built by Adolph Sutro in 1896, was by far the classiest version. It contained art galleries, dining rooms, and an observation deck. It survived the 1906 earthquake but was destroyed by fire the following year. The 1909 replacement, which still stands, is a dud by comparison, but its dining rooms and bar are still popular, despite unexciting food. Sunset over the Pacific can be worth the price of a drink. Seal Rocks, just offshore from the Cliff House, is washed by crashing waves but is not as densely populated by seals as it once was.

Musée Mécanique MAP 15
1090 Point Lobos Ave ☎ 415-386-1170
$ free ⌚ 11am-7pm Mon-Fri, 11am-8pm Sat-Sun 🚌 18, 38 Muni
W www.museemecanique.citysearch.com

The brilliantly whimsical Musée Mécanique makes the trip to the Cliff House worthwhile. The collection, assembled and restored by Edward Galland Zelinsky and Daniel Galland Zelinsky, spotlights early-20th-century arcade games, risqué Mutoscope motion pictures ('See what the belly dancer does on her day off!') and self-playing pianos. Odd, ingenious,

Laughing Sal greets visitors to the Musée Mécanique.

coin-operated 'automata' displays – mechanical folk art, really – include a spinning Ferris wheel built of toothpicks and a fully operational miniature opium den in which thumb-size hopheads loll on their floor mats while a dragon peeks from behind a curtain. By pumping quarters into the machines, you'll get more amusement than you bargained for.

Camera Obscura MAP 15
1090 Point Lobos Ave ☎ 415-750-0415 $ $1
⌚ 10am or 11am-sunset daily 🚌 18, 38 Muni

On the deck below the Cliff House, this giant

Victorian invention projects the view outside onto a parabolic screen.

Sutro Baths MAP 15
$ free ⌚ sunrise-sunset daily 🚌 18, 38 Muni ♿ limited

In the cove just north of the Cliff House are the remains of these baths. At the same time that he built the Cliff House, in 1896, the wealthy Adolph Sutro built a magnificent indoor swimming pool complex that could accommodate 25,000 visitors a day. But despite

ANTHONY PIDGEON
Sutro Bath ruins

the initial splash they made, the pools never made money. An ice-skating rink was added in 1937, and the whole complex was converted to ice skating in 1952. Demolition began in 1966, but a fire finished the structure off before the wreckers could. Period prints at the GGNRA's Cliff House visitors' center show what an amazing creation the six-pool (some saltwater, some freshwater), 3-acre palace must have been.

Palace of the Legion of Honor MAP 15
100 34th Ave ☎ 415-863-3330 $ adult $8, senior $6, teen $5, under 12 free; 2nd Wed of the month free ⌚ 9:30am-5pm Tues-Sun 🚌 1, 18, 38 Muni ♿
w *www.legionofhonor.org*

One of San Francisco's best art museums sits amid the trees and golf links of Lincoln Park.

Sugar magnate Adolph Spreckels' name pops up regularly around San Francisco, and this magnificent art museum was the creation of his wife, Alma Spreckels. The French pavilion for the 1915 Panama-Pacific Exposition in the Marina was a replica of the Palais de la Légion d'Honneur in Paris and was stocked with French art. The exposition buildings were temporary, but Mrs Spreckels decided she wanted to construct a permanent replica. Architect George Applegarth, who also built the Spreckels Mansion in Pacific Heights, built it here.

The museum opened in 1924 and includes an excellent collection of medieval to 20th-century European art, including many works by the impressionists and a huge Rodin collection. The museum also has well-conceived exhibits, often bringing in major works from other institutions.

If you took the bus here, flash your Muni transfer at the museum to receive a $2 discount.

Park Lands

Northwest from the Cliff House, the Golden Gate National Recreation Area oversees parks and beaches that extend to the Presidio. There is some excellent hiking here.

Golden Gate National Recreation Area Visitors Center MAP 15
☎ 415-556-8642 $ free ⌚ 10am-5pm daily 🚌 18, 38 Muni ♿
w *www.nps.gov/goga*

This information center, hidden away downstairs from and behind the Cliff House, dispenses information about all the GGNRA coastal parks, so it's a good place to stop before hiking any of the nearby trails.

Lincoln Park MAP 15
☎ 415-221-9911 $ free ⌚ sunrise-sunset daily 🚌 1, 18, 38 Muni ♿ limited

John McLaren, best known as Golden Gate Park's superintendent for 56 years, took time out from his day job to establish lovely Lincoln Park. There's a fine walking path, part of the 9-mile Coastal Trail that winds along this surprisingly rugged stretch of coast from the Cliff House to Lands End. The park's path offers terrific views of the Golden Gate, and it takes about an hour roundtrip – and it's worth it, fog or no fog. The walk starts by the remains of the gigantic Sutro Baths and passes the USS *San Francisco* memorial which looks out over the ocean from Point Lobos. The ship sank during the WWII battle of Guadalcanal, in the Solomon Islands, and its bridge is preserved on the clifftop. Also see Golf, later.

Coastal Trail MAP 15
sunrise-sunset daily 18, 28 Muni

The 9-mile Coastal Trail starts at Fort Funston and ends at Fort Mason. Four miles of it are sandy Ocean Beach (see the Sunset section in this chapter). You can catch the trail midway at Lincoln Park.

Lands End & Fort Miley MAP 15
415-556-8371 Fort Miley ranger station sunrise-sunset daily 18, 38 Muni limited

Lands End and adjacent Fort Miley offer some spectacular hikes along nearly pristine coastal cliffs. Ruins of old defense batteries offer a respite from the hustle and bustle of nature.

Sutro Heights Park MAP 15
free sunrise-sunset daily 18, 38 Muni limited

Across the street from the Cliff House, tourists are welcome to stroll around the grounds of the Adolph Sutro Estate, now known as Sutro Heights Park. The mansion is gone, but some of the walls and gardens remain, and there are wonderful views.

GOLDEN GATE PARK MAP 15

free sunrise-sunset daily 5, 7, 29, 44, 71 Muni

San Francisco's biggest park stretches almost halfway across the 7-mile-wide peninsula. In 1866 Mayor Frank McCoppin led the push to create the park, at a time when San Francisco's meteoric gold-fueled growth had left little time to think about such civic niceties. In 1870, a 24-year-old civil engineer named William Hammond Hall won the competition to design the park, and a year later he commenced the task of turning 1017 acres of dunes into the largest human-made park in the world. (Initial inspiration for Golden Gate Park came from Frederick Law Olmsted, designer of New York's Central Park, but he quickly decided that reclaiming the dunes was an impossible task – and was suitably astonished when Hall accomplished the feat.)

Battles with land speculators forced Hall to resign five years later, but by the 1880s the park had become the city's most popular attraction. Hall was recalled in 1886, but a year later he handed over the park's management to John McLaren, who administered the park for the next 56 years. As astute at managing politicians as he was at growing plants, the indestructible Scottish-born gardener lived to be 97, remaining in charge of his beloved park 'til the day he died.

Apart from gardens, groves, lakes, sporting facilities, and trails, the park also has a host of museums and other indoor attractions. Toward the eastern end of the park, the Academy of Sciences, MH de Young Memorial Museum, Asian Art Museum, and Japanese Tea Garden cluster around the Music Concourse, where the Midwinter International Exposition of 1894 was held. They can be a welcome escape on days when the fog rolls in and the temperature plummets. A $10 'Culture Pass' includes admission to all the park attractions that charge entry fees, offering a $5.50 savings. The pass can be used over a number of days.

McLaren Lodge (Park Headquarters)
415-831-2700, 415-263-0991 information on free walking tours free 9am-5pm Mon-Fri 21, 33 Muni

Park information, including a detailed map of the park, is available from McLaren Lodge, at the eastern entrance to the park. Built in 1896, this was park administrator John McLaren's home. It now holds the offices of the Friends of Recreation & Parks, which organizes free walking tours of the park.

Japanese Tea Garden
Hagiwara Tea Garden Dr 415-831-2700 adult $2, child $1; green tea and fortune cookies $2 9am-6:30pm daily summer, 8:30am-6pm daily winter 44 Muni limited

The park's most popular tourist attraction, the Japanese Tea Garden was originally built for the 1894 Midwinter International Exposition. The garden features a pagoda, gates, bridges, a variety of statues, and a nice little teahouse where you can enjoy green tea and fortune cookies. The garden has had an interesting, and at times rather sad, history. Makoto Hagiwara, who constructed the original garden for the fair, lived there until 1925, during which time he extended it from 1 to 5 acres. After his death, the garden remained in the Hagiwara family's care until 1942, when anti-Japanese prejudice resulted in their eviction from the garden, the demolition of a number of structures, and even a name change to 'Oriental Tea Garden.' Things gradually improved after the war; the original name was reinstated, the large 1790 bronze Buddha was installed, and in the early '50s the dry, stone Zen Garden was added.

RICHARD CUMMINS

Japanese Tea Garden in Golden Gate Park

Conservatory of Flowers

☎ 415-831-2700 ⏰ sunrise-sunset daily 🚌 21, 33 Muni

This elegant frame and glass structure, the oldest building in the park, is being completely rebuilt afer a storm damaged it a few years ago. Faithfully recreating its original design, modeled after a greenhouse in London's Kew Gardens, is proving to be painstaking work. The conservatory was brought from Ireland in 1876 for millionaire James Lick's San Jose property, but he died while it was still in its packing crates. A group of San Francisco businessmen bought it and donated it to Golden Gate Park, where it was assembled in 1878.

Music Concourse

⏰ sunrise-sunset daily 🚌 44 Muni ♿

The Music Concourse, with its surrounding museums (see below), is the cultural nexus of the park. The Golden Gate Park Band performs regularly on summer Sundays at 1pm in the Spreckels Temple of Music, at the west end of the concourse.

MH de Young Memorial Museum

Hagiwara Tea Garden Dr ☎ 415-863-3330 🚌 44 Muni
w www.thinker.org/deyoung

A gift to the city from *San Francisco Chronicle* founder MH de Young, this once stately museum grew out of the 1894 Midwinter International Exposition. Seriously damaged in the 1989 earthquake, the old de Young is currently closed so that it can be completely rebuilt. The new museum is scheduled to open in spring 2005. Until then, selections from the museum's fine holdings of American art, much of it from the collection of Mr and Mrs John D Rockefeller III, will be displayed at the Palace of the Legion of Honor.

California Academy of Sciences

55 Concourse Dr ☎ 415-750-7145 $ adult/senior $8.50, teen/student $5.50, ages 4-12 $2; 1st Wed of the month free ⏰ 10am-5pm daily Jan-May & Oct-Dec, 9am-6pm daily Jun-Sep, 1st Wed of every month open until 8:45pm 🚌 44 Muni ♿
w www.calacademy.org

This 'academy' is really an educational museum complex that includes a natural history museum, an aquarium, and a planetarium (see below). Together, these museums cover the gamut, from Earth to oceans to space, in a variety of fascinating exhibits.

The main building houses the Natural History Museum, with a variety of exhibits that are designed to make valuable impressions on children. The Life through Time exhibit traces the development of life on earth and includes some superb dinosaur models. Wild California, with displays of California wildlife, is particularly of local interest. Easily the most unsettling exhibit is the earthquake platform, where you watch an earthquake video while the platform shakes beneath your feet, simulating increasingly larger tremors building up to the Great Quake of 1906. The academy has a shop and a café.

Show a Muni transfer or pass to get a $2.50 discount.

Steinhart Aquarium

55 Concourse Dr ☎ 415-750-7145 $ admission to the academy includes entry to the aquarium ⏰ 10am-5pm daily Jan-May & Oct-Dec, 9am-6pm daily Jun-Sep, 1st Wed of the month open until 8:45pm 🚌 44 Muni ♿
w www.calacademy.org

This aquarium, famous for the terrifying (from a tiny-tot perspective) alligator pit in its entryway, features a 'fish roundabout' 180 feet in diameter, as well as some smaller tanks with an assortment of very strange fish. The aquarium's seals and dolphins are fed every two ours. Feeding begins at 10:30am every day xcept Wednesday, when feeding begins at 2:30pm.

Morrison Planetarium
5 Concourse Dr ☎ 415-750-7141 $ (in ddition to admission to the California Academy of Sciences) adult $2.50, senior/child 1.50; under 6 free ⏲ vary 🚌 44 Muni ♿
w www.calacademy.org

he trippy light shows here – including Neighbors in Space' and 'Worlds Unseen' – re worth catching.

Stow Lake
☎ 415-752-0347 ⏲ sunrise-sunset daily
🚌 29, 44 Muni ♿

edal boats, row boats, and electric motor oats are available at the boat-rental house on tow Lake. The island in the middle of Stow ake, Strawberry Hill, is a nice spot for walking nd for watching the boats. Huntington Falls umbles down the hill into the lake. A pretty Chinese pavilion stands at the foot of the falls.

Pioneer Log Cabin
ohn F Kennedy Dr ⏲ sunrise-sunset daily
🚌 29 Muni

his log cabin was built in 1911. Redwood logs, ut in Humboldt County, were fashioned into a aft and floated down the coast to San Francisco.

Lloyd Lake
ransverse Dr 🚌 29 Muni

hese waters reflect the Portals of the Past, he entrance portico to a Nob Hill mansion hat was destroyed in the 1906 earthquake. 's the city's only memorial to that quake.

Golden Gate Park Stadium
🚌 29 Muni ♿

lso known as the Polo Fields, these grounds re furnished with football and soccer fields nd a trotting track. The great hippie-fest of 967, the 100,000-strong Gathering of the ribes–Human Be-In, took place here.

Spreckels Lake
🚌 5 Muni ♿

eople of all ages launch their miniature achts and sailboats here. Across the street, a uilding houses a model boat club.

Bison paddock
🚌 5 Muni

ere's a park surprise. Buffalo have inhabited olden Gate Park on and off since 1894. The urrent herd arrived in 1984.

Dutch & Murphy windmills
🚌 18 Muni

Past the archery field and the golf course stands the 1902 Dutch windmill, which once pumped water to the Strawberry Hill reservoir, atop the Stow Lake island. Near the southwest corner of the park, the Murphy windmill (1905) is more run-down.

Beach Chalet
1000 Great Hwy ☎ 415-386-8439 $ free
⏲ 8am-10pm daily 🚌 18 Muni ♿
w www.beachchalet.com

This building, with a microbrewery now upstairs (see the boxed text 'Brewpubs' in Places to Eat), went up in 1925. Its interior was painted with murals during the Great Depression. (See the boxed text 'Public Art in the City' in Facts about San Francisco.)

Children's Playground
Kezar Dr $ free ⏲ sunrise-sunset daily
🚌 71 Muni ♿

Built in 1888, this playground was the first ever in a US park. It features a 1912 carousel and a variety of swings, jungle gyms, and other fun apparatuses.

Park Gardens

There are a host of groves and gardens within Golden Gate Park.

Strybing Arboretum and Botanical Gardens
☎ 415-661-1316 $ free ⏲ 8am-4:30pm Mon-Fri, 10am-5pm Sat-Sun 🚌 44, 71 Muni ♿
w www.strybing.org

These 70-acre gardens include a Garden of

Fragrance, designed to have a special appeal for the visually impaired, and a garden of California native plants that explodes with color when the native wildflowers bloom in early spring. There's also a redwood nature trail. Free tours of the arboretum take place every day; for details, stop by the little bookstore just inside the arboretum entrance.

AIDS Memorial Grove
☎ 415-750-8340 $ free ⏲ sunrise-sunset daily 🚌 44 Muni ♿
w www.aidsmemorial.org

This stately grove was inaugurated in 1991 and is a quiet, peaceful spot for reflection and remembrance of those who have died with AIDS.

Shakespeare Garden
$ free ⏲ sunrise-sunset daily 🚌 44 Muni ♿

This 1928 garden has 150-odd plants, all of which are featured in Shakespeare's writings. The park also has Dahlia Dell, Fuchsia Dell, Rhododendron Dell, Rose Garden, and – beside the Dutch windmill – the Queen Wilhelmina Tulip Garden.

Redwood Memorial Grove
$ free ⏲ sunrise-sunset daily 🚌 44 Muni ♿

This grove of redwood trees was planted in the 1930s and already towers over the rest of the park's flora. The grove commemorates the dead of the 1898 Spanish-American War and WWI.

Sporting Facilities

The park is packed with sporting facilities, including 7½ miles of bicycle trails, many miles of jogging trails, and 12 miles of horseback-riding trails. John F Kennedy Dr east of Crossover Dr is closed to motor vehicles on Sunday to allow more space for cyclists, skateboarders, in-line skaters, joggers, and others engaged in human-powered transport.

The park has an archery range, baseball and softball diamonds, fly-casting pools, a cramped nine-hole golf course, greens for lawn bowling, horseshoe pitching, four soccer fields, and 21 tennis courts. Oh, and there's also a bocce green.

Stow Lake Boathouse
Stow Lake ☎ 415-752-0347 $ hourly rate: row boats $11, pedal boats $15, motorboats $18 ⏲ 10am-4pm daily 🚌 29 Muni

You can rent a rowboat, pedal boat, or electric boat at the Stow Lake boathouse. Boats must have at least one person 16 or older aboard. If you brought a dog, you can take it on a rowboat.

Golden Gate Park Stables
John F Kennedy Dr ☎ 415-668-7360 $ 1-hr guided trail ride $30 ⏲ 9am-5pm daily 🚌 5 Muni

To ride a horse with a trail guide for one hour, call the Golden Gate Park Stables. Reservations are required.

THE SUNSET & TWIN PEAKS

South of Golden Gate Park, the city's hilly terrain makes three final skyward lunges at Twin Peaks, Mt Sutro, and Mt Davidson and from there rolls westward in block after uniform block to the ocean. Formerly known as El Pecho de la Chola, 'The Breasts of the Indian Girl,' the summits of the 900-foot Twin Peaks afford a superb vista over the whole Bay Area, especially at night. Northwest of Twin Peaks is Mt Sutro (918 feet), topped by the triple-pronged antennae of Sutro Tower, which broadcasts most of the city's TV and radio. To the southwest is Mt Davidson (938 feet).

The area south of the park down to Sloat Blvd (which runs past the San Francisco Zoo and Stern Grove) and from about 7th Ave to the ocean is known as the Sunset District, a mostly residential area filled with pastel-colored stucco homes built between the 1930s and the 1950s. The Inner Sunset, centered around 9th Ave at Irving and Judah Sts, has the most to offer, with a variety of ethnic restaurants and cafés only a block or two from Golden Gate Park. Ocean Beach bounds the district on the west, and the San Francisco Zoo, Lake Merced, and Fort Funston all lie to the south.

Ocean Beach MAP 15
☎ 415-556-8371 🚌 18, 23, 31, 38, 48, 71, N Muni

Ocean Beach stretches for 4 miles along the coast, from the Cliff House to the cliffs of Fort Funston. On sunny days, you'll find a classic California beach scene, packed with sunbathers, surfers, and picnickers. Unfortunately sunny days are few and far between. From

June to September, Ocean Beach is often covered by thick, cold fog or equally demoralizing coastal clouds, and as a result it tends to be deserted except for fisherfolk and indomitable surfers.

RICK GERHARTER

Ocean Beach and the Cliff House

San Francisco Zoo

☎ *415-753-7061* $ *adult $10, senior/teen $7, ages 3-11 $4; 1st Wed of the month free* ⌚ *10am-5pm daily* 🚌 *18, 23 Muni* ♿ **w** *www.sfzoo.org*

San Francisco's Fleischacker Zoo is sandwiched between Lake Merced and the ocean. Though not one of the country's best zoos, it has some fine attractions, including the Primate Discovery Center and Gorilla World, one of the largest gorilla enclosures in the world. The big cats (lions and tigers) are fed daily at 2pm except Monday. There's also a children's petting zoo, where kids can mingle with farm animals in a barnyard, a gorgeous Dentzel carousel ($2), and nice playgrounds and picnic areas.

San Francisco residents carrying picture ID get a $2 discount.

Fort Funston MAP 1

☎ *415-556-8371* ⌚ *6am-9pm daily* ♿ *limited*

A mile south of the zoo, the grassy dunes of Fort Funston suggest what the western part of San Francisco may have looked like before it was paved over in the early part of the 20th century. The park is protected as part of the Golden Gate National Recreation Area, and it attracts butterflies and migrating birds. Not many native plants thrive here (much of the ground is smothered by ice plant, a pervasive nonnative succulent), but at the far northern end of the park the National Park Service is running a restoration project in which volunteers are removing exotic vegetation and replacing it with native plants such as dune sagebrush *(Artemisia pycnocephala)*, coast buckwheat *(Eriogonum latifolium)*, and sand verbena *(Abronia latifolia)*. One of the most thrilling aspects of the park is that hang gliders launch and land from there. To the observer who has never actually tried the sport, watching other human beings take off in flight is exhilarating.

The Coastal Trail (see the Richmond) and the much shorter Sunset Trail are the best way to take in the dramatic landscape, which includes beaches, 200-foot cliffs, and a WWII gun battery where 146-ton guns still point out to sea. During the early cold-war period, Nike missiles were kept where the parking lot is now. Obviously, after more than half a century of military use, Fort Funston is not a pristine preserve.

To get to Fort Funston you must drive, bike, or walk; follow the Great Hwy south and turn right on Skyline Blvd; the entrance to the park is past Lake Merced, on the right-hand side.

THE BAY

San Francisco is a contender for any 'city by the bay' beauty contest, but it's a curiously shy bay. San Francisco Bay is not a living, breathing part of the city, the way Sydney Harbor is, or even a working part of a hard-working city, as is Hong Kong Harbor. San Francisco Bay always seems to be around the corner, glimpsed in the distance, seen from afar, spanned by bridges, and dotted with sails and fast-moving ferries.

The bay is the largest on the California coast, stretching about 60 miles in length and up to 12 miles in width. It's fed by the Sacramento and San Joaquin Rivers and enters the ocean through the Golden Gate. It is, however, very shallow, averaging only 6 to 10 feet in depth at low tide. In the heyday of the ferries, before the bridges were built, the pier at Berkeley had to be built 3 miles out into the bay in order to reach water deep enough for the ferries to dock.

The shape of the bay has been radically altered by landfill. Since 1969 the Bay Conservation and Development Commission has put the brakes on any further landfill.

Golden Gate Bridge MAP 1

Fort Point Lookout Marine Dr ☎ 415-556-1693 ⓢ traveling southbound car $3, rush hour carpools free (5am-9am and 4pm-6pm with 3 or more passengers) ⏲ 24 hours 🚌 28, 29 Muni; Golden Gate Transit buses (see below for transportation details) ♿ w www.goldengate.org

Commenced in January 1933 and opened in May 1937, the beautiful Golden Gate Bridge links San Francisco with Marin County, and despite competition from modern constructions such as the Transamerica Pyramid, it remains the symbol of the city. The bridge is nearly 2 miles long, with a main span of 4200 feet. At the time of its completion, it was the longest suspension bridge in the world, and the 746-foot suspension towers were higher than any construction west of New York. The bridge tested the limits of Depression-era engineering, with the tricky harbor currents causing special difficulties. Joseph B Strauss, the bridge's builder, was a specialist in steel-bridge design who had built more than 400 bridges all over the world. The bridge's name comes from the nickname given the entrance to the harbor by early visitors, but its actual color is 'international orange.' Painting the bridge is a never-ending job. A team of 25 painters adds another thousand gallons every week.

A prime starting point for bridge appreciation is the Fort Point Lookout. The lookout offers excellent views and has a gift center, a statue of Strauss, and a sample of the 3-foot-thick suspension cable. There are even better views from the lookout at Vista Point, on the north side of the bridge, because from there San Francisco forms part of the backdrop.

It's estimated that more than 100,000 cars cross the bridge every day.

The 29 Muni runs to the lookout and the toll plaza; the 28 Muni runs just to the toll plaza. Any Golden Gate Transit bus bound for Marin County stops at the toll plaza as well. Unlike the Bay Bridge, the Golden Gate Bridge provides access to walkers and cyclists. From the Fort Point Lookout a pathway leads up to the toll plaza, and then it's a couple of miles across to the other side. If you're riding a bike, simply follow the 49-Mile Dr signs along Lincoln Blvd through the Presidio to the parking lot right before the toll plaza. Beyond the lot is a paved bike path, which begins just past a sign showing a map of Fort Point; it

Death at the Golden Gate

Eleven men died during construction of the Golden Gate Bridge, and it has continued to chalk up a steadily rising number of fatalities ever since: it is San Francisco's favorite suicide site.

It's a 220-foot drop from the bridge to the water. If the impact doesn't kill you immediately, the swift current will carry you out to sea, where a diver stunned by such a fall faces the likelihood of either drowning or being eaten by sharks. Despite these factors, some have survived bridge jumps, including an 18-year-old woman who jumped twice in 1988; she survived the first time but died on her second attempt two months later. At least one jumper wasn't attempting suicide: a German stunt man made the jump in 1980 intending to survive. He didn't.

According to the official count maintained by bridge authorities, the thousandth suicide made the leap sometime in 1995. (The authorities had stopped announcing the tally of suicides as it approached 1000, fearing there would be a rush to be the thousandth.) But no one will ever know exactly how many people have leaped over the orange fence: countless 'unofficial' suicides – those who disappeared, without witness, in the fog of the Golden Gate – have no doubt occurred over the years.

Since the 1950s, proponents for a suicide barrier have been unable to get a proposal past the bridge authorities, who maintain that the aesthetic appeal of the bridge should be preserved. Others, defending the right to die, have supported that argument. In the meantime, the only preventive measure to be installed on the bridge is a series of emergency telephones, which connect callers directly with crisis counselors. The phones went up in the highly publicized anticipation of the thousandth jumper.

Ironically, proponents of the suicide barrier once included the Rev Jim Jones, whose moving antisuicide speech in 1977 was undermined a year later, when Jones himself led a mass suicide in Guyana.

takes you under the bridge and around to the sidewalk on the westbound side, which is reserved for bikes only.

Bay Bridge MAP 1

$ westbound $2, rush hour carpools free (with 3 or more passengers; see Golden Gate Bridge, above, for hours) Buses that cross the Bay Bridge depart the Transbay Terminal

The Bay Bridge, connecting San Francisco and Oakland, is considerably longer than the Golden Gate Bridge, carries far more traffic, and predates it by six months, but it has never enjoyed the same iconic fame.

The Bay Bridge was built between April 1933 and November 1936 and actually consists of three separate parts: a double suspension bridge leads from San Francisco to the mid-bay Yerba Buena Island; a tunnel then cuts straight through the rocky island, and a series of latticework spans connects Yerba Buena Island to Oakland. The bridge spans 4½ miles of water.

The 1989 earthquake revealed that the bridge was not 100% earthquake-proof: a 50-foot piece of the top deck on the Yerba Buena–Oakland section slumped to the lower deck, killing a motorist. Like the Golden Gate Bridge, the San Francisco–Yerba Buena section of the Bay Bridge is pinned to solid rock, but the Oakland side is based on bay-bottom clay, not the best foundation when a temblor comes along. This stretch of bridge will be replaced eventually, and state transportation authorities went back and forth for quite some time, trying to settle on an appropriate design. In mid-1998, a single-tower suspension design was selected by Caltrans, the main state transportation authority, and although the decision was apparently final, several Bay Area mayors immediately began protesting the design, which from early models does not look nearly so striking as the bridge's San Francisco half.

The best views are from the top deck (westbound), which grants a nice view of the bay and downtown San Francisco. There's a toll westbound. During the morning and evening rush hours, a car with three occupants counts as a carpool and not only crosses free but also avoids the toll-booth lines.

Treasure Island MAP 1

108 Muni

The rock cut out from the Yerba Buena tunnel

RICHARD CUMMINS

Bay Bridge, from the Embarcadero

formed the basis of adjacent Treasure Island, which lies halfway between San Francisco and Oakland. Named after the Robert Louis Stevenson novel, the island was the site of the International Golden Gate Exposition of 1939–40, which celebrated the completion of the two bridges. Beginning with WWII, the islands were occupied by the US Navy and Coast Guard, which only recently departed. Civilians have begun to inhabit the island. There's a worthwhile museum (currently closed; see below) and superb views of the downtown skyline.

Treasure Island Museum

410 Palm Ave 108 Muni
w dictyon.com/treasure

This museum, which is currently closed, occupies an art moderne structure that went up for the Expo and was slated to become the terminal for San Francisco International Airport, which according to original plans would have been on the island. Following the US entry to WWII, the navy took over the island in exchange for land south of the city, which is where the airport is now.

This museum showcased the PanAm China Clippers that took off and landed on Treasure Island during the 1930s. There were also displays about the 1939–40 World's Exposition. Keep your ears to the ground for word on its reopening.

Alcatraz

☎ 415-705-5555 Blue & Gold Fleet Ferries
$ general $14.50, senior $13, ages 5-11 $9.50; evening tours: adult $22, senior/teen $19, 5-11 $13 ⏲ 9:30am-6:30pm daily summer, 9:30am-4:30pm winter; booking office 8am-5pm daily reservations required ♿ limited
w www.blueandgoldfleet.com

For 30 years, from 1933 to '63, the little rocky island in the middle of San Francisco Bay was the most famous prison in the US. The 12-acre island was named Isla de Alcatraces (Isle of the Pelicans) by Lieutenant Juan Manuel de Ayala, commander of the *San Carlos,* the first European vessel to enter the bay. It remained uninhabited until a military fortification was begun there in 1853 and a lighthouse was built in 1854. (The current lighthouse dates from 1909.) During the Civil War, the fort was used as a military prison.

RICK GERHARTER

'The Rock,' San Francisco's biggest tourist attraction

Alcatraz became the prison of choice for serious offenders for a simple reason – 'the Rock' was believed to be escape-proof, until the Anglin brothers and Frank Morris floated away in a raft they made in 1962 and were never seen again. That enigmatic escape was made famous by the 1979 movie *Escape from Alcatraz,* starring Clint Eastwood. Remarkably, Alcatraz was never packed to capacity; there were 450 cells, but the population averaged 264, and only 1576 convicts were imprisoned there over the island's entire penal history.

After its closure, the island was more or less forgotten for six years, and then it was taken over by Native Americans who conducted a protest sit-in from 1969 to 1971. Although the island has been a major tourist attraction since 1973, only basic repairs have been made to the prison buildings and discussion continues about the island's long-term future.

Al Capone spent 4½ years in Alcatraz, but the exact cell he occupied is not known. The tour does point out the cells occupied by other famous residents, such as 'Machine Gun' Kelly, the Anglin brothers (with replicas of the dummies they used to foil prison guards on the eve of their escape), and Robert Stroud, the so-called Birdman of Alcatraz.

It's said that Stroud, contrary to Burt Lancaster's big-screen depiction of him, was actually a thoroughly difficult person and spent most of his 17 years on the Rock in the unpleasant D-block solitary cells. During his lifetime, he was known as the 'Bird Doctor of Leavenworth,' referring to the federal penitentiary in Leavenworth, Kansas, where he'd kept canaries. Truth be told, Stroud wasn't allowed to keep birds after his transfer to Alcatraz in 1942.

The park ranger station has information on the island and its history; visit www.nps.gov/alcatraz

It's wise to phone ahead and book or pick up tickets well in advance, because the boats can be sold out days ahead of time in the summer. A 5pm evening tour is less crowded and is guided by a knowledgeable park ranger but costs an arm and a leg. Prices given above include ferry, phone order fee, and audio tour save up to $5 by purchasing tickets at Pier 41 and forgoing the audio tour.

Angel Island

Angel Island State Park

☎ *415-435-1915* Ⓢ *roundtrip adult $12, ages 6-12 $6.50, under 6 free* ⌚ *8am-sunset daily* ⛴ *Blue & Gold Fleet Ferry & Angel Island–Tiburon ferry*
w *www.angelisland.org*

Angel Island's mild Mediterranean-like climate and fresh ocean breezes make it a perfect bicycling spot, and spreading out a picnic in a protected cove overlooking the close but immeasurably distant urban surroundings is a unique treat. The island's varied history – it has served as a military base, an immigration station, a WWII Japanese internment camp, and a Nike missile site – has left it with some interesting and thought-provoking old forts and bunkers to poke around in. Most recently it has been the site of a native-plant restoration project.

There are 12 miles of roads and trails around the island, including a hike to the summit of 781-foot Mt Livermore (no bikes) and a 5-mile perimeter trail. On weekends and holidays, the Immigration Station, which operated from 1910 to 1940, is open and staffed with docents. Camp Reynolds, the East Garrison Chapel, and the Guard House at Fort McDowell offer guided tours. At 1pm and 2pm a Civil War cannon is fired from the shore near Camp Reynolds.

There are nine campsites on the island (see Places to Stay). The *Cove Café* at Ayala Cove, where the ferries dock, has limited choices; bring everything you might need – it is an island, after all. You can also rent bicycles at Ayala Cove for $10 an hour or $25 for the day, and there are tram tours around the island from May to September.

You can reach Angel Island by ferry from either Fisherman's Wharf, in San Francisco, or from Tiburon in Marin County, on the opposite side of the bay.

Cove Café
Ayala Cove ☎ 415-435-0358 ⏲ 8am-sunset daily Sat-Sun Apr-Nov Ⓒ cash only ⛴ Blue & Gold Fleet Ferry ♿

This café has limited food and ice cream choices.

Tram tours
☎ 415-897-0715 $ adult $11.50, senior $10.50, ages 6-12 $7.50 ⏲ 10:30am, 12:15pm, 1:30pm daily May-Sep & 3:15pm Sat-Sun year-round

One-hour tram tours are a relaxed way to explore the island's military history and cultural past.

Sea Trek
☎ 415-488-1000 $ 2½-hr tour $75, all-day tour $130 ⏲ 10am-4pm daily
W www.seatrekkayak.com

You can explore Angel Island from the unique perspective of a stable, two-person sea kayak. Guided tours last 2½ hours or all day; reservations are essential.

Blue & Gold Fleet Ferries MAP 8
☎ 415-705-5555 $ roundtrip adult $12, ages 5-12 $6.50, under 6 free ⏲ call or check website for departure times 🚌 32, F Muni ♿
W www.blueandgoldfleet.com

A Blue & Gold Fleet Ferry leaves from San Francisco's Pier 41 two or three times daily.

Angel Island–Tiburon Ferry
21 Main St ☎ 415-435-2131 $ adult $5.50, child $4.50 ⏲ call or check website for departure times ♿
W www.angelislandferry.com

The ferry from Tiburon to Angel Island runs several times a day, more frequently than the ferry from San Francisco to the island.

ACTIVITIES

San Franciscans are an energetic lot, and there are plenty of opportunities to burn calories even within the city limits.

Bicycling

If the city's contours are more of a challenge than even many local bicyclists care to take on (although, of course, a good many San Franciscans are *not* deterred by 10% grades), the more common complaint is automobile traffic. The city seems to have a lot more motorists than it did even five years ago, and, of course, more cars means a lot more tension on the roads for drivers and bicyclists alike. To avoid the hazards, head to Golden Gate Park or the Presidio. For the clearest evidence that this is a bicycling city, join Critical Mass on the last Friday of the month (see the boxed text 'Critical Mass' in Getting Around).

Marin County, just across the Golden Gate Bridge from the city, is much more attractive for cyclists – it is, after all, the birthplace of mountain biking. A classic San Francisco ride takes you across the bridge to the Marin Headlands. You can also take your bike on the ferry to Tiburon, Angel Island, or within riding distance of Mt Tam – the Bay Area's supreme mountain-biking challenge. See Excursions for more information.

There are several good books for Bay Area cyclists, including *Bay Area Bike Rides,* by Ray Hosler (1994), and *Cycling the San Francisco Bay Area: 30 Rides to Historic Sites and Scenic Places,* by Carol O'Hare (1993). For information on renting a bicycle, see Getting Around.

Golf

There are three public golf courses in San Francisco; if you're economizing, most of them have twilight fees.

Harding Park MAP 1
cnr Harding Rd and Skyline Blvd ☎ 415-664-4690 $ Mon-Fri $26, Sat-Sun $31; 9-hole course $13 ⏲ 6:30am-7pm daily 🚌 18 Muni

This is a beautiful 18-hole course near the ocean. Also on the site is the Jack Fleming nine-hole course.

Lincoln Park course MAP 15
34th Ave and Clement St ☎ 415-750-4653 $ Mon-Fri $23, Sat-Sun $27 ⏲ sunrise-sunset daily 🚌 18 Muni

For spectacular views, the hilly, 18-hole Lincoln Park course wraps around the California

Palace of the Legion of Honor and runs along the coast west of the Golden Gate Bridge.

Golden Gate Park course MAP 15
John F Kennedy Dr and 47th Ave ☎ 415-750-4653 ⓢ Mon-Fri $8, Sat-Sun $11 ⏲ 6am-8pm Mon-Fri 🚌 5 Muni

Golden Gate Park has a challenging nine-hole, par-27 course.

Presidio Golf Course MAP 16
☎ 415-561-4653 ⓢ without cart Mon-Fri $35, without cart after 3pm Mon-Fri $25, without cart Sat-Sun $55, without cart after 3pm Sat-Sun $35 ⏲ sunrise-sunset daily 🚌 28 Muni

In the summer of 1995, this golf course opened to the public after a century of exclusive use by US military personnel. Now operated by the National Park Service, the gorgeous course runs along the bay and is considered one of the country's best. Book far in advance.

Mission Bay Golf Center MAP 4
1200 6th St ☎ 415-431-7888 ⏲ 7am-11pm daily ♿

You can hit a bucket of balls into the twilight here.

Running & Skating

In San Francisco, **Marina Green (Map 9)** has a 2½-mile jogging track and fitness course, and there are many running paths through **Golden Gate Park (Map 15)**. There are a couple of routes all the way from the Panhandle to the ocean, covering about 3 miles, and on Sunday motor vehicles are banned from a good part of John F Kennedy Dr. **The Presidio (Map 16)** is another great park for running.

Bay to Breakers
☎ 415-808-5000 ext 2222 ⓢ adult $25, child $20 Ⓜ Embarcadero BART & Muni station
W www.baytobreakers.com

The race, held in May, is as much a festival as a run, with tens of thousands of often wildly costumed participants making their way from the Embarcadero across the city to the ocean.

Skates on Haight MAP 11
1818 Haight St ☎ 415-752-8375 ⓢ skate rental: $6/hour, $24/day ⏲ 11am-7pm Mon-Fri, 10am-6pm Sat-Sun 🚌 33, 43 Muni ♿
W www.skates.com

MORGAN KONN

Some of the less debaucherous Bay to Breakers participants

You can rent skates here and cruise directly into Golden Gate Park, half a block away.

Sailing & Windsurfing

Any view of the bay, dotted with sails in every season, shows this is prime sailing country. It's not, however, the easiest stretch of water to sail on, and much of the year the wind can be as chilly as the water. It's also extremely important to pay attention to the tides. If you go out in a small boat at ebb tide, you might just find yourself waving goodbye to San Francisco as you're sucked out to sea. The bay is at its best from April through August, when the west winds blow.

Spinnaker Sailing MAP 4
Pier 40 ☎ 415-543-7333 ⓢ sunset cruise $25, brunch cruise $40, sailing lessons $295 ⏲ 10am-5pm daily 🚌 32 Muni ♿
W www.spinnaker-sailing.com

The easiest way to get out on the water – in a snazzy old brigantine, no less – is to take one of the cruises offered by this company. It also offers sailing lessons.

Swimming & Surfing

The sunny California image does not apply to San Francisco. The waters in the Bay Area, bay side or ocean side, are cold and plagued with currents. Swimming is often unsafe and never very pleasant. Walking, jogging, and sunbathing (buck naked in some areas) are the popular shoreline activities.

There's a tiny patch of beach at Aquatic Park, just west of Fisherman's Wharf, where you often see hardy swimmers in the chilly waters.

Each year in July, the truly hardy are ferried out to Alcatraz Island, where they dive into the water and make the 1½-mile swim to Aquatic Park. Entry to this event, officially called the Alcatraz Sharkfest Swim, costs $60 to $75. Reserve a spot at least a month in advance.

Envirosports
PO Box 1040, Stinson Beach, CA, 94970
☎ 415-868-1829 $ $60-75
w www.envirosports.com

Contact Envirosports for race information and registration forms for the Alcatraz Sharkfest Swim.

Baker Beach, on the ocean immediately south of the Golden Gate Bridge, is popular with sunbathers, walkers, and surf fishers; nudists lay out at the northern (Presidio) end. There are great views from China Beach, south of Baker Beach, and more nudity at the tiny beach below Lands End.

Past Point Lobos is Ocean Beach, starting at Geary Blvd just north of Golden Gate Park, and heading south for 4 miles. Swimming there is not advised. Ocean Beach is one of the most challenging and exhausting places to surf in California, especially in winter, when the powerful, cold swells can reach 12 feet or more. There are no lifeguards, and you should never surf alone or without at least a 3mm full-length wetsuit.

Wise Surfing
☎ 415-665-9473 ⌚ 24 hours

For a recorded message of the latest surfing conditions at Ocean Beach, call Wise Surfing.

Bowling

To partake in one of the world's least rigorous sports and revel in the sound of ricocheting pins, head to the Presidio.

The Presidio Bowling Center
Montgomery St ☎ 415-561-2695 $ rates vary ⌚ 9am-midnight Sun-Thurs, 9am-2am Fri-Sat 🚌 42 Muni ♿

Tennis

There are free public tennis courts all over San Francisco. The courts at **Mission Dolores Park (Map 14)** are popular.

San Francisco Recreation & Park Dept
☎ 415-831-2700 ⌚ 9am-5pm daily
w parks.sfgov.org

For other free public tennis courts, call the San Francisco Recreation & Park Dept or check its website.

The 21 courts in **Golden Gate Park (Map 15)** charge a fee.

Walking Tours

Many neighborhood experts guide walks, and their tours are as varied as the city's parts.

Chinese Heritage Walk & Chinese Culinary Walk and Luncheon
Chinese Culture Center, 750 Kearny St (Map 5) ☎ 415-986-1822 $ Chinese Heritage Walk $15, Chinese Culinary Walk and Luncheon $30 ⌚ 10am-4pm Tues-Sat, noon-4pm Sun 🚌 15 Muni ♿
w www.c-c-c.org

You can tag along on a Chinese Heritage Walk (Saturday afternoon) or a Chinese Culinary Walk and Luncheon (Friday morning) from the Chinese Culture Center.

Mission District Mural Walk
Precita Eyes Mural Arts Center, 2981 24th St (Map 14) ☎ 415-285-2287 $ tours: adult $10, senior $5, under 18 $2 ⌚ 10am-5pm Mon-Fri, 10am-4pm Sat, noon-4pm Sun 🚌 48 Muni ♿
w www.precitaeyes.org

Precita Eyes conducts the Mission District Mural Walk. The Saturday afternoon walk is led by a muralist, lasts two hours, and takes in some 75 murals.

Cruisin' the Castro
375 Lexington St; tours meet at Harvey Milk Plaza, cnr Market and Castro (Map 12) ☎ 415-550-8110 $ $40 includes brunch ⌚ 10am Tues-Sat & most holidays Ⓜ Castro St Muni station 🚌 37, F Muni
w www.webcastro.com/castrotour

For history and a behind-the-scenes peek into San Francisco's gay mecca, try Cruisin' the Castro, a four-hour walk led by local resident Trevor Hailey. Reservations required.

Victorian Home Walk
Meet at Westin St Francis Hotel lobby, cnr Powell and Geary (Map 2) ☎ 415-252-9485 $ $20 ⌚ 11am daily 🚌 38, 76 Muni 🚋 Powell-Mason cable car w www.victorianwalk.com

This 2½-hour walk tours Pacific Heights and Cow Hollow. The guide discusses the architectural details that distinguish Victorian houses and enters some of the homes.

Haight-Ashbury Flower Power Walking Tour
Meet in front of New Main Library, 100 Larkin St (Map 3) ☎ 415-863-1621 $ $15 ⌚ 9:30am Tues & Sat

This 2½-hour walking tour points out all the spots where the '60s flowered. Call to reserve.

Dashiell Hammett Tour
Meet at northwest cnr of New Main Library, 100 Larkin St (Map 3) ☎ 510-287-9540 $ $10 ⌚ noon Sat spring & summer M Civic Center BART; Van Ness & Civic Center Muni stations 🚌 5, 6, 19, 21, 47, 49 Muni w www.donherron.com

One of San Francisco's best-known walks is led by author Don Herron. The four-hour tour gumshoes up and down the streets of the Tenderloin and Union Square, sniffing clues left by the great crime fiction writer Dashiell Hammett. You can't make reservations; just show up or call to schedule a tour.

San Francisco Public Library MAP 3
100 Larkin St ☎ 415-557-4266 $ free ⌚ tour times vary M Civic Center BART; Van Ness & Civic Center Muni stations 🚌 5, 6, 19, 21, 47, 49 Muni w www.sfpl.lib.ca.us

The library offers an eclectic variety of walking tours led by savvy local historians. Possibilities include the Art Deco Marina Tour, Victorian San Francisco, Cityscapes and Roof Gardens, and Coit Tower Murals. Check out the website for more information.

Whale Watching

Mid-October through December is the peak season for whale watching in the Bay Area, as gray whales make their annual migration south from the Bering Sea to Baja California. It's the longest annual mammal migration in the world, and because the whales tend to cruise along the coastline, they're easy to spot from land. Point Reyes, to the north, is a prime whale-watching spot. The whales pass by on their way home in March but are farther from shore on the northward leg of the journey.

Oceanic Society Expeditions
Fort Mason Center, Building A (Map 9) ☎ 415-474-3385 $ whale-watching cruise $48-52/person, to Farallon Islands $60-65 ⌚ 8:30am-4:30pm Fri-Mon 🚌 28 w www.oceanic-society.org

The Oceanic Society runs boats out on the ocean – sometimes to the Farallon Islands – during both migration seasons. They depart from Fort Mason, and tours last all day. Kids must be 10 or older. Reservations are required.

Places to Stay

San Francisco has the full range of accommodations, from exorbitant presidential suites to bug-ridden flops. We'll assume readers of this book have their sights set somewhere between those parameters and dispense with the extremes.

What you get for $60 a night in San Francisco won't measure up to what $60 gets you in, say, Portland, Oregon. Considering what property values are in the city these days, it's miraculous that some hotels can still offer rooms at $40. We list a few that we find acceptable, but bear in mind that your sense of good fortune at finding such a sweet deal may diminish during your stay. Service may be indifferent; nighttime street noise might be worse than imagined. But such accommodations might suit you just fine.

Also beware that the city takes an additional bite out of your pocketbook with a hefty 14% room tax on top of the quoted rates. (Hostels are exempt.) Absurd fees for making local calls from your room can add another hidden cost. Make your first call to the front desk, and ask what outside calls will cost you. You're often better off going downstairs to a pay phone.

Apart from the numerous backpacker hostels, the categories in this chapter are divided by neighborhood. But first, we offer a brief description of your options.

CAMPING Camping choices in San Francisco proper are limited to two group sites in the Presidio that are often booked as early as a year in advance. Angel Island, with stunning nighttime views of the city and of shipping traffic in the bay, is equally popular. The selection broadens considerably once you start considering Marin County, north of the Golden Gate, or the peninsula, toward Half Moon Bay. See Excursions for additional listings.

HOSTELS San Francisco has a surprising number of hostels, some of them quite central. The level of guest satisfaction seems to vary, however. Lonely Planet receives a lot of angry mail from unhappy hostel guests, whose complaints range from bed bugs to grumpy service to humping bunkmates making it impossible to sleep. Of course, the happy customer is less likely to write, so when we checked out the hostels listed in this chapter, we tried to keep an open mind. But the unfortunate truth is that when you're looking for cheap digs, your own attitude often has as much to do with how comfortable you will be. For the price, your only other option is a room on skid row.

Hostelling International (HI) is the long-term survivor of the hostel business, and in San Francisco the two best hostels are run by this organization. You don't have to be an HI member to stay in the hostels, although membership ($25 a year in the US) gives you a discount and other advantages. The city's other hostels are independents.

Many hostels offer kitchen and laundry facilities, meeting rooms, TV lounges, and other useful conveniences. Their notice boards can be great sources of local information and travel hints. A bed in a hostel typically costs $18 to $20 and may be in a dormitory (with four to eight beds) or a double room. In San Francisco, resident laws force hostels to maintain a two-week limit on stays – that's two weeks *per year.* For longer stays, you'll have to move around a bit.

HOTELS There are inexpensive hotels in San Francisco, but the cheapest places are no fun at all. If you're really economizing, you'll find the hostels are a better bet. That said, safe, comfortable hotels can cost as little as $40 to $100 for a double. Mid-range hotels run $100 to $200, and once you get over $200 a night, you're in the 'top end' category.

MOTELS A city motel room typically costs $50 to $100. There are some convenient ones South of Market just a short stroll from Union Square, in the Fisherman's Wharf area, and along Lombard St in the

Marina. The big advantage of these motels is the free parking they offer – a great incentive if you're traveling by car. Consider that overnight parking in city garages can cost $30 or so a night!

B&Bs San Francisco has lots of comfortable and romantic B&Bs, with prices for two typically ranging from $80 to $150. A reservations network exists that can make finding a B&B easier for you.

Bed & Breakfast Reservations
PO Box 282910 ☎ 415-696-1690, 800-872-4500 c cash only

Bed & Breakfast Reservations can make free bookings at B&Bs throughout California.

CAMPING

Camping in the Presidio or on Angel Island is an unforgettable experience. It will either be a jolly night of campfires, barbecue, booze, and song, or of bone-chilling winds that prohibit fires and force you and your friends to huddle up for warmth and to prevent the tents from blowing away, in which case your memories won't be so positive.

Rob Hill Campground MAP 16
Washington St ☎ 415-561-5444
$ $10/night high season, $7 low season
c cash only year-round 27 Muni
w www.nps.gov/prsf

To stay a night in the Presidio, you'll have to assemble a group, make your plans and reservations way ahead, and be flexible enough to take what's available. There are only two sites, both accommodating groups of up to 30 people.

Angel Island Camp Sites (ParkNet)
☎ 800-444-7275 $ $10/night high season, $7 low season c cash only Blue & Gold Fleet Ferry from Pier 41 2 or 3 times daily; also from Tiburon in Marin County
w www.angelisland.org

Angel Island's nine campsites accommodate up to eight people. Sites 4, 5, and 6 offer spectacular views of San Francisco at night. All sites are 2 miles from the ferry launch, so pack only what you can carry in on your back. Wood fires are not permitted.

HOSTELS

General information about hostels here and elsewhere can be found on the Web at www.hostels.com.

Reservation Services & Discounts

Hotel reservation services are a convenient way to shop for mid-range rooms, simplifying what would otherwise require multiple phone calls. Some also serve as clearinghouses for hotel bookings during low-occupancy periods, in which case they can offer lower rates than the hotel would quote you. If you are flexible, you might be able to save big bucks on rooms that are generally priced out of your range. The service is free to the customer, but sometimes prepayment is required, and cancellation fees may apply.

User-friendly websites are becoming an increasingly popular way to choose your accommodations. You can cross-check between the hotel reviews in this book and the up-to-date (or discounted) rates available on the Web. Or call to get personable attention. Some of the following companies can reserve rooms in several hundred hotels.

Topaz Hotel Services
360 22nd St, Suite 300, Oakland, CA 94612 ☎ 510-628-4440, 800-677-1550 c AE, D, DC, JCB, MC, V w www.hotelres.com

WorldRes, Inc
1510 Fashion Island Blvd, Suite 100, San Mateo, CA 94404 ☎ 650-372-1705 c AE, D, MC, V w www.placestostay.com

Turbo Trip
☎ 504-522-9234, 800-473-7829 c AE, D, MC, V w www.turbotrip.com

Hostel at Union Square MAP 2
312 Mason St ☎ 415-788-5604 $ $22/person members, $25/person nonmembers C *V, MC* 🚌 *5, 21, 38, F Muni* ♿
W *www.norcalhostels.org*

The main HI hostel's location, just a block from Union Square, is one that five-star hotels would kill for. It has 230 beds divided between dorms and double rooms. Dorms sleep three to six. The double rooms are available at the same per-person rates. Reservations are not accepted for beds or rooms, so at busy times there's always the chance you will show up only to find there's no room for you. When we dropped by, the hostel appeared to be efficiently run, but some guests have complained about bugs and unpleasant staff.

Globetrotters Inn MAP 2
225 Ellis St ☎ 415-346-5786 $ private rooms $27/person, dorms $15/person
C *cash only* M *Powell St BART & Muni station* 🚌 *5, 21, 38, F Muni*
e *globetrottersinn@yahoo.com*

This place is just around the corner from the HI hostel. Accommodations in this smaller, slightly run-down hostel are either in dorms for four or in private rooms. If you arrive by Greyhound, take a No 38 Muni bus from the Transbay Terminal and get off at Mason. If you arrive by Amtrak, take the free shuttle to the Ferry Building and a No 5 or 21 Muni bus, or an F streetcar, up Market St to Mason, then walk 3 blocks north.

New Central Hotel & Hostel MAP 3
1412 Market St ☎ 415-703-9988 $ singles $35/night shared bath, $45/night private bath, $230/week shared bath, $300/week private bath; doubles $45/night shared bath, $55/night private bath; dorms $17/night, $105/week C *V, MC, AE, DC, D* M *Civic Center BART & Muni station* 🚌 *Market St buses, F Muni*

New Central offers a variety of rooms and dorms. Guests must be able to show a passport or proof of travel. Linens are included, and guests can use the kitchen. There's no curfew.

San Francisco International Student Center MAP 4
1188 Folsom St ☎ 415-255-8800 $ dorms $15-17/night, $90/week C *cash only* 🚌 *12, 19 Muni*

Upstairs from the Cat Club, this small hostel (50 beds) may suffer from the occasional drum 'n' bass vibration. That shouldn't be a problem for clubhoppers, though. There are kitchen facilities – including a fridge and a microwave – and clean showers. Travelers must show a passport or student ID.

Globe Hostel MAP 4
10 Hallam St ☎ 415-431-0540
$ *singles/doubles $47 low season, dorms $19* C *cash only* 🚌 *12, 14 Muni*

This is a big hostel in the heart of the SoMa clubland (there's no curfew). The building overlooks Folsom St, but the entrance is on Hallam, a small side street. Well run and friendly, the rooms are surprisingly quiet. The hostel attracts an international crowd, and Americans wanting to stay here must show proof of travel plans. The dorm rooms (five beds) all have attached baths. Off-season, five of the rooms are rearranged to be private double rooms. There's a laundry, TV room, sun deck, café, and an Irish bar on the corner, but there's no kitchen. From the Transbay Terminal, take a No 12 Muni bus up Howard St and walk a block south to Folsom on 7th St or take a No 14 Muni bus up Mission St and walk 2 blocks south on 7th.

SoMa Inn MAP 4
1080 Folsom St ☎ 415-863-7522 $ singles $35/night, $175/week; doubles $49/night, $199/week; dorms $20/night, $100/week
C *V, MC, AE, D, DC* 🚌 *12, 19 Muni*

This is basically a flophouse – nothing fancy or particularly comfortable, but if you need a place to stay South of Market, try it. The desk is attended 24 hours, and there's no curfew.

Pacific Tradewinds Guest House MAP 5
680 Sacramento St ☎ 415-433-7970 $ $18-20/night, $108-120/week C *V, MC* 🚌 *1, 15 Muni* 🚋 *California St cable car*
W *www.hostels.com/pt*

In the fuzzy zone where Chinatown descends into the Financial District, this is the friendliest of the city hostels. This well-maintained 4th-floor hostel has four to eight bunks in dorms – no private rooms – and there's a fully equipped kitchen. Its social room is a great place to meet other travelers, and the owner, Darren Overby, is a wealth of information on the city (he also keeps files on California excursions). Guests can take advantage of free DSL internet access.

Green Tortoise Hostel MAP 6
494 Broadway ☎ 415-834-1000 $ singles/doubles $48, triples $56, quads $58,

dorms $19-22 Ⓒ *V, MC, AE, D* 🚌 *15 Muni*
Ⓦ *www.greentortoise.com*

On Broadway, North Beach's seedy strip-joint strip, this medium-size hostel is actually a clean and safe place to stay, and the street activity poses no real threat. The hostel is run by the same people who run those funky buses, so expect similarly relaxed, slightly offbeat accommodations here. It's just around the corner from scores of bars, restaurants, and cafés, and there's no curfew. Dorms have three to eight beds. There's free breakfast and free internet access, and a kitchen, laundry, and sauna are available. Luggage storage, lockers, and linen cost extra.

San Francisco International Hostel MAP 9
Fort Mason, Building 240 ☎ *415-771-7277*
Ⓢ *$21-23* Ⓒ *V, MC, JCB* 🚌 *30, 42, 47 Muni*
Ⓦ *www.norcalhostels.org*

This second HI hostel trades downtown convenience for a pleasantly quiet setting. However, dorms range from a manageable four beds to a whopping 24 beds, and some of the rooms are unisex. There's no curfew, but there is limited daytime access to the dorms. Limited free parking is available. Take Muni bus No 42 from the Transbay Terminal to the stop at Bay St and Van Ness Ave. Bus Nos 30 and 47 also stop there.

HOTELS, MOTELS & B&Bs

Union Square

For urban accommodations that won't blow your budget, Union Square, the Theater District, and the Tender Nob area are the places to look. You'll find youth-oriented pensiones in the Tender Nob and a number of 'designer'-type hotels scattered throughout the area.

BUDGET The area to the west of Union Square has San Francisco's greatest density of hotels, and along with the five-star luxury and mid-range hotels are some real bargains.

Grant Hotel MAP 2
753 Bush St ☎ *415-421-7540, 800-522-0979* Ⓢ *singles $49-60, doubles $49-80*
Ⓒ *V, MC, AE* Ⓜ *Powell St BART & Muni station* 🚌 *2, 3, 4, 76 Muni*
Ⓦ *www.granthotel.citysearch.com*

The Grant Hotel is another basic low-priced hotel, offering clean, simple accommodations. All rooms have private bathrooms. Service can be indifferent, depending on who's at the desk.

Adelaide Inn MAP 2
5 Isadora Duncan Lane ☎ *415-441-2261*
Ⓢ *singles $50, doubles $64* Ⓒ *AE, D, MC, V*
🚌 *27, 38, 76 Muni*

On a mysterious little alley, Adelaide Inn is an 18-room pensione that appeals to foreign visitors. Rooms have a shared bath, and prices vary depending on the room size and demand. A continental breakfast is included.

Foley's Inn MAP 2
235 O'Farrell St ☎ *415-397-7800* Ⓢ *singles $55-65 shared bath, $85-135 private bath; doubles $65-75 shared bath, $95-145 private bath; triples $125-165 private bath*
Ⓒ *V, MC, D* Ⓜ *Powell St BART & Muni station* 🚌 *Market St buses*
Ⓦ *www.foleysinn.com*

Foley's Inn, until recently a residence hotel, proclaims a modest but noble objective of offering affordable rooms in an expensive neighborhood. There's nothing fancy about the place – in fact, it appears to still have some permanent lodgers. But it's very central and the rooms we saw were decent. And one of the city's best fake Irish pubs is downstairs.

Herbert Hotel MAP 2
161 Powell St ☎ *415-362-1600* Ⓢ *singles $55-65 shared bath, $85-135 private bath; doubles $65-75 shared bath, $95-145 private bath; triples $125-165 private bath; quads $135-205 private bath* Ⓒ *V, MC, D* Ⓜ *Powell St BART & Muni station* 🚌 *38 Muni*
🚋 *Powell-Mason, Powell-Hyde cable cars*
Ⓦ *www.herberthotel.com*

A block south of Union Square, this hotel is about as cheap as they come. It's very basic, with no extra services, but the rooms are acceptable for the price.

Stratford Hotel MAP 2
242 Powell St ☎ *415-397-7080, 888-504-6835* Ⓢ *singles $55-70 shared bath, $89-119 private bath; doubles $55-70 shared bath, $89-145 private bath; family rooms $135-189* Ⓒ *V, MC, AE, D, DC* Ⓜ *Powell St BART & Muni station* 🚌 *38 Muni* 🚋 *Powell-Mason, Powell-Hyde cable cars*
Ⓦ *www.stratfordhotel.com*

Rooms here are cheap and basic – a very good value if location is a high priority. A free continental breakfast is served in the hotel's modest tearoom.

Sheehan Hotel MAP 2
620 Sutter St ☎ 415-775-6500, 800-848-1529 $ singles/doubles $65-99 shared bath, singles $89-109 private bath, doubles $99-169 private bath, triples $109-179 c V, MC, AE, D, DC, JCB bus 2, 3, 4, 76 Muni ♿ limited
w www.sheehanhotel.com

This 64-room hotel occupies a former YMCA building, and as a result it has good fitness facilities and an indoor swimming pool, unique among the city's lower-priced hotels. Otherwise, rooms are very basic but comfortable. Most rooms have private bath. Prices include a continental breakfast.

Mosser's Victorian Hotel MAP 2
54 4th St ☎ 415-986-4400, 800-227-3804 $ singles/doubles $69-89 shared bath, $129-209 private bath; triples $145-225 c V, MC, AE, D, DC M Powell St BART & Muni station bus Market St buses, 30 Muni
w www.victorianhotel.com

This elegant old hotel has basic rooms, some with shared bath at a reduced rate. It's not far from the Union Square shops, Yerba Buena museums, and Market St transit. Continental breakfast is included.

Dakota Hotel MAP 2
606 Post St ☎ 415-931-7475 $ singles $79, doubles $89-119, $395 week c V, MC M Powell St BART & Muni station bus 27, 38 Muni
e dakota606@hotmail.com

This is a small, very basic 40-room hotel from the 1920s. The elevator is a tribute to early-20th-century ingenuity, and rooms are equipped with steam radiators and claw-foot tubs. In some, you can still see where, long ago, Murphy beds – those ingenious contraptions that could be swung back into a wall during the day – were once bolted in. Modern amenities, such as cable TV, microwaves, and refrigerators, are also available. Modest renovation in recent years has brightened the place up a bit, but rates remain reasonable.

Golden Gate Hotel MAP 2
775 Bush St ☎ 415-392-3702 $ $78-85 shared bath, $115-130 private bath c V, MC M Powell St BART & Muni station bus 2, 3, 4, 76 Muni
w www.goldengatehotel.com

The Golden Gate is a friendly family-run hotel in a well-maintained old building. Rooms are small but clean and comfortable, and those that lack a private bath still come equipped with sink. Continental breakfast and afternoon tea reflect the establishment's simple hospitality.

Biltmore Hotel MAP 2
735 Taylor St ☎ 415-673-4277 $ singles $79-89, $425-525/week; doubles $89-99, $500-700/week; triples $99-109; quads $109-119 c V, MC, AE bus 2, 3, 4, 76 Muni
w www.biltmoresf.com

Under the same management as the Amsterdam Hotel, the Biltmore offers very similar amenities – it's an old building on the outside, with modest remodeled rooms on the inside – at a slightly lower price.

Halcyon Hotel MAP 2
649 Jones St ☎ 415-929-8033, 800-627-2396 $ $90-139, $540/week c V, MC, AE bus 2, 3, 4, 38, 76 Muni
w www.halcyonsf.com

This is a friendly little 25-room establishment. It's not fancy, but it is a great value, as each room has its own private bathroom and a little kitchen, local telephone calls are free, dataports are available, and the hotel has laundry facilities. Phone ahead, because the office is open for limited hours only and you may not be able to get in if they're not expecting you. In summer, only nightly rates are offered.

Alisa Hotel MAP 2
447 Bush St ☎ 415-956-3232, 800-956-4322 $ $89 shared bath, $159 private bath c V, MC bus 15 Muni cable car California St cable car
w www.alisahotel.com

This is an unpretentious hotel near Chinatown and Union Square. Rooms are clean and comfortable but on the small side.

Amsterdam Hotel MAP 2
749 Taylor St ☎ 415-673-3277, 800-637-3444 $ singles $99-129, $450/week; doubles $109-149; triples $119-159; quads $129-169 c V, MC, AE bus 2, 3, 4, 76 Muni

Built in 1909, the Amsterdam draws an international crowd looking for comfortable but not stylish accommodations. Rooms have remodeled bathrooms.

Mary Elizabeth Inn MAP 2
1040 Bush St ☎ 415-673-6768 c cash only bus 27 Muni

At press time, this women-only hotel, run by the United Methodist Church, was closed for renovation. It was due to reopen sometime in 2002. When we last visited, it had decent rooms at very reasonable prices. Call to ask about current rates.

If you find yourself in a pinch, there are a number of weekly/monthly hotels that stretch for several blocks on O'Farrell St; they're in passable condition and charge reasonable rates. But you wouldn't want to book in one without first checking out the room.

MID-RANGE Post St runs past the north side of Union Square, Geary St runs past the south, and many excellent mid-range hotels lie in the blocks to the west.

Hotel Bijou MAP 2
111 Mason St ☎ 415-771-1200, 800-771-1022 Ⓢ singles/doubles $109-179, triples $119-189 Ⓒ V, MC, AE, D, DC, JCB Ⓜ Powell St BART & Muni station 27, 31, N Muni ♿
w *www.hotelbijou.com*

A short block from Hallidie Plaza, Hotel Bijou stands out among the strip joints and peepshow parlors down the street. This is a 'budget' designer hotel with a cinematic theme – videos of films set in San Francisco screen nightly in a small art deco–style theater just off the lobby. Service is friendly and the rooms are neat and comfortable, though a bit gaudy in decore.

Hotel Beresford Arms MAP 2
701 Post St ☎ 415-673-2600, 800-533-6533 Ⓢ singles $135, doubles $145, triples $155, suites with Jacuzzi $169-199 Ⓒ V, MC, AE, D, DC, JCB 2, 3, 4, 27, 76 Muni ♿ roll-in shower
w *www.beresfordsfo.com*

The Beresford Arms is a well-kept 96-room hotel that has retained some of its antiquated charm without sacrificing comfort. Rooms are spacious and smartly furnished, and some of the suites have kitchens and Jacuzzis. You can breakfast on coffee and pastries in the lobby, and there's afternoon wine in the elegant lobby.

Hotel Beresford MAP 2
635 Sutter St ☎ 415-673-9900, 800-533-6533 Ⓢ singles $135, doubles/triples $145, quads $155 Ⓒ V, MC, AE, D, DC, JCB 2, 3, 4, 76 Muni ♿ limited
w *www.beresford.com*

This hotel of 114 rooms is the sister establishment to Hotel Beresford Arms and only a block from Union Square. Rooms are easy on the eyes, service is friendly, and the downstairs pub is an easygoing spot for a pint.

Maxwell Hotel MAP 2
386 Geary St ☎ 415-986-2000, 888-734-6299 Ⓢ $160-215 Ⓒ V, MC, AE, D, DC, JCB 38 Muni Powell-Mason, Powell-Hyde cable cars ♿
w *www.maxwellhotel.com*

This smartly restored 1908 hotel is part of the Joie de Vivre chain, which turns faded hotels into hip and lively places to stay. Rooms here are designed with a theatrical theme, playing on the proximity of the theater district.

York Hotel MAP 2
940 Sutter St ☎ 415-885-6800, 800-808-9675 Ⓢ singles/doubles $129-189, triples $145-205 Ⓒ V, MC, AE, DC, D, JCB 27, 76 Muni ♿
w *www.yorkhotel.com*

If this sharp 96-room hotel looks familiar, perhaps you recall scenes from Alfred Hitchcock's *Vertigo* that were shot here. (Nobody fell out any windows.) The York's opulent lobby and swanky Plush Room bar belie the understated elegance of the rooms upstairs. Modern accoutrements include an exercise facility and modem access.

Commodore Hotel MAP 2
825 Sutter St ☎ 415-923-6800, 800-338-6848 Ⓢ singles/doubles $139-179, triples $149-189 Ⓒ V, MC, AE, DC, D, JCB 2, 3, 4, 76 Muni
w *www.thecommodorehotel.com*

This restored hotel is a strikingly hip property that plays on an art deco steamship aesthetic. Rooms are custom furnished and comfortable, and the kitschy lobby, while not very conducive to lounging, yields to the hot little Red Room bar on one side and to the Titanic Cafe, a breakfast and lunch counter, on the other.

Cartwright Hotel MAP 2
524 Sutter St ☎ 415-421-2865, 800-227-3844 Ⓢ singles/doubles $139-199, suites $239-299 Ⓒ V, MC, AE, D, DC 2, 3, 4, 76 Muni Powell-Mason, Powell-Hyde cable cars
w *www.cartwrighthotel.com*

Attractive rooms, excellent service, and a convenient location (just a block from Union Square) make this a good value.

Hotel Union Square MAP 2
114 Powell St ☎ 415-397-3000, 800-553-1900 ⓢ $189 Ⓒ V, AE, MC, D, DC, JCB Ⓜ Powell St BART & Muni station 🚌 27, 31 Muni 🚋 Powell-Mason, Powell-Hyde cable cars ♿
w *www.hotelunionsquare.com*

This hotel, halfway between the Square and Market St, has been elegantly restored. Front rooms are exposed to street noise, including the clang of Powell St cable cars.

Petite Auberge MAP 2
863 Bush St ☎ 415-928-6000, 800-365-3004 ⓢ singles/doubles $135-245, triples $155-265 Ⓒ V, MC, AE, DC 🚌 2, 3, 4, 76 Muni
w *www.foursisters.com*

This nearby hotel is under the same management as the White Swan Inn, below, and offers similar facilities and an even more romantic look.

Savoy Hotel MAP 2
580 Geary St ☎ 415-441-2700, 800-227-4223 ⓢ $149-279 Ⓒ V, MC, AE, D, DC 🚌 27, 38 Muni
w *www.savoyhotel.net*

This is one of the Theater District's swank hotels. Sometimes rates are reasonable (depending on the season), but regardless, guests are given 1st-class treatment. Rooms come with extras like hair dryers, irons, and dataports; complimentary afternoon tea and sherry, continental breakfast, and shoe shines are offered. And as if that weren't enough, a snazzy French restaurant, the Brasserie Savoy, is just off the lobby.

White Swan Inn MAP 2
845 Bush St ☎ 415-775-1755, 800-999-9570 ⓢ singles/doubles $175-250, triples $195-270 Ⓒ V, MC, AE, DC 🚌 2, 3, 4, 76 Muni
w *www.foursisters.com*

If you have an English grandmother (who isn't in a wheelchair), and you're bringing her to San Francisco, try Petite Auberge's comely sister, the White Swan. It's quaint, it's old, it has B&B comfort, and it brings traditional English charm to San Francisco. The Swan's 26 spacious rooms all have fireplaces, sitting rooms, and antique furniture. Breakfast is served in the morning (the breakfast room opens onto a small garden), and tea and cookies are put out in the afternoon. There's also a fitness room and dataports – to help get granny up to date.

The Inn at Union Square MAP 2
440 Post St ☎ 415-397-3510, 800-288-4346 ⓢ singles/doubles $195-245, triples $215-265, quads $235-285, suites $245-350 Ⓒ V, MC, AE, D, DC Ⓜ Powell St BART & Muni station 🚌 2, 3, 4, 76 Muni 🚋 Powell-Mason, Powell-Hyde cable cars ♿ limited
w *www.unionsquare.com*

These 30 elegant rooms and suites are just a few steps from Union Square. Staff is helpful and knowledgeable – despite a policy requiring them not to accept gratuities. Rates include a daily continental breakfast served on each floor and afternoon tea and wine. Smoking is not allowed anywhere in the hotel.

Hotel Rex MAP 2
562 Sutter St ☎ 415-433-4434, 800-433-4434 ⓢ $215-225 Ⓒ V, MC, AE, D, DC 🚌 2, 3, 4, 76 Muni 🚋 Powell-Mason, Powell-Hyde cable cars ♿
w *www.sftrips.com*

This is a cool property with a swanky lobby and lounge reminiscent of New York's Algonquin in the 1920s. Each guest room is uniquely decorated, with art deco furniture, antique rotary telephones, and hand-painted lampshades. Services are completely up to date, with dataports, CD players, and health club access available to all guests.

Hotel Triton MAP 2
342 Grant Ave ☎ 415-394-0500, 800-433-6611 ⓢ $219-269 Ⓒ V, MC, AE, D, DC 🚌 2, 3, 4, 30, 45, 76 Muni ♿
w *www.hotel-tritonsf.com*

Only a few steps from the entrance to Chinatown and a stroll from Union Square, this hotel has 140 exotically designed guest rooms. Celebrity suites include the Carlos Santana Suite and the Jerry Garcia Suite. For nonrockers, there's the basic (and small) Zen Den. Complimentary morning coffee and evening wine are served in the lobby. Nightly tarot readings and internet access are available, and if you're in a dress-up partying kind of mood, the hotel rents feather boas.

TOP END San Francisco has dozens of hotels in the expense-account bracket, offering guests the sort of extravagant hotel experience that makes the city outside almost a side attraction. We include just a few here.

Sir Francis Drake Hotel MAP 2
450 Powell St ☎ 415-392-7755, 800-227-5480 ⓢ singles/doubles $160-245, triples $180-265, quads $200-285 Ⓒ V, MC, AE, D, DC, JCB 🚌 2, 3, 4, 76 Muni 🚋 Powell-Mason, Powell-Hyde cable cars ♿
W *www.sirfrancisdrake.com*

An old soldier near Union Square, the Drake outdoes many of its more expensive neighbors with an opulent lobby, beefeater-costumed doormen, and a swinging top-floor nightclub.

RICK GERHARTER

Meet Tom, the Drake's doorman for 20 years.

Westin St Francis Hotel MAP 2
335 Powell St ☎ 415-397-7000, 800-228-3000 ⓢ singles $229 standard room, $330 superior room (without view), $375 deluxe room (with view); doubles $229 standard room, $380 superior room (without view), $405 deluxe room (with view) Ⓒ V, MC, AE, D, DC, JCB 🚌 38 Muni 🚋 Powell-Mason, Powell-Hyde cable cars ♿
W *www.westin.com*

Occupying the entire west side of Union Square, the St Francis is probably the city's most famous hotel. It was built just before the 1906 earthquake and was burned out by the postquake fire. It was completely rebuilt, and more recently a tower was erected behind the original hotel, bringing the room count up to 1300. Renovations brought rooms up to date a few years back, and some of the more expensive rooms afford gorgeous views of downtown.

Hotel Monaco MAP 2
501 Geary St ☎ 415-292-0100, 800-214-4220 ⓢ $319-459 Ⓒ V, MC, AE, D, DC, JCB 🚌 38 Muni ♿
W *www.monaco-sf.com*

This is an opulently refurbished hotel on the edge of the Theater District. The decadent lobby, sweeping staircases, and colorfully decorated guest rooms are all reminiscent of an era of more stylish travel, and the luxury doesn't stop there. It's over-the-top hospitality, with evening wine, dataports, shoe shine, and chair massages. A posh restaurant and bar are downstairs.

Campton Place Hotel MAP 2
340 Stockton St ☎ 415-781-5555 ⓢ $325-450 Ⓒ V, MC, AE 🚌 2, 3, 4, 30, 45, 76 Muni ♿
W *www.camptonplace.com*

Catering to business travelers, this small and conservative hotel (110 rooms) qualifies as standard issue luxury accommodations. Understated efficiency and comfort are the objectives here.

Pan Pacific Hotel MAP 2
500 Post St ☎ 415-771-8600, 800-533-6465 ⓢ $340-440 Ⓒ V, MC, AE, D, DC, JCB 🚌 76 Muni 🚋 Powell-Mason, Powell-Hyde cable cars ♿
W *www.panpac.com*

The 'Pan Pac' offers luxury accommodations in full 1980s glory – there are telephones and small TV sets in the bathrooms. DSL lines, meeting lounges, and 24-hour room service allow guests to wheel and deal round the clock.

Civic Center & the Tenderloin

There are some good deals around the Civic Center, particularly along the sketchy Tenderloin periphery.

Aida Hotel MAP 3
1087 Market St ☎ 415-863-4141, 800-863-2432 ⓢ singles $33-53 shared bath, $44-71 private bath; doubles $56-81; triples $66-91 Ⓒ V, MC, AE, D, CB, JCB Ⓜ Civic Center BART & Muni station 🚌 5, 6, 71 Muni

This hotel is a little worn, with cigarette burns on the carpets and some mattresses more tired

Over-the-Top Opulence

If you step into the lobby of the St Francis Hotel, you may be tempted to ask the house detective (who calls attention to himself by carrying a walkie-talkie), 'What're you lettin' these cheap gunsels carry around so much hardware for?' That's a Humphrey Bogart line in *The Maltese Falcon,* from a scene set in a San Francisco hotel lobby that could have been modeled on the lobby of the St Francis. But like a lot of business-minded hotels, the St Francis lost much of its character over the years, and the hotel dick, rather than appreciate the Bogart reference, would probably show you the door for mouthing off.

In the years immediately following the 1906 earthquake, as San Francisco anticipated an influx of dignitaries and bons vivants for the 1915 Panama-Pacific International Exposition, many fashionable hotels were built in the city. Like the St Francis, most of these hotels were eventually stripped of their character to suit the bland tastes of business travelers. Others became faded residence hotels.

But now if you wander the streets that surround Union Square, you will find ample evidence of a growing trend: old hotels are exhibiting a panache that has been missing in local hostelry for a long time. As you might expect in California, hotel designers seem to have turned to the movies for inspiration, endowing their properties with a healthy dose of Hollywood kitsch.

MONICA J MEARES

Even the lobby at the Fairmont is worth a visit.

So, that Bogart litmus test is not necessarily bogus. Several Theater District hotels seem to be deliberately reminiscent of the exotic and intriguing backdrops of Bogart films. The Savoy and the Monaco hotels have old-style restaurant-bars that exhibit a solid arrangement of black and white tiles, dark wood paneling, and brass. The Maxwell and the Rex Hotel even offer classic rotary phones in their sleek, noirish guest rooms.

The outrageous Triton Hotel, on Grant Ave, introduced the designer hotel concept to San Francisco. Its mod interior motifs tend to dissolve into campy, psychedelic figures that may have been inspired by cartoons. The Triton is popular with rock stars, who are obviously comfortable with the hotel's imaginative excesses.

But none of these hotels match up to the real thing. The Fairmont Hotel, on Nob Hill, is a perfect remnant of the days of steamer-trunk travel. The Fairmont emerged from the ashes of the '06 quake and was recently refurbished to its original grandeur. It retains its swirling marble columns, its lushly carpeted lobby, its tiki bar, and its typical Americanness: at once impressive and gaudy, the Fairmont projects a naive imperialism that attempts to bring the world down to size.

So much opulence might seem pretentious – or even politically incorrect – in this day and age. But it admirably adds the surreal and the absurd to the otherwise staid hotel industry. And whereas the luxury of the past was the exclusive privilege of an elite class, these restored classics are generally priced within the means of common folk willing to splurge for a memorable night.

than the people sleeping on them, but it's tidy and well run and the rates are very reasonable. A continental breakfast is included.

Central YMCA Hotel MAP 3
220 Golden Gate Ave ☎ 415-885-0460 ⓢ singles $43 shared bath; doubles $61 shared bath, $72 private bath; triples $75 shared bath; dorms $25 ⓒ V, MC Ⓜ Civic Center BART & Muni station 🚍 19 Muni
w www.ymcasf.org

This is not the best address in town, but it offers simple, clean rooms with shared bathroom facilities (men and women welcome). The Y's fitness facilities are available for guests, and coffee and muffins are provided in the morning. Students with an ISIC card get a discount.

Edwardian San Francisco Hotel MAP 3
1668 Market St ☎ 415-864-1271, 888-864-8070 ⓢ singles $69-109 shared bath; doubles $79-109 shared bath, $89-169 private bath; triples $79-109 shared bath, $149-169 private bath; quads $149-169 private bath ⓒ MC, V, AE, D, DC Ⓜ Van Ness Muni station 🚍 26, 37, F Muni
w www.edwardiansfhotel.com

This is a presentable and charming little place with 'European-style' boutique rooms. The location is ideal for someone torn between the Castro/Mission area and downtown.

Embassy Hotel MAP 3
610 Polk St ☎ 415-673-1404 ⓢ singles/doubles $69-109, triples $79-119, quads $89-129 ⓒ MC, V, AE, D 🚍 19, 31, 47, 49 Muni ♿
w www.embassyhotelsf.com

On the edge of the 'Loin, this hotel offers basic but clean singles and doubles with private baths. Rooms were recently remodeled, and dataports are now available. Free parking and continental breakfast are pluses.

Abigail Hotel MAP 3
246 McAllister St ☎ 415-861-9728, 800-243-6510 ⓢ $99-169 ⓒ V, MC, AE, D, DC, JCB 🚍 5, 19 Muni
w www.abigailhotel.com

This hotel adds a little hipness to the Civic Center. Just around the corner from City Hall and the New Main Library, it was refurbished in 1990 by the Joie de Vivre chain. The 61 guest rooms, furnished with antiques, are reasonably priced, and the lobby opens up to Millennium, one of the city's most renowned vegetarian restaurants. Long-term rates are also available.

Days Inn MAP 3
895 Geary St ☎ 415-441-8220, 800-325-2525 ⓢ singles/doubles $99-109, triples $119-129, quads $129-139 ⓒ V, MC, AE 🚍 38 Muni

This is a basic motel convenient for families and groups traveling together. The neighborhood is a little sketchy. Parking is free.

Phoenix Motel MAP 3
601 Eddy St ☎ 415-776-1380, 800-248-9466 ⓢ singles/doubles $145-175, triples $160-190, quads $175-205 ⓒ AE, D, DC, MC, V 🚍 19, 31 Muni
w www.sftrips.com

While in the Tenderloin, this hotel is just a couple of blocks from the relative safety of Van Ness Ave. This is also a Joie de Vivre property, a recycled '50s motor lodge with an arty swimming pool and a faux-Vegas vibe. The ultra-hip nightclub Backflip occupies the adjacent former coffee shop. Free parking and a continental breakfast make the rooms a great value.

RICK GERHARTER

South of Market

SoMa has a variety of accommodations options, from youth hostels (see Hostels earlier) to luxury hotels.

Hotel Britton MAP 4
112 7th St ☎ 415-621-7001, 800-444-5819 ⓢ $85-119 ⓒ V, MC, AE, D, DC Ⓜ Civic Center BART & Muni station 🚍 14, 26 Muni ♿
w www.renesonhotels.com

The Best Western chain has three properties on a single block of 7th St, including the Hotel Britton. The Britton boasts phony European charm but it's clean and relatively convenient – basically, it's a notch above the chain's standard offerings at a still reasonable price. If the Britton's booked, the central reservations desk will try to place you in one of the other properties, but they're not as cheap.

The Pickwick MAP 4
85 5th St ☎ *415-421-7500, 800-437-4824* $ *singles/doubles $119-199, triples $139-219* C *V, MC, AE, D, DC* 🚌 *14, 26, 27 Muni* ♿

The Pickwick is a little overpriced, considering there's nothing special about the rooms or the service, but it's nice enough and very conveniently located, and rates do drop significantly during slow times. Dataports, irons, and parking are available.

Hotel Griffon MAP 4
155 Steuart St ☎ *415-495-2100, 800-321-2201* $ *$220-285* C *V, MC, AE, D, DC* 🚌 *14, 32, F Muni* ♿
W *www.hotelgriffon.com*

At a great location on the waterfront, close to the Embarcadero Center and the Ferry Building, the 59 rooms of the Griffin are modern, well designed, and comfortable. Prices include a light breakfast. Rooms facing the bay, with views of the Bay Bridge, are the most expensive.

Palace Hotel MAP 4
2 New Montgomery St ☎ *415-512-1111, 800-325-3535* $ *singles $300, doubles $340* C *V, MC* M *Montgomery St BART & Muni station* 🚌 *Market St buses, F Muni* ♿
W *www.sfpalace.com*

One of San Francisco's most famous and snobbish hotels, the original Palace was the ultimate in luxury when it opened in 1875. Opera star Caruso was staying here during the quake of 1906; one of the city's favorite tales has him running out of the hotel in his bath towel, vowing never to return to San Francisco – and he was true to his word. The postquake fire reduced the hotel to an ash pile, and it was rebuilt in 1909. It recently underwent a major renovation comprising 550 rooms. The central Garden Court, one of San Francisco's most elegant rooms, is worth seeing even if you don't stay here. The hotel also offers a range of suites, a pool, and a health club.

San Francisco Marriott MAP 4
55 4th St ☎ *415-896-1600* $ *$409* C *V, MC, AE, D, DC* M *Powell St BART & Muni station* 🚌 *14, 30 Muni* ♿
W *www.marriott.com*

This flashy, modern hotel looks across Yerba Buena Gardens and, more to the point, the Moscone Convention Center. The 1500 rooms cater to conventioneers and business travelers with discounts that cut into steep published rates for standard rooms. Weekend specials sometimes reduce the rate to under $200, even for nonbusiness travelers.

Financial District

A cheap night in the Financial District is pretty much impossible. However, the Pacific Tradewinds Guest House (see the Hostels section) is on the periphery of this district. Unless you're a business traveler, it doesn't really make sense to stay here anyway. The following listings qualify as 'top end' establishments.

Hyatt Regency MAP 5
5 Embarcadero Center ☎ *415-788-1234, 800-233-1234* $ *singles $290, doubles $315* C *V, MC, AE, D, DC* M *Embarcadero BART & Muni station* 🚌 *F Muni* ♿
W *www.hyatt.com/usa/san_francisco*

Ah, yes, *feel* the Hyatt Touch. That's their motto. This is probably San Francisco's most architecturally memorable hotel: its backward-leaning 20-story atrium gave Mel Brooks vertigo in the film *High Anxiety*. If you can stand the heights, there are 800 rooms to choose from. It also has business rooms with fax machines and other amenities.

Park Hyatt MAP 5
333 Battery St ☎ *415-392-1234, 800-492-8822* $ *singles $455-540, doubles $480-565* C *V, MC, AE, DC, D, JCB* 🚌 *1, 42 Muni* ♿
W *www.parkhyatt.com*

This is another, less exotic Hyatt, on the other end of the Embarcadero Center. It has 360 very businesslike rooms.

Chinatown

Chinatown offers a number of budget and mid-range accommodations.

Gum Moon Women's Residence MAP 5
940 Washington St ☎ *415-421-8827* $ *singles $26/night, $105/week, $372-387/month; doubles $22/night, $88/week, $300-312/month* C *cash only* 🚌 *1, 30, 45 Muni* 🚋 *Powell-Mason, Powell-Hyde cable cars*
W *www.gbgm-umc.org*

Gum Moon, operated by the Methodist Church, is an inexpensive alternative for women only. It has a fully equipped kitchen, laundry facilities, a charmingly dated parlor, and rooms with shared bath. Reservations are not accepted. English and Chinese are spoken.

Obrero Hotel MAP 5
1208 Stockton St ☎ 415-989-3960 $ $30-60 C V, MC 🚌 30, 45, 83 Muni

Situated on a bustling Chinatown block near North Beach, this hotel has just 12 rooms with shared bathrooms and rock-bottom prices.

YMCA Chinatown MAP 5
855 Sacramento St ☎ 415-982-4412, 415-576-9622 $ singles $32-35, doubles $43 C V, MC 🚌 1, 30, 45 Muni California St cable car W www.ymcasf.org

The YMCA offers basic lodging just steps away from busy Grant Ave. It takes only men, requires reservations well in advance, and keeps its office open only from 6:30am to 10pm on weekdays, 9am to 4pm on weekends, making check-in difficult if you arrive at an odd hour. All rooms have shared bath. If you can surmount the hurdles, it's one of the cheapest options a lone traveler will find in the city; your seventh night will be free!

Grant Plaza MAP 5
465 Grant Ave ☎ 415-434-3883, 800-472-6899 $ singles $55-63, doubles $69-109 C V, MC, AE, D, DC, JCB 🚌 1, 30, 45 Muni California St cable car W www.grantplaza.com

The Grant Plaza is on a busy corner, just a block from the Chinatown gate and the California St cable car. Rooms are neat and tidy.

Astoria Hotel MAP 5
510 Bush St ☎ 415-434-8889, 800-666-6696 $ $66/night, $390/week, $1500/month C V, MC, AE, D 🚌 2, 3, 4, 15, 30, 45 Muni ♿ W www.futton.com/astoria

This place is right by the Chinatown gate and only a couple of blocks from Union Square. It is not a fancy hotel and rooms are basic; for the cheapest rates, guests get a shared bath.

Royal Pacific Motor Inn MAP 5
661 Broadway ☎ 415-781-6661, 800-545-5574 $ singles $95-106, doubles $99-110, triples $107-112, quads $118 C V, MC, AE 🚌 30, 45 Muni W www.royalpacific.citysearch.com

This classic American motor lodge sticks out like a sore thumb on the Chinatown–North Beach border, but it's a good deal for families traveling with a car.

Sam Wong Hotel MAP 5
615 Broadway ☎ 415-362-2999 $ singles $95, doubles $139-149, triples $179 C V, MC 🚌 30, 45 Muni ♿

The recently refurbished Sam Wong Hotel is simple but stylish and very comfortable. Limited parking is available.

Holiday Inn Financial District MAP 5
750 Kearny St ☎ 415-433-6600, 800-424-8292 $ $149-269 C V, MC, AE, D, DC, JCB 🚌 15, 30, 41 Muni ♿ W www.holiday-inn-hotels-san-francisco-directory.com

Also known as the Chinatown Holiday Inn, since it's linked with Portsmouth Square by a pedestrian bridge, this is one of the city's least favorite architectural creations. But occasionally special deals make it worth considering, and you don't have to look at the building if you're staying here. There are 566 rooms and a swimming pool.

North Beach

There aren't many hotels in North Beach, although Fisherman's Wharf and Chinatown are both nearby. Parking in this area can be difficult.

Washington Square Inn MAP 6
1660 Stockton St ☎ 415-981-4220, 800-388-0220 $ singles/doubles $150-225, triples $175-250 C V, MC, AE, D, DC 🚌 39 Muni ♿

This quaint hotel opposite the park has 15 rooms. All rooms have private bath, and some have a view of the square (for which you pay more). Continental breakfast and afternoon wine included.

Hotel Boheme MAP 6
444 Columbus Ave ☎ 415-433-9111 $ singles/doubles $149-169, triples $174, quads $179 C V, MC, AE 🚌 30, 41, 45 Muni W www.hotelboheme.com

Right in the heart of North Beach is this small and very stylish hotel. The decor is a consistently subdued modern swank – an updated gangster-era look that makes subtle reference to the neighborhood's Beat history. All rooms have a private bath, and half of them overlook bustling Columbus Ave.

Nob Hill

Nob Hill is topped by some of the city's oldest and classiest hotels, but there are a few rela tively humble and less expensive options. A couple of the neighborhood's better choices are filed away under Long-Term Accommodations, covered later in this chapter.

Nob Hill Hotel MAP 7
835 Hyde St ☎ 415-885-2987
$ singles/doubles $79-150, triples $139-170 C V, MC 🚌 2, 3, 4, 27, 76 Muni ♿
W www.nobhillhotel.com

This small 1906 hotel was recently spiffed up, with neat and comfortable rooms dressed up in neo-Victorian attire. Rates fluctuate wildly from season to season.

Nob Hill Inn MAP 7
1000 Pine St ☎ 415-673-6080
$ singles/doubles $125-165, triples/quads $165-245, suite (up to 6 people) $275
C V, MC, AE, D, DC, CB 🚋 California St cable car

This is a pleasant 20-room hotel in an old Edwardian house. Rooms are very tastefully decorated with antiques. Continental breakfast is included, and some of the rooms have kitchen facilities.

Nob Hill Lambourne MAP 7
725 Pine St ☎ 415-433-2287, 800-275-8466 $ $220-285 C V, MC, AE, D, DC
🚌 30, 45 Muni
W www.nobhilllambourne.com

This small establishment (20 guest rooms) has all the amenities you might expect of a boutique business hotel. The rooms have computer, fax, and voice-mail facilities and some of the suites have kitchenettes. The hotel is conveniently central, close to Union Square, Chinatown, and the Financial District.

Fairmont Hotel MAP 7
950 Mason St ☎ 415-772-5000, 800-866-5577 $ singles $239-319, doubles $269-349 C V, MC, AE, D, DC, JCB 🚌 1 Muni
🚋 California St cable car ♿
W www.fairmont.com

The Fairmont's lobby was recently restored to its original over-the-top extravagance – you may want to hang out there, instead of in one of the hotel's rooms, which are just fine but pricey. An unfortunate casualty of the makeover was the panoramic top-floor restaurant-bar; people who like to gawk at the skyline over cocktails will have to sneak over to the Mark Hopkins, across the street (call it extended corridor creeping).

Huntington Hotel MAP 7
1075 California St ☎ 415-474-5400
$ singles $275-420, doubles $300-445 C V, MC, AE, D, DC 🚌 1 Muni 🚋 California St cable car
W www.huntingtonhotel.com

This is another of Nob Hill's seductively smooth and very expensive old-school hotels. It has luxuriant rooms, a stuffy restaurant, and a spa.

Renaissance Stanford Court Hotel MAP 7
905 California St ☎ 415-989-3500, 800-468-3571 $ singles/doubles $309-339, triples $329-359 C V, MC, AE, D, DC
🚌 1 Muni 🚋 Powell-Mason, Powell-Hyde, California St cable cars ♿
W www.renaissancehotels.com

This businesslike hotel, close to Union Square as well as Nob Hill, is noted for the Tiffany-style glass dome over the driveway. The overpriced rooms are characterized by understated elegance.

Mark Hopkins Inter-Continental Hotel MAP 7
999 California St ☎ 415-392-3434, 800-327-0200 $ $350-460 C V, MC, AE, D, DC
🚌 1 Muni 🚋 California St cable car ♿
W www.markhopkins.net

Another Nob Hill landmark, this hotel is also right up there in price. You get what you pay for, of course – outrageously beautiful rooms with furniture that smells like money. Upstairs, the Top of the Mark cocktail lounge is renowned for its superb views over the bay.

Ritz-Carlton San Francisco MAP 7
600 Stockton St ☎ 415-296-7465, 800-241-3333 $ $475-700 C V, MC, AE, D, DC
🚌 30, 45 Muni 🚋 California St cable car ♿
W www.ritzcarlton.com

This palatial, white-columned hotel was originally home to an insurance company. In 1991, it was converted into one of the city's poshest and most expensive hotels. Rooms and services offer more luxury than anyone really needs, but we suppose there are those times when you just feel you deserve it.

Fisherman's Wharf

Only the Union Square area downtown has more big hotels than Fisherman's Wharf. The Wharf area is where you'll also find all the standard mid-range hotel chains, from Holiday Inn to Travelodge, although their prices are high here, especially in summer when rates go sky high. (For most of these places, summer rates go into effect around April or May and stay in effect into October.) Package tours often put their groups in these hotels, which usually offer parking (sometimes at an additional fee) and are generally amenable to families.

San Remo Hotel MAP 8
2237 Mason St ☎ 415-776-8688, 800-352-7366 ⓢ singles $50-75, doubles $60-85, triples $85 ⓒ V, MC, AE, D, JCB 🚌 30 Muni 🚋 Powell-Mason cable car
ⓦ www.sanremohotel.com

Built immediately after the 1906 quake, this charming family-owned hotel has been refurbished with individually decorated rooms, none of them with private bathroom facilities. The location is midway between the North Beach and Fisherman's Wharf centers of activity, and there's some nice walking from here. For the price, this has to be considered one of the best deals in the city.

Travelodge MAP 8
1201 Columbus Ave ☎ 415-776-7070, 800-578-7878 ⓢ singles/doubles $89-150 low season, $150-210 high season; triples $99-220 ⓒ V, MC, AE, DC 🚌 30 Muni ♿

This hotel offers basic convenience. The location – between Fisherman's Wharf and North Beach – and cheap parking will suit many travelers. Families can relax here, since there's nothing fancy about the rooms.

Wharf Inn MAP 8
2601 Mason St ☎ 415-673-7411, 800-548-9918 ⓢ $99-169 low season, $135-205 high season ⓒ V, MC, AE, D, DC, CB 🚌 32, F Muni
ⓦ www.wharfinn.com

This is a very basic hotel – not a bad choice for those traveling with children – in the heart of the Wharf area. Rates fluctuate wildly with the tourist tide.

Dockside Boat & Bed MAP 8
Pier 39, C Dock ☎ 415-392-5526, 800-436-2574 ⓢ $140-340 ⓒ V, MC 🚌 32, F Muni
ⓦ www.boatandbed.com

Dockside Boat & Bed offers an unusual variation on the B&B theme. You can select from a variety of boats moored in the marina, from a 36-foot Catalina sailboat to a 51-foot bluewater motor yacht. Boats are decked out with traditional paneling and come with showers, toilets, and basic kitchens. At night, you'll be rocked to sleep by the tide and in the morning you'll get a wake-up call from the resident sea lions. Rates (which already include taxes) fluctuate depending on the boat, the season, and the night of the week. Inexpensive parking is available. The office is at the C Dock on Pier 39, but it's best to call ahead for an appointment.

Tuscan Inn MAP 8
425 North Point St ☎ 415-561-1100, 800-648-4626 ⓢ $179-259 low season, $269-339 high season ⓒ V, MC, AE, D, DC, JCB 🚌 39, 42 Muni ♿
ⓦ www.tuscaninn.com

This is a Best Western hotel that is actually larger (220 rooms) than it looks and feels. The rooms are nice and clean and come with Nintendo games and small refrigerators (some also have VCRs). There's complimentary tea and coffee in the lobby in the morning and wine in the afternoon.

Holiday Inn MAP 8
1300 Columbus Ave ☎ 415-771-9000, 800-942-7348 ⓢ singles/doubles $169-285, triples $189-305 ⓒ V, MC, AE, D, DC 🚌 30, 42 Muni ♿
ⓦ www.hiwharf.com

The fairly standard rooms offer no surprises but this Holiday Inn has a pool and exercise facilities, as well as an array of amenities for business travelers.

Suites at Fisherman's Wharf MAP 8
2655 Hyde St ☎ 415-771-0200, 800-227-3608 ⓢ singles/doubles $229-279, triples $249-299 ⓒ cash only 🚌 30, 42 Muni 🚋 Powell-Hyde cable car ♿

This place has one- and two-bedroom suites each with a full kitchen. Rooms are equipped with stereos, VCRs, and dataports and are practical and comfortable.

Radisson MAP 8
250 Beach St ☎ 415-392-6700, 800-333-3333 ⓢ $229-289 ⓒ V, MC, AE, D, DC, JCB 🚌 32, F Muni ♿
ⓦ www.radisson.com

This modern but very basic hotel is grossly overpriced, but call to see if special rates are available during your stay.

Hyatt at Fisherman's Wharf MAP 8
555 North Point St ☎ 415-415-563-1234, 800-233-1234 ⓢ $199-400 ⓒ V, MC, AE, D, DC, JCB 🚌 30, 39, 42 Muni ♿
ⓦ www.hyatt.com

Another place where you can 'feel the Hyatt touch' – it's modern and semiluxurious, with a pool, spa, and fitness facility.

The Marina & Cow Hollow

West of Van Ness Ave, Lombard St is a kaleidoscope of neon motel signs beckoning you to pull in. If you're driving into town without room reservations, a motel on this strip is a relatively hassle-free way to get yourself settled. On Van Ness Ave, you'll find more of the same type of accommodations.

Golden Gate City Motel MAP 9
2707 Lombard St ☎ 415-567-2425
$ singles/doubles $55-95, triples $65-105
C V, MC, AE 🚌 28, 43, 76 Muni

This inexpensive motel with very basic amenities is just a block from the Presidio gate.

Motel Capri MAP 9
2015 Greenwich St ☎ 415-346 4667
$ standard $70-100, rooms with kitchenette $132-160 C V, MC, D, DC 🚌 28, 76 Muni

This well-preserved '50s motor lodge is a relatively inexpensive option.

Bed & Breakfast Inn MAP 9
4 Charlton Court ☎ 415-921-9784
$ singles/doubles $90-125 shared bath, $175-280 private bath; garden suite $380
C V, MC 🚌 41 Muni
W www.thebandb.com

Just off Union St on a quiet dead-end alley, this privately owned Victorian inn has romantic, nicely furnished rooms. Guests can take their breakfast – fresh pastries, fruits, etc – out to pleasant garden tables.

Marina Motel MAP 9
2576 Lombard St ☎ 415-921-9406, 800-346-6118 $ singles/doubles $79-149, triples $89-159 C V, MC, AE, D 🚌 28, 43, 76 Muni
W www.marinamotel.com

The standout on Lombard St, toward the western end, is this pleasant, family-owned motel with a secluding courtyard. Built in 1939 to accommodate visitors arriving via the new Golden Gate Bridge, it has retained some of its vintage motor court charm. Some rooms have small but complete kitchens.

Travelodge MAP 9
1450 Lombard St ☎ 415-673-0691 $ singles/doubles $96-135, triples $110-150
C V, MC 🚌 30, 47, 49, 76 Muni ♿
W www.travelodge.com

True to its chain's aims, this motel offers predictable rooms at a reasonable rate. It's a short walk from here to Fisherman's Wharf.

Comfort Inn by the Bay MAP 9
2775 Van Ness Ave ☎ 415-928-5000, 800-228-5150 $ singles/doubles $120-180, triples $130-190 C V, MC, AE, D 🚌 30, 47, 49, 76 Muni ♿
W www.hotelchoice.com

This is another basic chain hotel that's close to the Marina and Fisherman's Wharf. Call the toll-free number to find out if special discounts apply.

Sherman House MAP 9
2160 Green St ☎ 415-563-3600 $ $460-545 C AE, CB, DC, D, MC, V 🚌 41 Muni ♿
W www.theshermanhouse.com

This is one of the most luxurious small hotels in the city, with just 14 rooms in a landmark 1876 Italianate Victorian. The rooms and parlors have been painstakingly restored to their original state of grace but with all the latest conveniences. Some rooms have bay views – one even has a rooftop deck. Breakfast is served either in your room or in the dining room.

Pacific Heights & Japantown

Pacific Heights and Japantown are not very convenient for visitors planning to explore the city thoroughly, but pleasant lodging can be found throughout the area.

Mansions Hotel MAP 10
2220 Sacramento St ☎ 415-929-9444, 800-826-9398 $ $139-225 C V, MC, AE 🚌 1 Muni
W www.themansions.com

This hotel, in a quirky old Victorian mansion, is refreshingly endowed with a sense of humor. The decor and attitude are seriously over the top. We're talkin' goofy, here. Bizarre objets d'art fill all available table and shelf space – one rather large ceramic item that caught our eye depicted a mother swine nursing half a dozen piglets – and evening dinner is followed by a campy, albeit extremely entertaining, magic show. The breakfast is excellent.

Queen Anne Hotel MAP 10
1590 Sutter St ☎ 415-441-2828, 800-227-3970 $ singles/doubles $139-199, triples $149-209 C V, MC, AE, D, DC, JCB 🚌 2, 3, 4 Muni ♿
W www.queenanne.com

The Queen Anne, in a fine 1890 Victorian, offers reasonable rates for a bed and breakfast in Frisco. All rooms, while not spectacular in decor, have private bath and antiques, and some have romantic wood-burning fireplaces and bay windows. A continental breakfast is included in daily rates.

Majestic Hotel MAP 10
1500 Sutter St ☎ 415-441-1100, 800-869-8966 ⓢ singles/doubles $159-269, triples $179-289 ⓒ AE, V, MC, D, DC 🚌 2, 3, 4 Muni ♿
ⓦ www.thehotelmajestic.com

Not far from Japantown, this hotel survived the 1906 earthquake and, despite lavish restorations, retains its antique feel.

ROBERTO SONCIN GEROMETTA

Queen Anne Hotel

Radisson Miyako Hotel MAP 10
1625 Post St ☎ 415-922-3200, 800-333-3333 ⓢ $209-259 ⓒ V, MC, AE, D, DC, JCB 🚌 2, 3, 4 Muni ♿
ⓦ www.radisson.com

This deluxe, businesslike hotel was designed with shoji screens on its windows and deep Japanese bathtubs in the bathrooms (with instructions on how to use them). It's worth asking about the many discounts offered here.

The Haight

With its many fine old Victorian houses, the Haight has a number of interesting B&Bs and one cheaper alternative.

Metro Hotel MAP 11
319 Divisadero St ☎ 415-861-5364 ⓢ singles/doubles $59-69, triples/quads $69-99 ⓒ V, MC, AE, D, DC 🚌 24 Muni

This hotel, on the edge of the Haight, offers cheap and clean rooms with private baths, a private garden patio, and overnight parking. It's a very good deal, especially for groups.

Red Victorian B&B MAP 11
1665 Haight St ☎ 415-864-1978 ⓢ singles/doubles $86-126, triples $101-141, quads $116-156 ⓒ AE, D, MC, V 🚌 7, 33, 37, 43 Muni
ⓦ www.redvic.com

This trippy B&B is a national landmark built ir 1904. The current owner, a young-at-hear septuagenarian artist named Sami Sunchild left a commune in the mid-'70s and bough the then-decrepit hotel. She has fully restorec the building, decorating each room to reflec her dedication to peace, ecology, and globa friendship. (You can choose from the Flowe Child Room, the Sunshine Room, the Rainbow Room, the Peace Room, and the Summer o Love Room, among others.) In keeping wit the spirit of the Summer of Love, Ms Sunchilc says the hotel functions as a sort of 'international commune.' The cheaper rooms come with shared bath; only four of the 18 rooms have a private bath. A complimentary continental breakfast and afternoon tea are servec in the Gallery of Meditative Art downstairs. I has reduced rates for longer stays.

Stanyan Park Hotel MAP 11
750 Stanyan St ☎ 415-751-1000 ⓢ singles/doubles $115-180, triples $135-200, suites $250-310 ⓒ AE, MC, V, D, DC 🚌 7, 71 Muni ♿
ⓦ www.stanyanpark.com

This old Victorian hotel, a block south o Haight St, has 36 guest rooms plus more expensive suites. Continental breakfast is included. Book well ahead. If you have a ca park it in a well-lit area at night.

Victorian Inn on the Park MAP 11
301 Lyon St ☎ 415-931-1830, 800-435-1967 ⓢ $159-199 ⓒ V, MC, AE, D, DC 🚌 21 Muni

This inn, with 12 stylish rooms (all with privat bath), is on the other side of the Panhandle The rooms have Victorian details and furnishings, and the color scheme, biased towar purple, suits the place, though it's a bit dark

Continental breakfast and afternoon wine are complimentary.

If you prefer holing up in grand old houses, check out the pair of beauties on Alamo Square, just a few blocks from the Haight.

Alamo Square Inn MAP 11
719 Scott St ☎ 415-922-2055, 800-345-9888 $ singles/doubles $90-155, suites/apartments $175-205 C V, MC, AE 🚌 5, 24 Muni
W www.alamoinn.com

The Alamo Square Inn occupies a swell pair of Victorian mansions – a Queen Anne and a Tudor Revival. Rooms, all restored with private bath, exhibit impeccable taste, and a back patio is nice for a leisurely smoke (which you can't do inside). There's afternoon wine, a full breakfast, and free off-street parking. All things considered, the rates are extremely reasonable.

Archbishop's Mansion MAP 11
1000 Fulton St ☎ 415-563-7872, 800-543-5820 $ singles/doubles $149-265, triples $169-285 C V, MC, AE, D, DC 🚌 5, 22 Muni
W www.archbishopsmansion

This French chateau was indeed built for the city's archbishop back in 1904. It is now one of the city's pearls, and visitors can sleep, and even honeymoon, in the archbishop's old room. The mansion's 15 guest rooms all have private bathrooms (though some lack an actual tub in which to bathe) and sturdy old furniture. There is limited off-street parking.

The Castro & Upper Market

There are several places to stay in the Castro and Upper Market area, if you want to be near the gay epicenter of the city. All of the following accommodations cater to a mixed gay and straight clientele. Also see the boxed text 'Gay & Lesbian Accommodations.'

Twin Peaks Hotel MAP 12
2160 Market St ☎ 415-863-2909 $ singles $49 shared bath, $65 private bath, $225-240/week; doubles $49 shared bath, $65 private bath, $260-280/week; triples $59 shared bath, $75 private bath C V, MC M Church St Muni station 🚌 37, F Muni

This is a basic and simple place with a good location and very low rates.

Beck's Motor Lodge MAP 12
2222 Market St ☎ 415-621-8212, 800-227-4360 $ singles/doubles $90-120, triples $100-130 C AE, V, D, MC M Castro St Muni station 🚌 37, F Muni

This is an old motel that was spruced up with a vibrant paint job. Rooms are pretty ordinary. The advantage, other than location, is free parking. It's gay friendly.

The Mission

The Mission District is a popular destination for young travelers on a tight budget, but beyond sleazy Mission St flophouses, the neighborhood surprisingly offers no inexpensive lodging. See the Castro and Civic Center sections for nearby alternatives to what's listed below.

Andora Inn MAP 14
2434 Mission St ☎ 415-282-0337, 800-967-9219 $ $79-109 shared bath, $119-169 private bath C V, MC 🚌 14, 49 Muni
W www.andorainn.com

If you strolled past this place, you'd never know what elegant accommodations are hidden from the street. The Andora occupies a restored Victorian with a peaceful courtyard. Rooms are neat and stylish without being at all fussy. Guests here are well situated for scoping out the Mission nightlife. The rates include breakfast, and reduced rates are offered for stays over 14 days.

Inn San Francisco MAP 14
943 South Van Ness Ave ☎ 415-641-0188, 800-359-0913 $ singles/doubles $105-145 shared bath, $175-205 private bath; triples $195-225; quads $215-245 C V, MC, AE 🚌 12, 14, 49 Muni
W www.innsf.com

It's worth spending a bit more to stay in this grand old hotel. The inn comprises two old houses – an 1872 Victorian and a 1905 country cottage – that have been lovingly restored and furnished with antiques and Persian rugs. Large bouquets of fresh flowers greet you at every turn. Deluxe rooms offer a redwood hot tub, spa, or fireplace. All rates include an extensive continental breakfast; bus lines run 2 blocks away.

The Richmond

Seal Rock Inn MAP 15
545 Point Lobos Ave ☎ 415-752-8000 $ singles $90-116, doubles $98-124, triples $106-132, quads $114-140; add $6 for

Gay & Lesbian Accommodations

These days, most San Francisco hotels are not likely to be too concerned about the sexual inclinations of their guests, but some places go out of their way to make same-sex couples welcome. Of course, the bulk of these are in or near the Castro. Be advised that accommodations in this part of town can be hard to find and more expensive during popular gay and lesbian events, such as Pride Week at the end of June or on Halloween.

24 Henry MAP 12
24 Henry St ☎ 415-864-5686, 800-900-5686 ⓢ singles $65, doubles $80-110, triples $100-120 C *V, MC, AE*
W *www.24henry.com*

Just a few blocks from the heart of the Castro, on quiet residential Henry St, this old Victorian house offers friendly, homey accommodations. It's gay-owned, and the clientele is primarily gay and lesbian, but 24 Henry is a pretty unassuming sort of place where a Castro denizen's older parents might also feel comfortable and where children are welcome. Some of the rooms have a private bath.

Village House MAP 12
4080 18th St ☎ 415-864-5686, 800-864-5686 ⓢ singles/doubles $80-$90 shared bath, $119 private bath, $119-$149 for special events C *V, MC, AE*
W *www.24henry.com*

Owned by the folks who run 24 Henry, this is another old house with a variety of rooms, some of which have private bath, and a similar welcoming atmosphere. The primary difference, of course, is that Village House is just a few paces from the corner of 18th and Castro – you can't get any closer to the center of the lively Castro.

Willows Inn MAP 12
710 14th St ☎ 415-431-4770 ⓢ singles $100-120, doubles $110-140, triples $120-150, quads $160 C *V, MC, AE, D, DC*
W *www.willowssf.com*

Willows is a comfortable 12-room B&B with shared bathrooms. The rooms have rustic handcrafted furnishings of bentwood willow, antique armoires, and fluffy comforters, and the continental breakfast is brought to your room in the morning. An international crowd – equally male and female – tends to convene here. A large suite can accommodate four people. As a plus, rates do not go up during special events.

kitchenette C *cash only* 🚌 *18, 38 Muni*
W *www.sealrockinn.com*

Near the ocean, the Seal Rock is a handsome example of late-'50s hotel design – given the natural surroundings, it resembles a national park lodge. The rooms are large and most sleep up to four people, so it's a good place for families who want to spend a lot of time on the beach and hiking the nearby cliff trails. All rooms have a small refrigerator, and some have full kitchens. The most popular rooms (call way ahead) are the 3rd-floor rooms with fireplaces. A heated pool and recreation facilities will keep the kids from getting too antsy.

San Francisco International Airport

If you need to stay near the airport, you'l find lots of possibilities along Hwy 101 from Burlingame to South San Francisco. There are direct-dial phones to many of these places in the baggage-claim area, and free shuttle buses pick up and drop off guests outside the terminals. There are more than 20 hotels around the airport, so competition is fierce.

Millbrae and Burlingame, just south of the airport, and South San Francisco, imme diately north of the airport, offer an array of chain hotels with mid-range rates.

Motel 6
111 Mitchell Ave ☎ 650-877-0770 ⓢ singles $70, doubles $76, triples $82, quads $88 ⓒ V, MC, AE ♿ ⓦ www.motel6.com

Two miles from SFO, Motel 6 offers an inexpensive pre-flight stay, especially for families (children stay free). There's no airport shuttle, but the car rental agencies are nearby, so dropping off the car and catching the rental firm's shuttle to the airport is easy enough. A cab to the airport costs about $12.

Clarion Hotel
401 E Millbrae Ave ☎ 650-692-6363, 800-391-9644 ⓢ $129-159 ⓒ V, MC, AE, D, DC 🚌 free airport shuttle ♿ ⓦ www.clarionhotel.com

Just a mile from SFO, and on the edge of the bay, the Clarion offers a modern and convenient last-night's stay before an early flight. The hotel has an exercise room and laundry, and wake-up calls and morning coffee are easily arranged. The free 24-hour airport shuttle simplifies getting away.

Embassy Suites
250 Gateway Blvd ☎ 650-589-3400 ⓢ $249-289 ⓒ V, AE, D, DC, CB, JCB 🚌 free airport shuttle ♿ ⓦ www.embassy-suites.com

Two miles from the airport, this expensive suites-only hotel might be the way to rest up before a long flight. It has a laundry, pool, and free airport shuttle.

LONG-TERM ACCOMMODATIONS

Many cheaper places around the city offer good deals on weekly and monthly rates. The Halcyon Hotel (see Union Square) is a good example.

Scan the classified ads in the *San Francisco Chronicle* or the *San Francisco Bay Guardian* for long-term rentals. If you're planning to stay for a few months, subletting an apartment or room in the neighborhood of your choice is a good way to go. Both papers list sublets. There are also a number of roommate-referral services; check in the papers and under Roommate Assistance Services in the yellow pages. Some are neighborhood specific and all of them charge a membership fee.

Other central places with long-term possibilities include the following:

Beresford Manor MAP 2
860 Sutter St ☎ 415-673-3330, 800-533-6533 ⓢ singles $60 shared bath, $75 private bath, $225/week shared bath, $350/week private bath; doubles $70 shared bath, $85 private bath, $320/week shared bath, $450/week private bath; triples $80 shared bath, $95 private bath, $420/week shared bath, $550/week private bath ⓒ V, MC, AE, DC, D 🚌 2, 3, 4, 76 Muni ⓦ www.beresford.com

This is the most affordable of the three Beresford properties in the area and specializes in long-term accommodations for foreign students. Breakfast and dinner, included in the price, are served Monday through Saturday, and a continental breakfast is served Sunday.

The Harcourt MAP 7
1105 Larkin St ☎ 415-673-7721 ⓢ singles $225/week shared bath, $275/week private bath; doubles $160 person/week shared bath, $185 person/week private bath ⓒ V, MC 🚌 2, 3, 4, 76 Muni

This old place offers nothing fancy, but for young travelers staying in the city for a period of time, the low weekly rates (which include two meals daily) and central location are attractive. The guests are a mix of international travelers and students, and student discounts are available. There's a TV lounge, a rudimentary community kitchen, and maid service. The shared room option is available to lone travelers willing to share a room with a stranger.

San Francisco Residence Club MAP 7
851 California St ☎ 415-421-2220 ⓢ singles $58-128, $350-700/week, $1100-2100/month; doubles $78-148, $500-800/week, $1400-2300/month; triples $98-168; quads $118-188 ⓒ V, MC 🚌 1 Muni 🚋 Powell-Mason, Powell-Hyde, California St cable cars

This friendly European-style pensione is a very attractive alternative to the expensive accommodations available in the area, and it will accommodate short-term as well as long-term visitors. Most rooms have shared bath, and a few afford stellar views. It's just a block downhill from the top of Nob Hill. Breakfast and dinner (every night but Sunday) are included.

Places to Eat

It is often said that San Francisco has more restaurants per capita than any other city in the USA. But the city's culinary distinction is by no means based on sheer quantity. For locals and visitors alike, San Francisco's true strengths are the diversity of its influences, which stretch from Europe to Asia, and its wealth of high-quality, moderately priced choices. You won't have to search long to find a creative, expertly prepared meal in comfortable surroundings for $10 to $20. But, of course, you can spend as much money as you want in one of the city's prestigious restaurants.

Before setting out with knife and fork in hand and a serviette tucked into your shirt collar, you might want to take a moment to survey the culinary landscape, which has been shedding its boundaries of late. If you think you must go to North Beach for Italian food, Chinatown for Chinese food, or the Mission for Mexican food, you might be ignoring excellent restaurants serving the same types of food elsewhere in the city – and you also risk overlooking some surprising gems in each of those parts of town. Trained chefs frequently open shop in unexpected spots, gaining exposure to a broader, more open-minded clientele than they would in their more 'traditional' neighborhoods. Further blurring the lines, chefs are increasingly helping themselves to ingredients and methods from a variety of ethnic cuisines.

Note that the better-known restaurants almost always require reservations at least two weeks in advance for dinner on a Friday or Saturday night, and for some places you must reserve a month or two ahead. Weeknights it's easier to secure a place at the table. Sometimes you can skirt around this by sitting at the bar, where some restaurants will serve anything off the menu.

In this book, budget restaurants are those where you can spend less than $10 per person on your meal. An entree at mid-range places will cost you approximately $10 to $15, and top end places are $15 and up.

California Cuisine

Put simply, 'California cuisine' refers to light and creative cooking that relies *strictly* on fresh produce, breads, and meats. This philosophy guides many chefs in San Francisco and it has been applied to European- and Asian-influenced cuisines alike.

By no means is fresh, light, and creative restricted to California, but it was in the Bay Area – at Alice Waters' Chez Panisse restaurant, in Berkeley – that this culinary approach was fully realized in the 1970s. (See Excursions for more on that fine establishment.) Waters and her crew rediscovered principles that had been lost in the freeze-dried, fast-food 20th-century way of life. Combined with a greater variety of fresh ingredients than had traditionally been available in a single kitchen – and a shrewd understanding of how to use them – the simple formula yielded something new.

Most modern restaurants in San Francisco have adopted at least some of the tenets of California cuisine, and in recent years many traditional restaurants have been rejuvenated by introducing new chefs and updating their menus with California touches.

Asian

San Francisco's cultural ties to Asia are stronger than ever, and this vital exchange is clearly evinced at many of the city's restaurants, where the steady influx of people from all over Asia has inspired a culinary renaissance.

Modern Chinese American chefs are serving up food more refined and authentic than it was in the days of chop-suey and chow-mein parlors. San Franciscans are discovering that few cultures can match the Asian understanding of how to handle fresh fish and seafood in the kitchen. The new wave of chefs is proving that traditional stir-fries and dim sum needn't be greasy or smothered in starchy sauces. And in the hands of a capable Chinese chef, a drip-fried crispy-skin chicken is a meal not soon forgotten.

A key bit of advice: if you're thinking the place for the city's best Chinese food is Chinatown, think again. There are some excellent choices in the city's oldest Chinese quarter, but many subpar restaurants reside there as well; increasingly, the city is looking to the Richmond District for its better Chinese food.

There is no longer a cohesive Japanese neighborhood in the city, but Japantown – a strictly commercial district – is home to a number of excellent noodle parlors, and great sushi houses appear in many of the city's quarters.

Waves of other Asian immigrants have further enriched the city's restaurant scene. Over the years, Vietnamese pho (beef noodle soup) houses have induced many hungry San Franciscans to venture into the troubled Tenderloin, and recently, excellent Vietnamese restaurants have turned up in other parts of the city, particularly around the Mission District. They are showing that Vietnam's culinary tradition goes far beyond pho.

The demand for light, spicy foods has made Thai restaurants ubiquitous in the city. There seem to be more Thai restaurants than there are Thais in San Francisco. Other Asian cuisines – Korean, Cambodian, Indian, and Burmese – are all represented in San Francisco but are more prominent in other parts of the Bay Area.

Mediterranean

The people of San Francisco's largest Mediterranean faction, the Italians, have obviously staked their territory on the local culinary map: nearly every storefront on Columbus Ave in North Beach is occupied by an inviting-looking Italian restaurant. Excellent Italian restaurants also appear elsewhere in the city, and Italian pastas and Italian-inspired pizzas fired in wood-burning ovens are turning up on menus in restaurants that identify themselves as Californian or Mediterranean.

The Spanish custom of grazing on tapas, or appetizer-size portions, is now prevalent in San Francisco. The term 'tapas' is sometimes used loosely, whether the cuisine is actually Spanish or of a more general Mediterranean bent. Where food is served this way, and the cuisine is strictly Italian, the correct term is antipasti. Either way, it makes for a very social dining experience.

For ages, the food-conscious citizens of San Francisco were devoted strictly to French cuisine, and all the finest restaurants in the city were French. For decades, the city's most respected restaurant was a place called the Poulet d'Or, which people unable to pronounce French – meaning almost everyone in the city – called the 'Poodle Dog.' During its heyday in the 1890s, it stood not far from where Café Claude stands now; it closed in 1922. A few haute establishments survive from those days. Today, more affordable French bistros far outnumber the pricey traditional places, and on Claude Lane and Belden St, casual alfresco dining is as much the norm as it is in Paris.

East-West Fusion

With so many creative Asian and European chefs thriving in such omnicultural cities as Honolulu, San Francisco, and Los Angeles, it was inevitable that an exchange of ideas

Call Ahead!

Note that the restaurant industry in San Francisco is volatile, with places coming and going on a weekly basis. With that in mind, before making a special trip to a restaurant, you might want to call ahead to verify that it's still open for business.

would begin to occur. The inspired combination of Asian and European flavors and cooking methods, which first started to appear on the West Coast in the 1980s and really took off in the '90s, has probably created the biggest impact locally since California cuisine.

Dishes on a single menu might reflect influences from Korea, China, and Italy, or France, China, and Louisiana's Cajun country. Even burritos are getting the fusion treatment in 'wraps' outlets throughout the city. As with any adventurous new approach, sometimes these experiments don't work. Some critics, and even some chefs, have taken up the mantra 'fusion is confusion.' By now, most of the trendy fusion restaurants that opened in the '90s have gone the way of the Poodle Dog, but a few standouts have survived. Diners will find traces of fusion cooking on menus all over town.

Mexican

Although the city has a large and culturally vital Mexican community, there is a surprising shortage of quality Mexican restaurants. The city's only acceptable excuse for this deficiency is that its great wealth of taquerías satisfies its needs. Taquerías have cafeteria-style assembly-line service and specialize in simple fare such as tacos and burritos. Food is commonly wrapped in aluminum foil, even if you don't plan to take it out.

The beauty of the taquería is that you rarely have to spend more than $5 for a San Francisco–style burrito (see the boxed text 'The Sacred Mission Burrito') or a pair of soft tacos washed down with Mexican beer or an agua fresca (fresh fruit punch). The Mission District is where you'll find the most – and best – taquerías.

New American

In San Francisco's creative environment, there's still a prominent place for savory standards. New York strip steak, pork loins, and braised lamb chops accompanied by buttery mashed potatoes are mainstays of many of the city's most highly admired menus, and in those restaurants such meat-and-potato staples are called 'New American' cuisine. Expect organic meats and produce (potato varieties include everything but the russet) seasoned with originality.

San Francisco Traditions

San Francisco has its own treasured culinary traditions. At sidewalk seafood stalls in Fisherman's Wharf, you will see live Dungeness crab take a dunk in a cauldron of boiling water. The delicious crustaceans will soon appear at your table, either whole or in the form of crab Louis or crab cakes. San Francisco's distinctive sourdough bread makes a perfect, hearty accompaniment.

And, ahem, there's another wharf tradition that catches many a tourist's fancy. We are, of course, referring to chowder served in a hollowed round of sourdough bread. However, if you're trying to attain that special brand of San Francisco cool, be warned that most sensible locals would rather call their city 'Frisco' than eat this dish. That's why it's not offered in any restaurant outside of Fisherman's Wharf.

UNION SQUARE

The area around Union Square offers some of the finest four-star dining experiences in the city: Postrio, Masa's, Fleur de Lys, and Farallon are all within blocks of the square. There are also a few places in which to grab a quick, inexpensive bite to eat.

Franciscan Croissants (French bakery) MAP 2
301 Sutter St ☎ 415-398-8276 ⏲ 7:30am-6pm Mon-Sat, 10am-5pm Sun $ breakfast $3-5, lunch $5-6, dessert $3-5 C *cash only 🚌 2, 3, 4, 76, 30, 45 Muni ♿*

When all you want is a simple bite between stops while sightseeing or shopping, this small café comes in handy. Its croissant sandwiches and pastries are popular, and lines sometimes extend out the door.

Titanic Cafe (American) MAP 2
817 Sutter St ☎ 415-928-8870 ⏲ 7am-2pm daily $ breakfast $5-9, lunch $6.50-11, dessert $5.50 C *V, MC, DC 🚌 2, 3, 4, 76 Muni ♿*

A clean and smart-looking little spot (just a counter and half-dozen tables), the Titanic is well within reach of many of Union Square's hotels. Come here for an omelet, a burger, o

sandwich prepared with focaccia. The selec-
on is small but good.

:afé Claude (French) MAP 2
' Claude Lane ☎ 415-392-3505 11:30am-0:30pm Mon-Sat lunch $6.50-10, appe-'zer $4.50-9.50, entrée $11-13, dessert $5 c ', MC, AE, D, DC 2, 3, 4, 15, 76 Muni
ɪ www.cafeclaude.com

: Café Claude looks and feels authentically 'arisian, it's because the owner stripped out a 'aris bistro, shipped it to San Francisco, and eassembled it here. A zinc-topped bar, live ızz, and classic bistro fare all conspire to put ou in that Montparnasse frame of mind. Start vith a bowl of the best French onion soup in ne city, then tuck into daube en croûte (beef raised in red wine baked in pastry with mush-ooms) or duck breast with macaroni and armesan gratin. Bring along someone you ave romantic feelings for.

STEPHEN SAKS

Sidewalk seating at Café Claude

:orobudur (Indonesian) MAP 2
:00 Post St ☎ 415-775-1512 11:30am-'0pm daily lunch $6-7.50, appetizer $4-.50, entrée $6-14, dessert $3-4 c V, MC, ·E, D 2, 3, 4, 27, 38, 76 Muni
ɪ www.borobudursf.com

Named after a famous Javanese Buddhist temple, Borobudur has reasonable lunch specials and serves a variety of Indonesian specialties and has a good selection of vegetarian plates.

Café de la Presse (French bistro) MAP 2
352 Grant Ave ☎ 415-398-2680 7am-11pm daily appetizer $5.50-11.50, lunch $8.50-15.50 c V, MC, AE, D, DC 2, 3, 4, 76 Muni

Directly across from the Chinatown Gate, Café de la Presse sells an international selection of newspapers, magazines, and books, along with breakfast dishes, sandwiches, and burgers.

Anjou (French) MAP 2
44 Campton Place ☎ 415-392-5373 11:30am-2:30pm & 6pm-10pm Tues-Sat lunch $13.50-18, appetizer $3-14.50, entrée $15-20, dessert $5-6 c V, MC, D, DC, JCB 2, 3, 4, 15, 30, 45, 76 Muni
w www.anjou-sf.com

The menu changes regularly, but Anjou consistently delivers the goods. Just down an alley that seems to lead to nowhere, the wooden doors give way to an elegant and comfortable dining room, where bistro favorites are served with an elevated flare. On a given night, selections might include a crab tartlette (a flaky crust piled with generous chunks of crab and tomato in a creamy tartar sauce), or a fillet of bluenose bass so moist it parts at the slightest prod of your fork. Save room for Anjou's signature dessert, a delectable composition of pears in a warm Cointreau sabayon.

Grand Cafe (French) MAP 2
501 Geary St ☎ 415-292-0101 11:30am-2:30pm daily, 5:30pm-10pm Sun-Thurs, 5:30pm-11pm Fri-Sat lunch $8.50-18, appetizer $7-14, entrée $14-25, dessert $6 c V, MC, AE, D, DC 27, 38 Muni

Few dining rooms are as dazzling to look at as this one. Set in an old hotel ballroom and furnished extravagantly with enormous lamps hanging from the room's vaulted ceiling, the place lives up to its name. If the food (at mid-range to top-end prices) takes a back seat, it does so capably, with bold bistro fixtures, grilled and roasted meats, and buttery whipped potatoes.

Oritalia (fusion) MAP 2
590 Bush St ☎ 415-346-1333 5:30pm-10:30pm daily appetizer/small plate $9-11, entrée $17-27, dessert $7-8 c V, MC, AE, DC 2, 3, 4, 30, 45 Muni Powell-Mason, Powell-Hyde cable cars

If spaghetti, an adaptation of Chinese noodles prepared with ingredients available in Italy, is the origin of East-West fusion cuisine, then Oritalia is only taking a familiar concept a little further. The menu changes often but typically features dishes – like Asian-influenced cioppinos and risottos – that astutely bring together natural, if unexpected, combinations. Portions are small – the idea is to order a few plates for the table and 'graze.' Reservations are advisable most nights.

Farallon (seafood) MAP 2
450 Post St ☎ 415-956-6969 ⌚ 11:30am-10:30pm Mon-Wed, 11:30am-11pm Thurs-Sat, 2:30pm-5pm bistro menu only, 5pm-10pm Sun $ lunch appetizer $7-14, lunch $10-18, entrée $25-32, dessert $7-14 C V, MC, AE, D, DC 🚭 🚌 2, 3, 4, 76 Muni 🚋 Powell-Mason, Powell-Hyde cable cars ♿ W www.farallonrestaurant.com

Farallon makes a big splash with its outrageous underwater decor. Jellyfish chandeliers float from the ceiling, columns of russet kelp are lit from within, and octopus legs support the bar stools. The effect is more surreal aquatic dream than Disneyland kitsch. But the food, which the chef categorizes as 'coastal cuisine,' will not be outshined by the dining room. For seafood lovers, this is one of the city's great dining experiences. Feast on exquisite house-made caviars and follow them with roasted walleye pike with English-pea ravioli and mint pesto or succulent gulf prawns grilled to perfection and served with savory mushrooms, gnocchi, and watercress in sorrel sauce. You also can order quail or beef, but what's the point? Farallon redefines seafood.

Postrio (fusion) MAP 2
545 Post St ☎ 415-776-7825 ⌚ 11:30am-2pm & 5:30pm-10pm daily, café open all afternoon $ lunch appetizer $8.50-13.50, lunch $14.50-16, dinner appetizer $9-22, entrée $26-34, dessert $8-12 C V, MC, AE, D, DC 🚭 🚌 2, 3, 4, 76 Muni 🚋 Powell-Mason, Powell-Hyde cable cars ♿ W www.postrio.com

Few restaurants in San Francisco will make you feel better about dropping the big bills. Chef Wolfgang Puck's San Francisco atelier might be described as equal parts California kitchen, Paris bistro, Tokyo noodle bar, Milanese trattoria, and New York steak house. Sautéed foie gras with onion jam and hoisin sauce makes an ambitious starter. Main courses, from quail to grilled lamb to pan seared tuna, are expertly prepared with unex pected ingredients and are dazzlingl presented. Reservations are essential, unles you just stop at the café for a light bite.

Fleur de Lys (French) MAP 2
777 Sutter St ☎ 415-673-7779 ⌚ 6pm-9:30pm Mon-Thurs, 5:30pm-10:30pm Fri-Sat $ appetizer $16-24, entrée $31-38, dessert $10 C V, MC, AE, DC 🚭 🚌 limos accepted, 2, 3, 4, 76 Muni if taken discreetly ♿

Fleur de Lys entertains absurd fantasies, suc as dining in a harem tent…or in Barbar Eden's genie bottle. There's enough fabri covering the walls to outfit an entire circu company and enough flowers to deck out princess' coffin – understatement seems not t be the idea here. But with chef Hubert Kelle at the helm, the kitchen yields classic Frenc fare that is innovative rather than experimen tal, complex but prepared with a light hand To top it off, the service is impeccable. If yo can't get in, Keller is reportedly opening a ne restaurant, called Brasserie Keller, in SoMa.

Masa's (French) MAP 2
648 Bush St ☎ 415-989-7154, 800-258-7694 ⌚ 6pm-9:30pm Tues-Sat $ prix fixe $75 (4 courses), $80 (5 courses) C V, MC, AE, D, DC, JCB 🚌 limousine preferably, 30, 45 Muni 🚋 Powell-Mason, Powell-Hyde cable cars

In laid-back California, Masa's gets away wit being conservative and pricey because fo decades it's been one of the city's fines restaurants. Men are *required* to wear jacket and keeping your voice down happens natu rally – the regal atmosphere seems to induc hushed tones. Fun it isn't, but the haute-to the-hilt menu, which changes nightly, sizzle Expect foie gras, caviar, lobster, truffles, an filet mignon so tender you can chew it wit your eyelashes.

CIVIC CENTER

The Civic Center, Hayes Valley, and th Tenderloin embody all the extremes Sa Francisco has to offer, from the staid to th cutting edge to the down-and-out. Conse quently, there are many excellent lunchin and dining choices in the area, running th gamut from cheap Vietnamese to celebrit chefdom.

Max's Opera Cafe (American) MAP 3
;01 Van Ness Ave ☎ 415-771-7301 no eservations ⌚ 11:30am-10pm Sun-Mon, 11am-11pm Tues-Thurs, 11am-midnight Fri-at $ appetizer $4-10, entrée $7-25, dessert $2-7 C AE, D, DC, MC, V ⓘ 🚌 5, 12, 47, 49 Muni ♿

\t this glossy branch of the Max's chain (also ee South of Market), the day job/night job dis-inction blurs, as waiters divide their time be-ween serving your table and singing arias and how tunes. The food here plays on tried and rue New York deli classics, with excessive por-ions and high prices designed to make New 'orkers feel right at home. The pastrami sand-vich ($11) won't win over Carnegie Deli devo-ees, but Max's is an easy, relatively inexpensive lternative for moviegoers and the post-opera rowd. (Singers take up the mic around 7pm.)

ndigo (American) MAP 3
;87 McAllister St ☎ 415-673-9353 ⌚ 5pm-1pm Tues-Sat, 5pm-9:30pm Sun $ appe-izer $6-10, entrée $16-19, dessert $6.50 C AE, MC, V ⓘ 🚌 5, 21, 31, 42, 47, 49 Muni

Comfortable and friendly Indigo gets boister-ous on opera nights, and the often-changing nenu can be hit or miss. New American com-inations such as portobello layered with oasted squash, chevre, and tomato-corn salsa $8), or chicken breast with home fries and moked applewood bacon ($16.50) can be nasterful, if occasionally overseasoned. The hree-course prix fixe dinner ($27) is a good argain, with a selection of three entrées. The vine list includes some affordable choices, and esserts are excellent.

tars (California) MAP 3
55 Golden Gate Ave ☎ 415-861-7827 ⌚ 11:30am-2:30pm Mon-Fri, 5:30pm-11pm aily $ lunch $18.50-30, appetizer $6-15, ntrée $18.50-30, dessert $5.50-10 C AE, DC, MC, V ⓘ 🚌 47, 49 Muni ♿

tars was the pearl of San Francisco restau-ants in the 1980s, when chef Jeremiah Tower shered in the California cuisine fad here and elebrities flocked in like sheep. More recently, he restaurant has lost some of its cachet, and ower has moved on, but Stars still offers an njoyable, if expensive, dining experience. The hanging menu still features an assortment of ishes influenced by Mediterranean, Middle astern, and African cuisine. Despite Stars' eputation and the prices, it is not a stuffed hirt sort of place.

Jardinière (French/California) MAP 3
300 Grove St ☎ 415-861-5555 ⌚ 5pm-midnight Tues-Sat, 5pm-10:30pm Sun-Mon $ appetizer $10-20, entrée $25-36, dessert $9 C AE, DC, MC, V ⓘ 🚌 21, 47, 49 Muni ♿

French-California cuisine is at its best at chef Traci Des Jardins' swanky namesake restaurant. Formerly of Rubicon, Des Jardins offers a creative seasonal menu that never misses a step. Tender and savory selections might include the likes of seared scallops with potatoes bathed in a truffle sauce, tuna tartare dressed in a soy-ginger vinaigrette, truffle chicken pot pies, or a very fine duck breast with blood oranges. Jardinière's streamlined interior, featuring a smartly curved bar (cosmopolitans are the signature drink) and intimate, velvet-upholstered booths, draws nearly as many comments as the food.

HAYES VALLEY

Hayes St and its many cross streets have lots of good restaurants that are just a spit and a holler from Civic Center. The adjacent blocks of Market St, just to the south, are included in this section as well.

Powell's Place (soul food) MAP 3
511 Hayes St ☎ 415-863-1404 ⌚ 9am-11pm daily $ appetizer $2-3, entrée $3-12, dessert $3 C AE, D, DC, MC, V 🚌 5, 21 Muni ♿

Gospel singer and fried-chicken genius Emmit Powell has been attracting a steady stream of devotees to these laid-back environs since 1972. Order fried chicken, corn muffins, and red beans and rice (all for just $8) and kick back while the jukebox churns out R&B and soul classics. Vegetables are of the canned variety – and at Powell's, you wouldn't expect anything less.

Vicolo Pizzeria (Italian) MAP 3
201 Ivy St ☎ 415-863-2382 ⌚ 11:30am-2pm Mon-Fri, 5pm-9pm Mon-Thurs, 5pm-10:30pm Fri, noon-10:30pm Sat, noon-9pm Sun $ pizza slice $3.50, pizza pie $19.50 C MC, V ⓘ 🚌 21, 47, 49 Muni ♿

Vicolo spins out basic and designer pizzas over the counter, whole or by the slice. Slices are slim and pricey, but whole pies come out to be a pretty good deal.

Caffé delle Stelle (Italian) MAP 3
330 Gough St ☎ 415-252-1110 ⌚ 11:30am-3pm daily, 5pm-10pm Mon-Thurs,

Vegetarian Food

The days are long past when a vegetarian had to have a private conference with a restaurant's chef before ordering that plate of steamed vegetables. More people than ever before are vegetarian, and almost every restaurant in San Francisco will have something vegetarian on its menu. But why settle for a token, uninspired menu item when there are so many great places in town where the kitchen specializes in vegetarian cooking?

Millennium MAP 3

246 McAllister St ☎ 415-487-9800 ⌚ 5pm-9:30pm daily $ appetizer $4-8, entrée $13-18, dessert $4-6 C DC, MC, V 🚭 🚌 5, 19, 42, 47, 49 Muni ♿

Inside the Abigail Hotel in the Civic Center, not far from City Hall, Millennium is one of the city's best vegan restaurants. The breaded pan-sautéed seitan medallions and rosemary polenta may convert hard-core carnivores.

Lucky Creation MAP 5

854 Washington St ☎ 415-989-0818 ⌚ 11am-9:30pm Thurs-Tue $ appetizer $4-6, entrée $4-6.50 C cash only 🚭 🚌 30, 45 Muni 🚋 Powell-Mason, Powell-Hyde cable cars ♿

You'll find some of the city's healthiest food in this little Chinatown dive. Fresh, colorful vegetables, prepared with all-natural ingredients, appear in soups and gluten puffs, or are sautéed and served over pan-fried noodles or rice. Meatless 'chicken' dishes serve as a reminder that Buddhist vegetarian chefs pioneered many techniques only recently adopted by their Western colleagues.

Greens MAP 9

Fort Mason, Building A ☎ 415-771-6222 ⌚ 11:30am-2pm Tues-Fri, 5:30pm-9:30pm Mon-Fri, 10am-2pm & 6pm-9pm Sat (prix fixe only); take-out 8am-4:30pm Tues-Sat, 9:30am-3:30pm Sun $ appetizer $5.50-10, lunch $6-12, entrée $14-19, dessert $3.50-7 C D, MC, V 🚭 🚌 22, 28, 30 Muni ♿

Greens, at Fort Mason on the edge of the Marina, is one of the USA's best-known vegetarian restaurants. There's real imagination at play in the dishes, and the results are generally terrific. On Friday and Saturday, Greens serves a fixed-price dinner, typically for about $36. There's also a bakery and take-out counter, so if you can't afford a full meal you can still enjoy a picnic on the waterfront.

Herbivore MAP 14

983 Valencia St ☎ 415-826-5657 ⌚ 11am-10pm Sun-Thurs, 11am-11pm Fri-Sat $ appetizer $2-6, entrée $5-13, dessert $2-3.50 C MC, V 🚭 🚌 14, 26, 49 Muni ♿

The efficient architectural lines of this Mission District restaurant's interior foreshadow the clean, healthful vegan dishes on the menu. Herbivore calls itself a grill, but soy- and gluten-based meat substitutes like tempeh and seitan sometimes dry out when cooked over an open flame. Regulars recommend the ravioli and lasagne. Sandwiches cost around $6.

The Ganges MAP 15

775 Frederick St ☎ 415-661-7290 ⌚ 5pm-10pm Tues-Sun $ appetizer $2-6, entrée $3-8, dessert $3, prix fixe $14 C MC, V 🚭 🚌 71, N Muni

Near the Haight and Golden Gate Park, The Ganges is an Indian vegetarian spot. Soothing lighting and soft raga music create an ambience that may induce you to go with the pillow-seating option (tables and chairs are also available). In order to experience the full range of the menu, go with a combination dinner ($11.50 to $15.50), which includes dahl, pappadam, chapati, and several main dishes – chana masala (garbanzo and mushroom curry) is a highlight. Reservations are recommended.

ṡpm-10:30pm Fri-Sun ⓢ lunch $8-10, ·ppetizer $4.50-8.50, entrée $8.50-15, lessert $4-5 ⓒ AE, D, DC, MC, V ⓟ ⓑ 21, 42, 47, 49 Muni ♿

Ɔelle Stelle is not so much a 'café of the stars' ıs a reasonably priced, always-packed trattoria vith simple, pleasant decor and friendly service. ·resh bread, a tasty dipping sauce, and pitchers ɔf sparkling water tide you over while you peuse a menu promising smartly prepared pastas. Ɔrder a bottle of the house wine, then begin vith fagottino, a delectable purse of grilled, nozzarella-stuffed cabbage doused in porcini. ·ollow that up with rich, savory gnocchi with ontina, honey, and chicken-apple sausage, or . lighter fresh asparagus-and-tomato ravioli.

ıuppenküche (German) MAP 3
ṡ01 Hayes St ☎ 415-252-9289 ⓗ 5pm-Opm daily, 10am-2:30pm Sat-Sun ⓢ appetizer $4.50-11.50, entrée $8-16, lessert $5 ⓒ AE, D, MC, V ⓑ 5, 21, 22 Muni

ι clean, well-lit, and sparsely decorated room vith long wooden tables and benches (you ıay have to share a table with other patrons) ıight sound a little severe, but it serves Sup·enkuche's stripped-down emphasis on food, rink, and satisfied souls. The specialty is Gerıanic comfort foods such as sautéed venison vith spaetzle and smoked pork chops with auerkraut – sustenance that goes well with all, frothy glasses of beer (18 choices on tap). lowever, the place does lack a solid round of eer-hall ballads.

ıbsinthe Brasserie & Bar French/California) MAP 3
98 Hayes St ☎ 415-551-1590 ⓗ 11:30am-am Tues-Fri, 10:30am-1am Sat, 10:30am-0:30pm Sun ⓢ lunch $9-22, appetizer 3-14, entrée $16-25, dessert $6-8 ⓒ AE, D, ɔC, MC, V ⓟ ⓑ 21, 42, 47, 49 Muni ♿

.bsinthe refashions Paris of the 1920s with hic velvet lounges, curling brass accents, and rt. The continental cuisine is hit-and-miss – eafood, meat, and pasta dishes are surprisıgly simple, portions are small, and prices are little steep. At the bar you can order from a easonably priced seafood menu. And no, ıey don't serve absinthe, the wormwoodased liqueur notorious (and outlawed) for riving belle époque roués mad.

uni Cafe (Mediterranean) MAP 3
658 Market St ☎ 415-552-2522 ⓗ 11:30am-midnight Tues-Sat, 11am-11pm un ⓢ lunch $10-18, appetizer $6-12, entrée $25-32, dessert $8-13 ⓒ AE, MC, V ⓟ ⓑ 6, 7, 26, 66, 71, F Muni ♿

Halfway through its third decade, stylish and casual Zuni remains a standard bearer in the San Francisco culinary parade. The modern menu changes daily but always features superb oysters (nearly two dozen varieties) and grilled and roasted meats and fish. Zuni's focaccia burger ($10; not available from 6pm to 10pm) is considered one of the city's best.

THE TENDERLOIN

Saigon Sandwiches (Vietnamese) MAP 3
560 Larkin St ☎ 415-474-5698 ⓗ 7am-4pm daily ⓢ $2.50 ⓒ cash only ⓑ 19, 31 Muni ♿

This little deli churns out simple Vietnamese sandwiches for less than $3 – an amazing deal, considering the sandwiches comprise of fresh French bread, tasty meats (barbecued chicken, pork, headcheese), sliced vegetables, and dressings.

Pho Hoa (Vietnamese) MAP 3
431 Jones St ☎ 415-673-3163 ⓗ 8am-8pm daily ⓢ $4.50-6 ⓒ cash only ⓑ 27, 38 Muni ♿

Pho's the way to go at Pho Hoa. The place is large and rarely crowded, but the soup is hot and satisfying.

Pho Thai Binh Duong (Pacific Restaurant; Vietnamese) MAP 3
337 Jones St ☎ 415-928-4022 ⓗ 10am-5pm Mon & Wed-Sun ⓢ appetizer $4.50-5, entrée $4.50-6.50 ⓒ cash only ⓑ 27, 31, 38 Muni ♿

A few years back, this dimly lit and unassuming restaurant was momentarily plucked from obscurity when Alice Waters began trumpeting its praises, but Pacific Restaurant has pretty much slinked back into its foxhole, serving a predominantly Vietnamese clientele. Here you can choose from a steaming bowl of pho, which rates among the best San Francisco has to offer, or barbecued meats with rice or noodles and piles of fresh basil and mint leaves.

Viet Nam II (Vietnamese) MAP 3
701 Larkin St ☎ 415-885-1274 ⓗ 8am-midnight daily ⓢ appetizer $4-9, entrée $4.50-7.50 ⓒ MC, V ⓟⓟ ⓑ 19, 38 Muni ♿

With one of the Tenderloin's most highly esteemed menus, Viet Nam II is no more expensive or fussy than its neighbors. In addition to good rice and noodle staples, the menu

PLACES TO EAT

includes fresh seafood specials and a variety of vegetarian plates. It's not on the menu, but inquire about the canh chua – a delicious catfish soup ladled out in an ambrosial pineapple and tamarind broth.

Tu Lan (Vietnamese) MAP 3
8 6th St ☎ 415-626-0927 ⌚ 11am-9:30pm Mon-Sat $ appetizer $4-5.50, entrée $4-11, dessert $1.50 C cash only ⓥⓥ 🚌 Market St buses, 14 Muni ♿

There are two things San Franciscans go to skid row for – to buy crack and to eat at Tu Lan. Some real surprises await beyond the grimy façade, at the frenzied counter, and in the cluttered little dining rooms: a whole pompano, deep-fried and drenched in a ginger sauce; 'ten things in a pot' ($11), which turns out to be a simple but soothing soup brimming with meat and vegetables; and myriad vegetarian choices. The stir-fries and imperial rolls can be greasy…but they're darn tasty.

Original Joe's (Italian/American) MAP 3
144 Taylor St ☎ 415-775-4877 ⌚ 10:30am-midnight Sun-Thu, 10:30am-12:30am Fri-Sat $ breakfast $4-14, appetizer $1-9, entrée $6-25, dessert $2-5 C AE, CB, D, DC, MC, V Ⓜ Powell St BART & Muni station 🚌 Market St buses ♿

Joe's dapper veteran staff and plush Naugahyde booths are a welcome escape from the trendy dining rooms of nearby Union Square. Rich, hearty Italian American standards, such as veal parmigiana ($14) and spaghetti bolognese ($8), and flame-grilled steaks and burgers may not always agree with delicate 21st-century stomachs (whatever happened to the sturdy models of the last century?), but Joe's is a righteous indulgence now and then.

SOUTH OF MARKET

The new money's in SoMa. Every month hot new restaurants open in this part of town, but the old standbys haven't necessarily suffered from the increased competition. When it comes to culinary variety, SoMa is a wide terrain.

Budget

Red's Java House (American) MAP 4
The Embarcadero ⌚ 6am-4pm Mon-Fri $ breakfast $1-2.50, lunch $2-3 C cash only 🚌 42, N Muni

A beloved relic of the old port, Red's (since

STEPHEN SAKS

Get jumpin' at Red's Java House.

1912) serves the cheapest lunch around. Th longshoremen are long gone, but the humbl shack still specializes in coffee-and-donu breakfasts and greasy double cheeseburger and Bud in a bottle for lunch.

Caffe Centro (Italian) MAP 4
102 South Park Ave ☎ 415-882-1500 ⌚ 7am-6pm Mon-Fri, 8am-4pm Sat $ breakfast $1-4.50, lunch $2-6.50, dessert $1-3.50 C V, MC ($10 minimum) ⓥ 🚌 15, 30, 42, 76 Muni ♿

What's sweet about Caffe Centro is that Sout Park is one little pocket in the city where side walk tables really make sense. The lack o noisy traffic, the South Park greenery, nic weather and a laid-back, secluded atmospher are reason enough to swing out here; goo strong coffee, simple but fine pastries, panin and healthful sandwiches cap it.

Caffe Museo (Mediterranean) MAP 4
151 3rd St ☎ 415-357-4500 ⌚ 11am-6pm Fri Tues, 11am-9pm Thurs $ entrée $5-9, desser $3 C V, MC, AE ⓥ 🚌 9, 14, 15, 30 Muni ♿

SFMOMA has a very California and ver pleasant café where pizzas, panini sandwiche soups, and salads are ordered at a counter an then served at your table. It's not merely con venient – the food is prepared with care an prices are not really out of line. On weekend a lively see-and-be-seen crowd adds interes to the sidewalk tables.

Mid-Range

Max's Diner (American) MAP 4
311 3rd St ☎ 415-546-6297 ⌚ 11am-10pm

un-Thurs, 11am-midnight Fri-Sat Ⓢ *break-ast $5-12, appetizer $3-13, entrée $6.50-4, dessert $3-5.50* Ⓒ *AE, DC, MC, V* ⓟ *Montgomery St BART & Muni station* 🚌 *12, 15, 30, 45 Muni* ♿

ighthearted fake '50s diner atmosphere and eavyweight American fare are served up in enerous portions at Max's. Ample booths are genuinely serviceable feature – over lunch or inner you'll feel your hind side growing into hat extra space. In truth, the menu includes ome health-conscious, low-fat items, but the narquee items are more along the lines of reat burgers, chicken-fried steak, pot roast, nd ice-cream sodas. Heaping homestyle reakfasts are served all day.

asil Thai (Thai) MAP 4
175 Folsom St ☎ *415-552-8999* ⏲ *11:30am-2:45pm Mon-Fri, 5pm-10pm aily* Ⓢ *lunch appetizer $3.50-8, lunch 6.50-10, entrée $8.50-14, dessert $3-6* *AE, MC, V* ⓟ 🚌 *12, 19, 27 Muni* ♿

)n a strip crowded with dance clubs and outh hostels, Basil Thai smartly combines arty oMa attitude and sophisticated Thai cuisine. hough familiar Thai classics are on the menu, e kitchen sets itself apart with the subtle fla-ors of dishes like goong-gra-bog (deep-fried arcels of succulent prawns), kang ped (a oney-roasted duck with pineapple curry), nd eggplant with tofu and vegetables in a asil-chili puree. Alas, it's also more expensive han the average Thai restaurant.

uca di Beppo (Italian) MAP 4
55 Howard St ☎ *415-543-7673* ⏲ *5pm-0pm Mon-Thurs, 5pm-11pm Fri, 4pm-1pm Sat, noon-10pm Sun* Ⓢ *appetizer 6-13, entrée $8-20, dessert $6-9* Ⓒ *V, MC, E, DC* 🚌 *12, 27, 30, 45, 76 Muni* ♿

omehow, without being noticed, Buca di eppo, a Minneapolis-based chain, has man-ged to take over America. (If you live in this ountry, chances are there's one in your own or in the nearest city.) Perhaps the acklash hasn't come yet because Buca di eppo was conceptualized by screwballs hose wiseassery verges on insanity. Its din-g rooms and toilets are irreverent galleries elebrating Italian Americana, Pope John aul II, and absurd comedy, among other ings, and a raucous party seems to be in rogress at each table. Surprisingly, the tchen staff takes its job quite seriously – esty pastas and chicken cacciatores are served on huge family-style platters (bring a large group and order about one dish for every three or four of you).

Julie's Supper Club (American/California) MAP 4
1123 Folsom St ☎ *415-861-0707* ⏲ *5pm-10pm Mon-Wed, 5pm-11pm Thurs-Sat* Ⓢ *appetizer up to $8, entrée up to $16, dessert $5.50* Ⓒ *V, AE, DC, MC* 🚌 *12, 19 Muni* ♿

An old-timer on the SoMa scene (since 1987), Julie's is still alive and kicking. Its whimsical 1950s interior (note the Marlin Room that resembles a fish tank) and swing-ing piped-in music set an upbeat tone. The California-cuisine dinner menu is uneven, so come during happy hour (weekdays 5pm to 7pm) for $3 martinis and lemon drops and for stellar appetizers that are on the house. It's an economical way to fuel up and get gassed.

Infusion Bar & Restaurant (American) MAP 4
555 2nd St ☎ *415-543-2282* ⏲ *11:30am-3pm Mon-Fri, 5pm-10pm Mon-Thurs & Sat, 5pm-11pm Fri* Ⓢ *lunch appetizer $6-8, lunch $5.50-11, dinner appetizer $4-11, entrée $9-22, dessert $4-6* Ⓒ *AE, DC, MC, V* 🚌 *15, 42 Muni* ♿

Infusion has a gimmick, to be sure. The name refers to the place's signature item – yucky drinks that mix Russian booze with exotic fruits. However, the restaurant has some very solid offerings, like tequila filet mignon ($22) served with chipotle mashed potatoes, and a traditional cheeseburger with fries ($9). Pacific Bell Park is a short walk from here.

South Park Cafe (French) MAP 4
108 South Park Ave ☎ *415-495-7275* ⏲ *7:30am-11am & 11:30am-2:30pm Mon-Fri, 5:30pm-10pm Mon-Sat* Ⓢ *lunch appetizer $2.50-9.50, lunch $6.50-12.50, dinner appe-tizer $4.50-8.50, entrée $12.50-18.50, dessert $2-4* Ⓒ *AE, MC, V* 🚌 *15, 30, 42, 45 Muni* ♿

SoMa's hip and energetic interpretation of the French bistro, South Park Cafe packs in a lively multimedia crowd for lunch and a more so-phisticated crowd in the evening. The lure is a pleasant (at night romantic) atmosphere and solid traditional French fare, including steamed mussels soaked in white-wine sauce and served with wonderful fries, steak frites, roasted duck breast, French 'tapas,' a nice se-lection of reasonably priced wines, and deli-cious desserts.

Restaurant LuLu (French/Italian) MAP 4
816 Folsom St ☎ 415-495-5775 11:30am-10:30pm Sun-Thurs, 11:30am-11:30pm Fri-Sat lunch $8-18, appetizer $2-11, entrée $12-23, dessert $7-11 C AE, DC, MC, V 12, 30, 45 Muni

Occupying a stylishly converted auto-repair shop, LuLu overwhelms diners with its constant motion and noisy scene-makers. The open kitchen is a hive of activity, with several flaming ovens dedicated to cooking rotisserie meats – the pork and chicken are particularly tender and tasty – and flaky pizzas. In all the hustle and bustle, it's no wonder plates of mashed potatoes sometimes go cold before they make it to your table. Diners can also assemble a satisfying meal of oysters from the raw bar and antipasti and other small plates for the table.

Fringale (French) MAP 4
570 4th St ☎ 415-543-0573 11:30am-3pm Mon-Fri, 5:30pm-10:30pm Mon-Sat lunch appetizer $3.50-16, lunch $9-20, dinner appetizer $5.50-18, entrée $14.50-23, dessert $6-7 C AE, MC, V 9, 15, 30, 45 Muni

Crowded and noisy Fringale is an unassuming little place with very French waiters to go with its exceptional French-Basque food. The restaurant has built a strong reputation on dishes like a mashed-potato cake studded with shredded duck confit. Fish specials, steamed mussels, pork loins, and steak frites will have you coming back for more. To cap it off, desserts are fantastic and prices very reasonable.

Top End

Azie (fusion) MAP 4
826 Folsom St ☎ 415-538-9444 5:30pm-10:30pm Sun-Thurs, 5:30pm-11:30pm Fri-Sat appetizer $9-20, entrée $25-32, dessert $8-13 C AE, DC, MC, V 12 Muni

Azie presents creative Asian/French cuisine with polish. A cool, soothing atmosphere is established with subdued lighting and intimate and modern decor, though an odd experiment currently has a trip-hop DJ spinning on weekend evenings. Prices are high, but the exquisite food coming out of the kitchen – spicy fish parfait ($13) or half a dozen tender medallions of roast duck in blood-orange sauce ($26) – lives up to expectations.

ANTHONY PIDGEON

Azie – so cool it's hot

Dine (American) MAP 4
662 Mission St ☎ 415-538-3463 5:30pm 10pm Mon-Thurs, 5:30pm-11pm Fri-Sat appetizer $7-12, entrée $17-26, dessert $7-9 C AE, MC, V Montgomery St BART & Muni station 14, 15, 30, 45 Muni

Earthy tones and dark wood lend a surprisingly warm feeling to this hip SoMa spot nea Yerba Buena Gardens. The welcoming amb ence is a suitable complement to the moder and flavorful food. The butter-lettuce sala accompanied by a tangy blue cheese dress ing, is large enough for two, and light seared scallops are a memorable warm-u act for a perfectly seasoned risotto or tend lamb entrée.

Boulevard (contemporary American) MAP 4
1 Mission St ☎ 415-543-6084 11:30am-2pm Mon-Fri, 5:30pm-10pm Sun-Wed, 5:30pm-10:30pm Thurs-Sat lunch $12.50-17, appetizer $8.50-18, entrée $26-34, dessert $9-12.50 C AE, D, DC, M, V Embarcadero BART & Muni station 14, F Muni

Boulevard's exquisite belle époque ambience raises expectations for a highly spirited evening and superb food, and the restaurant delivers. Chef Nancy Oakes has a truly fine way with savory pork loins, lamb chops, duck, fish, and mounds of buttery mashed potatoes. Of course, living it up like this will cost you big bucks, and reservations are essential.

Hawthorne Lane (California/Asian fusion) MAP 4
22 Hawthorne St ☎ 415-777-9779 11:30am-2pm Mon-Fri, 5:30pm-10pm Sun-Thurs, 5:30pm-10:30pm Fri-Sat lunch appetizer $7-10, lunch $11.50-16, dinner appetizer $9-17.50, entrée $26-34, dessert $7-8.50 CB, D, DC, JCB, MC, V 12, 15, 30, 45, 76 Muni

Hidden away in a beautifully converted warehouse on an alley near SFMOMA, Hawthorne Lane is one of the city's most highly regarded restaurants. Its oft-shifting menu of California-Asia fusion emphasizes top-notch ingredients and dishes that are exquisitely presented and flavorful. Seafood entrées shine and might include miso-glazed scallops paired with taro-shrimp dumplings ($30) or a simple preparation of pan-roasted monkfish with lentils ($28). A more economical alternative is grazing on the bar's appetizers. Reservations are essential.

FINANCIAL DISTRICT

Although the Financial District dies at night, there are a surprising number of interesting dinner places along its outer edges. On Sunday, many of these places will be closed.

Budget

The area has a wealth of small places where you can grab a quick bite, and there are a few very good cafés here, too. However, most of the inexpensive joints shut down before dinner.

Palio Paninoteca (Italian) MAP 5
505 Montgomery St ☎ 415-362-6900 6am-4pm Mon-Fri breakfast $2-4, lunch $6-10 V, MC, AE, D 1, 15 Muni

This busy, well-lit café makes excellent coffee and panini sandwiches, along with salads, soup, lasagne, and polenta.

Il Massimo del Panino (Italian) MAP 5
441 Washington St ☎ 415-834-0290 7:30am-3pm Mon-Fri lunch $3.50-6.50, dessert $1-2 V, MC, D 12, 42 Muni

Basically a cafeteria, Il Massimo draws businesspeople in droves for Italian sandwiches at very fair prices. The half-hungry can order half-sandwiches at a bargain price. The crudo sandwich on focaccia is certain to please prosciutto lovers, and if you'd rather picnic outdoors you're only a block from Redwood Plaza, in the shadow of the Transamerica Pyramid.

360° Gourmet Burritos (Mexican fusion) MAP 5
359 Kearny St ☎ 415-989-8077 10am-8:30pm Mon-Fri, 11am-4pm Sat $5-8 V, MC, AE 15, 41 Muni

The 'gourmet' burrito is dangerous – it tampers unnecessarily with the burrito concept. But some people really go for 'em. Imagine – artichokes, goat cheese, or roasted duck in a burrito. All right, we're picking on the most unusual ones. Traditional varieties are also available. Our thumb's not all the way up, but it's not down either.

PLACES TO EAT

Mid-Range

One of the city's liveliest restaurant zones is the 'French Ghetto' that straddles the Financial District and Union Square line. Just off Bush in this transition zone is tiny Belden St, which is closed to traffic to allow alfresco Mediterranean dining from end to end. Belden St draws office workers during the lunch rush; on warm afternoons and evenings, it's a great place to enjoy a leisurely late lunch or dinner, although some people complain that with the warmer weather comes a faint odor from this ancient alleyway (you can ask for a table indoors if you prefer). During the rush, you might want to wait until you see where seating is available before deciding which restaurant to patronize. At all of these places, you can eat well for $10 to $15 at lunch, although if you're drinking, the tab will easily double.

Metropol (Italian-Austrian) MAP 5
168 Sutter St ☎ 415-732-7777 7:30am-9pm Mon-Fri, 11:30am-4pm Sat breakfast $4-9, entrée $9-16, dessert $3-6 V, MC, AE, D, DC 2, 3, 4, 15, 30, 41 Muni

This smart and locally favored Austrian-owned café does a brisk lunchtime business, and the

Frisco Classics

Well into the 20th century, San Francisco's mainstay establishments were those that offered varied but basic menus built on steaks, chops, simple pastas, and local fruits of the sea – crabs, oysters, sole, and salmon. Surprisingly, many of these old restaurants continue to thrive in spite of – or perhaps because of – the city's continuously revolving door of trendy new restaurants.

John's Grill MAP 2

63 Ellis St ☎ 415-986-3274 ⌚ 11am-10pm Mon-Sat, 5pm-10pm Sun $ lunch $8-15, appetizer $7-14, entrée $17-28, dessert $6-7 C V, MC, AE, DC M Powell St BART & Muni station 🚌 27, 30, 45 Muni ♿

W www.johnsgrill.com

John's has been offering up traditional grill food since 1908. The restaurant received a break in the 1930s, when Dashiell Hammett gave John's a brief mention in his novel *The Maltese Falcon* (Hammett dined here frequently while working next door for the Pinkerton agency). John's has been boasting the connection ever since – the food takes second billing to the history and atmosphere of the place. On the extensive menu, fresh fish is a safe bet. Prices are steep for food of this quality, but this is an essential stop if you're tailing Hammett.

House of Shields MAP 4

39 New Montgomery St ☎ 415-392-7732 ⌚ 11:30am-10pm daily C MC, V M Montgomery St BART & Muni station 🚌 Market St buses, 14, F Muni

Nailed to a wall over one of the mahogany booths in this amazing relic (since 1908) is a framed newspaper column that comments on what an old-fashioned place House of Shields is – and *that* was written half a century ago. Patrons line the long mahogany bar and squeeze into narrow wood booths, waiters follow a series of well-worn paths on the tile floor, and an ancient stuffed moose's head overlooks the scene with an air of contentment (he and his companions, a bull and a stag, were dusted off only a few years ago). There's live jazz music some nights. House of Shields serves fish and meat classics, and the burgers are excellent.

Sam's Grill & Seafood Restaurant MAP 5

374 Bush St ☎ 415-421-0594 ⌚ 11am-9pm Mon-Fri $ appetizer $4-12, entrée $9-25, dessert $3.50-6 C V, MC, AE, JCB M Montgomery St BART & Muni station 🚌 1, 5, 30, 31, 38, 69 ♿

Sam's first opened its doors in 1867, and it hasn't changed a bit since moving to its present location in 1946. The historic atmosphere and Financial District location mean Sam's is still a clubby, manly sort of place, with private booths and starched white tablecloths. The food is a trip down memory lane – fresh fish offerings like petrale sole and salmon, pasta on the side, and heaps of sourdough bread.

Tadich Grill MAP 5

240 California St ☎ 415-391-1849 ⌚ 11am-9:30pm Mon-Fri, 11:30am-9:30pm Sat $ appetizer $4-13, entrée $12-42, dessert $3-4 C V, MC M Embarcadero BART & Muni station 🚌 1, F Muni 🚋 California St cable car ♿

If Tadich, San Francisco's oldest restaurant, weren't so damn busy all the time, it would pass as the sort of place Edward Hopper liked to paint. It has that 1930s brand of unfussy class: a long counter for solitary diners, tables in the window, hat and coat hangers, and older, gentlemanly waiters. Even the loud, puffed-up businessmen who jam into the narrow wooden booths can't spoil the atmosphere. The menu, with its standard grill fare, is also a San Francisco relic, although it has a few Mediterranean-style seafood surprises. Ask which fish is fresh before you order. Reservations are not taken, so come early if you don't want to wait long for a table.

asual but efficient service helps keep prices own. Soups and sandwiches are all gourmet uality – zesty specialties include roasted pork oin and grilled eggplant – and they make a atisfying meal for less than $10. More in-olved fare, making for a hearty dinner, is also vailable, like oven-roasted salmon and rose-nary chicken and a selection of pizzas and astas.

:afe Tiramisù (Italian) MAP 5
elden St ☎ 415-421-7044 ⌚ 11:30am-3:30pm Aon-Fri, 5pm-11:30pm Mon-Sat $ appetizer 6-11.50, entrée $11-24, dessert $7 C *V, MC, E, D, DC* 🚌 *2, 3, 4, 15, 41, 76 Muni* ♿

t this warm and convivial basement restau-ant, the waitstaff often greet diners with a earty *'Buona sera!'* The food is equally grat-ying and innovative – a carpaccio appetizer, oasted pork chops with blackberry currant auce, smoked-venison, and blackberry ravi-li may appear on the ever-changing menu.)ccasionally, the kitchen overreaches for that ndescribable new flavor. The hot dessert em, of course, is that rich, chocolate, creamy iramisù.

'louf (French/seafood) MAP 5
elden St ☎ 415-986-6491 ⌚ 11:30am-3pm Aon-Fri, 5:30pm-10pm Mon-Wed, 5:30pm-nidnight Thurs-Sat $ lunch $13-17, appe-izer $5.50-13.50, entrée $13.50-24, dessert 7 C *V, MC, AE* 🚌 *2, 3, 4, 15, 41, 76 Muni*

'louf is French for 'splash,' and that's the ound you'll hear when you plunge into ome of the seafood dishes served here. Snorkeling sounds are discouraged.) The hip ut casual bistro atmosphere and tables out n the alley make this a popular lunch spot n sunny days, and the house specialty, teamed mussels, is great for sharing with a mall group. The chubby mollusks are eaped in iron cauldrons and bathed in your ick of eight sauces, all of which go wonder-ully with crisp, slender fries. Additional fruits e la mer include clams, swordfish, ahi tuna, nd sautéed monkfish.

:afé Bastille (French) MAP 5
2 Belden St ☎ 415-986-5673 ⌚ 11:30am-0pm Mon-Sat $ lunch $8-11, appetizer 5-9, entrée $13-18, dessert $5 C *V, MC, E* 🚌 *2, 3, 4, 15, 41, 76 Muni* ♿ *limited*

his happening little bistro offers some inter-sting table choices – basement or alley? astille anchors the Belden St scene, and each uly it hosts the French Ghetto's annual Bastille Day celebration. The standard bistro fare (steak frites, etc) and savory crepes are of un-even quality, but a European expat crowd and jazz combos make it a lively joint most nights of the week.

Top End

Naturally, the Financial District has its share of prestigious expense-account restaurants, many of which tempt noncorporate types to venture into this part of town for that some-thing special on the menu.

Rubicon (California/French) MAP 5
558 Sacramento St ☎ 415-434-4100 ⌚ 11:30am-2:30pm Mon-Fri, 5:30pm-10:30pm Mon-Thurs, 5:30pm-11pm Fri-Sat $ lunch appetizer $7-11, lunch $14-17, dinner appetizer $9-17, entrée $21-29, dessert $7-13 C *V, MC, AE, DC* 🚌 *1, 9, 15, 42 Muni* ♿

Although some longtime devotees of Rubicon insist it is no longer up to snuff, the restaurant hasn't yet forfeited its national reputation for serving up exciting gourmet cuisine. French sauces dress up the daily selection of fish and meat dishes. Rubicon's bustling parade of servers and somewhat boisterous atmosphere are better suited for a celebration than an in-timate dinner. Wine connoisseurs will enjoy poring over the 24-page wine list.

Aqua (seafood) MAP 5
252 California St ☎ 415-956-9662 ⌚ 11:30am-2:30pm Mon-Fri, 5:30pm-10:30pm Mon-Thurs, 5:30pm-11pm Fri-Sat $ lunch appetizer $11-20, lunch $18-25, dinner appetizer $11-60, entrée $28-42, dessert $9 C *V, MC, AE, DC* Ⓜ *Embarcadero BART & Muni station* 🚌 *1, 8 Muni* *California St cable car* ♿

With its emphasis squarely on seafood, Aqua is by many accounts San Francisco's best restaurant. French traditions with subtle Cali-fornia twists underlie many of the dishes, and truffles, foie gras, and rich sauces figure prominently. Appetizers include delectable caviar, and entrées range from medallions of ahi tuna with seared foie gras in a pinot noir sauce to Maine lobster with fresh shavings of black truffle. Indecisive diners can opt for the tasting menu – five signature dishes for $68 (the vegetarian version is $55). The extensive wine list commendably includes choices as low as $15. Reserve your table four to six weeks ahead of time.

JACKSON SQUARE

The Jackson Square Historic District is home to some of the city's most stylish restaurants. But the eating's not cheap here.

Bix (American) MAP 5
56 Gold St ☎ 415-433-6300 ⏰ 11:30am-11pm Mon-Thurs, 11:30am-midnight Fri, 5:30pm-midnight Sat $ appetizer $7-16, entrée $14-30, dessert $6.50 [C] V, MC, AE, D, DC 🚌 15, 42 Muni

Hidden away on a narrow alley, Bix sports stylized art deco trimmings that evoke early-20th-century steamship luxury. The American menu offers a few contemporary twists, like a tender and juicy chicken stuffed with prosciutto served on wild rice. The best tables, on the mezzanine level, overlook a swank mahogany bar and a dining room that resembles a 1930s dance hall. You'll want to look sharp and start with serious cocktails.

Cypress Club (American) MAP 5
500 Jackson St ☎ 415-296-8555 ⏰ 5:30pm-10pm Sun-Thurs, 5:30pm-11pm Fri-Sat $ appetizer $9-17, entrée $24-37, dessert $8-10 [C] V, MC, AE, DC 🚌 15, 30, 41, 45 Muni ♿

The Cypress Club's dining room takes some getting used to. It looks like it was designed by a cartoonist, with bulbous columns, strange parachutelike lights hanging from above, and a shocking orange-and-gold color scheme. Stylishly presented New American offerings, like steak in a tangy wine-reduction sauce with mashed potatoes with truffle oil, aren't spectacular, but they do add flair to the good-time atmosphere.

CHINATOWN

Chinatown is packed with hole-in-the-wall hash houses and cavernous but economical dim sum parlors. Most Chinatown restaurants have separate Chinese and English menus, and the difference isn't just in the semantics. Often, Chinese-speaking patrons are getting different food from English-speakers – stuffed pork belly and such. Sometimes fresh seafood items are not on the menu either. If you're an adventurous eater looking for a more intense dining experience, it sometimes pays to chat up your waiter – ask questions and point discreetly toward that steaming sea bass sitting on your neighbor's table if that's what you want.

Kam Po (HK)K (Chinese) MAP 5
801 Broadway ☎ 415-982-3516 ⏰ 10am-8pm daily $ $2-4 [C] cash only 🚌 30, 45, 83 Muni

If you're on a tight budget, the nondescrip and mysteriously named Kam Po (HK)K is you ticket. Good, basic victuals await those wh venture past the dead ducks and less-familia items that hang in the window. Steamin wonton soups and a variety of rice plates ca be had for under $4. The chopped roast pork a house specialty, is addictive. Kam Po close early on slow nights.

Star Lunch (Chinese) MAP 5
605 Jackson St ☎ 415-788-6709 ⏰ 11am-6:30pm Tues & Thurs-Fri, 11am-5:30pm Wed, 10:30am-7pm Sat-Sun $ $3-5 [C] cash only 🚌 15, 41 Muni

This bona fide 'Shanghai-style' greasy spoo might be too intense for some people. Bu there's something inviting about its hand painted sign and worn-out lunch counter, es pecially if you're running out of funds. Th kindly folks here sling some cheap and tast hash – seasoned pork chops and spice braised beef accompanied by steamed ric and the occasional vegetable.

Viet Nam Restaurant (Vietnamese) MAP 5
620 Broadway ☎ 415-788-7034 ⏰ 8am-midnight daily $ appetizer $2-3.50, entrée $4-5 [C] cash only 🚌 15, 30, 41, 45 Muni ♿

This little hash house introduced Vietnames truck-stop fare to San Francisco. You'll under stand what this means if you've traveled i Vietnam and stopped at the roadside stal where filling pho soups and barbecued-meat and-rice plates are churned out at very lo prices. It's greasy but tasty and loaded wit protein and carbohydrates.

Sam Wo's (Chinese) MAP 5
813 Washington St ☎ 415-982-0596 ⏰ 11am-3am Mon-Sat $ appetizer $2.50-4.50, entrée $3-6 [C] cash only 🚌 15, 30, 41 45 Muni

This legendary chow house owes its notoriet to an abusive waiter named Edsel Ford. Forc a Chinese American who adopted the name c an unpopular car model, insulted his cus tomers to no end, but they couldn't help com ing back for more. Today's waiters just put th grub on the table. You won't find many veg etables on your plate here, and those you d

Dim Sum

San Francisco rivals Hong Kong in the popularity and quality of its dim sum restaurants. In the Canton province of China, where dim sum originated, the act of eating dim sum is called yum cha, or 'drink tea,' because the little snacklike dishes first appeared in teahouses. Chinese businessmen used to spend so many hours in teahouses that the restaurants served as virtual extensions of their offices, so the teahouses began serving snacks for them to graze on. Though dim sum continues to be served during business hours (typically from 10am to 3pm), it is no longer just for businessmen.

Typically, dim sum consists of bite-size pastrylike items filled with pork, shrimp, taro root, or vegetables, which have been steamed, fried, or baked. Steamed vegetables and hearty congee soup (rice porridge with ingredients such as shrimp, fish, peanuts, or pork giblets) are commonly offered as well. Two or three items are served on small plates for $2 to $4. The best way to enjoy as many different dishes as possible is to eat with a group of people.

In a typical dim sum parlor, waiters roll carts between crowded tables that are crammed from wall to wall in a cavernous dining room. Patrons simply select the plates they'd like from the passing carts. A running tab is kept at your table.

There are good dim sum restaurants in many parts of San Francisco, but for an authentic experience, go to Chinatown. Dim sum is popular every day, but on weekends the crowds and the excitement level reach their peak.

Yank Sing MAP 4

201 Spear St, Rincon Center ☎ 415-781-1111 ⌚ 11am-3pm Mon-Fri, 10am-4pm Sat-Sun $ $2.75-4.50 C V, MC, AE, DC M Embarcadero BART & Muni station Market St buses, F Muni ♿

It may be true that Yank Sing has the best dim sum this side of Hong Kong, but it's a little more expensive than the Chinatown parlors and some people miss the chaotic atmosphere.

Dol Ho MAP 5

808 Pacific Ave ☎ 415-392-2828 ⌚ 7am-5pm Thurs-Tue $ $1.50-2.50 C cash only 30, 45, 83 Muni ♿

Small and relaxed by Chinatown standards, Dol Ho prepares very good dim sum. Try the silky shrimp crepe, dipped in a special soy blend.

Gold Mountain MAP 5

644 Broadway ☎ 415-296-7733 ⌚ 10:30am-3pm Mon-Fri, 8am-3pm Sat-Sun, 5pm-9:30pm daily $ appetizer $2-4, entrée $7-16 C V, MC 15, 30, 41, 45 Muni ♿

This Chinatown establishment embodies the raucous spirit of dim sum. A formidable armada of dim sum carts wends its way through the noisy aisles, bearing fresh and finely prepared dim sum.

Harbor Village MAP 5

4 Embarcadero Center, 2nd floor ☎ 415-781-8833 ⌚ 11am-2:30 Mon-Fri, 10:30am-2:30pm Sat-Sun, 5:30pm-9:30pm daily $ $2.50-4.50 C V, MC, AE, DC M Embarcadero BART & Muni station 1, 41, F Muni ♿

Great dim sum turns up in unexpected places. Sleek and stylish Harbor Village is hidden away in the Embarcadero Center, in the Financial District.

Ton Kiang Restaurant MAP 15

5821 Geary Blvd ☎ 415-387-8275 ⌚ 10:30am-10pm Mon-Thurs, 10:30am-10:30pm Fri, 10am-10:30pm Sat, 9am-10:30pm Sun $ $2.50-4 C AE, D, DC, JCB, MC, V 38 Muni ♿

Ton Kiang's delicious dim sum is served day or night, and in addition to the roving carts, dim sum can be cooked to order, ensuring freshness. It's way out in the Richmond but worth the trip.

find certainly won't be fresh. Sam Wo's is a hot spot for past-midnight refueling.

House of Nanking (Chinese) MAP 5
919 Kearny St ☎ 415-421-1429 ⌚ 11am-10pm Mon-Fri, noon-10pm Sat, 4pm-10pm Sun $ appetizer $5-8, entrée $5-12 C cash only 15, 41 Muni ♿

If you're looking for a respite from the hustle and bustle of Chinatown, step inside the House of Nanking, where it's relative mayhem. The line stretching outside is a reflection of the good food coming out of the steaming open kitchen. But the line moves quickly, mostly because the waiters make sure the patrons inside order quickly, are served quickly, and eat quickly. They'll even order for you if you're indecisive. Helpful, aren't they? Worry not – they know what's good.

Lichee Gardens (Chinese) MAP 5
1416 Powell St ☎ 415-397-2290 ⌚ 7am-9:30pm daily $ lunch $4.50-7.50, appetizer $5-14, entrée $6.50-14 C V, MC 30, 45 Muni

Lichee Gardens is an unassuming family-style place where the food can be outstanding on some nights but oddly lackluster on others. The steamed bean cake stuffed with shrimp mousse is always good, as is mixed-vegetable chow mein Hong Kong–style. Add the fried, crispy-skin chicken and you've got one of the best meals Chinatown has to offer for a moderate price. Dim sum carts circulate until 3pm daily.

Yuet Lee Seafood Restaurant (Chinese seafood) MAP 5
1300 Stockton St ☎ 415-982-6020 ⌚ 11am-3am Wed-Mon $ $5-20 C cash only 30, 45 Muni

Walking up Broadway in the wee small hours ('til 3am), you're likely to notice this active corner eatery with the bright windows. And though it looks like a dive and is cheap like a dive, the seafood here – whether cooked in a clay pot or roasted with salt and pepper – is consistently good. You can also warm yourself with satisfying noodle soups (about $4) chock full of wontons, dumplings, and chopped meats. Most dishes cost just $5 or $6.

R&G Lounge (Chinese) MAP 5
631 Kearny St ☎ 415-982-7877 ⌚ 11am-9:30pm daily $ appetizer $6-13, entrée $8.50-15 C AE, D, DC, MC, V 9, 15 Muni

One of Chinatown's most respected and popular eateries, R&G Lounge serves capably prepared Cantonese food at low prices. Go for the clay pot dishes or salt-and-pepper roasts whether it's prawns, crab, or chicken you're hungering for. The downstairs decor is no more exciting than any other Chinatown restaurant, but the upstairs dining room is a favorite haunt of local Chinese VIPs and visiting Hong Kong suits. You can easily eat for $15 or less.

Far East Cafe (Chinese) MAP 5
631 Grant Ave ☎ 415-982-3245
⌚ 11:30am-10pm daily $ lunch $5-10, appetizer $4-12, entrée $8-25 C V, MC, AE 1 Muni California St cable car ♿

People generally head to the Far East Cafe for the atmosphere, and they're never disappointed. Its swanky dining room, designed in 1920, is a rare glimpse of the privileged side of Chinatown's intriguing past. You'll want to admire the crazy carved-wood chandeliers and the dragon gateway that separates the eating area from the bar and to snoop inside one of the private wooden booths. The food's nothing special – no surprises on this menu – but heaping $5 lunch specials mean you don't have to pay extra for the atmosphere.

Empress of China (Chinese) MAP 5
838 Grant Ave ☎ 415-434-1345
⌚ 11:30am-3pm & 5pm-11pm Mon-Sat, 12:30pm-11pm Sun $ appetizer $4-13.50, entrée $6.50-38, dessert $2.50-4.50 C AE, CB, D, DC, JCB, MC, V 1, 30, 45 Muni ♿

Before taking the elevator to this top-floor restaurant, pause to assess the snapshots of glamorous people who have dined here. Their ranks include Jayne Mansfield, Ricardo Montalban, Sammy Davis Jr, Mick Jagger, and, of course, Thomas Kean, the former governor of New Jersey. Upstairs, classic plush dining rooms and stellar views reinforce the place's laudable history, but the food is dragged down by 1950s American housewife shortcuts – canned veggies and such. Stick to the less expensive basics and appreciate the atmosphere.

NORTH BEACH

North Beach, San Francisco's Italian enclave, has been experiencing something of a gastronomic renaissance in recent years. It still has great neighborhood Italian American places that serve meatball sandwiches and plates of heavily sauced pastas and it has more than its share of mediocre tourist-trap eateries, but these establishments now share their turf with the new breed of chefs cooking up light and innovative variations on the Italian repertoire.

Budget

Liguria (Italian) MAP 6
1700 Stockton St ☎ 415-421-3786 ⌚ 8am-4pm Mon-Fri, 7am-4pm Sat-Sun $ half-sheet focaccia $3 c cash only 🚌 15, 30, 39, 45 Muni ♿

If you're at the park, you'll probably smell the aroma of a great snack baking in the ovens of Liguria. This admirably no-frills bakery produces one thing and one thing only: focaccia (with tomato sauce or without). Get there before lunchtime, as it nearly always sells out and shuts down early (1pm or 2pm).

Molinari's Delicatessen (Italian) MAP 6
373 Columbus Ave ☎ 415-421-2337 ⌚ 8am-6pm Mon-Fri, 8am-5pm Sat $ $4.50-7.50 c V, MC 🚌 15, 30, 41, 45 Muni ♿

For bonzer hero sandwiches, North Beach dwellers head to Molinari's. It's been around for 100 years, but the cold cuts and sweet peppers are fresh and of a high quality. A vegetarian delight is Joe's Special, with fresh mozzarella, dried tomatoes, sweet peppers, and basil garlic. There are a few plastic sidewalk tables; better yet, Washington Square is just a few blocks away.

Golden Boy Pizza (pizza) MAP 6
542 Green St ☎ 415-982-9738 ⌚ 11:30am-11:30pm Sun-Thurs, 11:30am-1:30am Fri-Sat $ pizza slice $2-3, pizza pie $22.50-34 c cash only 🚌 15, 30, 39, 41, 45 Muni

Golden Boy has an edgy punk attitude and there's not a comfortable seat in the place and a whole pie is absurdly expensive – but the pizza here *rocks*. Our advice is order a slice or two, wash it down with beer (there's a nice selection on tap) or cider, and get on with your day. All you will spend is $5 to $8, depending on the number of slices and toppings.

Malvina (Italian) MAP 6
1600 Stockton St ☎ 415-391-1290 ⌚ 7am-5pm Mon-Sat, 8am-4pm Sun $ breakfast $4.50-8, lunch $6-8.50, dessert $2-4 c V, MC, AE 🚌 15, 30, 39, 41, 45 Muni ♿

Old-world elegance and ample daylight shining through windows along two sides make Malvina a comfortable place to stop for a light bite. The menu is simple: omelets and pastries for breakfast, focaccia sandwiches and a few warm plates for lunch. The staff aren't in the habit of rushing you through a meal, and footloose locals often while away the morning here.

Mo's Burgers (American) MAP 6
1322 Grant Ave ☎ 415-788-3779 ⌚ 11am-10pm Sun-Thurs, 11am-11:30pm Fri-Sat $ breakfast $4-9, entrée $5.50-10 c MC, V 🚌 15, 30, 41, 45 Muni ♿

Mo's makes a legitimate claim to the city's best burger by preparing freshly ground beef patties over a revolving grill and serving 'em up with homemade mayonnaise. *Three Stooges* fans and cow-lovers will appreciate the artwork on the walls.

Brandy Ho's (Chinese) MAP 6
217 Columbus Ave ☎ 415-788-7527 ⌚ 11:30am-11pm Sun-Thurs, 11:30am-midnight Fri-Sat $ appetizer $2-10, entrée $4.50-14.50, dessert $1.50-5 c AE, D, MC, V 🚌 15, 41, 83 Muni

Although its name is reminiscent of a prostitute's, Brandy Ho's is a respectable restaurant dishing out authentic Hunan cuisine. The snazzy decor and the pyrotechnics in the open kitchen make for a colorful and festive night out. Highly recommended are the sizzling rice shrimp ($10), tapioca-marinated shrimp poured over crispy rice cakes, and the hot-and-sour beef ($7), featuring a unique Hunan vinegar sauce.

Mario's Bohemian Cigar Store (Italian) MAP 6
566 Columbus Ave ☎ 415-362-0536 ⌚ 10am-11pm daily $ $6.50-11.50 c cash only 🚌 15, 30, 41, 45 Muni

The cigar inventory was liquidated long ago, and the old men have yielded to a slightly younger, more mixed crowd, but this old fave has retained its unique name and its classic North Beach feel. Now a relaxed café-bar, Mario's offers a great vantage of the busy street scene around Washington Square, plus fresh focaccia sandwiches, tap beer, and wine.

Mid-Range

L'Osteria del Forno (Italian) MAP 6
519 Columbus Ave ☎ 415-982-1124 ⌚ 11:30am-10pm Sun-Mon & Wed-Thurs, 11:30am-10:30pm Fri-Sat $ lunch $4-13, appetizer $4.50-7.50, entrée $7-11, pizza

pie $10-17, dessert $4.50 Ⓒ *cash only* Ⓟ 🚌 *15, 30, 41, 45 Muni* ♿

This little gem is crammed amid Columbus Ave's overabundance of touristy Italian restaurants. It's romantic, small (10 tables), and run by two pleasant Italian women who craft tasty thin-crust pizzas, sophisticated antipasti, and dinners such as lamb skewers in Northern Italian style. This is also a great place to stop at midday for sandwiches on fresh focaccia. Everything is reasonably priced.

North Beach Pizza (Italian) MAP 6
1499 Grant Ave ☎ 415-433-2444 ⌚ 11am-1am Sun-Thurs, 11am-3am Fri-Sat $ appetizer $2.50-3.50, pizza pie $8-20, entrée $9-12 Ⓒ *V, MC, AE, D, DC* Ⓟ 🚌 *15, 30, 39, 41, 45 Muni* ♿

San Francisco isn't famous for its pizza, which perhaps explains the success of this mediocre chain. The home branch, in the heart of North Beach, is a cramped and dark tavern that stays open late every night. Stick with the pizza.

Caffé Macaroni (Italian) MAP 6
59 Columbus Ave ☎ 415-956-9737 ⌚ 5pm-10pm Mon-Sat $ appetizer $4-11, entrée $7.50-16, dessert $4.50 Ⓒ *cash only* Ⓟ 🚌 *12, 15, 41 Muni* ♿

Cramped Macaroni is a lively spot that churns out some of the neighborhood's best Italian food. The handsome and ebullient waiters turn on the charm for every woman who walks by, whether she's stopping to eat or not, and they'll gladly teach you an Italian phrase or two. The squid-ink pasta with shellfish is deservedly acclaimed, and the pork medallions, while a bit salty, are well balanced with fennel-infused tomato sauce and served over polenta. Reservations are not accepted, and there is usually a wait. An alternative is Macaroni Express, across the street, with a similar but more economical menu.

Ideale (Italian) MAP 6
1309 Grant Ave ☎ 415-391-4129 ⌚ 5:30pm-10:30pm Tues-Thurs, 5:30pm-11pm Fri-Sat, 5pm-10pm Sun $ appetizer $4.50-9, entrée $9-18, dessert $5.50-6.50 Ⓒ *AE, D, DC, MC, V* Ⓟ 🚌 *12, 15, 30, 41, 45 Muni* ♿

Ideale's inviting, modern look is matched by its exemplary service and its highly tempting Italian menu. The kitchen shines a little brighter when you order the more traditional pasta and meat offerings and lay off some of the more fanciful inventions. Large portions make most entrées suitable for sharing. The justifiably famous tiramisu is not to be missed, no matter how much you've overeaten.

Fog City Diner (New American) MAP 6
1300 Battery St ☎ 415-982-2000 ⌚ 11:30am-11pm Sun-Thurs, 11:30am-midnight Fri-Sat $ lunch $8-19, appetizer $2-11, entrée $8-27, dessert $4-7 Ⓒ *V, MC, D, DC* Ⓟ 🚌 *42, F Muni* ♿

On the bay side of Telegraph Hill, Fog City Diner is the glitziest of the city's fake '50s diners. There's no claim to greasy-spoon authenticity here. But do chrome, neon, and the mu shu pork burrito belong together? Well, why not. The menu, while containing many surprises, shines brightest when it sticks to the basics – real diner fare does benefit from capable hands in the kitchen. There's an oyster bar, and a wide variety of wines are available by the glass. If you haven't made dinner reservations, the wait can be long.

Helmand (Afghani) MAP 6
430 Broadway ☎ 415-362-0641 ⌚ 5:30pm-10pm Tues-Thurs, 5:30pm-11pm Fri-Sat $ appetizer $4, entrée $10-16, dessert $4 Ⓒ *V, MC, AE* ⓅⓅ 🚌 *12, 15, 30, 41, 42 Muni* ♿

Well hidden from bawdy Broadway, this rather somber restaurant serves competent Afghani food. While that usually means a heavy emphasis on meat, this place offers some good vegetarian items as well. Try the kaddo borawni, a sweet appetizer of baked pumpkin served with a light yogurt sauce. Charbroiled lamb kebabs and cumin rice reign supreme.

The House (on Grant) (fusion) MAP 6
1230 Grant Ave ☎ 415-986-8612 ⌚ 11am-3pm Mon-Fri, 5:30pm-10pm Mon-Thurs, 5:30pm-11pm Fri, 5pm-11pm Sat $ lunch $8-15, appetizer $6-9, entrée $12-19, dessert $4.50-7 Ⓒ *AE, DC, MC, V* Ⓟ 🚌 *12, 15, 30, 41, 45 Muni*

The House is slick and modern rather than homey, and the fusion cuisine on the menu probably isn't the sort of cooking that came out of your mother's kitchen. But why dwell on the name, when the place successfully combines Asian and European ingredients to create scintillating, original dishes? We'll admit a preference for the more straightforward offerings, like the outstanding Chilean sea bass (so fresh, we had to slap it), the vibrant seafood salads, and the grilled beef with sensuous, sesame-flecked noodles.

Top End

Moose's (American) MAP 6
1652 Stockton St ☎ 415-989-7800 ⌚ 11:30am-2:30pm Thurs-Sat, 10am-2:30pm Sun, 5:30pm-10pm Sun-Thurs, 5:30pm-11pm Fri-Sat $ breakfast/brunch $9-13, lunch $7.50-17, appetizer $5-14, entrée $11-30, dessert $7-8 C AE, DC, JBC, MC, V 🚭 🚌 15, 30, 39, 41, 45 Muni ♿

The decor may be slightly dated '80s corporate chic, but big ol' loveable Moose is one of the friendliest restaurants in town and is still worth going to. While the Mooseburger ($11) always garners praise, the halibut with crab-potato rösti and fennel-tangerine salad ($22), accented with a sweet-and-tart lemon ribbon, is more representative of the chef's creative abilities. This is also a lively spot for Sunday brunch with piano accompaniment.

Rose Pistola (Italian) MAP 6
532 Columbus Ave ☎ 415-399-0499 ⌚ 11:30am-3pm daily, 5:30pm-11pm Sun-Thurs, 5pm-midnight Fri-Sat $ appetizer $5-11.50, entrée $7.50-27, dessert $4.50-7.50 C AE, D, DC, MC, V 🚌 15, 30, 39, 41, 45 Muni ♿

One of San Francisco's most popular restaurants, Rose Pistola fuses updated Beat-pop style (a Ferlinghetti poem appears on the menu, and jazz combos play in the evening) with creative Ligurian dishes. Chef Reed Hearon has a reputation for bringing together the finest ingredients and hardest-to-find herbs – which leads to the question, 'Why did my fish taste like a boiled hotdog?' It is acceptable to build a meal out of antipasti, for which the restaurant is justifiably famous. Prices are reasonable. Reservations are advisable in the evening but not necessary for lunch.

Enrico's Supper Club (Mediterranean) MAP 6
504 Broadway ☎ 415-982-6223 ⌚ 11:30am-11pm Sun-Thurs, 11:30am-12:30am Fri-Sat $ appetizer $5-12, entrée $11-25, dessert $6 C AE, MC, V 🚭 🚌 12, 15, 30, 41, 45, 83 Muni ♿

The Broadway striptease strip has long been home to Enrico's, the city's oldest sidewalk café. The menu includes some creative over-reaching – delicate pizzas, unique antipasti, and traditional seafood and meat dishes prepared with original twists make this a great spot to stop by for lunch, an afternoon snack, or a special dinner. Evening jazz combos and the front patio's proximity to an unpredictable street scene add pizzazz to the dining.

Black Cat (French) MAP 6
501 Broadway ☎ 415-981-2233 ⌚ 5:30pm-11:15pm Mon-Thurs, 5:30pm-12:15am Fri-Sat $ appetizer $7-9.50, entrée $12-20, dessert $6-7.50 C AE, DC, MC, V 🚭 🚌 12, 15, 30, 41, 45, 83 Muni ♿

Reed Hearon's second North Beach restaurant, the Black Cat, is a high-toned statement in bohemian style, with cool, subdued colors that cast a romantic glow on references to the neighborhood's Beat history. After several incarnations, the kitchen has settled on French bistro fare. Start with the niçoise croquettes ($7) of veal and rice in a pool of garlicky tomato sauce. The seafood mixed grill ($18), with calamari, mussels, and delicately charred tuna, is highly recommended, as is the rotisserie roasted leg of lamb, served with baby carrots, mashed potatoes, and lemony spinach ($18).

Caffe Sport (Italian) MAP 6
574 Green St ☎ 415-981-1251 ⌚ 5pm-10:30pm Tues-Sat, noon-2:30pm Fri-Sat $ lunch $7-11, entrée $15-24 C cash only 🚌 15, 30, 41, 45 Muni

Restaurateur Antonio La Tona is a woodcarver and painter, and over the past three decades he has decorated his Sicilian seafood restaurant with his own intricately carved and intensely colorful benches, chairs, tables, and ornamental beams. The result is almost hallucinatory. The food, with a commendable seafood-and-pasta emphasis, isn't quite so unique, but the large family-style platters will feed two or three people. Come in a large group – dining at Caffe Sport is meant to be a boisterous experience.

Fior D'Italia (Italian) MAP 6
601 Union St ☎ 415-986-1886 ⌚ 11:30am-10:30pm daily $ appetizer $5-14.50, entrée $13.50-36 C V, MC, AE, D, DC 🚭 🚌 15, 30, 39, 41, 45 Muni ♿

On Washington Square, Fior D'Italia claims to be the oldest Italian restaurant in the entire country (it was founded in 1886), and indeed the wall hangings and starched curtains exude an old-fashioned vibe. The extensive menu requires careful decision making: order conservatively and you'll make out all right, though you'll have to drop a bigger wad than the food merits.

RUSSIAN HILL & NOB HILL

Hyde St and Polk St run along the western edge of Russian and Nob Hills. There are pleasant places to enjoy a nice lunch after hiking up and down the area's scenic stairways, and some of the area's restaurants are worth specifically seeking out for dinner.

The Bagelry (bagels) MAP 7
2134 Polk St ☎ 415-441-3003 ⌚ 6:30am-5pm Mon-Tues & Thurs-Sat, 6:30am-noon Wed, 6:30am-4pm Sun $ $3-6 C cash only 🚭 🚌 19, 42, 47, 76, 83 Muni ♿

Along a busy shopping strip, the Bagelry represents a quick and inexpensive breakfast or lunch. A bagel with lox spread ($3) is a filling snack, while a variety of bagel sandwiches can make a more substantial midday meal. Of course, bagels are also good without anything on them. There are a few tables, but primarily it's a take-out operation.

Pancho's Salsa Bar & Grill (Mexican) MAP 7
1639 Polk St ☎ 415-474-2280 ⌚ 11am-10pm Sun-Thurs, 11am-11pm Fri-Sat $ $3.50-7 C cash only 🚭 🚌 1, 19, 42, 47, 49, 76 Muni

Pancho's is the best taquería in the central part of San Francisco. A respectable salsa bar and quality grilled meats make it worth seeking out, though, alas, there's no pork on the menu.

U-Lee (Chinese) MAP 7
1468 Hyde St ☎ 415-771-9774 ⌚ 11am-9pm Tues-Sun $ appetizer $3-6, entrée $4-7.50 C cash only 🚭🚭 🚌 12, 27, 83 Muni 🚋 Powell-Hyde cable car ♿

For cheap and decent Chinese grub, U-Lee is friendly and charmingly nondescript. Pot stickers, rice plates, and many vegetarian choices are highlights on the menu, and big portions make it a good idea to share with friends.

Cordon Bleu (Vietnamese) MAP 7
1574 California St ☎ 415-673-5637 ⌚ 11:30am-2:30pm & 5pm-10pm Tues-Sat, 4pm-10pm Sun $ lunch $4.50, appetizer $3, entrée $6-7.50 C cash only 🚌 1, 19, 42, 47, 49, 76 Muni 🚋 California St cable car ♿

Simple and inexpensive Vietnamese barbecued chicken, smothered in a sweet sauce and served over rice, is the specialty at this tiny eatery. Hefty fried imperial rolls are greasy but tasty and constitute a small meal. Eight counter seats and a couple of small tables fit just a small crowd, but take-out service is available. It's a convenient place to sup before or after seeing a movie at the adjacent Lumiere Theater.

Grubstake (American/Portuguese grub) MAP 7
1525 Pine St ☎ 415-673-8268 ⌚ 5pm-4am Mon-Fri, 10am-4am Sat-Sun $ breakfast $5-7.50, appetizer $1.50-5, entrée $4.50-14.50 C cash only 🚌 19, 42, 47, 49, 76 Muni

In an old Key Line rail car, this greasy spoon is most popular among late-night partyers seeking cheap sustenance. Burgers and breakfasts are the main attractions, but a few Portuguese selections might also tempt you.

Zarzuela (Spanish) MAP 7
2000 Hyde St ☎ 415-346-0800 ⌚ 5:30pm-10pm Tues-Sat $ appetizer (tapas) $3-7.50, entrée $7.50-14, dessert $4.50 C MC, V 🚭 🚌 41, 45 Muni 🚋 Powell-Hyde cable car ♿

One of the biggest dining attractions on Russian Hill is Zarzuela, an unassuming eatery that always draws a crowd willing to wait on the sidewalk before eating (no reservations). In a city full of so-so tapas bars, this place stands out for its authentic Spanish tapas and paellas.

Hyde St Bistro (French) MAP 7
1521 Hyde St ☎ 415-441-7778 ⌚ 5:30pm-10:30pm Tues-Sun $ appetizer $5.50-9, entrée $12-16, dessert $4.50-8.50, prix fixe $25 (3 courses) C V, MC, D, DC, AE, JCB 🚭 🚌 12, 27 Muni 🚋 Powell-Hyde cable car

This relaxed and friendly little bistro is refreshingly devoid of trendiness – only solid traditions are observed here. The venison pâté and caramelized-onion goat-cheese tart are long on robust flavor and country charm, and the duck confit is a marvel of crisp, crackly skin concealing tender meat that falls off the bone. A house specialty is escargot with gnocchi bouillabaisse.

I Fratelli (Italian) MAP 7
1896 Hyde St ☎ 415-474-8240 ⌚ 5:30pm-10pm daily $ appetizer $3.50-7, entrée $11-19, dessert $4-6 C AE, MC, V 🚭 🚌 41, 45 Muni 🚋 Powell-Hyde cable car ♿

I Fratelli's large portions of wonderful Italian fare and its friendly atmosphere are popular among Russian Hill denizens. Dishes like rich fettucine alla carbonara and a nicely seasoned crispy-skinned roasted half chicken are prepared by capable hands, and bottles of Chianti make for a merry crowd. Reservations are recommended.

Swan Oyster Depot (seafood) MAP 7
1517 Polk St ☎ 415-673-1101 ⌚ 8am-5:30pm Mon-Sat ⓢ appetizer $2.50-10, entrée $12-32 c cash only 🚌 1, 19, 42, 47, 49, 76 Muni 🚋 California St cable car ♿

The historic charm and fresh seafood at Swan Oyster Depot have claimed a highly devoted clientele. It's really an old fish market – occupying this spot since 1912 and now operated by the gregarious Sancimino brothers – with a long marble counter for those who prefer to eat and run. A half-dozen fresh, sea-salty oysters on the half shell ($7), excellent clam chowder ($4.50), and a variety of fresh seafood salads all reflect San Francisco's strong seafood traditions.

FISHERMAN'S WHARF

Don't come to Fisherman's Wharf looking for cheap eats. The one inexpensive option you can count on would be the take-out stalls selling fresh seafood, a Fisherman's Wharf specialty, around the waterfront parking lot and Jefferson St. If you're here during the crab season (mid-November to June), enjoy Dungeness crab and sourdough bread, which is about as San Franciscan as you can get.

Pier 39 restaurants mainly cash in on their touristy location, and their food is usually good enough not to detract from the view. Some of them are blatant theme-park enterprises. If you don't mind the banality of these places, they might be your best option if you're toting the family.

Buena Vista Café (American) MAP 8
2765 Hyde St ☎ 415-474-5044 ⌚ 9am-2am Mon-Fri, 8am-2am Sat-Sun ⓢ breakfast $6-8.50, appetizer $3-4, entrée $4.50-11.50, dessert $3 c V, MC, AE, D, DC, CB 🚌 19, 30, 42 Muni 🚋 Powell-Hyde cable car

Buena Vista Café is a historic bar with a few tables and a menu offering seafood dishes, breakfast, and burgers. The establishment introduced Irish coffee to the US, so naturally it would be wise to partake of that tradition while you're here.

McCormick & Kuleto's (seafood) MAP 8
900 North Point St ☎ 415-929-1730 ⌚ 11:30am-11pm Mon-Sat, 10:30am-11pm Sun ⓢ appetizer $5-12, entrée $10-23 c MC, V 🚭 🚌 19, 30, 42 Muni 🚋 Powell-Hyde cable car ♿

Overlooking the water, this is your best bet for good seafood at Ghirardelli Square. Its informal, busy Crab Cake Lounge, upstairs, offers the best value, with appetizers such as pizzas from a wood-fired oven, oysters on the half shell, and crab cakes. Entrées include Parmesan-coated petrale sole and traditional crab Louis. The downstairs dining room is more formal and has a more extensive seafood menu.

Tarantino's (seafood) MAP 8
206 Jefferson St ☎ 415-775-5600 ⌚ 11am-11pm daily ⓢ lunch $5-13, appetizer $7-13, entrée $13-25 c V, MC 🚌 42, F Muni ♿

This is another of the Wharf's old-time family establishments where uninspired fish dishes are overpriced. But the sidewalk café in front is a good spot to tuck into clam chowder dished into hollowed-out sourdough rounds.

Alioto's (seafood) MAP 8
8 Fisherman's Wharf ☎ 415-673-0183 ⌚ 11am-11pm daily ⓢ lunch $8-13.50, appetizer $8-12.50, entrée $13-26 c V, MC 🚌 42, F Muni ♿

There are far better seafood restaurants in other parts of the city, but if you decide to eat in this area, Alioto's upstairs dining room has a view of docked fishing boats. Alioto's was one of the old fish stalls that turned into a restaurant back in the 1920s, sparking the tourist trade on Fisherman's Wharf. In the 1960s, the restaurant employed a nattily dressed midget as maitre d' to stimulate business, but the place lacks flash these days.

No 9 Fisherman's Grotto (seafood/Italian) MAP 8
9 Fisherman's Wharf ☎ 415-673-7025 ⌚ 11am-11pm daily ⓢ lunch $12-14, appetizer $9-13.50, entrée $14.50-28, dessert $4-7 c V, MC, AE, D, DC 🚌 42, F Muni ♿

If you're doing the Fisherman's Wharf thing, why not plunge all the way in? The quintessential wharf tourist trap has the virtue of being so outdated it's starting to look cool again (the hipsters will never discover it, though). Dining in the candy-colored Venetian booths downstairs is a perverse thrill (the food can be really awful), while the faded '50s upstairs dining room offers the standard wharf views. The neglected swanky cocktail lounges and the seemingly forgotten gift shop are time-warp treasures.

PLACES TO EAT

THE MARINA & COW HOLLOW

Most of the Marina's eating options cling close to the Chestnut St axis, but there are a few choices elsewhere. Lombard St has quite a few fast-food eateries.

Lucca Ravioli Co (Italian) MAP 9
2120 Chestnut St ☎ 415-921-7873 ⌚ 9am-6:30pm Mon-Fri, 9am-6pm Sat-Sun $ $4-6 C V, MC 🚌 28, 30, 43, 76 Muni ♿

For a hefty Italian hero that you can take to the Marina Green, stop by this busy little deli.

Mel's Drive-In (American) MAP 9
2165 Lombard St ☎ 415-921-3039 ⌚ 6am-2am Sun-Thurs, 24 hours Fri-Sat $ breakfast $4.50-10.50, entrée $5-14, dessert $3.50 C cash only 🚭 🚌 22, 30, 43, 76 Muni ♿

Mel's is an authentic '50s diner that played a significant supporting role in the George Lucas film *American Graffiti*. The decor and food remain true to diner tradition, with burgers, fries, milkshakes, and a few healthy concessions (salads).

Cafe Marimba (Mexican) MAP 9
2317 Chestnut St ☎ 415-776-1506 ⌚ 5:30pm-10pm Mon-Tues, 11:30am-10pm Wed-Thurs & Sun, 11:30am-11pm Fri-Sat $ appetizer $5.50-9, entrée $6.50-16.50, dessert $5-5.50 C AE, MC, V 🚭 🚌 28, 30 Muni ♿

Named for the Yucatecan xylophone-like instrument, Marimba indeed has a ringing vibe. The garish decor and the peppy margarita-fueled crowd are more reminiscent of Cancun tourist traps than authentic cantinas, but the food clearly rises above the clamor. Regional seafood dishes and the restaurant's signature mole sauces are Marimba's well-disguised strengths.

Balboa Cafe (American) MAP 9
3199 Fillmore St ☎ 415-921-3944 ⌚ 11:30am-2am Mon-Fri, 11am-2am Sat-Sun $ appetizer $5-12, entrée $8-27 C cash only 🚌 22, 28, 43, 76 Muni ♿

One of the city's historic bar and grills, the Balboa has more to offer than its famous yapping singles nighttime bar scene. Now owned by the proprietors of the PlumpJack Cafe, it features pretty solid grill fare. The relaxed pace during the day is more consistent with Balboa's antique interior – the bar was established in 1914 and retains its original wooden iceboxes – but at night the noise level rivals a chorus of walruses and holler monkeys.

Liverpool Lil's (English) MAP 9
2942 Lyon St ☎ 415-921-6664 ⌚ 11am-midnight Mon-Fri, 10am-midnight Sat-Sun $ appetizer $8-13, entrée $9-19 C MC, V 🚌 28, 43 ♿

A cozy old English-style pub with a neighborhood vibe, Liverpool Lil's is probably the most down-to-earth spot for food and drink in the Marina. Solid seafood, burgers, and pub fare are mainstays of the menu. It's just across the street from the Presidio Gate and not far from the Palace of Fine Arts and the Exploratorium.

Bistro Aix (French) MAP 9
3340 Steiner St ☎ 415-202-0100 ⌚ 6pm-10pm Mon-Thurs, 6pm-11pm Fri-Sat, 5:30pm-9:30pm Sun $ appetizer $4.50-8, entrée $10-18, dessert $6 C V, MC, AE, DC 🚌 22, 28, 30, 41, 43, 45, 76 Muni ♿

Warm atmosphere and heartening bistro fare are what make Aix a popular neighborhood place. Stylishly tasty meals include papardelle pasta with fava beans and snap peas or grilled ahi with mashed potatoes in a fruity red-wine reduction and topped with fried spinach. The weeknight prix fixe, with crispy roasted chicken and steak options, is a bargain at $15.

Betelnut (Asian) MAP 9
2030 Union St ☎ 415-929-8855 ⌚ 11:30am-11pm Sun-Thurs, 11:30am-midnight Fri-Sat $ appetizer $5-10, entrée $14-17, dessert $5-7 C V, MC, D, DC 🚭 🚌 22, 41, 45 Muni

Betelnut seductively combines pan-Asian cuisine with an exotic 1930s film noir atmosphere. Of course, the Marina beautiful people scene can sometimes be a distraction, but the heady mix of flavors from Southeast Asia and Japan will ultimately command your attention. Start off with a home-brewed beer and some 'little plates' – miniservings of such things as green papaya salad and chili-crusted calamari. Among the varied entrées, don't miss the sea bass with black sesame seeds. Reservations are a must.

PlumpJack Cafe (Mediterranean) MAP 9
3127 Fillmore St ☎ 415-563-4755 ⌚ 11:30am-2pm Mon-Fri, 5:30pm-10pm Mon-Sat $ lunch $12-15, appetizer $5-14, entrée $18-25, dessert $5-7 C AE, D, DC, MC, V 🚭 🚌 22, 41, 45 Muni ♿

Elegant and simple, PlumpJack serves sophisticated fare with an emphasis on Mediterranean-California techniques. Tender pork loins feature an apple sweetbread crepinette in a mustard-based sauce. The organic roasted chicken is spruced up with a tangerine and olive dressing. There's also a superb list of wines by the glass or you can bring in a bottle from nearby PlumpJack wine shop and not pay a corkage fee.

PACIFIC HEIGHTS & JAPANTOWN

The stretch of Fillmore St between Sutter and Jackson Sts, just north of Japantown, is home to a motley host of inviting restaurants serving an array of cuisines. Japantown, of course, is more focused, with noodle soups and sushi being the primary enticements.

Jackson Fillmore (Italian) MAP 10
2506 Fillmore St ☎ 415-346-5288 ⌚ 5:30pm-10pm Mon-Thurs, 5:30pm-10:30pm Fri-Sat, 5pm-10pm Sun $ appetizer $7-8, entrée $10-17, dessert $5-7 C V, MC, AE 🚭 🚌 3,12, 22, 24 Muni ♿

This tiny trattoria has only eight tables, serves fine southern Italian food at reasonable prices, and will accept reservations only for parties of three or more – so getting in can require perseverance. But gratification awaits in the form of tasty zucchini carpaccio and wonderful garlicky, olive-oily chicken. There are also many nonvegan veggie items.

Elite Cafe (Cajun) MAP 10
2049 Fillmore St ☎ 415-346-8668 ⌚ 5pm-11pm Mon-Sat, 5pm-10pm Sun $ appetizer $4.50-10.50, entrée $17.50-28, dessert $6.50-7.50 C AE, D, DC, MC, V 🚌 1, 3, 22 Muni

What the Elite Cafe lacks in that 'down on the bayou' feel it makes up for with its beautifully preserved 1920s dining room, replete with tile floors, wooden booths, and art deco hanging lamps. The Cajun and Creole seafood is good but can be shockingly expensive. Appetizers like Cajun popcorn (lightly breaded and fried shrimp) and crab cakes are excellent, while the jambalaya with duck confit is a bit naughty. Reservations aren't accepted, so if you have to wait, enjoy a mint julep at the bar and soak up the atmosphere.

Japan Center

The Japan Center is packed with restaurants, particularly in the Kintetsu Building. More Japanese restaurants can be found along Post St and in the Buchanan Mall, across Post St.

Isobune (Japanese) MAP 10
Kintetsu Mall, 1737 Post St ☎ 415-563-1030 ⌚ 11:30am-10pm daily $ sushi $1.50-3.50 C V, MC, JCB 🚭 🚌 22, 38 Muni ♿

As in the floating sushi bars so popular in Japan, the sushi chefs at Isobune prepare food and place it on wooden boats that sail around the inner perimeter of an oval counter. Patrons seated at the counter simply lift the dishes they want off the bobbing boats. Your bill depends on the number of empty dishes you're left with. It's fun, cheap, and delicious.

On the Bridge (Japanese) MAP 10
1581 Webster St ☎ 415-931-2743 ⌚ 11:30am-10pm daily $ $5.50-9 C V, MC, JCB 🚭 🚌 2, 3, 4, 22, 38 Muni ♿

This ultra-cute little eatery, on the bridge connecting the Kintetsu and Kinokuniya Buildings, specializes in an intriguing Euro-Japanese and Indo-Japanese hybrid cuisine called yoshoku, which has been popular in Japan for more than 100 years. Japanese 'pastas' and curried rice plates take on unexpected but delightful flavors.

Mifune (Japanese) MAP 10
Kintetsu Mall, 1737 Post St ☎ 415-922-0337 ⌚ 11am-9:30pm Sun-Thurs, 11am-10pm Fri-Sat $ appetizer $2.50-8, noodle soup $4-8, entrée $9.50-17 C V, MC, AE, D 🚭🚭 🚌 22, 38 Muni ♿

Looking like a '60s movie-set depiction of a Japanese house, Mifune is one of San Francisco's most popular noodle parlors. A mere $5 will set you up with a hearty bowl of udon or soba noodles, either in a bowl of hot broth or served cold with seaweed and shrimp. Many delicious vegetarian selections are available.

Van Ness Ave

Van Ness Ave is the sort of wide thoroughfare that divides neighborhoods rather than serves their needs. The street still has some of the old auto showrooms that once made it San Francisco's 'Auto Row,' and the highest concentration of steak restaurants in the city is here, too. Going out for a Cadillac and a steak surely qualifies as the ultimate in American extravagance, and you can have it all on Van Ness Ave.

Tommy's Joynt (American) MAP 10
1101 Geary St ☎ 415-775-4216 ⌚ 11am-1:45am daily $ appetizer $2, entrée $4-6.50 C cash only 🚌 38, 42, 47, 49 Muni ♿
If, instead of beef, you prefer buffalo meat with your Cadillac, Tommy's Joynt is the place for you. You'll recognize it by the swirly and colorful Victorian-style paintings that cover its exterior. Tommy's has a hofbrau sort of arrangement, whereby inexpensive soups, stews (here's where the buffalos enter the picture), and an extensive list of sandwiches on sourdough rolls are served over a counter. The bar at this San Francisco institution has an equally impressive variety of beers from all over the world.

Golden Turtle (Vietnamese) MAP 10
2211 Van Ness Ave ☎ 415-441-4419 ⌚ 5pm-10:30pm Tues-Sun $ appetizer $5-9, entrée $7-13, dessert $3.50 C AE, DC, MC, V 🌿 🚌 42, 49, 47, 76 Muni ♿
Golden Turtle's reputation as one of the city's best Vietnamese restaurants keeps large crowds coming on the weekend. The spring rolls, clay pot dishes, and sizzling beef fondue are clearly of a higher standard than the Vietnamese chow in the Tenderloin, and the atmosphere is an improvement, too. Of course, prices are also higher, but it's worth it.

Harris' Restaurant (American) MAP 7
2100 Van Ness Ave ☎ 415-673-1888 ⌚ 5:30pm-9:30pm Mon-Thurs, 5:30pm-10pm Fri, 5pm-10pm Sat, 5pm-9:30pm Sun $ appetizer $8-12, entrée $25-35, dessert $7 C V, MC 🚌 12, 42, 47, 49 Muni ♿

RICK GERHARTER

Tommy's has the best buffalo stew in town.

One of San Francisco's best steak houses, Harris' is as straightforward as they come. A martini, a caesar salad, and a New York cut probably won't leave room for pecan pie. The Cadillac dealership is just down the street.

THE HAIGHT

Reflecting the experimental nature of the local clientele, Haight St offers an eclectic international array of cuisines. This is a good part of town to head to for inexpensive food. The restaurants in Cole Valley, south of Haight St, cater to more refined palates.

Ben & Jerry's (ice cream) MAP 11
1403 Haight St ☎ 415-249-4685 ⌚ noon-10pm Mon-Thurs, noon-11pm Fri, 11am-11pm Sat, 11am-10pm Sun $ cone $2.50 C cash only 🌿🌿 🚌 6, 7, 33, 43, 66, 71 Muni
Ben and Jerry, two hippies from Vermont who struck the ice-cream mother lode, have an outlet of their namesake chain here, on the prestigious hippie corner of Haight and Ashbury. All the standard flavors are available, as are sparkly originals like 'Rainforest Crunch,' 'Cherry Garcia,' and a few other bad ideas.

Pork Store Cafe (American) MAP 11
1451 Haight St ☎ 415-864-6981 ⌚ 7am-3:30pm Mon-Fri, 8:30am-4pm Sat-Sun $ breakfast $3-8, lunch $4.50-7.50 C cash only 🌿 🚌 6, 7, 43, 66, 71 Muni ♿
This busy little diner has been slinging truck-stop slop since 1919: eggs, bacon, hash browns, pancakes, and weak coffee for breakfast; burgers, fries, and other fat-and-carbo combos for lunch, all served up on a well-worn counter and on rickety tables by waiters who look like they just rolled out of bed.

Zona Rosa (Mexican) MAP 11
1797 Haight St ☎ 415-668-7717 ⌚ 11am-10pm daily $ burritos $4.50-6, platters $5.50-7 C cash only 🌿 🚌 7, 33, 43, 66, 71 Muni ♿
Zona Rosa serves up good, cheap Mexican food in the assembly-line Mission District manner. Burritos are the place's forté.

Kan Zaman (Middle Eastern) MAP 11
1793 Haight St ☎ 415-751-9656 ⌚ 5pm-midnight Sun-Thurs, noon-2am Fri-Sat $ appetizer $2.50-5, entrée $7-11, dessert $2 C V, MC 🌿🌿 🚌 7, 33, 43, 66, 71 Muni ♿
In the category of trippy Haight-Ashbury dining experiences, Kan Zaman takes the prize. You'll be transported by funky Arabian-night

decor, fake palms, cushion-on-the-floor seating, late-night belly dancers working the floor for tips, and patrons getting goofed on the house hookah ($7). Decent, reasonably priced Middle Eastern food includes spicy falafels, hummus, baba ghanoush, and kebabs – vegetarian shish kebabs are a specialty.

Massawa Restaurant (East African) MAP 11
1538 Haight St ☎ 415-621-4129 ⌚ 11:30am-10pm Sun-Thurs, 11:30am-11pm Fri-Sat $ appetizer $2-4, entrée $6-11.50 C V, MC, AE, DC 🚭 🚌 6, 7, 66, 71, 43 Muni ♿

You and your tablemates can dig into shared platters such as the kelwa (chopped beef sautéed with spiced clarified butter, specially seasoned hot pepper, jalapenos, onions, and tomatoes and served with a dollop of yogurt). There are numerous veggie options as well. Dishes are served with spongy injera bread for scooping and, if you like, African beer.

Cha Cha Cha (Caribbean) MAP 11
1801 Haight St ☎ 415-386-5758 ⌚ 11:30am-4pm daily, 5pm-11pm Sun-Thurs, 5pm-11:30pm Fri-Sat $ appetizer $3.50-8.50, entrée $11-13.50, dessert $4 C V, MC 🚭 🚌 7, 33, 43, 66, 71 Muni ♿

The fun, lively, loud, and extremely popular Cha Cha Cha offers spicy Caribbean tapas (under $10) and main dishes like red snapper steamed in banana leaf. The food, while mostly very good, can be of uneven quality, and since the restaurant doesn't take reservations, most nights you'll have to wait up to an hour for your table. If the wait is going to be that long, duck into a nearby bar. Cha Cha Cha's own bar is a crowded waiting room with a slim selection of wines and beers – but have some sangria after you're seated.

Cole Valley

A couple of blocks south of Haight St, Cole Valley's eateries are upscale refuges for the professionals who have colonized the neighborhood. Cole Valley also has quick stops for a do-it-yourself lunch in Golden Gate Park.

Say Cheese (delicatessen) MAP 11
856 Cole St ☎ 415-665-5020 ⌚ 10am-7pm Mon-Sat, 10am-5pm Sun $ $5.50-6 C V, MC, D, DC 🚭 🚌 6, 37, 43, N Muni

Order a vegetarian or meat sandwich to go – the park is just a few blocks from here – and select from an impressive list of international cheeses.

Zazie (French) MAP 11
941 Cole St ☎ 415-564-5332 ⌚ 8am-2:30pm Mon-Fri, 9am-3pm Sat-Sun, 6pm-9:30pm Mon-Thurs, 6pm-10pm Fri-Sat, 5:30pm-9:30pm Sun $ breakfast $5-9, lunch $5-10, appetizer $4-10, entrée $11-15, dessert $4-6 C MC, V 🚭 🚌 6, 37, 43, N Muni ♿

Zazie, with its warm Provençal tones and narrow sky-lit dining room, is about as pleasant a spot for breakfast or lunch you could hope to find. Eggs, pancakes, and gourmet sandwiches are the order of the daytime. If it's a sunny day, try to get a table out on the flowery back patio. It's also open for dinner, when the menu focuses on heartwarming Provençal fare – roasted salmon seasoned with basil-tomato vinaigrette is served on a bed of sautéed spinach and mashed potatoes.

Eos Restaurant & Wine Bar (fusion) MAP 11
901 Cole St ☎ 415-566-3063 ⌚ 5:30pm-10pm Mon-Sat, 5pm-10pm Sun $ appetizer $8-12, entrée $22-28, dessert $7 C AE, MC, V 🚭 🚌 6, 37, 43, N Muni ♿

Eos is one of San Francisco's most highly regarded East-West fusion restaurants. Its self-conscious, postindustrial dining room is too noisy for intimate conversation. Impressively designed appetizers, such as the seared ahi tuna tower, get the palate warmed up with a variety of intriguing flavors. Main courses, such as roast Alaskan halibut and quail stuffed with steamed lotus rice, are arranged beautifully with fresh local produce and can keep you pleasantly occupied for a couple of hours. The adjoining wine bar makes an extensive wine list available to diners – but few offerings cost less than $8 a glass or $40 a bottle.

Lower Haight

Ten blocks east of the Haight-Ashbury, the Lower Haight is bar-central, but when the party crowd needs sustenance, they can turn to a number of international restaurants. There are also several morning-after refueling spots in the neighborhood.

Axum Cafe (Ethiopian) MAP 11
698 Haight St ☎ 415-252-7912 ⌚ 5pm-10:30pm Mon-Fri, 1pm-10:30pm Sat-Sun $ $4.50-8 C AE, D, DC, MC, V 🚭 🚌 6, 7, 66, 71 Muni ♿

Lower Haight hipsters have embraced this unassuming Ethiopian restaurant that offers a nice selection of lamb and vegetarian dishes. Large portions, low prices, and zesty flavors draw a crowd nearly every night.

Squat & Gobble Cafe (American) MAP 11
237 Fillmore St ☎ 415-487-0551 ⌚ 8am-10pm daily $ breakfast $4-6, entrée $5-7 C cash only 🚌 6, 7, 22, 66, 71 Muni ♿

It has a stupid name, but Squat & Gobble wins people over with exceedingly huge portions and very reasonable prices. Its large, sunny, woodsy interior is nice for whiling away the morning or afternoon with a paper and inexpensive crepes, omelets, salads, and sandwiches.

Kate's Kitchen (American) MAP 11
471 Haight St ☎ 415-626-3984 ⌚ 8am-9pm Mon-Fri, 9am-9pm Sat, 9am-4pm Sun $ breakfast $4-8, lunch $5-6.50, appetizer $3-6, entrée $6-9.50 C cash only 🚌 6, 7, 22, 66, 71 Muni ♿

A neighborhood breakfast favorite, Kate's serves platter-size pancakes piled with fruits, plus other breakfast standards with Southern influences.

Thep Phanom (Thai) MAP 11
400 Waller St ☎ 415-431-2526 ⌚ 5:30pm-10:30pm daily $ appetizer $7-9, entrée $8-12, dessert $5 C AE, D, DC, MC, V 🚌 6, 7, 22, 66, 71 Muni ♿

Cramped little Thep Phanom, just a short walk from Haight St or Market St, has long been recognized as one of San Francisco's best Thai restaurants. Order from the list of specials,

All-American Breakfasts

Most San Franciscans have a favorite restaurant for basic hearty breakfasts, but for short-term visitors the special places are not always so easy to find. Out-of-towners looking for a smart start to their day would do well to consider any of the following quality breakfast spots:

Sears Fine Foods MAP 2
439 Powell St ☎ 415-986-1160 ⌚ 6:30am-2:30pm daily $ breakfast $5.50-13 C cash only 🚌 2, 3, 4, 76 Muni 🚋 Powell-Mason, Powell-Hyde cable cars ♿

This nondescript eatery was founded in 1938 by a retired circus clown named Ben Sears – which may be all the recommendation you need. Rest assured, they don't clown around with the food. The joint's in every tourist guidebook (uh, including this one…), and all the local concierges seem to recommend it. As a result, Sears' rather ordinary pancakes have become 'world famous,' and while this should just be your basic place to grab a quick bite, in reality you may have to wait on the sidewalk before being seated.

Dottie's True Blue Café MAP 3
522 Jones St ☎ 415-885-2767 ⌚ 7:30am-3pm Thurs-Mon $ breakfast $6-9, lunch $6-7.50 C D, V 🚌 27, 38 Muni

This bright and friendly Tenderloin spot serves up hefty hotcakes, a variety of tasty sausages (apple chicken, andouille, etc), eye-popping omelets, and strong coffee. The staff are real cordial, and the busy grill is run by hash-slinging professionals. Don't expect to waltz in and be seated, though: on weekends, there's a line out the door.

Mama's MAP 6
1701 Stockton St ☎ 415-362-6421 ⌚ 8am-3pm Tues-Sun $ breakfast $8-12 C cash only 🚌 15, 30, 39, 41, 45 Muni ♿

It's a little on the cute side and the prices are a bit steep, but Mama's is a genuinely cozy spot, where window-side tables are warmed by the morning sun and the straightforward breakfast and lunch fare is topnotch. Omelets, hotcakes, and an exemplary French toast rule the breakfast menu, while sandwiches (veggie options), soups, and burgers headline for lunch. But the line down the sidewalk on weekend mornings may test your desire to get in.

which change nightly, as they are where the restaurant really shines.

THE CASTRO

In the past few years, many fine restaurants have opened in the hub of San Francisco's gay community. Meanwhile, cruisy quick-bite joints and 24-hour diners continue to add to the hustle and bustle of the Castro.

Hot 'n' Hunky (American) MAP 12
4039 18th St ☎ 415-621-6365 ⌚ 11am-midnight Sun-Thurs, 11am-1am Fri-Sat $ $3-5.50 C cash only Ⓜ Castro St Muni station 🚌 33, F Muni ♿

A Castro standby since 1980, Hot 'n' Hunky flips cheap burgers in an eat-and-run environment.

California Harvest Ranch Market (grocery/delicatessen) MAP 12
2285 Market St ☎ 415-626-0805 ⌚ 8:30am-11pm daily $ $5-6 C AE, MC, V Ⓜ Castro St Muni station 🚌 24, 37, F Muni ♿

At this gourmet grocery store and deli, there are no tables, but the outdoor sidewalk benches provide a perfect resting spot while you indulge in the market's amazing assortment of improv edibles. You can choose among sandwiches, trays of sushi, fresh produce, bins of dried fruit, vegan baked goods, salads, and much more.

Baghdad Cafe (American) MAP 12
2295 Market St ☎ 415-621-4434 ⌚ 24 hours $ breakfast $3-12, entrée $4.50-9, dessert $3-5 C cash only Ⓜ Castro St Muni station 🚌 24, 37, F Muni ♿

All-American Breakfasts

Doidge's Cafe MAP 9
2217 Union St ☎ 415-921-2149 ⌚ 8am-12:30pm Mon-Fri, 8am-1:30pm Sat, 8am-2:30pm Sun $ breakfast $7-11 C V, MC, D, DC 🚌 22, 41, 45 Muni

Hungry patrons at this homey Marina eatery know to call ahead for reservations, which is a pain in the ass but also telling. The breakfasts are indeed good – the French toast is fine, as are the eggs Benedict. Some weekend mornings are so busy that even if you have a reservation you may have to wait out on the sidewalk before being seated.

Ella's MAP 10
500 Presidio Ave ☎ 415-441-5669 ⌚ 7am-2pm Mon-Fri, 9am-2pm Sat-Sun $ breakfast $3-7.50 C AE, MC, V 🚌 1, 3, 4 Muni

Ella's is a clean and friendly establishment that's known for its sticky buns, served piping hot out of the oven, and for its high-quality breakfasts. It's so well known, there's almost always a line down the sidewalk on weekends, and tables are scarce on weekdays, too.

Chloe's Café MAP 13
1399 Church St ☎ 415-648-4116 ⌚ 8am-3pm Mon-Fri, 8am-4pm Sat-Sun $ breakfast $5-9, lunch $5-9 C cash only 🚌 J Muni

Tiny Chloe's is a Noe Valley neighborhood favorite where hefty portions pretty much take care of you 'til dinner. The bustling engine room of a kitchen churns out the city's heftiest, tastiest pecan pancakes, and eggs and home fries are hearty and fresh. On any given day, you may have to wait for a table, but the wait's always long on weekends.

Boogaloo's MAP 14
3296 22nd St ☎ 415-824-3211 ⌚ 8am-3pm daily $ breakfast $5-7 C V, MC Ⓜ 24th St BART station 🚌 14, 26, 49 Muni ♿

If you've tied one on in the Mission the night before, breakfast at this cheerful spot will bring you back to life. Many of the dishes have Cajun and Caribbean accents (andouille sausages and jerked pork chops, for example), and heaps of food appear on every plate.

The best of the neighborhood's 24-hour eateries, Baghdad Cafe makes an effort to provide relatively healthful diner food. Triple-decker turkey sandwiches, full-on breakfasts, and panoramic windows overlooking the street are what people come here for.

Sparky's Diner (American) MAP 12
242 Church St ☎ 415-626-8666 ⌚ 24 hours $ lunch specials $5.50, entrée $3.50-11.50 C CB, D, DC, MC, V 22, 37, F, J Muni

If you're hankering for breakfast at 4am, head to Sparky's, another place that serves the coffee-shop classics 'round the clock. In the early evening, it's not a bad place for families, but it hops late into the night, when barhoppers, clubhoppers, hairhoppers, and hopheads descend on the place.

It's Tops (American) MAP 12
1801 Market St ☎ 415-864-9352 ⌚ 8am-3pm Sun-Fri, 8pm-3am Wed-Fri, 8am-3am Sat $ breakfast $5-12, lunch $5-11 C MC, V 37, F Muni

Somewhat removed from the Castro stands It's Tops, an authentic museum-piece diner dating to the 1930s. Prices are somewhat inflated, no doubt because of the atmosphere. The food is standard greasy spoon. Always popular for breakfast, it draws barhoppers seeking a late-night bite during the latter half of the week.

Chow (American/Italian) MAP 12
215 Church St ☎ 415-552-2469 ⌚ 11am-11pm Sun-Thurs, 11am-midnight Fri-Sat $ appetizer $2-7, entrée $6-10.50, dessert $3-5 C MC, V 22, 37, F, J Muni ♿

A few doors off Market, Chow offers affordable and tasty pizzas, pastas, and grilled and roasted meats. High ceilings, traditional decor, solid beer and wine selections, and a friendly energetic staff make it a pleasant place to share a meal with friends.

Orphan Andy's (American) MAP 12
3991 17th St ☎ 415-864-9795 ⌚ 24 hours $ breakfast $4-8.50, lunch $6-8.50, entrée $6-11 C V, MC, AE Ⓜ Castro St Muni station 24, 37, F Muni ♿

Orphan Andy's is a 'round-the-clock Castro institution that primarily serves the needs of hungry clubhoppers. Filling diner classics – greasy lunch and breakfast – are what's cookin'.

Tin-Pan Asian Bistro (Pan-Asian) MAP 12
2251 Market St ☎ 415-565-0733 ⌚ 11am-11pm Sun-Thurs, 11am-midnight Fri-Sat $ appetizer $6-10, entrée $7-10 C AE, DC, MC, V 22, 37, F, J Muni ♿

Tin-Pan, a friendly and busy cross-cultural noodle house, freely blends Asian influences in a dizzying variety of noodle dishes. The noodles are made on the premises and are quite good, but sometimes the overambitious blend of ingredients devolves into the flavor equivalent of brown.

Tita's Hale 'Aina (Hawaiian) MAP 12
3870 17th St ☎ 415-626-2477 ⌚ 5pm-10pm Tues-Fri, 10am-10pm Sat-Sun $ lunch $6-10, appetizer $5-11, entrée $7-11, dessert $2.50-4 C MC, V Ⓜ Castro St Muni station 24, 33, F Muni ♿

It has all the comfort of a casual neighborhood café, but Tita's is in fact a Hawaiian outpost, where Kahlua pig and aku tuna are prepared the multicultural Hawaiian way. Ti leaves, ginger, and sweet fruit flavors set the tone, while Hawaiian music (piped in) and exotic decor help transport diners to the islands.

Mecca (fusion) MAP 12
2029 Market St ☎ 415-621-7000 ⌚ 6pm-11pm Mon-Wed, 5:30pm-midnight Thurs-Sat, 5pm-10pm Sun $ appetizer $2-18, entrée $16-26, dessert $7.50 C AE, DC, MC, V Ⓜ Church St Muni station 22, F, J Muni ♿

In a dimly lit postmodern structure, Mecca is as much a nightclub as it is a restaurant. There's a DJ or live music every night of the week, and the cocktails are as famous as are the celebrities who often walk though the doors. But the kitchen turns out well-respected entrées and small plates, such as pancetta-wrapped roasted monkfish and wood-roasted split chicken. At the bar, you can order tasty pizzas and a wide variety of California wines.

NOE VALLEY

Being an urbane, livable sort of neighborhood, Noe Valley has great places for breakfast, and there are a couple of stellar restaurants for dinner too.

Savor (American/French) MAP 13
3913 24th St ☎ 415-282-0344 ⌚ 8am-10pm Sun-Thurs, 8am-11pm Fri-Sat $ breakfast $5.50-8, entrée $5.50-9, dessert $4.50-5 C V, MC 48, J Muni ♿

Savor packs them in for light breakfast standards, savory and sweet crepes, and healthful sandwiches and salads. On sunny days, the back courtyard is where everyone wants to sit.

Firefly (California) MAP 13
4288 24th St ☎ 415-821-7652 ⏱ 5:30pm-10pm daily $ appetizer $7-9.50, entrée $15-20, dessert $6-8 C AE, MC, V ⊘ 🚌 35, 48 Muni ♿

Noe Valley's best restaurant, Firefly, is an innovator that's well appreciated but free of all the buzz of similarly creative restaurants in San Francisco. The menu changes regularly but always evinces the kitchen's versatile adeptness in European, Asian, and American cuisine (including the occasional Southern barbecue), and the food benefits from a creative blend of ingredients and select local produce. This place earns harmonious raves from both carnivores and vegetarians.

THE MISSION

Always one of San Francisco's more idiosyncratic neighborhoods, the Mission District has nevertheless taken a seat at this food-mad city's dining table. Between Valencia and Dolores Sts, 16th St is bustling with affordable restaurants that explore an intriguing array of cuisines. Valencia and Guerrero are both hopping with restaurants at the corners of 21st and 22nd Sts. Italian, Vietnamese, East-West fusion, and tapas have all established a presence in the neighborhood.

But the signature food of the Mission District remains the burrito. Traditional Mission-style burritos, with little corruption wrought by the recent 'wraps' trend, are prepared at countless taquerías along Mission St. But, surprisingly, restaurants serving quality traditional Mexican fare in more comfortable eat-in environs are few and far between.

At Mexican eateries, credit cards are frequently not accepted, but ATMs proliferate in the neighborhood's bars, so getting a cash fix is always easy.

Budget

Mitchell's Ice Cream (ice cream)
688 San Jose Ave (at 29th St) ☎ 415-648-2300 ⏱ 11am-11pm daily $ cones $2 C cash only 🚌 14, 24, 26, J Muni ♿

At surreal Mitchell's, cones and tubs filled with ice cream of every flavor and stripe are served through bullet-proof windows. The ice cream is made daily on the premises. Unusual but natural enough flavors like mango, lichee, and avocado all have their devotees, and traditional chocolate, vanilla, and coffee flavors are also very good.

La Palma Mexica-tessen (Mexican delicatessen) MAP 14
2884 24th St ☎ 415-647-1500 ⏱ 10:30am-9pm Sun-Fri, 11:30am-9pm Sat $ $2-4 C V, MC 🚌 27, 48 Muni

La Palma is a Mexican grocery with a take-out counter in back that's famous for its handmade tamales. You can also order burritos and tacos or, if you have a kitchen at your disposal, get goods to prepare your own Mexican fiesta.

St Francis Fountain (American) MAP 14
2801 24th St ☎ 415-826-4200 ⏱ 11am-9pm Mon-Fri, 11:30am-8pm Sat-Sun $ $4-6 C MC, V 🚌 27, 48 Muni ♿

A Mission District treasure, the St Francis Fountain has been in operation since 1918 and has maintained its impeccable soda-fountain appearance. Inexpensive burgers and sandwiches are on the menu, but the St Francis' forté is its ice cream and malted milkshakes. Old-timers from Brooklyn will relish the opportunity to order old-fashioned egg cream sodas.

Truly Mediterranean (Middle Eastern) MAP 14
3109 16th St ☎ 415-252-7482 ⏱ 11am-midnight Mon-Sat, 11am-10pm Sun $ $4-6 C cash only ⊘⊘ Ⓜ 16th St BART station 🚌 14, 22, 26, 49 Muni ♿

Denizens of the Mission have discovered that meatless falafels are perfectly suited for scarfing between bars, and Truly Med is well situated to fill the need. Inexpensive falafels, shawermas, hummus, and kebabs are also available on a mostly take-out basis (the place has just a few chairs).

Atlas Café (American) MAP 14
3049 20th St ☎ 415-648-1047 ⏱ 7am-10pm Mon-Fri, 8am-10pm Sat, 8am-8pm Sun $ breakfast $2-3, entrée $4-7 C cash only ⊘⊘ 🚌 27 Muni ♿

Atlas Café, deep in the Mission, is emblematic of the district's ongoing gentrification – just a few years back, there was no place around here that specifically appealed to white slackers and dot-commers. But the place has its virtues. It's a casual, mixed scene, and live

PLACES TO EAT

acoustic music (no cover) draws folks from around town on Thursday night and Saturday afternoon. Inexpensive breakfasts, sandwiches (veggie choices and Cuban pork, among others), strong coffee, and tap beers are reason enough to come any time.

We Be Sushi (Japanese) MAP 14
538 Valencia St ☎ 415-565-0749 ⌚ noon-10pm Sun-Thurs, noon-11pm Fri-Sat $ appetizer $2, entrée $6 C V, MC (minimum $10) M 16th St BART station 🚌 14, 22, 26, 49 Muni

We Be is a local favorite. The sushi's nothing to write home about, but it's good and very affordable. There are two locations in the neighborhood (see below).

We Be Sushi (Japanese) MAP 14
1071 Valencia St ☎ 415-522-0129 ⌚ noon-10pm Sun-Thurs, noon-11pm Fri-Sat $ appetizer $2, entrée $6 C V, MC (minimum $10) 🚌 14, 26, 49 Muni ♿

See above.

Chava's (Mexican) MAP 14
3248 18th St ☎ 415-552-9387 ⌚ 6am-6pm

The Sacred Mission Burrito

The Mission District burrito is a perfect rolled-up meal: rice, beans, grilled meat, salsa, guacamole, and sour cream contained in a flour tortilla and wrapped in aluminum foil. The rice is what sets it apart from other regional varieties, although in truth few locals would insist on this definition.

The flour tortilla originated in Sonora, Mexico (where maize was scarce), and its purpose evolved as it spread north. California's 19th-century agricultural laborers, most of whom were Mexican, utilized the tortilla's glutinous flexibility to create self-contained, easily transported rice-and-bean lunches. Burrito historians trace the burrito's San Francisco roots to the early 1960s, when retailers first began selling the fortifying foodstuff for take-out consumption. Gradually, incredible local competition – there are about 100 taquerías in the Mission – has forced cooks to perfect their grilling techniques, select quality ingredients, create original salsas, and develop efficient systems of assembly to ensure a consistently fresh and tasty product.

Old hands at devouring burritos usually stand the entire package on end and peel down just enough foil before biting (the foil, not the tortilla, is usually what holds the burrito together). It is permissible for neophytes to remove all the foil, lie the burrito on a plate, and dig in with a knife and fork.

For many San Franciscans, inexpensive burritos are a staple food for at least some period of their life. Overindulgence in burritos is common, leading to the uniquely San Franciscan condition of being 'burritoed out.'

One burrito, costing $4 to $6, is often more food than a single person can chow down in a sitting.

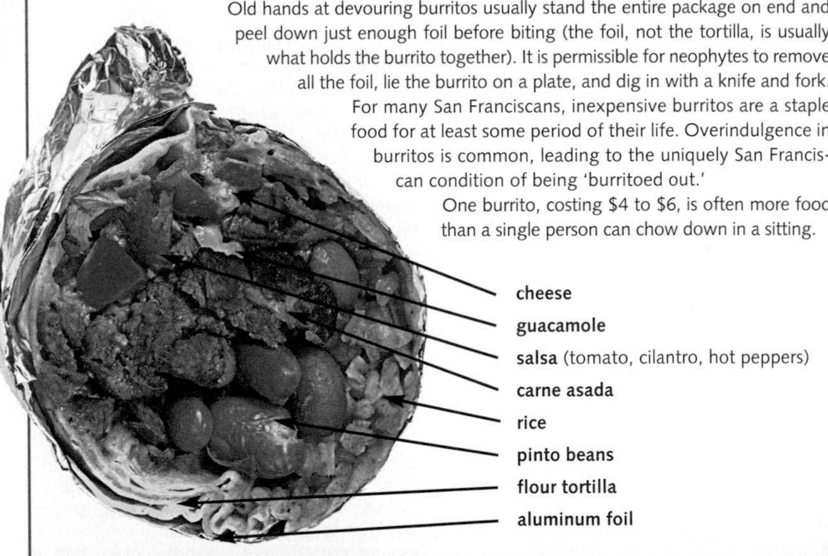

daily $4-9.50 cash only 16th St BART station 12, 48 Muni

Chava's, a slightly disheveled but convivial Mexican eatery, is several blocks from the hubbub of Mission St, but if you are fanatical about menudo (beef tripe soup), then you'll agree it's worth the walk. Chava's homemade tortillas also rate among the city's best, and they go great with menudo and the restaurant's other soups. The hot chile colorado is another draw, but most of the combo platters are churned out pretty carelessly.

La Rondalla (Mexican) MAP 14
901 Valencia St 415-647-7474 11:30am-3:30 Tues-Sun appetizer (to share) $10, entrée $3.50-10, dessert $2 cash only 14, 26, 49 Muni

La Rondalla, a Mission District fixture with festive decor, is another place where mediocre Mexican food and cheap margaritas go together. If tequila makes you hallucinate, you'll get off on the joint's year-round Christmas lights, velvet paintings, and mariachi bands, as many a Mission denizen has over the past few decades.

The Sacred Mission Burrito

Here's a selection of popular taquerías, all of which are on Map 14:

La Cumbre Taquería
515 Valencia St 415-863-8205 11am-9pm daily $3.75-5 MC, V 16th St BART station 14, 22, 49 Muni

Once the most popular taquería in the neighborhood, La Cumbre has lost its edge. But the burritos are small and inexpensive, which suits diminutive appetites.

La Taquería
2889 Mission St 415-285-7117 11am-9pm Mon-Sat, 11am-8pm Sun $3-4.50 cash only 24th St BART station 14, 48, 49 Muni

The best taquería in town? A lot of people think so. This place has no rice cooker, but makes up for that lack with superb meats – try the carnitas.

Taquería Can-Cun
2288 Mission St 415-252-9560 10am-1am Sun-Thurs, 10am-2am Fri-Sat $3.50-4 cash only 16th St BART station 14, 49 Muni

This popular taquería is known for its delicious vegetarian burrito, packed with fresh avocado, and its tortillas are flaky and delicious.

Taquería El Farolito
2779 Mission St 415-826-4870 9am-2:30am daily $3-4 cash only 24th St BART station 14, 48, 49 Muni

This popular and narrow little place feels like a side-street Tijuana dive. The staff grill, rather than steam, their tortillas, and some locals stand by their salsas.

Taquería Pancho Villa
3071 16th St 415-864-8840 10am-midnight daily $5-10 cash only 16th St BART station 14, 22, 49 Muni

Here you'll find some of the best and biggest burritos in town. The constant line out the door ensures the ingredients are always fresh.

Taquería San José
2830 Mission St 415-282-0203 8am-midnight Sun-Thurs, 8am-4am Fri-Sat $3-4.50 cash only 24th St BART station 14, 48, 49 Muni

This place has possibly the world's tastiest al pastor (spicy barbecued pork) burrito.

Puerto Alegre (Mexican) MAP 14
546 Valencia St ☎ 415-255-8201 ⌚ 11am-10pm Mon, 5pm-11pm Tues, 11am-11pm Wed-Sun $ breakfast $4, appetizer $5-10, entrée $3.50-13 C V, MC, DC M 16th St BART station 🚌 14, 22, 26, 49 Muni ♿

Puerto Alegre is a cheap Mexican cantina that is known more for its margaritas than for its rather ordinary tacos, burritos, and combo platters. But in all honesty, the food starts to taste awfully good once you've got some booze under your belt. Happy hour (3pm-6pm Monday and Wednesday to Friday) is always a good time to show up.

Burger Joint (American) MAP 14
807 Valencia St ☎ 415-824-3494 ⌚ 11am-11pm daily $ $6-7 C cash only 🚭 🚌 14, 26, 33, 49 Muni ♿

The retro-contemporary stylings of Burger Joint's interior, with its colorful Formica tables and vinyl booths, somehow look, well, *dated* – they're the retro-contemporary stylings of five years ago, not the retro-contemporary stylings of today. But never mind that, the handmade organic patties, golden crispy fries, and ultra-rich milkshakes are top-notch.

Bitterroot (American) MAP 14
3122 16th St ☎ 415-626-5523 ⌚ 7am-5pm Mon-Fri, 8am-4pm Sat-Sun $ appetizer $4-8, entrée $5-9, dessert $3.50-5 C V, MC 🚭 M 16th St BART station 🚌 14, 22, 26, 49 Muni ♿

When Bitterroot proclaims itself an 'American restaurant,' it doesn't quite come off with the same iconic authority as, say, Johnny Cash does when he titles an album 'American Recordings.' But the place does a commendable job with inexpensive and hearty American meals. Breakfast comes closer to chuck-wagon standards, but a burger and fries will do you for lunch. Stay away from the barbecue.

Mid-Range & Top End

Keur Baobab (Senegalese) MAP 14
3388 19th St ☎ 415-643-3558 ⌚ 6am-midnight Tues-Thurs, 6am-2am Fri-Sun $ appetizer $3.50-7, entrée $7-10, dessert $2.50-5 C V, MC, D 🚭 🚌 14, 33, 49 Muni

A convenient and festive pit stop in a night of Mission barhopping is Keur Baobab, where the cuisine of Senegal has been introduced to hordes of people who had never tried it before. The verdict is usually favorable. Delicious entrees include yassa (grilled chicken and onions in lemon garlic), shrimp or fish tchou (a spicy tomato sauce), and vegetarian mafe (veggies with peanut sauce over rice). Also stop by its new location, right around the corner on Mission St.

Esperpento (Spanish) MAP 14
3295 22nd St ☎ 415-282-8867 ⌚ 11am-3pm Mon-Fri, 11am-4pm Sat, 5pm-10pm Mon-Thurs, 5pm-11pm Fri-Sat, noon-10pm Sun $ lunch $7, tapas $4-8, entrée $9, paella (2 people) $26, dessert $3 C V, MC, AE, D, DC, JCB 🚭 M 24th St BART station 🚌 14, 26, 49 Muni ♿

A lively and colorful tapas bar, Esperpento is the place to go for a social evening of grazing on small but inexpensive portions of piquant ropa vieja and rabbit stew and swilling the house sangria ($14 a pitcher). Esperpento also specializes in savory seafood paellas – saffron rice simmering with tomatoes, peppers, mussels, and shrimp. On Friday and Saturday, the bar is also popular.

El Nuevo Frutilandia (Cuban/Puerto Rican) MAP 14
3077 24th St ☎ 415-648-2958 ⌚ 11:30am-3pm & 5pm-9pm Tues-Fri, noon-10pm Sat, noon-9pm Sun $ tapas $1.50-8, entrée $7-13, dessert $3 C V, MC 🚭🚭 M 24th St BART station 🚌 12, 48 Muni ♿

At this Caribbean pit stop, the tapas can be uneven – stick to the alcapurrias (meat-filled yucca fritters) or fried plantains – but the nightly meat specials, which might include roast pork or chicken fricassée, always excel. The carne guisada con papas (beef and potato stew) is also really good. On weekends, guitar music livens the joint up.

Sunflower (Vietnamese) MAP 14
3111 16th St ☎ 415-626-5023 ⌚ 11:30am-3pm Mon-Fri, 5pm-10:30pm Mon-Thurs, 5pm-11pm Fri, noon-11pm Sat, noon-10:30pm Sun $ lunch $5-7, appetizer $6-7.50, entrée $8-16, dessert $3 C V, MC 🚭🚭 M 16th St BART station 🚌 14, 22, 26, 49 Muni ♿

If you are unable to gain admittance to the ultra-chic Slanted Door (below), take heart. Just a block away, Sunflower is a very down-to-earth but no less pleasant Vietnamese alternative. The goods emerging from the kitchen are authentic and quite delicious. Flaming beef and prawns are about as dramatic as the place gets, but the steamed sea bass fillet is fresh and subtly seasoned, and the imperial rolls are fried to perfection. Budget lunch specials are another reason to stop by.

Ti Couz (French) MAP 14
3108 16th St ☎ 415-252-7373 ⏲ 11am-11pm Mon-Wed, 11am-midnight Thurs-Fri, 10am-midnight Sat, 10am-11pm Sun ⓢ appetizer $2-10, entrée $3-20, dessert $2-5.50 Ⓒ MC, V Ⓜ 16th St BART station 🚌 14, 22, 26, 49 Muni ♿

This authentic Breton creperie turns out a huge variety of sweet and savory crepes and a nice selection of soups and salads. It also has a good selection of cider, another specialty of Brittany.

Pauline's Pizza Pie (pizza) MAP 14
260 Valencia St ☎ 415-552-2050 ⏲ 5pm-10pm Tues-Sat ⓢ appetizer $6.50, pizza pie $13-22, dessert $5 Ⓒ MC, V 🚌 26 Muni ♿

In the shadow of the old Levi's factory, Pauline's has been quietly making some of the best pizza in town for many years now. Nontraditional toppings such as feta cheese, squash, and andouille sausage don't overshadow the requisite ingredients for great pizza: a delicate and tasty crust, fresh and well-seasoned sauce, and cheese that does not turn to rubber when it cools. You can also order more familiar – but no less excellent – pizzas with pesto, Italian sausage, or vegetable combinations. Prices are not out of line.

Slanted Door (Vietnamese) MAP 14
584 Valencia St ☎ 415-861-8032 ⏲ 11:30am-3pm & 5:30pm-10pm Tues-Sun ⓢ lunch $5.50-13, appetizer $5-8.50, entrée $8.50-18, dessert $6 Ⓒ V, MC Ⓜ 16th St BART station 🚌 14, 22, 26, 49 Muni ♿

The Slanted Door, a Vietnamese restaurant with some cross-cultural touches, played a central role in igniting the Mission District's current culinary boom. The name's reference to the building's oblique portal, as well as a very modern and pleasant interior, reflects chef-owner Charles Phan's training as an architect, while the food reflects his Vietnamese heritage, as well as his good taste and originality. Garlic 'shaking beef,' startlingly fresh Chilean sea bass with shiitake mushrooms and ginger, and caramelized clay pot chicken with mild chiles are unforgettably good. Lunches – also worth coming for – are more traditional rice plates.

Mangiafuoco (Italian) MAP 14
1001 Guerrero St ☎ 415-206-9881 ⏲ 5:30pm-10:30pm Wed-Mon ⓢ appetizer $6-9, entrée $12-18 Ⓒ V, MC 🚌 26, 48 Muni ♿

The slightly loud but attractive dining room at Mangiafuoco is decorated with icons from the Italian folktale of the Fire Eater (whose mouth was as big as an oven) and awash with the aromas of some of the city's best Northern Italian cuisine. Outstanding dishes include the antipasto misto (including sautéed fungi and carpaccio), a perfect risotto, mezzaluna (handmade ravioli filled with squash and crushed amaretto cookies and bathed in brown butter and sage), and angello (small racks of lamb drizzled in a sauce of balsamic vinegar, mustard, and huckleberry). There's an excellent list of Italian and Californian wines.

Foreign Cinema (French) MAP 14
2534 Mission St ☎ 415-648-7600 ⏲ 5:30pm-11pm Tues-Sat, movies & bar open 'til 2am ⓢ appetizer $6-10, entrée $14-21, dessert $5-7 Ⓒ AE, MC, V 🚌 14, 26, 49 Muni ♿

For dinner and a movie in a single stop, the Mission District gives you Foreign Cinema. The food is French, and the films, projected against a screen overlooking the back patio, are all of the non-Hollywood variety. It's a clever idea, even if the films sometimes merely add to the atmosphere. For meat eaters, the menu is a mouthwatering scene-stealer: entrées include grilled filet mignon with caramelized vegetables and foie gras sauce, and red-wine-braised lamb shank with pancetta-garlic flageolet.

Flying Saucer (fusion) MAP 14
1000 Guerrero St ☎ 415-641-9955 ⏲ 6pm-10pm Mon-Thurs, 6pm-10:30pm Fri-Sat ⓢ appetizer $5-13, entrée $17-30, dessert $7-15 Ⓒ AE, MC, V 🚌 26, 48 Muni ♿

Flying Saucer's dining room, with its vinyl booths and replica of Venus de Milo, is a cross between retro diner and faux Roman playboy mansion – it's the work of a screwball visionary. Similarly, the chef has created a surprisingly original and highly lauded cuisine that plays on Californian and Asian tastes. The menu changes constantly, but portions are always large, artfully arranged, and endowed with inspired ingredients (jicama, shiitake mushrooms, and fresh herbs often appear in unexpected combinations). Reservations are essential for weekend dinners.

BERNAL HEIGHTS

Bernal Heights, an out-of-the way neighborhood to the south of the Mission, rarely draws tourists, but the neighborhood does have an excellent restaurant that often lures San Franciscans to these parts.

Liberty Cafe
410 Cortland Ave ☎ 415-695-8777 ⌚ 11:30am-3pm Tues-Fri, 5:30pm-9pm Tues-Thurs & Sun, 5:30pm-9:30pm Fri-Sat, 10am-2pm Sat-Sun $ lunch $6-13, appetizer $5-9.50, entrée $12.50-15.50, dessert $5-6 C AE, MC, V 24 Muni ♿

The Liberty Cafe stakes it reputation on chicken pot pie, made to order and served piping hot. The cozy little restaurant's seasonal menu is also highly regarded for home-style dishes featuring fresh, organic ingredients.

POTRERO HILL

This part of town isn't a huge destination for dinner, although there are some fine restaurants up here. But if you're headed for the Bottom of the Hill nightclub, at the base of Potrero Hill, you might want to grab a bite to eat first.

Goat Hill Pizza (Italian) MAP 14
300 Connecticut St ☎ 415-641-1440 ⌚ 11:30am-10:30pm daily $ appetizer $3.50, pizza pie $9-23 C V, MC, AE, DC, D 22, 53 Muni ♿

A longtime neighborhood favorite, Goat Hill Pizza serves up thin-crust pizzas with a nice tomato sauce and draught Anchor Steam by the glass or pitcher. There's a great view, and local art hangs on the walls. This joint even has soy cheese, if you want it.

THE RICHMOND

When you're looking for great food in San Francisco, do not overlook the Richmond. Clement St east of Park Presidio Blvd is the cultural axis of New Chinatown. There's a slew of Chinese restaurants, but you'll also find Korean, Cambodian, Japanese, Thai, Vietnamese, and other Asian restaurants here. Asian places have moved farther west on Geary Blvd, where they mingle with Russian and kosher delis. Some of the city's finest Chinese restaurants are in this neighborhood.

Taiwan Restaurant (Chinese) MAP 15
445 Clement St ☎ 415-387-1789 ⌚ 11am-10pm Sun-Thurs, 11am-midnight Fri, 10am-midnight Sat $ lunch $3.50, appetizer $2.50-9, entrée $4-18 C V, MC 2, 4, 38, 44 Muni ♿

At Taiwan Restaurant, the specialties are noodles, wontons, and pot stickers, all of which are handmade in the glassed-in kitchen near the entrance. Highly recommended are the noodle soups – especially the 'beef soup noodles with own gravy' (filed away under Rice & Noodles on the detailed menu). Taiwan Restaurant also has the cheapest lunch special around: $3.50 for rice plates.

Tommy's Mexican Restaurant (Mexican) MAP 15
5929 Geary Blvd ☎ 415-387-4747 ⌚ 11am-11pm daily $ appetizer $3-6.50, entrée $5-17, dessert $3.50 C AE, MC, V 29, 38 Muni ♿

Tommy's has been run by the same family for decades and has a loyal following. The service is as good as the food is tasty. The menu features familiar Mexican combos and regional Yucatecan dishes – try the pollo pibil (chicken wrapped and cooked in banana leaves and served with rice and black beans). Fresh-squeezed lime margaritas are a specialty.

Lucky Penny (American) MAP 15
2670 Geary Blvd ☎ 415-921-0836 ⌚ 24 hours $ breakfast $2.50-8, lunch $4-6, appetizer $1.50-3, entrée $6.50-11, dessert $2-5 C MC, V 38, 43 Muni ♿

A traditional American coffee shop with standard decent fare, Lucky Penny never closes. Breakfast is clearly the best meal of the day in this busy spot.

La Vie (Vietnamese) MAP 15
5830 Geary Blvd ☎ 415-668-8080 ⌚ 11am-10pm Tues-Sun $ lunch $5.50-7.50, appetizer $5.50-12, entrée $6-16, dessert $3 C D, DC, MC, V ($15 minimum) 29, 38 Muni ♿

For solid Vietnamese dishes – but no pho – head to La Vie. The canh sua (catfish in pineapple and tamarind broth) is fine, and flaming meats and seafood cooked at your table are outstanding. The prices are reasonable – two might eat well for $25.

Louis' Restaurant (American) MAP 15
902 Point Lobos Ave ☎ 415-387-6330 ⌚ 6:30am-4:30pm Mon-Fri, 6:30am-6pm Sat-Sun $ breakfast $5-8, entrée $7-12, dessert $2.50 C cash only 18, 38 Muni ♿

Just in back of the Cliff House, you can get the same superb views at Louis', a humble coffee shop where panoramic windows overlook the remains of the Sutro Baths. Hot open-faced roast beef sandwiches, burgers, and standard breakfasts are the ticket here. Tables are crammed together, but the people are friendly in this no-frills joint.

Ton Kiang Restaurant (Chinese) MAP 15
5821 Geary Blvd ☎ 415-387-8275 ⌚ 10:30am-10pm Mon-Thurs, 10:30am-10:30pm Fri, 10am-10:30pm Sat, 9am-10:30pm Sun $ appetizer $3.50-12.50, entrée $7.50-11, dessert $3 C AE, D, DC, JCB, MC, V 🚌 38 Muni ♿

Ton Kiang is one of the city's best Chinese restaurants. Often praised for its dim sum, which is superbly cooked to order, Ton Kiang has a versatile menu that's consistently good. It specializes in Cantonese cuisine inspired by the migratory Hakka people, and dishes such as black cod with black-bean sauce are succulent and impressively presented.

RICK GERHARTER

Multi-decker steamers in Ton Kiang's kitchen

Angkor Wat (Cambodian) MAP 15
4217 Geary Blvd ☎ 415-221-7887 ⌚ 11am-2:30pm Mon-Sat, 5pm-10pm daily $ appetizer $3-6, entrée $7-15, dessert $2.50-5 C AE, MC, V 🚌 2, 31, 38 Muni ♿

Angkor Wat serves terrific Cambodian food in a very friendly atmosphere at inexpensive prices. On Friday and Saturday night, the Cambodian Royal Ballet performs two shows here.

Cliff House (seafood/American) MAP 15
1090 Point Lobos Ave ☎ 415-386-3330 ⌚ 11am-10:30pm Sun-Thurs, 11am-11pm Fri-Sat $ lunch appetizer $5-13, lunch $9-11, dinner appetizer $6-10.50, entrée $17-30 C V, MC, AE, D, DC 🚌 18, 38 Muni ♿

The Cliff House is known for its colorful history and great views (if you can snag a window seat) but not for its food, which consists of ordinary sandwiches, burgers, and seafood.

Kabuto Japanese Restaurant (Japanese) MAP 15
5116 Geary Blvd ☎ 415-752-5652 ⌚ 5:30pm-11pm Tues-Sat, 5:30pm-10pm Sun $ appetizer/sushi $2-7, entrée $9-13, dessert $1.50-4 C MC, V 🚌 28, 38 Muni ♿

More than a few serious sushi enthusiasts have proclaimed Kabuto the best sushi bar in the city. It's an unatmospheric but intimate little place, and it gets crowded on weekends.

THE SUNSET

South of Golden Gate Park, the Sunset District has a large collection of budget ethnic eating places, particularly along Irving St from 5th Ave all the way to 25th Ave. The up-and-coming Inner Sunset, concentrated around the intersection of 9th Ave and Irving St, has a healthy mix of traditional neighborhood establishments and fashionable new eateries.

Pluto's Fresh Food for a Hungry Universe (American) MAP 15
627 Irving St ☎ 415-753-8867 ⌚ 11:30am-10pm Sun-Thurs, 11:30am-11pm Fri-Sat $ appetizer $1.50-3.50, entrée $3.50-6, dessert $2 C MC, V 🚌 6, 43, 44, 66, N Muni ♿

Pluto's nerdy atomic-age decor doesn't hinder the food, which comes in large portions at unbelievably low prices. For $5 or less, you get heaping salads composed of fresh organic produce, or meat and potato fixings, or a hefty sandwich. A signature item is the roast chicken, served either on a dinner plate or between two slices of bread.

Park Chow (American/Italian) MAP 15
1240 9th Ave ☎ 415-665-9912 ⌚ 11am-10pm Mon-Thurs, 11am-11pm Fri, 10am-11pm Sat, 10am-10pm Sun $ appetizer $2-7, entrée $6-10.50, dessert $3-5 C MC, V 🚌 6, 43, 44, 71, N Muni ♿

Half a block from Golden Gate Park's 9th Ave gate, Park Chow offers affordable and tasty pizzas, pastas, and grilled and roasted meats. Simple decor, solid beer and wine selections, and a friendly, energetic staff make it a pleasant place to share a meal with friends.

Ebisu (Japanese) MAP 15
1283 9th Ave ☎ 415-566-1770 ⌚ 11:30am-2pm Mon-Fri, 5pm-10pm Mon-Wed, 5pm-midnight Thurs-Fri, 11:30am-midnight Sat, 11:30am-10pm Sun $ lunch $5.50-13.50, appetizer $2.50-8.50, entrée $9-17, dessert $3 C AE, DC, MC, V 🚌 6, 43,44, 66, N Muni ♿

Lines of people wait to get into Ebisu, a Japanese restaurant that offers a choice of three dining experiences. At the energetic front sushi bar, the chefs perform their tasks with dramatic flair; in the traditional Japanese dining room, diners remove their shoes and sit on tatami mats; and finally, there are some tables and chairs to accommodate patrons who are too American or too stiff-kneed to sit on the floor.

House (fusion) MAP 15
1269 9th Ave ☎ 415-682-3898 ⌚ 5pm-10pm Sun-Thurs, 5pm-11pm Fri-Sat $ lunch $8-15, appetizer $6-9, entrée $12-19, dessert $4.50-7 C AE, DC, MC, V 🚭 🚌 6, 43, 44, 66, N Muni ♿

House offers innovative East-West fusion at lower prices than more highly celebrated fusion restaurants, and its baked Chilean sea bass rivals that of Cole Valley's Eos. Delicious noodles and starters also shine, as they do at the original branch in North Beach.

Thanh Long (Vietnamese/seafood) MAP 15
4101 Judah St ☎ 415-665-1146 ⌚ 4:30pm-10pm Tues-Thurs & Sun, 4:30pm-11pm Fri-Sat $ appetizer $6-9, entrée $11-34, dessert $4.50-6 C AE, D, DC, JCB, MC, V 🚭 🚌 18, N Muni ♿

Believe it or not, every night people go way out to the Outer Sunset to eat at Thanh Long. The main attractions are the whole roast Dungeness crab (around $30), large enough to be shared by two, and garlic noodles ($7). Reservations are recommended.

Entertainment

San Franciscans like to get out. The city may be known for its restaurants, but its citizens spend even more of their time in cafés and bars. In recent years, an all-out invasion of twenty-somethings, their pockets weighed down with dot-com cash, has certainly done little to change that trend. The city probably benefits from the general prosperity of the entire region – at night and on weekends people from neighboring cities converge on San Francisco to enjoy its big-city amusements, and the added business helps support a far greater number of entertainment spots than a city as small as San Francisco could maintain on its own.

Still, San Francisco is no match for New York or Los Angeles. There's far less going on in this burgh. Closing time in the bars is 2am, and the after-hours scene, while picking up of late, is not a big deal here. And, ironically enough, the soaring economy of the 1990s has not spurted a corresponding growth in every aspect of the city's cultural life. As rents have gone sky-high, struggling artists and musicians have been forced to move out of town in search of cheaper studio spaces. As the real estate boom continues to gentrify the old South of Market warehouse district, many of the noise-generating clubs that sparked SoMa's first revival have been forced to close their doors to appease the area's touchy new population. It's been the same story across the artistic spectrum: from dance companies to old movie houses, the city's old entertainments are finding it increasingly difficult to stay afloat here. (Ah, it reminds one of the mimes. What happened to all the mimes? Used to be one on every corner….)

Of course, San Francisco's not Omaha, Nebraska, either. The city remains one of the cultural capitals of the USA, and does so in a style all its own. Entertainment here is not dominated by the industry machinery that controls the creative energies of Los Angeles and New York, and in some ways it actually benefits from its low-key atmosphere. Established musicians and actors often sojourn here to hone their talents beyond the glare of LA's industry spotlight, and the dance clubs and live-music venues are refreshingly free of big-time flash and attitude – no Puff Daddy trials here.

CAFÉS

In San Francisco, cafés sometimes straddle several categories. Many places that call themselves cafés serve the function more of a bar or restaurant than a coffeehouse and so are not listed in this section. By the same token, most of the following places serve alcohol and at least a smattering of edibles. See the Bars section of this chapter, and the Places to Eat chapter, for additional coffee sources.

A note on the coffee itself: San Franciscans are coffee achievers from way back. The city was coffee-mad long before Starbucks hit the scene. Local roasters, such as Berkeley-based Peet's, introduced the Bay Area to strong, slightly overroasted coffee, and that's pretty much the local taste. For visitors, San Francisco coffee might taste a little burnt. Also, for no good reason, cafés here and elsewhere in the US serve coffee at a scalding temperature, which explains why people are always blowing on their coffee before they drink it. Boiling-hot coffee is particularly hazardous in cardboard take-out cups – hence, the little cardboard 'jackets' that must be slipped 'round your cup to protect your hands. When freshly poured steaming-hot coffee spurts through the lid of your take-out coffee, it can put the tip of your tongue out of commission for the rest of your trip – so drink with caution!

Union Square

The area is teeming with hotel guests, and the neighborhood's cafés give these people ample opportunity to spend their downtime somewhere besides their hotel rooms. Most of the following places are also good for a light bite.

Café de la Presse MAP 2
352 Grant Ave ☎ 415-398-2680 ⌚ 7am-11pm daily 🚌 2, 3, 4, 76 Muni ♿

Busy with a mostly tourist clientele, Café de la Presse is a modern, European-style café with an international selection of newspapers and magazines.

Caffe Espresso MAP 2
462 Powell St ☎ 415-395-8585 ⌚ 6:30am-10pm daily 🚌 2, 3, 4, 76 Muni ♿

As ersatz 1920s Parisian cafés go, this one's not bad. In addition to good, strong coffee, wines and aperitifs are also available.

Borders Books & Music MAP 2
400 Post St, 2nd floor ☎ 415-399-1633 ⌚ 9am-11pm Mon-Thurs, 9am-midnight Fri-Sat, 9am-9pm Sun Ⓜ Powell St BART & Muni station 🚌 2, 3, 30, 45, 49, 76 Muni 🚋 Powell-Mason, Powell-Hyde cable cars ♿ w www.borders.com

The advantage really big bookstores have is that they don't have to clutter all that space up with books. Up the Borders escalator, past one of San Francisco's most extensive magazine sections, you'll find the café, where patrons are permitted to read the first few chapters of their next purchase over a cappuccino. Windows overlook the bustling square.

Cup-A-Joe Coffee House MAP 2
896 Sutter St ☎ 415-563-7745 ⌚ 6am-8pm Mon-Fri, 7am-8pm Sat-Sun 🚌 2, 3, 4, 76 Muni ♿ w www.cupajoecoffeehouse.com

Out in the Tender Nob, Cup-A-Joe provides caffeine-deprived souls with a chance to feed their habit while surfing the Net ($2 for 15 minutes). Large windows make it an airy and well-lit spot to relax in.

Hayes Valley

Momi Toby's Revolution Cafe & Art Bar MAP 3
528 Laguna St ☎ 415-626-1508 ⌚ 7:30am-10pm Mon-Fri, 8am-10pm Sat-Sun 🚌 21 Muni

Despite the name suggesting militant artiness, Momi's is a cool and casual hangout with a small but airy room that features wood-frame windows and a marble-top bar. Coffee, beer, wine, pizzettas, and focaccia sandwiches draw you in; the comfortable vibe of the place makes you want to stay.

Chinatown

The Chinatown equivalent of the coffee house is typically a busy little pastry shop where old men who live in SRO apartments spend their days. It's a pretty insular social scene, and there's rarely a chair to spare in any of these places, so a hapless tourist in search of an espresso will stick out like a sore thumb. Head to North Beach for coffee. There is, however, a good tea parlor on the Chinatown/North Beach edge.

Imperial Tea Court MAP 5
1411 Powell St ☎ 415-788-6080 ⌚ 11am-6:30pm daily 🚌 30, 45 Muni w www.imperialtea.com

A tea break at the serene Imperial Tea Court, where birdcages hang above antique tables, is meant to be a relaxed, cultured experience. The helpful staff, whose knowledge and appreciation for tea rivals that of your average wine snob, will help you to select from an amazing variety of aromatic green and black leaves. Then, if you're taking your tea on the premises, they will prepare your brew and answer any questions you might have. Some precious varieties are extremely expensive (exceeding $100 per pound), but a pot of refreshing keemu mao feng costs just a few dollars.

North Beach

North Beach's cafés, emanating the enticing aroma of beans roasted in the back rooms, are what give the neighborhood its laid-back, European character. Sidewalk coffee sippers along busy Columbus Ave are as much a part of the action as they are observers of it. On weekday afternoons, you can really absorb the old North Beach neighborhood feel, which is not so evident on the weekend, when out-of-towners seem to crowd every doorway.

Caffe Trieste MAP 6
601 Vallejo St ☎ 415-392-6739 ⌚ 6:30am-11pm Sun-Thurs, 6:30am-midnight Fri-Sat 🚌 15, 30, 41, 45 Muni ♿ w www.caffetrieste.com

Trieste harks back to the Beat days and feels like the comfortable old gathering place that has no need to prove itself. It opened in 1956 and the mural on the back wall, depicting a quiet Sicilian port scene, dates to 1957. On Saturday afternoon, the singing proprietors of his family-owned café, with accordion and brass accompaniment, break out bel canto standards.

Caffè Greco MAP 6
423 Columbus Ave ☎ 415-397-6261
7am-midnight daily 🚌 15, 30, 41, 45 Muni
Greco's friendly crew prepare fine espressos, but only if you're lucky will you snag one of the sidewalk tables on a warm Saturday afternoon.

Caffe Puccini MAP 6
411 Columbus Ave ☎ 415-989-7033
6am-11:30pm Sun-Thurs, 6am-1am Fri-Sat 🚌 15, 30, 41, 45 Muni ♿
Puccini's sidewalk tables collide with nearby Greco's. Inside the tiny café, recorded arias create an operatic atmosphere.

Caffè Roma MAP 6
526 Columbus Ave ☎ 415-296-7942 6am-7pm Mon-Thurs, 6am-8pm Fri, 7am-midnight

Chinatown Dirge

Granted, funerals don't generally qualify as live entertainment, but when esteemed Chinatown residents pass into the afterlife, an intriguing spectacle often ensues. The usual hubbub along Grant Ave pauses as the initial strains of a somber hymn, performed by the mobile Green St Mortuary Band, become audible. The music grows louder until nothing else can be heard within the narrow thoroughfare, and traffic parts to give the funeral cortege right of way. Shopkeepers and their customers poke their heads out of doorways, and tenants peer from upstairs windows to witness a familiar sight. Tourists, unsure what is happening, stop in their tracks and take photos. The musicians, wearing military caps ('US Coast Guard surplus,' admits bandleader Lisa Pollard), march past in step, pointing the way with their horns.

Funeral marches are a venerable tradition in Chinatown, going back to the arrival of the Chinese during the gold rush. The original funeral bands played traditional Chinese instruments and music. But during the early 20th century, American-born Chinese developed a preference for Western music, and funeral bands began to play Christian hymns and dirges. John Coppola, who plays trumpet and arranges the band's music today, theorizes that British military funerals in Hong Kong may also have been influential. Other innovations have become part of the Green St funeral tradition, including the black Cadillac convertible that follows the band, bearing an enlarged photograph of the deceased.

For the musicians, many of whom spend their evenings performing in jazz combos or the San Francisco Symphony, playing funeral marches is not a bad gig, and it yields union-scale pay. But playing marches through the streets of one of the city's oldest neighborhoods can be truly inspiring – the music is often imbued with pathos as cherished members of the community are ushered out of Chinatown.

RICK GERHARTER

The Green St Mortuary Band

The band can be called to play any day of the week, rain or shine. Sometimes it plays as many as three funerals in a day. The musical processions, which always begin at the Green St Mortuary (649 Green St), typically start around 11:30am and can follow a variety of routes, often including Grant Ave in the heart of Chinatown.

Sat, 7am-8pm Sun 15, 30, 41, 45 Muni
www.cafferoma.com

The neighborly staff at Roma, one of North Beach's roasteries, make a proper cup of java, and the café's gregarious patrons often carry on conversations, between several tables, in English and Italian.

Stella Pastry MAP 6
446 Columbus Ave 415-986-2914 7:30am-6pm Mon-Thurs, 7:30am-midnight Fri-Sat, 8:30am-5pm Sun 15, 30, 41, 45 Muni

For an Italian pastry and coffee, Stella is a nice, quiet little spot, free from the lively social scene that defines so many of the neighborhood's cafés.

The Haight

This part of town – especially upper Haight St – overflows with comfortable cafés where you can enjoy a coffee while watching the entertaining street action.

Blue Front Cafe MAP 11
1430 Haight St 415-252-5917 8am-10pm Sun-Thurs, 8am-11pm Fri-Sat 7, 71 Muni

This is a cool hangout that serves Middle Eastern food and beer, as well as coffee, until late at night and often has live music.

Cafe International MAP 11
508 Haight St 415-552-7390 8am-10pm Tues-Thurs, 8am-midnight Fri, 8am-9pm Sat-Sun 6, 7, 22, 71 Muni

This café attracts Rastas and neo-hippies – overall, it's quieter and more introspective than most of its lower Haight neighbors and serves salads, sandwiches, and light Middle Eastern meals. There's live music some evenings.

Horse Shoe MAP 11
566 Haight St 415-626-8852 7am-midnight daily 6, 7, 71 Muni

The sprawling Horse Shoe attracts the slacker crowd. Internet access and foosball tables are more of an attraction than the coffee.

People's Cafe MAP 11
1419 Haight St 415-553-8842 7am-10pm daily 7, 71 Muni

People's Cafe is a nice enough spot for breakfast, a sandwich, and light vegetarian meals. You can also just get a coffee and a table by a window, optimal for people-watching.

The Castro & Upper Market

The increasingly commercial Castro has a number of chain coffee outlets, but there are a few distinguished independent cafés in the neighborhood.

Peet's Coffee & Tea MAP 12
2257 Market St 415-626-6416 6:30am-9pm Mon-Wed, 6:30am-10pm Thurs-Sat, 7am-8pm Sun Castro St & Church St Muni stations F Muni
www.peets.com

On busy Market St, there's a Peet's outlet serving the local chain's famously strong French roast. There are just a few tables, so it's mostly a take-out operation.

Cafe Flore MAP 12
2298 Market St 415-621-8579 7am-11pm Sun-Thurs, 7am-midnight Fri-Sat Castro St Muni station F Muni

Cafe Flore has a lot of what you might expect in a San Francisco hangout. It's rustic, fashionable, offers healthful counter food and strong coffee, and has a large street-side patio that gets *extremely* cruisy on sunny days. It's always busy, since many of the Castro's creative types have flexible schedules, and they work Flore into their routine. The menu of breakfast specials, lunch sandwiches, and simple pasta dishes is extensive, and prices are reasonable.

Orbit Room Cafe MAP 12
1900 Market St 415-252-9525 7am-2am Mon-Fri, 7:30am-1am Sat, 7:30am-10pm Sun F Muni

A fashionable mixed crowd is attracted to the Orbit Room, a postindustrial jazz-age café where a striking art deco pressed-tin ceiling contrasts with a bare, pockmarked concrete floor. It stays open late and boasts a good jukebox and panoramic windows, and its sidewalk tables make it well suited to lingering over coffee or draught beer or a very light meal. There's live jazz on Sunday afternoon.

The Mission

Mission District coffeehouses tend to offer bohemian atmosphere and lousy coffee. They're good for holding court at a table for hours without spending a lot of money, but if what you need is a serious pick-me-up you may need to venture elsewhere.

**he Bearded Lady
ruck Stop Cafe** MAP 14
*85 14th St ☎ 415-626-2805 7am-7pm
ʼlon-Fri, 9am-10pm Sat-Sun 16th St
ART station 14, 22, 26, 49 Muni*

)n a quiet, out-of-the-way street, the Bearded ady is a lesbian-run coffeehouse that doubles s a gallery and hosts various readings and vents on weekend evenings. Light meals are erved as well.

afé Istanbul MAP 14
*25 Valencia St ☎ 415-863-8854 noon-
ıidnight daily, until 1am Fri-Sat 16th St
ART station 14, 22, 26 Muni*

trong Arabian teas are the specialty at Istanul, where pillows and low-lying tables invite ou to take your shoes off and get comfortble. Light Middle Eastern fare, including ıazas, salads, and pita sandwiches, and cofe, beer, and wine are available. Belly dancers erform on Saturday night (8pm).

afe La Boheme MAP 14
*318 24th St ☎ 415-285-4122 6am-10pm
ʼlon-Fri, 7am-10pm Sat, 7am-9pm Sun
24th St BART station 14, 48 Muni*

s the name perhaps suggests, Cafe La Boeme is filled with fire-sale furniture. It's priıarily a lefty Latino hangout but attracts a ıixed clientele.

afe Macondo MAP 14
*159 16th St ☎ 415-863-6517 10am-
0pm Mon-Fri, 11am-10pm Sat-Sun 16th
t BART station 14, 22, 26, 49 Muni*

afe Macondo is a model bohemian literary nvironment, with old couches, an odd assemblage of tables and reading lamps, and ftist Latin American political posters on the all. Faithful patrons come to read, talk, or njoy a game of chess rather than to drink eak coffee and eat uninspired CentralAmeran dishes.

afe Qué Tal MAP 14
*005 Guerrero St ☎ 415-282-8855 7am-8pm
ʼlon-Fri, 8am-8pm Sat-Sun 26, 48, J Muni*

un by women who make a very nice espresso rink, Qué Tal is a well-lit and airy spot. These ualities are enhanced by good acoustics and s ceiling mural of parrots flying overhead.

otrero Hill

arley's MAP 14
*315 18th St ☎ 415-648-1545 6:30am-
10pm Mon-Fri, 8am-10pm Sat-Sun 22,
53 Muni*

Mission denizens often venture out to Potrero Hill to have their coffee at Farley's. Weekly poetry readings, local art displays, a welcoming atmosphere, and good opportunities for people- and dog-watching make this neighborhood joint stand out.

BARS

For a city of its size, San Francisco has a phenomenal selection of bars. The variety is staggering, especially if you've already had a few: downtown has its historic old bars, Nob Hill boasts its views, North Beach offers a

No Smoking!

In California, it is against the law to smoke in bars. When the smoking ban went into effect New Year's Eve 1998 – smack in the middle of the citywide rendering of 'Auld Lang Syne' – it was difficult to imagine that any bar would refuse to allow smoking. But most bars *are* enforcing the law, as the clusters of smokers standing outside on the city's sidewalks attest.

For those who absolutely must smoke while drinking, the ban does make exceptions. Owner-operated bars where the owner is the sole employee are exempt. And some other places simply interpret the law loosely – ashtrays are not provided and 'no smoking' signs are posted, but bar staffers shrug when

patrons ignore the signs. In some bars the 'no smoking' signs are written in every language but English, and empty shot glasses are filled to the brim with cigarette ash. And some bars have back patios where people are free to puff away to their hearts' content.

boozy literary bender, the Marina promises libidinous libations for those of the hetero persuasion, the Castro delivers nonstop gay action, SoMa is open to any scene that doesn't object to the postindustrial converted warehouse setting, and the Lower Haight pursues the postpunk stupor.

Of course, in pretty much every part of town, there's a bevy of ersatz Irish pubs, old neighborhood dives, and swanky nouveaux lounges. SoMa has the biggest concentration of bars doubling as clubs and music venues, and the Mission and the Haight can never seem to get their fill of gin mills and taprooms for the savvy crowds that stamp in those grounds on a Saturday night. It's often a fuzzy line between bars, clubs, and concert venues, with many nightspots playing alternate or dual roles on any given night of the week.

Licensing laws in California are comparatively liberal (you can get a drink almost anywhere), but to be served you have to be 21, and if you look at all youthful you may well be asked to prove your age. The bars in San Francisco all close at an unreasonable 2am. To stretch your evening, you'll have to switch to clubs.

Union Square

A lot of the nightlife around Union Square is based in hotels, but the action here is by no means limited to the tourist trade. Some of the hotel bars have stunning interiors, while others afford impressive views, and local socialites are drawn to them all, favoring a swinging bar that consistently attracts new faces. Recent additions have certainly reinvigorated the neighborhood, particularly the Tender Nob area, where the Red Room has elevated hipness to a new level of perfection. But the more assured traditional bars retain their favored status without having to try so hard.

Blue Lamp MAP 2
561 Geary St ☎ 415-885-1464 ⏲ 2pm-2am daily $ cover $3-5 (when there's music) 🚌 38 Muni ♿
w www.bluelamp.com

On more than one occasion, an old-timer from the Midwest or Great Plains has wandered into this faded but noble old bar and ordered a bottle of Bud. After swilling half the bottle, h catches the bartender's attention again an tells him the last time he's been in this joint wa during WWII. And, if he's not mistaken, the haven't changed the wallpaper since ther (Them WWII vets always remember the wall paper.) The Blue Lamp draws a crowd ofter because among so many ritzy Geary St hotel it's a taste of something real without being de pressing. It books blues bands most nights, th fireplace gets good use, and a friendly game c pool can always be had here.

C Bobby's Owl Tree MAP 2
601 Post St ☎ 415-776-9344 ⏲ 6pm-2am daily 🚌 2, 3, 4, 76 Muni ♿

Old C Bobby has a single-mindedness t match the Red Room's, but the focus here i owls. The walls are covered with photos c owls and display cases of owl statuettes, an there are a few stuffed specimens hangin from the ceiling as well. The clientele consist mostly of silver-haired men, but there's alway a smattering of curious youngsters of either se swiveling in their Naugahyde chairs to admir the sundry examples of Bobby's favorite birc

Gold Dust Lounge MAP 2
247 Powell St ☎ 415-397-1695 ⏲ 6am-2am daily Ⓜ Powell St BART & Muni station 🚌 38 Muni ♿

The good old Gold Dust Lounge has bee serving Irish coffee and cheap booze sinc Prohibition ended. Haughty locals refuse t heed the inviting call of its swinging doors, it movie-set Gold Rush interior, and the inau thentic Dixieland jazz that's performed her every night. Their loss. In this burgh, there's n more agreeable place in which to get juiced.

Harry Denton's Starlight Room MAP 2
450 Powell St, 21st floor ☎ 415-395-8595 ⏲ 4:30pm-2am daily Ⓜ Powell St BART & Muni station 🚌 2, 3, 4, 76 Muni 🚋 Powell-Mason, Powell-Hyde cable cars ♿
w www.harrydenton.com

The Drake Hotel's swank top-floor lounge with-a-view draws an upbeat crowd dresse to the nines. The nightly live music menu typ ically features a cool jazz starter, a mor swinging main course, and something emi nently danceable for dessert.

Lefty O'Doul's MAP 2
333 Geary St ☎ 415-982-8900 ⏲ 10am-2am daily Ⓜ Powell St BART & Muni station

38 Muni *Powell-Mason, Powell-Hyde :able cars*

.ong before fusion cuisine became a local :ulinary trend, Lefty O'Doul's pioneered the :ross-cultural concept: an Irish sports bar and ι German hofbrau all in one! You can saddle ıp on a bar stool supported by baseball-bat egs and talk baseball until they start turning he lights out. In fact, you can even do this over ι bottle of cheap beer (or finer draughts) and ι hot open-face turkey sandwich lathered in a asteful pale gravy. If you're lucky, old folks ;athered 'round the piano will be singing ılong to show tunes.

Red Room MAP 2
327 Sutter St ☎ 415-346-7666 ⌚ 5pm-2am daily 2, 3, 4, 76 Muni

This extravagant study in reds – red vinyl, red ɔottles, red bar, red light – is something to behold. It looks like a splitting headache and eels like a Dean Martin bender, but the small oom gets packed late in the week.

Redwood Room MAP 2
496 Geary St ☎ 415-775-4700 Ⓜ Powell St BART & Muni station 38 Muni

The somberly lit, art deco Redwood Room, off he lobby of the Clift hotel, is arguably the city's nost elegant room. Sadly, it's currently on the :ity's endangered species list because the hotel

s shamelessly toying with the idea of stripping he lounge. The room's exquisiteness transcends ts primary function as a bar – you wouldn't vant to show up here in sightseeing shorts ınd hiking shoes. But before dinner or after seeıg a play, you just might feel like a martini, and his would be the place to have it. It won't be :heap – the cost of indulging in the house pecialty is $8.50. To soften the blow, a pianist ɔlays standards in the early evening.

Hayes Valley

Hayes Valley is in some respects a fashion-conscious extension of the Castro, but the bars in the vicinity attract a pretty laid-back gay clientele.

Marlena's MAP 3
488 Hayes St ☎ 415-864-6672 ⌚ noon-2am Mon-Fri, 10am-2am Sat-Sun 21 Muni

This not-so-fancy gay bar opens early and is never empty. It has been around since the '60s and draws a mature crowd. It's very casual, until Friday night, when the place holds its midnight drag show.

The Tenderloin

Smack dab in the heart of the 'Loin, where every corner seems to be occupied by a down-and-out bar, you'll find some of the city's very best watering holes.

Backflip MAP 3
601 Eddy St ☎ 415-771-3547 ⌚ 7pm-2am Tues-Thurs & Sat, 5pm-2am Fri 19, 31 Muni
w *www.backflipsf.citysearch.com*

Backflip has drawn inspiration from the swimming pool on its back patio and elevated the idea to an unimaginable level of surreal, cinematic perfection. The fashion victims occupying the vinyl chairs in this underwater hallucination somehow enhance the overall effect. (Backflip once served dinner – until it realized wannabe supermodels don't eat – but appetizers are still available.) Ultracool DJs pack 'em in late evenings.

Edinburgh Castle MAP 3
950 Geary St ☎ 415-885-4074 ⌚ 5pm-2am daily 19, 38 Muni

There is no exaggerating about the likes of this place, as it is large enough to house two pool tables, several dart boards, a theatrical production company, some loud rock bands, private rooms, tables upstairs and downstairs bending under the weight of so many drinks and elbows, and walls laden with portraits of Scottish noblemen ready for the Sunday foxhunt. Occasionally, a bagpiper passes through and simply blows the roof off. An extensive list of Scotch whiskeys, a fine selection of tap beers, and fish-and-chips delivery service are all the excuse you need to cancel your plans to see Coit Tower or whatever it was that made you come to San Francisco. Sometimes, the crowd can be predominantly of the just-old-enough-to-drink set.

Of course, the Tenderloin is at its best when you aim a little lower. Local dives, where even the bartender is sometimes too drunk to conduct business, include **The Ha-Ra Club** (☎ 415-673-3148, 875 Geary St), with Bukowski atmosphere and a pool table, and **The High Tide** (☎ 415-771-3145, 600 Geary St), with a pool table and a portrait of a topless Polynesian woman behind the bar.

South of Market

Contemporary SoMa entrepreneurs never seem content with just opening a basic bar. See the Dance Club listings, later in the chapter, for a more extensive listing of what's going on in this part of town. Wha[t] follows is a lineup of places where you ca[n] quietly work on your drinking.

The Eagle Tavern MAP 4
398 12th St ☎ 415-626-0880 ⌚ noon-2am daily 🚌 12 Muni ♿

The quintessential gay biker/leather bar, th[e] Eagle pretty much keeps the Folsom St Fa[ir] torch glowing year-round. Its back patio is th[e] site of occasional Sunday afternoon bee[r] busts, and every now and then lesbian leathe[r] nights are held here.

Garden Court MAP 4
2 New Montgomery St ☎ 415-512-1111 ⌚ 6:30am-10:30am & 11:30am-2pm daily, 6pm-10pm Tues-Sat Ⓜ Montgomery St BART & Muni station 🚌 Market St buses, 14, F Muni ♿

Brewpubs

Brewpubs are always worth knowing about when you're traveling. The atmosphere tends to be casual, the waiters are usually friendly, the food is generally good without being too adventurous, and there's almost always a selection of microbrews that you won't get to try anywhere else. Brewpubs also make it possible for mom and dad to swill a few beers without having to leave the kids with a babysitter. San Francisco has an excellent variety of brewpubs.

Gordon Biersch Brewery MAP 4
2 Harrison St ☎ 415-243-8246 ⌚ 11:30am-1am daily Ⓒ AE, D, DC, MC, V 🚌 N Muni ♿

The Bay Bridge sails right over this immensely popular after-work hangout. Biersch serves a broad range of quality microbrews – the marzen is especially popular – and you can eat beer battered appetizers and other surf-and-turf selections.

Thirsty Bear Brewing Company MAP 4
661 Howard St ☎ 415-974-0905 ⌚ 11:30am-10:30pm Mon-Thurs, 11:30am-midnight Fri, noon-midnight Sat, 5pm-10pm Sun Ⓒ AE, DC, MC, V 🚌 14, 15, 30, 45 Muni ♿

Thirsty Bear adds variety to the local brewpub scene by offering an array of hot and cold Spanish tapas dishes, in addition to the usual sandwiches and grill fare.

21st Amendment MAP 4
563 2nd St ☎ 415-369-0900 ⌚ 11:30am-9pm Mon-Tue, 11:30am-10pm Wed-Fri, noon-10pm Sat, noon-9pm Sun Ⓒ AE, D, DC, MC, V 🚌 15, 42 Muni ♿

This brewpub, near South Park, is just a short walk from the ballpark. The menu includes pizzas and surf-and-turf specials that go down easy when you're swilling the house pale ale.

San Francisco Brewing Company MAP 6
155 Columbus Ave ☎ 415-434-3344 ⌚ 11:30am-1am Mon-Thurs, noon-1:30am Fri-Sat, noon-1am Sun 🚌 12, 15, 30, 41, 45 Muni ♿

One of the city's oldest brewpubs occupies the site of a former Barbary Coast saloon, built in 1907. The space retains much of its historic aesthetic – flame mahogany, beveled glass, and 'he Palace's airy and elegant Garden Court, a lesignated landmark with a vaulted glass ceil-ng and potted tropical plants, is the hotel's primary tourist draw. It's not really a bar – here's no counter or stools, and the live harp nusic is definitely not of the blues-harmonica 'ariety. But it's still a choice spot for an after-noon drink or a pot of tea.

Iouse of Shields MAP 4
'9 New Montgomery St ☎ 415-392-7732
Ɔ 11:30am-10pm daily Ⓜ Montgomery St BART & Muni station 🚌 Market St buses, 4, F Muni

'he common folk wet their whistles at this nanly little joint just across from the Palace Hotel. It looks and feels like a hunting lodge, omplete with decorative taxidermy and dark nahogany booths, but it's classy enough to qualify as a historic treasure. It opened in 1908. There's live jazz some nights, and lunch and dinner are available off the grill. It closes absurdly early – at 10pm.

Julie's Supper Club MAP 4
1123 Folsom St ☎ 415-861-0707 ⏲ 5pm-10pm Mon-Wed, 5pm-11pm Thurs-Sat
🚌 12, 19 Muni ♿
W www.juliessupper.citysearch.com

Retro '50s Julie's Supper Club (see Places to Eat for more on the restaurant) has a weekday happy hour (5pm to 7pm) that features $3 martini specials. The bar's a class operation – mixed drinks are the way to go.

Kate O'Brien's MAP 4
579 Howard St ☎ 415-882-7240 ⏲ 11:30am-1:30am daily 🚌 12, 15, 76 Muni ♿
W www.kateobriens.citysearch.com

An energetic SoMa crowd hangs at Kate

Brewpubs

an odd overhead contrivance of oars that fan the room. Sidewalk tables are popular on warm afternoons, and a nightly crowd, mostly office workers, comes for live jazz combos, decent pub food, and the joint's handcrafted brews.

Magnolia Pub Brewery MAP 11
1398 Haight St ☎ 415-864-7468 ⏲ 11am-11pm Mon-Fri, 10am-11pm Sat-Sun C V, MC, AE, D 🚌 6, 7, 43, 66, 71 Muni ♿

Great food and great beer are an irresistible combination. Magnolia is a friendly brewpub with an extensive menu offering honey-mustard pork chops, melt-in-your-mouth fontina-stuffed risotto cakes, pizzas, and organic hamburgers. But the raison d'etre of this place is finely crafted English beer, with taps pumping directly from the basement brewery.

ANDREW DEAN NYSTROM

Potrero Brewing Company MAP 14
535 Florida St ☎ 415-552-1967 ⏲ 11:30am-midnight Mon-Wed, 11:30am-2am Thurs-Fri, 10:30am-2am Sat, 10:30am-midnight Sun C AE, DC, MC, V 🚌 22, 27, 33 Muni ♿

In the industrial zone that joins the Mission and Potrero Hill, this brew pub draws new-media types and beer fanatics from all over town. The house wheat ale is a standout, and it goes well with the kitchen's solid American offerings.

Beach Chalet
1000 Great Hwy ☎ 415-386-8439 ⏲ 11:30am-10pm Sun-Thurs, 11:30am-11pm Fri-Sat C MC, V 🚌 5, 31, 38 Muni ♿

At the western end of Golden Gate Park, across from Ocean Beach, the bustling Beach Chalet offers great bistro food (moderate in price), house-brewed beers, live jazz and blues, and spectacular sunsets over the Pacific. Reservations are recommended, especially on sunny days. Be sure to check out the WPA murals downstairs while you're waiting for a table.

O'Brien's, a large but comfortable Irish pub where DJs spin on Saturday night. The bartenders pull a nice Guinness, and pub food is served for lunch and dinner.

Pied Piper Bar MAP 4
2 New Montgomery St ☎ 415-512-1111 ⏲ 11:30am-11pm daily Ⓜ Montgomery St BART & Muni station 🚌 Market St buses, 14, F Muni ♿

Deep within the opulent Palace Hotel, the Pied Piper is in a class of its own. Mahogany walls and plush seating are nice enough, but what really sets this place apart is the 1909 Maxfield Parrish painting, from which the place gets its name, that hangs over the bar. Prices are steep, but the Pied Piper is worth stopping by for a quick one.

Financial District

Most of the bars in the Financial District are places where business travelers and other suits unwind, but a few of these may be of interest to the common tourist.

Carnelian Room MAP 5
555 California St, 52nd floor ☎ 415-433-7500 ⏲ 3pm-11pm Mon-Thurs cocktails, 3pm-midnight Fri-Sat cocktails, 6pm-10pm dinner daily 🚌 1, 15 Muni 🚋 California St cable car ♿
W www.carnelianroom.com

If your main objective for the evening is to get really high, the Carnelian Room, atop the Bank of America Building, affords a truly spectacular 52nd-floor view, and the cocktail hour is just the time to enjoy it. Drink prices are *(natch!)* also high.

Equinox MAP 5
5 Embarcadero Plaza ☎ 415-788-1234 ⏲ 4pm-midnight Mon-Fri, 4pm-1am Fri, noon-1am Sat, 10:30am-midnight Sun Ⓜ Embarcadero BART & Muni station 🚌 1, F Muni 🚋 California St cable car ♿

The rotating circular restaurant-bar atop the bay-front Hyatt Regency Hotel shows off San Francisco from multiple angles. It's really not that great a thrill – it doesn't move fast enough to make you dizzy or to even knock your drink off your table, and drinks are expensive. Do not order the overpriced food.

London Wine Bar MAP 5
415 Sansome St ☎ 415-788-4811 ⏲ 11:30am-10pm daily 🚌 1, 15, 42 Muni
W www.londonwinebar.citysearch.com

If you came to San Francisco looking for a cozy English-pub-style bar with an extensive wine list, this is it.

Chinatown

If stories about Chinatown's lurid past have gotten you all excited, duck into one of the neighborhood's dark little caverns for a few cold ones. You won't meet slinky barmaids in silk dresses or any of that jazz, but Chinatown's bars seem to have retained a certain passé seaminess that hearkens back to WWII, if not the Barbary Coast.

Buddha Lounge MAP 5
901 Grant Ave ☎ 415-362-1792 ⏲ 2pm-2am daily 🚌 1, 9, 15, 30, 41, 45 Muni ♿

This sleepy little den of iniquity feels like a South Pacific shore leave. The Buddha is staunchly of another era, from its irreverent name and shapely bar stools to the grumpy barkeeps.

ANTHONY PIDGEON

Find enlightenment at the Buddha Lounge.

Li Po MAP 5
916 Grant Ave ☎ 415-982-0072 ⏲ 2pm-2am daily 🚌 1, 9, 15, 30, 41, 45 Muni ♿

Named for a Chinese poet, Li Po is furnished with

urid 1960s-era plush red booths and bar stools ust waiting to be sat on by anyone in the mood or nursing a Bud or a Tsingtao. The jukebox has some funky surprises, but the bipolar atmosphere – varying between sedate and frenzied – pretty much depends on whether or not the regulars are slamming dice on the bar.

North Beach

North Beach's old Beat taverns, Italian American neighborhood joints, and snazzy new lounges offer barhoppers a nice variety within a walkable area. Many bars n North Beach are open in the afternoon, f not all day, and some double as cafés and restaurants.

Bamboo Hut MAP 6
479 Broadway ☎ 415-989-8555 ⌚ 8pm-2am Wed, 5pm-2am Thurs-Fri, 8pm-2am Sat 🚌 12, 15, 30, 41, 45 Muni ♿
w www.maximumproductions.com/bamboo

The good-lookin' lil' Bamboo Hut's where the unior Vegas Grind set goes for cheap tropical drinks. When there's a swingin' show on at the HiBall Lounge, next door, there's usually some nattily dressed spillover. Naturally, nothing but the most exotic sounds comes out of this lil' hut's sound system.

North End Caffè MAP 6
1402 Grant Ave ☎ 415-956-3350 ⌚ 8am-midnight Mon-Thurs, 8am-1am Fri, 9am-1am Sat, 9am-midnight Sun C cash only 🚌 15, 30, 41, 45 Muni
w www.northendcaffe.com

A hip little café-bar off the main drag, North End Caffè is another of the neighborhood's great afternoon diversions. It's casual and funky and has a flock of devoted regulars. Selected light fare is posted on a chalkboard menu, and when the firebreathing bartenders are on duty, things really get cooking.

The Saloon MAP 6
1232 Grant Ave ☎ 415-989-7666 ⌚ noon-2am daily $ live music cover $2-5 🚌 15, 30, 41, 45 Muni ♿

The worn-out Saloon, which first opened its doors in 1861, looks like it hasn't had a coat of paint since it was built. One of San Francisco's oldest bars, it is a rare North Beach survivor of the 1906 quake and fire, and despite its historic appeal it commendably lacks preciousness or any of the ersatz antique 'enhancements' that all too typically mar old places. A mix of disheveled old-timers, street people, and local hipsters hang here, and blues and rock bands perform nightly and on Sunday afternoon.

Savoy Tivoli MAP 6
1434 Grant Ave ☎ 415-362-7023 ⌚ 5pm-2am daily 🚌 15, 30, 41, 45 Muni ♿

The large Savoy Tivoli somehow feels part Montmartre brasserie, part American frat house. Its patio café tables looking out onto the street and its dark mahogany interior attract an upbeat mix of American college kids, young professionals, and European tourists.

Specs' MAP 6
12 William Saroyan Place ☎ 415-421-4112 ⌚ 4:30pm-2am daily, opens 5pm Sat-Sun 🚌 12, 15, 30, 41, 45 Muni ♿

Hidden away on tiny William Saroyan Place (formerly Adler Place), Specs' is a dark, cave-like dive enjoyed by barflies in the afternoon and a mix of hipsters and loosened-tie types in the evening. It's also known as the 'Adler Museum,' a nod to the intriguing hodgepodge of memorabilia, culled from ports around the globe, that has ended up on the place's walls. The taps are limited to Budweiser, but better brews are served in bottles.

Tony Nik's MAP 6
1534 Stockton St ☎ 415-693-0993 ⌚ noon-2am Tues-Sun 🚌 15, 30, 41, 45 Muni ♿

When old Tony Nik's suddenly introduced longer hours, after years of closing its doors before dinner, a whole new generation of North Beach denizens discovered the bar's hidden charms. A small but genuinely swanky lounge, its Rat Pack interior mostly intact, Tony Nik's is a mature, neighborly sort of place with consummate barkeeps who know their mixology.

Tosca Cafe MAP 6
242 Columbus Ave ☎ 415-391-1244, 415-986-9651 ⌚ 5pm-2am daily 🚌 12, 15, 30, 41, 45 Muni ♿

Had Francis Ford Coppola taken the liberty of setting *The Godfather* in San Francisco, he would have surely set an operatic bloodbath or a quiet strangling in Tosca. The place has that self-assured Italian American brusqueness, with a smoke-stained ceiling, a worn linoleum floor, red vinyl booths, and an all-opera jukebox (with genuine 45rpm platters). The polished professional bartenders make a snappy martini, but – in yet another suitable detail – the bar's signature bev, lined up across the bar in advance of anticipated orders, is an unremarkable cappuccinolike concoction. Local literati, filmmakers, and politicos unwind here, but they usually head straight to the backroom, which is off limits to you, pal.

Vesuvio MAP 6
255 Columbus Ave ☎ 415-362-3370 ⌚ 6am-2am daily 🚌 12, 15, 30, 41, 45 Muni ♿

Afternoons are the perfect time to head for Vesuvio, an idiosyncratic pub with upstairs windows overlooking Jack Kerouac Alley. Grab a table and a beer and pore over the books you just bought at City Lights Bookstore, just a few paces away. At night, this old Beat hangout can get crowded with tourists and after-work revelers, but the bar continues to have its local regulars.

Nob Hill

Making the Nob Hill bar rounds is pretty straightforward. This really isn't one of the city's more popular stomping grounds, but there are a couple of outstanding hotel bars worth going to, even if you're staying somewhere else.

Tonga Room MAP 7
950 Mason St ☎ 415-772-5278 ⌚ 5pm-midnight Sun-Thurs, 5pm-1am Fri-Sat $ cover $3 🚌 1 Muni 🚋 California St cable car ♿
W www.tongaroom.com

In a room deep within the Fairmont Hotel, civilization as we know it has been completely stripped away, leaving us with…the horror! Or is it paradise? The Tonga room's thatch-covered tables and bamboo chairs are arranged around a built-in lagoon, and every half-hour an artificial monsoon strikes. (Inner voice, through megaphone: *Everyone please remain calm!*) To help you forget the lost comforts of the Western world, intrepid waitpersons, seemingly oblivious to the weather, serve expensive fruity rum cocktails in coconut shells. You'll be talking like a pirate by midnight, guaranteed. Happy hour (5pm to 7pm weeknights) is popular. At 8pm, a stage floats out onto the lagoon bearing a cheesy cover band.

Top of the Mark MAP 7
999 California St ☎ 415-392-3434 ⌚ 3pm-5pm Mon-Fri, 8:30pm-12:30am Sun-Thurs, 9pm-1am Fri-Sat $ cover $8-10 🚌 1 Muni 🚋 California St cable car ♿
W www.topofthemark.citysearch.com

San Francisco's preeminent 'skylounge,' the Top of the Mark is perfect for that classy night on the town. In the evening, the cover charge is steep and a stuffy dress code goes into effect, but jazz and swing combos play in the swanky space, and there's a dance floor, a light menu, and, of course, unbeatable views. You can also come in the afternoon for the more casual tea time.

Fisherman's Wharf

Being a hard-core tourist can be really exhausting, as we found out while researching the Fisherman's Wharf area for this book. Fortunately, the neighborhood has several decent places in which to refresh yourself.

Buena Vista Café MAP 8
2765 Hyde St ☎ 415-474-5044 ⌚ 9am-2am Mon-Fri, 8am-2am Sat-Sun 🚌 30, 42 Muni 🚋 Powell-Hyde cable car

The Buena Vista Café, near the cable car turnaround, is so popular you may have to wait in line to get in. Try an Irish coffee, which became a San Francisco tradition after this bar introduced that beverage to the city. See Places to Eat for more information.

Jack's Cannery Bar MAP 8
2801 Leavenworth St ☎ 415-931-6400 ⌚ 10am-2am daily 🚌 30, 42 Muni 🚋 Powell-Hyde cable car ♿

On a warm evening, Jack's patio, in the Cannery's closed-in brick courtyard, is probably the most agreeable spot in the general vicinity. The bar also has one of the longest lineups of taps in town – 110 draft ales, lagers, stouts, porters, and ciders. There's usually live music on the courtyard stage.

The Marina & Cow Hollow

The Marina still has the city's highest concentration of singles' bars, long after the now-legendary yuppie 1980s.

Bus Stop MAP 9
1901 Union St ☎ 415-567-6905 ⌚ 10am-2am Mon-Fri, 9am-2am Sat-Sun 🚌 41, 45 Muni ♿

Ya gotta love bars with names that sound like excuses for getting home late from work – 'Baby, I musta been standin' at the Bus Stop for an *hour*.' This little joint has been around since 1900, closing just long enough sometime in the '70s to be stripped of any historic charm it might once have had. It's a hard-core sports bar, with some 17 TV sets.

Perry's MAP 9
1944 Union St ☎ 415-922-9022 ⌚ 11am-10pm Mon-Tues, 11am-11pm Thurs, 11am-midnight Fri, 9pm-midnight Sat, 9pm-10pm Sun 🚌 41, 45 Muni ♿
w www.perrysunionst.citysearch.com

Perry's is an old-timey establishment, with well-worn tile floors telling the tale of so many trips between the tables and the latrine. But the clientele has gone through changes over the years. Since the 1980s, this has been a bona fide cruising spot – the archetypal San Francisco 'breeder' bar, as Armistead Maupin describes it. Burgers and pub grub are served.

The Haight

The Haight's bars are curiously unsentimental about the area's past. Neighborhood joints, where local alcoholics pass for local color, are probably as close as you'll get to the Haight's glory days. But, oddly, Haight St has several choice retro '50s bars, where swinging attire and serious cocktails pretty much suggest that the '60s never happened.

An Bodhran MAP 11
668 Haight St ☎ 415-431-4724 ⌚ 4pm-2am daily, opens 6pm Sat 🚌 6, 7, 71 Muni ♿
w www.anbodhran.citysearch.com

On lower Haight St, An Bodhran is one of the city's better nouveau Irish pubs, with a low-key crowd, pints a-flowing, and live Irish music performances on Wednesday night and Sunday afternoon.

Club Deluxe MAP 11
1509 Haight St ☎ 415-552-6949 ⌚ 4pm-2am Mon-Fri, 3pm-2am Sat, 2pm-2am Sun $ live music cover $3-5 🚌 7, 71 Muni ♿
w www.clubdeluxe.com

Just a few paces from the corner of Haight and Ashbury, the very picturesque Club Deluxe is in emphatic denial that the '60s ever happened. The place's ambience is vintage 1949 from floor to ceiling, and many of the rather snooty people who spend their time here come dressed to the nines, 1940s style. The barkeeps are famous for making good bloody Marys and other mixed concoctions, and jazz combos perform Wednesday through Sunday nights.

John Murio's Trophy Room MAP 11
1811 Haight St ☎ 415-752-2971 ⌚ noon-2am daily 🚌 7, 71 Muni ♿

Murio's sort of sounds like a sports bar, but it isn't. It's a friendly neighborhood tavern in which you are likely to encounter the same cast of characters on any given night, and it's a good place to overhear conversations revealing just what a strange neighborhood the Haight is.

Mad Dog in the Fog MAP 11
530 Haight St ☎ 415-626-7279 ⌚ 11:30am-2am Mon-Fri, 10am-2am Sat-Sun 🚌 6, 7, 22, 71 Muni
w www.themaddoginthefog.com

Though it's a British-style pub, Mad Dog in the Fog doesn't go out of its way to seem 'authentic.' Dartboards, a wide variety of beers, pub grub, and a young crowd of heavy drinkers pretty much define the place. In keeping with British tradition, the bar hosts popular quiz nights twice a week, and on weekends it books live bands and DJs. Soccer is an obsession, and the bar adjusts its hours to accommodate live satellite broadcasts of European matches (then it opens at 6am).

Noc Noc MAP 11
557 Haight St ☎ 415-861-5811 ⌚ 5pm-2am daily 🚌 6, 7, 22, 71 Muni ♿

The Noc Noc is a lower Haight dinosaur from the early '80s, when things were just starting to happen on this now-active block, but it's still one of the street's more interesting bars. Its dark and moody cavelike interior attracts a mellow crowd, but the bar doesn't serve hard booze – just beer and wine and a few non-alcoholic choices.

Toronado MAP 11
547 Haight St ☎ 415-863-2276 ⌚ 11:30am-2am daily 🚌 6, 7, 22, 71 Muni ♿

The Toronado, named for an obsolete car model, exudes a certain masculine style that's somewhat misleading. To be sure, the afternoon crowd is mostly male, with a large biker contingent – but San Francisco bikers are, on the whole, a gentle lot. In the evening the bar is one of the Lower Haight's more popular destinations, and a mixed crowd comes for the casual atmosphere and one of the best tap selections in town.

Zam Zam MAP 11
1633 Haight St ☎ 415-861-2545 ⌚ 2pm-2am daily 🚌 7, 71 Muni ♿

If Zam Zam's seductive Moroccan portal strikes your fancy, follow that impulse. The place was once notorious for its rude, now dearly departed owner (who would, in all seriousness, kick patrons out for ordering the 'wrong' drink or sitting in the 'wrong' chair), but Zam Zam is now a very hospitable and swanky den of dissolution. The retro atmo and a jukebox spinning Sinatra tunes surely call for a mixed bev of some sort.

The Castro

If you've come to San Francisco to cruise the Castro, you may find the neighborhood is perhaps more affluent and polished than you expected. But the neighborhood has more than enough bars.

Detour MAP 12
2348 Market St ☎ 415-861-6053 ⌚ 2pm-2am daily Ⓜ Castro St Muni station 🚌 24, F Muni ♿

Detour has one of the city's longest happy hours, from 2pm to 8pm. But what makes this dark, all-male bar one of the Castro's most popular gathering spots is its DJs, a superior sound system, chain-link urban playground decor, male go-go dancers, and a diverse and cruisy crowd.

Harvey's MAP 12
500 Castro St ☎ 415-431-4278 ⌚ 11am-2am Mon-Fri, 9am-2am Sat-Sun Ⓜ Castro St Muni station 🚌 24, 33, F Muni ♿

The peachy, suburban exterior and the gay memorabilia on the walls of Harvey's are clear indications that this is a theme-oriented, tourist-friendly place. Windows overlook the 18th and Castro crossroads, affording great people-watching opportunities. Standard bar food is available. The name is a tribute to slain city supervisor Harvey Milk.

Martuni's MAP 12
4 Valencia St ☎ 415-241-0205 ⌚ 2pm-2am daily 🚌 F Muni
Ⓦ www.martunis.citysearch.com

A little way down Market St from the heart of the Castro, this gay-friendly cocktail lounge is a certifiably swank place. Martuni's has someone tinkling the ivories every night, and the patrons all seem to have committed the great Broadway songbook to memory. Martinis are de rigueur, of course.

Metro MAP 12
3600 16th St ☎ 415-703-9750 ⌚ 2:30pm-2am Mon-Fri, 1pm-2am Sat-Sun Ⓜ Castro St Muni station 🚌 24, F Muni

Metro is a more urbane gathering spot than some of its high-energy neighbors. From the street, you'll see men in collared shirts and sometimes a few women in power clothing standing on its upstairs balcony, watching the activity on the busy corner from above. The bar has margarita nights and karaoke nights and a kitchen that cooks up Chinese appetizers and dishes.

SF Badlands MAP 12
4121 18th St ☎ 415-626-9320 ⌚ 2pm-2am daily Ⓜ Castro St Muni station 🚌 24, 33, F Muni ♿

One of the Castro's biggest pick-up spots, Badlands packs 'em in, especially after 10pm. The Sunday afternoon (4pm to 9pm) beer bust attracts lines that stretch halfway down the block. The diverse gay crowd includes leather men, businessmen, and punky kids.

Twin Peaks MAP 12
401 Castro St ☎ 415-864-9470 ⌚ noon-2am daily Ⓜ Castro St Muni station 🚌 24, F Muni ♿

Twin Peaks, with its large front windows, was the first gay bar where the patrons weren't hidden from the street. An older male crowd hangs out in this conversation-oriented bar.

Upper Market

Down Market St, the Castro fuses with the Mission and the Lower Haight in a transition zone. A diverse crowd is drawn to a great mix of unusual drinking spots.

Lucky 13 MAP 12
2140 Market St ☎ 415-487-1313 ⌚ 4pm-2am Mon-Thurs, 2pm-2am Fri-Sun Ⓜ Church St Muni station 🚌 22, F Muni ♿

The Castro meets the Lower Haight in this smart and edgy hangout. An urban-cool crowd – lotsa tattoos and leather here – gets good use out of the loud, hard-rockin' jukebox, a pool table and pinball machines, and the barkeeps are always busy pouring Chimay and a selection of European brews.

Mecca MAP 12
2029 Market St ☎ 415-621-7000 ⌚ 5pm-midnight Sun-Wed, 5pm-1:30am Thurs-Sat Ⓜ Church St Muni station 🚌 22, F Muni ♿
Ⓦ www.sfmecca.com

You can get expertly mixed cocktails at the oh-so-contemporary, chic Mecca. Jazz and soul music is performed live once or twice a week and DJs spin slick mixes most other nights.

ENTERTAINMENT

The Mission

The Mission is a barhopper's mirage. A heavy concentration of nightspots is clustered around the corner of 16th and Valencia, and there are ample others along 22nd St and on Mission St. The choice is staggering: DJ lounges, bohemian slacker watering holes, jazz supper clubs, fashion-victim poseur scenes, bike-messenger bars, lesbian neighborhood bars, and low-key dives offering your basic three-quarter-size pool table and tap beer. Mission crowds tend to mix fairly freely, although there has been some grousing about the Friday and Saturday night infusion of mainstream professionals, mostly from other parts of town or from out of town. The following listing is a mere sampling of what the Mission has to offer.

Albion MAP 14
3139 16th St ☎ 415-552-8558 ⌚ 1pm-2am Mon-Fri, noon-2am Sat-Sun Ⓜ 16th St BART station 🚌 22, 26 Muni ♿

Long ago the nucleus of the Inner Mission scene, the Albion now seems content to live out its days as a casual and slightly disheveled neighborhood dive. A quirky crowd assembles here to drink good tap beers and make use of the bar's pool tables and pinball machines. Weekday happy 'hour' runs all the way from 2pm to 7pm.

Beauty Bar MAP 14
2299 Mission St ☎ 415-285-0323 ⌚ 5pm-2am Mon-Fri, 7pm-2am Sat-Sun 🚌 14, 49 Muni ♿
W www.beautybar.citysearch.com

Now the hairhoppers and glamour pusses have a bar of their own. Stylistically, San Francisco's Beauty Bar (there's another in Manhattan) is a throwback to the early 1960s, when men wore sharkskin suits and women dried their bouffants in atomic, cone-shaped hair dryers. A martini and a manicure will set you back $10. Relatively un-cuckoo DJs spin several nights a week.

Casanova Lounge MAP 14
527 Valencia St ☎ 415-863-9328 ⌚ 4pm-2am daily Ⓜ 16th St BART station 🚌 22, 26 Muni ♿

The Casanova feels a little like a Quentin Tarantino set brought to life, with velvet paintings (a cohesive retrospective on '60s and '70s cheese) and a plastic incandescent fireplace, and the bar crew, known for mixing kick-ass martinis, is equal to the trendy environs. The crowd swings from hip locals during the week to invading young professionals on the weekend. Free pool on Sunday afternoon brings the place back down to earth.

Dalva MAP 14
3121 16th St ☎ 415-252-7740 ⌚ 4pm-2am daily Ⓜ 16th St BART station 🚌 22, 26 Muni ♿
W www.dalva.com

The dimly lit, Spanish alley interior of the Dalva is unimpressive, but this is one of 16th St's better bars. It has a long happy hour (from 4pm to 7pm weekdays) and a great jukebox (free during happy hour), serves cheap drinks, and is generally conducive to conversation in the early evening. After 9:30pm, DJs spin obscure records for lovers of jazz, Latin music, film soundtracks, and exotic tiki pop.

Doc's Clock MAP 14
2575 Mission St ☎ 415-824-3627 ⌚ 4pm-2am Mon-Fri, 6pm-2am Sat, 8pm-2am Sun 🚌 14, 49 Muni ♿

The large neon sign over the entrance to Doc's Clock has always been an attention grabber, even for those whizzing through the Mission St traffic. But this is one of the district's more relaxed dives and is not a bad place to duck into when the more popular bars nearby are just too much to take.

Dylan's MAP 14
2301 Folsom St ☎ 415-641-1416 ⌚ 3pm-2am daily 🚌 12 Muni ♿

Dylan's is an old Mission District tavern that, in

RICK GERHARTER

Former speakeasy Dylan's

ENTERTAINMENT

its current incarnation, celebrates Welsh culture. Dylan Thomas photos and Tom Jones album covers grace the walls. Live music (jazz and rockabilly), odd theater performances, and regular visits by a tamale vendor make this a great spot to hang out. Check out the sparsely furnished backroom – it was a speakeasy during Prohibition, and you can still sense that some serious drinking was done there in those days.

500 Club MAP 14
500 Guerrero St ☎ 415-861-2500 ⌚ 10am-2am Mon-Fri, 6am-2am Sat-Sun Ⓜ 16th St BART station 🚌 22, 26 Muni ♿

The 500 Club's giant neon martini sign shines like a beacon on an otherwise undistinguished corner. On weekday afternoons and evenings, this is a casual neighborhood bar, complete with pool tables, a working fireplace, run-down tables, and an odd assemblage of elderly alcoholics and laid-back hipsters. On weekends, it is overrun with younger scenesters.

Hush Hush Lounge MAP 14
496 14th St ☎ 415-241-9944 ⌚ 5pm-2am daily $ cover $3-5 after 10pm 🚌 14, 26, 49 Muni ♿

The Hush Hush is a sophisticated yet quirky little bar that becomes a DJ club with an admission charge late at night. The DJs spin an eclectic mix of dance grooves and more ambient sounds, but there's no dance floor to speak of.

Kilowatt MAP 14
3160 16th St ☎ 415-861-2595 ⌚ 4pm-2am Mon-Fri, 1pm-2am Sat, 10am-2am Sun Ⓜ 16th St BART station 🚌 22, 26 Muni ♿

Kilowatt, in a converted firehouse, draws a diverse crowd – punky Mission denizens most of the time, a smattering of neo-yuppies on the weekend. Sometimes the crowd even includes a few dogs. During the NFL season, a football-loving crowd takes over on Sunday.

Latin American Club MAP 14
3286 22nd St ☎ 415-647-2732 ⌚ 6pm-2am Sun-Thurs, 5pm-2am Fri, 4pm-2am Sat 🚌 14, 26, 49 Muni ♿

The popular Latin American Club is amply lit by high windows in the predusk hours, and its funky decor and casual mismatched tables and chairs make this a pleasing place to settle into any time. The bartenders controlling the house stereo have a varied and informed taste in music, which certainly adds to the place's appeal.

Lexington Club MAP 14
3464 19th St ☎ 415-863-2052 ⌚ 3pm-2am daily 🚌 14, 49, 26 Muni ♿ limited

The Lexington's friendly confines draw a young and predominantly pierced dyke crowd – in fact, surprisingly, this is the only bar in the city that caters specifically to lesbians (Wild Side West, in Bernal Heights, is also lesbian-owned and lesbian-friendly but attracts a more general neighborhood crowd). A pool table and a good jukebox add to a busy but relaxed milieu.

Lone Palm MAP 14
3394 22nd St ☎ 415-648-0109 ⌚ 6pm-2am Mon-Thurs & Sat, 5pm-2am Fri, 7pm-2am Sun 🚌 14, 26, 49 Muni ♿
W www.lonepalm.citysearch.com

The Lone Palm has that sexy desert oasis ambience, with bas relief Egyptian motifs, seductive lighting, cool piped-in jazz, and leafy palms. A polished, professional crowd claims the place most of the time, and the sophisticated dames tending the bar are frequently called upon to mix cosmopolitans and martinis.

Make-Out Room MAP 14
3225 22nd St ☎ 415-647-2888 ⌚ 6pm-2am daily $ live music cover $6 🚌 14, 26, 49 Muni ♿

The Make-Out Room, another Mission favorite (brought to you by the folks who own the Latin American Club), is furnished with velvet curtains, a mahogany bar, and an assortment of vintage Formica tables. But it's not at all fussy about its style – the floor is bare concrete. Weeknights are the best time to come, before the usual weekend revelers take over, and on some nights live music (indie rock, cowpunk, and experimental stuff) provides another reason to come here.

Zeitgeist MAP 14
199 Valencia St ☎ 415-255-7505 ⌚ 9am-2am daily Ⓜ 16th St BART station 🚌 22, 26 Muni ♿

ENTERTAINMENT

Social headquarters for the city's motley crowd of bike messengers and urban bikers, the Zeitgeist is always worth going to. On warm afternoons and evenings, regulars (and smokers) head straight to the bar's graveled 'beer garden,' which is practically under a freeway ramp. The ramshackle interior keeps busy with pool tables and TV broadcasts of *The Simpsons.*

Bernal Heights

Laid-back, out-of-the-way Bernal Heights is home to an intriguing mix of people. There are several neighborhood watering holes on Cortland Ave, but only one regularly attracts people from other parts of town.

Wild Side West
424 Cortland Ave ☎ 415-647-3099 ⌚ 1pm-2am daily 🚌 24 Muni

Wild Side West, on the ground floor and in the back garden of a Victorian house, is a very casual neighborhood spot that always draws an interesting crowd. It's owned and operated by (and popular with) lesbians, but the eclectic neighborhood has embraced the place as its local dive. With its cluttered interior and friendly vibe, this bar is one of the city's gems.

The Richmond

The Richmond District is home to San Francisco's highest concentration of Irish bars. There are more of them than we care to mention – most are quiet little neighborhood bars, and we wouldn't want to upset a tranquil scene. The faux-Irish-pub trend hasn't reached this part of town yet.

Pat O'Shea's Mad Hatter MAP 15
3848 Geary Blvd ☎ 415-752-3148 ⌚ 10am-2am daily 🚌 38 Muni ♿

On the face of it, Pat O'Shea's is nothing special, but friendly people and surprisingly good bar food are a winning combination. The bar takes sports more seriously than its Guinness – a dozen TV sets will tune you into sporting from 'round the world.

The Plough and the Stars MAP 15
116 Clement St ☎ 415-751-1122 ⌚ 4pm-2am Mon, 2pm-2am Tues-Thurs, noon-2am Fri-Sun $ cover $4 Fri-Sat 🚌 1, 2, 4, 38 Muni ♿ W www.whatwasit.com/plough

You're likely to be treated to a memorable and distinctly Irish experience at the Plough and Stars, where blue-collar Irish expats come to knock a few back after work. Most nights, musicians perform Irish music, and a few people in the crowd even know how to jig to it.

Trad'r Sams MAP 15
6150 Geary Blvd ☎ 415-221-0773 ⌚ 10am-2am daily 🚌 38 Muni ♿

For fake-tiki exotica, circa 1940, some San Franciscans will head way out into the foggy avenues to Trad'r Sam's. The old bamboo canopies and bamboo telephone booth that are crammed into this tiny bar leave hardly enough room for the young drunkards who hang out here on Saturday night. Come on a woebegone weeknight for a more sedate tropical vacation. And tip well – making fruity drinks is hard work.

LIVE MUSIC

In San Francisco, the emphasis is on small and medium-size theaters that are not big enough for the type of major stage show put on by 'supergroups' like the Rolling Stones and U2, or even the latest greatest thing like Destiny's Child.

San Francisco's tastes tend to be more cultish, anyway. Alt rock, grunge, post-punk, twang-pop, and less easily pegged musical genres are more the city's style. And while local bands always seem to be getting major recording deals, the city's local scene isn't exactly thriving these days. The number of bars and other small venues that book unsigned bands has dwindled in recent years, and musicians unable to keep up with the city's soaring cost of living have moved on to less expensive parts of the world. Many bars that once featured live music now just hire DJs – the kids seem to like it, and it's cheaper that way.

That said, there's still a lot of music in San Francisco by both locals and visiting out-of-towners. There's no shortage of jazz supper clubs and blues bars, and if a little headbanging is what you need, you'll find it easily enough. The listings in the *Bay Guardian,* the *SF Weekly,* and the Sunday *Chronicle's* 'Pink Section' will fill you in on what's happening in town.

Music Festivals

In the past few years, San Francisco has hosted an alternative music event called

Noise Pop, loosely modeled on Austin's popular South by Southwest festival. Held in late February and early March, Noise Pop features plenty of bands from here and around the country, many of them unsigned, for a marathon of shows in clubs around town. Other festivals include the following:

San Francisco Blues Festival
Great Meadow ☎ 415-979-5588 $ advance ticket $25, gate ticket $30 ⌚ 🚌 22, 47, 49 Muni ♿
w www.sfblues.com

Two days of blues take place on Fort Mason's Great Meadow in mid- or late September.

San Francisco Jazz Festival
☎ 415-788-7353, 800-627-5277 outside California
w www.sfjazz.org ♿

The renowned SF Jazz Fest packs 'em in for shows in clubs and larger venues throughout the city for two weeks in October and November.

Music Halls

San Francisco has a great selection of auditoriums that book touring acts. The type of music featured in these theaters can vary widely.

Great American Music Hall MAP 3
859 O'Farrell St ☎ 415-885-0750 ⌚ box office 10am-4pm Sun-Mon, noon-6pm Tues-Sat, noon-9pm on show nights $ $10-35 🚌 19, 38 Muni ♿
w www.musichallsf.com

Long ago a bordello, the Great American Music Hall shifted its focus to less seamy forms of live entertainment, and it's one of the classiest places to see a show. A balcony with table seating rims the main standing area, the sound system is top-notch, and food and beverages are available. The music ranges over a wide terrain that includes rock, alt, country, jazz, and blues.

The Warfield MAP 3
982 Market St ☎ 415-775-7722 ⌚ doors open at 7pm $ $18-35 Ⓜ Civic Center BART & Muni station 🚌 Market St buses, F Muni ♿
w www.thefillmore.com/warfield.asp

The old Warfield was originally a vaudeville theater. It's now managed by Bill Graham Presents, which often books accomplished artists looking for an intimate (compared to an arena) concert venue. Musical forms include rock, pop, world, and singer-songwriter, among others. There's a restaurant and bar.

Maritime Hall MAP 4
450 Harrison St ☎ 415-974-0634 ⌚ doors open at 8pm $ $15-27 🚌 42 Muni ♿
w www.maritimehall.com

Maritime Hall, which started as headquarters for the Sailors' Union of the Pacific, has acquired a rough and rowdy reputation as a music hall. The bookings tend to favor bands typically overlooked by more established promoters, with hip-hop, reggae, the occasional heavy metal outfit, and C&W outlaws like Willie Nelson and Merle Haggard featured. Balcony seating hangs over a large dance floor, and the staff here are notoriously rude.

Masonic Auditorium MAP 7
1111 California St ☎ 415-776-4917 ⌚ doors open at 8pm $ $20-50 🚌 1 Muni 🚋 California St cable car ♿
w www.sfmasoniccenter.com

This theater, atop Nob Hill, seats about 2000 (no standing) and mostly features major jazz shows. A recent schedule had Max Roach one night and Wayne Shorter the next, but occasionally the mellower classic rock and established country singers will perform here.

Fillmore Auditorium MAP 10
1805 Geary Blvd ☎ 415-346-6000 ⌚ box office 10am-4pm Sun, 7:30pm-10pm on show nights $ $18-35 🚌 22, 38 Muni ♿
w www.thefillmore.com

Opened by rock impresario Bill Graham in the '60s and famed for its highly collectible psychedelic posters, the legendary Fillmore Auditorium is going strong. The grand old hall, with its dim chandeliers hanging over the audience, hosts an eclectic calendar of events, from big-name rock shows to punk gigs to wild wrestling matches. The theater's general admission policy means you don't have to buy your tickets as soon as they go on sale, unless a show is likely to sell out quickly.

Rock Clubs

Small-label and unsigned bands usually play in small clubs and bars around town, and some intimate clubs bring in touring groups with a national following.

The Cellar at Johnny Foley's MAP 2
243 O'Farrell St ☎ 415-954-0777 ⌚ 11:30am-2am daily $ $10-15 Ⓜ Powell St BART & Muni station 🚌 Market St buses, 27, 38 Muni

Powell-Mason, Powell-Hyde cable cars
www.johnnyfoleys.com

In the cozy basement of a handsome nouveau Irish pub, Foley's Cellar usually features traditional Irish ensembles. Occasionally, the promoters from Slim's (see above) book touring rock and folk acts here. These are very low-key environs for bands that are just an eyelash shy of reaching the big time – jump at the chance to get in on the action.

Covered Wagon Saloon MAP 4
911 Folsom St ☎ 415-974-1585 ⌚ 4:30pm-

Getting Tickets

Popular events often sell out far in advance, but out-of-town visitors are not at a disadvantage since most tickets can easily be purchased over the phone or on the internet. The following ticket agents distribute tickets to a wide range of events, including theater, opera, cinema, museum exhibits, concerts, and sporting events. If you've arrived in town without tickets to the theater or symphony, you may actually be in luck, since discount tickets are sometimes available on the day of performances.

BASS & Tickets.com
☎ 415-776-1999 ⌚ phone operator 8:30am-9pm Mon-Sat, 10am-9pm Sun C *AE, MC, V*
W *www.tickets.com*

BASS and Tickets.com sell tickets, via a website or over the phone, to many events in San Francisco. Bass also maintains ticket outlets throughout the Bay Area. There's a surcharge on each ticket purchased.

Mr Ticket
2065 Van Ness Ave ☎ 415-292-7328 ⌚ phone operator 9am-5:30pm Mon-Fri, 10am-2pm Sat
C *AE, D, MC, V*
W *www.mrticket.com*

This ticket broker, which charges whatever price the market can bear (which can be astronomical for, say, a postseason sports event), is worth calling if tickets are sold out for the event you want to see.

Ticketmaster
☎ 415-421-8497 C *MC, V, AE*
W *www.ticketmaster.com*

This company also sells tickets, via a website or over the phone, to all types of events in San Francisco. Ticketmaster outlets can be found throughout the Bay Area. There's a surcharge on each ticket.

Ticketweb
C *AE, D, MC, V*
W *www.ticketweb.com*

Ticketweb sells tickets through the internet to most events in the city, and most of the theaters' websites have links to it. A surcharge is added to the price of each ticket.

TIX Bay Area MAP 2
Union Square Garage ☎ 415-433-7827 ⌚ 11am-6pm Tues-Thurs, 11am-7pm Fri-Sat C *MC, V (cash only for half-price tickets)* M *Powell St BART & Muni Station* *38 Muni*
W *www.theatrebayarea.org*

Discount theater tickets are available on the day of each performance at the TIX Bay Area booth. Half-price tickets are available for selected events, with an additional service charge. You can also order half-price tickets in advance by mail through the organization's Tix by Mail program. TIX Bay Area sells tickets in advance at full price.

2am Tues-Fri, 8pm-2am Sat, 5pm-2am Sun $3-7 12, 27 Muni

The CW Saloon serves the multifarious needs of bike messengers and SoMa hipsters as it evolves each day from an afternoon and early evening bar to a venue hosting thrash rock bands and DJs at night. A backroom features karaoke, and on Thursday night 'Sinky's Peepshow,' featuring plump go-go dancers and other lewd and lascivious forms of entertainment, has lasted much longer than anyone could have foreseen.

Hotel Utah MAP 4
500 4th St ☎ 415-421-8308 11:30am-2am Mon-Fri, 6pm-2am Sat-Sun $4-7 30, 45, 76 Muni

An old South of Market favorite on the ground floor of a Victorian residence hotel, the Utah has a small side room for live music. Local or touring indie rock and punk bands play several nights a week. When the music doesn't move you, the old mahogany bar's always a great place to grab a bite and down a few pints.

Paradise Lounge MAP 4
308 11th St ☎ 415-621-1912 3pm-2am daily $4-11 9, 42 Muni

Paradise, for some, is a noisy, crowded, youthful hangout spread out over two floors and three stages. There may be as many as five different shows on some nights, ranging from hard rock and punk to jazz and poetry readings. Earlier in the day, from 3pm to 7pm, there's free pool for all.

Slim's MAP 4
333 11th St ☎ 415-621-3330 shows at 8pm $12-25 9, 42 Muni
www.slims-sf.com

Slim's is partly owned by '70s rock star Boz Scaggs, but the club's listings are always worth a look. Along with a steady stream of roots-oriented rock bands, an edgier brand of singer-songwriters often performs here – Frank Black, formerly of the Pixies, usually stops at Slim's while touring, and Lloyd Cole has appeared here. The large club has tables and a dinner menu, but it's strictly standing-room-only if a popular show is on. Its hours of operation and show times vary.

Kimo's MAP 7
1351 Polk St ☎ 415-885-4554 8am-2am daily live music cover $5 19, 42, 47, 49 Muni California St cable car

Kimo's is a laid-back gay bar with a rock club upstairs. It features alt, punk, and experimental rock and roll units.

Bottom of the Hill MAP 14
1233 17th St ☎ 415-621-4455 information, 510-601-TWEB tickets 3pm-2am Sun-Thurs, 2pm-2am Fri, 8:30pm-2am Sat $5-12 19, 22 Muni
www.bottomofthehill.com

At the base of Potrero Hill, Bottom of the Hil is a small club that presents live music sever nights a week. The bill ranges from jazzy funk to folky punk. A small patio and a late-nigh kitchen ensure a good crowd at this otherwise out-of-the-way hot spot. The Sunday afternoon all-you-can-eat barbecue is always popular, and this is a key venue for the Noise Pop Fest in February and March.

Jazz & Blues Clubs

Sophisticated nightclubs peddling expensive liquor and dishing out nightly servings of savvy sounds are a San Francisco specialty. Some of the following clubs diverge from the musical formula now and then, bu for the most part they stick with a sexy blend of suave jazz and urban blues. It may be that the city's taste for this sort of thing is waning, and some of the hipper places have started to book more alt rock and DJs.

Biscuits & Blues MAP 2
401 Mason St ☎ 415-292-2583 5pm-2am Mon-Fri, 6pm-2am Sat-Sun cover $5-12.50 Powell St BART & Muni station 2, 3, 4, 38, 76 Muni Powell-Mason, Powell-Hyde cable cars
www.biscuitandblue.citysearch.com

With a steady lineup of blues and jazz talent Biscuits & Blues has earned a reputation as a dependable entertainment choice in the Union Square area. A menu features Southern cooking.

HiBall Lounge MAP 6
473 Broadway ☎ 415-397-9464 7pm-1am Tues-Thurs, 8:30pm-2am Fri-Sat, 8pm-1am Sun $2-8 12, 15, 30, 41, 45 Muni
www.hiball.com

A few years ago, when the swing revival was at its peak, the HiBall was ground zero for the zoot-suit and pedal-pusher set. How quickly retro scenes die. The HiBall is still up and running, albeit with less emphasis on swing. The swanky Vegas-style lounge has a certain timeless appeal, and you can still catch a contemporary swing unit here, but the weekly calendar now includes alt rock bands and DJs.

Jazz at Pearl's MAP 6
256 Columbus Ave ☎ 415-291-8255
🕒 8pm-midnight Mon, 8pm-2am Tues-Sun
$ no cover 🚌 12, 15, 30, 41, 45 Muni ♿
w www.jazzatpearls.citysearch.com

A no-nonsense jazz club with a friendly vibe, Pearl's features modern jazz talent every night but Sunday. The club enforces a two-drink minimum but rarely charges a cover.

Lou's Pier 47 MAP 8
300 Jefferson St ☎ 415-771-0377 🕒 4pm-midnight Mon-Thurs, 3pm-1am Fri-Sat
$ $2-10 🚌 F Muni ♿
w www.louspier47.com

Something of a respite from the mass-market tourist zone, Lou's is a restaurant-nightclub that books live blues artists seven days a week, beginning in the afternoon and going on 'til midnight or later.

Rasselas MAP 10
2801 California St ☎ 415-567-5010 🕒 5pm-10pm Sun-Thurs, 5pm-11pm Fri-Sat, shows at 8pm $ $2-5 🚌 1, 24 Muni ♿

Rasselas has two rooms, with an Ethiopian restaurant in one room and a funky little jazz club in the other. A well-worn hardwood floor and mismatched tables and chairs create a 1950s Village feel, perfect for grooving to snappy rhythms and cool, twisted sax solos.

Cafe du Nord MAP 12
2170 Market St ☎ 415-861-5016 🕒 6pm-2am Sun-Tues, 4pm-2am Wed-Sat $ cover $5-10
M Church St Muni station 🚌 22, F Muni
w www.cafedunord.com

Cafe du Nord still looks the way it must have in the 1930s, when the basement parlor served well as a speakeasy. On weekends, the place jumps with an alcohol-fueled exuberance rarely seen since Prohibition was repealed. The two front rooms offer a sophisticated setting for drinking and dining, and every night the club's dimly lit back music chamber offers live music of various interesting stripes, including jazz, salsa, lounge-abilly, and space-pop.

Bruno's MAP 14
2389 Mission St ☎ 415-550-7455 🕒 6pm-2am Tues-Sat $ $7-9 🚌 14, 49 Muni ♿
w www.brunoslive.com

It may be impossible to ignore Bruno's well-dressed patrons as they brush past each other in the club's multiple chambers – including the slender, often cramped Cork Club, furnished with a Hammond organ for funk nights, or the equally crowded (and genuinely swanky) main lounge, equipped with a grand piano. But don't overlook the fact that the club books talented jazz groups in both rooms nearly every night (other types of music round out the weekly schedule). To swing with the place, throw the scene down the hatch and chase it with a Scotch. Next to the bar, a portal leads to the club's dining room, where a reputable dinner trade is carried out.

Elbo Room MAP 14
647 Valencia St ☎ 415-552-7788 🕒 5pm-2am daily $ $7-10 M 16th St BART station
🚌 22, 26 Muni
w www.elbo.com

The Elbo Room has a swank curved bar that's always packed with scenesters. DJs and live musicians perform upstairs, playing anything from experimental jazz to hip-hop.

Pier 23 Cafe
Pier 23 ☎ 415-362-5125 🕒 5pm-close daily, music starts 8pm or 10pm $ cover $5 (sometimes free) 🚌 42, F Muni ♿
w www.pier23cafe.citysearch.com

The old waterfront restaurant on Pier 23 regularly features jazz, R&B, reggae, and Latin bands at night. It's an upbeat, very casual scene, and on warm evenings it's always nice to step out onto the back patio, overlooking the bay. A dinner menu, with standard seafood and pasta choices, is available.

DANCE CLUBS

San Francisco's club scene isn't as heavily hyped as LA's, New York's, or Miami's. The city does have large, multilevel dance venues, but most places are actually pretty intimate. Reflecting the rave influence, the scene is by turns characterized by an Ecstasy-fueled idealism and a monomaniacal self-indulgence. On the whole, the club scene is defined more by the people who come to hang out than by big-time promoters and celebrities and their bodyguards. You'll encounter a cross section not just of the city but of the entire Bay Area, with gays, straights, blacks, Latinos, whites, and Asians frequently mixing.

As is typical everywhere these days, dance venues combine forces with various promoters to put on different parties each night of the week. So the atmosphere, musical emphasis, and crowd in a given place can sometimes undergo dramatic transformation from night to night. Some independent promoters present roving clubs that turn up weekly or monthly at a different venue each time. One result of the shifting landscape is that weeknights are a big thing, as clubs of all sizes try to establish niches.

If you want to keep going 'round the clock, after-parties and Sunday tea dances are not hard to come by. As clubs close (anywhere between 2am and 6am), representatives from other clubs are often standing outside the door, handing out invitations to after-parties, which generally begin at 5am or 6am and can continue on through the afternoon. Full-moon raves, which take place outdoors under a full moon and go to the wee hours, are still reputed to go on around the Bay Area, but you'll have to put your ear to the ground to hear about them.

South of Market has the largest concentration of dance clubs, but there are some notable clubs in other parts of town as well.

Information

It's a wise idea to check up-to-date sources to see what's going on during your stay. The single best source of up-to-date club information is the monthly *Flyer Urban Culture Guide,* a pocket-size pamphlet that's available free in coffee shops, bars, and clubs in SoMa. The Flyer is also online at www.flyersf@amalgammedia.com. Another good website for club nights and underground parties in the city is www.sfstation.com. The ever accessible *Bay Guardian* and *SF Weekly* are also useful sources, as is the gay publication, the *Bay Times.*

You can also call the 'Be-At' information hotline (☎ 415-626-4087). Updated every day, the Be-At Line relays information at a rapid clip, in the often cryptic clubby language.

Venues

Most of the city's dance clubs are South of Market, and the rest are dispersed around town. Of course, the club scene is always volatile, and there will no doubt be newer and hotter clubs around town by the time you read this.

Ruby Skye MAP 2
420 Mason St ☎ 415-675-4874 ⌚ 9pm-3am Wed & Fri-Sat, special events scheduled other nights $ $10-15 Ⓜ Powell St BART & Muni station 🚌 2, 3, 4, 38, 76 Muni 🚋 Powell-Mason, Powell-Hyde cable cars W www.rubyskye.com

The ultra-high-tech and plush Ruby Skye, in the heart of Union Square, offers a variety of entertainments, including cirque-style performers, fire-breathers, and dancing. This is not an edgy, underground sort of thing: Ruby Skye is designed to thrill well-heeled professionals, and expensive-looking clothes are expected of all guests.

Polly Esther's Culture Club MAP 3
181 Eddy St ☎ 415-885-1977 ⌚ 9pm-2am Thurs, 8pm-4am Fri-Sat $ $5-15 Ⓜ Powell St BART & Muni station 🚌 Market St buses, 27, 31, F Muni ♿ W www.pollyesthers.com

Polly Esther's is basically the fast-food franchise of dance clubs, with outlets across the US. A mostly tourist and bridge-and-tunnel crowd comes to shake its collective fanny to all the great K-tel hits of the '70s and '80s. It's very convenient to guests staying in Union Square hotels, although the immediate surroundings – the Tenderloin – may not be the best for walking back to your room in the wee hours.

The Cat Club MAP 4
1190 Folsom St ☎ 415-431-3332 ⌚ 9pm-3am Wed-Sat (sometimes later) $ $4-6 🚌 12, 19 Muni ♿

A very popular SoMa spot, the Cat Club hosts a variety of parties. San Francisco's perennial Bondage A Go Go (featuring a fully functional 'punishment area') holds court here on Wednesday night.

EndUp MAP 4
995 Harrison St ☎ 415-543-7700 ⌚ 10pm-4:30am Thurs, 10pm Fri-4pm Sat, 9pm-2am Sat, 6am-2am Sun $ $5-10 🚌 27, 42 Muni W www.theendup.citysearch.com

The EndUp is a SoMa institution that keeps going strong. Its intimate club nights attract a very mixed crowd, although Fag Fridays make an obvious pitch for the gay male set. The Sunday T-Dance, which begins early but gets going around midday, is one of the coolest things going, particularly when the sun is out and the back patio really gets into the swing of things. The club rocks 'round the clock all weekend.

Where to Shoot Stick

As many a traveler with chalk between his or her fingers can tell you, shooting a good game of pool is not a bad way to pass the time in a strange bar in a new city. Plenty of San Francisco's watering holes are prepared to accommodate just such a traveler. Although many – if not most – bars are equipped with the token bar-size pool table, a few stand out as particularly welcoming to the eight-ball enthusiast.

Hollywood Billiards MAP 3
61 Golden Gate Ave ☎ 415-252-9643 ⌚ 6pm-2am daily $ $5-10 C cash only M Powell St BART & Muni station 🚌 Market St buses, F Muni

Hollywood Billiards is an old-school establishment with no fewer than 37 tables and a full bar. Wednesday night is 'Ladies' Night' – very popular with lesbian pool sharks!

Chalkers MAP 4
201 Spear St, Rincon Center ☎ 415-512-0450 ⌚ 11:30am-1am Mon-Wed, 11:30am-2am Thurs-Fri, 2pm-2am Sat, 3pm-11pm Sun C AE, DC, MC, V M Embarcadero BART & Muni station 🚌 Market St buses ♿ W www.chalkers.citysearch.com

For a yuppie evening of pool, there's always Chalkers. This civilized pool parlor even offers 'informal instruction from a roving pro.'

Paradise Lounge MAP 4
308 11th St ☎ 415-621-1912 ⌚ 3pm-2am daily 🚌 9, 42 ♿

Come to this SoMa standby during happy hour, 3pm to 8pm daily, for cheap drinks and some serious eight ball in the upstairs pool room.

Amusement Center MAP 6
447 Broadway ☎ 415-398-8858 C cash only 🚌 12, 15 Muni

This no-nonsense billiards parlor, upstairs from a noisy arcade on North Beach's Broadway strip, has more than a dozen tables. This place is straight out of a '50s melodrama, complete with troubled youth.

500 Club MAP 14
500 Guerrero St ☎ 415-861-2500 ⌚ 10am-2am Mon-Fri, 6am-2am Sat-Sun C cash only M 16th St BART station 🚌 22, 33 Muni ♿

This seedy little Mission District dive has a pair of tables in a room that's dedicated to the game.

111 Minna Gallery MAP 4
111 Minna St ☎ 415-974-1719 ⏲ 4pm-2am Tues-Fri, 9pm-2am Sat $ $3-10 🚌 12, 14, 15, 76 Muni ♿
W *www.111annex.com*

An art gallery doubling as a club, 111 Minna is a cool space that draws a smart SoMa crowd.

1015 Folsom MAP 4
1015 Folsom St ☎ 415-431-1200 ⏲ 10pm-6am Thurs-Sun, varying closing time other nights $ $10-20 🚌 12 Muni
W *www.1015.com*

Long one of the city's foremost dance clubs, 1015 has three levels and features superstar DJs and the best in local spinning talent. This is where some of the city's most happening parties take place (Nikita on Friday night, Spundae on Sunday night), and the club is so popular that some nights it's impossible to get in until after 2am.

Sound Factory MAP 4
525 Harrison St ☎ 415-979-8686 ⏲ 9pm-4am Sat, special events scheduled other nights $ $5 and up 🚌 42 Muni
W *www.thesoundfactory.citysearch.com*

The Sound Factory is the amusement park of dance clubs, with 15,000 sq feet of dance space in many rooms on many levels. Musical persuasions run the gamut, from house and jungle to Top 40. On Saturday night, the club attracts college students, but some nights it's strictly 21 and up.

The Stud MAP 4
399 9th St ☎ 415-252-7883 ⏲ 5pm-3am daily $ $5-7 🚌 19, 27, 42 ♿
W *www.thestud.citysearch.com*

The legendary Stud is an elder statesman among SoMa clubs. Though some straight people frequent it, the Stud remains first and foremost a gay establishment. Trannyshack, which takes place Tuesday night, is a transgender and cross-dresser cabaret at which a few honest-to-gosh singers join the usual lip-synch artists. Funk and '80s nights draw relatively mainstream crowds.

330 Ritch MAP 4
330 Ritch St ☎ 415-522-9558 ⏲ 5pm-1am Wed-Fri, 10pm-2am Sat-Sun & Tues $ cover $5-7 🚌 30, 42, 45, 76 Muni

A spacious nightclub with tables around a dance floor, 330 Ritch has an eclectic weekly lineup designed to get you shaking your booty to varying tempos, from the latest jungle music to R&B grooves, and downshifting to a mellower loungecore vibe. A live swing combo plays early Wednesday night. The multichambered club includes a restaurant and a pool room.

Up & Down Club MAP 4
1151 Folsom St ☎ 415-626-2388 ⏲ 9pm-2am Mon-Tues, 8pm-2am Wed-Thurs, 9:30pm-2am Fri-Sat $ $5-7 (sometimes free) 🚌 12, 19 Muni

The 'up' portion of the Up & Down Club has a very small dance floor, and DJs spin hip-hop there most nights. Meanwhile, the swanky lounge downstairs usually features live music (jazz and other styles). Admission allows guests to move freely between the two levels.

VSF MAP 4
278 11th St ☎ 415-621-4863 ⏲ 9pm-3am Mon-Thurs, 9pm-4am Fri-Sat, 9pm-6am Sun $ $5-15 🚌 9, 12, 42 Muni

VSF, in the heart of the old 11th St SoMa club district, offers several small rooms for heating up and a rooftop deck for cooling off. The musical mix includes R&B, soul, dub, house, and trance, and occasionally live samba combos perform.

Broadway Studios MAP 6
435 Broadway ☎ 415-291-0333 ⏲ 7pm-2am Wed, 9pm-2am Thurs-Sat, 5pm-2am Sun $ $10-15 🚌 12, 15, 30, 41, 45 Muni
W *www.broadwaystudios.com*

If you're looking for an alternative to the young and hip SoMa scene, move your rump to Broadway Studios, where ballroom dancing and the hustle rule. The intriguing old room, built in 1919, has three bars, a restaurant, a 40-foot-high ceiling, balcony tables, and a spacious dance floor. Many nights the music is performed by capable combos and orchestras.

Club 238 MAP 6
238 Columbus Ave ☎ 415-402-0000 ⏲ 10pm-5am Thurs, 9pm-4am Fri-Sat, 9pm-6am Sun $ $15 🚌 12, 15, 30, 41, 45 Muni

Club 238, a large North Beach space, keeps going after hours. It draws a lot of out-of-towners and usually has them shakin' their hinds to all the house and hip-hop they can stand.

Justice League MAP 11
628 Divisadero St ☎ 415-289-2038 ⏲ 9pm-2am when events scheduled $ $5-18 🚌 21, 24 Muni ♿

Justice League is one of the city's more serious spin-culture clubs, bringing DJs from around the world to San Francisco on a regular basis. Live bands also sometimes play here.

Nickie's MAP 11
460 Haight St ☎ 415-621-6508 ⏲ 9pm-2am daily $ $3-5 🚌 6, 7, 22, 71 Muni
w www.nickies.com

Nickie's is one of the city's more eclectic and down-to-earth DJ bars, featuring reggae, Grateful Dead, funk, disco, and ambient music on different nights. It's usually packed with a party crowd from all over town.

The Top MAP 11
424 Haight St ☎ 415-864-7386 ⏲ 5pm-2am daily $ $3-5 🚌 6, 7, 22, 71 Muni ♿

Some of San Francisco's biggest DJs got their start at The Top. The small club offers pretty straightforward turntable fare: all the hip-hop, house, disco, and breaks you can shake your booty to.

The Café MAP 12
2367 Market St ☎ 415-861-3846
⏲ 12:30pm-2am daily $ no cover Ⓜ Castro St Muni station 🚌 F Muni

The population at the hugely popular Café is young and ethnically mixed and gets more gay as the night goes on. This is one of the only places in the Castro that has a dance floor, and the long deck overlooking Market St is a good place to cool off. In the afternoon, it's a relatively relaxed Castro hangout.

El Rio MAP 14
3158 Mission St ☎ 415-282-3325 ⏲ 3pm-2am daily $ $4-7 (sometimes free) 🚌 14, 49 Muni ♿

El Rio is in some ways the ultimate Mission District dive. A large, upbeat bar and dance club with very generous happy hour specials and a spacious outdoor patio, it attracts a diverse crowd of gay men, lesbians, and straights, all of varying ethnicities and walks of life. The Sunday afternoon barbecue, when a live salsa band performs, is the most popular event here, while Thursday's 'Arabian Nights,' when belly-dancing lessons are offered, is a measure of the club's diversity.

Liquid MAP 14
2925 16th St ☎ 415-431-8889 ⏲ 9pm-2am Mon-Sat $ $2-5 (sometimes free) Ⓜ 16th St BART station 🚌 14, 22, 49 Muni ♿

A narrow bar on a seamy block in the Mission, Liquid hosts a different party every night of the week, but the place is always jam-packed and the vibe is consistently good.

26Mix MAP 14
3024 Mission St ☎ 415-826-7378 ⏲ 5pm-2am Tues-Fri, 9pm-2am Sat-Sun $ $3-6 (sometimes free) 🚌 14, 49 Muni ♿
w www.26mix.com

It looks like an ordinary cocktail lounge, but 26Mix is clearly all about DJs and dancing. (Its owners have been promoting the place as a 'sound bar.') In the heart of the Mission District, 26Mix showcases the talents of local DJs every night of the week.

CINEMA

The Bay Area is a terrific region for moviegoers, with wonderful old cinemas, discerning local film buffs, plenty of foreign-film and art-house venues, and several world-class film festivals. Typically admission is $7.50 to $9 to see a movie, though weekday matinees tend to drop prices to $5 or $6. See the daily papers for the most reliable schedules.

Film Festivals

The city's many film festivals are all very popular, and tickets generally sell out before the screenings. This makes it difficult but not impossible for out-of-town visitors to attend the films. The best approach is to check out festival websites, offered below, several weeks before the festival begins. Often, tickets can be purchased through the festival's website or at www.tickets.com.

Asian American Film Festival
☎ 415-255-4299
w www.naatanet.org/festival

The festival is hosted by NAATA (National Asian American Telecommunications Association) in March at the Kabuki 8 Theater and in Berkeley. There are also screenings at other times of the year.

Jewish Film Festival
☎ 415-621-0556
w www.sfjff.org

The world's largest Jewish film festival is held in July and August at the Castro Theatre and elsewhere around the Bay Area.

San Francisco Independent Film Festival
☎ *415-820-3907*
W *www.sfindie.com*

This nine-day event in mid-January promotes artistic underground films. Animated shorts are often a highlight.

San Francisco International Film Festival
☎ *415-929-5000*
W *www.sfiff.org*

This very popular festival takes place in April, mainly at the Kabuki 8 Theater and the Castro Theatre. Tickets almost always sell out in advance, so check out the website or call to get advance information.

San Francisco International Lesbian & Gay Film Festival
☎ *415-703-8650*
W *www.frameline.org*

Frameline hosts the queer film festival in June, at the Castro, Roxie, and Victoria theaters.

San Francisco Silent Film Festival
☎ *415-777-4908*
W *www.silentfilm.org*

Psst! For many years now, San Francisco has very quietly held an annual silent film festival, showcasing classic pretalkie cinema. The films are screened at the wonderful Castro Theatre in early July.

ENTERTAINMENT

Movie Theaters

Listings for all of the following theaters appear in the daily papers, but what the listings don't tell you is if the theater itself adds or detracts from your viewing enjoyment.

AMC 1000 MAP 3
1000 Van Ness Ave ☎ 415-931-9800 $ general $8.50, matinee $5.50 🚌 38, 42, 47, 49 Muni ♿
W *www.amctheatres.com*

An enormous multiplex (14 screens) in a cleverly converted auto showroom, 1000 Van Ness mostly shows mainstream Hollywood releases. The state-of-the-art theaters feature 'surround sound' and luxurious stadium seating, and the lobby has a stylish café-bar.

Opera Plaza Cinema MAP 3
601 Van Ness Ave ☎ 415-771-0102 $ general $8.50, matinee $5 🚌 5, 19, 31, 42, 47, 49 Muni ♿
W *www.landmarktheatres.com*

Art-house and foreign films screen at Opera Plaza, with two full-size theaters. The tiny 'screening rooms,' where good movies that have been out for a while always seem to end up, will leave you feeling cheated – the screens are far too small and the admission price is not reduced. The theater's newspaper listings specify which room films will show in – be sure to check.

Loews Theatres Metreon MAP 4
101 4th St ☎ 415-369-6000 $ general $8.50, matinee $5 🚌 14, 15, 30, 45, 76 Muni ♿
W *www.metreon.com*

Once you get past the city's admirable skepticism toward modern chain theaters, the flashy Metreon is hard to knock. It's a state-of-the-art cineplex, with enormous screens, comfortable stadium seating, and great sound to enhance your viewing pleasure. Almost all of the current blockbusters play here.

Embarcadero Center Cinema MAP 5
Embarcadero One, promenade level ☎ 415-352-0810 $ general $8.50, matinee $5 Ⓜ Embarcadero BART & Muni station 🚌 1, 41 Muni ♿
W *www.landmarktheatres.com*

This comfortable five-screen multiplex shows a commendable mix of new international and art-house releases.

Lumiere Theater MAP 7
1572 California St ☎ 415-885-3200 $ general $8.50, matinee $5 🚌 1, 19, 42, 47, 49 Muni 🚋 California St cable car ♿
W *www.landmarktheatres.com*

The Lumiere has one large screening room and two smaller rooms and shows a mix of first-run art-house and foreign films.

Metro Theater MAP 9
2055 Union St ☎ 415-931-1685 $ general $8.50, matinee $5 🚌 41, 45 Muni ♿

The enormous art deco Metro Cinema was restored in the late '90s. It has cushy new seats and a modern sound system, and it shows first-run, big-budget Hollywood flicks.

AMC Kabuki 8 Theaters MAP 10
1881 Post St ☎ 415-931-9800 $ general $8.75, matinee $5.50 🚌 22, 38 Muni ♿
W *www.amctheatres.com*

The Kabuki, just outside Japan Center (read: plenty of restaurants nearby), is a multiplex that mostly shows blockbusters but sometimes features quality exclusive engagements that are worth trekking out this way for. The city's film festivals usually use this theater for some screenings. The Kabuki offers validated parking.

Clay Theater MAP 10
2261 Fillmore St ☎ 415-346-1123 $ general $8.50, matinee $5 1, 22 Muni ♿
w www.landmarktheatres.com

In business since 1913, the Clay is a single-screen cinema that regularly features independent and foreign films. Midnight Saturday screenings are fun events.

Red Vic Movie House MAP 11
1727 Haight St ☎ 415-668-3994 $ general $6.50, matinee $4.50 7, 71 Muni ♿
w www.redvicmoviehouse.com

The small Red Vic has an unorthodox arrangement of padded benches for your viewing comfort. The cinema screens the odd first-run independent, but its calendar is mostly filled with rare cult films and interesting classics and re-releases.

Castro Theatre MAP 12
429 Castro St ☎ 415-621-6120 $ general $7.50, matinee $4.50 M Castro St Muni station 24, F ♿ limited
w www.thecastro.com

The Castro Theatre, one of the city's cultural treasures, has all the velvet, Grecian columns, and fake plants any vintage cinema buff could ever hope for, and seeing a show here is always an event. On the magnificent Wurlitzer organ that rises in front of the stage, David Hegarty plays popular tunes before the show starts, as he has done for the last 20 years. Sometimes he even accompanies silent films. Of course, gay and lesbian cinema always has a home at the Castro, but restored Hollywood classics and foreign films also frequently screen here.

Roxie Cinema MAP 14
3117 16th St ☎ 415-863-1087 $ general $7, matinee $4 M 16th St BART station 22, 26 Muni ♿
w www.roxie.com

The funky old Roxie, a single-screen theater with lumpy old seats, features an adventurous, eclectic selection of films, with many classic long-forgotten old flicks thrown into the mix.

COMEDY

San Francisco's (and America's) comedy scene has declined over the past 10 or 15 years. At one time, local comics such as Robin Williams and Paula Poundstone made this one of the world's funniest cities. Now it sometimes hurts to watch the city's comics overreach for laughs. Still, the touring talent rarely passes the city up, and the city has a pair of clubs that book 'em.

The Punch Line MAP 5
444 Battery St ☎ 415-397-4337 ⌚ 9pm, 11pm (approximately) $ $8-15 plus a 2-drink minimum 1, 42 Muni
w www.punchlinecomedyclub.com

The Punchline regularly books this (and last) year's hot comics, with one show most nights, two shows Friday and Saturday.

Cobb's Comedy Club MAP 8
2801 Leavenworth St ☎ 415-928-4320 ⌚ 8pm, 11pm $ $7-15 plus a 2-drink minimum 30, 42, F Muni Powell-Hyde cable car ♿

Cobb's is a comfy little comedy club that mostly features lesser-known talents. It has several showcase nights a week that put the spotlight on 12 to 15 up-and-coming comics.

THEATER

Theater isn't sparking the level of interest it did in the 1960s and '70s, when San Francisco was at the center of radical changes introduced to the art form. But that doesn't mean there isn't a lot going on these days, and when it comes to drama, SF is still one of the more dynamic cities in the US.

Local Companies

In the 1960s, several cutting-edge companies opened in San Francisco, and most of them are still around. The American Conservatory Theater (ACT) is the city's most prominent company, and the Magic Theatre, once home to playwright Sam Shepard, continues to put on important works.

American Conservatory Theater (Geary Theater) MAP 2
Geary Theater, 415 Geary St ☎ 415-749-2228 $ $15-60 M Powell St BART & Muni station 38 Muni ♿
w www.act-sfbay.org

San Francisco's most accomplished theater company, the American Conservatory Theater (ACT) has been a training ground for many famous actors over the years, and its productions are top-notch. Each Christmas season, ACT puts on Dickens' *A Christmas Carol*. As a bonus, ACT's home is the historic Geary Theater.

Beach Blanket Babylon MAP 6
678 Green St ☎ 415-421-4222 ⏱ 3pm Sun, 7pm Fri-Sun, 8pm Wed-Thurs, 10pm Fri-Sat $ $25-60 🚌 15, 30, 41, 45 Muni ♿
w www.beachblanketbabylon.com

'Beach Blanket Babylon,' at Club Fugazi in North Beach, is San Francisco's longest-running comedy extravaganza. The show is basically a fun spoof on current events (in 1999, for instance, an oversized Monica Lewinsky wig got a big chuckle). Now into its third decade, BBB is still packing them in. All audience members must be over 21 years of age, except at matinees.

Magic Theatre MAP 9
Fort Mason Center, Building D ☎ 415-441-8822 ⏱ box office noon-5pm Tues-Sat $ $25-30 🚌 28, 30 Muni ♿
w www.magictheatre.org

The Magic gained a national reputation in the 1970s, when Sam Shepard was the theater's resident playwright, and this is still one of the city's most important theaters. The Magic occasionally produces star-studded shows, as it did in late 2000 with Shepard's The *Late Harry Moss,* starring Sean Penn and Nick Nolte.

Big Houses

Many of the city's theaters are housed in historic and architecturally significant buildings. Some of the more spectacular are also described in Things to See & Do.

Alcazar Theatre MAP 2
650 Geary St ☎ 415-441-6655 business office ⏱ show times vary 🚌 27, 38 Muni ♿

The Theater on the Square company produces some of its plays in this old Masonic lodge.

Curran Theatre MAP 2
445 Geary St ☎ 415-551-2000 ⏱ show times vary Ⓜ Powell St BART & Muni station 🚌 38 Muni ♿

The big spectaculars – like the Andrew Lloyd Webber musicals – show at the Curran.

Golden Gate Theatre MAP 3
1 Taylor St ☎ 415-551-2000 ⏱ show times vary Ⓜ Powell St BART & Muni station 🚌 Market St buses, F Muni ♿

Touring productions of Broadway shows play here, sometimes featuring major stars.

Orpheum Theatre MAP 3
1192 Market St ☎ 415-551-2000 ⏱ show times vary Ⓜ Civic Center BART & Muni station 🚌 Market St buses, F Muni ♿

Recently renovated, the Orpheum has been substantially enlarged so it can accommodate big Broadway musicals along the lines of *Show Boat* and *Miss Saigon.*

Alternative Theater

The true measure of a city's drama scene, of course, is the quality, depth, and diversity of its small theater spaces. In that capacity, it can be said that San Francisco is rather hospitable to the art form. Theater Artaud and the Exit Theatre always have something new and exciting going on, as do a wide variety of other small, alternative theater companies.

Cable Car Theater MAP 2
430 Mason St ☎ 415-982-5463, 800-660-8462 ⏱ shows at 7:30pm Fri-Sat, 3pm Sun $ $20-75 Ⓜ Powell St BART & Muni station 🚌 38 Muni 🚋 Powell-Mason, Powell-Hyde cable cars

This theater caters mostly to tourists, with long-running off-Broadway shows, such as the comedy *Tony 'n' Tina's Wedding.*

Mason St Theatre MAP 2
340 Mason St ☎ 415-982-5463 ⏱ shows at 3pm & 7:30pm Sun, 8pm Tues-Fri, 6:30pm & 9:30pm Sat $ $34 Ⓜ Powell St BART & Muni station 🚌 38 Muni 🚋 Powell-Mason, Powell-Hyde cable cars
w www.shearmadness.com

For years, the popular and zany barbershop who-dunnit *Shear Madness* has been playing at this little theater.

Theatre on the Square MAP 2
450 Post St ☎ 415-433-9500 ⏱ shows at 8pm Tues-Thurs, 8:30pm Fri, 3pm & 8:30pm Sat, 3pm & 7pm Sun $ $30-50 🚌 2, 3, 4, 76 Muni 🚋 Powell-Mason, Powell-Hyde cable cars ♿
w www.theatreonthesquare.com

Some notable off-Broadway productions have passed through this sizable theater, and many big artists have played on its stage, including Sandra Bernhardt, John Leguizamo, and the world's greatest mime, Marcel Marceau.

Exit Theatre MAP 3
156 Eddy St ☎ 415-673-3847 ⏱ shows at 8pm Fri-Sat $ $15-25 Ⓜ Powell St BART & Muni station 🚌 Market St buses, 31, F Muni ♿
w www.sffringe.org

Free & Outdoors

The high cost of living in San Francisco doesn't mean visitors have to reach for their wallet for everything. Free outdoor entertainment abounds in San Francisco, especially in summer, when the city's big dance, theater, and music companies – and some of its smaller ones – put on performances in the open air. Stern Grove (in the Sunset District) and Golden Gate Park host a variety of events, as do Justin Herman Plaza and other public squares downtown.

Stern Grove Festival MAP 1

Sloat Blvd ☎ 415-252-6252 ⏲ 2pm Sun mid-June to mid-Aug $ free Ⓜ Stonestown Muni station 🚌 28 Muni ♿

W *www.sterngrove.org*

The Stern Grove Festival presents 10 free Sunday afternoon concerts in the Stern Grove Amphitheater. The grove's open-air amphitheater, sunken into a meadow surrounded by eucalyptus and redwood trees, is a beautiful spot to enjoy a picnic while listening to music. The annual calendar (which appears on the website before each season) usually includes performances by the San Francisco Symphony, the San Francisco Opera, the San Francisco Ballet, big-name jazz artists, and other musicians from around the world. Take the K or M Muni streetcar to Stonestown Muni station, then catch the No 28 bus to the corner of Sloat, near the park entrance.

Justin Herman Plaza MAP 5

Embarcadero Center ⏲ noon Fri in summer $ free Ⓜ Embarcadero BART & Muni station ♿

On Fridays during the summer there are lunchtime jazz concerts in Justin Herman Plaza, at the Embarcadero Center.

Old St Mary's Church Concerts MAP 5

660 California St ☎ 415-288-3800 ⏲ 12:30pm Tues $ free (donations) 🚌 1, 9, 31 Muni 🚋 California St cable car ♿

Old St Mary's Church puts on a varied repertoire of free classical music performances.

Redwood Plaza MAP 5

Transamerica Pyramid ⏲ noon Fri in summer $ free ♿

On Friday during the summer, there are lunchtime jazz concerts in the shade in Redwood Plaza, near the Transamerica Pyramid.

San Francisco Shakespeare Festival MAP 15

Golden Gate Park ☎ 415-422-2222 park information ⏲ 1:30pm Sat-Sun in Sept $ free ♿

The Shakespeare performances in Golden Gate Park are among the city's most popular outdoor events. Each year one play is performed throughout the month of September, starting on Labor Day. Performances are put on in the grove opposite the Conservatory of Flowers, and the crowds usually show up about two hours early.

Opera in the Park MAP 15

Sharon Meadow, Golden Gate Park ☎ 415-864-3330 ⏲ 1:30pm-3:30pm 2nd Sun in Sept $ free ♿

This noncostumed concert celebrates the opening of the opera season and draws huge crowds.

San Francisco Mime Troupe

☎ 415-285-1720 ⏲ weekend afternoons $ donations (free) ♿

W *www.sfmt.org*

This roving theater troupe performs at parks throughout San Francisco and the East Bay all summer. Don't expect any silent, white-faced mimes – this is political musical theater in the commedia dell'arte tradition. It's big, it's loud, it's free (though donations are appreciated), and it's a lot of fun.

The Exit has one of the city's best programs, with an exciting experimental atmosphere. It has two theaters, and usually two shows run simultaneously. The Exit also manages the Fringe Festival (see Theater Festivals, below).

Bayfront Theatre MAP 9
Fort Mason Center, Building B ☎ 415-824-8220, 415-474-8935 box office ⌚ shows at 8pm Thurs-Sun, 10:30pm Fri-Sat $ $6-15 🚌 28, 30 Muni ♿
w www.improv.org

This small space is home to Bay Area Theatresports, which calls itself BATS. And what on earth is 'theatresport'? Basically, improvisation is the name of the game, and big laughs are the goal. This doesn't always come off so well – as when Shakespeare gets butchered – but the goofy 'tournaments' are certainly a novel idea, so get out and root for your favorite improv players.

The Marsh MAP 14
1062 Valencia St ☎ 415-641-0235 ⌚ shows at 8pm Thurs-Sun $ $12-17 🚌 14, 26, 49 Muni ♿
w www.themarsh.org

The Marsh considers itself a 'breeding ground' for creativity. It succeeds in always putting on events of interest – from solo performances to experimental 'works in progress' – and has a loyal following.

Theater Artaud MAP 14
450 Florida St ☎ 415-621-7797 ⌚ shows at 8pm Tues-Sat, 7pm Sun $ $15-25 🚌 22, 27 Muni ♿
w www.theaterartaud.org

The Artaud opened its live-work space in 1972 – way before live-work spaces became common – and although it has developed into a sophisticated and highly successful operation, it remains one of the city's most adventurous houses. (They like gettin' nekkid here.) Occasionally, the space creates a buzz with performances by the inimitable Karen Finley or Artaud's former house band, the Kronos Quartet.

Theatre Rhinoceros MAP 14
2926 16th St ☎ 415-861-5079 ⌚ show times vary $ $15-20 M 16th St BART station 🚌 14, 22, 49 Muni
w www.therhino.org

Theatre Rhino is the nation's longest-running lesbian, gay, bisexual, and transgender theater company. Productions here are by turns edgy, bawdy, serious, and experimental.

A Traveling Jewish Theatre MAP 14
470 Florida St ☎ 415-399-1809 ⌚ show times vary $ $12-25 🚌 22, 27 Muni ♿
w www.atjt.com

A Traveling Jewish Theatre, founded in 1978, presents a variety of entertainment genres focusing on Jewish and American cultural issues. Borscht Belt comedy, music, storytelling, and serious and comic drama are all explored.

Theater Festivals

San Francisco has an interesting theater festival that takes place every September at theaters around Union Square.

Fringe Festival
☎ 415-931-1094 $ $8 or less
w www.sffringe.org

If you're in town in September, check out the Fringe Festival, a marathon of uncensored plays and live performances – 52 shows, 250 performances, in five theaters over the course of 11 days. It's produced by the ever-exciting Exit Theatre – see Alternative Theater for more on the company.

CLASSICAL MUSIC & OPERA

The city of San Francisco makes a commendable effort to bring high cultcha to the uncouth masses. Its symphony and opera are top-notch.

Herbst Theatre MAP 3
401 Van Ness Ave ☎ 415-392-4400 M Civic Center BART; Van Ness & Civic Center Muni stations 🚌 42, 47, 49 Muni ♿

There are classical music performances, as well as dance performances by the San Francisco Ballet, at the Herbst.

San Francisco Symphony (Davies Symphony Hall) MAP 3
201 Van Ness Ave ☎ 415-864-6000 $ $10-85 M Civic Center BART; Van Ness & Civic Center Muni stations 🚌 42, 47, 49 Muni ♿
w www.sfsymphony.org

San Francisco's highly regarded symphony, under the directorship of Michael Tilson Thomas, performs from September to May in Davies Symphony Hall. A limited number of discount tickets go on sale at the box office two hours before performances (cash only).

San Francisco Opera (War Memorial Opera House) MAP 3
301 Van Ness Ave ☎ 415-864-3330 $ $50-500 M Civic Center BART; Van Ness & Civic

ENTERTAINMENT

Center Muni stations 42, 47, 49 Muni
w *www.sfopera.com*

The acclaimed San Francisco Opera Company is the second largest in the US, and it performs at the lovely War Memorial Opera House from June to January. Standing-room tickets, available for some shows, are $8 and go on sale two hours before the performance. The opera also puts on free performances in Golden Gate Park and Stern Grove during the summer. Check out the company's website or call for dates.

Yerba Buena Center for the Arts
700 Howard St ☎ *415-978-2787* Ⓜ *Powell St BART & Muni station* *12, 15, 30, 45, 76 Muni*
w *www.yerbabuenaarts.org*

The YBCA's eclectic mix of performing arts includes symphonies, ballet, theater, and folk and experimental art forms.

Pocket Opera Company
☎ *415-575-1102* $ *general $27, child/student $13*
w *www.pocketopera.org*

The Pocket Opera was founded in 1978 by a local character named Donald Pippin. Pippin translates librettas into English but remains faithful to the original score, and his company performs in halls around the Bay Area from February to June. In San Francisco, performances are at the Florence Gould Theater in the Palace of the Legion of Honor and at the Temple Emanu-El in the Richmond District.

BALLET

San Francisco Ballet
455 Franklin St ☎ *415-861-5600 information, 415-865-2000 tickets* $ *$7-100, senior/student tickets sometimes available for half-price* Ⓜ *Civic Center BART & Muni station* *42, 47, 49 Muni*
w *www.sfballet.org*

Now under the directorship of Helgi Tomasson, the San Francisco Ballet is one of the USA's oldest ballet companies. The company mostly performs at the War Memorial Opera House, but each season several shows are staged at the Yerba Buena Center for the Arts. Other dance performances take place at a variety of venues around the city, including the Herbst Theatre.

SPECTATOR SPORTS

San Francisco is a Big League city, bub. To clam up the naysayers, the city is home to two long-established professional sports teams. For information on Oakland's teams, see Excursions.

San Francisco 49ers
3Com Park ☎ *415-656-4900* *box office 9am-5pm Mon-Fri, 9am-1pm Sat* $ *$25-100* *Muni shuttles*
w *www.sf49ers.com*

San Francisco's National Football League team, the 49ers, is one of the most successful teams in league history, having brought home no fewer than five Super Bowl championships. In recent years, the team has not been very strong, but fan loyalty has not flagged and tickets can be hard to come by. If you don't get tickets well in advance (try Ticketmaster), your best hope of getting in is by paying high prices to a ticket broker or scalper.

By car, take Hwy 101 south from downtown to the exit for 3Com Park; from there the stadium is easy to find. On game days, Muni operates special bus services from downtown to the stadium.

San Francisco Giants MAP 4
Pacific Bell Park ☎ *415-467-8000* *box office 9am-5pm Mon-Fri, 9am-1pm Sat* $ *$10-45* *15, 30, 42, 45, N Muni*
w *giants.mlb.com*

The city's National League baseball team plays 81 home games from April to October. The team played well in its first season in its intimate new ballpark, Pacific Bell Park, taking the National League West title in 2000. Games are almost always sold out, but season-ticket holders often sell unwanted tickets through the team's website. It's also worth checking Internet auctions like eBay.com and craigslist.org.

ENTERTAINMENT

Shopping

San Francisco's shopping is best and most interesting when you focus on small, quirky, unusual items. Sure, there are big department stores and an international selection of name-brand boutiques, but the oddities of Hayes Valley, the Haight, and the Mission are a lot more fun.

Most stores, especially the tourist-oriented ones, are open every day (though some are closed on Sunday), typically from 9am or 10am to 6pm. Department stores keep later hours, often staying open 'til 8pm or 9pm.

Visitors should not forget the 8.25% San Francisco sales tax, which is lumped on to every item sold and is not, like the European VAT (value-added tax), refundable to foreign visitors. A price 10% lower than the prices back home is going to be almost as expensive, once sales tax is added.

WHERE TO SHOP

Union Square

San Francisco's downtown shopping area is concentrated around Union Square and along nearby Market St, and it is home to some of the most expensive and exclusive retailers. Many of the world's premier designers own shops in the area. This is also where the city's major department stores and one of its largest shopping centers are located.

Macy's MAP 2
170 O'Farrell St ☎ 415-397-3333 ⌚ 10am-8pm Mon-Wed, 10am-9pm Thurs-Sat, 11am-7pm Sun Ⓜ Powell St BART & Muni station 🚍 30, 38, 45 Muni ♿

Macy's, the surviving king of the old guard of American department stores, has several floors of merchandise, with an emphasis on clothing and cosmetics. The men's department is in a separate building across the street.

Neiman-Marcus MAP 2
150 Stockton St ☎ 415-362-3900 ⌚ 10am-7pm Mon-Sat, 10am-6pm Sun Ⓜ Powell St BART & Muni station 🚍 30, 38, 45 Muni ♿

Overlooking Union Square, Nieman-Marcus is an upscale department store. The store's grand entryway and top-floor restaurant lure in those who aren't in need of clothes or cosmetics.

Nordstrom MAP 2
865 Market St ☎ 415-243-8500 ⌚ 9:30am-9pm Mon-Sat, 10am-7pm Sun Ⓜ Powell St BART & Muni station 🚍 Market St buses, F Muni ♿

Nordstrom is a high-end department store in the San Francisco Shopping Centre.

Saks Fifth Avenue MAP 2
384 Post St ☎ 415-986-4300 ⌚ 10am-7pm Mon-Sat, 11am-6pm Sun Ⓜ Powell St BART & Muni station 🚍 30, 38, 45 Muni ♿

The New York–based fashion retailer has a large store on Union Square.

San Francisco Shopping Centre MAP 2
865 Market St ☎ 415-495-5656 ⌚ 9:30am-8pm Mon-Sat, 11am-6pm Sun Ⓜ Powell St BART & Muni station 🚍 Market St buses, F Muni ♿

San Francisco's only central shopping mall, the San Francisco Shopping Centre has 65 stores on nine floors. Nordstrom is the mall's anchor store, and numerous clothing boutiques and a variety of other shops round it out. There's also a food court. A huge new Bloomingdale's is supposed to open next door to the San Francisco Shopping Centre sometime in the next few years.

Hayes Valley

Hayes St between Franklin and Laguna Sts near the Civic Center is a trendy little enclave with a subcultural feel. Most of the shops are stylish little boutiques featuring local and international designers, but there are also stores selling tasteful furniture and housewares. There's no better place to come looking for that interesting Italian glass vase you've been hankering after.

Embarcadero Center

Spanning 4 blocks in the Financial District between Clay and Sacramento Sts not far from the waterfront, the Embarcadero Center is a not altogether successful attempt at mall-making. It's worth a stop if you're in he area, but don't make a special trip – the shops here are generally outposts of larger stores around Union Square, including Banana Republic and the Gap.

South of Market

South of Market is not generally a great shopping part of town – there are specialty stores scattered throughout the area, but the area is not conducive to walking or window-shopping. Close to Market St, the Metreon entertainment complex has a variety of shops worth perusing while waiting for a movie.

Metreon MAP 4
101 4th St ☎ 800-638-7366 ⏲ 10am-10pm Sun-Thurs, 10am-11pm Fri-Sat Ⓜ Powell St & Montgomery St BART & Muni stations 🚌 14, 30, 45 Muni ♿

As a shopping mall, the slick and modern Metreon seems to be modeled on airport terminals where there are no clear divisions between the walkway and the shops – merchandise shelves and cashier stands sort of pop up in your way as you walk through. The mall also creates – probably deliberately – the sense of strolling through an internet browser. Shops are definitely niche-oriented. The **Chronicle Bookstore** carries only esoteric titles by the local publisher. **Wild Things** sells the books of Maurice Sendak, as well as toys inspired by his characters. **Moebius** is an assortment of clothing racks, which at press time featured the graphic design work of J Otto Siebold (Space Monkey T-shirts, etc). At **microsoftSF** (☎ 415-369-6030), patrons can test drive the latest software and video games. For a broader selection of games, head to **PlayStation** (☎ 415-369-6040).

Chinatown

Only Fisherman's Wharf rivals Chinatown for sheer quantity of tourist junk. A stroll down Grant Ave will supply all the postcards, Golden Gate snow globes, and novelty T-shirts you could possibly want. But it's not all tacky souvenirs: many of these stores also sell paper lanterns, silk slippers, jade jewelry, and embroidered tablecloths. Explore the back streets and alleys for bargain-priced cookware and herbal pharmaceuticals.

Fisherman's Wharf

For San Francisco souvenirs, there's no better – or worse – place than Fisherman's Wharf. This garish tourist strip is at its most intense in the claustrophobic shops of Pier 39. The Cannery, Ghirardelli Square, and the Anchorage are other, less frenetic, wharf-front shopping centers.

The Marina & Cow Hollow

Union St in Cow Hollow is dotted with designer boutiques and gift shops. Only a few blocks down toward the bay is Chestnut St in the Marina, where a host of chain stores like the Gap and Pottery Barn cater to a yuppie crowd.

Pacific Heights

Fillmore St north of Geary Blvd and Japantown is lined with cafés, classy clothing shops, and upscale home-furnishing stores. Those with less cash to splash come here for the few secondhand stores, and either way, Fillmore St is a pleasant zone for browsing and window-shopping.

The Haight

Haight St tries hard to sustain its role as a youth-culture mecca; these days it's the place to come for superchunky platform shoes and glam costumes rather than hippie sandals. It's especially good for vintage clothing and music, especially secondhand and older CDs and vinyl. Bear in mind that it can get very crowded on weekends.

The Castro

Castro St and Market St nearby have a bit of everything, including chichi antique shops, men's clothing stores, leather stores, bookshops, and novelty stores, all aimed to one degree or another at an affluent gay crowd. Come as much for the vibe as for what's in the stores.

Noe Valley

Noe Valley's main street is 24th St. This thoroughly San Franciscan strip is far from the tourist throng and is packed with a selection of clothes, books, and food. Since the neighborhood is favored by well-to-do

RICK GERHARTER

Fillmore St in Pacific Heights

families, you'll also find a preponderance of shops filled with maternity wear, kids' recycled clothes, and toys.

The Mission

Valencia St is a hot spot for recycled clothing and secondhand objets d'art. Some stores here specialize in overpriced junky fire salvage, but there are a few places where curios of the past are sold at reasonable prices. The interesting shops are spread out along the strip between 16th and 24th Sts and are interspersed with café-restaurants and household appliance stores selling all the antique stoves and washing machines you might care to bring back home with you. Mission St is lined with Latin American and Chinese shops, some of which are worth perusing for unusual inexpensive imports, like tortilla irons and mariachi CDs.

Farmers' Markets

The local farmers' markets are a true reflection of the region's inventive culinary spirit. The markets are where aspiring chefs can talk produce with local growers, and they're often a good place to grab a tasty, inexpensive snack.

Farmers' Market MAP 3
United Nations Plaza ☎ 415-558-9455 ⌚ 7am-2pm Wed & Sun Ⓜ Civic Center BART & Muni station 🚌 Market St buses, F Muni ♿

This market, more down-to-earth than the one at Ferry Plaza (see below), has stalls stacked with whatever is in season, some of which is organic. Go early to get the best stuff, or late for bargain bags of the tailings.

Ferry Plaza Farmers' Market
MAP 5 & MAP 6
Justin Herman Plaza on Tues; cnr Embarcadero & Green St on Sat ☎ 415-353-5650 ⌚ 10:30am-2:30pm Tues, 8am-1:30pm Sat Ⓜ Embarcadero BART & Muni station 🚌 F Muni ♿

This farmers' market, with two locations and a fluctuating schedule, is a lively and eye-catching event. It's a ramshackle cornucopia of organic produce from local growers, an uncommon assortment of familiar and unusual varieties of fruits and vegetables. Although most tourists won't have immediate access to a kitchen, they will surely agree that this is a great place to get an inside look at what's happening on the local culinary scene. Ready-to-eat foods are also sold.

San Francisco Flower Mart MAP 4
640 Brannan St ☎ 415-781-8410 ⌚ 10am-3pm Mon-Sat 🚌 27, 42 Muni

Although you won't find food here, you will find fresh flowers. This market, bringing more than 80 florists and plant vendors together in a single venue, is the city's best place to buy fresh-cut flowers, but it's quite a trek from downtown. Some vendors accept credit cards.

WHAT TO BUY

Books

San Francisco is a bookish city, and the Bay Area is second only to New York as a publishing center. There are many interesting specialty stores in the city, but true bibliophiles should also venture to the East Bay to explore Berkeley's superb selection of bookshops (see Excursions).

GENERAL BOOKSTORES The national chain bookstores have established them selves in San Francisco, but the city contin-ues to support its independent booksellers. Many bookstores are open late every night of the week.

Borders Books and Music MAP 2
400 Post St ☎ 415-399-1633 ⌚ 9am-11pm Mon-Thurs, 9am-midnight Fri-Sat, 9am-9pm Sun Ⓜ Powell St BART & Muni station 🚌 2, 3, 76, 30, 45 Muni 🚋 Powell-Mason, Powell-Hyde cable cars ♿

The national chain superstore is San Francisco's largest bookstore. Escalators quietly whisk patrons from floor to floor. The top floor is devoted to CDs, and there's a café on the 2nd floor.

Rizzoli Bookstore MAP 2
117 Post St ☎ 415-984-0225 ⌚ 10am-7pm Mon-Sat, 10:30am-6pm Sun 🚌 15, 30, 45 Muni, Market St buses ♿

Rizzoli, specializing in art, photography, and architecture books, is a pleasant place to spend some time. There's a quiet café and a small selection of world music CDs on the top floor.

A Clean Well-Lighted Place for Books MAP 3
601 Van Ness Ave ☎ 415-441-6670 ⌚ 10am-11pm Mon-Sat, 10am-9pm Sun 🚌 42, 47, 49 Muni ♿

This is one of the city's better general bookstores, selling new copies only, and it holds many author readings.

City Lights MAP 6
261 Columbus Ave ☎ 415-362-8193 ⌚ 10am-midnight daily 🚌 12, 15, 30, 41, 45 Muni

San Francisco's most famous bookstore was the first paperbacks-only bookshop in the USA and has always been at the cutting edge of writing and literature. It was the center of the Beat scene in the '50s and is still owned by its founder, poet Lawrence Ferlinghetti. It's a wonderful place to browse late at night, and the poetry room upstairs has the best selection around.

Books Inc MAP 12
2275 Market St ☎ 415-864-6777 ⌚ 9:30am-11pm Mon-Sat, 9:30am-10pm Sun Ⓜ Castro St Muni station 🚌 F Muni ♿

The western USA's oldest independent bookstore, Books Inc has an impressive array of new titles and a particularly sizable selection of gay and lesbian titles.

Garage & Sidewalk Sales

On spring and summer weekends, garage sales and sidewalk sales spring up in many parts of San Francisco; with the possible exception of Pacific Heights, all residential neighborhoods make good hunting grounds. The Mission, particularly along Dolores St, is especially worth checking out. The best way to find a garage sale is simply to head out for a stroll on a sunny Saturday or Sunday.

Book Passage
51 Tamal Vista Blvd, Corte Madera ☎ 415-927-0960, 800-999-7909 ⌚ 10am-10pm Sun-Thurs, 10am-11pm Fri-Sat ♿

If you find yourself in Marin, stop by Book Passage. One of the best bookstores in the Bay Area, it has a nice cafe, an especially good travel section, and in the evenings the store often hosts author readings and slide shows.

USED BOOKSTORES San Francisco has several decent used bookstores but lacks the really great emporium that you might expect of a booksmart city such as this one.

Acorn Books MAP 7
1436 Polk St ☎ 415-563-1736 ⌚ 10:30am-8pm Mon-Sat, noon-7pm Sun 🚌 1, 19 Muni 🚋 California St cable car ♿

Acorn is the best place to find rare San Franciscana. Otherwise, despite the impressive space, this isn't a great store – unpleasant staff and high prices don't help.

Dog Eared Books MAP 14
900 Valencia St ☎ 415-282-1901 ⌚ 10am-10pm Mon-Sat, 10am-8pm Sun 🚌 14, 26, 49 Muni ♿

Dog Eared Books has strong selections of mysteries and gay and lesbian titles and a decent rack of alternative magazines and adult comic books.

Green Apple Books MAP 15
506 Clement St ☎ 415-387-2272 ⌚ 10am-10:30pm Sun-Thurs, 10am-11:30pm Fri-Sat 🚌 1, 2, 4, 38 Muni ♿ limited

Green Apple is one of the best bookstores in the city, with a large selection of new and used titles shelved in an odd assortment of rooms. This is a good place to find interesting books you weren't even looking for.

RICK GERHARTER

You'll spend hours browsing in Green Apple.

SPECIALTY BOOKSTORES There are plenty of places around town where you can browse and buy books on your esoteric hobby.

Kayo Books MAP 3
814 Post St ☎ 415-749-0554 ⏲ 11am-6pm Wed-Sun 🚌 2, 3, 4, 76 Muni ♿ limited

If you're fresh off the Dashiell Hammett tour of the Tenderloin and Union Square area, you might want to stop by here for some supplementary reading. Kayo's always has a great stock of vintage mystery paperbacks, along with an indecent selection of pulp sleaze and other esoteric genres.

Friends of Photography Bookstore MAP 4
655 Mission St ☎ 415-495-7242 ⏲ 11am-6pm daily 🚌 14, 15, 30, 45 Muni ♿

Just off the entrance to the Ansel Adams Museum, this store specializes in large-format photography books.

Rand McNally MAP 4
595 Market St ☎ 415-777-3131 ⏲ 9am-7pm Mon-Fri, 10am-6pm Sat, 11am-5pm Sun Ⓜ Montgomery St BART & Muni station 🚌 Market St buses, F Muni ♿

The Rand McNally store is a great source for travel books and maps.

William Stout Design Books MAP 4
27A South Park Ave ☎ 415-495-6757 ⏲ 11am-5:30pm Tues-Fri, 11:30am-5pm Sat 🚌 15, 30, 45 Muni

Stout's SoMa shop offers a choice selection of art and design books, including hard-to-find imports.

Thomas Bros Books and Maps MAP 5
550 Jackson St ☎ 415-981-7520 ⏲ 9:30am-5:30pm Mon-Fri 🚌 15, 41 Muni ♿

Thomas Bros, a company noted for its detailed maps, operates this store near North Beach and Chinatown. It specializes in travel books and, of course, maps.

William Stout Architectural Books MAP 5
804 Montgomery St ☎ 415-391-6757 ⏲ 10am-6:30pm Mon-Fri, 10am-5:30pm Sat 🚌 15, 41 Muni

This stylish little shop is jam-packed with a rich and comprehensive collection of books on architecture and industrial design.

Builders Booksource MAP 8
900 North Point St ☎ 415-440-5773 ⏲ 10am-9pm Mon-Sat, 10am-6pm Sun 🚌 19, 30, 42 Muni ♿

This store has an inspiring range of books on architecture, gardening, and interior design.

Kinokuniya Bookshop MAP 10
1581 Webster St ☎ 415-567-7625 ⏲ 10:30am-8pm daily 🚌 22, 38 Muni ♿

In Japantown, this store features a huge assortment of books in Japanese, including plenty of manga comic books, and a wide assortment of Asia-related titles in English.

Marcus Books MAP 10
1712 Fillmore St ☎ 415-346-4222 ⏲ 10am-7pm Mon-Sat, noon-5pm Sun 🚌 2, 3, 4, 22 Muni ♿

Marcus Books specializes in books by authors from Africa or of African descent. It's been around since 1960 and is an important force in the local African American community.

Bound Together Anarchist Collective Bookstore MAP 11
1369 Haight St ☎ 415-431-8355 ⏲ approximately 11:30am-7:30pm daily 🚌 6, 7, 71 Muni

If you're an anarchist, here's where you go to recharge your rebellious spirit and stock up on radical literature.

Comix Experience MAP 11
305 Divisadero St ☎ 415-863-9258 ⏲ 11am-7pm Mon-Sat, noon-5pm Sun 🚌 6, 7, 24, 66, 71 Muni ♿

Geared toward the interests of mature comic

RICHARD CUMMINS

Bound Together: A radical intellectual's heaven

book aficionados, Comix Experience carries alternative and underground work by the likes of Crumb, Clowes, and Sala, as well as the latest (and reissued) portrayals of some of your favorite action heroes.

A Different Light Bookstore MAP 12
489 Castro St ☎ 415-431-0891 ⊙ 10am-10pm Sun-Thurs, 10am-11pm Fri-Sat Ⓜ Castro St Muni station 🚌 24, F Muni ♿

A Different Light is the largest gay and lesbian bookseller in the US and features author readings many nights at 7:30pm.

Get Lost MAP 12
1825 Market St ☎ 415-437-0529 ⊙ 10am-7pm Mon-Fri, 10am-6pm Sat, 11am-5pm Sun Ⓜ Church St Muni station 🚌 F Muni ♿

Travelers will want to get to Get Lost, a personable little gem of a shop specializing in travel books, maps, and atlases; it also stocks globes and luggage.

San Francisco Mystery Bookstore MAP 13
4175 24th St ☎ 415-282-7444 ⊙ 11:30am-5:30pm Tues-Thurs, 11:30am-8pm Fri-Sat 🚌 24, 35, 48 Muni ♿

Detective-fiction freaks should head to the SF Mystery Bookstore, where new and used, in-print and out-of-print titles are stocked.

Books & Periodicals MAP 14
2929 24th St ☎ 415-282-2994 ⊙ 11am-4pm Tues-Sat 🚌 27, 48 Muni ♿

This is the place to head for books in Chinese, as well as books in English about China. Of particular interest is the selection of Chinese folklore books for children.

Newspapers & Magazines

If the local presses don't give you all you're looking for, the variety offered by San Francisco's news- and magazine-focused shops will be more satisfying.

Café de la Presse MAP 2
352 Grant Ave ☎ 415-398-2680 ⊙ 7am-11pm daily 🚌 2, 3, 4, 76 Muni ♿

This pleasant café sells European newspapers and magazines.

Harold's International Newsstand MAP 2
454 Geary St ☎ 415-441-2665 ⊙ 7am-11pm daily Ⓜ Powell St BART & Muni station 🚌 38 Muni 🚋 Powell-Mason, Powell-Hyde cable cars ♿

A block away from Union Square, Harold's offers the city's best selection of newspapers from around the country and the world, and it also has a wide offering of magazines of all types.

Records & CDs

San Francisco has a few chain superstores that emphasize current rock, pop, and hip-hop releases and strive to offer a well-rounded selection of all musical styles. But the city's strength is in small independent stores that cater to more marginal tastes.

Virgin Megastore MAP 2
2 Stockton St ☎ 415-397-4525 ⊙ 9am-11pm Mon-Thurs, 9am-midnight Fri-Sat, 10am-11pm Sun Ⓜ Powell St BART & Muni station 🚌 30, 45, F Muni ♿

If sheer scale is what you're after, visit Virgin's downtown store, with two floors of CDs, a floor of games and DVDs, listening stations, and a café.

Tower Records MAP 7
2525 Jones St ☎ 415-885-0500 ⊙ 9am-midnight daily 🚌 30, 42 Muni ♿

For a large, general selection of CDs, Tower is the ever-dependable standby. It also offers a good selection of periodicals and 'zines, and the classical annex, across the street from the main store, is exceptional.

Amoeba Records MAP 11
1855 Haight St ☎ 415-831-1200 ⊙ 10:30am-10pm Mon-Sat, 11am-9pm Sun 🚌 7, 66, 71 Muni ♿

This huge emporium, in a former bowling alley, is the city's best source for interesting new and used records and CDs in nearly every genre. Thoroughly inspecting three or four of its better sections (rock, jazz, blues, hip-hop, reggae) will keep you occupied for hours. The store often features live performances.

Jack's Record Cellar MAP 11
254 Scott St ☎ 415-431-3047 ⏲ noon-7pm Wed-Sun 🚌 6, 7, 24, 66, 71 Muni ♿

The city's longest-running record store still specializes in 78rpm discs. For jazz and R&B enthusiasts, it's a great place to browse, even if you sold your turntable years ago.

Open Mind Music MAP 11
342 Divisadero St ☎ 415-621-2244 ⏲ 11am-9pm Mon-Sat, noon-8pm Sun 🚌 6, 7, 24, 66, 71 Muni ♿

Open Mind primarily fulfills the needs of DJs and electronica fanatics, with a broad selection of birth, school, house, death, and ambient LPs.

Spundae Reckords + CDs MAP 11
678 Haight St ☎ 415-575-1580 ⏲ 1pm-7pm Mon, noon-8pm Tues-Sat, 1pm-6pm Sun 🚌 6, 7, 22, 66, 71 Muni ♿

Spundae Reckords is the place to go if you need to have the latest house mixes on 12-inch singles. The store also carries some CDs.

Grooves MAP 12
1797 Market St ☎ 415-436-9933 ⏲ 11am-7pm Mon-Tues & Thurs-Sun, 1pm-7pm Wed 🚌 F Muni ♿

Dedicated solely to the LP and emphasizing jazz, blues, country, and rock, the bins at Grooves are always worth perusing. The store also offers a free search service for rare finds.

Tower Records MAP 12
2280 Market St ☎ 415-621-0588 ⏲ 9am-midnight daily Ⓜ Castro St Muni station 🚌 37, F Muni ♿

A small Tower store with a general selection is located in the Castro.

Streetlight Records MAP 13
3979 24th St ☎ 415-282-3550 ⏲ 10am-10pm Mon-Sat, 10:30am-9pm Sun 🚌 24, 48 Muni ♿

The Noe Valley branch of Streetlight, a Northern California chain, has a healthy mix of new and used records, CDs, and tapes. No section stands out, but it's worth a look for the odd marked-down item. Another good branch is in the Castro (see Map 12).

Aquarius Records MAP 14
1055 Valencia St ☎ 415-647-2272 ⏲ 10am-9pm Mon-Wed, 10am-10pm Thurs-Sun 🚌 14, 26, 49 Muni ♿

For underground music, check out Aquarius, which stocks a limited but choice selection of punk, garage, experimental, and odd import CDs, among other things. Staff are helpful.

Discolandia MAP 14
2964 24th St ☎ 415-826-9446 ⏲ 11:30am-

Welcome to the Fun House

San Francisco demolished its amusement park, Playland on the Beach, decades ago, but the city seems to long for the days when amusements were meant to delight, terrify, and horrify all at the same time. A number of shops in the city are cashing in on that oft-neglected side of human nature.

Quantity Postcards MAP 6
1441 Grant Ave ☎ 415-986-8866 ⏲ 11am-6pm Sun-Thurs, 11am-11pm Fri-Sat (hours can vary) Ⓒ MC, V 🚌 15, 30, 41, 45 Muni ♿
Ⓦ www.tiltpix.com

Quantity is a purveyor of rare and weird – OK, sometimes very weird – postcards. It's impossible to visit this shop without developing an overwhelming urge to send a card to some long-lost friend. The antique pinball machines and arcade relics (not for sale) are enough reason to drop by.

Happy Trails MAP 11
1615 Haight St ☎ 415-431-7232 ⏲ 11am-7:30pm daily 🚌 7, 66, 71 Muni ♿

Happy Trails sells reproductions of American pop curios, tiki novelties, and a lot of other things you don't need but might want anyway.

Uncle Mame MAP 12
2241 Market St ☎ 415-626-1953 ⏲ 2pm-7pm Mon, noon-7pm Wed & Fri-Sat, noon-5pm Sun Ⓒ MC, V 🚌 F Muni ♿
Ⓦ www.unclemame.com

This Castro District store specializes in the nostalgic and the scatological. It's a naughty, Pee Wee Herman-esque take on the past, with Charlie's Angels lunch boxes, Pez dispensers, and gay Ken dolls.

6:30pm Mon-Sat, noon-4pm Sun 🚌 *27, 48 Muni* ♿

Deep in the Mission, Discolandia is the oldest Latin-music store in the Bay Area, and it's a good source for merengue, salsa, and Tejano CDs. It also sells Spanish-language periodicals, comics, and pulp novels.

Flat Plastic Sound MAP 15
24 Clement St ☎ *415-386-5095* 🕘 *11am-7pm Mon-Sat, noon-6pm Sun* 🚌 *1, 2, 4, 38 Muni* ♿

Flat Plastic Sound stocks classical, jazz, and country vinyl.

Rock Memorabilia

As you would expect, San Francisco's not a bad place to shop for rock and roll posters and artwork from the '60s onward. In addition to the following listing, Amoeba (see Records & CDs, earlier) has a nice selection of vintage and reprint concert posters.

Rock Posters & Collectibles MAP 6
1851 Powell St 🕘 *10am-6pm Tues-Sat* 🚌 *15, 30 Muni* ♿

This small shop has many of the famous '60s concert posters from the Fillmore Auditorium, as well as handbills and some original artwork. The shop also carries more recent memorabilia from the punk era and later.

Musical Instruments

Like any music-minded city, San Francisco has the usual powerhouse guitar store where rockers can gather all their rad gear. For these, check the yellow pages. But the city offers a pair of unique shops worth highlighting for their selections of international folk instruments.

Clarion Music Center MAP 5
816 Sacramento St ☎ *415-391-1317* 🕘 *11am-6pm Mon-Fri, 9am-5pm Sat* 🚌 *1, 30, 45 Muni* ♿

In the middle of Chinatown, this fascinating shop sells an array of merchandise, including Asian string instruments, African congas, Central American marimbas, an indescribable variety of percussion instruments, and gongs galore.

Lark in the Morning MAP 8
2801 Leavenworth St ☎ *415-922-4277* 🕘 *10am-6pm daily* 🚌 *30, 42 Muni* 🚋 *Powell-Hyde cable car* ♿

Lark in the Morning is a world musician's fondest wish, with a staggering assortment of instruments and recordings, from gypsy guitars and accordions to bagpipes and experimental noisemakers.

Fashion

San Francisco is a stylish city where the style spectrum is far-ranging and diverse. Anything goes, from sharp tailored suits to retro to drag extravagance, and everything in between.

For mainstream fashions, Union Square department stores (see earlier in this chapter) can take care of pretty much all your needs. If money's no object, that neighborhood's streets are lined with designer outlets and boutiques.

Additionally, San Francisco is the hometown of Levi Strauss and the Gap chain stores, which include Banana Republic and Old Navy.

Banana Republic MAP 2
256 Grant Ave ☎ *415-788-3087* 🕘 *9:30am-8pm Mon-Sat, 11am-7pm Sun* 🚌 *2, 3, 4, 30, 45, 76 Muni* ♿

The Gap's upmarket cousin occupies the huge White House building and capably fills it with sleek, toned-down styles – Gap clothing you can wear to the office – as well as a limited selection of housewares.

The Gap MAP 2
890 Market St ☎ *415-788-5909* 🕘 *9:30am-9pm Mon-Sat, 10am-7pm Sun* Ⓜ *Powell St BART & Muni station* 🚌 *Market St buses, F Muni* 🚋 *Powell-Mason, Powell-Hyde cable cars* ♿

This is ground zero for the Gap, the international clothing company. It's an enormous store, with two floors and a children's wing loaded with those familiar Gap styles and Gap colors and shelf after shelf of khakis.

The Levi's Store MAP 2
300 Post St ☎ *415-501-0100* 🕘 *10am-8pm Mon-Sat, 11am-6pm Sun* 🚌 *30, 45, 76 Muni* 🚋 *Powell-Mason, Powell-Hyde cable cars* ♿

Levi's huge new flagship store is really just a three-dimensional, interactive commercial, as oversized flagship stores tend to be. You don't really need to come here if you're just looking for a standard pair of 501s, but if you're after that funky cut that no one else has or a style

Levi Strauss

San Francisco's most famous contribution to sartorial elegance is a reliable pair of Levi's jeans. A German gold-rush immigrant, the 21-year-old Levi Strauss arrived from New York in 1850 burdened with materials from his brothers' store. When he'd sold everything except the sailcloth, he struck on the idea of using it to make indestructible pants for hard-working miners. He founded Levi's with his brothers in 1853. The riveted-pockets idea was patented in 1873, and the word 'denim' was also a Levi Strauss invention: when *serge* from Nîmes, France, was substituted for sailcloth, the *'serge de Nîmes'* became 'denim.'

the company fazed out decades ago, and are willing to pay Soviet black-market prices for it, then this place is hog heaven.

Old Navy MAP 2
801 Market St ☎ 415-344-0375 ⌚ 9:30am-9pm Mon-Sat, 11am-8pm Sun Ⓜ Powell St BART & Muni station 🚌 9, 30, 45, F Muni ♿
When the Gap ceased being a cheap clothing chain, the company opened up Old Navy to fill the need. Reasonably priced everyday clothing is the specialty here. Of all Union Square's stores this one, resplendent with campy '50s slogans, is perhaps the most visually entertaining.

DESIGNER CLOTHING Of course, all the international designers – Versace, Armani, and their snazzy ilk – have a presence in the high-profile Union Square area. Without going into great detail, what follows is a selective list of some lesser-known but equally chic fashion moguls with boutiques in San Francisco.

Agnès B MAP 2
33 Grant Ave ☎ 415-772-9995 ⌚ 11am-7pm Mon-Sat, 11am-5pm Sun Ⓜ Montgomery St BART & Muni station 🚌 9, 15, 30, 45, F Muni
This shop carries simple but pretty styles for women.

Betsey Johnson MAP 2
160 Geary St ☎ 415-398-2516 ⌚ 10am-6pm Mon-Sat, noon-5pm Sun Ⓜ Powell St BART & Muni station 🚌 9, 30, 38, 45 Muni ♿
These racks are alive with the New York–based designer's exuberant styles.

MAC (men's store) MAP 2
5 Claude Lane ☎ 415-837-0615 ⌚ 11am-6pm Mon-Sat, noon-5pm Sun 🚌 2, 3, 4, 15, 76 Muni
This is MAC's men's shop filled with designer and retro gear, natty ties, and a selection of vintage French garments.

Wilkes Bashford MAP 2
375 Sutter St ☎ 415-986-4380 ⌚ 10am-6pm Mon-Sat 🚌 2, 3, 4, 30, 45, 76 Muni ♿
Wilkes Bashford has seven flights of expensive, conservative, high-quality clothes for men and women.

Manifesto MAP 3
514 Octavia St ☎ 415-431-4778 ⌚ 10am-6pm Wed & Fri, 10am-7pm Thurs, 11am-6pm Sat, noon-5pm Sun 🚌 21 Muni
The shop sells original, retro-inspired handmade clothes and accessories for women and men.

Nomads MAP 3
556 Hayes St ☎ 415-864-5692 ⌚ 11am-7pm Mon-Sat, 11am-6pm Sun 🚌 21 Muni ♿
Casual menswear by local designers is sold at Nomads.

Jeremy's MAP 4
2 South Park Ave ☎ 415-882-4929 ⌚ 11am-7pm Mon-Fri, 11am-6pm Sat, 11am-5pm Sun 🚌 15, 30, 42, 45, 76 Muni
Last season's big-name designer duds and select secondhand threads are at jaw-dropping bargain prices (for men and women).

Martha Egan MAP 5
1 Columbus Ave ☎ 415-397-5451 ⌚ 11am-6pm Tues-Sat 🚌 1, 15, 41 Muni
A local designer fashions contemporary clothes with vintage fabrics and designs for women and men.

MAC (women's store) MAP 6
1543 Grant Ave ☎ 415-837-1604 ⌚ 11am-6pm Mon-Sat, noon-5pm Sun 🚌 15, 30 41, 45 Muni
MAC's women's branch has some exquisite outfits.

Uko MAP 9
2070 Union St ☎ 415-563-0330 ⌚ 11am-6:30pm Mon-Sat, noon-5:30pm Sun 🚌 41, 45 Muni ♿

Uko has garments for men and women, made from lovely fabrics, and carries a good range of accessories.

Ambiance MAP 11
1458 Haight St ☎ 415-552-5095 ⌚ 10am-7pm Mon-Sat, 11am-7pm Sun 🚌 6, 7, 66, 71 Muni ♿

Ambiance has casual and dressy women's clothing, plus period-inspired hats and jewelry.

Rabat MAP 13
4001 24th St ☎ 415-282-7861 ⌚ 10am-6:30pm Mon-Fri, 10am-6pm Sat, 11am-5:30pm Sun 🚌 24, 48 Muni ♿

You'll find snazzy shoes for guys and gals and drapey, sumptuous clothes for women.

VINTAGE CLOTHING When Aunt Louise and Uncle Ernie put on weight and had to get entirely new wardrobes, their old dresses, slacks, shoes, and hats ended up in a number of shops around town. This is why in San Francisco you're better off shopping for old clothes than new. Haight St is bumper-to-bumper with hand-me-down boutiques, and others can be found scattered all over the city.

560 Hayes St MAP 3
560 Hayes St ☎ 415-861-7993 ⌚ noon-7pm Mon-Fri, 11am-6pm Sat-Sun 🚌 21 Muni ♿

Known only by its street address, 560 Hayes is jam-packed with a particularly classy selection of recycled clothes.

Buffalo Exchange MAP 7
1800 Polk St ☎ 415-346-5726 ⌚ 11am-7pm Mon-Sat, noon-6pm Sun 🚌 1, 19, 27 Muni ♿

Buffalo's Polk St branch has the same appeal as its Haight St store.

Leopard Room MAP 7
1825 Polk St ☎ 415-923-0175 ⌚ noon-7pm Mon-Fri, noon-5pm Sat, noon-6pm Sun 🚌 12, 19 Muni ♿

These snazzy threads are left over from the FDR years on through the Eisenhower years.

American Rag MAP 10
1305 Van Ness Ave ☎ 415-474-5214 ⌚ 10am-9pm Mon-Sat, noon-7pm Sun 🚌 2, 3, 4, 42, 47, 49, 76 Muni ♿

This is a huge store with shoes and new and recycled clothes. Prices can be outrageous, but it's a good place for one-stop shopping.

Aardvark's MAP 11
1501 Haight St ☎ 415-621-3141 ⌚ 11am-7pm daily 🚌 6, 7, 66, 71 Muni ♿

Here you'll get all the funky '70s garb you need to get the attention of the people you're trying to impress.

Buffalo Exchange MAP 11
1555 Haight St ☎ 415-431-7733 ⌚ 11am-7pm Mon-Sat, noon-7pm Sun 🚌 6, 7, 66, 71 Muni ♿

This is the sort of place where you might trade in the clothes you're wearing for an entirely new outfit (though you'll probably have to drop a few bills, too). It's a good spot to grab a well-worn pair of jeans or a smart-looking shirt.

Held Over MAP 11
1543 Haight St ☎ 415-864-0818 ⌚ 11am-7pm Sun-Thurs, 11am-8:30pm Fri-Sat 🚌 7, 66, 71 Muni ♿

For serious vintage-fashion victims, Held Over is well stocked in leather jackets, tuxedos, concert T-shirts, and wild-and-crazy plaid slacks.

La Rosa Vintage MAP 11
1171 Haight St ☎ 415-668-3744 ⌚ noon-7pm daily 🚌 7, 66, 71 Muni ♿

La Rosa features very select, high-class merchandise of movie-set caliber – no bargains here.

Sparky's Trading Co MAP 11
1732 Haight St ☎ 415-387-5053 ⌚ 11am-7pm daily 🚌 7, 66, 71 Muni ♿

Sparky's features vintage swingwear and uptight salespeople.

Wasteland MAP 11
1660 Haight St ☎ 415-863-3150 ⌚ 11am-7pm Sun-Thurs, 11am-8pm Fri-Sat 🚌 7, 66, 71 Muni ♿

This emporium-sized grab bag is packed with bargain-priced hand-me-downs from the '70s onward.

Guys & Dolls MAP 13
3789 24th St ☎ 415-285-7174 ⌚ 11am-7pm Mon-Fri, 11am-6pm Sat, noon-6pm Sun 🚌 48, J Muni ♿

Pick up some well-preserved clothes and accessories from the Swing Era.

Clothes Contact MAP 14
473 Valencia St ☎ 415-621-3212 ⌚ 11am-7pm Mon-Sat, noon-7pm Sun Ⓜ 16th St BART station 🚌 22, 26 Muni ♿

This place is a grab bag that sells rumpled clothing by the pound ($8 per pound). A single item of clothing usually costs $8 or less.

OUTRÉ CLOTHING With a large gay population and many public events requiring people to dress outrageously, it's little surprise San Francisco has its share of costume shops, where drama queens, disco kings, glamour-pusses, cowpokes, and circus clowns are guaranteed to find exactly what they're looking for.

Costumes on Haight MAP 11
735 Haight St ☎ 415-621-1356 ⌚ 11am-7pm Mon-Sat, noon-6pm Sun 🚌 6, 7, 22, 66, 71 Muni ♿

This isn't a bad place to search for that unique new or used psychedelic shirt or a mask, wig, or clown suit.

Adults Only

If the shops listed under the 'Outré Clothing' heading don't quite address all of your very adult needs, there's a very mature store in the Mission District.

Good Vibrations MAP 14
1210 Valencia St ☎ 415-974-8980, 800-289-8423 ⌚ 11am-7pm Mon-Tues, 11am-8pm Wed-Sun Ⓒ AE, D, MC, V Ⓜ 24th St BART station 🚌 14, 26, 48, 49 Muni ♿ Ⓦ www.goodvibes.com

In the Mission District, this tasteful shop sells all the various tools, toys, and accessories you will need for your adult entertainment needs. It specializes in vibrators of all types and sizes, as well as other paraphernalia, such as sex toys, books, and videos. It also has the most inexpensive condoms in the city. The antique vibrator exhibit, with many outdated models resembling 1950s kitchen appliances, is quite fascinating.

Piedmont Boutique MAP 11
1452 Haight St ☎ 415-864-8075 ⌚ 11am-7pm daily 🚌 7, 66, 71 Muni ♿

For totally outrageous glam attire – pink feather boas, purple wigs, Travolta disco suits, and imaginative undergarments – and all the chintzy accessories you'll need to customize your get up, head straight to this happening little shop.

Positively Haight St MAP 11
1400 Haight St ☎ 415-252-8747 ⌚ 10am-8pm Mon-Sat, 11am-7pm Sun 🚌 6, 7, 66, 71 Muni ♿

This is your one-stop shop for tie-dye T-shirts and hippie pants for die-hard Deadheads.

Image Leather MAP 12
2199 Market St ☎ 415-621-7551 ⌚ 9am-10pm Mon-Sat, 11am-7pm Sun Ⓜ Church St Muni station 🚌 22, F Muni ♿

Image Leather is a hard-core leather and fetish gear shop with a dildo exhibit down in its 'dungeon.'

Stormy Leather MAP 12
582C Castro St ☎ 415-671-1295 ⌚ noon-7pm Mon, Wed-Thurs, & Sat-Sun, noon-8pm Fri Ⓜ Castro St Muni station 🚌 24 Muni

This is the place to go for far-out and standard leather duds. Another branch is South of Market at 1158 Howard St.

Worn Out West MAP 12
582 Castro St ☎ 415-431-6020 ⌚ noon-7pm Mon-Thurs & Sat-Sun, noon-8pm Fri Ⓜ Castro St Muni station 🚌 24 Muni

This is the place to find Stetson hats, western shirts, chaps, cowboy boots, and, er, gas masks.

Foxy Lady Boutique MAP 14
2644 Mission St ☎ 415-285-4980 ⌚ 10am-6pm Mon-Thurs, 10am-7pm Fri-Sat 🚌 14, 49 Muni ♿

If you're a lady, but not quite foxy, maybe you just need to visit this store. Some wild lingerie, a pair of knee-high boots, and a fake fur will make you irresistible.

SHOES San Francisco has some wonderful shoe shops.

Niketown MAP 2
278 Post St ☎ 415-392-6453 ⌚ 10am-8pm Mon-Sat, 11am-7pm Sun Ⓜ Powell St BART & Muni station 🚌 2, 3, 4, 30, 45 Muni ♿

This is an absurdly large temple to the sporting gear gods.

Bulo MAP 3
418 Hayes St ☎ 415-255-4939 ⌚ 11:30am-6:30pm Mon-Sat, noon-6pm Sun 🚌 21 Muni ♿

The women's store carries exotic little numbers imported from Italy; Bulo's men's shop is across the street.

Gimme Shoes MAP 3
416 Hayes St ☎ 415-864-0691 ⌚ 11am-6:30pm Mon-Sat, noon-6pm Sun 🚌 21 Muni ♿

Gimme Shoes has a nice assortment of European imports; another shop is in Pacific Heights (see Map 10).

Insolent MAP 6
1418 Grant Ave ☎ 415-788-3334 ⌚ 11am-7pm Mon-Sat, 11am-6pm Sun 🚌 15, 30, 41, 45 Muni ♿

Head here for stylish and flashy Italian and Portuguese footwear.

Kenneth Cole MAP 9
2078 Union St ☎ 415-346-0285 ⌚ 10am-8pm Mon-Sat, 11am-6pm Sun 🚌 41, 45 Muni ♿

The New York designer has styles for men and women, from dressy to outdoorsy.

John Fluevog Shoes MAP 11
1697 Haight St ☎ 415-436-9784 ⌚ 11am-7pm Mon-Sat, noon-6pm Sun 🚌 7, 66, 71 Muni ♿

If you want platforms, Fluevog carries the classiest of wild styles.

HATS Mayor Willie Brown has angered a lot of San Franciscans, but there's still no denying the man looks great in a hat. The dashing mayor may inspire you to dash into the nearest haberdashery.

Mrs Dewson's Hats MAP 10
2050 Fillmore St ☎ 415-346-1600 ⌚ 11am-6pm Tues-Sat, noon-4pm Sun 🚌 1, 22 Muni ♿

Mrs Dewson sells hats for men and for women, including some beautiful numbers imported from Italy. The pricey 'Willie Brim,' favored by Mayor Brown ($275 a pop), is very stylin' indeed.

Antiques & Bric-a-Brac

If you're furnishing a 17th-century chateau in the South of France or if you just like to pretend you are, the city's prime shopping area for upmarket antiques is Jackson Square. For antiques with less polish and more quirk – the sort of thing that wouldn't look sorely out of place in a walk-up apartment – stroll the stretch of Market St that runs through the Civic Center district. Also try along Gough St near Market, and along Valencia St in the Mission. (You might also want to rummage thrift stores, listed later in this chapter.)

De Vera MAP 2
580 Sutter St ☎ 415-989-0988 ⌚ 10am-6pm Mon-Sat 🚌 2, 3, 4, 76 Muni ♿

In an elegant gallery, you'll find lovely hand-blown glassware from Italy and elsewhere. There's also an interesting array of jewelry and trinkets.

Folk Art International MAP 2
140 Maiden Lane ☎ 415-392-9999 ⌚ 10am-6pm Mon-Sat Ⓜ Powell St BART & Muni station 🚌 30, 45 Muni ♿

This mix of antique and contemporary handmade objects comes from Africa, Asia, and elsewhere.

Gump's MAP 2
135 Post St ☎ 415-982-1616 ⌚ 10am-6pm Mon-Sat Ⓜ Montgomery St BART & Muni station 🚌 2, 3, 4, 15, 30, 45, 76 Muni ♿

This San Francisco institution has two floors of home furnishings, glassware, ceramics, and some wonderful Asian art pieces.

Zeitgeist Timepieces & Jewelry MAP 3
437B Hayes St ☎ 415-864-0185 ⌚ noon-6pm Tues-Sat 🚌 21 Muni ♿

This is the city's best source for vintage watches and repair.

J Goldsmith Antiques MAP 7
1924 Polk St ☎ 415-771-4055 ⌚ noon-6pm Mon-Fri, noon-5:30pm Sat 🚌 12, 19, 27 Muni ♿

Prices are pretty reasonable on thoughtfully assembled Americana, with lots of old toys, 19th-century photos, World's Fair collector's items, and tools.

Naomi's MAP 7
1817 Polk St ☎ 415-775-1207 ⌚ 11am-6pm Tues-Sat 🚌 12, 19, 27 Muni ♿

A great range of vintage American tableware and crockery is for sale, including thousands of art deco teapots. Delivery service is available.

Cradle of the Sun MAP 13
3848 24th St ☎ 415-821-7667 ⏲ 10am-6pm Tues-Sat, 1pm-4pm Sun 🚌 48, J Muni ♿
This tiny shop has all the stained-glass vases, lamps, and window adornments you need for that Victorian fixer-upper you just bought.

Studio 24 MAP 14
2857 24th St ☎ 415-826-8009 ⏲ noon-6pm Wed-Sun 🚌 27, 48 Muni ♿
Studio 24 is next to Galería de la Raza and sells top-notch Mexican handicrafts.

X-21 Modern MAP 14
890 Valencia St ☎ 415-647-4211 ⏲ noon-6pm Mon-Thurs, noon-7pm Fri & Sun, noon-8pm Sat 🚌 14, 26, 49 Muni ♿
Most of the antique furniture sold here won't fit in an airline's carry-on luggage compartment, but some of the sleek and pricey art deco objets d'art will.

Thrift Stores

Stores selling used clothing and household wares can be found in every neighborhood in the city. During economic booms, shopaholics wishing to clear out overstuffed closets dump good-as-new castoffs on the city's thrift stores, which in turn sell the items at dramatically marked-down prices. A few thrift stores are listed here.

Goodwill Store MAP 4
1580 Mission St ☎ 415-575-2240 ⏲ 9am-8pm Mon-Sat, 11am-6pm Sun 🚌 14, 26, 42, 47, 49 Muni ♿
Goodwill's largest SF store has a huge showroom, mostly for clothes, plus an annex filled with bargain bins (entrance around the corner). There are smaller Goodwill shops all over town.

Community Thrift Store MAP 14
623 Valencia St ☎ 415-861-4910 ⏲ 10am-6:30pm daily 🚌 22, 26 Muni ♿
This is a bargain bonanza for clothing and kitchen utensils.

Salvation Army Thrift Store MAP 14
1501 Valencia St ☎ 415-643-8040 ⏲ 9:30am-9pm Mon-Fri, 9:30am-6pm Sat 🚌 14, 26, 48, 49 Muni ♿
Two large showrooms display clothing, cocktail glasses, and old pianos, and there's a large section with 'select' items.

Thrift Town MAP 14
2101 Mission St ☎ 415-861-1132 ⏲ 9am-8pm Mon-Fri, 10am-7pm Sat, 11am-6pm Sun Ⓜ 16th St BART station 🚌 14, 22, 49 Muni ♿
Two big floors are full of clothes, furniture, and bowling trophies.

Food & Drink

SOURDOUGH BREAD If you don't leave San Francisco with an appreciation for sourdough bread, you haven't tried enough. San Francisco sourdough is less sour than the Parisian variety. For a simple pleasure, buy a round loaf fresh out of the oven, tear off a hunk, apply butter, and eat it as the butter melts.

Boudin Bakery MAP 8
156 Jefferson St ☎ 415-928-1849 ⏲ 7:30am-5pm Mon-Fri, 7:30am-7pm Sat-Sun 🚌 F Muni ♿
The home store for the Boudin chain will suit people on their way to Aquatic Park for a picnic.

COFFEE & TEA San Francisco was a big coffee-drinking town, and rather quiet about it, long before Seattle and Starbucks hit the caffeine scene. The Berkeley-based Peet's chain has several stores in San Francisco. In recent years, San Franciscans have been turning increasingly to tea for a mellower lift, and a number of stores feature specialty teas to feed the demand.

Imperial Tea Court MAP 5
1411 Powell St ☎ 415-788-6080 ⏲ 11am-6:30pm daily 🚌 30, 45 Muni
With a helpful staff whose knowledge and appreciation for tea rivals that of your average wine snob, Imperial Tea Court will help you to select from an amazing variety of aromatic green and black leaves. Some precious varieties are extremely expensive (exceeding $10/lb), but a pot of refreshing keemun mao feng costs just a few dollars. Children are welcome.

Ten Ren Tea Co MAP 5
949 Grant Ave ☎ 415-362-0656 ⏲ 9am-9pm daily 🚌 12, 15, 30, 45 Muni ♿
This intense Chinatown shop sells everything from expensive gift-boxed oolong teas to economical packs of ti kyan yin (iron goddess of mercy) tea bags and bulk teas.

Peet's Coffee and Tea MAP 7
2139 Polk St ☎ 415-474-1871 ⌚ 6:30am-7pm Mon-Fri, 7am-7pm Sat-Sun 🚌 12, 19 Muni ♿

Peet's roasts aren't for everyone – they make dark, very strong, and slightly bitter brews. But many San Franciscans have acquired a taste for them, and many local cafés and roasters have tried to emulate them. Other Peet's stores are on Market St in the Castro, on Fillmore St in Pacific Heights, and on Battery St in the Financial District.

CHOCOLATE As the lasting success of Ghirardelli attests, San Franciscans have always been fond of chocolate. In addition to Ghirardelli, there are small gourmet chocolatiers all over town.

Teuscher Chocolates of Switzerland MAP 2
255 Grant Ave ☎ 415-398-2700 ⌚ 10am-6pm Mon-Sat 🚌 2, 3, 4, 76 Muni ♿

Teuscher's delectables are flown in every week from Zurich.

Ghirardelli Soda Fountain & Chocolate Shop MAP 8
900 North Point St ☎ 415-474-3938 ⌚ 9am-11pm Sun-Thurs, 9am-midnight Fri-Sat 🚌 19, 30, 42 Muni ♿

The stacks of chocolate bars on display here will make chocolate fiends delirious.

Joseph Schmidt Confections MAP 12
3489 16th St ☎ 415-861-8682 ⌚ 10am-6:30pm Mon-Sat 🚌 22, F, J Muni ♿

This small shop is chocablock with artfully designed gourmet chocolates.

RoCocoa Faerie Queene Chocolates MAP 12
415 Castro St ☎ 415-252-5814 ⌚ 11am-7pm Tues-Sun Ⓜ Castro St Muni station 🚌 24, F Muni ♿

Chocolate decadence can be found at this tiny shop purveying homemade chocolates.

WINE The best way to shop for wine is to take a trip to Napa or Sonoma Valley – see Excursions if the Wine Country is on your itinerary. If time doesn't allow it, however, San Francisco has more than enough stores with great selections of California wines, sometimes with great bargains. Overseas visitors should check their home country's import regulations before taking a case of wine back home.

Napa Valley Winery Exchange MAP 2
415 Taylor St ☎ 415-771-2887 ⌚ 10am-7pm Mon-Sat, 10am-5pm Sun 🚌 38 Muni

This is not a big store, but it has a specialized selection of local wines, and its central location means visitors in Union Square hotels won't have to haul their purchases far.

K&L Wines and Spirits MAP 4
766 Harrison St ☎ 415-896-1734 ⌚ 9am-7pm Mon-Fri, 9am-6pm Sat, 10am-5pm Sun 🚌 30, 45, 76 Muni ♿

This large shop carries a wide range of California wines.

Trader Joe's MAP 4
555 9th St ☎ 415-863-1292 ⌚ 9am-9pm daily 🚌 19, 27, 42 Muni ♿

This chain carries excellent deals on local and imported wines and is also a great place for groceries.

Wine Club MAP 4
953 Harrison St ☎ 415-512-9086, 800-966-7835 ⌚ 9am-7pm Mon-Sat, 11am-6pm Sun 🚌 27, 42 Muni ♿

This store has discounted prices on a huge selection of wines.

PlumpJack Wines MAP 9
3201 Fillmore St ☎ 415-346-9870, 888-415-9463 ⌚ 11am-8pm Mon-Sat, 11am-6pm Sun 🚌 22 Muni ♿

PlumpJack has a great selection from all over the world, and its staff can make excellent recommendations.

Bicycles

For a hilly town, San Francisco sports a surprisingly strong contingent of cyclists. The biggest posse of bicycle shops is on and around Stanyan St by Golden Gate Park in the Haight.

American Cyclery MAP 11
510 Frederick St ☎ 415-664-4545 ⏲ 11am-7pm Mon-Fri, 10am-6pm Sat, 10am-5pm Sun 🚌 7, 66, 71 Muni ♿

One of the city's best bike shops, American Cyclery carries contemporary mountain and hybrid bikes, as well as antique bikes. Staff will work with customers to tailor a bike to very specific needs.

Valencia Cyclery MAP 14
1077 Valencia St ☎ 415-550-6601 ⏲ 10am-6pm Mon-Sat, 10am-4pm Sun 🚌 14, 26, 49 Muni

This shop carries a nice selection of bikes and will do repairs for a price.

Outdoor Gear

Many outdoor-gear stores sell not only clothing but also the necessary equipment for outdoor adventure, and they can give good advice on what to buy. If you're headed for the Sierra Nevadas, San Francisco lacks a truly great mountaineering source (high quality East Bay retailers are listed in the yellow pages). San Francisco is much better for those exploring the urban outdoors.

The North Face MAP 2
180 Post St ☎ 415-433-3223 ⏲ 10am-8pm Mon-Sat, 11am-6pm Sun 🚌 2, 3, 4, 15, 30, 41, 45, 76 Muni ♿

Come here for high-quality outdoor and adventure gear. There's another store South of Market.

Patagonia MAP 8
770 North Point St ☎ 415-771-2050 ⏲ 10am-6pm Mon-Sat, 11am-5pm Sun 🚌 30, 42 Muni 🚋 Powell-Hyde cable car ♿

This is a respected name in outdoor gear and clothing.

FTC Skateboarding MAP 11
622 Shrader St ☎ 415-386-6693 ⏲ 10am-7pm Mon-Sat, 11am-6pm Sun 🚌 7, 66, 71 Muni

Here you'll find state-of-the-art skateboard gear and snazzy skate-punk attire.

SFO Snowboarding MAP 11
618 Shrader St ☎ 415-386-1666 ⏲ 10am-7pm Tues-Sat, 11am-6pm Sun 🚌 7, 66, 71 Muni

State-of-the-art snowboards and boots, and racks of the latest baggy outerwear, are the thing here.

DLX SF MAP 12
1831 Market St ☎ 415-626-5588 ⏲ 11am-7pm Mon-Sat, 11am-6pm Sun 🚌 F Muni ♿

This is a skate shop with custom-designed boards and way-out garb.

Piercings

Getting a pin through it is a San Francisco specialty. Numerous piercing professionals can add a little sparkle and tingle to pretty much any part of your body, as the quantity of bejeweled noses, eyebrows, lips, nipples, navels, and tongues you'll see around town attest. Of course, these visible piercings only hint at what's going on in more private areas….

Anubis Warpus MAP 11
1525 Haight St ☎ 415-431-2218 ⏲ 11am-7pm Mon-Fri, 11am-8pm Sat-Sun 🚌 7, 66, 71 Muni ♿

Anubis Warpus addresses many of your alternative lifestyle needs, with a selection of jewelry, books, and periodicals in addition to piercing services. Prices start at $25 for a navel, nipple, or tongue, and the cost of the jewelry is on top of that.

Cold Steel America MAP 12
2377 Market St ☎ 415-621-7233 ⏲ noon-8pm daily Ⓜ Castro St Muni station 🚌 24, F Muni

These piercing specialists aren't likely to balk at any request.

SHOPPING

Body Manipulations MAP 14
3234 16th St ☎ 415-621-0408 ⌚ noon-7pm daily Ⓜ 16th St BART station
🚌 22, 26 Muni

Since 1989, this mellow, friendly 'piercing studio' has been offering inexpensive piercing ($10 to $25), branding, and scarification services.

Tattoos

If you have that appreciation for art on skin, save a little room for one of San Francisco's reputable tattoo artists.

Lyle Tuttle Tattooing MAP 7
841 Columbus Ave ☎ 415-775-4991
⌚ noon-9pm Mon-Sat, noon-8pm Sun
🚌 30 Muni 🚋 Powell-Mason cable car

Needle artist Tuttle keeps a small but fascinating tattoo museum to inspire your choice of classic tattoo designs.

Black & Blue Tattoo MAP 14
483 14th St ☎ 415-626-0770 ⌚ noon-7pm daily 🚌 26 Muni
w www.black-n-blue-tattoo.com

Some girls might prefer this women-owned and -operated tattoo parlor – and guys should appreciate the ladies' work as well. It can get pretty busy, so be sure to call for an appointment.

Excursions

East Bay

Linked to San Francisco by the Bay Bridge, the East Bay mostly consists of dense suburbs that range from residential and industrial neighborhoods on the bay-side flats to pricey residential real estate cushioned in lush vegetation high in the hills. Gritty Oakland and opinionated Berkeley, each with its own distinct personality, dominate the area, and surprisingly pristine hills rise behind them. Miles of parks cover the ridgeline, beyond which lie the bedroom communities of Contra Costa County, sprawled at the base of towering Mt Diablo.

Getting There & Away

Logistically, driving to the East Bay from San Francisco is simple, though traffic over the Bay Bridge may make you wish you'd taken BART. To reach Oakland, cross the Bay Bridge and take I-880, following signs for downtown Oakland. For downtown Berkeley, cross the Bay Bridge and bear left on I-80 to the exit for University Ave; for the Southside, take I-80 to Hwy 13 (Ashby Ave), then drive east to Telegraph Ave, where you turn left.

AC Transit Buses
☎ *510-817-1717* Ⓢ *adult $1.35, senior/disabled/child 65¢* ♿ *limited*
Ⓦ *www.actransit.dst.ca.us*

AC Transit runs a number of convenient buses from San Francisco's Transbay Terminal, at Mission and 1st Sts, to downtown Oakland and Berkeley, especially during commute hours. The trip takes 30 minutes.

Buses also run between Berkeley and downtown Oakland and between various East Bay BART stations and the downtown areas; check with AC Transit or at the BART stations for connections.

BART (Bay Area Rapid Transit)
☎ *510-464-6000* ⏲ *4am-1am Mon-Fri, 6am-1am Sat, 8am-1am Sun* ♿
Ⓦ *www.bart.org*

BART is the most convenient way to get from San Francisco to the East Bay and back. Trains run like clockwork (that is, if you're using a clock that hiccups every now and then). Trains run every 15 minutes Monday to Friday outside of commute hours and more frequently during morning and evening hours on most lines; they run every 15 or 20 minutes on Saturday and Sunday, depending on the route. Check exact times by picking up a schedule at any station.

To downtown Oakland, catch a train on the Richmond or Pittsburg/Bay Point line and take it to the 12th or 19th St stations. For North Oakland, go to Rockridge. To Berkeley, catch a Richmond-bound train to one of three BART stations: Ashby, Berkeley (this main station is at Shattuck Ave and Center St), and North Berkeley. BART fares vary depending on the length of the trip; check at the station. A BART-to-Bus transfer ticket, available from white AC Transit machines near station exits, costs $1.15 for adults, 55¢ for seniors and children.

See the Bicycles & Public Transportation section of the Getting Around chapter for information on taking a bike on BART.

Alameda/Oakland Ferry MAP 5 & DOWNTOWN OAKLAND MAP
☎ *510-522-3300* ⏲ *approximately 6am-9:30pm, schedules vary with season* Ⓢ *adult $4.75, senior $3, ages 5-12 $2* Ⓜ *Embarcadero BART & Muni station (San Francisco)*
Ⓦ *www.eastbayferry.com*

The ferry sails from San Francisco's Ferry Building to Jack London Square, where it docks at Clay and Water Sts. The ride takes about 20 minutes, and if the day is calm and sunny, it's delightful. See the Getting Around and Things to See & Do chapters for other ferry destinations, including Alameda, Alcatraz, and Angel Island.

OAKLAND

With a climate generally warmer and less foggy than San Francisco's, some sizable parks, a large downtown lake, some thriving neighborhoods and plenty of good restaurants, Oakland is a low-key, livable, and somewhat underappreciated city.

The Oakland area's earliest inhabitants were Ohlone Indians. In 1820, the land was

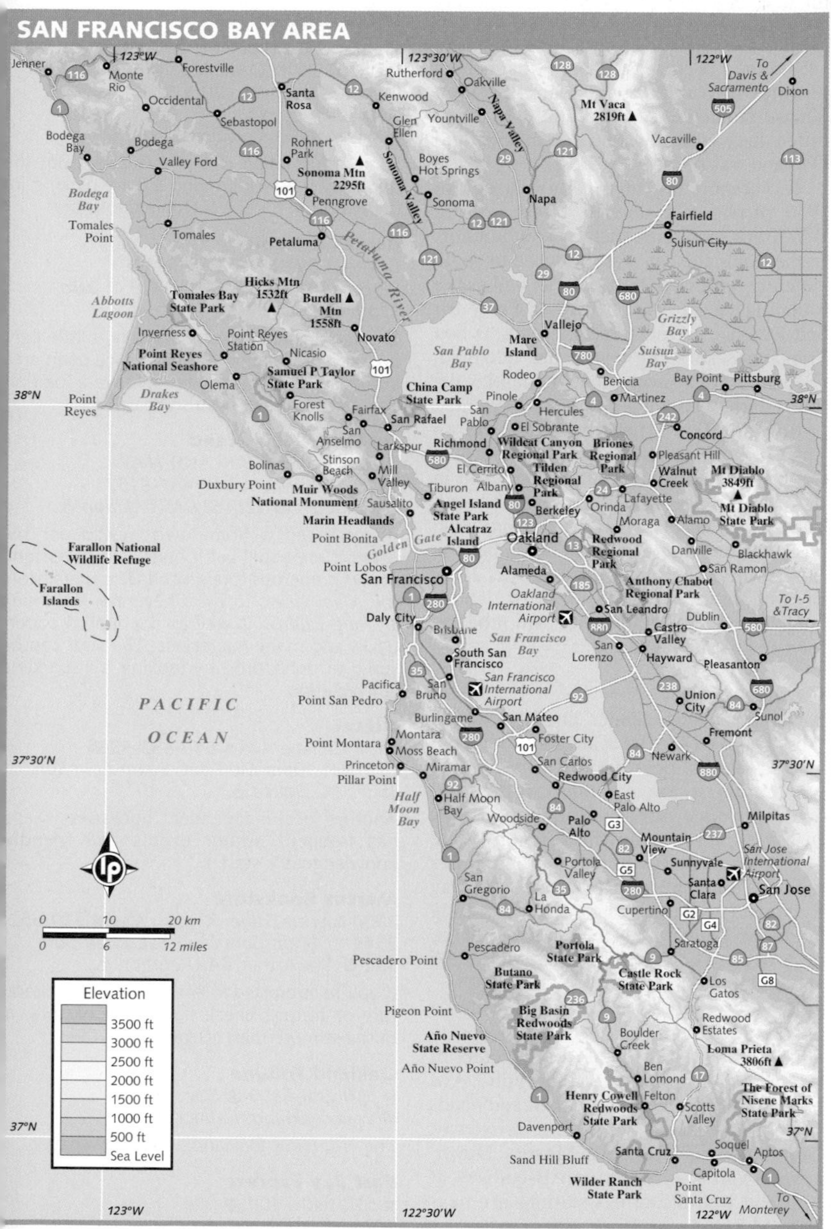
SAN FRANCISCO BAY AREA
Jenner
Monte Rio
Forestville
Occidental
Sebastopol
Santa Rosa
Kenwood
Rutherford
Oakville
Yountville
Glen Ellen
Napa Valley
Sonoma Valley
Bodega Bay
Bodega
Valley Ford
Rohnert Park
Sonoma Mtn 2295ft
Boyes Hot Springs
Sonoma
Napa
Penngrove
Petaluma
Petaluma River
Tomales
Tomales Point
Abbotts Lagoon
Tomales Bay State Park
Hicks Mtn 1532ft
Burdell Mtn 1558ft
Novato
Inverness
Point Reyes Station
Nicasio
Point Reyes National Seashore
Samuel P Taylor State Park
Olema
Drakes Bay
Point Reyes
Forest Knolls
Fairfax
San Anselmo
San Rafael
Larkspur
China Camp State Park
San Pablo Bay
Mare Island
Vallejo
Rodeo
Pinole
San Pablo
Hercules
El Sobrante
Richmond
Mt Vaca 2819ft
Vacaville
Dixon
To Davis & Sacramento
Fairfield
Suisun City
Grizzly Bay
Suisun Bay
Benicia
Martinez
Bay Point
Pittsburg
Concord
Pleasant Hill
Walnut Creek
Mt Diablo 3849ft
Mt Diablo State Park
Wildcat Canyon Regional Park
Briones Regional Park
Tilden Regional Park
El Cerrito
Albany
Berkeley
Orinda
Lafayette
Moraga
Alamo
Danville
Blackhawk
San Ramon
Bolinas
Stinson Beach
Mill Valley
Tiburon
Duxbury Point
Muir Woods National Monument
Sausalito
Angel Island State Park
Marin Headlands
Point Bonita
Golden Gate
Alcatraz Island
Oakland
Redwood Regional Park
Farallon National Wildlife Refuge
Farallon Islands
Point Lobos
San Francisco
Alameda
Anthony Chabot Regional Park
Oakland International Airport
San Leandro
Daly City
Brisbane
South San Francisco
San Francisco Bay
San Lorenzo
Castro Valley
Dublin
To I-5 & Tracy
Hayward
Pleasanton
Pacifica
Point San Pedro
San Bruno
San Francisco International Airport
Union City
Sunol
PACIFIC OCEAN
Burlingame
San Mateo
Foster City
Fremont
Montara
Moss Beach
Point Montara
Princeton
Pillar Point
Miramar
San Carlos
Newark
Redwood City
Half Moon Bay
East Palo Alto
Woodside
Palo Alto
Milpitas
Mountain View
Portola Valley
Sunnyvale
San Jose International Airport
Santa Clara
San Jose
San Gregorio
La Honda
Cupertino
Pescadero
Pescadero Point
Portola State Park
Saratoga
Butano State Park
Castle Rock State Park
Los Gatos
Pigeon Point
Big Basin Redwoods State Park
Redwood Estates
Año Nuevo State Reserve
Año Nuevo Point
Boulder Creek
Loma Prieta 3806ft
Ben Lomond
Henry Cowell Redwoods State Park
Felton
Scotts Valley
The Forest of Nisene Marks State Park
Davenport
Sand Hill Bluff
Santa Cruz
Soquel
Aptos
Capitola
Wilder Ranch State Park
Point Santa Cruz
To Monterey
123°W
123°30'W
122°W
122°30'W
38°N
37°30'N
37°N
0 10 20 km
0 6 12 miles
Elevation
3500 ft
3000 ft
2500 ft
2000 ft
1500 ft
1000 ft
500 ft
Sea Level

included in the enormous rancho granted to Mexican soldier Luis Maria Peralta, but in 1850 three US citizens 'leased' what is now downtown Oakland and Jack London Square from the Peralta family. In short order, they sold the land off in lots, and Oakland was born.

The completion of the Bay Bridge in 1936 provided a needed boost, as did WWII-era industries such as shipbuilding. In the 1960s, the city was the scene of some violently repressed draft riots, as well as the founding of the Black Panther Party for Self-Defense. In more recent years, as San Francisco's shipping traffic has declined, Oakland's has grown; today, Oakland is the fourth-largest container port in the country.

Revitalization efforts have spruced up some of downtown Oakland, but much of that area is still somewhat forlorn, and in the evenings the whole area empties out. There are indications that the city may soon be on the upswing, especially if you believe the promises of Oakland's mayor, Jerry Brown, a former California state leader laughingly called 'Governor Moonbeam' for some of his way-out ideas.

Orientation

Oakland is a long, slender city. Historically, West Oakland has been heavily industrial with residential pockets, but with the new millennium it has exploded with high-density, upscale offices and housing stock. Just east are the downtown and Lake Merritt areas. North Oakland includes upscale Piedmont and Rockridge. East Bay Regional Parks run along the hills, forming its eastern border. I-880 traces the bay at the city's western edge, and I-580 parallels I-880 about 1½ miles inland.

Broadway is the backbone of downtown Oakland, running from Jack London Square at the waterfront north to Piedmont Ave and Rockridge. Telegraph Ave branches off Broadway at 15th St and heads straight to Berkeley; east from Broadway, Grand Ave runs to Lake Merritt. Downtown BART stations are on Broadway at 12th and 19th Sts; others stations are near Lake Merritt and in Rockridge.

Information

Oakland Convention & Visitors Bureau
DOWNTOWN OAKLAND MAP
475 14th St, Suite 120 ☎ 510-839-9000
⏲ 8:30am-5pm Mon-Fri ♿
W www.oaklandcvb.com

Some information is also available from the booth by the Jack London Square parking lot (beneath the Barnes & Noble bookstore).

Barnes & Noble
DOWNTOWN OAKLAND MAP
98 Broadway ☎ 510-272-0120 ⏲ 9am-11pm daily 🚌 59 AC Transit ♿

This large chain store sheds only a little light on local information but has a nice open area in front where you can briefly take a load off and enjoy a break from sightseeing.

De Lauer Newsstand
DOWNTOWN OAKLAND MAP
1310 Broadway ☎ 510-451-6157
⏲ 24 hours Ⓜ 12th St BART station ♿

If you need a hometown newspaper fix, chances are you'll get it here. This newsstand carries numerous foreign and US papers (from the *Maui News* to the Cheyenne, Wyoming *Tribune-Eagle*), as well as discounted paperbacks and many magazines. The staff can be surly, so don't drop by looking for sparkling conversation.

Diesel
5433 College Ave ☎ 510-653-9965
⏲ 10am-10pm Mon-Sat, 10am-6pm Sun
🚌 51 AC Transit ♿

Another local independent bookstore, Diesel has frequent author events and friendly knowledgeable staff.

Marcus Bookstore
3900 Martin Luther King Jr Way ☎ 510-652-2344 ⏲ 10am-6pm Mon-Sat, noon-5pm Sun Ⓜ MacArthur BART station ♿

If you're interested in African American literature or history, check out this bookstore, in business more than 40 years.

Oakland *Tribune*
☎ 510-208-6300 $ 50¢
W www.oaklandtribune.com

The *Tribune* is Oakland's daily newspaper.

East Bay Express
☎ 510-540-7400 $ free
W www.eastbayexpress.com

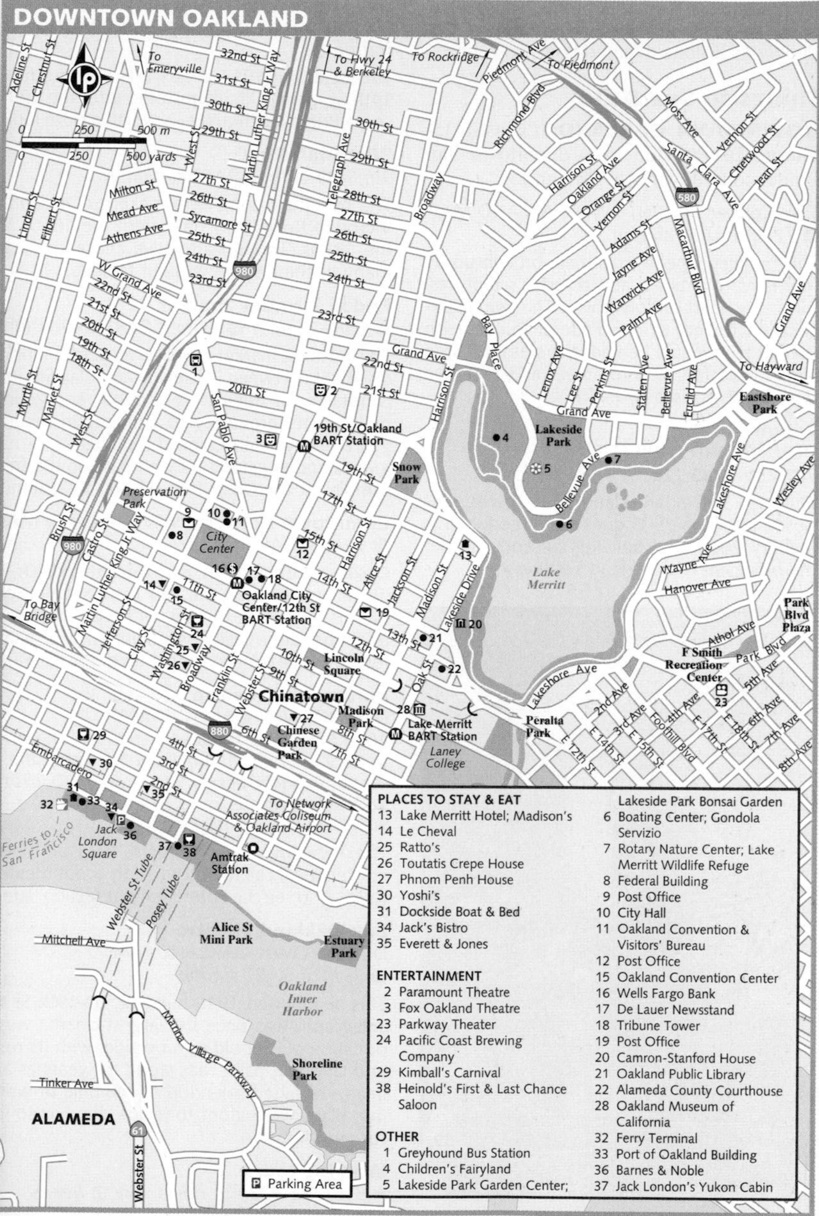

PLACES TO STAY & EAT
13 Lake Merritt Hotel; Madison's
14 Le Cheval
25 Ratto's
26 Toutatis Crepe House
27 Phnom Penh House
30 Yoshi's
31 Dockside Boat & Bed
34 Jack's Bistro
35 Everett & Jones

ENTERTAINMENT
2 Paramount Theatre
3 Fox Oakland Theatre
23 Parkway Theater
24 Pacific Coast Brewing Company
29 Kimball's Carnival
38 Heinold's First & Last Chance Saloon

OTHER
1 Greyhound Bus Station
4 Children's Fairyland
5 Lakeside Park Garden Center; Lakeside Park Bonsai Garden
6 Boating Center; Gondola Servizio
7 Rotary Nature Center; Lake Merritt Wildlife Refuge
8 Federal Building
9 Post Office
10 City Hall
11 Oakland Convention & Visitors' Bureau
12 Post Office
15 Oakland Convention Center
16 Wells Fargo Bank
17 De Lauer Newsstand
18 Tribune Tower
19 Post Office
20 Camron-Stanford House
21 Oakland Public Library
22 Alameda County Courthouse
28 Oakland Museum of California
32 Ferry Terminal
33 Port of Oakland Building
36 Barnes & Noble
37 Jack London's Yukon Cabin

This alternative weekly, published Fridays, has good coverage of Oakland and Berkeley, including its 'Billboard' entertainment section.

Things to See & Do

DOWNTOWN OAKLAND It's just a 15-minute BART ride from downtown San Francisco to downtown Oakland.

City Center DOWNTOWN OAKLAND MAP

M *12th St BART station*

This multilevel pedestrian mall, broken up by fountains, plantings, and colorful sculptures, forms the heart of downtown. The twin glass-encased towers of the Federal Building on Clay St rise up just behind it. It's easy to stop here for coffee or a full meal as you arrive from San Francisco by BART.

Tribune Tower

DOWNTOWN OAKLAND MAP

401 13th St M *12th St BART station*

This 1923 Oakland landmark tower was closed after the 1989 quake and reopened in January 2000. The building currently houses the offices of the Oakland *Tribune*.

RICK GERHARTER

Oakland City Center

City Hall DOWNTOWN OAKLAND MAP

1 Frank Ogawa Plaza M *12th St BART station* ♿

This beautiful 1914 beaux arts building near 14th St, painstakingly restored after the 1989 Loma Prieta earthquake, is worth a close look.

'Victorian Row'

9th St M *12th St BART station* ♿

The buildings along here make up Oakland's Victorian Row. They date from the 1860s to the 1880s. Though attractive and appealing, many of them stand without tenants.

Friday farmers' market

🕘 *8am-2pm Fri* M *12th St BART station* ♿

This bustling market takes up most of 2 blocks on 9th St (between Broadway and Clay St) and is notable for the variety of foods and goods on sale. Its proximity to Chinatown means you'll always find colorful mounds of exotic greens and vegetables. Don't pass up the free samples at the Great Harvest Bread Co stand.

Chinatown DOWNTOWN OAKLAND MAP

M *12th St BART station*

Oakland's Chinatown, here since the 1870s, is much smaller than the San Francisco version but nevertheless bustles with commerce. It might better be called Asiatown, since its many residents hail from every corner of the Far East.

Paramount Theatre

DOWNTOWN OAKLAND MAP

2025 Broadway ☎ *510-465-6400* 🕘 *show times vary, tours 10am 1st & 3rd Sat of the month* $ *show tickets vary, tour $1* M *19th St BART station* ♿

W *www.paramounttheatre.com*

The Paramount is a restored 1931 art deco masterpiece; call for information about theater tours. Also see the Entertainment section, later.

Fox Oakland Theatre

DOWNTOWN OAKLAND MAP

M *19th St BART station*

This abandoned 1928 building, on 19th St at Telegraph, was once the largest cinema west of Chicago. The old sign outside, with its rust and chipping paint, has stood for years as an image of faded splendor. At the time of writing, plans were afoot to restore the Fox to its former glory.

Walking tours

☎ *510-238-3234* 🕘 *hours vary* $ *free* ♿

W *www.oaklandnet.com*

The City of Oakland Community Development Agency leads free 90-minute tours of historic downtown streets and City Hall. Reservations are recommended.

JACK LONDON SQUARE The waterfront where writer and adventurer Jack London once raised hell now bears his name. It has been difficult converting a decaying industrial area into a tourist zone, but local developers have recently boosted property values around the square by building numerous apartments, condos, and live-work lofts.

A new Amtrak station opened here in 1995. Also in the mid-1990s, the city and the Port of Oakland poured $4 million into the renovation of the space where swanky jazz club Yoshi's now resides. Several chain restaurants dot the area, and there's a farmers' market in the square every Sunday morning.

Heinold's First & Last Chance Saloon
DOWNTOWN OAKLAND MAP
56 Jack London Square ☎ 510-839-6761
noon-midnight daily 🚌 59 AC Transit ♿

It is said that London was a regular patron of this 1880 building, maintained in all its period glory and still open for business. It's just seedy enough to feel authentic.

Jack London's Yukon cabin
DOWNTOWN OAKLAND MAP
free 🚌 59 AC Transit

Across from the saloon is a replica of London's cabin, and if ever a building looked out of place, it's this one. In front of the cabin, there's a bronze sculpture of a wolf (think *Call of the Wild*) that gives a surreal aura to the whole scene.

LAKE MERRITT Oakland's visual centerpiece was once a tidal marsh teeming with waterfowl. It became a lake in 1869 with the damming of an arm of the Oakland estuary, and the following year the state legislature designated it a wildlife refuge, the first in the US. It still supports migratory waterfowl, and it's still connected to the estuary, so its 155 acres are briny. If you look too closely you'll see the water isn't the cleanest, but Lake Merritt is still an urban jewel, a popular place to stroll or run (a 3.1-mile path circles the lake). At night, it's ringed with a graceful necklace of white lights.

The two main commercial streets bordering Lake Merritt are Lakeshore Ave, on the eastern edge, and Grand Ave, running along the north. Their stores offer more to locals than to visitors, but both have some nice spots for eating or drinking – see Places to Eat and Entertainment, later, for suggestions.

Lakeside Park
DOWNTOWN OAKLAND MAP
free 🚌 58 AC Transit

This 122-acre park on the north side of Lake Merritt is the site of the garden center, the sailboat house, and the Rotary Nature Center, and it's right by Children's Fairyland. There's parking at the entrance ($2 on weekends, free weekdays), or you can park on Grand Ave and walk in.

Lakeside Park Garden Center
DOWNTOWN OAKLAND MAP
666 Bellevue Ave ☎ 510-238-3208
10am-4pm daily free 🚌 58 AC Transit ♿

This large and lovely enclosure contains a variety of landscaped areas, including community gardens, a fire-resistant demonstration garden, a vegetable and fruit garden, and an herb and fragrance garden.

Lakeside Park Bonsai Garden
DOWNTOWN OAKLAND MAP
☎ 510-763-8409 11am-3pm Wed-Fri, 10am-4pm Sat, noon-4pm Sun donations (free) 🚌 58 AC Transit ♿

Bonsai aficionados won't want to miss this peaceful, circular enclosure with its fantastic miniature plants, rock garden, and dry waterfall. Friendly, knowledgeable docents make it hard to get away without learning something. Don't miss the suisekis, found stone 'sculptures' of animals, birds, humans, and natural objects.

Children's Fairyland
DOWNTOWN OAKLAND MAP
699 Bellevue Ave ☎ 510-452-2259 hours vary $6 🚌 58 AC Transit ♿
www.fairyland.org

Established in 1950, this finely landscaped 10-acre kiddie amusement park features live animals, rides, and daily puppet shows.

Rotary Nature Center
DOWNTOWN OAKLAND MAP
552 Bellevue Ave ☎ 510-238-3739 9am-5pm daily free 🚌 58 AC Transit ♿
www.lakemerritt.com

This is the interpretive center for the Lake Merritt Wildlife Refuge. There's usually a naturalist on hand, and there's a daily bird feeding at 3:30pm behind the center. Call the center or check its website for information about special historical talks and ecological boat tours of the lake.

Boating Center
DOWNTOWN OAKLAND MAP
568 Bellevue Ave ☎ 510-444-3807 ⌚ 9am-6pm Mon-Fri June-Sept, 9am-7pm Sat-Sun June-Sept, 10:30am-5pm Tues-Sun Jan-May & Oct-Dec $ canoes or rowboats $6/hour, kayaks and pedal boats $8/hour 🚌 58 AC Transit ♿
W www.oaklandsports.org

For a jaunt on the lake, rent a pedal boat at the park's Boating Center.

Gondola Servizio
DOWNTOWN OAKLAND MAP
568 Bellevue Ave ☎ 510-663-6603
⌚ 10am-10pm daily, weather permitting
$ basic cruises $55/hour, small picnic cruises $65/hour, wedding cruises $225/hour 🚌 58 AC Transit
W www.gondolaservizio.com

For an offbeat but relaxing diversion, try a lake cruise in an accurate replica of a Venetian gondola.

Camron-Stanford House
DOWNTOWN OAKLAND MAP
1418 Lakeside Dr ☎ 510-444-1876 ⌚ tours 11am-4pm Wed, 1pm-5pm Sun $ adult $4, senior $2, child $1 🚌 11 AC Transit ♿ 1st level only

In the late 19th century, Lake Merritt was lined with fine homes, but only this one (built in 1876) still remains. You can go on a tour, but the best aspect of the house is really its lakeside setting and the hint it gives of how Oakland looked in its Victorian heyday.

Oakland Museum of California
DOWNTOWN OAKLAND MAP
1000 Oak St ☎ 510-238-2200 ⌚ 10am-5pm Wed-Sat, noon-5pm Sun, 10am-9pm 1st Fri of each month $ adult $6, senior/student $4, child free; free 2nd Sun of the month
Ⓜ Lake Merritt BART station ♿
W www.museumca.org

This museum, opened in 1969, is in a graceful building not far from the lake. It has three parts: one on the environment, one on California history, and one devoted to art. The museum owns a fine permanent collection of works by California photographers (Ansel Adams, Dorothea Lange, and the like), so look for what's on display when you visit. There's a café, a store, and a quiet, multilevel rooftop garden.

North Oakland

As you head northeast up Broadway, this main thoroughfare becomes a strip of car dealerships so lengthy it has its own name 'Broadway Auto Row.' Once you get past the gas guzzler displays, there are a number of places of interest worth exploring as you move away from the downtown area.

Piedmont Ave
🚌 59 AC Transit

The 4- or 5-block commercial strip of Piedmont Ave has some interesting antique shops, coffeehouses, and fine restaurants.

Rockridge
Ⓜ Rockridge BART station

College Ave, which bustles with prosperous people and their well-behaved dogs, runs into Berkeley, and the whole length of it is lined with boutiques, bookstores, cafés, and upscale restaurants.

Oakland Hills

East of downtown, the streets become more convoluted, winding through exclusive communities such as Montclair before reaching the ridgeline, where a series of parks crown the hills.

For a nice day hike without traveling far, the large East Bay parks are ideal.

East Bay Regional Parks District
☎ 510-562-7275
W www.ebparks.org

Call or visit online for details about individual parks (there are 50 in the system, along with 20 regional trails); also available is the excellent Regional Parks booklet, as well as information on the East Bay Skyline National Trail, which runs for 31 miles along the hills from Richmond in the north to Castro Valley in the south.

Redwood Regional Park
⌚ 5am-10pm daily $ free 🚌 60 AC Transit

A mountain-bike ride or a run or a hike on th

:rails, through the groves, and along the hill- :ops of the 1840-acre Redwood Park will nake you forget you're in an urban area.

:habot Space & Science Center
'0000 Skyline Blvd ☎ 510-336-7300
⊙ 10am-5pm Tues-Sat, noon-5pm Sun; planetarium & theater also open 7pm-9pm :ri-Sat $ $5.50-20 🚌 53 AC Transit ♿
w www.chabotspace.org

'his 86,000-sq-foot planetarium, observatory, ınd surround-view theater, which sits on 13 ıcres at the edge of Redwood Regional Park, ›pened in August 2000. Wander through the ıiry, three-story space, which features exhibits ın every level, including a 3-D tour of 'Your 'lace in the Universe.'

SARAH JH HUBBARD

Chabot Space & Science Center

The planetarium show is usually fun, but if ou have to choose between it and the ʼlegaDome movie, go for the flick. The 360- egree theater, specializing in science films, oasts the latest technology and is guaranteed ɔ induce a lovely vertigo as you tip back in our seat and willingly suspend all disbelief. If our Bay Area visit is blessed with clear skies, isit Friday or Saturday evening between 7pm nd 9:45pm, when you can explore stars, 'anets and far-flung nebulae with 8- and 20- ıch refractor telescopes and a 36-inch reflec- ɔr telescope – one of the largest in the ɔuntry regularly open to the public.

.nthony Chabot Regional Park
› 7am-10pm daily $ free

his 4972-acre park offers bucolic trails and a 15-acre lake to fish in (do you like rainbow out and largemouth bass?). You can reach ıe lake by car from I-580. Exit in San Leandro : Fairmont Dr and go east (uphill); the marina entrance will be to the left. Call regional park headquarters for boating and fishing fees.

Places to Stay

Staying in San Francisco is hard to top, and the convenient BART service makes a day trip to Oakland a breeze. But if you'd like to experience a bit of East Bay luxury, Oakland offers a couple of choice options.

Dockside Boat & Bed
DOWNTOWN OAKLAND MAP
57 Clay St ☎ 510-444-5858 fax 510-444-0420 $ doubles $125-340 C MC, V, AE
🚌 59 AC Transit

This unusual 'hotel' is actually five or six individual boats, available dockside for your bunking pleasure and ranging from 32 to 65 feet long. Continental breakfast is included in the rate, which is charged per couple.

Lake Merritt Hotel
DOWNTOWN OAKLAND MAP
1800 Madison St ☎ 510-832-2300 $ $159-259 C AE, MC, V, DC ♿

This clean, comfortable, elegant hotel was remodeled in April 2000. The decor features plush loveseats, wicker chairs, potted palms, and a baby grand in the lobby (shades of 1927, the year the hotel was built). Genteel Madison's, a lovely space with a glass wall overlooking Lake Merritt, is the restaurant off the lobby.

Places to Eat

DOWNTOWN The downtown area is about a 10-minute walk from Jack London Square or the Oakland Museum.

Ratto's (Italian deli)
DOWNTOWN OAKLAND MAP
821 Washington St ☎ 510-832-6503
⊙ 9am-6pm Mon-Fri, 9:30am-5pm Sat
C MC, V Ⓥ Ⓜ 12th St BART station ♿

This one's an Oakland institution (since 1897) serving generous salads and great sandwiches (try the roast beef). It has a full deli selling olives, cheese, and international delicacies, as well as an impressive selection of wines.

Toutatis Crepe House (French)
DOWNTOWN OAKLAND MAP
719 Washington St ☎ 510-465-6984
⊙ 11:30am-2pm Mon-Fri, 10am-2pm Sat-Sun, 6pm-9pm Tues-Thurs, 6pm-10pm Fri-Sat
$ appetizer $2-8, entrée $6-9, dessert $2-6
C cash only Ⓥ Ⓜ 12th St BART station ♿

Owner and Normandy native Eric Leroy specializes in every kind of crepe imaginable, tenderly wrapping spicy or sweet fillings in delicate pancakes made from special organic buckwheat flour. For something different, try the caramelized apple dessert crepe, or the one made with chocolate Häagen Dazs ice cream (don't worry, you'll walk it off).

Le Cheval (Vietnamese)
DOWNTOWN OAKLAND MAP
1007 Clay St ☎ 510-763-8495 ⌚ 11am-9:30pm Mon-Sat, 5pm-9:30pm Sun $ lunch $5.50-7.50, appetizer $4-8.50, entrée $5-9.50 C V, MC, AE, CB Ⓥ Ⓜ 12th St BART station ♿

Popular at lunchtime, Le Cheval (the horse) serves delicious Vietnamese food in spacious environs; the clay pot dishes are excellent. Go in a good mood because, as the menu warns, prices are 'subject to change depending on customer attitude.'

Phnom Penh House (Cambodian)
DOWNTOWN OAKLAND MAP
251 8th St ☎ 510-893-3825 ⌚ 11am-9:15pm daily $ $6-8 C MC, V Ⓥ Ⓜ 12th St BART station ♿

This is an excellent, affordable Cambodian restaurant.

JACK LONDON SQUARE Good food, some cheap and some not very, is plentiful in the square area.

Everett & Jones (barbecue)
DOWNTOWN OAKLAND MAP
126 Broadway ☎ 510-663-2350 ⌚ 11am-10pm Mon-Wed, 11am-11pm Thurs, 11am-midnight Fri, noon-midnight Sat, noon-10pm Sun $ lunch $6-7, entrée $10-17 C MC, V, AE 🚌 59 AC Transit ♿

This large, friendly barbecue joint is a branch of a Bay Area institution. Opened in 1999, it features plastic-covered tablecloths and quasi-antique furnishings that give it an old-time feel, which is modified by high ceilings and picture windows all around. The ribs, mashed potatoes, and cole slaw are authentic and mighty tasty.

Yoshi's (Japanese)
DOWNTOWN OAKLAND MAP
510 Embarcadero West ☎ 510-238-9200 ⌚ restaurant: 11:30am-2pm Mon-Fri, noon-2:30pm Sat-Sun, 5:30pm-9:30pm Sun-Thurs, 5:30pm-10pm Fri-Sat; sushi bar: 5:30pm-10:30pm Sun-Mon, 5:30pm-11pm Tues-Thurs, 5:30pm-11:30pm Fri-Sat $ lunch $8-12, entrée $15-20 C MC, V Ⓥ 🚌 59 AC Transit ♿

Yoshi's is deservedly well known as a major jaz venue, but travelers could do worse than to drop by just to eat. Often, particularly a lunchtime, you can get a table immediately and the service is quick and courteous. Sushi i a specialty (with a vegetarian sushi meal available), and the tempura is light, fluffy, and tasty

Jack's Bistro (Mediterranean)
DOWNTOWN OAKLAND MAP
1 Broadway ☎ 510-444-7171 ⌚ 7am-10pm $ breakfast $4-8.50, lunch $8-14, appetizer $9-14.50, entrée $14-17 C MC, V, AE Ⓥ 🚌 59 AC Transit ♿

If you're feeling flush, try this mellow bistro serving up California-style Mediterranean seafood and poultry dishes; it's got a wood-fire rotisserie. Watching the boats slip by at sunset could justify the expense.

LAKE MERRITT After you've walke around the lake, you've earned a goo dinner – or lunch at the very least. Luckily good food can be found not far away.

Arizmendi (pizza)
3265 Lakeshore Ave ☎ 510-268-8849 ⌚ 7am-7pm Tues-Sat $ $3-11 C cash only Ⓥ 🚌 13 AC Transit ♿

This bakery co-op sells scrumptious gourme pizza by the slice or the pie. If you miss th pizza, try the equally good focaccia or any c the hearty pastries or breads. None will ru you more than a few dollars.

Autumn Moon Café (California)
3909 Grand Ave ☎ 510-595-3200 ⌚ 7:30am-2pm & 5pm-9pm Sun-Thurs, 8:30am-2pm & 5 pm-9:30pm Fri-Sat $ breakfast/lunch $6-10, appetizer $4-10, entrée $11-18 C MC, V Ⓥ 🚌 12 AC Transit ♿

In an old house, this comfortable café serve breakfast, lunch, and dinner. The risotto an the polenta are especially good, although th meat dishes definitely pass the taste test (try th char-grilled lamb with potato fritters). All ingredients are fresh, and the staff are gracious. Th place can be very crowded on weekends.

NORTH OAKLAND You'll find plenty c places to eat on either Piedmont Ave c

College Ave, both attractive commercial streets.

Gaylord's Caffe Espresso (café fare)
4150 Piedmont Ave ☎ 510-658-2877 ⌚ 6am-midnight daily $ $1.50-8 C cash only 59 AC Transit ♿

This small, independent neighborhood café is a Piedmont institution. Open long hours, Gaylord's features an array of coffee drinks, plus a small food menu featuring some tasty soups and chilies. It feels good to patronize an anti-Starbucks – and you can get ice cream.

Barney's Gourmet Hamburgers (burgers)
4162 Piedmont Ave ☎ 510-655-7180 ⌚ 11am-9:30pm Mon-Thurs, 10am-10pm Fri-Sat, 10am-9pm Sun $ $4-6 C MC, V 59 AC Transit ♿

If you're searching for something simple, this upscale joint serves the best burgers you'll find anywhere – and that goes for the veggie burgers, too. There's also a Barney's in Rockridge (☎ 601-0444, 5819 College Ave).

Tropix Backyard Café (Creole & Jamaican)
3814 Piedmont Ave ☎ 510-653-2444 ⌚ 11:30am-9pm Mon-Thurs, 11:30am-10pm Fri, 10am-10pm Sat-Sun $ lunch $7-11.50, entrée $12-14 C V, MC, AE 59 AC Transit ♿

Here you can get good food served on the colorful back patio.

Bay Wolf (California/Mediterranean)
3853 Piedmont Ave ☎ 510-655-6004 ⌚ 11:30am-2pm & 6pm-9pm Mon-Fri, 5:30pm-9pm Sat-Sun $ lunch $9.50-16, appetizer $6.50-12.50, entrée $16-20, dessert $3-7 C MC, V 59 AC Transit ♿

This is one of the best-known restaurants in the East Bay. The menu changes monthly, but the emphasis is always Mediterranean. Appetizers are creative – buckwheat crepes with smoked trout and horseradish crème fraîche, for example. Beef and chicken are regularly represented, and the fish is always excellent, as are various pastas (such as butternut squash ravioli). Join the matrons of Piedmont at lunch as they gossip about their nannies and their houses at Tahoe, or opt for dinner outside on the plant-shrouded, heated front porch, even on chilly evenings.

Oliveto (Italian)
5655 College Ave ☎ 510-547-5356 ⌚ café: 7am-10pm Mon-Sat, 8am-9pm Sun; restaurant: 11:30am-2:30pm Mon-Fri, 5:30pm-9pm Mon, 5:30pm-9:30pm Tues, 5:30pm-10pm Wed-Sat, 5pm-9pm Sun $ appetizer $8-16, entrée $16-27, dessert $3.50-8 C MC, V, AE M Rockridge BART station ♿

You can sip coffee or wine in the downstairs café (sidewalk tables are nice on a balmy day) or go upstairs for a good Northern Italian meal; specialties are house-cured meats and handmade pastas.

Entertainment

BARS If you're in the mood for a cold brew, try one of the following:

Cato's Ale House
3891 Piedmont Ave ☎ 510-655-3349 ⌚ 11:30am-midnight Mon-Wed, 11:30am-1am Thurs-Sun $ $2.50-4.50/pint 59 AC Transit ♿

Cato's is often quite crowded, but if you can get a seat, you'll have your choice of microbrews. In autumn, it serves a delicious pumpkin ale. Appetizers, stews, and pizzas are hearty and available for $15 and less.

Pacific Coast Brewing Company
DOWNTOWN OAKLAND MAP
906 Washington St ☎ 510-836-2739 ⌚ 11:30am-midnight Mon-Thurs, 11:30am-1am Fri-Sat, 11:30am-11pm Sun $ bar food $6-9.50, pint of beer $4 M 12th St BART station ♿

If you're downtown and thirsting for a brew, try the Gray Whale Ale. It's great with the meat loaf and other tasty comfort foods on the substantive bar menu.

MUSIC If you're near Jack London Square and want to dance or hear good music, you're in luck. (Yoshi's is worth the trip from San Francisco.)

Kimball's Carnival
DOWNTOWN OAKLAND MAP
522 2nd St ☎ 510-444-6979 ⌚ 7pm-midnight Wed-Sat, box office 1pm-6pm Mon-Sat $ $10 Wed, $15 Fri-Sat ♿

This place has 6000 square feet of dance floor where you can boogie to live salsa and merengue bands four nights a week; dance lessons (from 8pm to 9pm) are part of the evening. Call for show information and reservations.

Yoshi's DOWNTOWN OAKLAND MAP
510 Embarcadero West ☎ *510-238-9200*
shows at 8pm & 10pm, some 2pm matinees *$12-26*
www.yoshis.com

For live music, this is Oakland's most famous venue. It bills itself as a world-class jazz club, and that's no lie. The biggest, brightest names, from the legendary to the up-and-coming, play here, and the acoustics are terrific. Recent acts at the time of writing included Nancy Wilson and the Mingus Big Band.

A Cultural Triad

So. You're in the 'Paris of the West,' and while you're in the area you'll want to go to the ballet and the opera and probably take in an art exhibit and tour the campus of a major university. Yachting on the bay would also be an enriching experience, suitably capped off by dinner in a world-class restaurant.

On the off chance that all this culture gives you a cramp in the pinkie finger (and other places), we'll let you in on a little secret: you can take in some ball-cracking and some head-whacking at the Coliseum in Oakland, which is home to three big-time professional sports teams.

Tickets to Oakland Athletics' baseball are cheaper than to that stuck-up other Bay Area baseball club, and here you'll be watching a four-time world championship team. Oakland Raiders football fans are more fun than fans of that red-and-gold San Francisco team that plays in Hurricane – excuse me, I mean 3Com – Park. As for pro basketball, Oakland's Golden State Warriors are the only show in town.

All three teams call the Network Associates Coliseum/Oakland Arena their home, and you can leave your San Francisco hotel and take BART directly there in less than an hour. Call for Athletics tickets at ☎ 510-568-5600, Oakland Raiders Tickets at ☎ 800-949-2626, and Golden State Warriors tickets at ☎ 510-762-2277. And check out the Coliseum's website at www.stadianet.com. The place is definitely not Davies Symphony Hall, but it can still show you a good time.

– Elaine Merrill, a biased A's fan

THEATERS & CINEMAS In Oakland it's easy to avoid the massive cineplexes that are increasingly common in San Francisco.

Paramount Theatre
DOWNTOWN OAKLAND MAP
2025 Broadway ☎ *510-465-6400* *show times vary* *movies $5, prices vary for other events* *19th St BART station*
www.paramounttheatre.com

They don't show movies real often here, but when they do it's an experience. Some titles from a recent program of film classics: *To Kill a Mockingbird, The Birds, My Little Chickadee*.

Periodically, there are big-name musicians in concert, as well as live theater productions. The Paramount is home to the venerable Oakland Ballet (☎ 510-452-9288) and also the Oakland East Bay Symphony (☎ 510-444-0801), which puts on six Friday concerts from November to May. Programs run the gamut from classical to contemporary.

Parkway Theater
DOWNTOWN OAKLAND MAP
1834 Park Blvd ☎ *510-814-2400* *$5* *1[illegible] AC Transit* *downstairs only*
www.picturepubpizza.com

You get the best of both worlds: the comforts of home and a movie on the big screen. You can watch second-run films from comfy couches with a beer, slice of pizza, or sandwich in your hand. Call for show times; note there are weekly special 'baby brigade' shows when infants are welcome.

Getting Around

Downtown Oakland is small enough that you can walk from one place to the next. You even can walk to the Oakland Museum or Lake Merritt, if you're not in a hurry. Biking is definitely an option, but watch for multiple stoplights and heavy traffic in places. If you're auto-less, AC Transit buses and BART can pretty much take you where you need to go. See the Getting There & Away section at the beginning of this chapter for public transit information.

ERKELEY

)ominated by its enormous University of :alifornia campus and long renowned for :s mixture of bizarre street life and acivist politics, Berkeley is a fascinating, nultifaceted small city that maintains an dentity quite distinct from San Franisco's. Birthplace of both the Free Speech Aovement and the California culinary evolution, home to both buttoned-down rofessors and amped-up wastrel youth, he beautiful, hill-backed city is anything ut one-dimensional.

The first Spanish explorers came to the rea in 1772 and were greeted by the local)hlone, whose language and culture soon vere nearly decimated. By the mid-19th entury, the immigrants' land was domiated by farms and the tiny town of)cean View, built on the place where 4th t shops and restaurants now thrive. 3erkeley's defining moment arrived in 866, with the decision to found the ollege here. The first students arrived in 873, and the place hasn't been the same ince.

Today, Berkeley, filled with coffeeouses, eateries, museums, cinemas, record hops, and bookstores, offers visitors the hance to play in its lovely parks and anyons, dine on gourmet cuisine, watch he latest foreign films, or simply gawk at s witch's brew of pierced urchins, street endors, Nobel laureates, and Patagoniavearing yuppies.

)rientation

3erkeley is bordered by the bay to the west, he hills to the east, Oakland to the south, nd Albany and Kensington to the north. -80 runs along the town's western edge, ext to the marina; from here, University Ave heads east to the campus.

Shattuck Ave crosses University Ave a lock west of campus, forming the main rossroads of the downtown area. To the orth is the Northside, including the Gourmet Ghetto' district; to the south is he downtown Berkeley BART station. outhside, including Telegraph and College Ives, is south of campus.

Information

Berkeley Convention & Visitors Bureau
BERKELEY MAP
2015 Center St ☎ 510-549-7040, 510-549-8710 24-hour recorded information, 800-847-4823 ⌚ 9am-5pm Mon-Fri Ⓜ Downtown Berkeley BART station ♿ Ⓦ www.berkeleycvb.com

The friendly staff at this office can offer a wealth of information on what to do and see around town; they also have accommodations information.

Berkeley Historical Society
BERKELEY MAP
1931 Center St ☎ 510-848-0181 ⌚ 1pm-4pm Thurs-Sat $ free Ⓜ Downtown Berkeley BART station ♿ Ⓦ www.ci.berkeley.ca.us/histsoc

This Berkeley history museum offers occasional but excellent Saturday and Sunday walking tours of town; call for a schedule.

Berkeley *Daily Planet*
☎ 510-841-5600 $ free

This small daily has an events calendar and some local news.

Daily Californian
☎ 510-548-8300 $ free Ⓦ www.dailycal.org

This paper comes out Monday to Friday during the academic year; it emphasizes campus news and carries a daily calendar of UC-related events.

University of California, Berkeley

The Berkeley campus of the University of California is the oldest and second-largest

ANDREW DEAN NYSTROM

Only in Berkeley...

university in the state. It has more than 32,000 students, more than 1000 professors, and more Nobel laureates than you could point a particle accelerator at. Among its more interesting offerings are the Museum of Paleontology, with its Tyrannosaurus rex skeleton; the Bancroft Library, which has some interesting California history exhibits; and the Phoebe Hearst Museum of Anthropology. To locate various university sites, go to UC Berkeley Visitor Services or check maps posted at various locations throughout the campus.

The Campus BERKELEY MAP
☎ *510-642-6000* Ⓜ *Downtown Berkeley BART station* 🚌 *52, 64 AC Transit*
w *www.berkeley.edu*

From Telegraph Ave, enter the campus via Sproul Plaza and Sather Gate, a center for people-watching, soapbox oration, and drumming. Or enter campus from Center and Oxford Sts, near the downtown Berkeley BART station.

UC Berkeley Visitor Services
BERKELEY MAP
101 University Hall, 2200 University Ave
☎ *510-642-5215* ⌚ *10am-4pm Mon-Fri, 10am-5pm Sat-Sun* $ *free* 🚌 *64 AC Transit* ♿
w *www.berkeley.edu/visitors*

Campus maps and information are available here. The center, staffed by students cheery enough to charm the grumpiest curmudgeon, offers free campus tours at 10am from Monday to Saturday and at 1 pm Sunday, as well as dorm tours for prospective students.

Campanile
☎ *510-642-4636* ⌚ *10am-4pm Mon-Fri, 10am-5pm Sat-Sun* $ *adult $2, child $1*

This landmark structure is officially named Sather Tower. Modeled on St Mark's Basilica in Venice, the 307-foot spire offers fine views over the Bay Area. At the top, you can stare up into a carillon of 61 bells – ranging in size from a cereal bowl to a Volkswagen – and, at noon, watch a carillonist play one of three booming daily recitals.

Berkeley Art Museum BERKELEY MAP
2626 Bancroft Way ☎ *510-642-0808*
⌚ *11am-5pm Wed & Fri-Sun, 11am-9pm Thurs* $ *adult $6, senior/student/child $4; free 11am-noon & 5pm-9pm Thurs* 🚌 *7, 51,*

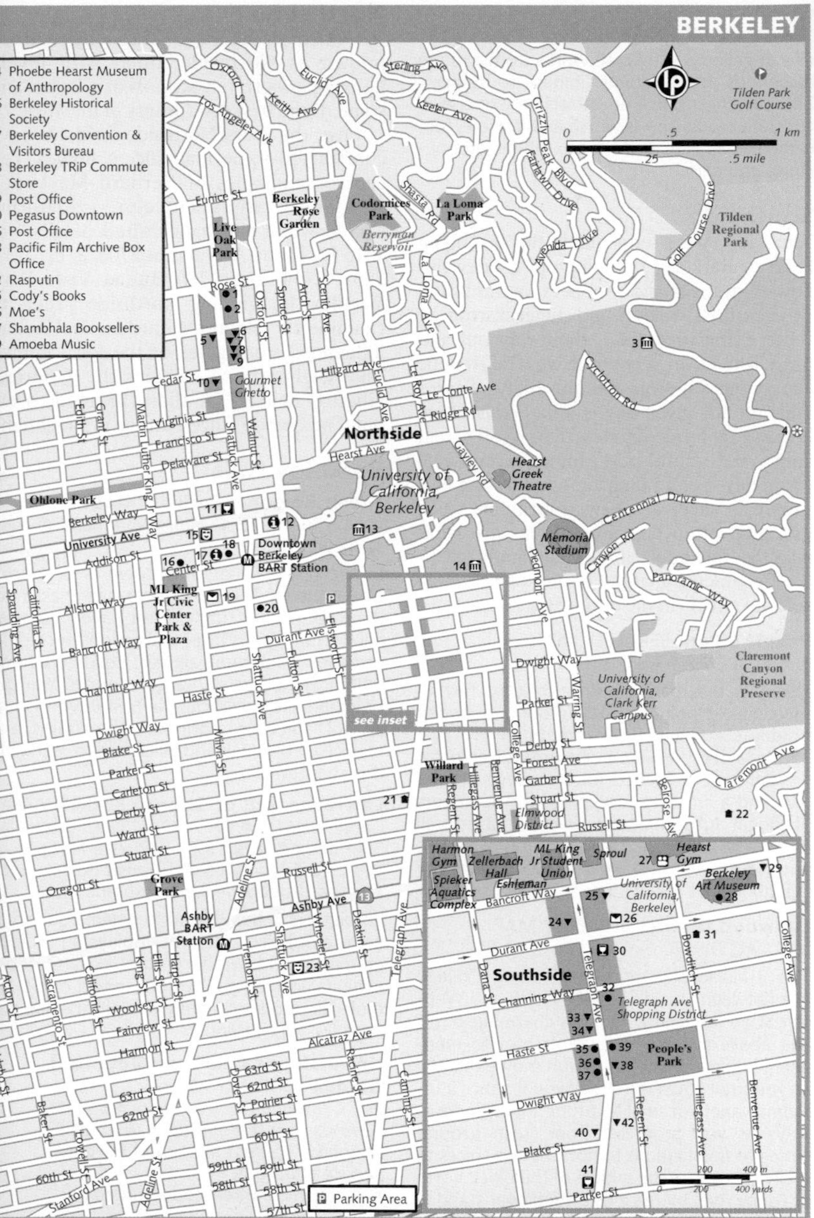
BERKELEY
4 Phoebe Hearst Museum of Anthropology
6 Berkeley Historical Society
7 Berkeley Convention & Visitors Bureau
8 Berkeley TRiP Commute Store
9 Post Office
0 Pegasus Downtown
5 Post Office
8 Pacific Film Archive Box Office
2 Rasputin
5 Cody's Books
6 Moe's
7 Shambhala Booksellers
9 Amoeba Music
Tilden Park Golf Course
0
.5
1 km
0
.25
.5 mile
Tilden Regional Park
Berkeley Rose Garden
Codornices Park
La Loma Park
Berryman Reservoir
Live Oak Park
Gourmet Ghetto
Northside
University of California, Berkeley
Hearst Greek Theatre
Memorial Stadium
Ohlone Park
Downtown Berkeley BART Station
ML King Jr Civic Center Park & Plaza
see inset
University of California, Clark Kerr Campus
Claremont Canyon Regional Preserve
Willard Park
Elmwood District
Grove Park
Ashby BART Station
Harmon Gym
Zellerbach Hall
ML King Jr Student Union
Sproul
Hearst Gym
Spieker Aquatics Complex
Eshleman
University of California, Berkeley
Berkeley Art Museum
Southside
Telegraph Ave Shopping District
People's Park
0
200
400 m
0
200
400 yards
Parking Area

64 AC Transit
www.bampfa.berkeley.edu

Eleven galleries showcase works from a range of periods, from ancient Chinese to modern. The building itself – an attractive exercise in concrete brutalism – is worth a visit. Here, too, is the Pacific Film Archive box office, a bookstore, and café.

Southside

Telegraph Ave is undeniably the throbbing heart of Berkeley, pumping out a sidewalk-flow of students and shoppers, vagrants and vendors, brisk walkers and sluggish strollers, those trying to squeeze their way out and those who never seem to leave. The frenetic energy buzzing from the university's Sather Gate on any given day is a mix of honking horns and loud debates over God's real name, of youthful post-hippies reminiscing about days before their time and young hipsters who sneer at tie-dyed nostalgia. Such different, often opposing, forces are what give the Telegraph area its distinctly rebellious character, making it one of the most colorful streets in the entire Bay Area.

People's Park BERKELEY MAP
free *51 AC Transit*

This park is a marker in local history, having served as a political battleground between residents and city government in the late 1960s. Since then it's been ground zero for dissidents, a residence for Berkeley's homeless, and a lucrative workplace for purveyors of illegal substances. It holds a basketball court, a sandy volleyball area, and a tot lot, but you'll never mistake it for your everyday neighborhood green.

Elmwood District BERKELEY MAP
51 AC Transit

This 3-block-long retail area, along College Ave between Stuart St on the north and Webster St on the south, contains charming shops and above-average restaurants, not to mention a bookstore and a first-run movie theater. As you stroll down the street, you'll notice a titillating variety of smells wafting through doorways as you progress: from fresh ground coffee to floral lotions to hot Chinese spices to sticky candies. In the middle of the block north of Ashby Ave, there's a colorful flower stand in an alleyway that leads to a public parking lot.

Northside

Just north of campus is the neighborhood known as Northside, filled with lovely homes, parks, stately schools of religion, and some of the best restaurants in the West.

Over the years, Northside residents have constructed some magnificent homes. You can see examples of Bernard Maybeck's Arts and Crafts architecture – featuring carved wood and handcrafted details – at 1515 La Loma Ave and at 2704, 2711, 2733, 2751, 2754, and 2780 Buena Vista Way. Wander the winding Northside streets to examine the elaborate gardens and Asian-influenced front gates of the local homes. The neighborhood includes the 'Gourmet Ghetto,' heaven for those inclined to eat out. The deified Chez Panisse is a highlight.

Berkeley Hills

Tilden Regional Park BERKELEY MAP
510-562-7275 *8am-10pm daily* *free*
67 AC Transit

In the hills east of downtown is Berkeley's crown jewel. This 2079-acre park has more than 30 miles of trails, from paved paths to hilly scrambles. Other attractions include a carousel, miniature railroad, children's farm, botanical garden, and a golf course. You can swim in Lake Anza; call the East Bay Regional Parks District for information, brochures, and maps (see the Oakland Hills section, earlier in this chapter).

Lawrence Hall of Science BERKELEY MAP
Centennial Dr *510-642-5132* *10am-5pm daily* *adult $7, senior/student $5, ages 3-6 $3* *8, 65 AC Transit*
www.lhs.berkeley.edu/lhshome.html

Youngsters in tow? Head to where you can all enjoy a huge collection of displays on subjects ranging from lasers to earthquakes. Outdoor exhibits, including a 60-foot model of a DNA molecule, compete with a breathtaking bay view for your attention.

University of California Botanical Garden BERKELEY MAP
200 Centennial Dr, No 5045 *510-642-3343* *9am-4:45pm daily* *adult $3, senior $2, student free, child $1* *Hill Service Shuttle*
www.mip.berkeley.edu/garden

Here you'll find 34 acres containing more than

3,000 plant species from all over the world, ne of the most varied collections in the US. ick up a self-guided tour at the gift shop; here's a different one for every season. Gardening junkies may deliberately get lost here.

West Berkeley

4th St Shopping District BERKELEY MAP

Hidden near the freeway in West Berkeley lies he glitz of this 3-block street mall. Background music is supplied by screaming seagulls and the moaning whistles of long freight rains that clatter by day and night.

Berkeley Marina BERKELEY MAP

free *51 AC Transit* ♿

f your credit cards are maxed or you don't want to shop, take a stroll around the marina, built on reclaimed land as a WPA project. Fragments of a 3-mile-long pier still jut into the bay; overhead, shorebirds defend their air space from an almost daily blitz of colorful kites.

Places to Stay

If you decide to stay the night, the Berkeley Convention & Visitors Bureau can help with lodging suggestions (see the Information section, earlier).

Berkeley and Oakland Bed & Breakfast Network

☎ *510-547-6380*

This hotline has information on private homes that offer lodging, from private suites to garden cottages.

Fido Ratings

If you're traveling with Fido, the East Bay offers room to ramble for both you and your pooch. There are a couple of small parks where unleashed dogs rule, and the East Bay Regional Parks are pretty much doggie heaven. East Bay Park regulations stipulate:

> Dogs may run at large within District parklands provided the owner, keeper or person exercising the dog(s) has a leash capable of fixed six-foot length in their [*sic*] possession and keeps their [*sic*] animal(s) under control at all times….Dogs may be off-leash in open space and other undeveloped areas of parklands, provided they are under control at all times.

Redwood Regional Park, in the Oakland hills east of the Montclair neighborhood, is particularly bucolic, with its 4-mile-long East Ridge Trail providing a wide, tree-shaded path with plenty of room for Fido to run while you look for hawks riding the wind currents. There's a view, thrown in for free, of Mt Diablo rising majestically in the distance. Fido rates this one four woofs.

The Ohlone Greenway, a swath of open space bordering a path that runs through Berkeley and north into Albany, has a small off-leash area next to Hearst Ave just east of Milvia St. This one, little more than half a square city block of dog-soaked turf, attracts mainly neighborhood regulars. Canines may find themselves a bit cramped; owners may find themselves deep in existential discussion with UC Berkeley professors who've dropped by to exercise their mutts. Fido rates this one two woofs (the company is great, but there's not a lot of running room and no view).

Cesar Chavez Park, at the Berkeley Marina (follow University Ave to the bay and bear right all the way to the end), also has a dog park. This one is on a gentle hill, with bay views and a fair amount of space for chasing tennis balls. To get to the off-leash area, you must walk a quarter mile or so from the street on a paved path. Fido, who does like to run, gives it three and a half woofs.

Point Isabel Regional Shoreline, an East Bay Regional Parks property on the San Francisco Bay Trail, at the north end of the East Bay (take I-80 to the Central Ave exit in El Cerrito), is what dog owners mean when they ask 'Have you been to the dog park?' Every dog who is *any* dog ends up at Point Isabel sometime, cavorting along a looping waterside path while a mandatory accompanying human takes in the amazing three-bridge view (Bay Bridge, Golden Gate, Richmond–San Rafael). Fido rates this one at the max – five woofs.

Rose Garden Inn BERKELEY MAP
2740 Telegraph Ave ☎ 510-549-2145
$ singles $119, doubles $229 C *MC, V, AE*
52, 43 AC Transit
e *info@rosegardeninn.com*

This charmer is quaint and close to campus, with pretty gardens, rooms, and suites. Breakfast and afternoon tea are included in the rates.

Hotel Durant BERKELEY MAP
2600 Durant Ave ☎ 510-845-8981 $ $140-195 C *MC, V 51 AC Transit*
e *durant@sfo.com*

This 140-room hotel is close to campus and offers a restaurant as well as a sports bar and a newsstand.

Claremont Resort & Spa BERKELEY MAP
41 Tunnel Rd ☎ 510-843-3000
$ singles/doubles $260-390, suites $450-950; 4-day spa packages: singles $1499, doubles $2399 C *MC, V, AE 6, 7 AC Transit*
e *reservations@claremontresort.com*

Opened in 1915 as a destination for fog-bound San Franciscans looking for a brief escape, the Claremont offers modern travelers (at least the well-heeled ones) the same option. You can drop in to Jordan's for lunch (try the roasted vegetable ravioli in a delicate yellow squash puree). Or spend a day or four at the spa, where services range from a Reflexology foot massage to a Spa Celebration package that includes the use of the whirlpool, steam room, deluge showers, and swimming pools and body scrubs. The spa offers body pampering of all kinds, from facials to body wraps to a therapeutic flotation tank.

Places to Eat

TELEGRAPH AVE Here you'll find the best variety of international cheap eats, catering mainly to the ravenous student seeking to fuel brilliant mind and burly body without breaking the bank.

Blondie's (pizza) BERKELEY MAP
2340 Telegraph Ave ☎ 510-548-1129
10am-1am Mon-Thurs & Sat, 10am-2am Fri, 11am-midnight Sun $ $2.50-5 C *cash only 40 AC Transit*

Fast-moving lines and a hefty pizza slice for $2 to $3 make Blondie's among the area's best lunch stops.

Cafe Intermezzo (café fare)
BERKELEY MAP
2442 Telegraph Ave ☎ 510-849-4592
coffee: 8:30am-10pm, food: 10:30am-10pm $ $3.50-5.50 C *cash only 64 AC Transit*

This longtime Telegraph Ave standout hold the title for the biggest sandwiches (on fres bread) and the most impressive salads.

Mario's La Fiesta (Mexican)
BERKELEY MAP
2444 Telegraph Ave ☎ 510-848-2588
10:30am-10:30pm daily $ $2-9 C *cash only 64 AC Transit*

Mario's is *the* Southside place for large serv ings of Mexican food.

Better sit-down meals are found down Tele graph Ave past Dwight Way.

Blue Nile (Ethiopian) BERKELEY MAP
2525 Telegraph Ave ☎ 510-540-6777
11:30am-10pm Tues-Sat, 5pm-10pm Sur
$ lunch $9-10, dinner $10-12 C *MC, V*
64 AC Transit

Eating finger-licking good Ethiopian food wit your hands gets easier as you sip your glass c honey wine.

On the corner of Telegraph Ave and Blak St sits The Village, a wooden structur housing an indoor mall with a handful c stores and surprisingly decent restaurants.

Norikonoko (Japanese) BERKELEY MAP
2556 Telegraph Ave ☎ 510-548-1274
11:30am-2pm & 5:30pm-9:30pm Wed-Mon $ $10-15 C *MC, V 64 AC Transit*

This is the place for home-style Japanese dishe

ELMWOOD DISTRICT The stretch o College Ave that passes through Elmwoo boasts some fine restaurants.

La Méditerranée (Mediterranean)
2936 College Ave ☎ 510-540-7773
10am-10pm Mon-Thurs, 10am-11pm Fri Sat, 10am-9:30pm Sun $ lunch $7, appetizer $4.50-7.50, entrée $7.50-9, dessert $4
C *MC, V 51 AC Transit*

This moderately priced restaurant offers tempting selection, including a vegetaria Middle Eastern plate with Grecian spinach an feta cheese, a rolled Levant sandwich, chees karni, and a grape leaf–wrapped dolma. Twangy background music and framed Greek posters complete the experience.

Shen Hua (Northern Chinese)
2914 College Ave ☎ 510-883-1777
⌚ 11:30am-2:30pm Mon-Sat, 5pm-9:30pm Sun-Thurs, 5pm-10pm Fri-Sat $ appetizer $5.50-11, entrée $8-15 C MC, V, AE 🚌 51 AC Transit ♿

This Chinese restaurant feels special, partly because of the airy main dining room and partly because it offers non–meat eaters a large selection of tofu and seafood dishes.

Trattoria La Siciliana (Sicilian)
2993 College Ave ☎ 510-704-1474 ⌚ 5pm-10pm Tues-Sun $ $13-25 C cash only 🚌 51 AC Transit ♿ downstairs only

An Italian food itch could (happily) lead you here. The pasta dishes are always creative and are always cooked by one of the owners. The charming decor includes interior balconies.

NORTHSIDE & DOWNTOWN The Northside, or the Gourmet Ghetto as it's known by Bay Area food devotees, is the birthplace of so-called California cuisine.

Cheese Board (cheeses, breads, pizza) BERKELEY MAP
1504 Shattuck Ave ☎ 510-549-3183
⌚ 7am-1pm Mon, 7am-6pm Tues-Fri, 7:30am-5pm Sat $ $8-16 C cash only 🚌 7, 51 AC Transit ♿

This Gourmet Ghetto mainstay has an amazing variety of cheeses; try a killer goat cheese pizza for a satisfying lunch.

Cha-Am (Thai) BERKELEY MAP
1543 Shattuck Ave ☎ 510-848-9664
⌚ 11:30am-3:30pm Mon-Sat, 5pm-9:30pm Sun-Thurs, 5pm-10pm Fri-Sat $ lunch/appetizer $5-6, entrée $6-9 C MC, V, AE 🚌 7, 51 AC Transit

This Thai restaurant has succulent curries and vegetarian offerings.

Cafe de la Paz (Spanish) BERKELEY MAP
1600 Shattuck Ave ☎ 510-843-0662
⌚ 11:45am-2:30pm Mon-Fri, 11am-3pm Sat-Sun, 5:30pm-9:30pm Mon-Thurs, 5:30pm-10pm Fri, 5pm-10pm Sat, 5pm-9:30pm Sun; express burrito bar: noon-2pm Mon-Sat $ appetizer $1.50-8, entrée $12-20 C MC, V 🚌 51 AC Transit ♿

This is a warm and cheerful place. Specialties are tapas and other Spanish and Latin American dishes, from a good paella to an Argentina-style barbecued beefsteak. Bonus: call to see when the next community musical event is scheduled.

César (tapas, desserts) BERKELEY MAP
1515 Shattuck Ave ☎ 510-883-0222
⌚ kitchen: 4pm-11pm, bar: 4pm-midnight $ tapas $4-8.50, dessert $4 C MC, V 🚌 43 AC Transit ♿

This airy tapas bar routinely makes every 'best-of' list, turning out simple and delicious small dishes and providing an impressive selection of wines and liquors. But don't let the small prices of the tapas plates fool you into thinking that this is a budget restaurant; those plates add up, and you could drop quite a bit of money here.

Chez Panisse (California) BERKELEY MAP
1517 Shattuck Ave ☎ 510-548-5525
⌚ café dinner: 11:30am-3pm & 5pm-10:30pm Mon-Thurs, 11:30am-3:30pm & 5pm-11:30pm Fri-Sat; restaurant 1st seating: 6pm-6:30pm Mon-Sat; restaurant 2nd seating: 8:30pm-9:30pm Mon-Sat $ café entrée $15.50-17; café dessert $4-6; fixed-price restaurant (15% service added) $45-75 C MC, V 🚌 7, 51 AC Transit ♿

Got a suitcase full of cash? Worship at the feet of Alice Waters, inventor of California cuisine.

Food guru Alice Waters

Chez Panisse, where menus change nightly, is in a lovely Arts and Crafts house. Downstairs you're served phenomenal prix fixe meals – pasta in shellfish broth, beef tenderloin with black truffles (the price of a meal rises as the week progresses). The upstairs café offers à la carte fare such as oven-baked calamari or grilled swordfish. For a world-famous temple of gastronomy, the place has retained a welcoming atmosphere. Make your reservations several weeks in advance.

WEST BERKELEY Mixed among the shops in the 4th St Shopping District are a couple of great spots for fresh food.

Café Rouge (Continental)
1782 4th St ☎ 510-525-1440 ⌚ 11:30am-3pm Mon, 11:30am-9:30pm Tues-Thurs & Sun, 11:30am-10:30pm Fri-Sat $ lunch $9-14, appetizer $8-12, entrée $15-32, dessert $6-8 C MC, V, AE ⊘ 🚌 9 AC Transit ♿

This café, rustic in a most genteel way, covers all the bases by offering an oyster bar as well as specialty meats from its own organic meat market. The menu changes weekly, based on seasonal fresh fruits and vegetables. Try a mean martini at the convivial center-of-the-room bar.

O Chamé (nouveau Japanese)
1830 4th St ☎ 510-841-8783 ⌚ 11:30am-3pm Mon-Sat, 5:30pm-9pm Mon-Thurs, 5:30pm-9:30pm Fri-Sat $ lunch $10.50-16.50, appetizer $6-9.50, entrée $16.50-20, dessert $3-5 C MC, V, AE ⊘ 🚌 9 AC Transit ♿

This upscale pseudo-Japanese place specializes in bowls of savory udon or soba noodles served in clear fish broth.

Entertainment

COFFEEHOUSES A mainstay for students and locals alike, coffeehouses dot every neighborhood, and the smell of fresh grounds wafts through the air above Berkeley from early morning 'til late at night. Some of the more notable include **Cafe Milano** (☎ 510-644-3100, 2522 Bancroft Way), **International House** (☎ 510-642-9932, 2299 Piedmont Ave), and **Caffe Strada** (☎ 510-843-5282, 2300 College Ave).

Mediterraneum Caffe (café fare)
BERKELEY MAP
2475 Telegraph Ave ☎ 510-549-1128 ⌚ 7am-midnight daily $ $1-6 C cash only ⊘ 🚌 64 AC Transit ♿

'The Med' is a Telegraph legend, known as a haven for intellectual mavericks clear back to the Free Speech days of the '60s. Espresso drinks are the main fare, but don't dismiss getting a meal of eggs or pancakes; later in the day the soups, salads, and pasta dishes may tempt you. If you want to buy a 'F**k the Police' T-shirt, they're often on sale right outside.

Peet's Coffee & Tea (espresso drinks, tea) BERKELEY MAP
2124 Vine St ☎ 510-841-0564 ⌚ 7am-7pm Mon-Sat, 8am-7pm Sun C MC, V, AE, DC ⊘ 🚌 7, 51 AC Transit ♿

Pick up fine teas and coffees at Peet's (just step over the dogs that loll around outside as if they owned the place). This is the original store in this local chain; there's another at the center of the 4th St Shopping District.

BARS & CLUBS There are lots of college watering holes near the campus, but unless you're a student, Berkeley isn't the best place for bar-hopping.

Bison Brewery Co BERKELEY MAP
2598 Telegraph Ave ☎ 510-841-7734 ⌚ bar 11am-1am Tues-Sun; kitchen: noon-10pm Tues-Thurs & Sun, noon-midnight Fri-Sat $ $3.50 🚌 64 AC Transit ♿ W www.bisonbrew.com

This lively place serves its own brews and has a pool table, live music on weekends, and a decent menu featuring hearty tacos and pizza.

Blake's BERKELEY MAP
2367 Telegraph Ave ☎ 510-848-0886 ⌚ 11:30am-2am Mon-Fri, noon-2am Sat, noon-1am Sun $ $3-6 🚌 64 AC Transit W www.blakes.citysearch.com

This one's *the* Berkeley nightspot for live music, notably blues (downstairs; cover charge), with bars on three floors, a menu of tolerable eats, and two pool tables.

Spats BERKELEY MAP
1974 Shattuck Ave ☎ 510-841-7225 ⌚ 4pm-1am Mon-Thurs, 4pm-2am Fri-Sat $ $3-10 🚌 43, 52 AC Transit ♿ W www.spats.citysearch.com

This saloon is Berkeley's best place for a mixed drink. It's filled with antique and cushy furniture and offers a long menu of exotic alcoholic beverages.

nited Capoeira Association & :apoeira Arts Cafe
'26 Addison St ☎ 510-666-1255 ⌚ 7am-'pm Mon-Fri, 7am-5pm Sat; introductory lass 5pm-6pm Mon-Fri ⓢ introductory class 5 Ⓜ Downtown Berkeley BART station ♿ W www.capoeiraarts.com

)rop in at this lively, colorful space for a class ı capoeira, the Brazilian martial art/dance orm done to lively music. Or order a 'Mind 'our Brain' smoothie off the café menu and ettle in to watch.

HEATERS & CINEMAS This university own has some terrific venues for live theater nd film (all within walking distance of ARТ).

erkeley Repertory Theatre ERKELEY MAP
025 Addison St ☎ 510-845-4700 ⓢ ticket 42.50-52 Ⓜ Downtown Berkeley BART tation ♿
W www.berkeleyrep.org

his respected theater mounts seven producons a year (July to September) of classic, conemporary, and new plays. A 600-seat facility vith a proscenium stage, opened in March 001, has generated new excitement for an lready vibrant venue.

a Peña Cultural Center BERKELEY MAP
105 Shattuck Ave ☎ 510-849-2568
Ⓜ Ashby BART station 🚌 43 AC Transit ♿
W www.lapena.org

a Peña offers music, theater, and other culıral events imbued with Latin American flaor. Friday night in the café, there's live music arting at 8pm.

acific Film Archive Theater ERKELEY MAP
575 Bancroft Way (theater); 2621 Durant ve (box office) ☎ 510-642-1412 ⌚ 11am-om box office ⓢ adult $7, senior/child $4, C student $4.50 Ⓜ Downtown Berkeley ART station 🚌 7, 51, 64 AC Transit ♿
W www.bampfa.berkeley.edu

red of Leonardo DeCaprio? The PFA is inernationally known as an educational center ıd exhibition venue for all types of cinema. features daily film and video screenings on l subjects from all eras and most countries. 'ograms change daily as the archive pursues s stated goals of increasing the understandg and appreciation of the art of cinema. Don't come here looking for the run-of-the-mill flick.

Zellerbach Hall BERKELEY MAP
☎ 510-642-9988 Ⓜ Downtown Berkeley BART station 🚌 51 AC Transit ♿
W www.calperfs.berkeley.edu

Dance and music of all types and styles, performed by national and international groups, are featured here. It's also the location of the Cal Performances Ticket Office, which sells tickets to all kinds of campus events.

Shopping

TELEGRAPH AVE Telegraph Ave offers everything from handmade sidewalk-vendor jewelry to head-shop paraphernalia, but its most appealing shops are its terrific book and music stores. The city has a reputation as a haven for bookstores, both near and not so near to campus.

Amoeba Music BERKELEY MAP
2455 Telegraph Ave ☎ 510-549-1125
⌚ 10:30am-10pm Mon-Sat, 11am-9pm Sun
🚌 40, 64 AC Transit ♿

Here's another gold mine for mass quantities of new and used CDs, tapes, and vinyl platters.

Cody's Books BERKELEY MAP
2454 Telegraph Ave ☎ 510-845-7852
⌚ 10am-10pm daily 🚌 40, 64 AC Transit ♿

Cody's carries one of the widest selections of new books in the world and regularly hosts author appearances. The floor staff are refreshingly knowledgeable – if you're lucky,

RICK GERHARTER

Tie-dyes and trinkets for sale on Telegraph Ave

you'll get waited on by Beth Ann. Look for the 4th St shop at 1730 4th St (☎ 510-559-9500).

Moe's BERKELEY MAP
2476 Telegraph Ave ☎ 510-849-2087
10am-11pm Sun-Thurs, 10am-midnight Fri-Sat 40, 64 AC Transit

Moe's offers four floors of new and used book-browsing; check out the art and antiquarian section – there's a large array of photography books.

Rasputin BERKELEY MAP
2401 Telegraph Ave ☎ 510-848-9004
10am-11pm Mon-Sat, 11am-11pm Sun 40, 64 AC Transit

Music, mass quantities of new and used CDs, tapes, and records (yes, lots of vinyl) can be found here.

Shambhala Booksellers BERKELEY MAP
2482 Telegraph Ave ☎ 510-848-8443
11am-8pm daily 64 AC Transit

This bookstore presents a serene setting for perusing metaphysical, spiritual, and New Age books. Take note of the tarot cards, too.

ELMWOOD DISTRICT Scattered between restaurants are specialty shops selling delightfully indulgent products.

Body Time
2911 College Ave ☎ 510-845-2101
10am-6:30pm Mon-Sat, 11am-6pm Sun 51 AC Transit

This local chain, established 30 years ago as a self-described 'hippy-dippy family soap business,' now peddles heavenly lotions – many unscented for the allergy-prone. Go ahead, treat your face.

Sweet Dreams
5709 College Ave ☎ 510-549-1211
51 AC Transit

You'll be drawn by your nose to this good-smelling shop, and you'll stay to check out the unusual jewelry and gift items.

NORTHSIDE & DOWNTOWN Some excellent bookstores will draw you in if you wander around the Gourmet Ghetto.

Pegasus Downtown BERKELEY MAP
2349 Shattuck Ave ☎ 510-649-1320
10am-10pm Sun-Thurs, 10am-10:45pm Fri-Sat Downtown Berkeley BART station

Pegasus carries a wide-ranging selection of new and used books and a noteworthy assortment of hard-to-find CDs. There's another branch in North Berkeley (☎ 510-525-6888, 1855 Solano Ave).

Black Oak Books BERKELEY MAP
1491 Shattuck Ave ☎ 510-486-0698
10am-10pm daily 43 AC Transit

Northside bibliophiles love this place, with new and used books and a full calendar of author appearances.

Easy Going BERKELEY MAP
1385 Shattuck Ave ☎ 510-843-3533
10am-7pm Mon-Fri, 10am-6pm Sat, noon-6pm Sun 43, 52 AC Transit

This long-standing and excellent travel bookstore also sells travel-related luggage and gizmos and sponsors author events.

FOURTH ST SHOPPING DISTRICT This area offers the finest in upscale shopping from urban-industrial home gadgetry to handmade papers.

Hear Music
1809B 4th St ☎ 510-204-9595 10am-8pm Mon-Thurs, 9am-9pm Fri-Sat, 9am-8pm Sun 9 AC Transit

When this store opened in the early 1990s it made the news by re-introducing the '50s practice of letting customers listen to their selections before buying them. Its listener booths are still crowded, and a wide range of music – jazz, contemporary, and classics – is for sale.

Restoration Hardware
1733 4th St ☎ 510-526-6424 10am-7pm Mon-Sat, 11am-6pm Sun 9 AC Transit

This elegant and quirky home accessory emporium, right across the street from Cody Books, specializes in retro bathroom hardware; you can also pick up such goodies as a $3 chrome-headed hammer.

Stained Glass Garden
1800 4th St ☎ 510-841-2200 10am-5:30pm Mon-Wed & Fri, 10am-7pm Thurs, 10am-5pm Sat, noon-4pm Sun 9 AC Transit

This airy indoor garden of sparkling glass offers everything from heavy-duty serving plates to sparkling earrings. For the craftsperson, a full range of glass-working tools and equipment is also available.

ur La Table
806 4th St ☎ 510-849-2252 ⏲ 9am-6pm aily 🚌 9 AC Transit ♿

his trendy kitchen store, right across the ɔurtyard from Peet's, conducts business with French accent – it offers cooking classes, ɔo. The genteel sign that greets you at the oor says all you probably need to know bout the store and about the chichi neighorhood it inhabits: 'We kindly request that ou carry your pet while you are in the store. Merci.'

;etting Around

'ublic transit and your feet are the best ptions for getting around crowded entral Berkeley. Parking near campus is ifficult. University-run parking areas – ne on College Ave between Durant Ave nd Channing Way, the other on Bancroft Vay between Telegraph Ave and Dana St – harge $1 up to one hour, $3 for one to wo hours, $5 for two to three hours, and n up. In the evenings and on weekends, ıere are other university lots open to the ublic for varying fees – usually about $3.

;erkeley TRiP Commute Store
ERKELEY MAP
033 Center St ☎ 510-644-7665 ⏲ noon-:30pm Tues-Fri Ⓜ Downtown Berkeley ART station ♿
www.public-safety.berkeley.edu/trip

his commute store has all sorts of public and lternative transportation information, which ıakes its short business hours a real shame. Vhen it's open, come here to purchase tickts and passes for various Bay Area transit ptions.

AC Transit operates public buses in Berkeεy; see the Getting There & Away section t the beginning of this chapter.

;ampus Transit
510-642-5149 $ 25¢-50¢ ♿ limited
www.public-safety.berkeley.edu ɔ&t/transit.html

he university's bus service runs all kinds of huttles – day and night – within the campus, round the perimeter, in the hills, and to ART stations and other points. Just telehone or check the website for complete chedules.

AROUND BERKELEY

San Francisco Bay Trail
$ free ♿ limited
W www.abag.ca.gov/bayarea/baytrail

At the time of writing, the East Bay portion of this projected nine-county 400-mile-plus ring trail around San Francisco Bay stretched from Richmond Harbor to Emeryville. It's a great way to see the bay. Biking, hiking, jogging, skating – any mode not involving motors – will get you up and down this long paved path that passes through a variety of locales including fishing piers, marinas, and parks.

Rosie the Riveter Memorial
$ free 🚌 74 AC Transit ♿
W www.ci.richmond.ca.us/~arts/art /rosie_dedication_photos.html

This memorial to women laborers of WWII was dedicated in 2000 at the former location of Kaiser Shipyards in Richmond, at the northern end of the East Bay section of the San Francisco Bay Trail. It is a 441-foot walkway (the length of a liberty ship) accented with images and text. Stroll the length of the memorial to the water's edge; you'll hear the laughter of children in the nearby park as you ponder historic photos etched on porcelain, follow a time line and read quotations from the women who kept the country running when the men went off to war.

Marin County

If there's a part of the Bay Area that consciously tries to live up to the California dream, it's Marin (pronounced muh-**rin**) County. Just a short drive across the Golden Gate Bridge from San Francisco, Marin's breathtaking views of San Francisco, abundance of hiking and biking trails, and great climate make it a wonderful day trip from the city. Visitors come to Marin for the splendor of Mt Tamalpais, Muir Woods, Point Reyes, and the wild Pacific coastline, as well as for the charm of its well-kept artsy communities, such as waterfront Sausalito and woodsy Mill Valley.

Getting There & Away

Even though Marin can be reached by ferry or bus, there are few public transportation

MARIN COUNTY

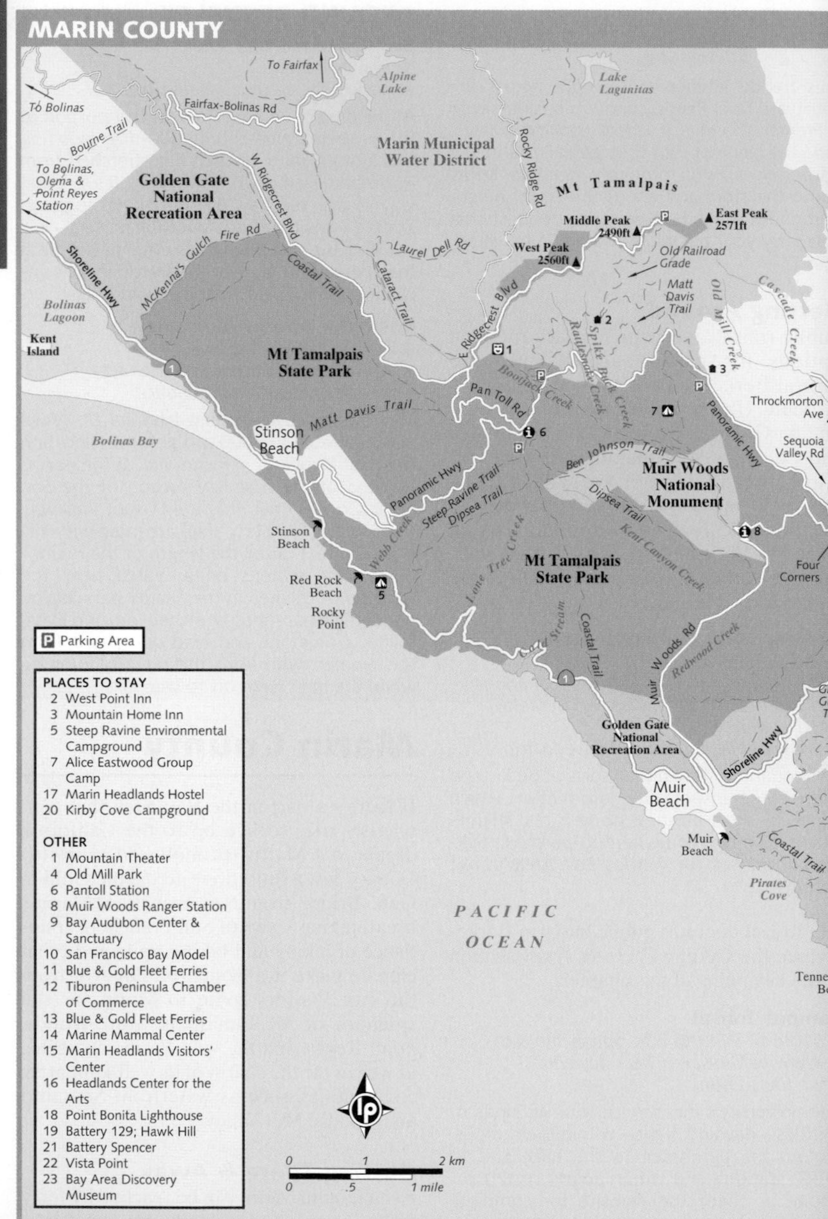
To Fairfax
Alpine Lake
Lake Lagunitas
To Bolinas
Fairfax-Bolinas Rd
Bourne Trail
Marin Municipal Water District
To Bolinas, Olema & Point Reyes Station
Golden Gate National Recreation Area
W Ridgecrest Blvd
Rocky Ridge Rd
Mt Tamalpais
Middle Peak 2490ft
East Peak 2571ft
West Peak 2560ft
McKenna's Gulch Fire Rd
Laurel Dell Rd
Old Railroad Grade
Shoreline Hwy
Coastal Trail
Cataract Trail
Matt Davis Trail
Old Mill Creek
Cascade Creek
Bolinas Lagoon
E Ridgecrest Blvd
Kent Island
Mt Tamalpais State Park
Rattlesnake Creek
Spike Buck Creek
Bootjack Creek
Pan Toll Rd
Throckmorton Ave
Panoramic Hwy
Stinson Beach
Matt Davis Trail
Bolinas Bay
Sequoia Valley Rd
Ben Johnson Trail
Muir Woods National Monument
Steep Ravine Trail
Dipsea Trail
Kent Canyon Creek
Webb Creek
Lone Tree Creek
Stinson Beach
Red Rock Beach
Rocky Point
Mt Tamalpais State Park
Four Corners
Cold Stream
Coastal Trail
Muir Woods Rd
Redwood Creek
Parking Area
Golden Gate National Recreation Area
Shoreline Hwy
Muir Beach
Muir Beach
Coastal Trail
Pirates Cove
PACIFIC OCEAN
PLACES TO STAY
2 West Point Inn
3 Mountain Home Inn
5 Steep Ravine Environmental Campground
7 Alice Eastwood Group Camp
17 Marin Headlands Hostel
20 Kirby Cove Campground
OTHER
1 Mountain Theater
4 Old Mill Park
6 Pantoll Station
8 Muir Woods Ranger Station
9 Bay Audubon Center & Sanctuary
10 San Francisco Bay Model
11 Blue & Gold Fleet Ferries
12 Tiburon Peninsula Chamber of Commerce
13 Blue & Gold Fleet Ferries
14 Marine Mammal Center
15 Marin Headlands Visitors' Center
16 Headlands Center for the Arts
18 Point Bonita Lighthouse
19 Battery 129; Hawk Hill
21 Battery Spencer
22 Vista Point
23 Bay Area Discovery Museum
0 1 2 km
0 .5 1 mile

MARIN COUNTY

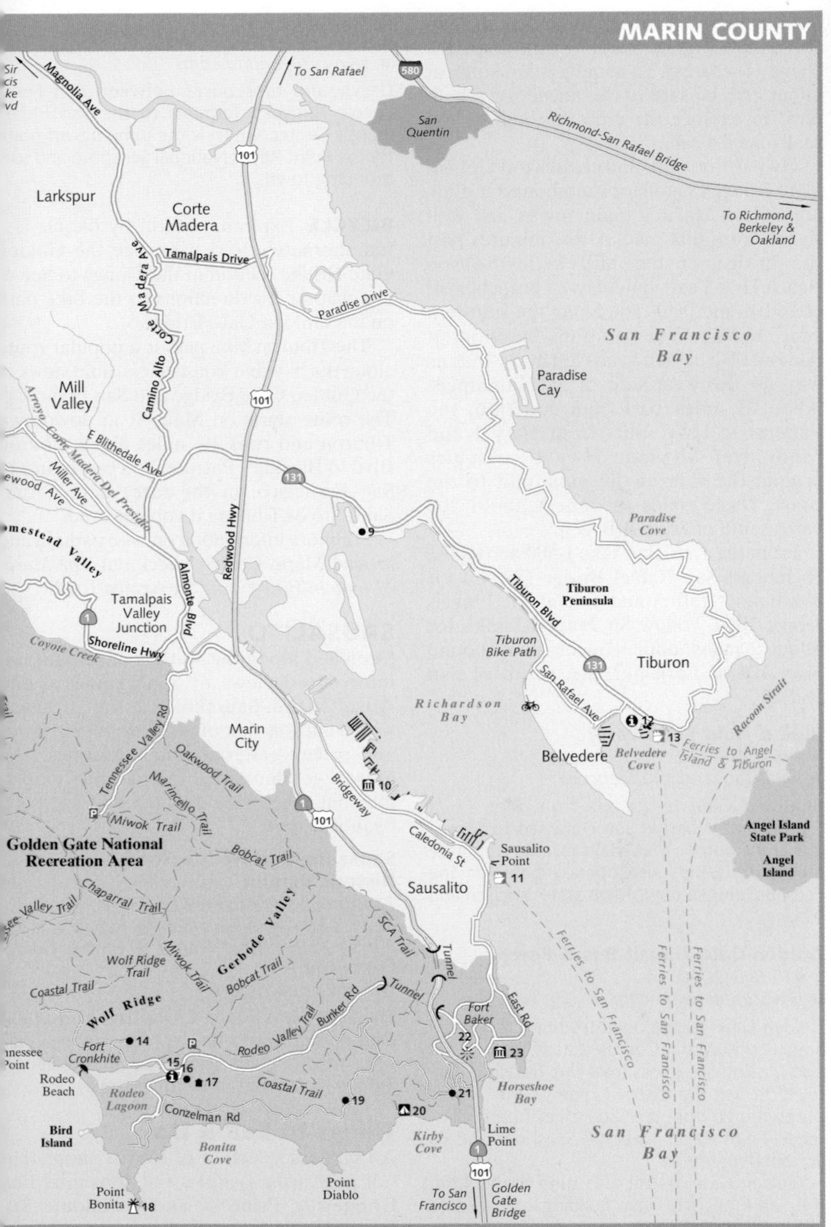
To San Rafael
San Quentin
Richmond-San Rafael Bridge
To Richmond, Berkeley & Oakland
Magnolia Ave
Larkspur
Corte Madera
Corte Madera Ave
Tamalpais Drive
Paradise Drive
San Francisco Bay
Paradise Cay
Mill Valley
Camino Alto
Arroyo Corte Madera Del Presidio
E Blithedale Ave
Miller Ave
Redwood Hwy
Almonte Blvd
Tamalpais Valley Junction
Shoreline Hwy
Coyote Creek
Paradise Cove
Tiburon Blvd
Tiburon Peninsula
Tiburon Bike Path
Tiburon
San Rafael Ave
Richardson Bay
Racoon Strait
Belvedere
Belvedere Cove
Ferries to Angel Island & Tiburon
Marin City
Tennessee Valley Rd
Oakwood Trail
Marincello Trail
Miwok Trail
Bridgeway
Caledonia St
Sausalito Point
Sausalito
Golden Gate National Recreation Area
Bobcat Trail
Chaparral Trail
Gerbode Valley
SCA Trail
Tunnel
Wolf Ridge Trail
Coastal Trail
Wolf Ridge
Bunker Rd
Rodeo Valley Trail
Fort Baker
East Rd
Fort Cronkhite
Rodeo Beach
Rodeo Lagoon
Conzelman Rd
Horseshoe Bay
Bird Island
Bonita Cove
Kirby Cove
Lime Point
Point Bonita
Point Diablo
To San Francisco
Golden Gate Bridge
Ferries to San Francisco
Angel Island State Park
Angel Island

options between towns, so getting around by bus takes some planning (and the right change for fares). To avoid getting stuck at either end, be sure to call ahead for schedules. To explore the area thoroughly, you really need a car.

Hwy 101 northbound crosses the Golden Gate Bridge ($3 toll for southbound traffic), and all of Marin's main towns are well signed from this road. A few minutes past the bridge, at the Mill Valley/Stinson Beach/Hwy 1 exit, quiet Hwy 1 branches off Hwy 101 and leads you along the southern edge of Mill Valley to Tam Junction, at Almonte Blvd, then heads left and winds its way up the west side of Mt Tamalpais. About 3 miles past Tam Junction, the Panoramic Hwy splits from Hwy 1 and winds over Mt Tam; Hwy 1 continues around the side of the mountain to the coast. These roads reconnect about 200 yards south of Stinson Beach.

From the East Bay, take I-580 across the Richmond–San Rafael Bridge ($2 toll for westbound traffic) and exit at Sir Francis Drake Blvd. Follow Sir Francis Drake for about 2 miles, until it meets southbound Hwy 101 at Larkspur, just south of San Rafael.

Blue & Gold Fleet Ferry
☎ *415-773-1188*
w *www.blueandgoldfleet.com*

Blue and Gold ferries sail from Pier 41 at Fisherman's Wharf in San Francisco to Sausalito and Tiburon. Weekdays during commute hours, the ferries also operate between the Ferry Building in downtown San Francisco and Tiburon.

Golden Gate Transit Bus & Ferry
☎ *415-923-2000*
w *www.goldengate.com*

Golden Gate Transit operates buses from San Francisco to Marin County. Catch them at 1st and Mission Sts across from the Transbay Terminal in San Francisco. Golden Gate Transit buses also go from the San Rafael Transit Center to Point Reyes National Seashore and its surrounding towns.

Golden Gate Transit also runs ferries from the San Francisco Ferry Building to Sausalito and Larkspur Landing.

Greyhound
☎ *800-229-9424*
w *www.greyhound.com*

Greyhound runs buses between San Fran cisco's Transbay Terminal to the San Rafae Transit Center, which is the jumping-off poin for the Point Reyes National Seashore and sur rounding towns.

BICYCLE Exploring Marin by bicycle is fun alternative to driving. See the Golde Gate Bridge section in the Things to See & Do chapter for directions to the bike pat on the Golden Gate Bridge.

The Tiburon bike path is a popular rout along the bay that boasts incredible views o the Golden Gate Bridge and San Francisc The route starts on Main St in downtow Tiburon and runs 2½ miles along Tiburo Blvd to Blackie's Pasture. You can return t San Francisco on the ferry from eithe Sausalito or Tiburon if you get tired.

For more information on bike paths in an around Marin County, check out *The Mari Mountain Bike Guide,* by Armor Todd.

SAUSALITO

Stretched along the water's edge with un interrupted views of San Francisco an Angel Island, Sausalito is a tourist have with a curious mix of junky souvenir shop and pricey galleries and boutiques. Th crowds get dense and the parking imposs ible, but there's no denying Sausalito is beautiful spot.

Sausalito Visitors' Center & Historic Exhibit
780 Bridgeway Blvd ☎ *415-332-0505*
11:30am-4pm Tues-Sun $ *free* *2, 10, 20, 50 Golden Gate Transit* *Blue & Gold Fleet Ferry*
w *www.sausalito.org*

The Sausalito Visitors' Center has a small ex hibit on the town's history. You can also pic up a walking guide booklet to make wander ing the waterfront more interesting.

Things to See & Do

An endless selection of tourist shops tha sell postcards, T-shirts, and souvenirs lin Bridgeway, Princess, and Caledonia Sts Don't forget to bring your camera, sinc

;ausalito's biggest attraction is its bay-side etting, with sailboats silhouetted against he shimmering city across the water. A ew other sites throughout town are worth hecking out.

;an Francisco Bay Model
ΛARIN COUNTY MAP
Λarinship Way ☎ 415-332-3871 9am-'pm Tues-Sat free 2, 10, 20, 50 ;olden Gate Transit ♿
www.baymodel.org

'he US Army Corps of Engineers created a cale model of the San Francisco Bay to test he effects of human activities on bay and lelta waters. A video explains how the model ; used. The building also houses a local art ollection and interesting displays on Sausa-to's nautical history.

Bay Area Discovery Museum
ΛARIN COUNTY MAP
557 McReynolds Rd ☎ 415-487-4398
10am-5pm Tues-Sun winter; 9am-4pm 'ues-Thurs, 10am-5pm Fri-Sun summer
adult/child $7, senior $6 76 Muni, hen a half-mile walk from the bus ♿
www.badm.org

'his hands-on children's museum is just under he north tower of the Golden Gate Bridge. 'ermanent exhibits include an underwater ea tunnel, a ceramic studio, a media center, nd a science lab. The museum has a café and store.

Houseboats
☎ 415-332-1916 free 2, 10, 20, 50 ;olden Gate Transit ♿
www.floatinghomes.org

'ausalito is renowned for its houseboat community, one of the world's largest and most diverse. These floating homes range from mansions to hippie havens. You can take a peek from the marina's dock or sign up for the Floating Homes Association annual tour. Check its website for details.

RICHARD CUMMINS

Sausalito's floating homes

Places to Eat

Sausalito is packed with cafés and restaurants, all catering to tourists. Although they don't offer the best prices, nor in some cases the best food, many offer fabulous views.

Waterfront Cafe (bakery)
85 Liberty Ship Way ☎ 415-332-5625
7:30am-5:50pm daily breakfast $1.50-4, lunch $4.50-6, salads $2.95/lb, entrée $4.50-6, dessert $1.50-4 AE, DC, D, MC, V 2, 10, 20, 50 Golden Gate Transit ♿

Have a seat with a coffee and a big sandwich and watch the boats.

Danish Diner (Danish)
37 Caledonia St ☎ 415-331-3034
6:30am-3pm Mon-Fri, 7am-3pm Sat-Sun breakfast $3-10, lunch $6-14 MC, V 2, 10, 20, 50 Golden Gate Transit

You can spot the windmill atop the Danish Diner from a mile away. Whether you yearn for Norwegian smoked salmon or a fluffy waffle topped with seasonal fruit, this tiny restaurant filled with locals will satisfy.

Caffe Tutti (Italian)
12 El Portal Dr ☎ 415-332-0211 6:45am-11pm daily breakfast $6-7.50, lunch $6-9, appetizer $4-8.50, entrée $6-9 AE, D, MC, V 2, 10, 20, 50 Golden Gate Transit Blue & Gold Fleet Ferry ♿

This is a convenient stop for sandwiches, pizza and pasta dishes, plus a wide variety of coffees.

Arawan (Thai)
47 Caledonia St ☎ 415-332-0882
11:30am-2pm Mon-Fri, 5pm-10pm Sat-Sun lunch $8, appetizer $6-10, entrée $7.50-12, dessert $3-4.50 AE, CB, DC, MC, V 2, 10, 20, 50 Golden Gate Transit ♿

For excellent and reasonably priced Thai food, check out Arawan. The lunchtime combo plate is a particularly good deal.

Gatsby's (seafood)
39 Caledonia St ☎ 415-332-4500
10am-10pm Mon-Fri, 9am-10pm Sat-Sun breakfast (weekends only) $6-11.50, lunch $7-17, appetizer $6-13, entrée $12-19

AE, DC, MC, V 2, 10, 20, 50 Golden Gate Transit

Gatsby's serves up scrumptious seafood and has live music most Friday and Saturday nights.

Getting There & Away

By car, take the Alexander Ave exit, the first after the Golden Gate Bridge (not counting Vista Point). Bridgeway Blvd, which runs along the waterfront, is the main drag leading into downtown.

If you're up for a little adventure, try walking to Sausalito by going across the Golden Gate Bridge, through Sausalito's luxurious hillside neighborhoods, and on into downtown. It's also a relatively easy destination by bicycle, and a direct shot on the ferry or bus.

Blue & Gold Fleet Ferry
Sausalito Ferry Terminal 415-773-1188 10:40am-6pm daily roundtrip adult $12, child $6, ages 5 & under free, bikes $1
www.blueandgoldfleet.com

You can take the Blue & Gold ferry from San Francisco's Fisherman's Warf (Pier 41) to downtown Sausalito. Call for a current schedule, as arrival and departure times change seasonally.

Golden Gate Transit
415-923-2000 bus: adult $2.35, senior/disabled $1.15, child $1.75; ferry: adult $2.95, senior/disabled $1.45, child $2.55
www.goldengate.com

Golden Gate Transit buses 2, 10, 20, and 50 service downtown Sausalito from San Francisco. The ferries go from the San Francisco Ferry Building to the Sausalito Ferry Terminal.

TIBURON

Resting on a peninsula pointing out into the center of the bay, Tiburon is a bay-side community that, much like Sausalito, is noted for its gorgeous views. It's connected by ferry with downtown San Francisco and is also the Marin jumping-off point for nearby Angel Island. (See the section on Angel Island in the Things to See & Do chapter.)

Main St is where the old houseboats have taken root on dry land and metamorphosed into classy 'Ark Row' shops and boutiques.

Tiburon Peninsula Chamber of Commerce MARIN COUNTY MAP
96B Main St, lower level 415-435-5633 8am-4pm Mon-Thurs, 8am-1pm Fri free Blue & Gold Fleet Ferry 8, 9, 10, 11 Golden Gate Transit
www.tiburon.citysearch.com

Visitor information is available from the chamber of commerce, when it is open. It's closed on weekends.

Things to See & Do

Take the ferry from San Francisco, browse as you stroll past the shops on Main St, grab a bite to eat overlooking the bay, and you've seen Tiburon. For a closer look, pick up the *Walking Guide to Historic Tiburon,* which you'll find in mailboxlike dispensers throughout town. The self-guided tour starts at Main St and Paradise Dr.

Old St Hilary's Church
201 Esperanza 415-435-1853 1pm-4pm Wed & Sun Apr-Oct free

Great views and the botanical wildflower garden make this hillside church worth a visit, even when it isn't open. The structure, built in 1888, is a wonderful example of carpenter Gothic.

Bay Audubon Center & Sanctuary
MARIN COUNTY MAP
376 Greenwood Beach Rd 415-388-2524 9am-5pm Wed-Sun donations ($2)
www.bayaudubon.org

The Bay Audubon Center is home to a wide variety of waterbirds. You can explore the miles of trails independently or participate in a guided nature walk at 9am and 1pm Sunday.

Places to Eat

Sam's Anchor Café (California)
27 Main St 415-435-4527 11am-10pm Mon-Thurs, 11am-10:30pm Fri, 10am-10:30pm Sat, 9:30am-10pm Sun break-fast $8.50-15, lunch $8.50-15, appetizer $4.50-14, entrée $10-19, dessert $3.50-7 AE, DC, D, MC, V Blue & Gold Fleet Ferry 8, 9, 10, 11 Golden Gate Transit

Sam's Anchor Café is the oldest continuous-use restaurant in Tiburon. A secret trap door to the bay allowed its saloon to function throughout the Prohibition era. It's still a popular local hangout, and it has an unbeatable view.

;weden House Café Bakery (Swedish)
'7 Main St ☎ 415-435-9767 ⌚ 8am-5pm ɅIon-Fri, 8am-6pm Sat-Sun $ breakfast $6-; lunch $6-12, dessert $1.50-4 C AE, MC, / Blue & Gold Fleet Ferry 🚌 8, 9, 10, '1 Golden Gate Transit ♿

'his is where you'll find traditional vörtbröd :nd lussekattor, as well as a full selection of ›ther baked goods, coffee, sandwiches, and alads.

;uaymas (Mexican)
; Main St ☎ 415-435-6300 ⌚ 11:30am-'0pm Mon-Fri, 11:30am-11pm Sat, '0:30am-10pm Sun $ lunch $11-20.50, ·ppetizer $5.50-13, entrée $11-20.50, lessert $4.50-6 C AE, DC, D, MC, V Blue & Gold Fleet Ferry 🚌 8, 9, 10, '1 Golden Gate Transit ♿

Right on the waterfront, this festive restaurant erves fresh Mexican specialties. You can vatch them crank out tortillas at the back of he restaurant. The best seats are on the outide patio overlooking the bay.

;etting There & Away

)n Hwy 101, look for the exit for Tiburon 3lvd, E Blithedale Ave, and Hwy 131; it eads into town and intersects with Juanita ‿ane and charming Main St, which is also :nown as Ark Row. You can also take the erry or the bus from San Francisco directly o downtown Tiburon.

3lue & Gold Fleet Ferry
'iburon Ferry Terminal ☎ 415-773-1188 ⌚ 10:40am-6pm daily $ roundtrip adult ;12, child $6, ages 5 & under free, bike $1 ♿
W www.blueandgoldfleet.com

'ou can take the Blue & Gold ferry from San 'rancisco's Fisherman's Warf (Pier 41) or the 'erry Building to the Tiburon ferry landing. :all for a current schedule, as arrival and de›arture times change seasonally.

;olden Gate Transit
☎ 415-923-2000 $ adult $2.95, senior/ lisabled $1.45, child $2.25 ♿
W www.goldengate.com

;olden Gate Transit buses Nos 8, 9, 10, and 11 ervice downtown Tiburon from San Francisco.

ɅILL VALLEY

f Sausalito and Tiburon are too touristy for 'our taste, head inland to Mill Valley, a town in the redwoods that feels like an artists' retreat. Originally a logging town and named after a lumber mill, Mill Valley also served as the starting point for the scenic railway that carried visitors up Mt Tamalpais. Though the tracks were removed in 1940, the space of the former station still serves as a central meeting point, housing the Depot Bookstore & Cafe and the chamber of commerce.

Chamber of Commerce
85 Throckmorton Ave ☎ 415-388-9700 ⌚ 10am-noon & 1pm-4:30pm Mon-Tues & Thurs-Fri $ free 🚌 4, 5, 10, 21 Golden Gate Transit ♿
W www.millvalley.org

Mill Valley visitor information is available here. A town map and current events list are posted on the bulletin board outside.

Things to See & Do

Old Mill Park MARIN COUNTY MAP
$ free 🚌 4, 5, 10, 21 Golden Gate Transit, then a 1-mile walk from the bus

This wooded park with a stream running through it is a wonderful place for a picnic. Here you'll find a restored version of the mill for which the town was named. Built around 1835 and restored in 1950, it is the oldest standing mill in California. Just past the bridge over Old Mill Creek, the 671 Dipsea Steps mark the challenging start of the Dipsea Trail, which winds its way through Mt Tamalpais State Park to Stinson Beach.

Tennessee Valley Trail
$ free

Though part of the Marin Headlands area, the Tennessee Valley Trail can be accessed just south of Mill Valley. With beautiful views of the rugged coastline and easy access to the beach and the ocean, this short, flat 2-mile trail is one of the most popular hikes in Marin. Naturally, the trail can be crowded on weekends, and it's best to go on a clear, calm day, since it can be very windy.

From downtown Mill Valley, take Miller Ave to the Shoreline Hwy as if you were going back to the Golden Gate Bridge; turn right onto Tennessee Valley Rd and follow it to the parking lot, where you'll find the trailhead. From Hwy 101, take the Mill Valley/Stinson Beach/Hwy 1 exit and turn left onto Tennessee Valley Rd.

Along E Blithedale and Throckmorton Aves are an array of fine housewares stores and antiques shops. Most of them are incredibly expensive, but there's no charge for window shopping.

Pullman & Co
108 Throckmorton Ave ☎ 415-383-0847 ⏲ 10am-6pm Mon-Sat, 11am-6pm Sun 🚌 4, 5, 10, 21 Golden Gate Transit ♿

Pullman & Co specializes in beautiful home accessories, as well as friendly greetings by Bella, the owner's black lab.

Summer House
21 Throckmorton Ave ☎ 415-383-6695 ⏲ 10am-6pm Mon-Thurs, 10am-7pm Fri-Sat, 11am-6:30pm Sun 🚌 4, 5, 10, 21 Golden Gate Transit ♿

Summer House specializes in beautiful home accessories.

Places to Eat

Depot Bookstore & Cafe (American)
87 Throckmorton Ave ☎ 415-383-2655 ⏲ 7am-9pm daily $ breakfast $2-6, lunch $5-8, entrée $5-8, dessert $1.50-2 C cash only 🚭 🚌 4, 7, 10, 21 Golden Gate Transit ♿

There are plenty of cafés around the center of town, including the Depot Bookstore & Cafe, which occupies the space of the former station. It specializes in reasonably priced soups, sandwiches, salads, and baked treats.

Wine & Spirits Delicatessen (deli)
12 Corte Madera Ave ☎ 415-388-3222 ⏲ 7am-7:30pm Mon-Sat, 9am-7pm Sun C D, MC, V 🚭 🚌 4, 5, 10, 21 Golden Gate Transit ♿

Mill Valley's centrally located deli is the place to stock up on picnic fixings. Sandwiches are made to order and the baked goods are irresistible.

Jenny Low's (Chinese)
38 Miller Ave ☎ 415-388-8868 ⏲ 11:30am-3pm Mon-Sat, 4:30pm-9:30pm Sun $ lunch $6-7, appetizer $5-7, entrée $5-10, dessert $3 C AE, MC, V 🚭 🚌 4, 5, 10, 21 Golden Gate Transit ♿

Try Jenny Low's for unbeatable Chinese cuisine.

Piazza D'Angelo (Italian)
22 Miller Ave ☎ 415-388-2000 ⏲ 11:30am-10:30pm Mon-Thurs, 11:30am-midnight Fri, 10:30am-midnight Sat, 10:30am-11pm Sun $ breakfast $6-8, lunch $8-19, appetizer $5-10, entrée $8-19, dessert $7 C AE, DC, MC, V 🚭 🚌 4, 5, 10, 21 Golden Gate Transit ♿

This pizza joint serves Italian food at reasonable prices.

El Paseo (French)
7 El Paseo ☎ 415-388-0741 ⏲ 5:30pm-10pm Tues-Sun $ appetizer $5.50-11.50, entrée $16-25, dessert $6-7.50 C AE, MC, V 🚭 🚌 4, 5, 10, 21 Golden Gate Transit ♿

Tucked away in a little back courtyard, this charming but pricey restaurant specializes in French cuisine. The food is excellent and the wine list impressive – well worth the splurge for a special occasion.

Entertainment

Sweetwater
153 Throckmorton Ave ☎ 415-388-2820 $ varies ⏲ noon-12:30am daily 🚌 4, 5, 10, 21 Golden Gate Transit ♿ W www.sweetwatersaloon.com

This intimate setting for live music is a favorite spot for local musicians. Enjoy live jazz from 4pm to 8pm on Sunday afternoon. Happy hour prices prevail from noon to 7pm Monday to Saturday and all day on Sunday.

Getting There & Away

From San Francisco or Sausalito, take Hwy 101 north to the Mill Valley/Stinson Beach/Hwy 1 exit. Follow Hwy 1, here called the Shoreline Hwy, to Almonte Blvd, which turns into Miller Ave, and take Miller into downtown Mill Valley.

From Tiburon, take Tiburon Blvd west until it becomes E Blithedale Ave and follow E Blithedale into downtown Mill Valley.

Golden Gate Transit
☎ 415-923-2000 $ adult $2.35, senior/disabled $1.15, child $1.75 ♿ W www.goldengate.com

Golden Gate Transit buses Nos 4, 5, 10, and 21 service downtown Mill Valley from San Francisco.

MARIN HEADLANDS

The headlands rise majestically out of the water at the north end of the Golden Gate Bridge, their rugged beauty all the more striking given their proximity to the city. You can explore the few forts and bunkers left over from a century of US military occupation, but other than those structures and a few park buildings, the area is free of development. Hiking and biking trails, beaches and isolated campgrounds are all nestled within these rolling coastal hills.

Marin Headlands Visitors' Center
MARIN COUNTY MAP
Fort Barry, Building 948 ☎ 415-331-1540
🕘 9:30am-4:30pm daily ⓢ free 🚌 76 Muni (Sunday & holidays only) ♿
w www.nps.gov/goga/mahe/index.htm

Trail maps and historical information are available from the Marin Headlands Visitors' Center. If you want to camp in the park, stop here first for a free but mandatory permit.

If you want a more detailed map than the one the park provides for free, you can buy the Olmsted & Bros' map *A Rambler's Guide to the Trails of Mt Tamalpais and the Marin Headlands*, which shows all the trails and elevations.

Things to See & Do

Battery Spencer MARIN COUNTY MAP
Conzelman Rd ⓢ free 🚌 76 Muni (Sunday & holidays only) ♿

After a short drive from the park entrance, you can explore the remains of the never-completed battery and get amazing views of the Golden Gate Bridge from above.

Battery 129 & Hawk Hill
MARIN COUNTY MAP
Conzelman Rd ⓢ free 🚌 76 Muni (Sunday & holidays only), then a 1½-mile walk from the bus ♿

At Battery 129, you can see thousands of migrating birds of prey soaring on the updrafts along the cliffs from late summer to early autumn.

Point Bonita Lighthouse
MARIN COUNTY MAP
🕘 12:30pm-3:30pm Sat-Mon ⓢ free 🚌 76 Muni (Sunday & holidays only), then a 1-mile walk from the bus

Built in 1855, the lighthouse is a breathtaking half-mile walk from the parking area.

Marine Mammal Center
MARIN COUNTY MAP
1065 Fort Cronkhite ☎ 415-289-7325
🕘 10am-4pm daily ⓢ free 🚌 76 Muni (Sunday & holidays only), then a 1-mile walk from the bus
w www.tmmc.org

On the hill above Rodeo Lagoon is the Marine Mammal Center, which rehabilitates injured, sick, and orphaned sea mammals before releasing them to the wild.

Headlands Center for the Arts
MARIN COUNTY MAP
944 Fort Barry ☎ 415-331-2787 🕘 office: 9am-5pm Mon-Fri, noon-5pm Sat-Sun; studios: call for dates and details ⓢ free 🚌 76 Muni (Sunday & holidays only), then a 1-mile walk from the bus
w www.headlands.org

These refurbished barracks were converted into conference facilities and work spaces for artists. Three Sundays a year, the center and its artists-in-residence host open studios – an opportunity to see works in progress and talk to the people creating them. Two or three times a month, the center hosts talks, performances, and other events. Call ahead and find out if anything is going on, or just go and check out the digs. It's a beautiful spot.

Rodeo Beach MARIN COUNTY MAP
ⓢ free 🚌 76 Muni (Sunday & holidays only)

This scenic and sandy beach, protected from the wind by high cliffs, is a nice place to picnic when the weather is good.

HIKING & BIKING The headlands has a crisscrossed web of excellent hiking and mountain biking routes. You can traverse just one or connect several to form loop trails of varying lengths and levels of difficulty. If biking, be sure to stay on designated biking trails or walk your bike on hiking-only trails. You can pick up a biking trail map at the visitors' center.

From Rodeo Beach, the Coastal Trail meanders 2 miles north to the scenic Hill 88. Hikers can continue along the Coastal Trail for another 6 miles, past the popular Tennessee Valley Trail (see Mill Valley, earlier) and all the way to Muir Beach, viewing the ocean from the blustery headlands the whole way.

For a good 12-mile dirt loop, bikers can take the Coastal Trail west from the fork of Conzelman and McCullogh Rds, bumping and winding 1¾ miles down past Bunker

Rd where it meets the Bobcat Trail. After 3 miles, Bobcat joins Marincello Rd and descends steeply for 1½ miles into the Tennessee Valley parking lot. From there, the Old Springs and Miwok Trails take you to Bunker Rd a bit more gently than the Bobcat Trail does, though any attempt to avoid at least a couple of hefty climbs while riding through the headlands is futile.

For an equally thrilling road ride, try Conzelman Rd, which plunges 700 feet from the fork and loops back to meet Bunker Rd; take either Bunker Rd through the five-minute tunnel and back to the Golden Gate Bridge or go up McCullogh Rd for (another) challenging climb with (another) winding downhill ride back to the bridge.

Places to Stay

There are several free drive-up and hike-in campsites in the headlands. The Marin Headlands Visitors' Center accepts campsite reservations and provides mandatory permits. Campers can shower at the Marin Headlands Hostel for $2.

Marin Headlands Hostel

MARIN COUNTY MAP
Fort Barry, Building 941 ☎ *415-331-2777* Ⓢ *doubles (up to 2 adults and 2 children) $39; dorms: adult $13-15, child $6.50; linen rental $1* Ⓒ *D, MC, V* 🚌 *76 Muni (Sunday & holidays only)* ♿ *yes (request when reserving)*

The HI Marin Headlands, in two historic 1907 buildings, is near the visitors' center, beaches, and hiking trails. It's open year-round.

Getting There & Away

By car, take the Alexander Ave exit just after the Golden Gate Bridge and dip left under the freeway. Conzelman Rd, to the right, takes you up along the bluffs. By bicycle, cross the Golden Gate Bridge on the bike-only side (see the Golden Gate Bridge section in Things to See & Do chapter for directions) and head up Conzelman Rd.

Muni

☎ *415-673-6864* Ⓢ *adult $1, senior 35¢, ages 4 & under free* ♿
Ⓦ *www.sfmuni.com*

Muni's bus route 76 has hourly service to the Marin Headlands on Sunday and holidays only. Muni is exact change only, and you can get on the bus in San Francisco at the Caltrain station at 4th and Townsend; at the Transbay Terminal; at Sutter and Post; and at Van Ness and Lombard. It stops in the headlands at Battery Spencer, Battery Alexander, and Rodeo Beach.

MT TAMALPAIS

Affectionately called 'Mt Tam' by locals, Mt Tamalpais (pronounced **ta**-mul-**pie**-us) has been a popular recreation area since the mid-1800s. In 1907, a rail line was constructed to allow easy access from Mill Valley to Mt Tam's highest point, East Peak (2571 feet). The track's 281 curves were the reason it became known as the 'crookedest railroad in the world.'

Mt Tamalpais State Park

MARIN COUNTY MAP
801 Panoramic Hwy ☎ *415-388-2070* ⏲ *7am-6pm daily winter, 7am-10pm daily summer* Ⓢ *parking $2* 🚌 *63 Golden Gate Transit (weekends & holidays only)* ♿
Ⓦ *www.cal-parks.ca.gov*

The park was formed in 1928 from land donated by the naturalist William Kent. Mt Tam's 6300 acres of hill and dale are still home to deer, foxes, and bobcats. Hikers, bikers, and equestrian enthusiasts now traverse the park's 50 miles of diverse trails, including the old railroad grade.

Pantoll Station MARIN COUNTY MAP
801 Panoramic Hwy ☎ *415-388-2070* ⏲ *10am-sunset intermittently* Ⓢ *parking $2* 🚌 *63 Golden Gate Transit (weekends & holidays only)* ♿

Pantoll Station is the Mt Tamalpais State Park headquarters; you can pick up a park map for $1 here.

East Peak Summit Visitors' Center

⏲ *Sat-Sun intermittently* Ⓢ *parking $2* ♿

You can drive all the way to the visitors' center at East Peak, then hike the remaining quarter mile to the 2571-foot summit.

Mountain Theater MARIN COUNTY MAP
☎ *415-383-1100 g* ⏲ *1pm on 6 Sundays May-June* Ⓢ *adult $24, senior/child $17, ages 3 & under free* ♿
Ⓦ *www.mountainplay.org*

Officially called the Cushing Memorial Theater, this outdoor amphitheater was constructed in the 1930s. It seats 4500 people and features one musical each spring. Ask the rangers at Pantoll Station about the once-a-year astronomy lecture at the theater – it might just be your lucky night.

Hiking

More than 50 miles of trails lie within Mt Tamalpais State Park, connecting with an even larger 200-mile-long trail system on adjacent parkland. Pantoll is an excellent place to start a day hike – it's a beautiful 8½-mile hike to the East Peak summit and back.

The Steep Ravine Trail follows a wooded creek to the coast (about 2 miles each way); or you can hike a mile farther to Stinson Beach, where the trail connects with the Dipsea Trail, the course of the annual cross-country Dipsea Race, begun in 1904. You can return via the Matt Davis Trail for a good loop.

Cataract Trail runs along Cataract Creek from the end of Pantoll Rd; it's about 3 miles to Alpine Lake. The last mile is a spectacular rooty staircase as the trail descends alongside Cataract Falls. (See the boxed text 'Marin County Waterfall Hikes.')

Biking

Mt Tam is famous for its mountain biking. Be aware that the fun of Mt Tam mountain biking is tempered by strict speed limits of 15mph (5mph around blind curves), and access is limited to fire roads – no single-track riding is allowed. Violations can result in fines of up to $250.

Marin County Waterfall Hikes

You'll find a number of spectacular waterfall hikes within Marin County. Though they make for pleasant day hikes at any time of year, they are at their best in the spring, when winter's rains have filled the rivers and the falls are really gushing.

Stairstep Falls This 2½-mile hike (roundtrip) is within Samuel P Taylor State Park, just east of Olema on Sir Francis Drake Blvd. The trailhead is at Devil's Gulch Horse camp, a mile west of the park's main entrance. Park in the dirt pullout on the south side of Sir Francis Drake, walk across the road and up the paved path for about 150 yards 'til you see a trail leading off to the right along Devil's Gulch Creek. After a few hundred yards, turn right and cross the footbridge, then turn left to continue along the creek, following the signs for the Barnaby Peak Trail. After crossing a bridge over a side creek, look for the Stairstep Falls Trail cutting off to the left. The 40-foot-tall falls drop in three cascades, or stair steps, through the shady, fern-covered canyon. The rocks and trees at the fall's base make for a nice picnic area.

Cascade Falls These falls near the Fairfax suburbs are an easy 2 miles roundtrip. To get there, drive to Fairfax, off Sir Francis Drake Blvd. Heading northwest on Broadway, turn left onto Bolinas Rd. Drive three-tenths of a mile, then bear right on Cascade Dr. It is 1½ miles to the gated trail. Start walking upriver along the fire road, then veer off it onto the single-track trail. The trail follows San Anselmo Creek. About a quarter mile in, cross the footbridge over the creek and head right, up the creek. You'll start to hear the waterfall in less than a mile.

Cataract Falls This series of cascades stretches for more than 1½ miles along the aptly named Cataract Creek. Though you can hike as much or as little of it as you like, the moderately difficult roundtrip trail is 3¼ miles long. Lake views, redwoods, and fern-covered canyons are some of this hike's most pleasant features. The stairs, which climb more that 800 feet, are not. To get to the trailhead, drive to Fairfax, off Sir Francis Drake Blvd. Heading northwest on Broadway, turn left onto Bolinas Rd. Drive 7.8 miles to the dam at Alpine Lake, cross the dam, and park in the pullouts just past the hairpin turn. The trailhead is on the left. The trail can also be hiked top to bottom, starting at Mt Tamalpais' Ridgecrest Blvd – the trailhead is 1.6 miles from the intersection of Panoramic Hwy.

The *Old Railroad Grade* is among Mt Tam's most popular rides. For a good, sweaty, 6-mile, 2280-foot climb, start in Mill Valley at the end of W Blithedale Ave and climb to East Peak (2571 feet).

For an easier ride than the Old Railroad Grade, start part way up Mt Tam at the Mountain Home Inn. From the West Point Inn along Old Railroad Grade, take the Old Stage Road to the Coastal Trail for 9 more (roundtrip) miles of climbs and descents with stunning ocean views.

Places to Stay

Mt Tamalpais Campgrounds

☎ *415-388-2070, 800-444-7275* Ⓢ *cabins: Steep Ravine $15, Pantoll Station $15; camping: Steep Ravine $7, Pantoll Station $12, group site $18* Ⓒ *cash only* 🚌 *63 Golden Gate Transit (weekends & holidays only)* ♿ *yes (1 cabin)*

Mt Tam has several campgrounds. Pantoll Station is on a first-come, first-served basis. Pay for camping permits at the Pantoll Station. You can make reservations and prepay for Steep Ravine cabins and campsites and for campsites at the Alice Eastwood Group Camp.

West Point Inn MARIN COUNTY MAP

☎ *415-646-0702, 415-388-9955* Ⓢ *adult $30, child $15, ages 5 & under free* Ⓒ *MC, V* ♿ *yes (by arrangement)*

This rustic inn and its cabins are a 2-mile hike from Pantoll Station. Bring a flashlight, as there is no electricity and candles are not allowed. You may use the communal kitchen to cook.

Mountain Home Inn

MARIN COUNTY MAP

810 Panoramic Hwy ☎ *415-381-9000* Ⓢ *singles $159-289, doubles $159-289* Ⓒ *MC, V* 🚌 *63 Golden Gate Transit (weekends & holidays only)*

Mountain Home Inn is on the east side of Mt Tamalpais. The awesome views of the East Bay from the deck make this a great stop for a meal or posthike refreshment; hotel rates include breakfast.

Getting There & Away

To get to Mt Tam's Pantoll station, take Hwy 1 to the Panoramic Hwy and look for the Pantoll sign.

Golden Gate Transit

☎ *415-923-2000* Ⓢ *adult $2.35, senior/disabled $1.15, child $1.75* ♿ Ⓦ *www.goldengate.com*

On weekends and holidays, take Golden Gate Transit's bus No 63 from the Marin City Transit Center at Donahue and Terners Sts. It stops at the Mountain Home Inn and Pantoll Station.

MUIR WOODS NATIONAL MONUMENT

The old-growth redwoods at Muir Woods were saved from logging when naturalist and philanthropist William Kent lobbied President Theodore Roosevelt to preserve the area as a national monument in 1908. The 550-acre reserve, surrounded on all sides by Mt Tamalpais State Park, is the closest redwood stand to San Francisco, so it can get quite crowded. You can avoid the crowds by visiting during the week or by arriving early (or late) on the weekends. In general, a short hike will get you out of the densest crowds and onto trails with huge trees and stunning vistas.

Muir Woods MARIN COUNTY MAP

☎ *415-388-2595* 🕘 *8am-sunset daily* Ⓢ *adult $2, ages 17 & under free* ♿ Ⓦ *www.nps.gov/muwo*

The main entrance to the park is on Muir Woods Rd. There's no smoking on trails, and no dogs, camping, or picnicking are allowed in the park.

Muir Woods Ranger Station

MARIN COUNTY MAP

☎ *415-388-2595* 🕘 *9am-sunset daily*

Admission to the park is free if you arrive before the ranger station is open; it's at the main entrance to Muir Woods.

Hiking

A quick and easy way to see some of the most impressive redwood trees is by walking Redwood Canyon's paved, level loop trails. They meander along Redwood Creek to the thousand-year-old trees gracing Cathedral Grove, then return via Bohemian Grove, where the tallest tree in the park stands 254 feet high. These popular paths can get pretty crowded. For a quiet 3-mile loop trail, take Ocean View Trail to Lost Trail to Fern Creek and return through Redwood Canyon. The Dipsea Trail is a good 2-mile hike up to the top of Cardiac Hill.

Getting There & Away

The main entrance to the park is on Muir Woods Rd. Take Hwy 1 'til you reach a fork; take the right-hand fork onto Panoramic Hwy and follow that for about a mile to Four Corners, where you turn left onto Muir Woods Rd. There are no direct buses to Muir Woods.

MUIR BEACH MARIN COUNTY MAP

The turnoff to Muir Beach from Hwy 1 is marked by the longest row of mailboxes on the north coast. It's a quiet little town with a nice beach, but it has no direct bus service.

Muir Beach Overlook
$ free ♿

For a quiet picnic spot with a nice view of Muir Beach and the coast, turn off Hwy 1 onto Muir Beach Overlook, just a mile north of town.

Lindisfarne Guest House
1601 Shoreline Hwy ☎ 415-383-3134 $ singles $75-105, doubles $125-155, apartments $350/two nights, each additional guest $40 C none ♿

This Buddhist retreat in the hills above Muir Beach makes for a relaxing retreat; breakfast is included in the room rates.

Pelican Inn
10 Pacific Way ☎ 415-383-6000 $ $191-229 C AE, D, MC, V ♿

This ever-popular inn is the only commercial establishment in town and has a pleasant restaurant and bar; room rates include tax and breakfast.

STINSON BEACH

Downtown Stinson Beach flanks Hwy 1 for about 3 blocks. It's a densely packed cluster of galleries and shops, eateries, and B&Bs and serves as the gateway to the beach of the same name.

Stinson Beach MARIN COUNTY MAP
☎ 415-868-0942 $ parking $2 🚌 63 Golden Gate Transit (weekends & holidays only) ♿

The 3-mile beach is often blanketed with fog; when it's sunny, it's blanketed with people. But this sandy beach, with its views of Point Reyes and San Francisco on clear days, is long enough to accommodate people strolling, sunbathing, and surfing. To get to the beach, take Calle del Arroyo, the only big street going west out of town. For a local weather report, call ☎ 415-868-1922.

Red Rock Beach MARIN COUNTY MAP
$ free 🚌 63 Golden Gate Transit (weekends & holidays only), then a 1-mile walk from the bus

This nude beach is popular but attracts smaller crowds than Stinson Beach, as it requires a steep hike down from the road.

Shakespeare at Stinson
PO Box 301 ☎ 415-868-1115 $ adult $18, child $13 🚌 63 Golden Gate Transit (weekends & holidays only) ♿
W www.shakespeareatstinson.com

For an inexpensive injection of culture, get tickets to an outdoor performance of a Shakespeare play. The season runs from May to October.

Audubon Canyon Ranch
4900 Hwy 1 ☎ 415-868-9244 ⏲ 10am-4pm Sat-Sun mid-March to mid-July; by appointment 2pm-4pm Tues-Fri mid-March to mid-July $ donations (free) ♿
W www.egret.org

Set in the hills above the Bolinas Lagoon, this is a major nesting ground for great blue herons and great egrets. Visitors can get a bird's-eye view from the trail above the narrow canyon. There's a sign for the ranch on the east side of the road (just north of the sign for the 'Volunteer Canyon of Audubon Canyon Ranch'). Keep a sharp lookout for it, because turning around is difficult once you pass it.

Places to Stay & Eat

Redwoods Haus
PO Box 404 ☎ 415-868-9828 $ rooms $55-170, apartments $65-200 C AE, D, MC, V 🚌 63 Golden Gate Transit (weekends & holidays only)

This ramshackle home with a slightly nautical feel offers rooms of various sizes with shared bath and use of the kitchen. A private cabin is also available.

Stinson Beach Motel
3416 Hwy 1 ☎ 415-868-1712 $ doubles

$60-90 winter, $85-130 summer; apartments $80-140 winter, $130-200 summer C *D, MC, V* 🚌 *63 Golden Gate Transit (weekends & holidays only)*

This simple motel has reasonably priced, comfortable rooms.

Sandpiper Motel
1 Marine Way ☎ 415-868-1632 $ doubles $85-160, triples $100-195, quads $150-195 C *MC, V* 🚌 *63 Golden Gate Transit (weekends & holidays only)*

The Sandpiper Motel is close to the beach.

Parkside Café (New American)
43 Arenal Ave ☎ 415-868-1272 ⌚ 7:30am-2pm Mon-Fri, 8am-2pm Sat-Sun, 5:30pm-9:30pm daily $ breakfast $6-9.50, lunch $7-11.50, appetizer $7-16, entrée $14-21, dessert $3-5 C *AE, DC, MC, V* 🚌 *63 Golden Gate Transit (weekends & holidays only)* ♿

By the beach is the Parkside, famous for its hearty breakfasts, but it also offers Italian-style dinners, good fish, and filet mignon.

Sand Dollar Restaurant (California)
3458 Hwy 1 ☎ 415-868-0434 ⌚ 11am-10pm daily, brunch served 8:30am-2pm on summer weekends only $ lunch $4-14, appetizer $3.50-7, entrée $8-17, dessert $5 C *AE, MC, V* 🚌 *63 Golden Gate Transit (weekends and holidays only)* ♿

This popular local bar and restaurant serves a variety of innovative dishes, including organic greens and free-range beef.

Stinson Beach Grill (American)
3465 Hwy 1 ☎ 415-868-2002 ⌚ 11:30am-8pm Mon-Fri, 11am-9pm Sat-Sun winter; 11:30am-10pm Mon-Fri, 11am-10pm Sat-Sun summer $ lunch $9.50-19, appetizer $6.50-12, entrée $8-19, dessert $1-6 C *AE, MC, V* 🚌 *63 Golden Gate Transit (weekends & holidays only)* ♿

This cozy bar and grill serves up fresh local produce and has a host of vegetarian options.

POINT REYES NATIONAL SEASHORE

Point Reyes National Seashore has 110 sq miles of desolate ocean beaches, wind-tousled ridge tops, and diverse wildlife. The enormous peninsula, with its rough-hewn beauty and excellent hiking and camping opportunities, is one of the most pleasurable Bay Area excursions. It can be visited as a day trip, but it is worth extending your visit by staying at one of the nearby towns. Be sure to bring warm clothing, as even the sunniest days can quickly turn cold and foggy.

Bear Valley Visitors' Center
Bear Valley Rd ☎ 415-663-1092 ⌚ 9am-5pm Mon-Fri, 8am-5pm Sat-Sun $ free ♿ W *www.nps.gov/pore*

The Bear Valley Visitors' Center is the Point Reyes National Seashore park headquarters. It has a great deal of information and maps, making it a good place to begin exploring the park.

Kenneth C Patrick Visitors' Center
Drakes Beach ☎ 415-669-1250 ⌚ 9am-5pm Sat-Sun & holidays winter, 10am-5pm Fri-Tues summer $ free ♿

The visitors' center at Drakes Beach has general information and maps, as well as exhibits focusing on 16th-century maritime exploration, marine fossils, and marine environments. A 250-gallon salt-water aquarium highlights life in Drakes Bay.

Lighthouse Visitors' Center
☎ 415-669-1534 ⌚ 10am-4:30pm Thurs-Mon $ free 🚌 *shuttle (see below)* ♿

The Point Reyes Lighthouse Visitors' Center has information about the lighthouse, whales, and wildflowers. From January through April, use the nearby observation deck to look for migrating gray whales.

A shuttle from the Kenneth C Patrick Visitors' Center to the Lighthouse Visitors' Center operates 9am to 5pm weekends and holidays December to April. When the shuttle's running, the road is closed to private vehicles. The shuttle costs $2.50; children under 12 are free.

Things to See & Do

Point Reyes Lighthouse
⌚ 10am-4:30pm Thurs-Sun $ free 🚌 *see Lighthouse Visitors' Center, above*

This spot, with its wild terrain and ferocious winds, has the best whale-watching on the coast. There's also a sea-lion viewing area nearby. The lighthouse is set 300 feet – 433 stairs – below the top of the 600-foot headland so its light can shine out below the fog, which often blankets Point Reyes. The lighthouse lens room and clockworks area are open as staffing and weather conditions permit.

SARAH JH HUBBARD

Watch whales from the Point Reyes lighthouse.

Chimney Rock

Overlooking Drakes Bay, Chimney Rock is a favorite of wildflower enthusiasts. Wild cucumber, purple thistles with sharp thorns and flowers as soft as velvet, bright orange California poppies, and wild grasses tenaciously cling to the wind-pounded promontory, looking none the worse for their troubles.

Earthquake Trail

free ♿

Of all the trails at Point Reyes, one of the most awe-inspiring is the half-mile Earthquake Trail. Here you can view the 16-foot gap between the two halves of a once-connected fence line, a lasting testimonial to the power of the 1906 earthquake that was centered in this area.

Kule Loklo

free

A 1-mile trail from the Bear Valley Visitors' Center leads to Kule Loklo, a reproduction of a Miwok Indian village.

Limantour Beach

free ♿

Here you can stroll along the long sandy beach or follow the trail that runs along Limantour Spit, with Estero de Limantour on one side and Drakes Bay on the other.

Inverness Ridge Trail

free

This trail heads from Limantour Rd up to 1336-foot Point Reyes Hill, with spectacular views of the entire national seashore. You can drive almost to the top from the other side, so don't be surprised if after hours of hiking you see perfectly refreshed people enjoying the view.

Marshall Beach

free

About 2 miles past Inverness, Pierce Point Rd splits off to the right from Sir Francis Drake Blvd. From here you can get to two nice swimming beaches on the bay: Marshall Beach requires a 1-mile hike from the parking area.

Hearts Desire Beach

☎ *415-669-1140* *8am-sunset daily*
parking $2 ♿
www.cal-parks.ca.gov/north/marin/tbsp237.htm

Technically part of Tomales Bay State Park, this beach offers pleasant swimming conditions and convenient facilities.

Abbotts Lagoon

A drive along Pierce Point Rd will take you past the huge windswept sand dunes at Abbotts Lagoon, full of peeping killdeer and other shorebirds. You can hike to the shore from the parking area.

Kehoe Beach

Kehoe Beach is a bit farther out along Pierce Point Rd and has rip tides and sneaker waves; swimming is not advised.

Tule Elk Reserve

At the end of Pierce Point Rd is the restored Historic Pierce Point Ranch and the trailhead for the Tomales Point Trail, which meanders for 3½ miles through the Tule Elk Reserve. Male Tule elk are an amazing sight, standing regally with their big antlers against the backdrop of Tomales Point. In the late summer and early autumn, you can hear the elk 'bugling,' which is basically the males making a lot of noise at the beginning of the mating season to establish their harems.

McClures Beach

McClures Beach, a short walk west of the Historic Pierce Point Ranch, is a good place for beach-combing but is not suitable for swimming.

Bass Lake

Though less frequently visited, trails throughout the southern Point Reyes peninsula are quite rewarding. The easy 2-mile hike along the Coastal Trail from the Palomarin trailhead to Bass Lake can be fun. For an adrenaline rush, plunge into the cold deep waters from the rope swing on the west side of the lake.

Places to Stay & Eat

You'll find countless places to stay both within and around Point Reyes National Seashore – from park campgrounds to luxurious bed and breakfast inns. Several agencies assist visitors with finding appropriate accommodations.

Point Reyes Campsites
☎ 415-663-8054 (reservations accepted 9am-2pm Mon-Fri only) $ 1-6 people $10, 7-14 people $20, 15-25 people $30 C MC, V

There are no drive-in campsites in the Point Reyes reserve, but there are four hike-in campgrounds and one boat-in site, all with pit toilets. Camping permits must be obtained from the Bear Valley Visitors' Center. Reservations are recommended.

Point Reyes Hostel
PO Box 247 ☎ 415-663-8811 $ dorms $13-15 C MC, V ♿

This Hostelling International facility has a family room and kitchen facilities.

Coastal Lodging
☎ 415-663-1351 C cash only

Coastal Lodging has listings for B&Bs and cottages in Point Reyes Station, Inverness, and Bolinas.

Inns of Marin
☎ 415-663-2000 C cash only

This agency books B&Bs, cottages, and small hotels in Point Reyes Station, Inverness, Tomales, Bolinas, and Stinson Beach.

Point Reyes Lodging
☎ 800-539-1872 C cash only

Point Reyes Lodging specializes in booking cottages and small inns in the Point Reyes area.

Johnson's Drakes Bay Oysters (seafood)
☎ 415-669-1149 ⏲ 8am-4:30pm Tues-Sun C MC, V, AE ♿

Halfway from Inverness to the Point Reyes Lighthouse, look for the sign to Johnson's Drakes Bay Oysters for delicious, fresh, cheap Pacific oysters. Prices range from $5 to $9 per dozen, depending on their size.

Getting There & Away

By car, you can get to Point Reyes a few ways. The curviest is along Hwy 1, through Stinson Beach and up to Olema. The less winding way is to take Hwy 101 to San Rafael, then follow Sir Francis Drake Blvd all the way to Olema and into Point Reyes. For the latter route, take the Central San Rafael exit and head west on 4th St, which turns into Sir Francis Drake Blvd. By either route, it's about 1½ hours to Olema from San Francisco.

Just north of Olema, where Hwy 1 and Sir Francis Drake Blvd come together, turn left onto Bear Valley Rd. Less than a mile farther, on the left, is the Bear Valley Visitors' Center, with access to trails leading all over the southern portion of the national seashore. To get to the actual point of Point Reyes, pass the visitors' center and bear left at Sir Francis Drake Blvd; follow this road to the point, about an hour's drive. Don't get discouraged if it seems you may never get there – enjoy the scenery, and remember that you are actually *already in the park.*

Golden Gate Transit
☎ 415-923-2000 $ adult $3, senior/disabled $1.50, child $3 ♿
W www.goldengate.com

You can catch the Golden Gate Transit bus No 65 at the San Rafael Transit Center at 3rd and Hetherton. It runs weekends and holidays only. It stops at the Bear Valley Visitors' Center and in Inverness, but that's as close as the bus gets to the national seashore – it doesn't go out to the actual point.

BOLINAS

This beachside community became famous in the 1970s for its disappearing direction signs, removed from Hwy 1 by locals in a successful campaign to save the town from development (and from marauding tourists). The highway department finally tired of replacing the signs and agreed to leave Bolinas to its own devices. The turnoff from Hwy 1 is the first left past Audubon Canyon Ranch. You can enter the southern reaches of Point Reyes National Seashore just north of Bolinas. There are no buses to Bolinas, which is just the way they like it there.

Things to See & Do

For a town so plainly unexcited about tourism, Bolinas offers some fairly tempting attractions.

Bolinas Museum

48 Wharf Rd ☎ 415-868-0330 ⌚ 1pm-5pm Fri, noon-5pm Sat-Sun $ free ♿
W www.bolinasmuseum.org

The Bolinas Museum has exhibits on the art and history of coastal Marin.

Wildlife Gallery & Studio

48 Wharf Rd ☎ 415-868-0402 ⌚ by appointment Mon-Fri, noon-6pm Sat-Sun $ free ♿

Hidden within the courtyard of the Bolinas Museum, you'll find the studio of wildlife artist and avian expert Keith Hansen. Original artwork, prints, books, note cards, and other gifts are for sale.

Point Reyes Bird Observatory

Mesa Rd ☎ 415-868-0655 ⌚ 9am-5pm daily $ free ♿
W www.prbo.org

The Point Reyes Bird Observatory has bird-banding and -netting demonstrations, a visitors' center, and a nature trail. Guided bird walks, which cost $5, are held at 9am on the first Sunday of each month.

Places to Stay & Eat

Smiley's Schooner Saloon & Hotel

41 Wharf Rd ☎ 415-868-1311 $ doubles $64 weekdays, $74 weekends C AE, MC, V

This crusty old bar with a combination salty-Western feel was founded in 1851 – a Bolinas legend. The basic, clean, and comfortable rooms are in a quiet building behind the saloon.

Blue Heron Inn & Restaurant

11 Wharf Rd ☎ 415-868-1102 $ doubles $110 C AE, D, MC, V

The claw-foot bathtubs and intimate setting of this two-room B&B will transport you back to another era. The restaurant on the 1st floor is exceptional.

Coast Cafe (American)

46 Wharf Rd ☎ 415-868-2298 ⌚ 7:30am-2pm & 5pm-8pm Mon-Thurs, 7:30am-3pm & 5:30pm-9pm Fri-Sun $ breakfast $2-8, lunch $5.50-7.50, appetizer $6.50-8.50, entrée $5.50-22, dessert $2.50-4.50 C AE, DC, D, MC, V ♿

This comfortable café serves up hearty home-style meals. Breakfasts are especially popular. Be sure to check the specials board for some of its more unique offerings.

Blue Heron Inn & Restaurant (California)

11 Wharf Rd ☎ 415-868-1102 ⌚ 5pm-8:30pm Mon & Wed, 5:30pm-9pm Thurs-Sun $ appetizer $5-8, entrée $8-22, dessert $3-5 C AE, D, MC, V

The restaurant at the Blue Heron Inn serves some of the best food you'll find in Marin County. Its innovative menu relies heavily on fresh local organic produce and local meats and fish. Monday night is family night, with a simpler menu appealing to children's tastes.

OLEMA

Though it's basically a one-horse town today (population 175), Olema was West Marin's main settlement in the 1860s. There was stagecoach service to San Rafael and a weekly steamer to San Francisco, not to mention *six* saloons. In 1875, when the railroad was built through Point Reyes Station instead of Olema, the town's importance began to fade. In 1906, it regained distinction as the epicenter of the Great Quake. Though it has never recaptured its former vitality, it does serve as a nice base for exploring the Point Reyes National Seashore.

It takes about 1½ hours via either Hwy 1 or Sir Francis Drake Blvd to reach Olema, at the junction of Hwy 1 and Sir Francis Drake Blvd, from San Francisco. On weekends and holidays, take Golden Gate Transit bus No 65 from the San Rafael Transit Center at 3rd and Hetherton.

Hiking & Biking

Bolinas Ridge Trail

Sir Francis Drake Blvd $ free 🚌 65 Golden Gate Transit (weekends & holidays only), then a 1-mile walk from the bus
W www.nps.gov/goga/parknews/winter00/content4.htm

The Bolinas Ridge trailhead is about a mile west of Olema on Sir Francis Drake Blvd. This 12-mile series of ups and downs ends at Bolinas-Fairfax Rd above the Bolinas Lagoon. Whether you hike it partway or take it the full 24 miles roundtrip for a grueling mountain-bike ride, you'll see spectacular views.

Places to Stay & Eat

Olema Ranch Campground

10155 Hwy 1 ☎ 415-663-8001, 800-655-2267 $ $20 for 1 tent, 1 car & 2 people; $28 for RV including full hookups; extra person $3; extra car $2; dog $1 C AE, D, MC, V 65 Golden Gate Transit (weekends & holidays only)

For car campers, the Olema Ranch Campground offers a minimarket, laundry facilities, and acres of flat ground to pitch a tent. This is a popular spot for RVs (recreational vehicles) and large groups.

Olema Inn

10000 Hwy 1 ☎ 415-663-9559 $ $145-165 Mon-Fri, $125-145 Sat-Sun C AE, MC, V 65 Golden Gate Transit (weekends & holidays only)

This well-appointed Victorian inn offers guests a quiet place to retreat to after a day of exploring the seashore. Even nonguests can enjoy a meal at the inn. Lunch is served 11:30am to 3pm daily, dinner Wednesday to Sunday from 5pm to 9pm.

POINT REYES STATION

With a gas station and an ATM, Point Reyes Station is the hub of West Marin. Essentially a ranch town, in the '60s Point Reyes was the site of an influx of artists and intellectuals getting back to the land. Today, it's an interesting blend: Toby's Feed Barn is still a booming business, the Old Western Saloon whoops it up on weekends, and there is often the smell of cattle on the afternoon breeze. Interspersed are art galleries, shops serving tofu and mushroom sandwiches and specialty coffees, and even a store that sells tie-dyed underwear.

The weekly paper, the *Point Reyes Light,* has local news and listings of events, restaurants, and lodging. The *Light* also publishes the *Coastal Traveler,* a free quarterly with good local information.

Hwy 1, which becomes Main St in town, runs right past the post office, housed in the old train station. On weekends and holidays, take Golden Gate Transit bus No 65 from the San Rafael Transit Center at 3rd and Hetherton.

Toby's Feed Barn

11250 Hwy 1 ☎ 415-663-1223 9am-5pm Mon-Sat, 9:30am-4pm Sun 65 Golden Gate Transit (weekends & holidays only)

Toby's Feed Barn sells various and sundry items to local farmers and tourists alike.

Old Western Saloon

11201 Hwy 1 ☎ 415-663-1661 10am-2am daily $ live music cover $4 65 Golden Gate Transit (weekends & holidays only)

You'll find locals young and old bellied up to this rough-looking bar. Stop in when the DJ spins on Friday night or for live music on Saturday.

Dance Palace

503 B St ☎ 415-663-1075 9am-9pm Mon-Fri, check for weekend show times $ entry fee varies 65 Golden Gate Transit (weekends & holidays only) W www.dancepalace.org

The Dance Palace community center has weekend events, movies, and music.

Gallery Route 1

11101 Hwy 1 ☎ 415-663-1347 11am-5pm Wed-Mon $ admission varies 65 Golden Gate Transit (weekends & holidays only)

This collective art gallery shows local art.

Cycle Analysis

Hwy 1 ☎ 415-663-9164 10am-3pm Sat-Sun Apr-Nov $ $10-12/hour, $23-28/half-day, $28-35/day 65 Golden Gate Transit (weekends & holidays only) W www.cyclepointreyes.com

You can rent mountain bikes by the day, half-day, or hour, or take a guided tour.

Permaculture Institute of Northern California

PO Box 627 ☎ 415-663-9139 10am 1st Sunday of the month or by appointment $ entry fee varies W www.permacultureinstitute.com

In a town where organic produce is the norm, PINC takes things a step further by integrating food production, water and energy use, and building practices. Learn about permaculture at 10am the first Sunday of each month at the open house; call for directions.

Places to Stay & Eat

Holly Tree Inn

3 Silverhills Rd ☎ 415-663-1554 $ doubles

$120-175 Mon-Fri, $120-190 Sat-Sun; apartments $225-250 c AE, MC, V

The Holly Tree Inn books several cozy rooms in the main house (each with private bath), a garden cottage behind the house, and a few luxury cottages near Inverness. Rates include breakfast.

Cricket Cottage

PO Box 627 ☎ 415-663-9139 $ apartments $145 up to 4 people, each additional guest $20 c MC, V 65 Golden Gate Transit (weekends & holidays only), then a 2-mile walk from the bus ♿

You can relax completely at this secluded retreat for up to four people. The cottage includes fireplace, private hot tub, and kitchenette stocked with breakfast fixings. There's a minimum two-night stay on weekends.

Bovine Bakery (bakery)

11315 Main St ☎ 415-663-9420 ⏲ 6:30am-5pm Mon-Fri, 7am-5pm Sat-Sun $ breakfast 45¢-$3.50 c cash only 65 Golden Gate Transit (weekends & holidays only) ♿

For coffee and pastries, this is *the* spot. Its cinnamon buns are among the best.

Cowgirl Creamery and Indian Peach Food Co (California)

80 4th St ☎ 415-663-9335 ⏲ 10am-6pm Wed-Sun $ lunch/entrée $3.50-12, dessert $2-3.50 c AE, MC, V 65 Golden Gate Transit (weekends & holidays only) ♿

This local market in an old barn has a lunch and dinner counter (get your tofu mushroom sandwiches here), cheese, wine, and local organic produce.

Pine Cone Diner (California)

60 4th St ☎ 415-663-1536 ⏲ 8am-8:30pm Tues-Sun $ breakfast $4.50-9, lunch $4-9, appetizer $7.50-12.50, entrée $6.50-22, dessert $5 c cash only 65 Golden Gate Transit (weekends and holidays only) ♿

Formerly a truck stop, the Pine Cone Diner now serves soups and sandwiches, as well as haute cuisine, often made from local organic produce. At breakfast, a table in the corner is reserved for the old-timers who prefer greasy-spoon fare and dishwater coffee.

Station House Cafe (American)

11180 Main St ☎ 415-663-1515 ⏲ 8am-9pm Sun-Thurs, 8am-10pm Fri-Sat winter; 8am-10pm Sun-Thurs, 8am-11pm Fri-Sat summer $ breakfast/lunch $6-10, appetizer $2-7, entrée $10-15, dessert $1-6 c D, MC, V 65 Golden Gate Transit (weekends & holidays only) ♿

For delicious fare, including locally raised beef and seafood, this is a favorite stop with reasonable prices.

INVERNESS

The word 'charming' comes to mind when you arrive in this little town spread along the west side of Tomales Bay. The downtown has a few restaurants and a good grocery store with a deli counter, and you'll find several great beaches just a few miles north of town.

Sir Francis Drake Blvd leads straight into Inverness from Hwy 1. On weekends and holidays, Golden Gate Transit bus No 65 stops here.

Blue Waters Kayaking Tours & Rentals

12938 Sir Francis Drake Blvd ☎ 415-669-2600 ⏲ 8am-6pm summer, call for winter hours $ rental $25, tours $49 65 Golden Gate Transit (weekends & holidays only) ♿ w www.bwkayak.com

Blue Waters offers natural history tours of Tomales Bay, or you can rent a kayak and paddle around the bay on your own, exploring secluded beaches and rocky crevasses.

Places to Stay & Eat

Golden Hinde Inn

12938 Sir Francis Drake Blvd ☎ 415-669-1389 $ $90-130, each additional person $20 c AE, MC, V 65 Golden Gate Transit (weekends & holidays only) ♿ e reservations@goldenhindeinn.com

The Golden Hinde Inn offers basic accommodations on Tomales Bay.

Inverness Valley Inn

13275 Sir Francis Drake Blvd ☎ 415-669-7250 $ singles $85 Mon-Fri, $100 Sat-Sun; doubles $125 Mon-Fri, $170 Sat-Sun; each additional person $20 c MC, V 65 Golden Gate Transit (weekends & holidays only), then a 1-mile walk from the bus

This streamside inn, set on 15 acres at the edge of the park, has a pool, hot tub, and tennis court. Each condominium-style unit has a kitchen and fireplace.

Manka's Inverness Lodge
☎ *415-669-1034* $ *doubles $185-285, apartments $265-465* C *MC, V* 🚌 *65 Golden Gate Transit (weekends & holidays only), then a 1-mile walk from the bus* ♿ *call for accessibility details*
e *mankas@best.com*

Manka's was built as a hunting lodge in 1917. Today, you can choose to splurge on the comfortable, elegant, and expensive rooms or a delicious dinner at the restaurant, which serves seasonal game. Rates include breakfast.

Gray Whale Pizza (Italian)
12781 Sir Francis Drake Blvd ☎ *415-669-1244* ⏲ *11:30am-8pm Sun-Fri, 11:30am-9pm Sat* $ *lunch/entrée $5.50-19, dessert $2-4* C *MC, V* 🚌 *65 Golden Gate Transit (weekends & holidays only)* ♿

This is the best spot for food downtown, with reasonably priced whole pizzas (or order by the slice weekdays at lunch).

Wine Country

The glorious Northern California Wine Country is a feasible day trip from San Francisco, but an overnight stay will give you a much better taste of the region's wines and its other attractions. The best times to visit are the autumn, when the grapes are on the vine, or in spring, when the hills are brilliant green.

Wine has been produced in this region since 1857, but setbacks early this century, such as deadly phylloxera blights and Prohibition, slowed things down for a time. Beating France in a blind tasting in Paris in 1976 put California on the international wine map, and it has never looked back.

The two valleys, Napa and Sonoma, lie about 1½ hours' drive north of San Francisco. Napa Valley, the farther inland of the two, has more than 200 wineries. Sonoma Valley is low-key and less commercial but still boasts more than 100 wineries. Both offer the same rustic beauty of vineyards, wildflowers, and green and golden hills, but to do either of them justice, allow at least two days.

Getting There & Away

Though a car makes it much simpler to get to and around the Wine Country, with planning and patience you can negotiate the public transit system. Call for current schedules, as arrival and departure times change seasonally.

By car, take Hwy 101 north from San Francisco to the Hwy 37 exit at Novato. For Napa Valley, follow Hwy 37 for about 10 miles, until it connects with Hwy 29. For Sonoma Valley, take Hwy 37 to Hwy 121 north, and then Hwy 12 north. From the East Bay, you can get to Hwy 29 directly from I-80 via Vallejo. The routes to Napa and Sonoma are well marked.

If you drive, keep in mind that Hwy 29 backs up on weekend evenings between 4pm and 7pm, which will slow your return to the city.

Baylink Ferry
☎ *415-643-3779* ⏲ *8am-11:25pm daily*
$ *day pass $12* ♿
w *www.baylinkferry.com*

Baylink connects San Francisco's Ferry Building and Pier 41 with the Vallejo Ferry Terminal with frequent ferry boat and evening bus service.

Blue & Gold Fleet Ferry
☎ *415-773-1188* ⏲ *6am-9:40pm daily*
$ *one-way: adult $8, child $4, ages 5 & under free; day pass $12* ♿
w *www.blueandgoldfleet.com*

You can take the Blue & Gold ferry from San Francisco's Fisherman's Warf (Pier 41) or the Ferry Building to the Vallejo Ferry Terminal. Blue & Gold also runs daily guided Wine Country tours, offered to adults 21 and over, for $53.

Golden Gate Transit
☎ *415-923-2000* $ *adult $5.70, senior/disabled $2.80, child $4.25* ♿
w *www.goldengate.com*

Golden Gate Transit bus No 90 runs from San Francisco to Sonoma; catch it at 1st and Mission Sts, across from the Transbay Terminal.

Napa Vine
☎ *800-696-6443* ⏲ *buses run approximately 5:20am-8:45pm* $ *50¢-$2.50; day pass: adult $6, senior/disabled $3, student $4* ♿
w *www.napavalleyvine.com*

Napa Vine, a local bus company, covers the area between the Vallejo Ferry Terminal through Napa Valley to Calistoga with its Route 10 bus.

Sonoma County Transit
☎ *707-576-7433, 800-345-7433* ⌚ *hours vary* ♿
W *www.sctransit.com*

Once you're in Sonoma County, Sonoma County Transit has buses around the Sonoma Valley.

Vallejo Ferry Terminal
495 Mar Island Way ⌚ *7:30am-5:30pm daily* ♿

Baylink Ferries run from the Vallejo Ferry Terminal to San Francisco's Ferry Building and Pier 41.

NAPA VALLEY

Highway 29, or St Helena Hwy, between Napa and Calistoga is the principal route through the Napa Valley. Most towns have a

Wine Tasting

Stopping in at wineries throughout the Napa and Sonoma Valleys is not just about drinking wine but *tasting* it. Though most of us think we know how to taste food and drink, it is helpful to use a few special techniques when tasting wine. Wine is most fully appreciated when all three of its primary characteristics – color, nose, and taste – are evaluated. And you look like a real pro if you can describe it using some of the more common terms.

STEPHEN SAKS

Grapes on the vine in Napa Valley

Color The color of wine can indicate what kind of grapes were used to make it, how old it is, and even if it has gone bad. Assess the wine's color by tilting the glass of wine over a white background or holding it up to the light. White wine ranges from pale yellow (Chablis and Sauvignon Blanc grapes) to buttery yellow (Chardonnay), with dessert wines and aged whites taking on a golden honey hue. Red wines range from transparent to opaque and may be an inky purple (Petite Sirah), a deep red (Cabernet Sauvignon or Merlot), or a light red (Pinot Noir). Older wines tend to be brownish at the edge of a glass. If either a white or red wine appears cloudy, it may be spoiled, though some wines and most port naturally contain more sediment.

Nose The smell, also called the nose or bouquet, plays a large part in one's enjoyment of a wine. To release the bouquet, swirl the wine in the glass, put your nose to the edge, and take a long slow sniff. Common words used to describe a wine's bouquet are: fruity (peach, pear, green apple, berries, tropical fruits), earthy (mushrooms, cedar, nuts, wood smoke), floral (rose), and spicy (mint, black pepper, cloves, cinnamon). If the wine has gone bad, it may smell like vinegar, cabbage, rubber, or wet wool.

Taste To taste wine, take a small sip into your mouth and suck air between your teeth. Hold the wine at the center of your tongue for a few seconds to allow each of its characteristics to come forth. The flavors may resemble many of the smells listed above. A few other things to note are: the acidity and level of sweetness; tannins (for red wines), which give the wine an astringent, or mouth-puckering, quality; the body or thickness of the wine; any oak flavors, which indicate barrel fermentation; and the finish, or aftertaste, of the wine.

What constitutes a good wine is largely determined by your personal preferences. What tastes divine to one may be just sour grapes to another.

visitors' center. Napa is the region's main town, but it's of little interest.

Napa Visitors' Center
NAPA VALLEY MAP
1310 Napa Town Center ☎ 707-226-7459 ⌚ 9am-5pm daily $ free 🚌 Napa Vine Route 10 ♿
W *www.napavalley.com*

Stop at the Napa Visitors' Center for a detailed map to the wineries and continue on your way.

Napa County Historical Society Museum
NAPA VALLEY MAP
1219 1st St ☎ 707-224-1739 ⌚ noon-4pm Tues & Thurs $ free 🚌 Napa Vine Route 10

This museum is worth a quick peek.

Napa Museum NAPA VALLEY MAP
55 Presidents Circle in Yountville ☎ 707-944-0500 ⌚ 10am-5pm Wed-Mon $ adult $4.50, senior/student $3.50, ages 7-17 $2.50 ♿
W *www.napavalleymuseum.org*

The modernist Napa Museum chronicles Napa's cultural history and showcases local paintings and collections. Downstairs are a gift shop and an interactive display about winemaking.

St Helena

Just north of Yountville, St Helena makes a good stop on your Napa Valley tour. The quaint town features lots of interesting old buildings and plenty of restaurants.

St Helena Chamber of Commerce
NAPA VALLEY MAP
1010 Main St, Suite A ☎ 707-963-4456 ⌚ 10am-5pm Mon-Fri, 11am-4pm Sat $ free 🚌 Napa Vine Route 10 ♿
W *www.sthelena.com*

The chamber of commerce has maps and general information for St Helena and Napa Valley.

Silverado Museum NAPA VALLEY MAP
1490 Library Lane ☎ 707-963-3757 ⌚ noon-4pm Tues-Sun $ free 🚌 Napa Vine Route 10 ♿
W *www.napanet.net/vi/silverado*

This small museum has a fascinating collection

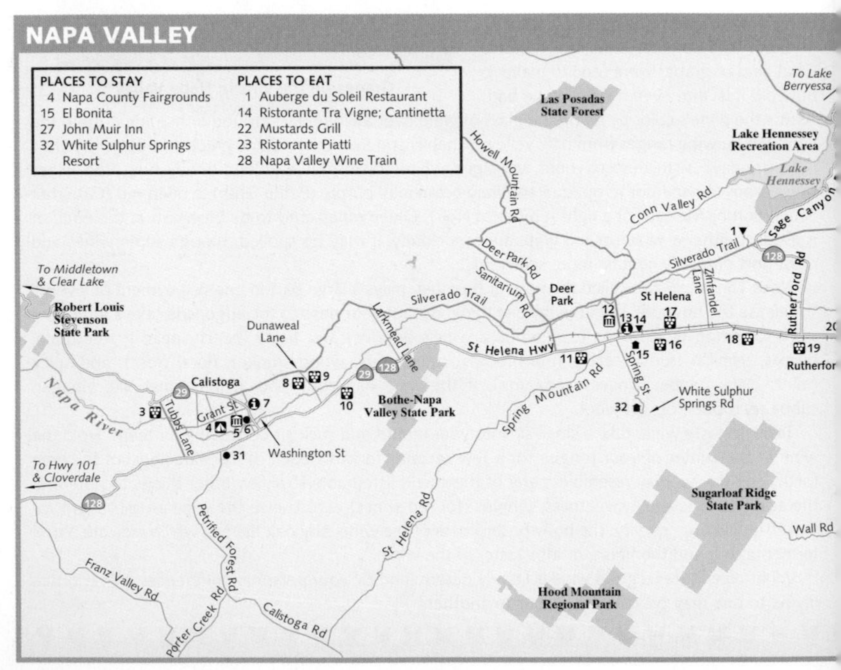

of Robert Louis Stevenson memorabilia. The writer honeymooned here in an abandoned mine bunkhouse in 1880 and lived for a time on Mt St Helena.

Calistoga

The farthest town to the north is Calistoga, known more for its mineral water than for its wine. This attractive town was founded in 1859 by Sam Brannan, the man who sounded the gold-rush alarm that brought prospecting '49ers in from all over the world. Filthy rich, Brannan envisioned building Calistoga into a sprawling resort, dependent on the nearby natural geysers and hot springs. Guiseppe Musante began bottling Calistoga mineral water here in 1924.

Calistoga Chamber of Commerce Visitors' Center

NAPA VALLEY MAP
1458 Lincoln Ave, Suite 9 ☎ 707-942-6333
🕘 10am-5pm Mon-Fri, 10am-4pm Sat, 11am-3pm Sun $ free 🚌 Napa Vine Route 10 ♿
w www.calistogafun.com

Stop at the chamber for information on the town's attractions and its many spas.

Sharpsteen Museum

NAPA VALLEY MAP
1311 Washington St ☎ 707-942-5911
🕘 11am-4pm daily $ donations (free)
🚌 Napa Vine Route 10 ♿
w www.sharpsteen-museum.org

Named after benefactor Ben Sharpsteen, animator, director, and producer for Walt Disney Studios for many years, this museum has Disneyesque dioramas portraying the town's history, as well as a detailed replica of Brannan's original resort town. Brannan's cottage is attached to the museum. Tours are available by appointment.

Old Faithful Geyser

1299 Tubbs Lane ☎ 707-942-6463 🕘 9am-5pm winter, 9am-6pm summer $ adult $6, ages 6-12 $2, ages 5 & under free 🚌 Napa Vine Route 10 ♿
w www.oldfaithfulgeyser.com

This geothermal geyser erupts approximately every 40 minutes. Learn more about geothermal activity and earthquakes at the

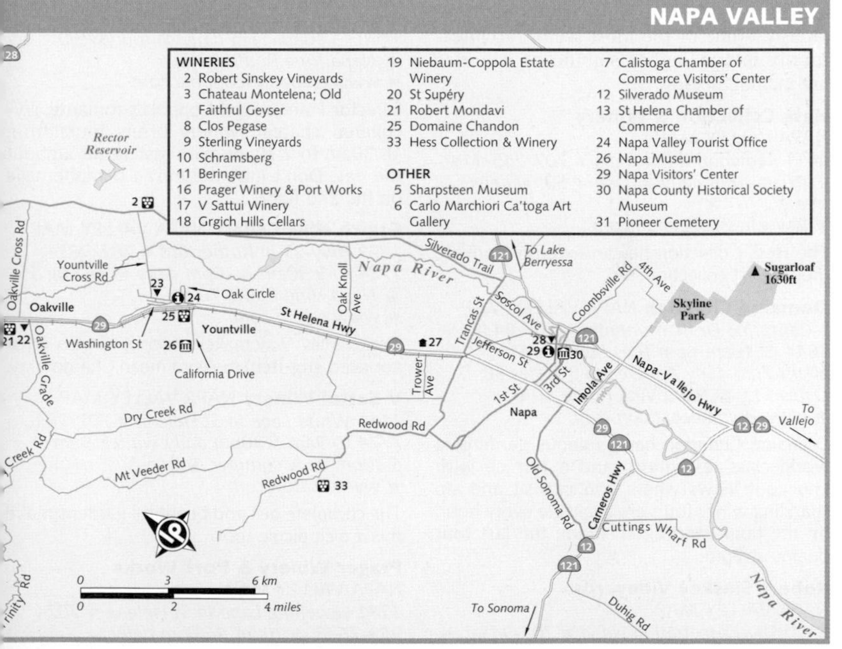

exhibit hall, in the video room, and on the self-guided tour.

Carlo Marchiori Ca'toga Art Gallery & Home NAPA VALLEY MAP
1206 Cedar St ☎ 707-942-3900 ⏲ tour 11am Sat May-Oct, gallery 11am-6pm Thurs-Mon (call ahead for winter gallery hours) $ tour $20, gallery free 🚌 Napa Vine Route 10 ♿
W www.catoga.com

Go to the fun-filled gallery to buy your ticket for a tour of Carlo Marchiori's surreally decorated home and garden, led by the artist himself.

Wineries

Most wineries charge a small fee for wine tastings. This is more prevalent a practice in Napa than in Sonoma, where many tastings are free. In Napa, expect to shell out anywhere from $3 to $10 to taste. Most wineries are open all day every day for tasting, but if you absolutely, positively don't want to miss a tasting or tour, call ahead.

For a complete guide to wineries, stop at one of the visitors' centers mentioned previously. Some of the most scenic, architecturally interesting, or significant wineries are included below.

Hess Collection & Winery
NAPA VALLEY MAP
4411 Redwood Rd in Napa ☎ 707-255-1144 ⏲ 10am-4pm daily $ tasting $3, gallery free ♿
W www.hesscollection.com

The Hess Collection has an extensive private modern art collection.

Domaine Chandon NAPA VALLEY MAP
1 California Dr in Yountville ☎ 707-944-8844 ⏲ 10am-6pm Tues-Sun Jan-Mar, 10am-7pm daily Apr-Dec $ 3 tastes $8, 5 tastes $12 🚌 Napa Vine Route 10 ♿
W www.domainchandon.com

Domaine Chandon has gorgeous gardens, a world-class restaurant, and a terrace with knockout views where you can sit and sip sparkling wine. Tours are available every hour, on the hour, starting at 11am; the last tour begins at 5pm.

Robert Sinskey Vineyards
NAPA VALLEY MAP
6320 Silverado Trail in Napa ☎ 707-944-9090 ⏲ 10am-4:30pm daily $ regular tasting $5, reserve wines $9 ♿
W www.robertsinskey.com

Robert Sinskey Vineyards grows grapes using biodynamic farming practices. The Pinot Noir is particularly noteworthy.

Robert Mondavi NAPA VALLEY MAP
7801 Hwy 29 in Oakville ☎ 800-666-3284 ⏲ 9am-5pm daily $ tasting $4, tour & tasting $10 🚌 Napa Vine Route 10 ♿
W www.robertmondaviwinery.com

The Robert Mondavi Winery, fronted by a stoic mission-style winery building and decorated with fun sculpture, offers informative tours and classes.

St Supéry NAPA VALLEY MAP
8440 Hwy 29 in Rutherford ☎ 707-963-4507 ⏲ 9:30am-5pm daily $ lifetime pass $5 🚌 Napa Vine Route 10 ♿
W www.stsupery.com

St Supéry's interactive and innovative displays on Napa Valley winemaking make this a great first stop for novice sommeliers.

Niebaum-Coppola Estate Winery
NAPA VALLEY MAP
1991 Hwy 29 in Rutherford ☎ 707-968-1100 ⏲ 10am-5pm daily $ tour $7.50 🚌 Napa Vine Route 10 ♿
W www.niebaum-coppola.com

Director Francis Ford Coppola's romantic ivy-covered chateau winery offers tours from 10:30am to 2:30pm, with tasting throughout the day. Don't miss the movie paraphernalia on the 2nd floor.

Grgich Hills Cellars NAPA VALLEY MAP
1829 Hwy 29 in Rutherford ☎ 707-963-2784 ⏲ 9:30am-4:30pm daily $ tasting $5 🚌 Napa Vine Route 10 ♿
W www.grgich.com

Grgich Hills' winemaker Mijenko Grgich (pronounced grig-**itch**) makes a mean Chardonnay.

V Sattui Winery NAPA VALLEY MAP
1111 White Lane in St Helena ☎ 707-963-7774 ⏲ 9am-5:30pm daily winter, 9am-6:30pm daily summer $ free ♿
W www.vsattui.com

The complete deli and beautiful gardens make this a nice picnic spot.

Prager Winery & Port Works
NAPA VALLEY MAP
1281 Lewelling Lane in St Helena ☎ 707-969-7678 ⏲ 10am-4:30pm daily

tasting $5
www.pragerport.com

f your palate is worn from wine tasting, try Prager Port Works. Ask when they last dusted the windowsill.

Beringer NAPA VALLEY MAP
2000 Main St in St Helena 707-963-4812 9am-5pm daily winter, 9am-6pm daily summer tasting $3, tour and tasting $5 Napa Vine Route 10
www.beringer.com

Beringer is the oldest continuously operating winery in the valley (it survived Prohibition by manufacturing sacramental wine).

Schramsberg NAPA VALLEY MAP
1400 Schramsberg Rd in Calistoga 707-942-6668 10am-3pm by appointment only tour & 3 tastings $10
www.schramsberg.com

The historic Schramsberg Vineyard was the first hillside winery of Napa Valley, founded in 1862. Now under the direction of the Davies family, the winery produces premier sparkling wines using the traditional méthode champenoise. Tours allow you to explore the wine caves, as well as learn the process of making sparkling wines.

Sterling Vineyards NAPA VALLEY MAP
1111 Dunaweal Lane in Calistoga 888-726-6136 10:30am-4:30pm daily $4
www.sterlingvineyards.com

An aerial tram carries you up to this hilltop winery, the first in Napa Valley to produce a vintage Merlot.

Clos Pegase NAPA VALLEY MAP
1060 Dunaweal Lane in Calistoga 707-942-4981 10:30am-5pm daily tasting $5, tour free
www.clospegase.com

Architecture, art, and wine form an enjoyable alliance at Clos Pegase. A free tour features the large collection of modern art, as well as the wine.

Chateau Montelena NAPA VALLEY MAP
1429 Tubbs Lane in Calistoga 707-942-5105 10am-4pm daily tasting $10 Napa Vine Route 10
www.montelena.com

Chateau Montelena is quite scenic – arched bridges lead over Jade Lake to intimate islands. Unfortunately, though, picnicking is not allowed.

Activities

A favorite way to see the valley is by biking. The Silverado Trail is a quieter road than Hwy 29. The region's early settlers originally used this route to get around.

Getaway Adventures
1117 Lincoln Ave 800-499-2453 prices vary Napa Vine Route 10
www.getawayadventures.com

For half- and full-day bicycle tours of the valley, check Getaway Adventures.

If you'd prefer to look down on the valley from above, several operators offer hot-air balloon trips.

Napa Valley Aloft
www.nvaloft.com person $180-225

This company represents Above the West Ballooning, Adventures Aloft, and Balloon Aviation services.

Napa Valley Balloons
800-253-2224 $175/person
www.napavalleyballons.com

Places to Stay

Accommodations range from campsites to motels to lovely B&Bs. In Calistoga, many places combine accommodations with spas. Call the Calistoga Chamber of Commerce for referrals.

Bothe-Napa Valley State Park
NAPA VALLEY MAP
3801 St Helena Hwy near Calistoga 707-942-4575, 800-444-7275 tent site $12 AE, MC, V Napa Vine Route 10

This park offers quiet campsites, with a swimming pool nearby and horseback riding in the summer and fall.

Skyline Park NAPA VALLEY MAP
2201 4th Ave in Napa 707-252-0481 $12 cash only

The campground is open in the summer only.

Napa County Fairgrounds
NAPA VALLEY MAP
1435 Oak St in Calistoga 707-942-5111 tent site $15, RV with hookup $22 MC, V

This city campground is more popular for RVs than tent campers.

Bed & Breakfast in Napa Valley
w *www.napalodging.com*

This web-based service provides contact information and prices for an extensive list of B&Bs throughout Napa Valley.

Bed & Breakfast Inns of Napa Valley
☎ *707-944-4444*

This service provides contact information and prices for B&Bs throughout Napa Valley.

John Muir Inn NAPA VALLEY MAP
1998 Trower Ave in Napa ☎ 707-257-7220, 800-522-8999 $ doubles $95-150 Mon-Fri, $105-$160 Sat-Sun; each additional guest $10 C AE, DC, D, MC, V Napa Vine Route 10

This modern hotel, just behind a Marie Callendar's restaurant, has 60 rooms.

El Bonita NAPA VALLEY MAP
195 Main St in St Helena ☎ 800-541-3284 $ doubles $107-179 Mon-Fri, $159-219 Sat-Sun; triples $139 Mon-Fri, $179 Sat-Sun; quads $169 Mon-Fri, $219 Sat-Sun; each additional guest $8 C MC, V Napa Vine Route 10

Comfortable and clean, this centrally located motel makes a good base for exploring the entire valley.

White Sulphur Springs Resort
NAPA VALLEY MAP
3100 White Springs Rd in St Helena ☎ 707-963-8588 $ doubles $110-225 Mon-Fri, $90-105 Sat-Sun; apartments $245 Mon-Fri, $205 Sat-Sun; each additional guest $30 C AE, MC, V

California's oldest resort is a peaceful place, with hot springs, a swimming pool, rustic cabins, and a redwood grove.

Places to Eat

There are some truly deluxe restaurants in the Napa Valley, where the rule is fresh, creative, and expensive cuisine accompanied by magnificent wines.

Mustards Grill (American)
NAPA VALLEY MAP
7399 Hwy 29 in Yountville ☎ 707-944-2424 11:30am-9pm Mon-Thurs, 11:30am-10pm Fri, 11am-10pm Sat, 11am-9pm Sun $ lunch $10-30, appetizer $6-11, entrée $10-30, dessert $5-7 C DC, D, MC, V Napa Vine Route 10

The casual atmosphere and savory food makes this restaurant popular with both locals and visitors.

Ristorante Piatti (Italian)
NAPA VALLEY MAP
6480 Washington St in Yountville ☎ 707-944-2070 11:30am-10pm Sun-Thurs, 11:30am-11pm Fri-Sat $ lunch $6-23, appetizer $6-9, entrée $12-23, dessert $6 C AE, DC, MC, V

You get a hearty traditional Italian meal at Ristorante Piatti.

Ristorante Tra Vigne (Italian)
NAPA VALLEY MAP
1050 Charter Oak Ave in St Helena ☎ 707-963-4444 11am-10:30pm daily $ appetizer $7-19, lunch/entrée $12-30, dessert $6-$8 C DC, D, MC, V Napa Vine Route 10

Tra Vigne is one of the finest Tuscan restaurants; for a cheaper meal, head across the patio to the Cantinetta, Tra Vigne's Italian deli, which serves light meals and more than 100 wines by the glass.

Auberge du Soleil Restaurant (California)
NAPA VALLEY MAP
180 Rutherford Hill Rd in Rutherford ☎ 707-963-1211 7am-2:30pm & 6pm-9:30pm daily; bar 7am-9:30pm daily $ breakfast $6-14, lunch $16-20, appetizer $2-12, 4-course menu $58, chef's menu $70, dessert $9 C AE, DC, D, MC, V

Hillside-terraced Auberge du Soleil is a quintessential Wine Country dining experience – and priced accordingly.

Napa Valley Wine Train (California)
NAPA VALLEY MAP
1275 McKinstry St in Napa ☎ 707-253-2111, 800-427-4124 8am-5pm Mon-Fri, 8am-6pm Sat-Sun C AE, DC, D, MC, V Napa Vine Route 10

Dine in a 1915 vintage Pullman dining car as it travels from Napa to St Helena and back. The 36-mile trip takes three hours and it's a beautiful ride. Champagne brunch ($59.50), served Saturday, Sunday, and holidays, departs at 8:55am. Lunch trips ($70) depart at 11:30am weekdays, 12:30pm weekends. Dinner trips ($78) depart at 6:30pm weekdays, 6pm weekends. A daily lunchtime deli car is more affordable ($30), but food costs extra.

SONOMA VALLEY

'Slonoma,' the locals' term for their relaxing, livable wine town, where family-owned wineries predominate, is a much more enjoyable place to wander around than Napa. In fact, if you have time to visit only one of the two wine valleys, definitely choose Sonoma. Also known as the 'Valley of the Moon,' Jack London's literary name for the region, it's a much less sterile, corporate county. The main highway through it is Hwy 12.

The unassuming Sonoma Valley is actually the birthplace of California wine. Hungarian count Agoston Haraszthy started producing wine here in 1855, and by the late 1860s there were already 50 vintners operating in the area.

The town of Sonoma, at the southern end of the 17-mile-long valley, is surrounded by vineyards and has a fascinating history. It's the site of an 1846 uprising of US settlers against the Mexican military command. The resulting 'Bear Flag Republic' was short-lived; when the Mexican-American War broke out a month later, the republic was absorbed into the expanded US territory. The revolt did, however, give California its state flag.

Sonoma Visitors' Bureau SONOMA VALLEY MAP
453 1st St E ☎ 707-996-1090 ⌚ 9am-5pm daily winter, 9am-7pm daily summer $ free 🚌 90 Golden Gate Transit ♿
w www.sonomavalley.com

Stop here for maps, local events lists, lodging information, and the 'Sonoma Walking Tour' booklet.

Things to See & Do

The State Park Service runs several historical sites within Sonoma. One ticket buys you entrance into the mission, barracks, and Lachryma Montis.

Mission San Francisco Solano de Sonoma SONOMA VALLEY MAP
☎ 707-938-9560 ⌚ 10am-5pm daily $ adult $1, ages 16 & under free 🚌 90 Golden Gate Transit ♿
w www.napanet.net/~sshpa

This 1823 building was the last of California's Franciscan missions and the only one built under Mexican rule (the rest were built by the Spanish).

Sonoma Barracks SONOMA VALLEY MAP
20 Spain St ☎ 707-939-9420 ⌚ 10am-5pm daily $ adult $1, ages 16 & under free 🚌 90 Golden Gate Transit ♿
w www.cal-parks.ca.gov

Used by Mexican troops under General Vallejo, the barracks also served as the capitol building of the short-lived California Republic.

Lachryma Montis SONOMA VALLEY MAP
☎ 707-938-9559 ⌚ 10am-5pm daily $ adult $1, ages 16 & under free 🚌 90 Golden Gate Transit ♿
w www.cal-parks.ca.gov

Lachryma Montis was General Vallejo's 500-acre farm and residence. The home, built in 1851–1852, was a far departure from the adobe construction typical of the time. Docent tours are given at 2pm daily.

Jack London State Historic Park SONOMA VALLEY MAP
2400 London Ranch Rd ☎ 707-938-5216 ⌚ park 9:30am-sunset daily, museum 10am-5pm daily $ parking $3, senior parking $2 ♿
w www.parks.sonoma.net/jlstory.html

North of Sonoma off Hwy 12 are the sleepy town of Glen Ellen and the Jack London State Historic Park, formerly the novelist's 800-acre ranch. The museum and the ruins of his grandiose home are worth a stop.

Wineries

Unlike in Napa Valley, free tastings and uncrowded tasting rooms are still the norm in Sonoma Valley.

Cline Cellars SONOMA VALLEY MAP
24737 Arnold Dr near Sonoma ☎ 800-546-2070 ⌚ 10am-6pm daily; tours at 11am, 1pm, 3pm daily $ free ♿
w www.clinecellars.com

The spacious Cline Cellars is still run by the Cline family. Tours are offered at 11am, 1pm, and 3pm.

Gundlach Bundschu Winery SONOMA VALLEY MAP
2000 Denmark St in Sonoma ☎ 707-938-5277 ⌚ 11am-4:30pm daily $ free ♿
w www.gunbun.com

The lighthearted Gundlach Bundschu, another

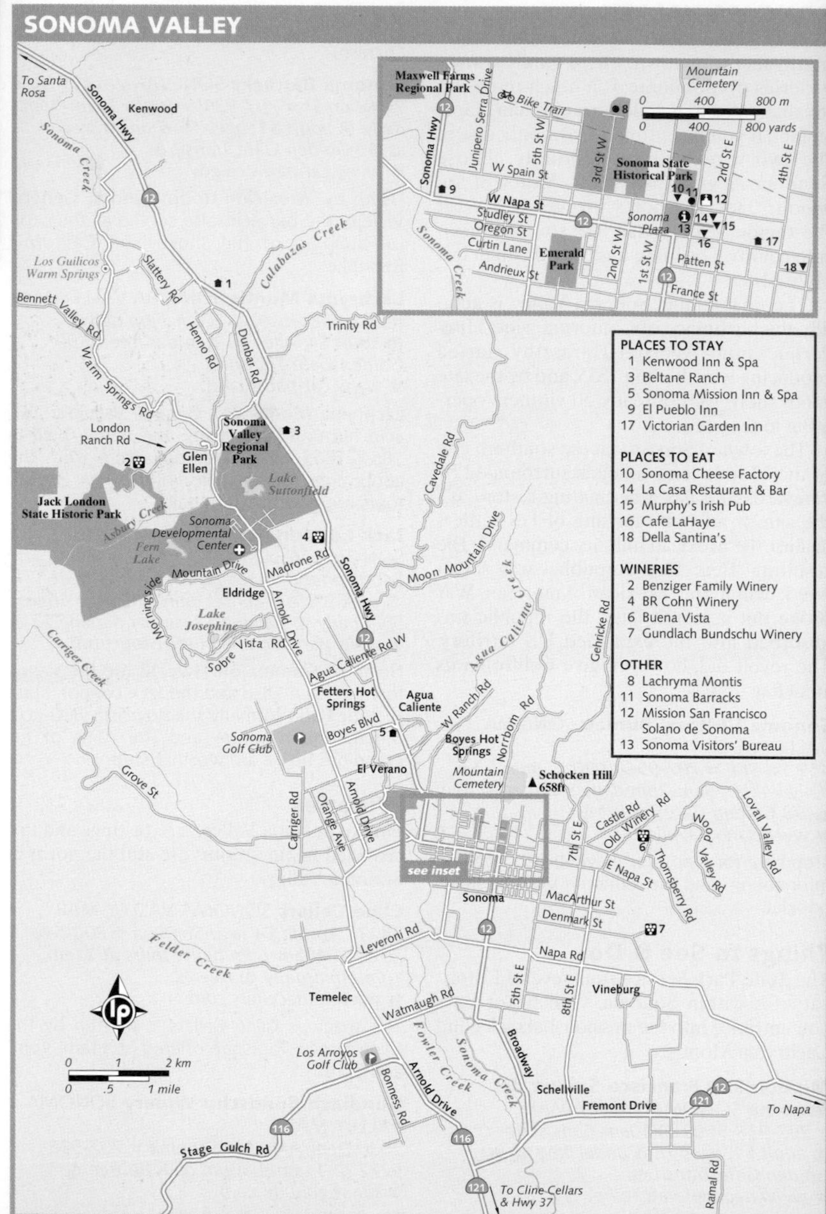
SONOMA VALLEY
PLACES TO STAY
1 Kenwood Inn & Spa
3 Beltane Ranch
5 Sonoma Mission Inn & Spa
9 El Pueblo Inn
17 Victorian Garden Inn
PLACES TO EAT
10 Sonoma Cheese Factory
14 La Casa Restaurant & Bar
15 Murphy's Irish Pub
16 Cafe LaHaye
18 Della Santina's
WINERIES
2 Benziger Family Winery
4 BR Cohn Winery
6 Buena Vista
7 Gundlach Bundschu Winery
OTHER
8 Lachryma Montis
11 Sonoma Barracks
12 Mission San Francisco Solano de Sonoma
13 Sonoma Visitors' Bureau
To Santa Rosa
Kenwood
Sonoma Hwy
Sonoma Creek
Los Guilicos Warm Springs
Slattery Rd
Calabazas Creek
Bennett Valley Rd
Henno Rd
Dunbar Rd
Trinity Rd
Warm Springs Rd
London Ranch Rd
Sonoma Valley Regional Park
Glen Ellen
Lake Suttonfield
Jack London State Historic Park
Asbury Creek
Sonoma Developmental Center
Fern Lake
Mountain Drive
Madrone Rd
Moon Mountain Drive
Cavedale Rd
Eldridge
Arnold Drive
Morning side
Lake Josephine
Sobre Vista Rd
Carriger Creek
Agua Caliente Rd W
Agua Caliente Creek
Gehricke Rd
Fetters Hot Springs
Agua Caliente
W Ranch Rd
Norrbom Rd
Sonoma Golf Club
Boyes Blvd
Boyes Hot Springs
El Verano
Mountain Cemetery
Schocken Hill 658ft
Grove St
Carriger Rd
Orange Ave
see inset
7th St E
Castle Rd
Old Winery Rd
Wood Valley Rd
Lovall Valley Rd
E Napa St
Thornsberry Rd
Sonoma
MacArthur St
Denmark St
Leveroni Rd
Napa Rd
Felder Creek
Temelec
5th St E
8th St E
Vineburg
Watmaugh Rd
Fowler Creek
Broadway
Los Arroyos Golf Club
Bonness Rd
Schellville
Fremont Drive
To Napa
Stage Gulch Rd
To Cline Cellars & Hwy 37
Ramal Rd
0 1 2 km
0 .5 1 mile
Maxwell Farms Regional Park
To Bike Trail
Junipero Serra Drive
5th St W
3rd St W
Mountain Cemetery
0 400 800 m
0 400 800 yards
Sonoma State Historical Park
2nd St E
4th St E
W Spain St
W Napa St
Studley St
Oregon St
Curtin Lane
Andrieux St
Emerald Park
2nd St W
1st St W
Sonoma Plaza
Patten St
France St

oldie dating to 1858, has a hillside cellar, peaceful lake, and sedate hiking trails.

Buena Vista SONOMA VALLEY MAP
18000 Old Winery Rd in Sonoma ☎ 800-926-1266 ⌚ 10am-5pm daily, tours 2pm daily $ free ♿
w www.buenavistawinery.com

The historic Buena Vista winery was Count Haraszthy's original vineyard, which helped launch the California wine industry.

Benziger Family Winery SONOMA VALLEY MAP
1883 London Ranch Rd in Glen Ellen ☎ 707-935-4046 ⌚ 10am-5pm daily $ free ♿
w www.benziger.com

Family-run Benziger is an appealing spot featuring vineyard tram tours.

BR Cohn Winery SONOMA VALLEY MAP
15140 Sonoma Hwy in Glen Ellen ☎ 707-938-4064, 800-330-4064 ⌚ 10am-5pm daily $ free ♿
w www.brcohn.com

This winery and olive oil hideout belongs to the manager of the Doobie Brothers. A concert-size stage overlooks the vineyard and is used for both weddings and rock music reunions.

Places to Stay

Sonoma Valley Concierge
453 1st St E in Sonoma ☎ 707-935-4300
e sonomaconcierge@sonomavalley.com

The Sonoma Valley Concierge makes bookings for accommodations within a wide price range.

Bed & Breakfast Association of Sonoma Valley
☎ 707-938-9513

For help finding a B&B, contact this local association.

El Pueblo Inn SONOMA VALLEY MAP
396 W Napa St in Sonoma ☎ 707-996-3651, 800-900-8844 $ doubles $105-165, each additional guest $10 c AE, D, MC, V 🚌 90 Golden Gate Transit ♿

This conveniently located motel is one of the cheapest options in the area.

Victorian Garden Inn
SONOMA VALLEY MAP
316 E Napa St in Sonoma ☎ 707-996-5339, 800-543-5339 $ doubles $109-185, apartments $199 c AE, D, MC, V
e info@victoriangardeninn.com

This classic B&B, filled with wicker and flowers, is a comfortable place to stay just a few blocks from downtown. Rates include breakfast.

Beltane Ranch SONOMA VALLEY MAP
11775 Hwy 12 in Glen Ellen ☎ 707-996-6501 $ $130-220 c cash only

This five-room B&B with a mountain backdrop and vineyard views offers volleyball and tennis courts, hiking trails, and wildlife viewing on its 1600-acre working ranch. Rates include breakfast.

JUDY BELLAH

Kenwood Inn & Spa
SONOMA VALLEY MAP
10400 Hwy 12 in Kenwood ☎ 707-833-1293, 800-353-6966 $ doubles $295-475, each additional guest $35 c AE, MC, V ♿

The incomparable Italian Kenwood Inn and Spa is a luxurious, romantic spot with 12 rooms. Nonguests may make an appointment to use the spa facilities.

Sonoma Mission Inn & Spa
SONOMA VALLEY MAP
18140 Hwy 12 in Boyes Hot Springs ☎ 707-938-9000, 800-862-4945 $ doubles $299-1200, each additional guest $50 c AE, D, MC, V 🚌 90 Golden Gate Transit ♿
e smi@smispa.com

The area's most expensive option may be this peacefully pink spa resort, the perfect spot for an indulgent weekend getaway. Nonguests can use the spa facilities on weekdays and Sunday afternoon (by appointment only).

Places to Eat

Sonoma Cheese Factory (deli)
SONOMA VALLEY MAP
2 W Spain St ☎ 707-996-1931, 707-996-

1000, 800-535-2855 ⌚ 8:30am-5:30pm Mon-Fri, 8:30am-6pm Sat-Sun Ⓒ *AE, D, MC, V* Ⓥ *90 Golden Gate Transit* ♿

If you're planning a picnic, the 'Home of Sonoma Jack' has everything you'll need, including free cheese tastings.

Murphy's Irish Pub (pub fare)
SONOMA VALLEY MAP
464 1st St E in Sonoma ☎ 707-935-0660 ⌚ 11am-11pm Mon-Fri, 11am-midnight Sat-Sun $ *no cover but $7 minimum purchase* *90 Golden Gate Transit* ♿ W *www.sonomapub.com*

Murphy's has good pub grub, beer, and live music Thursday through Sunday nights.

La Casa Restaurant & Bar (Mexican)
SONOMA VALLEY MAP
121 E Spain St in Sonoma ☎ 707-996-3406 ⌚ 11:30am-10pm daily (closed Mon in winter) $ *lunch $7-15, appetizer $6-13, entrée $7-15, dessert $2-6* Ⓒ *AE, DC, D, MC, V* *90 Golden Gate Transit* ♿

The region's Mexican roots shine here, a locals' inexpensive favorite near Mission San Francisco Solano de Sonoma.

Della Santina's (Italian)
SONOMA VALLEY MAP
133 E Napa St in Sonoma ☎ 707-935-0576 ⌚ 4pm-9:30pm daily $ *appetizer $4-8, entrée $9-20, dessert $3.50-6* Ⓒ *MC, V* *90 Golden Gate Transit* ♿

This small trattoria cooks up reasonably priced Tuscan food for dine-in or take-out.

Cafe LaHaye (New American)
SONOMA VALLEY MAP
140 E Napa St in Sonoma ☎ 707-935-5994 ⌚ 5:30pm-9pm Tues-Sat, 9:30am-2pm Sun $ *breakfast $6-10, appetizer $5-9, entrée $12-19, dessert $5-10* Ⓒ *MC, V* *90 Golden Gate Transit* ♿

This small café, decorated with local artwork, serves innovative cuisine in an intimate setting.

South of the City

San Francisco is on the tip of a 30-mile-long peninsula, sandwiched between the Pacific Ocean to the west and San Francisco Bay to the east. I-280 is the dividing line between a densely populated area running along the suburban eastern half of the peninsula and the rugged and more lightly populated Pacific coast.

San Francisco – with all its style, attitude and edge – disappears almost as soon as you head south. Along the Peninsula's other major north-south artery, Hwy 101, the city gives way to tract housing and strip malls that continue to San Jose and beyond. I-280 runs closer to the mountains and offers rural scenery and less traffic than Hwy 101. If you want a leisurely drive along the coast take Hwy 1. The scenery is breathtaking – especially looking down from the cliff-hugging stretch along Devil's Slide – and there are some interesting places along the way. Hwy 1 can be combined with I-280 or Hwy 101 for a loop back to San Francisco.

SAN FRANCISCO TO HALF MOON BAY

It's 28 miles from San Francisco to Half Moon Bay, and Hwy 1 winds south passing beach after beach – many of them unseen from the highway. All of them are more suitable for sunbathing than swimming, as the surf is unpredictable and the water is always cold. There's no access charge to the state beaches along the coast, but car parking usually costs $5. SamTrans buses go to many of the attractions listed in this section; see SamTrans listing, later, for contact information.

Pacifica & Devil's Slide

Pacifica and Point San Pedro, 15 miles from downtown San Francisco on Hwy 1, signal the end of the urban sprawl. The point also periodically marks the end of Hwy 1 at those times when Devil's Slide, an unstable cliff area a mile to the south, does just that – slides – after winter storms. The rebuilding and repairs always seem to be delayed by arguments between developers and conservationists about what should be done with this problem stretch – tunnel or bypass? – in the long term.

A word of warning: Pacifica has a well-deserved reputation as the fog capital of the Bay Area. When the sun shines, it's a pretty gorgeous place; when it's foggy, it's Polartec jacket city.

:altrans Highway Information Network
☎ 800-427-7623

t's always a good idea to call this service the o check on road conditions, especially during vet weather.

'acifica State Beach
'he main attraction here and at nearby Rock-.way Beach is catching some rays or a wave wear your wet suit).

iray Whale Cove to Miramar Beach

iray Whale Cove State Beach
'his spot is one of the area's popular 'clothing ptional' beaches.

Montara State Beach
'his is another sandy state beach.

McNee Ranch State Park
8am-sunset daily ⓢ free
plants.montara.com/mrsp.html

'his 700-acre park extends inland from Montara State Beach; trails into it climb up rom the Martini Creek parking lot. Follow ne paved road to the ranger's residence, rom where you can hike up to Montara Mountain.

ames V Fitzgerald Marine Reserve
his protected area encompasses many natu-al tidal pools that are exposed at low tide.

'illar Point Harbor
ishing boats bring in their catch here. You nay find yourself eating some of it if you hoose a surfside restaurant in Princeton.

Miramar
he beach at Miramar is home to one of the nost popular surfing breaks along the coast.

'laces to Stay & Eat

Montara has a number of B&Bs with lower rices than those in Half Moon Bay.

oint Montara Lighthouse HI Hostel
O Box 737 ☎ 650-728-7177 ⓢ dorms: $13 'I members, $15 nonmembers; private ooms: add a $10 room charge ⓒ MC, V
himontara@norcalhostels.org

his unusual lodging began as a fog station in 875; the hostel is adjacent to the current ghthouse, which dates from 1928. This very opular place has a living room, kitchen facil-ies, and even an outdoor hot tub ($5 per person). In summer, reservations are essential, especially on weekends.

Farallone Inn
1410 Main St in Montara ☎ 650-728-8200 ⓢ $110-195 ⓒ MC, V ♿ limited
ⓔ info@faralloneinn.com

This 1906-vintage Victorian B&B has nine cozy rooms.

Harbor View Inn
51 Alhambra Ave in Miramar ☎ 650-726-2329 ⓢ singles $90-135, doubles $110-155, quads $125-195 ⓒ cash only

The inn is close to Pillar Point Harbor.

Goose & Turrets
835 George St in Montara ☎ 650-728-5451 ⓢ $110-150 ⓒ MC, V, AE
ⓔ rhmgt@montara.com

Tea, included in the room rates, is served in the cheerful common room of this 1908 Italian villa. Amuse yourself playing the piano or reading in the rose garden as a fountain bubbles musically nearby.

Moss Beach Distillery (American)
☎ 650-728-5595 ⓘ noon-3:30pm Mon-Fri, noon-3pm Sat, 10am-3pm Sun, 4:30pm-8:30pm daily ⓢ $8-48 ⓒ MC, V, AE ♿

This restaurant is set on a cliff and claims to be haunted by the 'Blue Lady,' who wanders the bluffs awaiting the return of her piano-playing lover. Heavy-duty eaters may want to tackle the steak-and-lobster special ($48), a hefty meal in more ways than one.

SamTrans
1250 San Carlos Ave ☎ 800-660-4287, 650-508-6448 TDD
ⓦ www.samtrans.com

SamTrans runs buses down the coast to Half Moon Bay from the Daly City BART station during commute hours. The agency also operates limited service during the weekend; phone or visit the website for schedules.

HALF MOON BAY

The main town on the coast between San Francisco (28 miles north) and Santa Cruz (40 miles south), Half Moon Bay was a fishing and dairy village called Spanishtown until just after the turn of the 20th century. Today it has a population of around 9000, and its long stretches of beach, upscale shops, eateries, and B&Bs still attract weekenders.

Pumpkins are a major crop around here, and November's pre-Halloween harvest is celebrated in an annual festival featuring mouthwatering pies and hair-raising jack-o'-lanterns. There are a host of other local festivals and celebrations throughout the year.

Main St, with its shops, restaurants, and cafés, is the main drag. The surrounding blocks make up a historic district containing many 19th- and early-20th-century Victorian, craftsman, and art deco buildings.

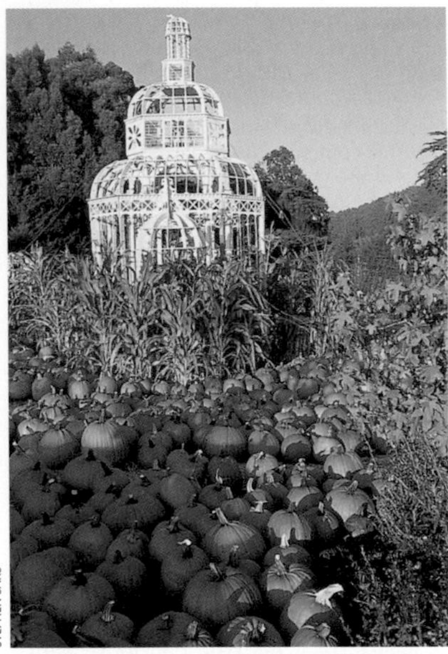

STEPHEN SAKS

A likely place to meet the Great Pumpkin

Inland there are trails through Purissima Creek Redwoods for cyclists and walkers.

Half Moon Bay Coastside Chamber of Commerce
520 Kelly Ave ☎ 650-726-8380 ⏲ 9am-4:30pm Mon-Fri winter; 9am-4pm Mon-Fri, 10am-3pm Sat summer ♿
w www.halfmoonbaychamber.org

Visitor information is available here, including details of HMB's signature pumpkin festival and other special events.

Half Moon Bay Review
714 Kelley Ave ☎ 650-726-4424
w www.hmbreview.com

Drop into the art deco offices and pick up a copy of the local paper for entertainment listings.

Half Moon Bay Jail
505 Johnston St ☎ 650-726-7084 ⏲ call for hours

This old two-cell jail exhibits articles and photographs of the town's earlier incarnation a the unusually cosmopolitan Spanishtown Visitor information is available.

Places to Stay & Eat

Overnighting at Half Moon Bay can be either very cheap or fairly expensive.

Francis State Beach
☎ 650-726-8820 $ $12 c cash only

The cheap options are the spartan campsite here, 54 of them. Sites, which do have communal warm-water showers, are available o a first-come, first-served basis only.

San Benito House
356 Main St ☎ 650-726-3425 $ $80-150
c MC, V, AE

This is one of the more moderately priced Ha Moon Bay B&Bs, with rates about as low a prices ever go around here.

Cameron's Restaurant & Inn
1410 S Cabrillo Hwy ☎ 650-726-5705
$ rooms $69-99 c MC, V, AE

This is a rather wacky English-style pub in century-old building with a large selection c beers and dishes that range from fish-and chips ($9) to roasted garlic and brie ($12 There's live music several nights a week and double-decker London bus in the parking lc just for smokers. The three rooms upstairs ar scant in luxuries but reasonably priced.

San Benito House (Mediterranean)
356 Main St ☎ 650-726-3425 ⏲ 5:30pm-9pm Thurs-Sat, 10:30am-1:30pm & 5:30pm 9pm Sun $ appetizer $5.50-9.50, entrée $13-18, dessert $4.50 c cash only

The restaurant here serves good Mediterranean cuisine in a charming dining room Choices range from the risotto cake to mesquite-grilled beef filet.

Three Amigos (Mexican)
200 N Cabrillo Hwy ☎ 650-726-6080
⏲ 9am-midnight daily $ $4-7 c MC, V

or an inexpensive meal, this is the best of the own's multitude of taquerías.

ANTA CRUZ

Vith its beach-town vibe, this town of 4,000 is serene most of the year. It's home o surfers, students, health-conscious restau-ants, and the Santa Cruz Beach Boardwalk. Ken Kesey launched his notorious acid dysseys here in the 1960s.

Restaurants and shops line parallel 'acific Ave and Front St, the unofficial main rags in Santa Cruz. To get to the beach and he Boardwalk, head south on Front St and urn left on Beach St.

anta Cruz Metropolitan Transit District
831-425-8600
www.scmtd.com

Call or check the website for Santa Cruz pub-c transit schedules and route information.

anta Cruz County Conference & 'isitors' Council
211 Ocean St ☎ 831-425-1234, 800-833-494 ⌚ 9am-4pm Mon-Sat, 10am-4pm un ♿
www.santacruzca.org

'ick up information from the friendly staff bout what to see and do here in the central oast's good-time city, whether it's for a day r for a week.

'hings to See & Do

anta Cruz Beach Boardwalk
831-423-5590 ⌚ 11am-8pm Sat-Sun vinter & public holidays (closed most of)ecember); 11am-11pm Mon-Sat, 11am-0pm Sun summer $ $1.80-3.60/rides, 22.95/unlimited ticket ♿
www.beachboardwalk.com

'he 1906 boardwalk is the oldest beachfront musement park on the West Coast and fea-ures the 1923 Giant Dipper roller coaster and he 1911 Looff carousel, both of them na-onal historic landmarks.

Auseum of Art & History
'05 Front St ☎ 831-429-1964 ⌚ 11am-5pm ues-Wed & Fri-Sun, 11am-7pm Thurs $ adult $4, senior/student $2, child free ♿
santacruzmah.org

'his museum focuses on regional history and nodern art and is definitely worth a quick ook around.

Surfing Museum
1305 E Cliff Dr ☎ 831-420-6289 ⌚ noon-4pm Thurs-Mon winter, noon-4pm Wed-Mon summer $ free ♿
W www.cruzio.com

This tiny museum is packed with surfing paraphernalia and memorabilia. It overlooks Steamer's Lane, Santa Cruz's most popular surfing break.

Freeline Design
821 41st Ave ☎ 831-476-2950 ⌚ 9am-6pm daily $ boards $6-15, wet suits $8

Hey dude, you can rent surfing gear, even those hard-to-find fiberglass boards, from this nifty surf shop.

Although there are no railway connections to modern Santa Cruz, there are two scenic historical train rides.

Santa Cruz Big Trees & Pacific Railway
☎ 831-335-4484 ⌚ call for current schedule $ adult $15, child $13

From the Boardwalk, these 1920s-style railway coaches take almost two hours to reach Roaring Camp, a re-created 1880s logging town.

Roaring Camp & Big Trees Railroad
☎ 831-335-4484 ⌚ call for current schedule $ $13.50

From Roaring Camp, narrow-gauge steam locomotives make 75-minute roundtrips to Big Trees Redwood Forest.

Places to Stay & Eat

The county visitors' bureau provides a 24-hour accommodations hotline at ☎ 800-833-3494. Motels (none of them especially cheap) line Hwy 1, which is known as Mission St within the city limits. Other good places to look are the streets running back from Beach St and the Boardwalk.

Carmelita Cottages Hostel
321 Main St ☎ 831-423-8304 $ dorms $15-18 C MC, V ♿

This one is one of the finest hostels in northern California, just 2 blocks from the beach and 5 blocks from downtown. Check-in is from 5pm to 10pm, and there's an 11pm curfew. Reservations are advised.

Sea & Sand Inn
201 W Cliff Dr ☎ 831-427-3400 $ $99-339 C MC, V, DC, AE

Since it's likely you're in Santa Cruz for the ocean, the views from this place will probably make the high prices seem justifiable.

Caffè Pergolesi (café fare)
418 Cedar St ☎ 831-426-1775 ⏲ 6:30am-midnight daily $ $1.50-4 C cash only
This student coffeehouse, which, interestingly enough, can also sell you sushi, lasagne, or beer, is a Santa Cruz landmark.

Zachary's (American)
819 Pacific Ave ☎ 831-427-0646 ⏲ 7am-2:30pm Mon-Sat $ $6.50-8.50 C MC, V, AE
Zachary's serves hearty, inexpensive breakfasts and lunches.

Gabriella Café (American)
910 Cedar St ☎ 831-457-1677 ⏲ 11:30am-9pm Sun-Thurs, 11:30am-10pm Fri-Sat $ lunch $8-11, entrée $16-22, dessert $6 C MC, V, AE
The menu changes seasonally in this comfy, candlelit restaurant. Order a local wine to complement your pasta or seafood.

Getting There & Away

Bus connections from the Caltrans/Amtrak station in San Jose take 45 minutes and cost $5, and the Greyhound Bus (☎ 800-229-9424) can also drop you in Santa Cruz.

By car, you can take the scenic route along the coast down Hwy 1 or the inland Hwy 101 or I-280 south to Hwy 17.

MONTEREY

Information

California's Spanish and Mexican history is encountered elsewhere, but its Latin heritage is richest in Monterey, a bustling town of about 30,000. There are numerous restored adobe buildings from the Spanish and Mexican eras, and it's enlightening to spend a day wandering about the town's historic quarter. Monterey offers a fine maritime museum and a world-famous aquarium, not to mention the relative tourist traps of Fisherman's Wharf and Cannery Row.

Things to See & Do

Monterey Bay

Here is one of the world's richest and most varied marine environments. It boasts a majestic coastline, famous kelp forests, and a di verse range of marine life, including mamma such as sea otters, seals, sea lions, elephan seals, dolphins, and whales. The protecte waters of the Monterey Bay National Marin Sanctuary extend approximately 50 miles ou to sea from San Simeon in the south to Sa Francisco in the north, where they merge int the Gulf of the Farallones National Marin Sanctuary.

Monterey Bay Aquarium
886 Cannery Row ☎ 831-648-4888, 831-648-8000 ⏲ 9:30am-6pm daily summer, 10am-6pm daily winter $ adult $15.95, senior/student $13.95, child/disabled $7.95 🚌 1 Monterey-Salinas Transit
W www.mbayaq.org
Cannery Row's one worthwhile attraction jus tifies a trip to the Monterey area all on its own Opened in 1984, it features state-of-the-ar exhibits devoted to the rich marine life of th Monterey Bay.

Life-size models of whales and other ma rine mammals hang from the beamed ceiling Star exhibits include the gigantic kelp fores where acrylic panels separate visitors fron more than 300,000 gallons of water, and ma rine creatures swim among the towerin fronds of kelp.

Children love the touch tanks, where the can pick up sea stars and other shallow-wate creatures, and the pool where bat rays can b gently stroked. Sea otter feeding is a prime at traction and usually takes place at 10:30am 1:30pm, and 3:30pm daily.

Places to Stay & Eat

A group of economical motels can be foun about 2½ miles east of Old Monterey on N Fremont St around the junction of Cas Verde, just south of Hwy 1 and just east o Hwy 68. Off-season prices can dip as low a $40 here, although you're looking at $70 t $100 in the Best Westerns and Travelodg category. This group includes the **Vagabon Motel** (☎ 831-372-6066, 2120 N Fremont St) **Travelodge** (☎ 831-373-3381, 2030 N Fremon St), and the **Ramona Inn** (☎ 831-373-244 2332 N Fremont St).

El Dorado Inn
900 Munras Ave ☎ 831-373-2921 $ $50-150 C MC, V, AE
Closer to downtown Monterey, El Dorado In

as fairly basic, old-fashioned rooms, some with fireplaces. Rates include a small in-room breakfast.

When mealtime rolls around, you'll find a number of decent choices. And, predictably, seafood restaurants abound along the wharf, including the **Bubba Gump Shrimp Co** (☎ 831-373-1884, 720 Cannery Row), and the rather snooty but excellent **Sardine Factory** (☎ 831-373-3775, 701 Wave St), where men will need to wear a jacket to get in.

Old Monterey Cafe (café fare)
489 Alvarado St ☎ 831-646-1021 ⏲ 7am-2:30pm daily $ $3-12 C MC, V, DC ♿

This café is resolutely old-fashioned, with plate-warping breakfasts served 'til closing, plus soups, sandwiches, and salads. It's a good choice for the budget-conscious.

Stokes Adobe (Mediterranean)
500 Hartnell St ☎ 831-373-1110 ⏲ 11am-10:30pm Mon-Sat, 4pm-10:30pm Sun $ lunch $5.50-9, appetizer $3-4.50, entrée $15.50-18, dessert $5.50 C none

The historic Stokes Adobe building houses a highly regarded restaurant of the same name, which was remodeled in March 2001. The updated menu focuses on the rich, rustic flavors of Mediterranean country cooking. A wood-burning stove in the bar area is used to smoke fish and to cook aromatic pizzas.

Getting There & Around

AIR & BUS The Monterey area is well-served by major airlines and buses.

Monterey Peninsula Airport
☎ 831-648-7000 🚌 21 Monterey-Salinas Transit ♿
W www.montereyairport.com

American Airlines, America West, and United Airlines all serve this airport. Call the individual airlines for information on direct flights to and from San Francisco and LA. The airport also is host to five national car rental companies.

Greyhound Bus Lines
☎ 800-229-9424 ♿
W www.greyhound.com

Call Greyhound's toll-free number for fares and schedules to and from Monterey and Carmel.

Monterey-Salinas Transit
1 Ryan Ranch Rd ☎ 831-899-2555 $ $1.50 ♿
W www.mst.org

The MST operates buses around the peninsula, inland to Salinas, and south to Big Sur. The whole peninsula (which includes Monterey, Pacific Grove, Pebble Beach, and Carmel) counts as one zone, and a single journey costs $1.50; a day pass good for all trips within one zone is $3. The fare from the peninsula south to Big Sur or inland to Salinas is $3. An all-zones day pass is $6.

CAR Rent a car at the airport or make the drive south from San Francisco – about 120 miles, give or take a scenic curve or two. Hwy 1 is the longer, more spectacular route; the alternative route, Hwy 101 south to Hwy 17 and then to Hwy 1, is pretty once you leave Hwy 101, but it's a long, traffic-choked haul down to San Jose.

CARMEL-BY-THE-SEA

Carmel began as a planned seaside resort in the 1880s and by the early 1900s had already established a reputation as a slightly bohemian retreat. The artistic flavor survives, but these days 'homogenous' and 'wealthy' are just as descriptive; Carmel positively glows with self-satisfaction. It's easy to see why this perfect vision of a California seaside village exerts such an attraction; woodsy Carmel has a neat grid of picturesque homes, an impressive coastal frontage, upscale shopping streets, and a beautiful Spanish mission.

Information

Carmel California Visitors' & Information Center
☎ 831-624-2522, 800-550-4333 fax 831-624-1329 ⏲ 9am-5pm Mon-Fri ♿
W www.carmelcalifornia.org

Comprehensive visitor information is available here. Between Memorial Day and Labor Day, the center also operates an information kiosk open noon to 5pm Thursday to Sunday at Ocean Plaza, at the corner of Ocean and Junipero Aves.

Things to See & Do

The town's picturesque appearance is ensured by local bylaws that forbid streetlights, sidewalks and, in the central area, mailboxes. But the onerous regulations sure do make for a pretty picture.

Mission San Carlos de Borromeo de Carmelo
3080 Rio Rd ☎ 831-624-1271 ⊙ 9:30am-4:30pm Mon-Sat, 10:30am-4:30pm Sun winter; 9:30am-7:30pm Mon-Sat, 10:30am-7:30pm Sun summer $ $2
The original Monterey mission was founded by Father Junípero Serra in 1769.The mission church was originally built of wood, then replaced by an adobe structure and, in 1793, by the present stone church. In the 19th century, the mission went into decline; it was secularized in 1834 and virtually abandoned in 1836 when the padre moved to Monterey. The ruin was roofed over in 1884, but restoration didn't really commence until 1931. Today, it is one of the most attractive and complete of the California missions, with a superb museum relating the story of Serra and the missions.

Places to Stay & Eat

The whole Monterey Peninsula has a reputation as an expensive place to stay, and prices reach their apogee in Carmel's selection of sleek small hotels and cozy B&Bs. Many places impose a two-night minimum stay on weekends, and rooms can be hard to find, particularly on summer weekends. A free room-finder service is offered at ☎ 800-847-8066.

Carmel restaurants can be surprisingly down to earth, and the prices are not always as outlandish as you might expect.

Caffe Cardinale (café fare)
Ocean Ave ☎ 831-626-2095 ⊙ 7am-6pm daily $ $1-6 C MC, V
For great coffees, locals swear by this place, which roasts its own beans on the premises. Soups and sandwiches are fresh and tasty. Sip your brew and indulge in a pastry on the balmy patio.

Forge in the Forest (American)
☎ 831-624-2233 ⊙ 11:30am-10pm Sun-Thurs, 11:30am-11pm Fri-Sat $ $12-25 C MC, V
Dine on the flower-filled patio or in the rustic interior, where there's an authentic blacksmith's forge. The California-influenced classic American food has won several awards, and there's a daily happy hour with free appetizers.

Getting There & Around

Carmel is only 5 miles south of Monterey b Hwy 1. See the Monterey section, earlie for bus information.

There's free unlimited parking at Vist Lobos Park, at 3rd Ave and Torres St.

Yosemite

A place of ravishing natural beauty shape by glaciers during the Ice Age, Yosemite Na tional Park encompasses vast and divers landscapes that are a boon to walkers, hiker trekkers, rock climbers, skiers, and natur lovers.

The first National Park in the worl (1890) thanks to the passionate campaign ing of naturalist John Muir, Yosemite i now one of the most visited spots in th USA, attracting more than four million vis itors each year.

The park's tourist hub is Yosemit Valley, where most of the facilities an campgrounds are based. The valley's ep center, Yosemite Village, has a visitor center, post office, restaurants, and severa museums. If you visit in the summer, th valley may seem brutally crowded, but yo need only hit the trails to find solitude an wilderness.

Yosemite National Park
PO Box 577 ☎ 209-372-0200 $ car $20, pedestrian $10
W www.nps.gov/yose, www.yosemitepark.com
You'll find visitors' centers in Yosemite Valle (open year-round) and Tuolumne Meadow (summer only). Information stations are lc cated in Wawona (spring, summer, and fal and Big Oak Flat (spring, summer, and fall).

Yosemite Valley Visitors' Center
☎ 209-372-0299 ⊙ 8am-4:30pm daily winter, 8am-6pm daily summer $ free
YARTS
This central information point has a kiosk ou front for simple questions and lodging info mation, a message board, museum-quality ex hibits, and a bookstore. The Wilderness Cente next door has wilderness permits and topc graphical maps.

THINGS TO SEE & DO

The 3000-foot, sheer granite walls towering above lush meadows and forests really let you know you're in Yosemite. Yosemite Village is a good starting point from which to see the valley's star attractions. YARTS, the free shuttle bus, makes getting from point to point fast and easy.

Yosemite Museum
☎ 209-372-0200 ⏲ 9am-4:30pm daily (closed for lunch) $ free 🚌 YARTS ♿

Displays at the museum interpret the cultural history of Yosemite's native Miwok and Paiute people from 1850 to the present. The Indian Village of Ahwahnee is a reconstructed Miwok village. Cultural demonstrations, such as basket-weaving, beadwork, and traditional games, are offered during the summer.

Half Dome

This is Yosemite's most distinctive monument. Climbers come from around the world to grapple with its legendary 'north face,' but good hikers can reach its summit via an 8½-mile trail from Yosemite Valley. The trail gains 2000 feet in elevation and has cable handrails for the last 200 yards. Though the hike can be done in one long day, it may be more enjoyable if you camp for a night. Little Yosemite Valley is a popular spot to overnight.

Tuolumne Meadows

At 8500 feet, Tuolumne Meadows is the largest subalpine meadow in the Sierra. The meadow's wide-open fields and clear blue lakes are a dazzling contrast to Yosemite's densely forested valley. In summer, it blooms with wild flowers, and in winter it is blanketed with snow.

Glacier Point
⏲ closed from October/November through May/June due to snow

One of the best views of the park is from Glacier Point, 3214 feet above the valley floor.

Yosemite Falls

The double-tiered stream of Yosemite Falls is visible from all over the valley. Together, the upper and lower falls cascade 2425 feet – the tallest waterfall in North America. The viewing point at the base shows only the lower falls, but the path leading to it gives a good view of both.

The Spirit of John Muir
☎ 209-372-1240 🚌 YARTS, Greyhound ♿
W www.yosemitepark.com

Throughout the summer, Lee Stetson does a one-man show about the life of John Muir. You can see several other performances about the lives of pioneers nightly at the Yosemite Lodge or the Valley Visitors' Center.

Hiking

Yosemite has more than 800 miles of trails that go far beyond the beaten tourist path. The best way to enjoy the park's natural splendor is to take to the backcountry, even if it is for just a few miles and only for half a day. Wilderness permits, available at visitors' centers and information stations, are free but required for all overnight trips.

Good for viewing waterfalls, Half Dome, and the valley, the Panorama Trail goes from Happy Isles Nature Center to Glacier Point. It's a challenging 8½ miles up, but coming down is a cinch. For $10, you can ride the bus one-way to/from Glacier Point.

At the valley's east end, a paved trail leads to Mirror Lake, which reflects Half Dome in the early evening and late afternoon. From here, a 3-mile trail makes a loop along Tenaya Creek, with nice views of its U-shaped canyon.

TOM DOWNS

The majestic Half Dome

You can hike to a few glacial lakes in Tuolumne Meadows. Trailheads to Cathedral Lakes, Sunrise Lakes, and May Lake Trails are all well marked from Tioga Rd. An easier option is to hike along a 2-mile section of the John Muir Trail, which has nice swimming holes, meadows, and dome views.

PLACES TO STAY & EAT

Yosemite Campgrounds
PO Box 1600, Cumberland MD 21502 ☎ 800-436-7275 reservations, 209-372-8502 information, 301-722-1257 international calls $ primitive sites $8; first-come, first-served $12; reserved sites $18 C *D, MC, V* *YARTS* ♿ *ask for accessible sites*

In Yosemite Valley, Upper Pines Campground is open year-round, Lower Pines Campground from March to October, and North Pines from April to October. Reservations are required at these valley campgrounds. Sunnyside Walk-In Campground is open year-round; sites are available on a first-come, first-served basis.

Yosemite Concession Services Corporation
☎ 559-252-4848 C *AE, D, MC, V YARTS* ♿ *ask for accessible accommodations*

Yosemite Concession Services Corporation operates a variety of lodging units in Yosemite. Rates range from as low as $38 per night at Curry Village for a basic tent cabin with nearby bathroom to over $250 per night for a room at the Ahwahnee Hotel.

Ahwahnee Hotel Dining Room (American)
☎ 209-372-1489 C *AE, D, MC, V* *YARTS* ♿

For an elegant meal, try the Ahwahnee, where the innovative menu is based on traditional American cooking. It's open for breakfast, lunch, and dinner.

Mountain Room (American)
☎ 209-372-1000 C *AE, D, MC, V* *YARTS* ♿

The Mountain Room at Yosemite Lodge features delicious steaks and seafood; it's open for dinner only.

White Wolf Lodge (Italian)
☎ 209-372-1000 C *AE, D, MC, V* *YARTS* ♿

This cozy dining room is set in Yosemite's breathtaking backcountry along Tioga Rd. Breakfast and dinner are served daily during the summer. Lunch is available at the lodge store. Dinner reservations are advised.

GETTING THERE & AROUND

Yosemite is about 200 miles from San Francisco. It takes 4½ hours to drive there - though it is possible as a day trip, staying overnight will allow you to see more of its attractions. Another option is to join a guided tour, which will get you there and back in a day without losing sleep, but you won't be able to explore the sites at your own pace.

Train & Bus

Amtrak
☎ 800-872-7245 $ $42
W *www.amtrak.com*

Amtrak's San Joaquin route will take you to Merced, linking with Amtrak and YARTS bus service to the park.

Blue & Gold Fleet Ferry
☎ 415-705-5555 ⏲ Tues, Thurs, Sun
$ adult $99, child $59 ♿
W *www.blueandgoldfleet.co*

Blue and Gold Fleet runs 13½-hour guided bus tours from San Francisco to Yosemite National Park.

Greyhound
☎ 800-229-9424 $ $24
W *www.greyhound.com*

Greyhound runs buses between San Francisco's Transbay Terminal and Merced, which is the jumping-off point for Yosemite-bound Amtrak and YARTS buses.

Yosemite Area Regional Transportation System (YARTS)
☎ 877-989-2787 $ $8 one-way, $15 roundtrip
W *www.yarts.com*

Visitors can ride YARTS buses from gateway communities outside the park into Yosemite Valley. YARTS buses connect with Amtrak and Greyhound in Merced. Riders need to obtain tickets from local ticket sellers before bus arrives.

Once you are in the park, the free Yosemite Valley shuttle system provides convenient access around eastern Yosemite Valley year-round. The bus stops at or near all overnight accommodations, stores, and the major vistas in eastern Yosemite Valley 'isitors are strongly encouraged to use the huttle bus instead of driving around eastern 'osemite Valley.

Car

3y car, take I-80 east across the Bay Bridge. ust across the bridge, take I-580 east toward Hayward/Stockton. From there, turn off onto I-205 east toward Tracy/Stockton, then take I-5 north to Hwy 120 and head toward Manteca/Sonora. At Manteca, follow Hwy 99 south toward Modesto/Fresno. At Merced, take the Hwy 140 east exit toward Mariposa/Yosemite and into the park.

Thanks

Many thanks to the travelers who used the last edition and wrote to us with helpful hints, useful advice, and interesting anecdotes:

Theodore C Bale, Martin Birnbach, Cameron Blackwood, Natasha Calvey, Verity Chegar, Angel Cuadras, Patricia Dorrington, Angelo Festa, Conner Gorry, Erik Jansen, Peter Jenkins, Gareth Jones, Michael Kluge, Magdalena Lachowska, Julie Manes, Ira Marks, Janette McClelland, Monica McManus, Richard Metcalfe, Frances Millane, Kerry Milsome, Stephanie Minns, Claire & Fiona Nash-Wortham, Tracey Nicholls, Alina Niemi, Amy Packer, Irina Pavlova, Christopher Race, BLH Ralph, Becky Robinson, Joaquin Sanz, Pauline Smith, Scott Smith, Melanie Thomas, Eileen Tran, Jodie Webber, Vicki West, and Eric Wilson

LONELY PLANET

You already know that Lonely Planet produces more than this one guidebook, but you might not be aware of the other products we have on this region. Here is a selection of titles which you may want to check out as well:

Out to Eat – San Francisco 2002
ISBN 1 74059 270 0
US$12.99 • UK£9.99

San Francisco City Map
ISBN 1 86450 014 X
US$5.95 • UK£3.99

California & Nevada
ISBN 0 86442 644 5
US$19.95 • UK£12.99

Los Angeles
ISBN 1 74059 021 X
US$15.99 • UK£9.99

San Diego & Tijuana
ISBN 1 86450 218 5
US$16.99 • UK£10.99

Seattle
ISBN 1 86450 304 1
US$14.99 • UK£8.99

Available wherever books are sold.

Index

Text

Bold indicates maps.

N

O

Bold indicates maps.

Bold indicates maps.

T

U

Places to Stay

Places to Eat

Boxed Text

San Francisco Map Section

To Marin County
Golden Gate Bridge
101
1
Fort Point
Crissy Field
Doyle Drive
San Francisco National Military Cemetery
THE PRESIDIO
MAP 16
0
1
2 km
0
.5
1 mile
Baker Beach
Lincoln Blvd
Presidio Golf Course
Mile Rock
China Beach
Laurel Heights
Lincoln Park Golf Course
25th Ave
Park Presidio Blvd
INNER RICHMOND
MAP 15
Fort Miley
Geary Blvd
Seal Rocks
Sutro Heights Park
OUTER RICHMOND
MAP 15
University of San Francisco
Masonic Ave
UPPER HAIGHT
MAP 11
Fulton St
Golden Gate Municipal Golf Course
GOLDEN GATE PARK
MAP 15
Stow Lake
Lincoln Way
COLE VALLEY
MAP 11
7th Ave
19th Ave
INNER SUNSET
MAP 15
University of California, San Francisco Medical Center
Great Hwy
Sunset Blvd
OUTER SUNSET
MAP 15
Noriega St
Laguna Honda
Midtown Terrace Recreation Center
904ft
Twin Peaks
922ft
PACIFIC OCEAN
Ocean Beach
West Sunset Playground
Sunset Reservoir
Golden Gate Heights Park
Laguna Honda Hospital
Taraval St
Vicente St
Mt Davidson 938ft
South Sunset Playground
Stern Grove
Sloat Blvd
San Francisco Zoo
Monterey Blvd
Skyline Blvd
Lake Merced
19th Ave
Muni M Oceanview line
City College of San Francisco
Harding Park Municipal Golf Course
San Francisco State University
Ingleside
35
Lake Merced
Park Merced
Brooks Park
Ocean View Recreation Center
Oceanview
Hang Glider Launch & Landing Site
Fort Funston
The Olympic Country Club
Brotherhood Way
San Francisco Golf Club

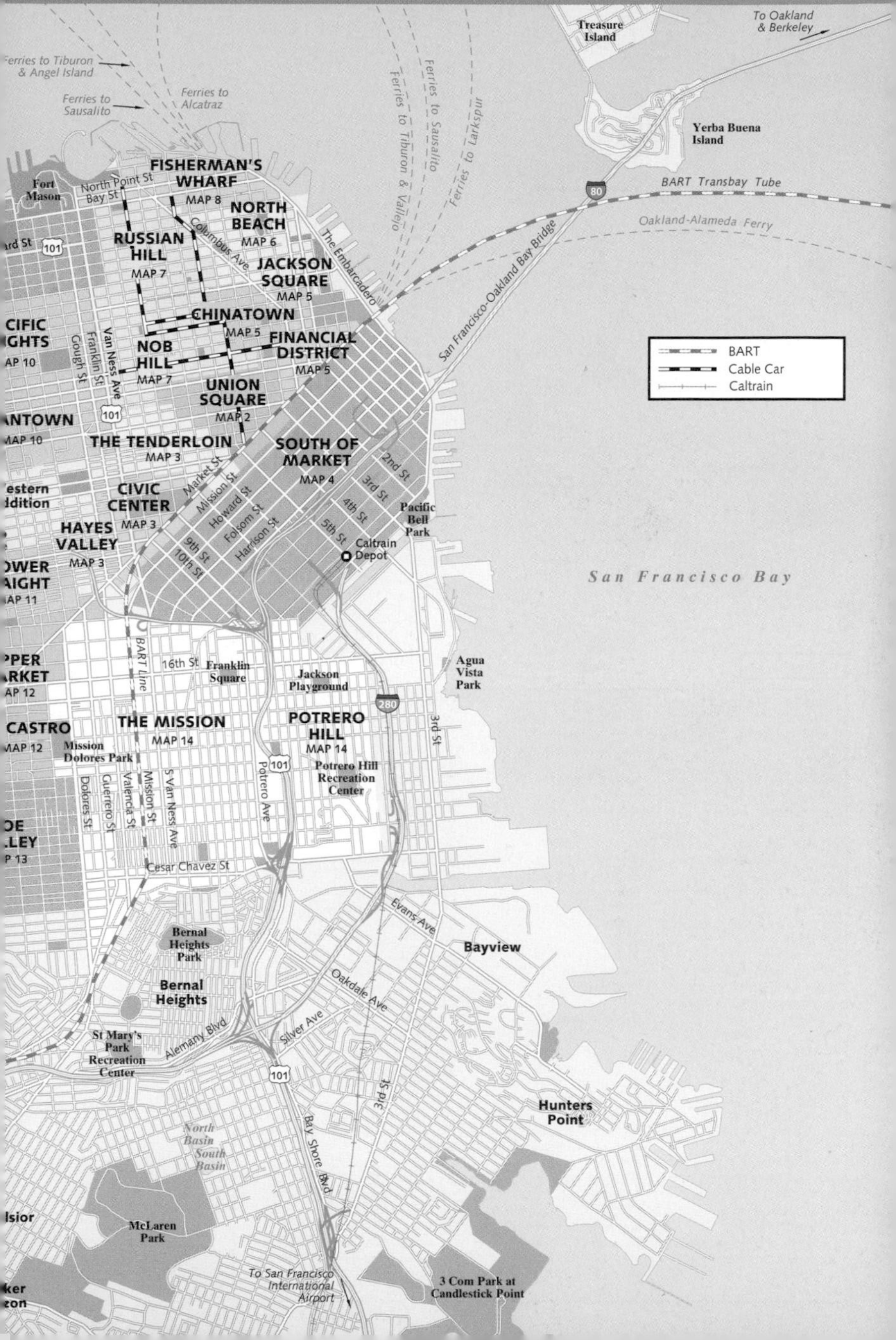

Treasure Island
To Oakland & Berkeley
Ferries to Tiburon & Angel Island
Ferries to Sausalito
Ferries to Alcatraz
Ferries to Tiburon & Vallejo
Ferries to Sausalito
Ferries to Larkspur
Yerba Buena Island
80
BART Transbay Tube
Oakland-Alameda Ferry
Fort Mason
North Point St
Bay St
FISHERMAN'S WHARF
MAP 8
NORTH BEACH
MAP 6
Columbus Ave
The Embarcadero
San Francisco-Oakland Bay Bridge
RUSSIAN HILL
MAP 7
JACKSON SQUARE
MAP 5
101
CHINATOWN
MAP 5
CIFIC
IGHTS
AP 10
NOB HILL
MAP 7
FINANCIAL DISTRICT
MAP 5
Gough St
Franklin St
Van Ness Ave

BART	
Cable Car	
Caltrain	

UNION SQUARE
MAP 2
ANTOWN
MAP 10
THE TENDERLOIN
MAP 3
SOUTH OF MARKET
MAP 4
2nd St
3rd St
4th St
5th St
Market St
Mission St
Howard St
Folsom St
Harrison St
9th St
10th St
estern
ddition
CIVIC CENTER
MAP 3
HAYES VALLEY
MAP 3
Pacific Bell Park
Caltrain Depot
OWER
AIGHT
AP 11
San Francisco Bay
BART Line
16th St
Franklin Square
Jackson Playground
Agua Vista Park
PPER
ARKET
AP 12
280
CASTRO
MAP 12
THE MISSION
MAP 14
POTRERO HILL
MAP 14
3rd St
Mission Dolores Park
101
Potrero Hill Recreation Center
Potrero Ave
Dolores St
Guerrero St
Valencia St
Mission St
S Van Ness Ave
OE
LEY
P 13
Cesar Chavez St
Evans Ave
Bernal Heights Park
Bayview
Bernal Heights
Oakdale Ave
Silver Ave
Alemany Blvd
St Mary's Park Recreation Center
101
3rd St
Hunters Point
Bay Shore Blvd
North Basin
South Basin
lsior
McLaren Park
To San Francisco International Airport
3 Com Park at Candlestick Point
ker
zon

MAP 2 UNION SQUARE
California St Cable Car Line
Nob Hill
see MAP 7
Pine St
Touchard St
Bush St
Austin St
Jones St
Leavenworth St
Hyde St
Larkin St
Polk St
Fern St
Sutter St
Cosmo Place
Post St
Colin Place
Shannon St
Hemlock St
to MAP 10
Cedar St
Geary St
O'Farrell St
Antonio St
Steveloe Pl
Ellis St
The Tenderloin
see MAP 3
Eddy St
Turk St
Golden Gate Ave
McAllister St
United Nations Plaza
0
100
200 m
0
100
200 yards
Parking Area
PLACES TO STAY
1 Mary Elizabeth Inn
2 Petite Auberge
3 White Swan Inn
4 Golden Gate Hotel
5 Grant Hotel
11 Hotel Triton
12 Alisa Hotel
15 York Hotel
17 Beresford Manor
18 Commodore Hotel; Titanic Cafe; Red Room
20 Amsterdam Hotel; Biltmore Hotel
21 Hotel Beresford
22 Sheehan Hotel
24 Hotel Rex
25 Cartwright Hotel
28 Sir Francis Drake Hotel; Harry Denton's Starlight Room
30 Campton Place Hotel
35 Hotel Beresford Arms
37 Dakota Hotel
39 Adelaide Inn
42 Pan Pacific Hotel
44 The Inn at Union Square
54 Halcyon Hotel
55 Savoy Hotel
57 Hotel Monaco; Grand Cafe
65 Maxwell Hotel
67 Westin St Francis Hotel; Compass Rose
70 Stratford Hotel
79 Hostel at Union Square
81 Foley's Inn; Foley's Irish House
82 Herbert Hotel
87 Globetrotters Inn
88 Hotel Union Square
91 Hotel Bijou
96 Mosser's Victorian Hotel
PLACES TO EAT
6 Masa's
8 Oritalia
10 Café de la Presse
13 Café Claude
19 Fleur de Lys
26 Sears Fine Foods
31 Anjou
33 Franciscan Croissants
36 Borobudur
41 Postrio
43 Farallon; Theatre on the Square
89 John's Grill
ENTERTAINMENT
16 Cup-A-Joe Coffee House
27 Caffe Espresso
38 C Bobby's Owl Tree
53 Alcazar Theatre
56 Blue Lamp
58 Redwood Room
60 Curran Theatre
61 Geary Theater
62 Biscuits & Blues
63 Ruby Skye
64 Cable Car Theater
66 Mason St Theatre
68 Lefty O'Doul's
69 Gold Dust Lounge
80 The Cellar at Johnny Foley's
OTHER
7 Miles Archer Plaque
9 Eglise Notre Dame des Victoires
14 MAC (Men's Store)
23 De Vera
29 Wilkes Bashford
32 Teuscher Chocolates of Switzerland
34 Banana Republic
40 Bohemian Club
45 Borders Books & Music
46 Saks Fifth Avenue
47 Children's Fountain
48 The Levi's Store
49 Niketown
50 The North Face
51 Gump's
52 Rizzoli Bookstore
59 Harold's International Newsstand
71 Dewey Monument
72 TIX Bay Area
73 Neiman-Marcus
74 Betsey Johnson
75 Folk Art International
76 De Vera
77 STA Travel
78 Napa Valley Winery Exchange
83 Macy's
84 Macy's Men's Store
85 Agnès B
86 CompUSA
90 Virgin Megastore
92 San Francisco Visitors Information Center
93 James Flood Building; The Gap
94 Nordstrom
95 Old Navy

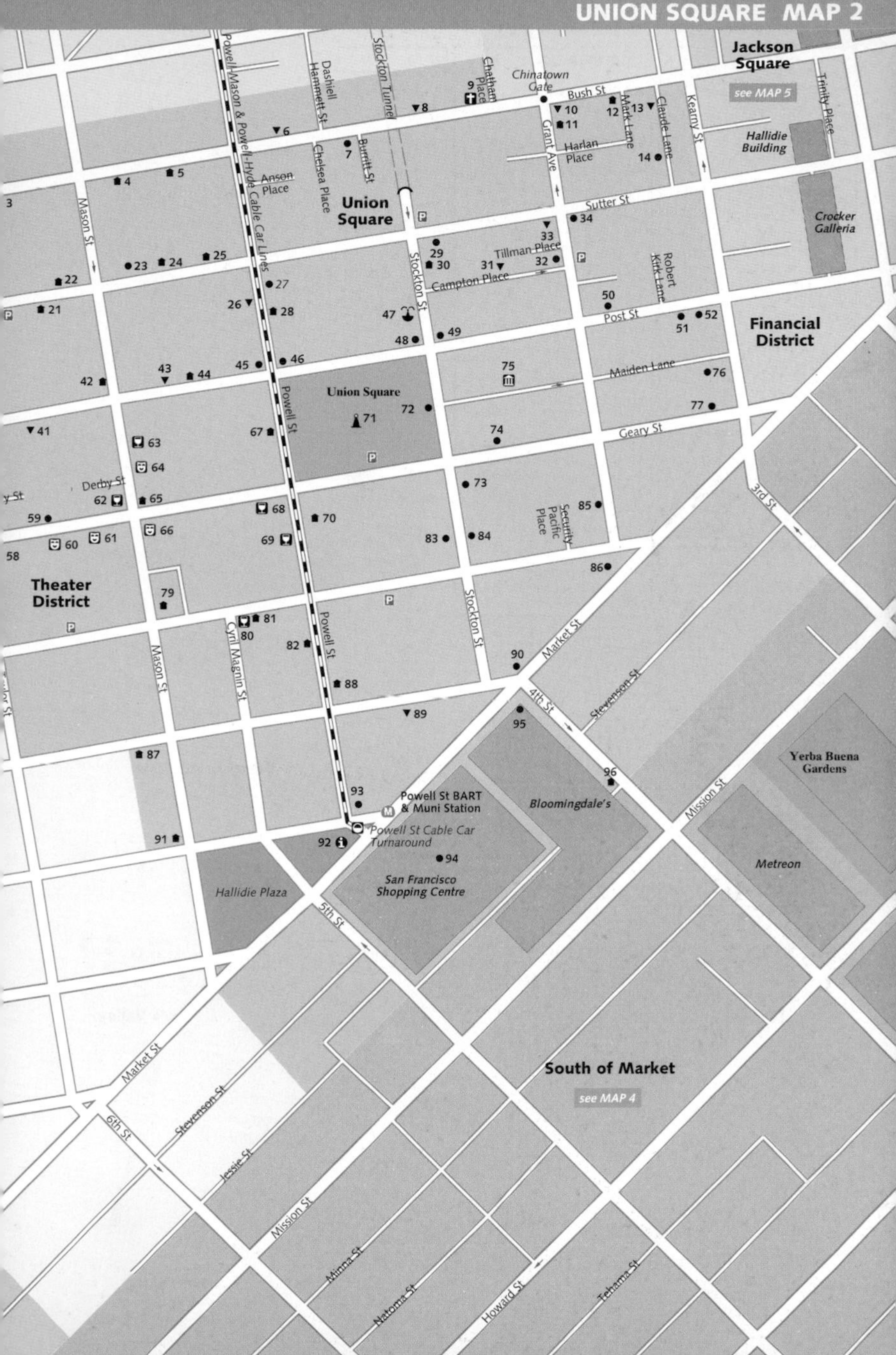
Jackson Square
see MAP 5
Chinatown Gate
Bush St
Chatham Place
Dashiell Hammett St
Stockton Tunnel
Powell-Mason & Powell-Hyde Cable Car Lines
Mark Lane
Claude Lane
Kearny St
Trinity Place
Hallidie Building
Grant Ave
Harlan Place
Anson Place
Chelsea Place
Burritt St
Union Square
Sutter St
Crocker Galleria
Mason St
Tillman Place
Campton Place
Stockton St
Robert Kirk Lane
Post St
Financial District
Maiden Lane
Union Square
Powell St
Geary St
Derby St
3rd St
Security Pacific Place
Theater District
Market St
Cyril Magnin St
Mason St
Powell St
Stockton St
4th St
Stevenson St
Yerba Buena Gardens
Mission St
Powell St BART & Muni Station
Powell St Cable Car Turnaround
Bloomingdale's
Metreon
Hallidie Plaza
San Francisco Shopping Centre
5th St
South of Market
see MAP 4
Market St
6th St
Stevenson St
Jessie St
Mission St
Minna St
Natoma St
Howard St
Tehama St

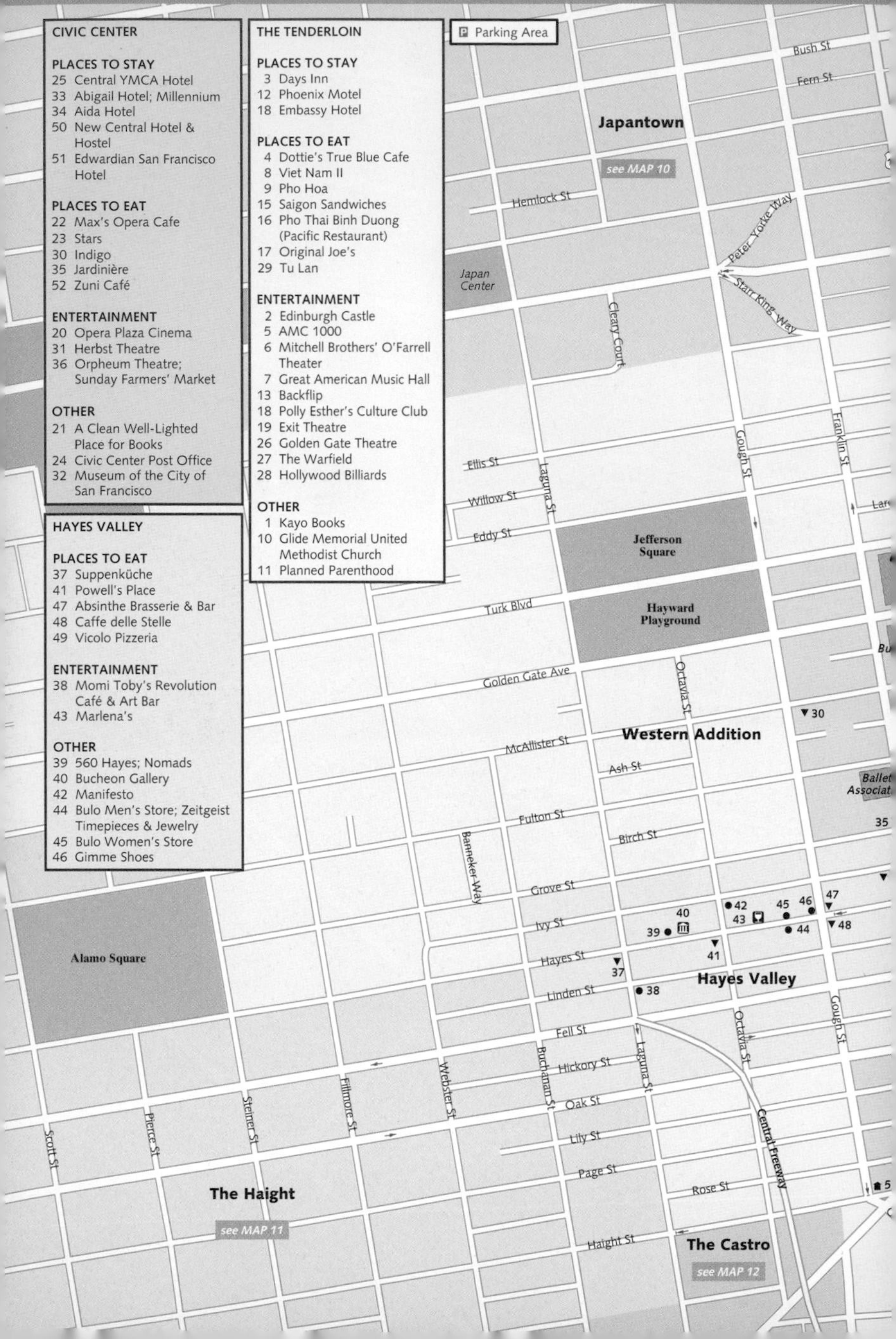

MAP 3 CIVIC CENTER, HAYES VALLEY & THE TENDERLOIN

CIVIC CENTER

PLACES TO STAY
25 Central YMCA Hotel
33 Abigail Hotel; Millennium
34 Aida Hotel
50 New Central Hotel & Hostel
51 Edwardian San Francisco Hotel

PLACES TO EAT
22 Max's Opera Cafe
23 Stars
30 Indigo
35 Jardinière
52 Zuni Café

ENTERTAINMENT
20 Opera Plaza Cinema
31 Herbst Theatre
36 Orpheum Theatre; Sunday Farmers' Market

OTHER
21 A Clean Well-Lighted Place for Books
24 Civic Center Post Office
32 Museum of the City of San Francisco

HAYES VALLEY

PLACES TO EAT
37 Suppenküche
41 Powell's Place
47 Absinthe Brasserie & Bar
48 Caffe delle Stelle
49 Vicolo Pizzeria

ENTERTAINMENT
38 Momi Toby's Revolution Café & Art Bar
43 Marlena's

OTHER
39 560 Hayes; Nomads
40 Bucheon Gallery
42 Manifesto
44 Bulo Men's Store; Zeitgeist Timepieces & Jewelry
45 Bulo Women's Store
46 Gimme Shoes

THE TENDERLOIN

PLACES TO STAY
3 Days Inn
12 Phoenix Motel
18 Embassy Hotel

PLACES TO EAT
4 Dottie's True Blue Cafe
8 Viet Nam II
9 Pho Hoa
15 Saigon Sandwiches
16 Pho Thai Binh Duong (Pacific Restaurant)
17 Original Joe's
29 Tu Lan

ENTERTAINMENT
2 Edinburgh Castle
5 AMC 1000
6 Mitchell Brothers' O'Farrell Theater
7 Great American Music Hall
13 Backflip
18 Polly Esther's Culture Club
19 Exit Theatre
26 Golden Gate Theatre
27 The Warfield
28 Hollywood Billiards

OTHER
1 Kayo Books
10 Glide Memorial United Methodist Church
11 Planned Parenthood

P Parking Area

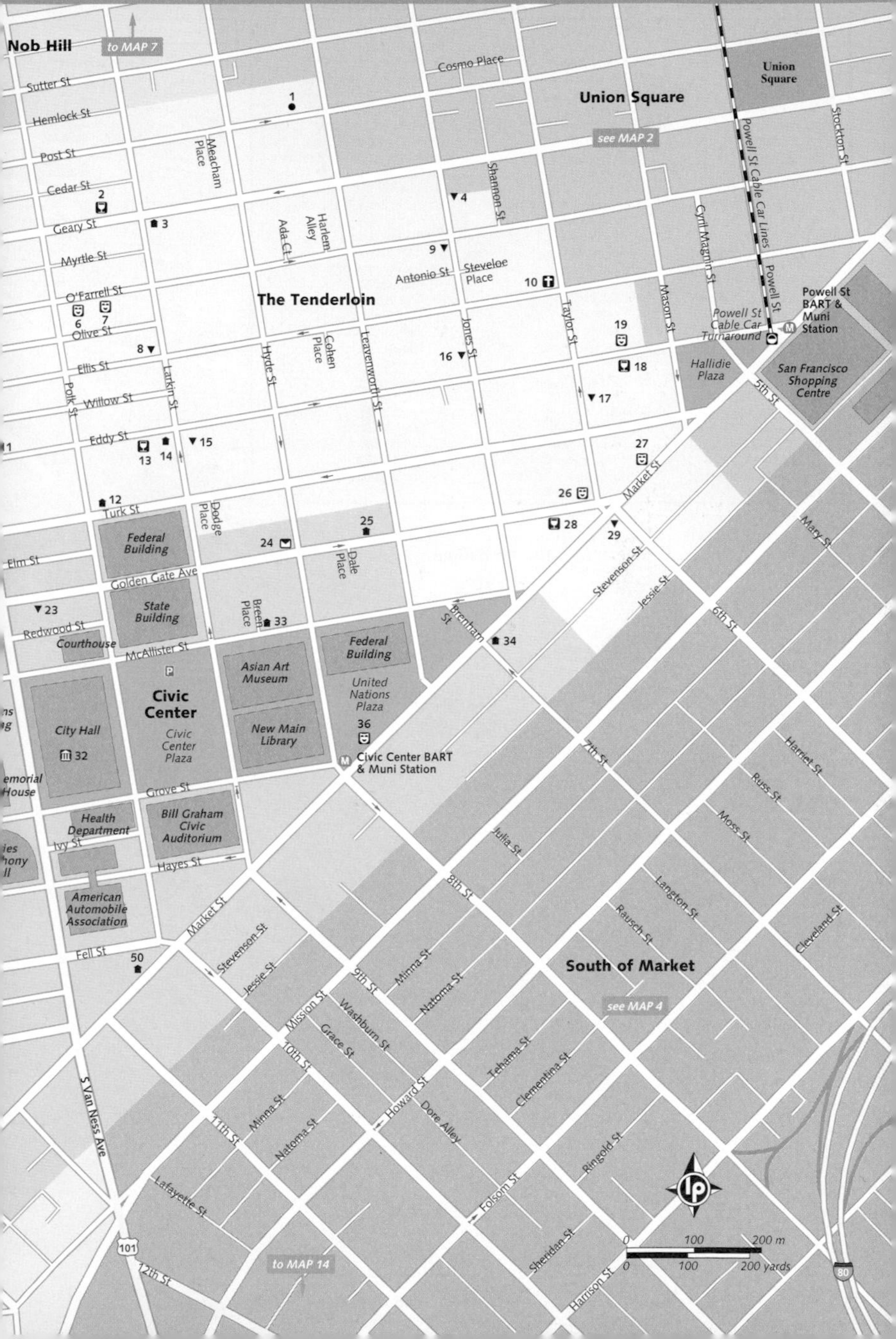

Nob Hill
to MAP 7
Union Square
see MAP 2
The Tenderloin
Civic Center
South of Market
see MAP 4
to MAP 14

Sutter St
Hemlock St
Post St
Cedar St
Geary St
Myrtle St
O'Farrell St
Olive St
Ellis St
Willow St
Eddy St
Turk St
Elm St
Golden Gate Ave
Redwood St
McAllister St
Grove St
Ivy St
Hayes St
Fell St
Cosmo Place
Meacham Place
Harlem Alley
Ada Ct
Shannon St
Antonio St
Steveloe Place
Cyril Magnin St
Powell St Cable Car Lines
Powell St
Stockton St
Mason St
Taylor St
Jones St
Leavenworth St
Cohen Place
Hyde St
Larkin St
Polk St
Dodge Place
Dale Place
Breen Place
Brenham St
Market St
Stevenson St
Jessie St
5th St
6th St
7th St
8th St
9th St
10th St
11th St
12th St
Mary St
Harriet St
Russ St
Moss St
Langton St
Rausch St
Cleveland St
Julia St
Minna St
Natoma St
Mission St
Washburn St
Grace St
Howard St
Dore Alley
Tehama St
Clementina St
Folsom St
Ringold St
Sheridan St
Harrison St
Lafayette St
S Van Ness Ave

Union Square
Powell St Cable Car Turnaround
Powell St BART & Muni Station
Hallidie Plaza
San Francisco Shopping Centre
Federal Building
State Building
Courthouse
City Hall
Civic Center Plaza
Asian Art Museum
New Main Library
Federal Building
United Nations Plaza
Civic Center BART & Muni Station
Health Department
Bill Graham Civic Auditorium
American Automobile Association

1, 2, 3, 4, 6, 7, 8, 9, 10, 12, 13, 14, 15, 16, 17, 18, 19, 23, 24, 25, 26, 27, 28, 29, 32, 33, 34, 36, 50

0 100 200 m
0 100 200 yards
101
80

PLACES TO STAY
2 Hotel Griffon
7 Palace Hotel; Pied Piper Bar; Garden Court
8 House of Shields
25 San Francisco Marriott
31 The Pickwick
43 Hotel Britton
44 Americania
55 SoMa Inn
56 San Francisco International Student Center
61 Globe Hostel

PLACES TO EAT
1 Boulevard
3 Yank Sing; Chalkers
10 Red's Java House
11 Dine
24 Hawthorne Lane
29 Max's Diner
32 Buca di Beppo
33 Restaurant LuLu; Azie
36 South Park Cafe
37 Caffe Centro
39 Infusion Bar & Restaurant
51 Fringale
58 Julie's Supper Club
60 Basil Thai

ENTERTAINMENT
6 Gordon Biersch Brewery
9 Kate O'Brien's
14 111 Minna Street Gallery
16 Maritime Hall
17 Sound Factory
21 Yerba Buena Center for the Arts
23 Thirsty Bear Brewing Company
40 21st Amendment
45 Covered Wagon Saloon
46 1015 Folsom
48 Endup
50 Hotel Utah
53 330 Ritch
57 Cat Club
59 Up & Down Club
64 The Stud
65 VSF
66 Paradise Lounge
67 Slim's
68 The Eagle Tavern

OTHER
4 Rand McNally
5 Transbay Terminal
12 Ansel Adams Center for Photography; Friends of Photography Bookstore
13 Pacific Bell Building
15 Adolf Gasser
18 Mexican Museum; California Historical Society
19 Jewish Museum of San Francisco
20 St Patrick's Church
22 San Francisco Museum of Modern Art (SFMOMA); Caffe Museo
26 Cartoon Art Museum
27 Zeum Art & Technology Center
28 Alamo Rent-a-Car
30 Old US Mint
34 Society of California Pioneers Museum
35 K&L Wines & Spirits
38 Jeremy's
41 William Stout Design Books
42 Spinnaker Sailing
47 Dubbelju
49 Wine Club
52 Jack London's Birthplace
54 Stormy Leather
62 San Francisco Flower Mart
63 Goodwill Store
69 Trader Joe's
70 Mission Bay Golf Center

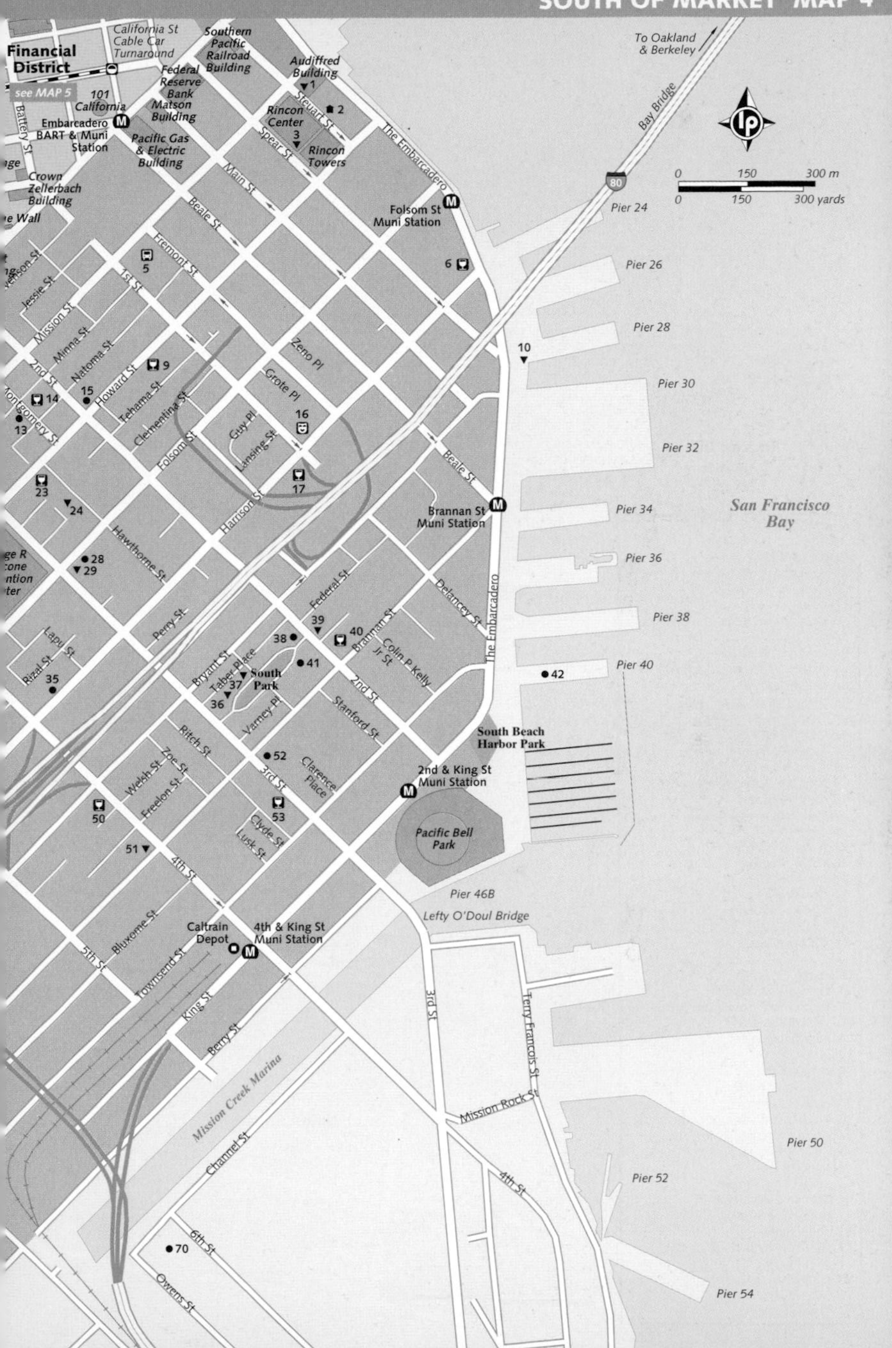

Financial District
see MAP 5
California St Cable Car Turnaround
Southern Pacific Railroad Building
Audiffred Building
Federal Reserve Bank
Matson Building
101 California
Embarcadero BART & Muni Station
Pacific Gas & Electric Building
Rincon Center
Rincon Towers
Crown Zellerbach Building
To Oakland & Berkeley
Bay Bridge
The Embarcadero
Folsom St Muni Station
Brannan St Muni Station
2nd & King St Muni Station
4th & King St Muni Station
Caltrain Depot
South Park
South Beach Harbor Park
Pacific Bell Park
Lefty O'Doul Bridge
Mission Creek Marina
San Francisco Bay
Pier 24
Pier 26
Pier 28
Pier 30
Pier 32
Pier 34
Pier 36
Pier 38
Pier 40
Pier 46B
Pier 50
Pier 52
Pier 54
0 150 300 m
0 150 300 yards
Battery St
Steuart St
Spear St
Main St
Beale St
Fremont St
1st St
2nd St
3rd St
4th St
5th St
6th St
Jessie St
Mission St
Minna St
Natoma St
Howard St
Tehama St
Clementina St
Folsom St
Harrison St
Bryant St
Brannan St
Townsend St
King St
Berry St
Channel St
Owens St
Zeno Pl
Grote Pl
Guy Pl
Lansing St
Hawthorne St
Perry St
Lapu St
Rizal St
Federal St
Delancey St
Colin P Kelly Jr St
Stanford St
Clarence Place
Taber Place
Varney Pl
Ritch St
Zoe St
Welsh St
Freelon St
Clyde St
Lusk St
Bluxome St
Terry Francois St
Mission Rock St
Montgomery St

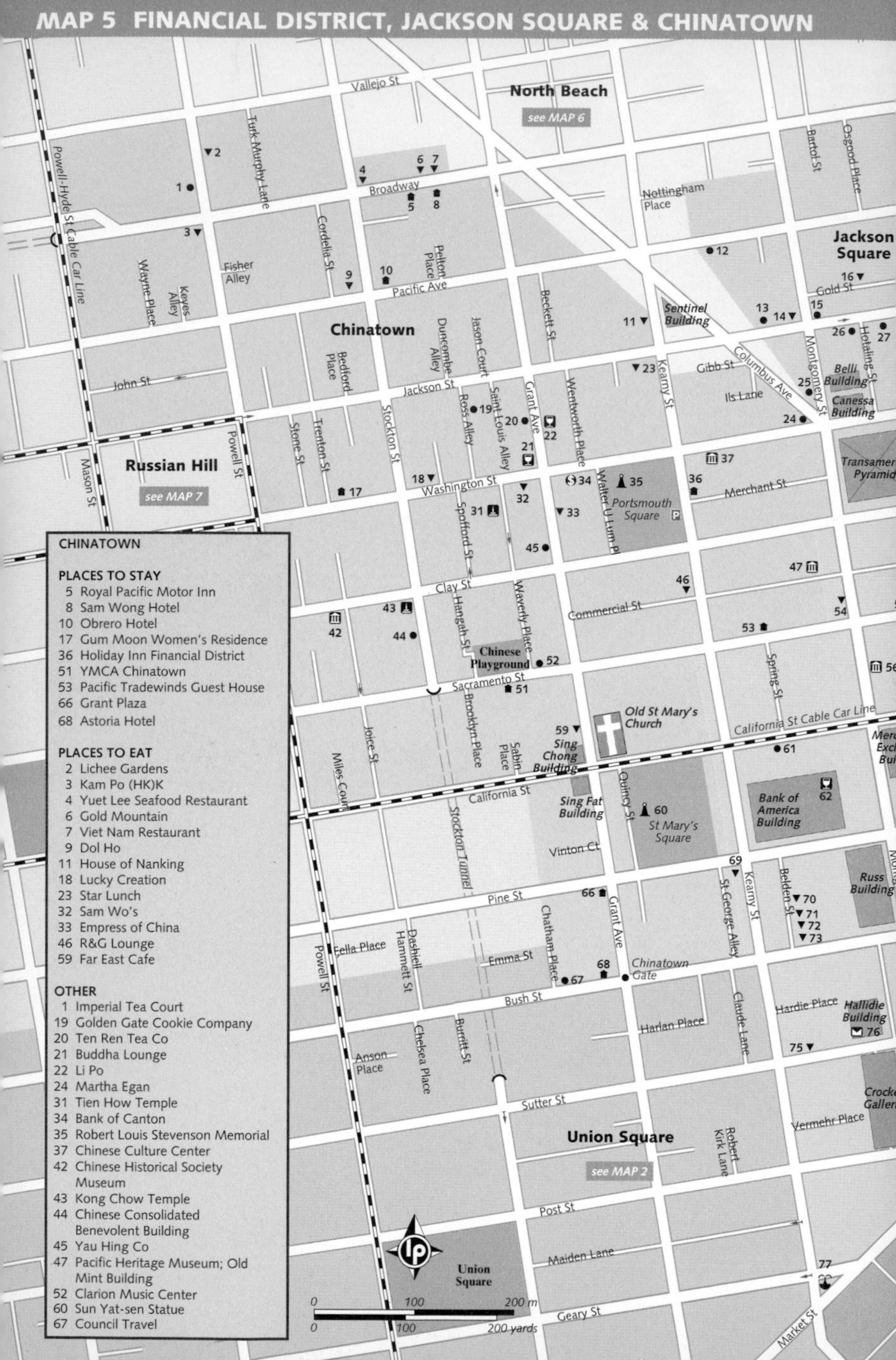
MAP 5 FINANCIAL DISTRICT, JACKSON SQUARE & CHINATOWN
North Beach
see MAP 6
Jackson Square
Chinatown
Russian Hill
see MAP 7
Union Square
see MAP 2
Vallejo St
Broadway
Pacific Ave
Jackson St
Washington St
Clay St
Sacramento St
California St
California St Cable Car Line
Pine St
Bush St
Sutter St
Post St
Maiden Lane
Geary St
Market St
Columbus Ave
Powell-Hyde St Cable Car Line
Powell St
Mason St
Stockton St
Stockton Tunnel
Grant Ave
Kearny St
Montgomery St
Turk Murphy Lane
Cordelia St
Pelton Place
Fisher Alley
Wayne Place
Keyes Alley
John St
Bedford Place
Duncombe Alley
Jason Court
Ross Alley
Saint Louis Alley
Beckett St
Wentworth Place
Walter U Lum Pl
Stone St
Trenton St
Spofford St
Waverly Place
Hangah St
Commercial St
Brooklyn Place
Sabin Place
Joice St
Miles Court
Quincy St
Vinton Ct
Fella Place
Dashiell Hammett St
Chatham Place
Emma St
St George Alley
Claude Lane
Belden St
Harlan Place
Hardie Place
Anson Place
Chelsea Place
Burritt St
Vermehr Place
Robert Kirk Lane
Nottingham Place
Bartol St
Osgood Place
Gold St
Gibb St
Ils Lane
Hotaling St
Merchant St
Spring St
Sentinel Building
Belli Building
Canessa Building
Transamerica Pyramid
Portsmouth Square
Chinese Playground
Old St Mary's Church
Sing Chong Building
Sing Fat Building
St Mary's Square
Bank of America Building
Russ Building
Hallidie Building
Chinatown Gate
Crocker Galleria
Union Square
0 100 200 m
0 100 200 yards
CHINATOWN
PLACES TO STAY
5 Royal Pacific Motor Inn
8 Sam Wong Hotel
10 Obrero Hotel
17 Gum Moon Women's Residence
36 Holiday Inn Financial District
51 YMCA Chinatown
53 Pacific Tradewinds Guest House
66 Grant Plaza
68 Astoria Hotel
PLACES TO EAT
2 Lichee Gardens
3 Kam Po (HK)K
4 Yuet Lee Seafood Restaurant
6 Gold Mountain
7 Viet Nam Restaurant
9 Dol Ho
11 House of Nanking
18 Lucky Creation
23 Star Lunch
32 Sam Wo's
33 Empress of China
46 R&G Lounge
59 Far East Cafe
OTHER
1 Imperial Tea Court
19 Golden Gate Cookie Company
20 Ten Ren Tea Co
21 Buddha Lounge
22 Li Po
24 Martha Egan
31 Tien How Temple
34 Bank of Canton
35 Robert Louis Stevenson Memorial
37 Chinese Culture Center
42 Chinese Historical Society Museum
43 Kong Chow Temple
44 Chinese Consolidated Benevolent Building
45 Yau Hing Co
47 Pacific Heritage Museum; Old Mint Building
52 Clarion Music Center
60 Sun Yat-sen Statue
67 Council Travel

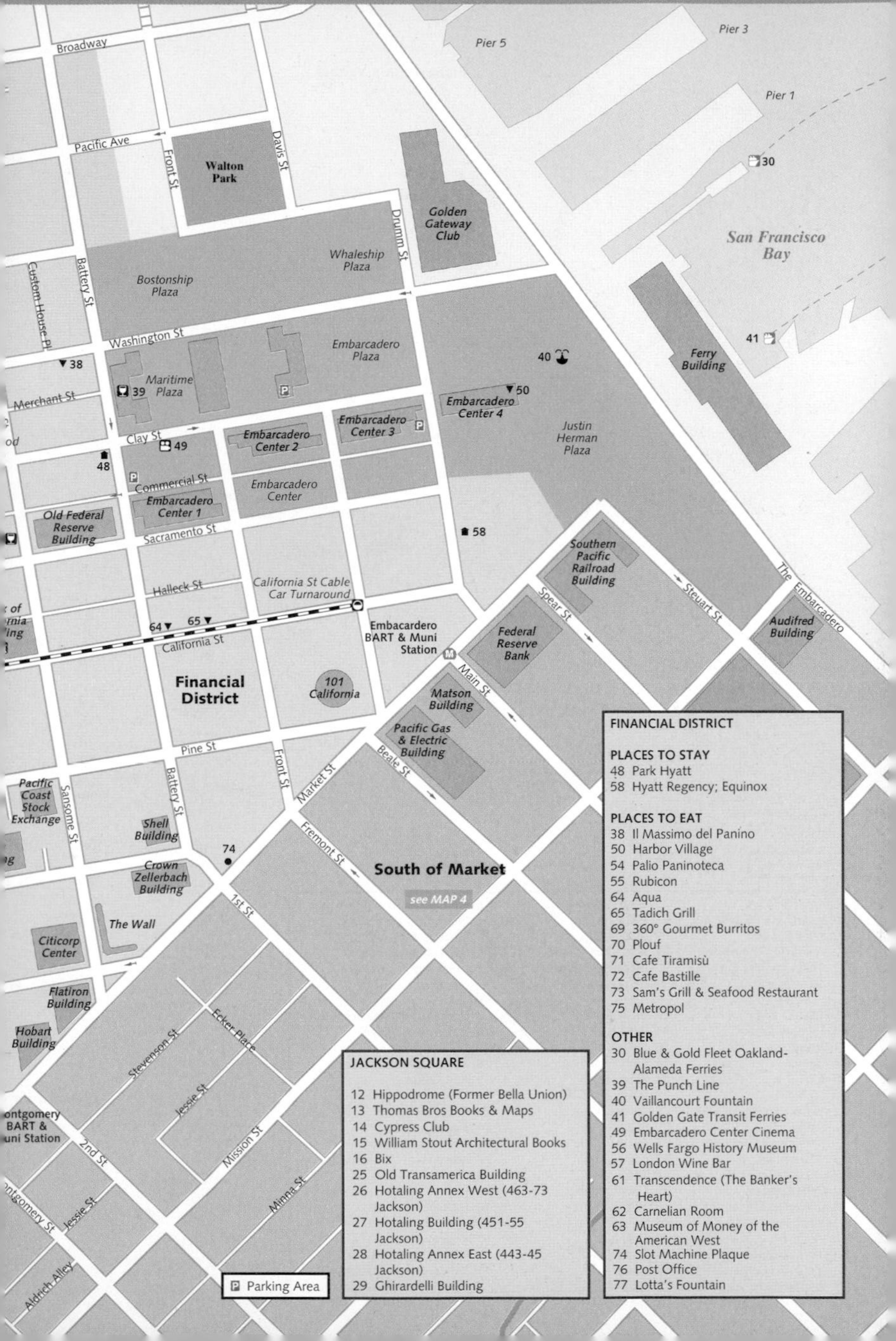
Broadway
Pier 5
Pier 3
Pier 1
30
Pacific Ave
Walton Park
Front St
Davis St
Golden Gateway Club
Drumm St
San Francisco Bay
Whaleship Plaza
Bostonship Plaza
Custom House Pl
Battery St
Washington St
Embarcadero Plaza
41
Ferry Building
40
38
Maritime Plaza
39
Merchant St
50
Embarcadero Center 4
Embarcadero Center 3
Embarcadero Center 2
Clay St
49
Justin Herman Plaza
48
Commercial St
Embarcadero Center
Embarcadero Center 1
Old Federal Reserve Building
Sacramento St
58
Southern Pacific Railroad Building
Halleck St
California St Cable Car Turnaround
Spear St
Steuart St
The Embarcadero
64
65
California St
Embarcadero BART & Muni Station
Federal Reserve Bank
Audifred Building
Main St
Financial District
101 California
Matson Building
Pacific Gas & Electric Building
Pine St
Beale St
Market St
Front St
Pacific Coast Stock Exchange
Sansome St
Battery St
Shell Building
Fremont St
74
South of Market
see MAP 4
Crown Zellerbach Building
1st St
The Wall
Citicorp Center
Flatiron Building
Hobart Building
Ecker Place
Stevenson St
Jessie St
Montgomery BART & Muni Station
2nd St
Mission St
Minna St
Montgomery St
Jessie St
Aldrich Alley
Parking Area
JACKSON SQUARE
12 Hippodrome (Former Bella Union)
13 Thomas Bros Books & Maps
14 Cypress Club
15 William Stout Architectural Books
16 Bix
25 Old Transamerica Building
26 Hotaling Annex West (463-73 Jackson)
27 Hotaling Building (451-55 Jackson)
28 Hotaling Annex East (443-45 Jackson)
29 Ghirardelli Building
FINANCIAL DISTRICT
PLACES TO STAY
48 Park Hyatt
58 Hyatt Regency; Equinox
PLACES TO EAT
38 Il Massimo del Panino
50 Harbor Village
54 Palio Paninoteca
55 Rubicon
64 Aqua
65 Tadich Grill
69 360° Gourmet Burritos
70 Plouf
71 Cafe Tiramisù
72 Cafe Bastille
73 Sam's Grill & Seafood Restaurant
75 Metropol
OTHER
30 Blue & Gold Fleet Oakland-Alameda Ferries
39 The Punch Line
40 Vaillancourt Fountain
41 Golden Gate Transit Ferries
49 Embarcadero Center Cinema
56 Wells Fargo History Museum
57 London Wine Bar
61 Transcendence (The Banker's Heart)
62 Carnelian Room
63 Museum of Money of the American West
74 Slot Machine Plaque
76 Post Office
77 Lotta's Fountain

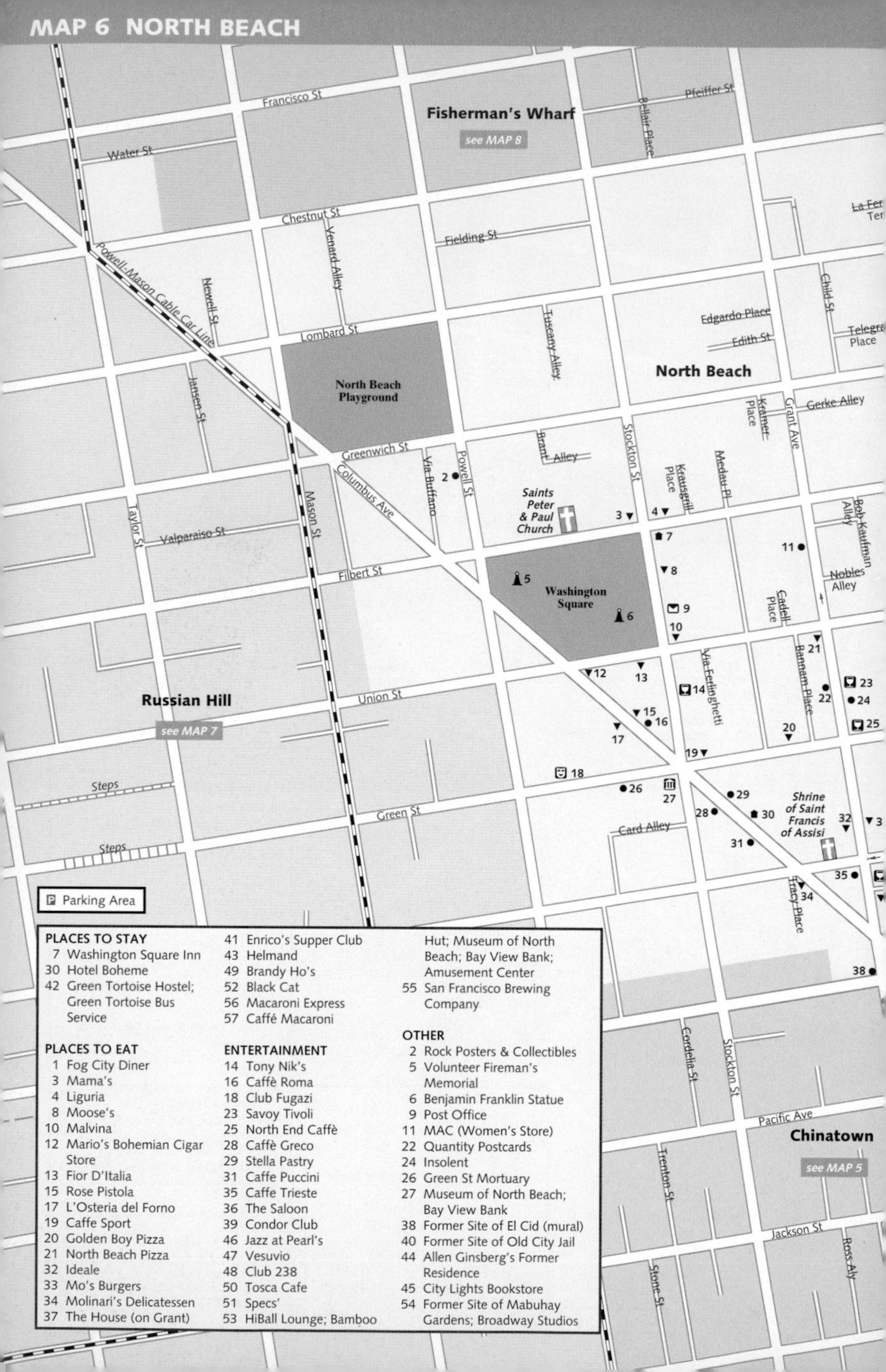
MAP 6 NORTH BEACH
Francisco St
Fisherman's Wharf
see MAP 8
Pfeiffer St
Bellair Place
Water St
Chestnut St
Fielding St
Venard Alley
La Fer
Ter
Powell-Mason Cable Car Line
Newell St
Tuscany Alley
Child St
Edgardo Place
Edith St
Telegra
Place
Lombard St
North Beach Playground
North Beach
Jansen St
Kramer Place
Grant Ave
Gerke Alley
Greenwich St
Brant Alley
Stockton St
Krausgrill Place
Medau Pl
Via Buffano
Powell St
Columbus Ave
Mason St
Taylor St
Valparaiso St
Saints Peter & Paul Church
Bob Kaufman Alley
Filbert St
Washington Square
Nobles Alley
Cadell Place
Bannam Place
Via Ferlinghetti
Russian Hill
see MAP 7
Union St
Steps
Green St
Card Alley
Shrine of Saint Francis of Assisi
Tracy Place
Steps
Parking Area
Cordelia St
Stockton St
Pacific Ave
Chinatown
see MAP 5
Trenton St
Jackson St
Ross Aly
Stone St
PLACES TO STAY
7 Washington Square Inn
30 Hotel Boheme
42 Green Tortoise Hostel; Green Tortoise Bus Service
PLACES TO EAT
1 Fog City Diner
3 Mama's
4 Liguria
8 Moose's
10 Malvina
12 Mario's Bohemian Cigar Store
13 Fior D'Italia
15 Rose Pistola
17 L'Osteria del Forno
19 Caffe Sport
20 Golden Boy Pizza
21 North Beach Pizza
32 Ideale
33 Mo's Burgers
34 Molinari's Delicatessen
37 The House (on Grant)
41 Enrico's Supper Club
43 Helmand
49 Brandy Ho's
52 Black Cat
56 Macaroni Express
57 Caffé Macaroni
ENTERTAINMENT
14 Tony Nik's
16 Caffè Roma
18 Club Fugazi
23 Savoy Tivoli
25 North End Caffè
28 Caffè Greco
29 Stella Pastry
31 Caffe Puccini
35 Caffe Trieste
36 The Saloon
39 Condor Club
46 Jazz at Pearl's
47 Vesuvio
48 Club 238
50 Tosca Cafe
51 Specs'
53 HiBall Lounge; Bamboo Hut; Museum of North Beach; Bay View Bank; Amusement Center
55 San Francisco Brewing Company
OTHER
2 Rock Posters & Collectibles
5 Volunteer Fireman's Memorial
6 Benjamin Franklin Statue
9 Post Office
11 MAC (Women's Store)
22 Quantity Postcards
24 Insolent
26 Green St Mortuary
27 Museum of North Beach; Bay View Bank
38 Former Site of El Cid (mural)
40 Former Site of Old City Jail
44 Allen Ginsberg's Former Residence
45 City Lights Bookstore
54 Former Site of Mabuhay Gardens; Broadway Studios

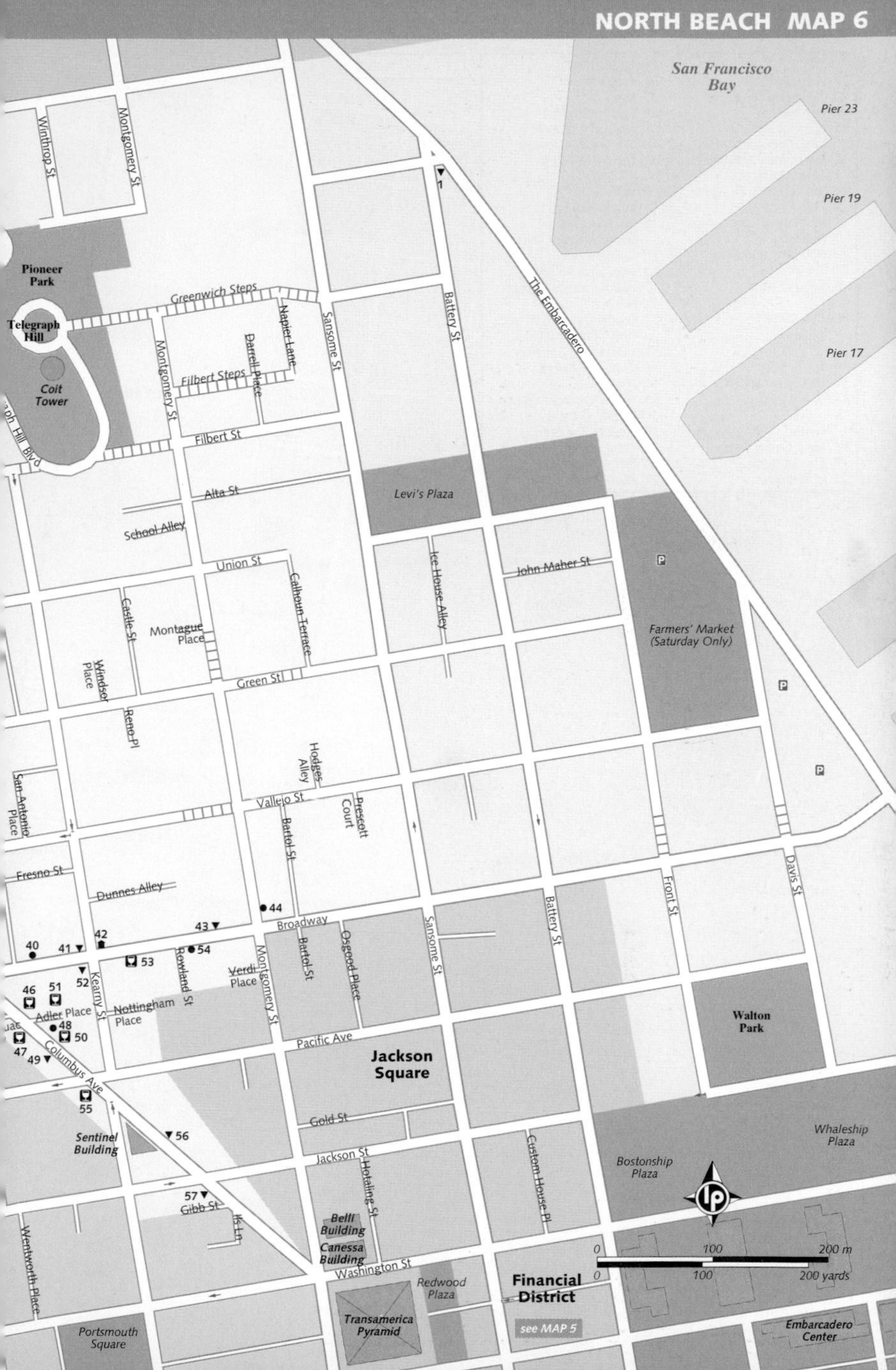
San Francisco Bay
Pier 23
Pier 19
Pier 17
The Embarcadero
Pioneer Park
Telegraph Hill
Coit Tower
Greenwich Steps
Filbert Steps
Winthrop St
Montgomery St
Napier Lane
Darrell Place
Sansome St
Battery St
Filbert St
Alta St
School Alley
Union St
Calhoun Terrace
Levi's Plaza
Ice House Alley
John Maher St
Farmers' Market (Saturday Only)
Castle St
Montague Place
Windsor Place
Reno Pl
Green St
Hodges Alley
Vallejo St
Prescott Court
Bartol St
San Antonio Place
Fresno St
Dunnes Alley
Broadway
Osgood Place
Front St
Davis St
Kearny St
Rowland St
Verdi Place
Adler Place
Nottingham Place
Columbus Ave
Pacific Ave
Jackson Square
Walton Park
Sentinel Building
Gold St
Jackson St
Hotaling St
Custom House Pl
Whaleship Plaza
Bostonship Plaza
Belli Building
Canessa Building
Washington St
Redwood Plaza
Gibb St
Wentworth Place
Financial District
Transamerica Pyramid
Portsmouth Square
see MAP 5
Embarcadero Center
0 100 200 m
0 100 200 yards
1
40
41
42
43
44
46
47
48
49
50
51
52
53
54
55
56
57

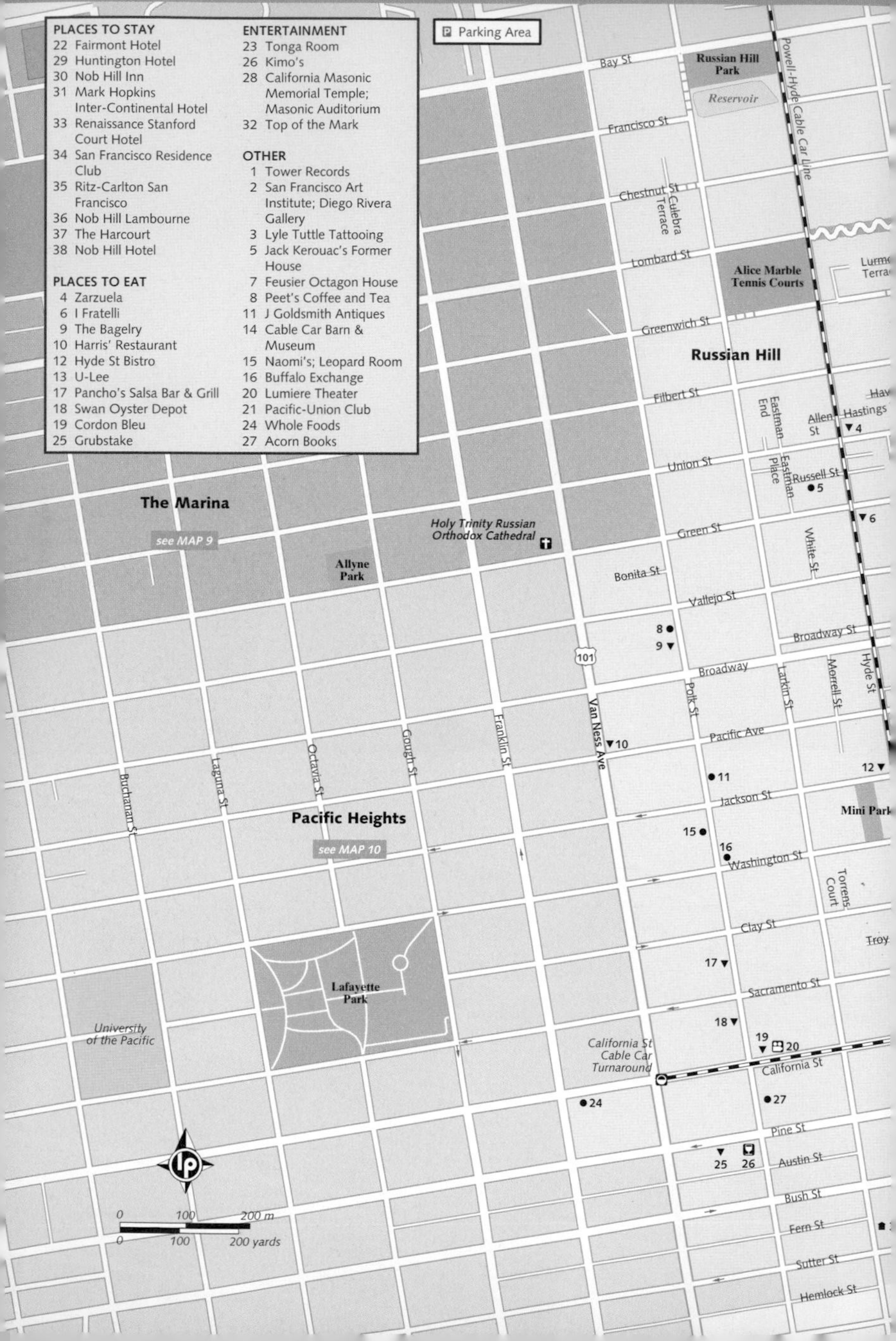

PLACES TO STAY
22 Fairmont Hotel
29 Huntington Hotel
30 Nob Hill Inn
31 Mark Hopkins Inter-Continental Hotel
33 Renaissance Stanford Court Hotel
34 San Francisco Residence Club
35 Ritz-Carlton San Francisco
36 Nob Hill Lambourne
37 The Harcourt
38 Nob Hill Hotel

PLACES TO EAT
4 Zarzuela
6 I Fratelli
9 The Bagelry
10 Harris' Restaurant
12 Hyde St Bistro
13 U-Lee
17 Pancho's Salsa Bar & Grill
18 Swan Oyster Depot
19 Cordon Bleu
25 Grubstake

ENTERTAINMENT
23 Tonga Room
26 Kimo's
28 California Masonic Memorial Temple; Masonic Auditorium
32 Top of the Mark

OTHER
1 Tower Records
2 San Francisco Art Institute; Diego Rivera Gallery
3 Lyle Tuttle Tattooing
5 Jack Kerouac's Former House
7 Feusier Octagon House
8 Peet's Coffee and Tea
11 J Goldsmith Antiques
14 Cable Car Barn & Museum
15 Naomi's; Leopard Room
16 Buffalo Exchange
20 Lumiere Theater
21 Pacific-Union Club
24 Whole Foods
27 Acorn Books

Parking Area

see MAP 8
Fisherman's Wharf
Water St
Houston St
Chestnut St
Bellair Place
Fielding St
Venard Alley
Lombard St
Winthrop St
Pioneer Park
Telegraph Hill
Coit Tower
Child St
North Beach Playground
Jansen St
3
Greenwich St
North Beach
see MAP 6
Alta St
Levi's Plaza
Powell-Mason Cable Car Line
Valparaiso St
Filbert St
Washington Square
Varennes St
Genoa Place
Sonoma St
Castle St
Calhoun Terrace
Ice House Alley
Aladdin Terrace
Union St
Jasper Pl
Bannam Pl
Marion Place
Black Place
Webb Place
Green St
Columbus Ave
Bartol St
condray Lane
7
Ina Coolbrith Park
Vallejo St
Fresno St
Romolo St
Osgood Pl
Sansome St
Montgomery St
Kearny St
Grant Ave
Stockton St
Broadway
Florence St
Glover St
Cordelia St
Jackson Square
Robert Levy Tunnel
Himmelmann Place
Salmon St
Mason St
Powell St
Gold St
Jones St
Taylor St
Pacific Ave
Sentinel Building
Beckett St
Chinatown
Leavenworth St
Bernard St
Trenton St
Belli Building
Hotaling St
John St
Auburn St
Jackson St
Stone St
Ross Alley
Place
Wentworth
Canessa Building
Transamerica Pyramid
Portsmouth Square
Washington St
Spofford St
Waverly Pl
14
Wetmore St
Codman Place
Clay St
Hang Ah St
Commercial St
Financial District
see MAP 5
Nob Hill
Reed St
Priest St
Sproule Ln
Chinese Playground
Sacramento St
Pleasant St
California St Cable Car Line
Merchant's Exchange Building
Kimball Place
Leroy Place
Huntington Park
22
23
California St
Quincy St
St Mary's Square
Bank of America Building
Grace Cathedral
21
Golden Court
32
33
34
Joice St
Stockton Tunnel
35
Acorn Alley
28
29
Nob Hill Place
31
Nob Hill Cir
Alley
St George
Russ Building
Helen St
Vine Terrace
Pine St
Hammett St
Dashiell
36
30
Claude Pl
Halliday Building
Touchard St
Bush St
Harlan Pl
Crocker Galleria
Sutter St
Campton Place
Union Square
see MAP 2
Post St
Cosmo Place
Maiden Lane
Union Square
he Tenderloin
Geary St

PLACES TO STAY
9 Dockside Boat & Bed
20 Wharf Inn
21 Radisson
27 Suites at Fisherman's Wharf
29 Holiday Inn
30 Hyatt at Fisherman's Wharf
31 Tuscan Inn
32 Travelodge
34 San Remo Hotel
PLACES TO EAT
11 No 9 Fisherman's Grotto
12 Alioto's
13 Tarantino's
23 McCormick & Kuleto's
26 Buena Vista Café
ENTERTAINMENT
7 Cinemax Theatre
10 Lou's Pier 47
17 Jack's Cannery Bar
18 Cobb's Comedy Club
OTHER
1 Sea Lions
2 Venetian Carousel
3 Blue & Gold Fleet Ferries
4 Blue & Gold Fleet Ferry Booking Office (for Alcatraz)
5 Blue & Gold Fleet Ferry Booking Office
6 San Francisco Seaplane Tours
8 Underwater World
14 Boudin Bakery
15 Ripley's Believe It or Not! Museum
16 Wax Museum
19 Lark in the Morning
22 San Francisco National Maritime Museum
24 Builders Booksource
25 Ghirardelli Soda Fountain & Chocolate Shop
28 Patagonia
33 Tower Classical Annex
Parking Area
Ferries to Alcatraz, Angel Island, Sausalito, Tiburon & Vallejo
Breakwater
Pier 45
Municipal Pier
USS Jeremiah O'Brien
Hyde St Pier
Alma
Fisherman's Wharf Seafood Center
USS Pampanito
Pier 43½ (Vista Pier)
Balclutha
Eureka
Eppleton Hall
CA Thayer
The Embarcad
Fisherman's Wharf
Aquatic Park
Jefferson St
The Cannery
Powell-Hyde Cable Car Turnaround
Beach St
Fisherman's Wharf
Golden Gate Promenade
Victoria Park
Ghirardelli Square
North Point St
Jones St
Taylor St
Leavenworth St
Hyde St
Bergen Place
Larkin St
Polk St
Van Ness Ave
Fort Mason
Powell-M Cable Ca Turnarou
Bay St
Bret Harte Terrace
Columbus Ave
Russian Hill Park
Reservoir
North View Court
Powell-Hyde Cable Car Line
Francisco St
Houston St
Water
The Marina
see MAP 9
Russian Hill
Chestnut St
see MAP 7
Culebra Terrace

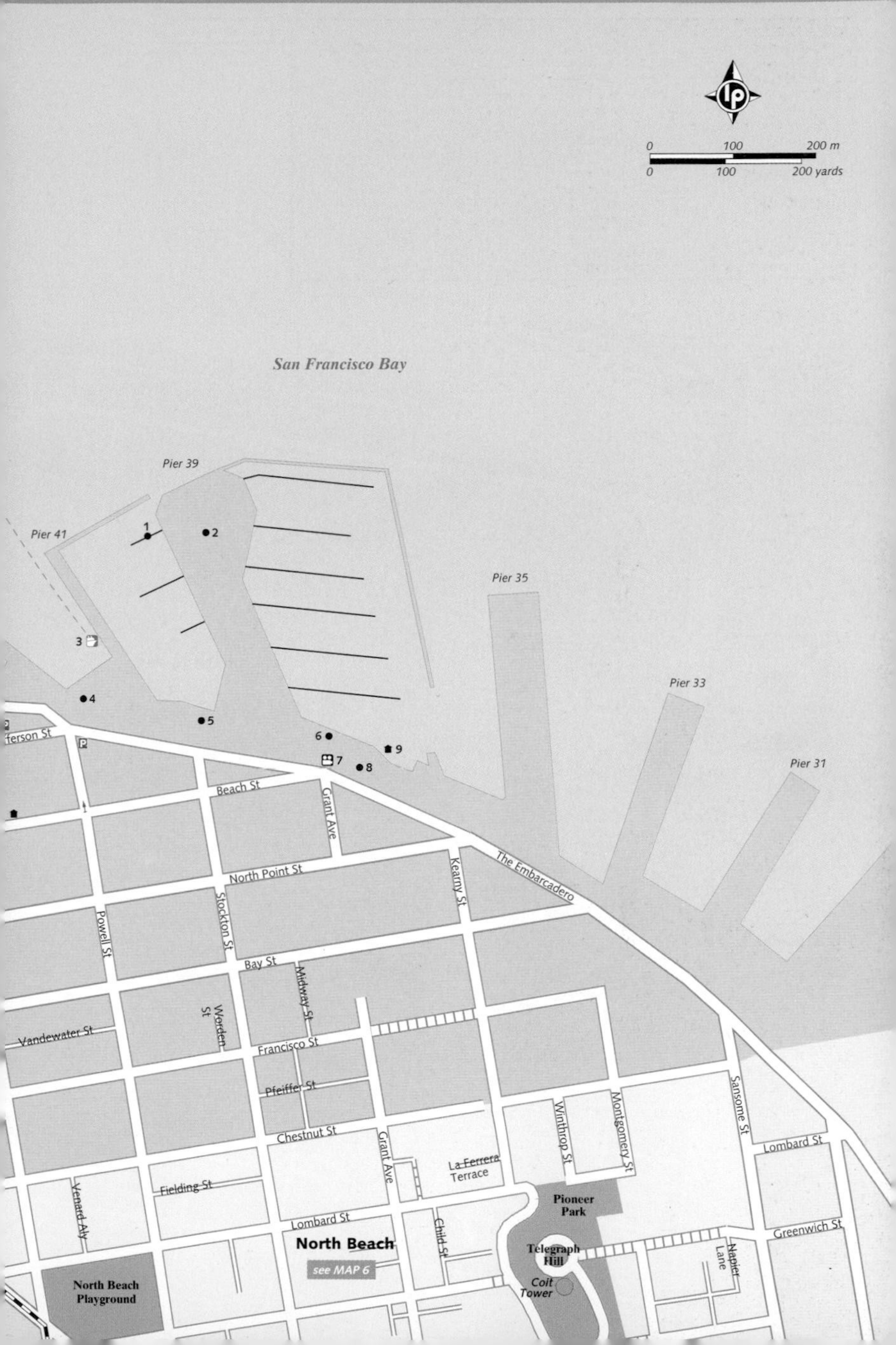

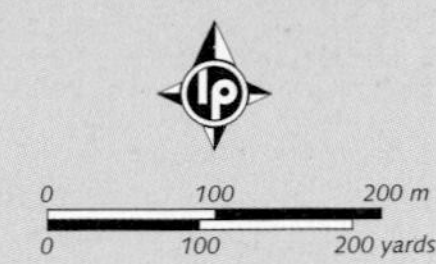

San Francisco Bay

Pier 39
Pier 41
Pier 35
Pier 33
Pier 31
1
2
3
4
5
6
7
8
9
Jefferson St
Beach St
Grant Ave
North Point St
Kearny St
The Embarcadero
Powell St
Stockton St
Bay St
Midway St
Worden St
Vandewater St
Francisco St
Pfeiffer St
Chestnut St
Winthrop St
Montgomery St
Sansome St
Lombard St
La Ferrera Terrace
Fielding St
Venard Aly
Lombard St
Child St
Pioneer Park
Greenwich St
North Beach
see MAP 6
Telegraph Hill
Napier Lane
Coit Tower
North Beach Playground

MAP 9 THE MARINA & COW HOLLOW

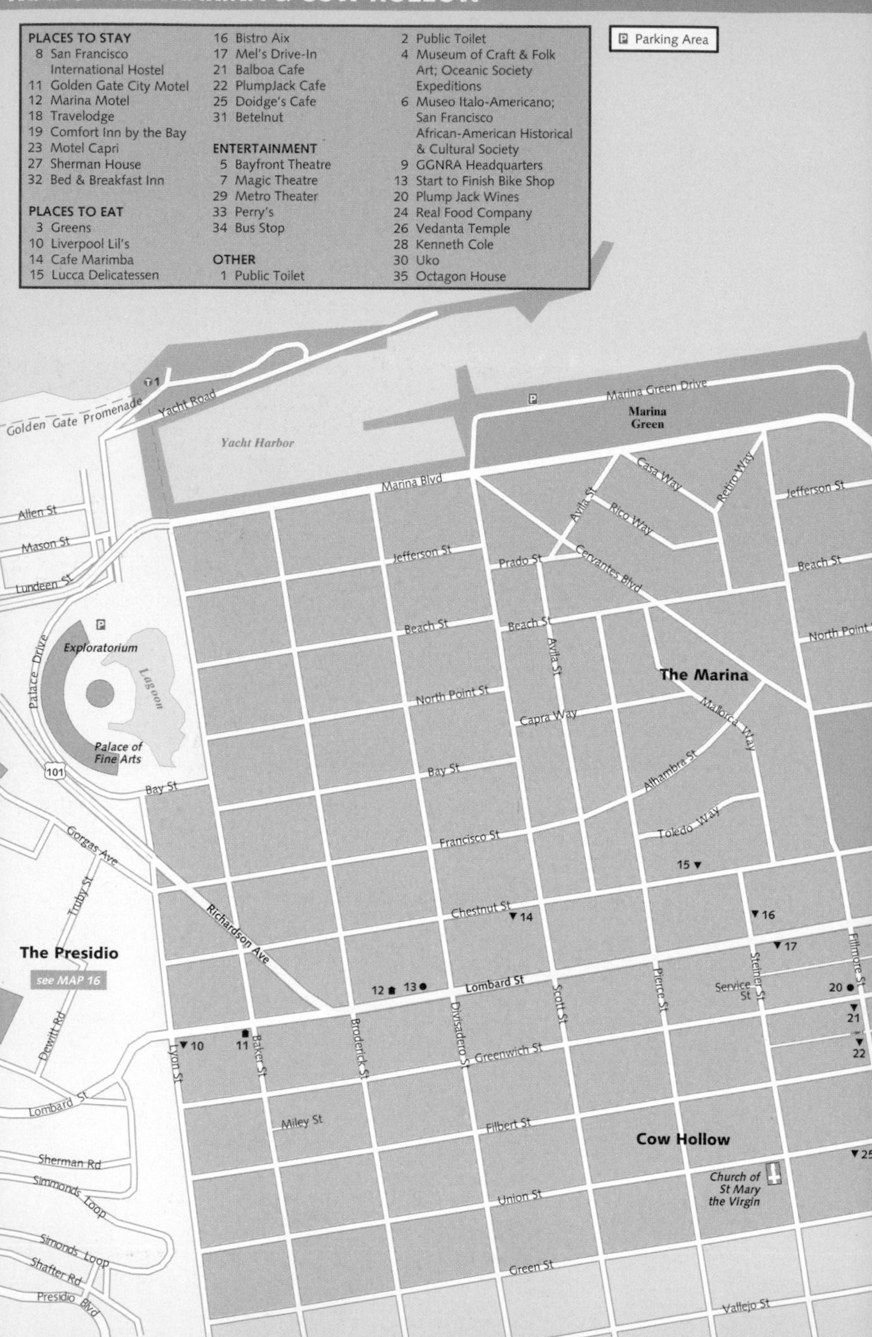
PLACES TO STAY
8 San Francisco International Hostel
11 Golden Gate City Motel
12 Marina Motel
18 Travelodge
19 Comfort Inn by the Bay
23 Motel Capri
27 Sherman House
32 Bed & Breakfast Inn
PLACES TO EAT
3 Greens
10 Liverpool Lil's
14 Cafe Marimba
15 Lucca Delicatessen
16 Bistro Aix
17 Mel's Drive-In
21 Balboa Cafe
22 PlumpJack Cafe
25 Doidge's Cafe
31 Betelnut
ENTERTAINMENT
5 Bayfront Theatre
7 Magic Theatre
29 Metro Theater
33 Perry's
34 Bus Stop
OTHER
1 Public Toilet
2 Public Toilet
4 Museum of Craft & Folk Art; Oceanic Society Expeditions
6 Museo Italo-Americano; San Francisco African-American Historical & Cultural Society
9 GGNRA Headquarters
13 Start to Finish Bike Shop
20 Plump Jack Wines
24 Real Food Company
26 Vedanta Temple
28 Kenneth Cole
30 Uko
35 Octagon House
Parking Area
Golden Gate Promenade
Yacht Road
Yacht Harbor
Marina Green Drive
Marina Green
Marina Blvd
Casa Way
Retiro Way
Avila St
Rico Way
Jefferson St
Prado St
Cervantes Blvd
Beach St
North Point St
Allen St
Mason St
Lundeen St
Exploratorium
Lagoon
Palace Drive
Palace of Fine Arts
101
The Marina
Mallorca Way
Capra Way
Alhambra St
Bay St
Toledo Way
Francisco St
Gorgas Ave
Truby St
Richardson Ave
Chestnut St
The Presidio
see MAP 16
Lombard St
Service St
Steiner St
Fillmore St
Pierce St
Scott St
Divisadero St
Broderick St
Baker St
Lyon St
Dewitt Rd
Greenwich St
Miley St
Filbert St
Cow Hollow
Church of St Mary the Virgin
Sherman Rd
Simmonds Loop
Simonds Loop
Shafter Rd
Presidio Blvd
Union St
Green St
Vallejo St

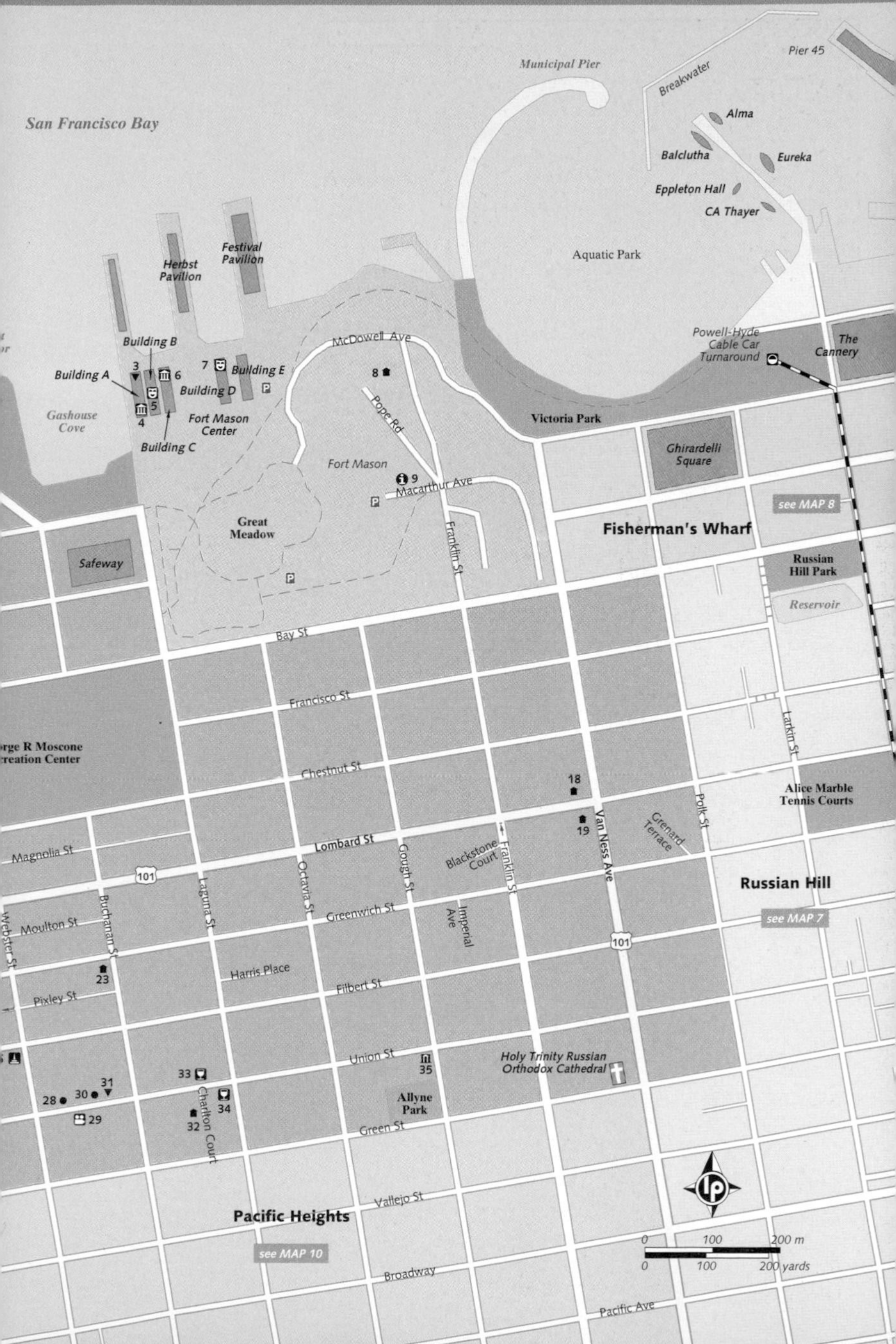
San Francisco Bay
Municipal Pier
Pier 45
Breakwater
Alma
Balclutha
Eureka
Eppleton Hall
CA Thayer
Aquatic Park
Festival Pavilion
Herbst Pavilion
Building B
Building A
Building E
Building D
Building C
Fort Mason Center
Gashouse Cove
McDowell Ave
Pope Rd
Fort Mason
Macarthur Ave
Great Meadow
Victoria Park
Powell-Hyde Cable Car Turnaround
The Cannery
Ghirardelli Square
see MAP 8
Fisherman's Wharf
Russian Hill Park
Reservoir
Safeway
Franklin St
Bay St
Francisco St
Chestnut St
Larkin St
Alice Marble Tennis Courts
Lombard St
Magnolia St
Moulton St
Pixley St
Webster St
Buchanan St
Laguna St
Octavia St
Gough St
Blackstone Court
Franklin St
Van Ness Ave
Grenard Terrace
Polk St
Russian Hill
see MAP 7
Greenwich St
Imperial Ave
Harris Place
Filbert St
Union St
Holy Trinity Russian Orthodox Cathedral
Allyne Park
Green St
Charlton Court
Vallejo St
Pacific Heights
see MAP 10
Broadway
Pacific Ave
0 100 200 m
0 100 200 yards

MAP 10 PACIFIC HEIGHTS & JAPANTOWN

PLACES TO STAY
15 Mansions Hotel
20 Queen Anne Hotel
21 Majestic Hotel
36 Radisson Miyako Hotel

PLACES TO EAT
5 Golden Turtle
7 Jackson Fillmore
16 Ella's
18 Elite Cafe
31 On the Bridge
38 Tommy's Joynt

ENTERTAINMENT
13 Clay Theater
17 Rasselas
27 Fillmore Auditorium
29 AMC Kabuki 8 Theaters

OTHER
1 Casebolt House
2 James Leary Flood's Second Mansion (2222 Broadway); Convent of the Sacred Heart
3 Bourn House
4 James Leary Flood Mansion (2120 Broadway)
6 Gibbs House
8 Whittier House
9 Spreckels Mansion
10 Haas-Lilienthal House
11 Gimme Shoes
12 California Pacific Medical Center Hospital
14 Temple Sherith Israel
19 Mrs Dewson's Hats
22 American Rag
23 UCSF Mt Zion Medical Center
24 Marcus Books
25 Goodwill Store
28 Kabuki Springs & Spa
30 Kinokuniya Building, Kinokuniya Bookshop
32 Maruwa Supermarket
33 Kintetsu Mall; Isobune; Mifune
34 Peace Pagoda
35 Miyako Mall
37 St Mark's Lutheran Church
39 Pacific Coast Hospital
40 Church of St John Coltrane

Parking Area

Cow Hollow
see MAP 9
Alta Plaza Park
Hamilton Square
University of San Francisco
to MAP 16
to MAP 15

Filbert St
Union St
Green St
Vallejo St
Broadway
Pacific Ave
Jackson St
Washington St
Clay St
Sacramento St
California St
Pine St
Bush St
Sutter St
Post St
Garden St
Geary Blvd
O'Farrell St
Ellis St
Eddy St
Turk St
Golden Gate Ave
Broderick St
Divisadero St
Scott St
Pierce St
Steiner St
Normandie Terrace
Raycliff Terrace
Perine Place
Presidio Ave
Lyon St
Baker St
Walnut St
Laurel St
Locust St
Mayfair Drive
Iris Ave
Manzanita Ave
Collins St
Masonic Ave
Lupine Ave
Wood St
Emerson St
Leona Terrace
St Josephs Ave
Beideman St
Terra Vista Ave
Encanto Ave
Fortuna Ave
Barcelona Ave
Anza Vista Ave
Nido Ave
Anza St
Ewing Terrace
Cook St
Blake St
Seymour St

0 100 200 m
0 100 200 yards

Union St
Allyne Park
Green St
Vallejo St
Broadway
Pacific Ave
Jackson St
Washington St
Clay St
Sacramento St
California St
Pine St
Austin St
Bush St
Fern St
Sutter St
Post St
Geary Blvd
O'Farrell St
Willow St
Turk St
Golden Gate Ave
McAllister St
Fulton St
Webster St
Buchanan St
Laguna St
Octavia St
Gough St
Franklin St
Van Ness Ave
Polk St
Morrell St
Larkin St
Fillmore St
101
Pacific Heights
Russian Hill
see MAP 7
Bromley Place
Lafayette Park
University of the Pacific
California St Cable Car Turnaround
Nob Hill
Orben Place
Wilmot St
Japantown
Hemlock St
Daniel Burnham Court
Cottage Row
Cedar St
Buchanan Mall
Peter Yorke Way
Starr King Way
Myrtle St
The Tenderloin
Japan Center
Cathedral of St Mary the Assumption
Avery St
Cleary Court
Olive St
Ellis St
The Fillmore
Hollis St
Eddy St
Larch St
Jefferson Square
Opera Plaza
Elm St
Hayward Playground
see MAP 3
Civic Center
Western Addition
to MAP 11
City Hall
Ballet Association
War Memorial Opera House
1 2 3 4 5 7 8 9 10 11 12 13 14 15 18 19 20 21 22 24 25 27 28 29 30 31 32 33 34 35 36 37 38 40

Turk Blvd
to MAP 10
Golden Gate Ave
University of San Francisco
McAllister St
Central Ave
Lyon St
Baker St
Masonic Ave
University of San Francisco
Fulton St
St Ignatius Church
Clayton St
Ashbury St
Grove St
St Mary's Hospital
Strader St
University of San Francisco
Cole St
Hayes St
3
Fell St
Panhandle
Oak St
5
Page St
Golden Gate Park
Stanyan St
Shrader St
Upper Haight
28
29
30
31
36
39
40
41
42
Haight St
43
Kezar Drive
21
22
25
32
33
34
35
37
38
11
14
26
27
Waller St
60
12
13
15
17
18
19
20
23
24
16
Buena Vista Park
58
Belvedere St
Downey St
Delmar St
59
Buena Vista Ave
Kezar Pavilion
Beulah St
61
Frederick St
Cole Valley
Java St
63
Buena Vista Ave
Piedmont St
Upper Terrace
Carl St
64
65
Masonic Ave
62
Roosevelt
States St
Parnassus St
Clifford Terrace
Ord Court
Willard St
Woodland Ave
Grattan St
Vulcan Stairw
Lower Terrace
Roosevelt Way
Upper Terrace
to MAP 15
Alma St
Saturn St
Rivoli St
Corbett Ave
17th St
Interior Park Belt
Market St

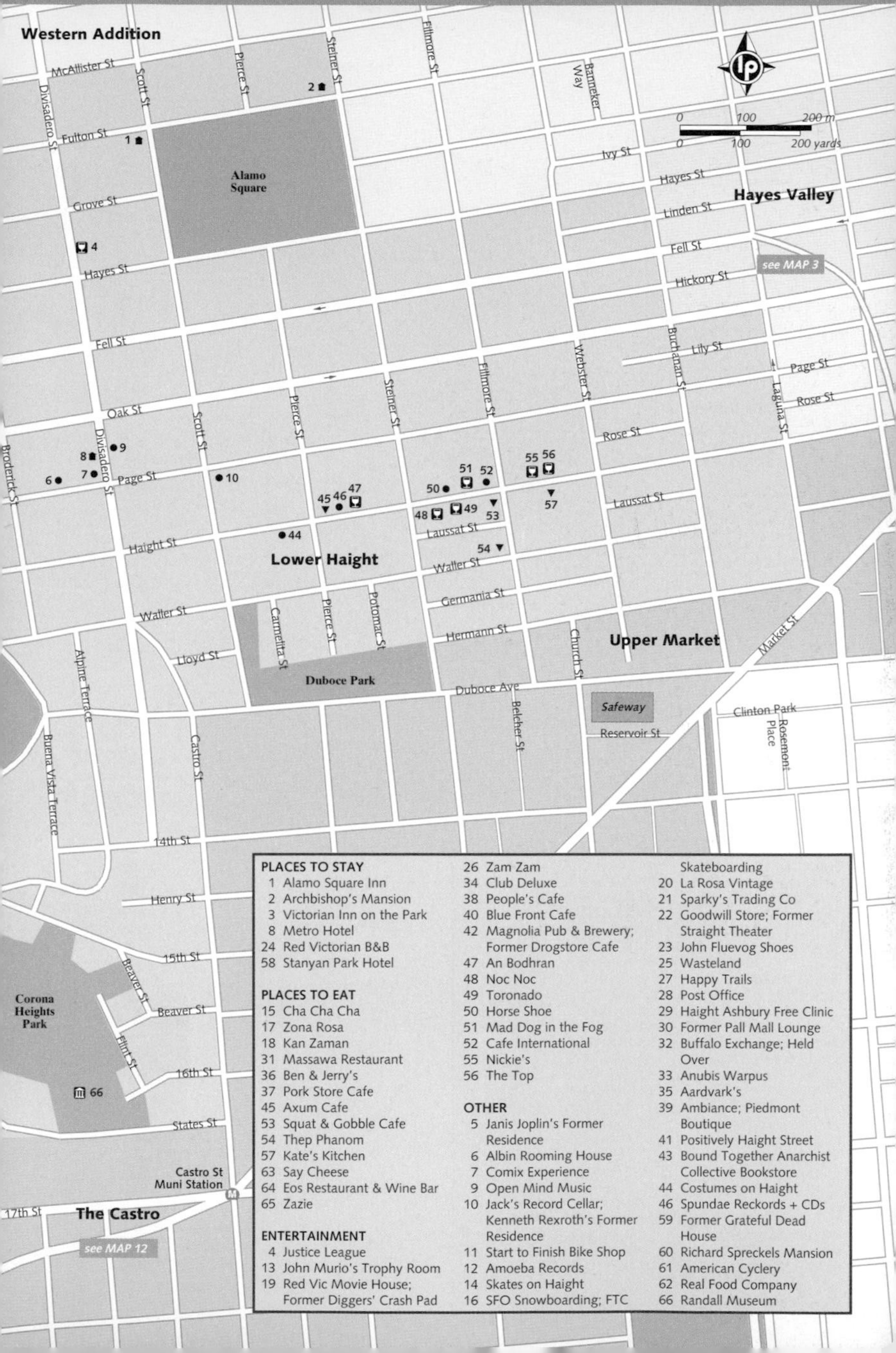

Western Addition

Alamo Square

Hayes Valley

Lower Haight

Upper Market

Duboce Park

Corona Heights Park

Castro St Muni Station

The Castro

see MAP 3

see MAP 12

PLACES TO STAY
1 Alamo Square Inn
2 Archbishop's Mansion
3 Victorian Inn on the Park
8 Metro Hotel
24 Red Victorian B&B
58 Stanyan Park Hotel

PLACES TO EAT
15 Cha Cha Cha
17 Zona Rosa
18 Kan Zaman
31 Massawa Restaurant
36 Ben & Jerry's
37 Pork Store Cafe
45 Axum Cafe
53 Squat & Gobble Cafe
54 Thep Phanom
57 Kate's Kitchen
63 Say Cheese
64 Eos Restaurant & Wine Bar
65 Zazie

ENTERTAINMENT
4 Justice League
13 John Murio's Trophy Room
19 Red Vic Movie House; Former Diggers' Crash Pad
26 Zam Zam
34 Club Deluxe
38 People's Cafe
40 Blue Front Cafe
42 Magnolia Pub & Brewery; Former Drogstore Cafe
47 An Bodhran
48 Noc Noc
49 Toronado
50 Horse Shoe
51 Mad Dog in the Fog
52 Cafe International
55 Nickie's
56 The Top

OTHER
5 Janis Joplin's Former Residence
6 Albin Rooming House
7 Comix Experience
9 Open Mind Music
10 Jack's Record Cellar; Kenneth Rexroth's Former Residence
11 Start to Finish Bike Shop
12 Amoeba Records
14 Skates on Haight
16 SFO Snowboarding; FTC Skateboarding
20 La Rosa Vintage
21 Sparky's Trading Co
22 Goodwill Store; Former Straight Theater
23 John Fluevog Shoes
25 Wasteland
27 Happy Trails
28 Post Office
29 Haight Ashbury Free Clinic
30 Former Pall Mall Lounge
32 Buffalo Exchange; Held Over
33 Anubis Warpus
35 Aardvark's
39 Ambiance; Piedmont Boutique
41 Positively Haight Street
43 Bound Together Anarchist Collective Bookstore
44 Costumes on Haight
46 Spundae Reckords + CDs
59 Former Grateful Dead House
60 Richard Spreckels Mansion
61 American Cyclery
62 Real Food Company
66 Randall Museum

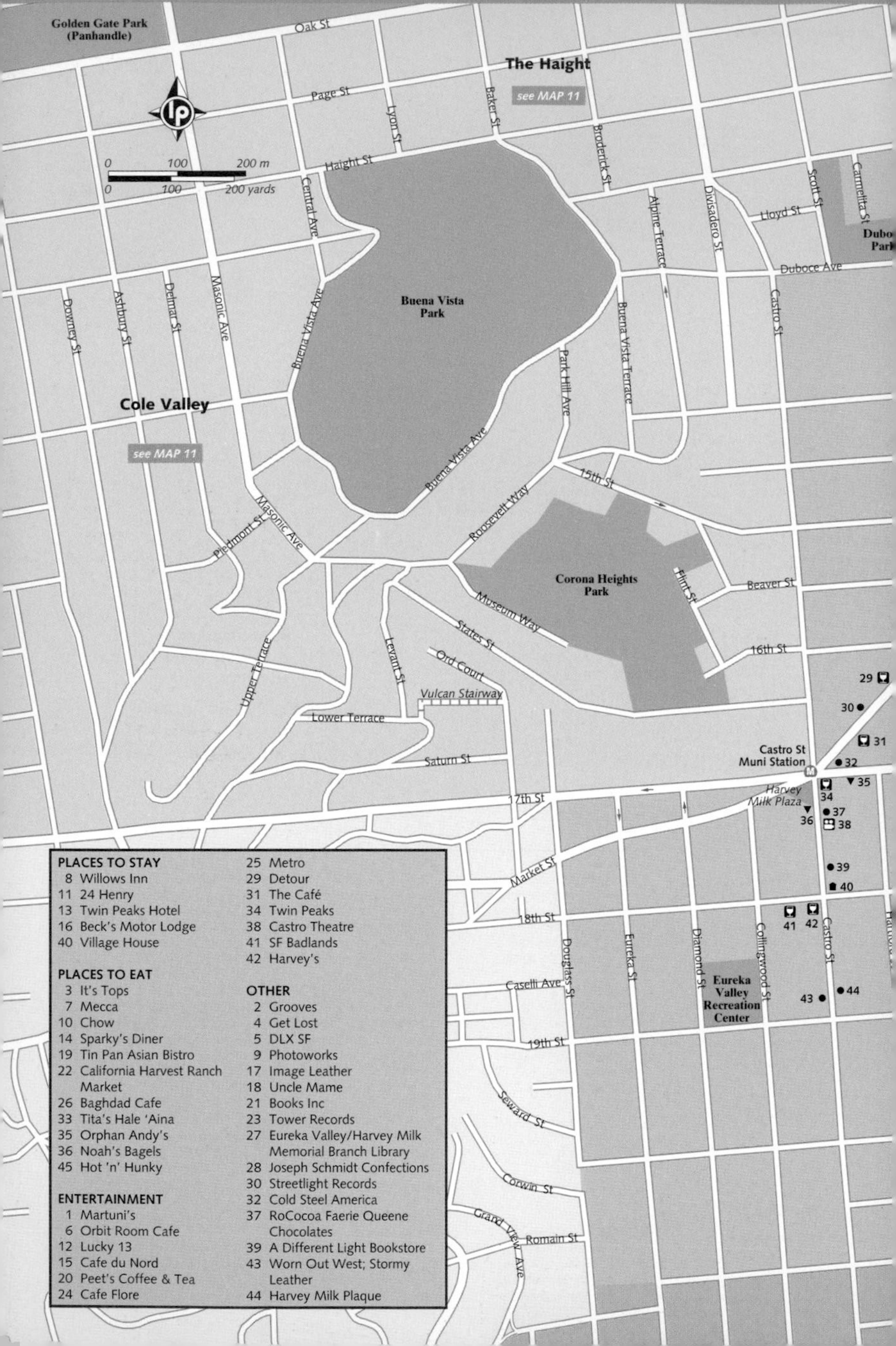

MAP 12 THE CASTRO & UPPER MARKET

Golden Gate Park (Panhandle)

The Haight

see MAP 11

Buena Vista Park

Cole Valley

see MAP 11

Corona Heights Park

Castro St Muni Station

Harvey Milk Plaza

Eureka Valley Recreation Center

PLACES TO STAY

8 Willows Inn
11 24 Henry
13 Twin Peaks Hotel
16 Beck's Motor Lodge
40 Village House

PLACES TO EAT

3 It's Tops
7 Mecca
10 Chow
14 Sparky's Diner
19 Tin Pan Asian Bistro
22 California Harvest Ranch Market
26 Baghdad Cafe
33 Tita's Hale 'Aina
35 Orphan Andy's
36 Noah's Bagels
45 Hot 'n' Hunky

ENTERTAINMENT

1 Martuni's
6 Orbit Room Cafe
12 Lucky 13
15 Cafe du Nord
20 Peet's Coffee & Tea
24 Cafe Flore
25 Metro
29 Detour
31 The Café
34 Twin Peaks
38 Castro Theatre
41 SF Badlands
42 Harvey's

OTHER

2 Grooves
4 Get Lost
5 DLX SF
9 Photoworks
17 Image Leather
18 Uncle Mame
21 Books Inc
23 Tower Records
27 Eureka Valley/Harvey Milk Memorial Branch Library
28 Joseph Schmidt Confections
30 Streetlight Records
32 Cold Steel America
37 RoCocoa Faerie Queene Chocolates
39 A Different Light Bookstore
43 Worn Out West; Stormy Leather
44 Harvey Milk Plaque

to MAP 3
South of Market
see MAP 4
Upper Market
Church St Muni Station
16th St BART Station
Safeway
Basilica
Mission Dolores Cemetery
Mission Dolores Park
The Mission
see MAP 14
The Castro
Noe Valley
see MAP 13
Haight St
Laussat St
Waller St
Germania St
Hermann St
McCoppin St
Market St
Reservoir St
Clinton Park
Brosnan St
Alert Alley
Gaiser Court
Camp St
Chula Lane
Clarion Alley
Dorland St
Hancock St
19th St
Cumberland St
20th St
Liberty St
21st St
Hill St
Steiner St
Fillmore St
Webster St
Buchanan St
Laguna St
Pearl St
Elgin Park
Stevenson St
Valencia St
Woodward St
Mission St
Guerrero St
Rosemont Place
Dolores St
Sanchez St
Belcher St
Church St
Boynton Court
Landers St
Ramona Ave
Albion St
Caledonia St
Julian Ave
Wiese St
Minna St
Natoma St
Capp St
Sharon St
Rondel Place
Hoff St
Dehon St
Harlow St
Abbey St
Prosper St
Dearborn St
Oakwood St
Linda St
Lapidge St
Lexington St
San Carlos St
Rayburn St
Quane St
Fair Oaks St
Ames St
Bartlett St
101

see MAP 12
The Castro
Noe Valley
Romain St
Market St
21st St
Worth St
Eureka St
Collingwood St
Hill St
22nd St
Alvarado St
23rd St
Elizabeth St
24th St
Jersey St
Fountain St
Hoffman Ave
Homestead St
Douglass St
Diamond St
Castro St
25th St
Clipper St
26th St
Carnelian Way
Douglass Playground
Diamond Heights Blvd
Red Rock Way
27th St
Newburg St
Duncan St
28th St
1
2
3
4

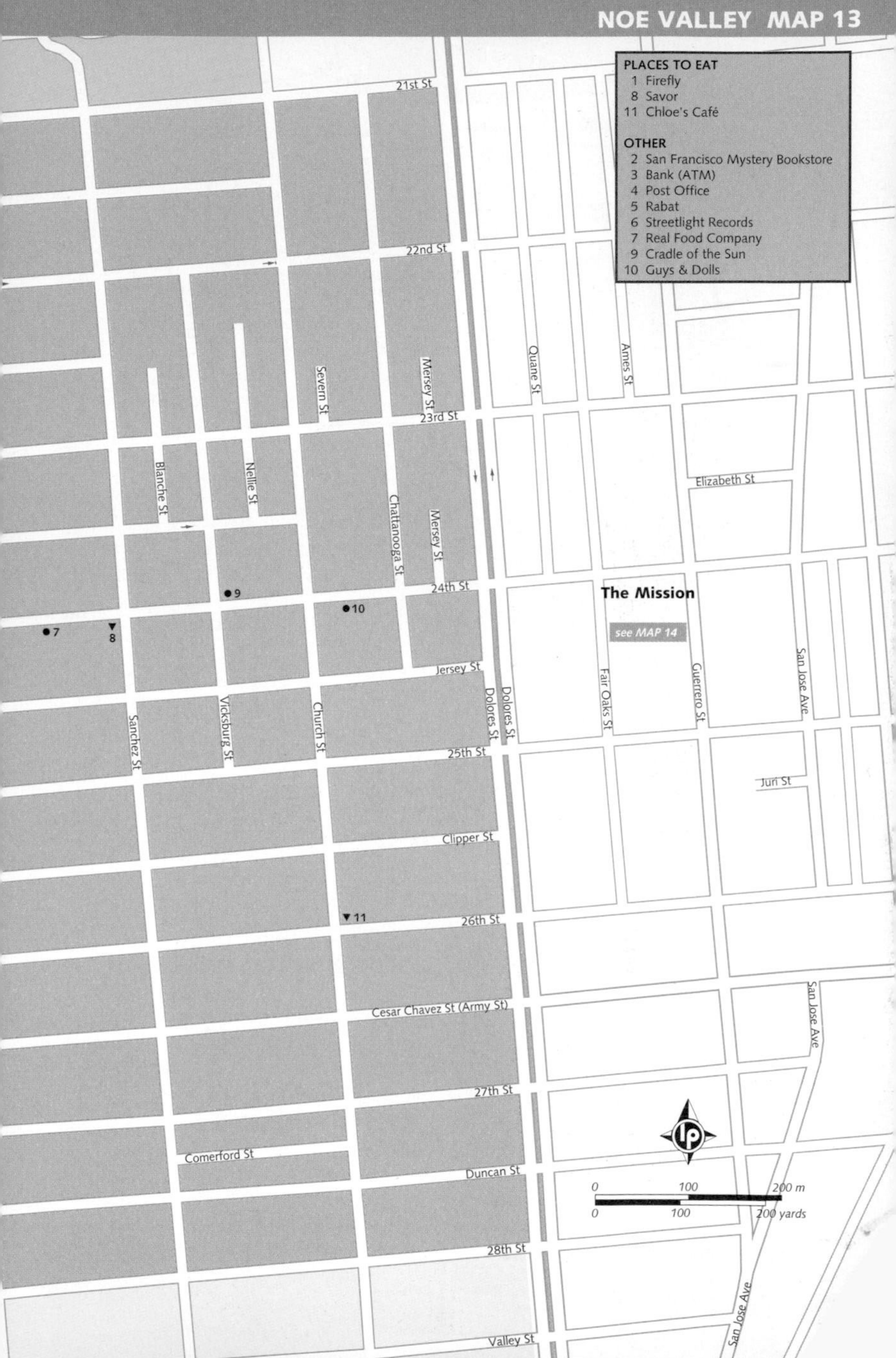
PLACES TO EAT
1 Firefly
8 Savor
11 Chloe's Café
OTHER
2 San Francisco Mystery Bookstore
3 Bank (ATM)
4 Post Office
5 Rabat
6 Streetlight Records
7 Real Food Company
9 Cradle of the Sun
10 Guys & Dolls
21st St
22nd St
23rd St
24th St
Jersey St
25th St
Clipper St
26th St
Cesar Chavez St (Army St)
27th St
Comerford St
Duncan St
28th St
Valley St
Severn St
Mersey St
Quane St
Ames St
Blanche St
Nellie St
Chattanooga St
Elizabeth St
The Mission
see MAP 14
Sanchez St
Vicksburg St
Church St
Dolores St
Fair Oaks St
Guerrero St
San Jose Ave
Juri St
0
100
200 m
200 yards

MAP 14 THE MISSION & POTRERO HILL

to MAP 11
Duboce Park
Duboce Ave
Safeway
Reservoir St
Clinton Park
Brosnan St
Walter St
Belcher St
Erie St
Stevenson St
Woodward St
14th St
Ramona Ave
Julian St
Caledonia St
Mission St
Natoma St
Church St Muni Station
Boynton Court
Henry St
15th St
Sharon St
Landers St
Spencer St
see inset
Adair St
16th St BART Station
Beaver St
16th St
Basilica
Mission Dolores
Chula Lane
Cemetery
Albion St
Rondel Place
Hoff St
Capp St
Enterprise St
see MAP 12
The Castro
Abbey St
17th St
Dolores Terrace
Dorland St
Bird St
Ford St
18th St
Oakwood St
Linda St
Lapidge St
Hancock St
Mission Dolores Park
19th St
The Missio
Cumberland St
Cumberland St
20th St
Valencia St
Lexington St
San Carlos St
Mission St
Capp St
S Van Ness Ave
Shotwell St
Folsom St
Treat Ave
Liberty St
Castro St
Noe St
Sanchez St
Church St
Dolores St
Guerrero St
21st St
Quane St
Fair Oaks St
Ames St
Hill St
Hill St
22nd St
Alvarado St
Alvarado St
Vicksburg St
Chattanooga St
23rd St
Elizabeth St
Elizabeth St
24th St
24th St BART Station
Noe Valley
Jersey St
see MAP 13
25th St
Poplar St
Orange Alley
Osage St
Lilac St
Cypress St
Virgil St
Horace St
Clipper St
26th St
Cesar Chavez St (Army St)
Mission St
27th St
San Jose Ave
Duncan St
28th St
Valley St
To Bernal Heights

0 200 400 m
0 200 400 yards

1 2 3 4 5 6 7 8 9 10 11 12 13 14 15 16 22 23 24 25 26 27 28 31 32 33 34 35 36 37 38 40 41 42 43 44 45 46 47 48 49 50 51 52 53 54 55 57 58 59 60 61 62 63 71 72 73

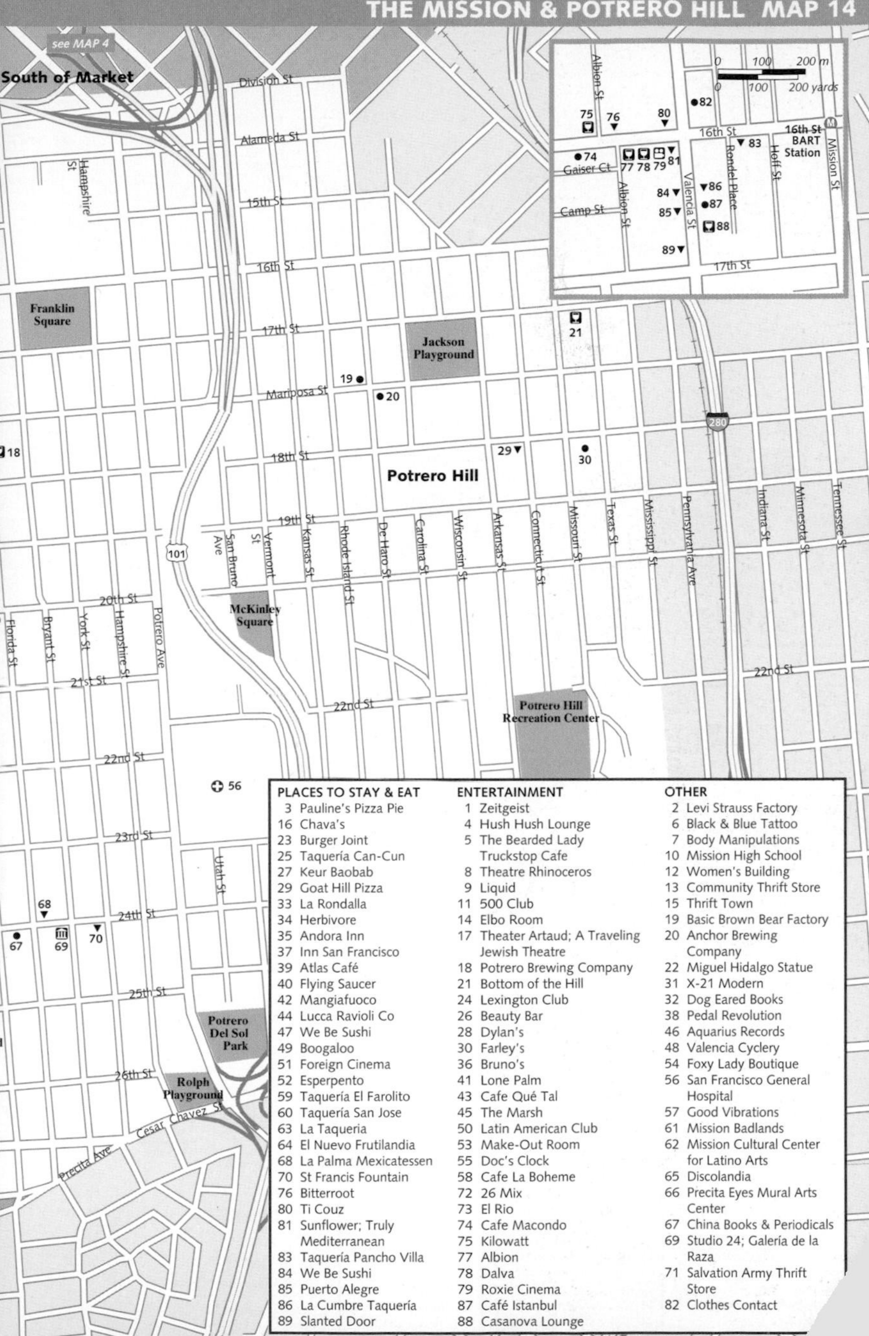
see MAP 4
South of Market
Division St
Alameda St
Hampshire St
15th St
16th St
17th St
Franklin Square
Jackson Playground
Mariposa St
18th St
Potrero Hill
19th St
Ave
San Bruno
St
Vermont
Kansas St
Rhode Island St
De Haro St
Carolina St
Wisconsin St
Arkansas St
Connecticut St
Missouri St
Texas St
Mississippi St
Pennsylvania Ave
Indiana St
Minnesota St
Tennessee St
101
280
20th St
McKinley Square
Florida St
Bryant St
York St
Hampshire St
Potrero Ave
21st St
22nd St
Potrero Hill Recreation Center
22nd St
23rd St
Utah St
24th St
25th St
Potrero Del Sol Park
26th St
Rolph Playground
Cesar Chavez St
Precita Ave
Albion St
Gaiser Ct
Camp St
Valencia St
Rondel Place
Hoff St
Mission St
16th St BART Station
17th St
0 100 200 m
0 100 200 yards
PLACES TO STAY & EAT
3 Pauline's Pizza Pie
16 Chava's
23 Burger Joint
25 Taquería Can-Cun
27 Keur Baobab
29 Goat Hill Pizza
33 La Rondalla
34 Herbivore
35 Andora Inn
37 Inn San Francisco
39 Atlas Café
40 Flying Saucer
42 Mangiafuoco
44 Lucca Ravioli Co
47 We Be Sushi
49 Boogaloo
51 Foreign Cinema
52 Esperpento
59 Taquería El Farolito
60 Taquería San Jose
63 La Taqueria
64 El Nuevo Frutilandia
68 La Palma Mexicatessen
70 St Francis Fountain
76 Bitterroot
80 Ti Couz
81 Sunflower; Truly Mediterranean
83 Taquería Pancho Villa
84 We Be Sushi
85 Puerto Alegre
86 La Cumbre Taquería
89 Slanted Door
ENTERTAINMENT
1 Zeitgeist
4 Hush Hush Lounge
5 The Bearded Lady Truckstop Cafe
8 Theatre Rhinoceros
9 Liquid
11 500 Club
14 Elbo Room
17 Theater Artaud; A Traveling Jewish Theatre
18 Potrero Brewing Company
21 Bottom of the Hill
24 Lexington Club
26 Beauty Bar
28 Dylan's
30 Farley's
36 Bruno's
41 Lone Palm
43 Cafe Qué Tal
45 The Marsh
50 Latin American Club
53 Make-Out Room
55 Doc's Clock
58 Cafe La Boheme
72 26 Mix
73 El Rio
74 Cafe Macondo
75 Kilowatt
77 Albion
78 Dalva
79 Roxie Cinema
87 Café Istanbul
88 Casanova Lounge
OTHER
2 Levi Strauss Factory
6 Black & Blue Tattoo
7 Body Manipulations
10 Mission High School
12 Women's Building
13 Community Thrift Store
15 Thrift Town
19 Basic Brown Bear Factory
20 Anchor Brewing Company
22 Miguel Hidalgo Statue
31 X-21 Modern
32 Dog Eared Books
38 Pedal Revolution
46 Aquarius Records
48 Valencia Cyclery
54 Foxy Lady Boutique
56 San Francisco General Hospital
57 Good Vibrations
61 Mission Badlands
62 Mission Cultural Center for Latino Arts
65 Discolandia
66 Precita Eyes Mural Arts Center
67 China Books & Periodicals
69 Studio 24; Galería de la Raza
71 Salvation Army Thrift Store
82 Clothes Contact

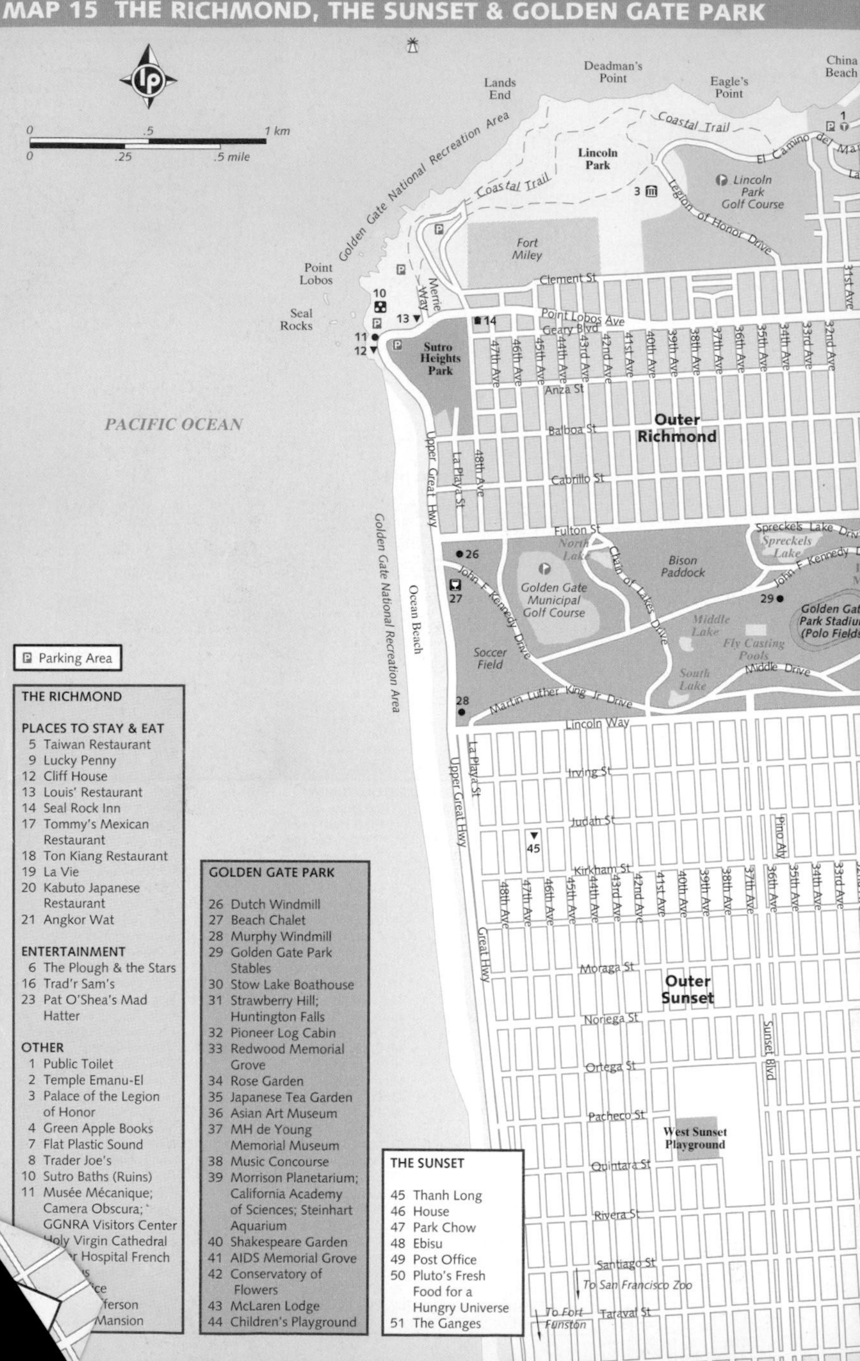

MAP 15 THE RICHMOND, THE SUNSET & GOLDEN GATE PARK
0 .5 1 km
0 .25 .5 mile
Lands End
Deadman's Point
Eagle's Point
China Beach
Coastal Trail
Golden Gate National Recreation Area
Lincoln Park
Lincoln Park Golf Course
Legion of Honor Drive
El Camino del Mar
Fort Miley
Point Lobos
Seal Rocks
Merrie Way
Clement St
Point Lobos Ave
Geary Blvd
Sutro Heights Park
Anza St
Balboa St
Cabrillo St
Fulton St
Outer Richmond
PACIFIC OCEAN
Upper Great Hwy
La Playa St
48th Ave
47th Ave
46th Ave
45th Ave
44th Ave
43rd Ave
42nd Ave
41st Ave
40th Ave
39th Ave
38th Ave
37th Ave
36th Ave
35th Ave
34th Ave
33rd Ave
32nd Ave
31st Ave
North Lake
Chain of Lakes Drive
Bison Paddock
Spreckels Lake Drive
Spreckels Lake
John F Kennedy Drive
Golden Gate Municipal Golf Course
Golden Gate Park Stadium (Polo Fields)
Middle Lake
Fly Casting Pools
Middle Drive
South Lake
Soccer Field
Martin Luther King Jr Drive
Ocean Beach
Golden Gate National Recreation Area
Lincoln Way
Irving St
Judah St
Kirkham St
Pino Aly
Great Hwy
Moraga St
Outer Sunset
Noriega St
Ortega St
Sunset Blvd
Pacheco St
West Sunset Playground
Quintara St
Rivera St
Santiago St
To San Francisco Zoo
To Fort Funston
Taraval St
Parking Area
THE RICHMOND
PLACES TO STAY & EAT
5 Taiwan Restaurant
9 Lucky Penny
12 Cliff House
13 Louis' Restaurant
14 Seal Rock Inn
17 Tommy's Mexican Restaurant
18 Ton Kiang Restaurant
19 La Vie
20 Kabuto Japanese Restaurant
21 Angkor Wat
ENTERTAINMENT
6 The Plough & the Stars
16 Trad'r Sam's
23 Pat O'Shea's Mad Hatter
OTHER
1 Public Toilet
2 Temple Emanu-El
3 Palace of the Legion of Honor
4 Green Apple Books
7 Flat Plastic Sound
8 Trader Joe's
10 Sutro Baths (Ruins)
11 Musée Mécanique; Camera Obscura; GGNRA Visitors Center
Holy Virgin Cathedral
Hospital French
fferson
Mansion
GOLDEN GATE PARK
26 Dutch Windmill
27 Beach Chalet
28 Murphy Windmill
29 Golden Gate Park Stables
30 Stow Lake Boathouse
31 Strawberry Hill; Huntington Falls
32 Pioneer Log Cabin
33 Redwood Memorial Grove
34 Rose Garden
35 Japanese Tea Garden
36 Asian Art Museum
37 MH de Young Memorial Museum
38 Music Concourse
39 Morrison Planetarium; California Academy of Sciences; Steinhart Aquarium
40 Shakespeare Garden
41 AIDS Memorial Grove
42 Conservatory of Flowers
43 McLaren Lodge
44 Children's Playground
THE SUNSET
45 Thanh Long
46 House
47 Park Chow
48 Ebisu
49 Post Office
50 Pluto's Fresh Food for a Hungry Universe
51 The Ganges

The Presidio
see MAP 16
To Golden Gate Bridge & Marin County
Presidio Golf Course
Mountain Lake
Pacific Heights
see MAP 10
Laurel Heights
Inner Richmond
University of San Francisco
Rossi Playground
St Ignatius Church
St Mary's Hospital
Panhandle
Lloyd Lake
Stow Lake
Elk Glen Lake
Mallard Lake
Strybing Arboretum & Botanical Gardens
Big Rec Ball Field
Lily Pond
Tennis Courts
Sharon Meadow
Kezar Pavilion
Kezar Stadium
The Haight
see MAP 11
Interior Park Belt
University of California, San Francisco Medical Center
Mt Sutro 918ft
Inner Sunset
Grand View Park
Laguna Honda Reservoir
Midtown Terrace Recreation Center
Twin Peaks
904ft
922ft
Sunset Reservoir
Golden Gate Heights Park
Forest Hill Muni Station
Laguna Honda Hospital
McCoppin Square
Glen Canyon Park
Mt Davidson

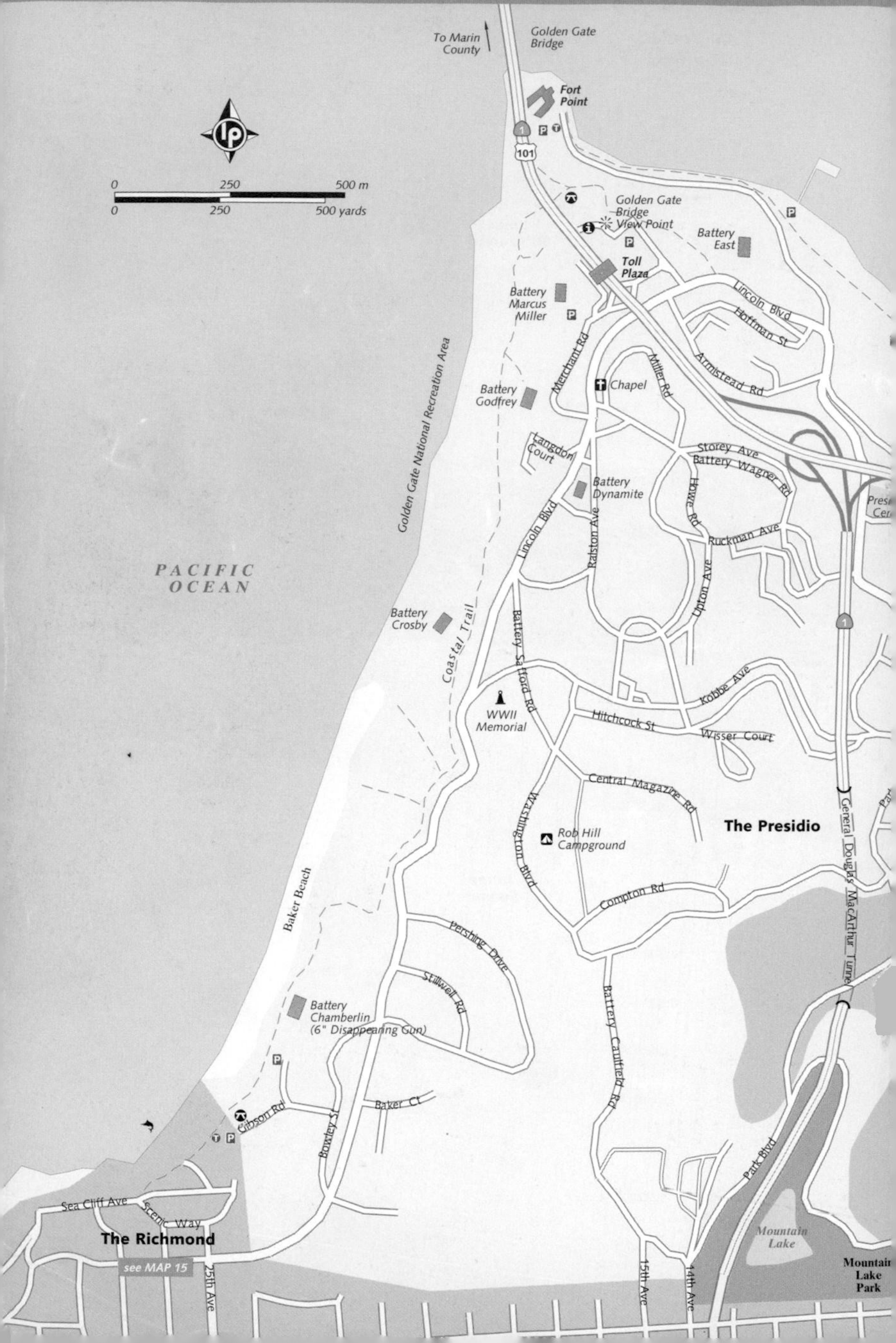

MAP 16 THE PRESIDIO

To Marin County
Golden Gate Bridge
Fort Point
1
101
0 250 500 m
0 250 500 yards
Golden Gate Bridge View Point
Battery East
Toll Plaza
Battery Marcus Miller
Lincoln Blvd
Hoffman St
Armistead Rd
Merchant Rd
Miller Rd
Chapel
Battery Godfrey
Golden Gate National Recreation Area
Langdon Court
Storey Ave
Battery Wagner Rd
Battery Dynamite
Howe Rd
Lincoln Blvd
Ralston Ave
Ruckman Ave
PACIFIC OCEAN
Upton Ave
Battery Crosby
Coastal Trail
Battery Safford Rd
Kobbe Ave
WWII Memorial
Hitchcock St
Wisser Court
Central Magazine Rd
The Presidio
Washington Blvd
Rob Hill Campground
General Douglas MacArthur Tunnel
Baker Beach
Compton Rd
Pershing Drive
Stillwell Rd
Battery Chamberlin (6" Disappearing Gun)
Battery Caulfield Rd
Baker Ct
Gibson Rd
Bowley St
Park Blvd
Sea Cliff Ave
Scenic Way
The Richmond
see MAP 15
25th Ave
15th Ave
14th Ave
Mountain Lake
Mountain Lake Park